ASIAN
AMERICAN
GENEALOGICAL
SOURCEBOOK

Genealogy Sourcebook Series

African American Genealogical Sourcebook

First edition

Asian American Genealogical Sourcebook

First edition

Hispanic American Genealogical Sourcebook

First edition

Native American Genealogical Sourcebook

First edition

ASIAN
AMERICAN
GENEALOGICAL
SOURCEBOOK

edited by
Paula K. Byers

 *Gale Research Inc.*

An International Thomson Publishing Company

I(T)P

Changing the Way the World Learns

NEW YORK • LONDON • BONN • BOSTON • DETROIT • MADRID
MELBOURNE • MEXICO CITY • PARIS • SINGAPORE • TOKYO
TORONTO • WASHINGTON • ALBANY NY • BELMONT CA • CINCINNATI OH

Staff

Editor: Paula K. Byers
Managing Editor: Neil E. Walker
Contributing Editor: Charles B. Montney
Associate Editors: Brian Escamilla, Christopher M. McKenzie, Geri J. Speace
Permissions Associate: Maria L. Franklin

Production Manager: Mary Beth Trimper
Production Assistant: Shanna Philpott Heilveil
Product Design Manager: Cindy Baldwin
Art Director: Pamela Galbreath
Macintosh Artist: Todd Nessel

Manager of Data Entry Services: Benita Spight
Data Entry Coordinator: Gwendolyn Tucker
Senior Data Entry Associate: Civie Ann Green

Systems and Programming Supervisor: Theresa A. Rocklin
Programmer: Charles Beaumont

I(T)P™   Gale Research Inc., an International Thomson Publishing Company.
ITP logo is a trademark under license.

Library of Congress Cataloging-in-Publication Data
Asian American genealogical sourcebook / edited by Paula K. Byers.
   p. cm. -— (Genealogy sourcebook series)
   Includes bibliographical references and indexes
   ISBN 0-8103-9228-3 (alk. paper)
   1. Asian Americans-—Genealogy-—Handbooks, manuals, etc.
   I. Byers, Paula K. (Paula Kay), 1954-   . II. Series.
   E184.06A828 1995
   929'.108985073-—dc20   95-31649

10 9 8 7 6 5 4 3 2 1

Asian American Genealogical Sourcebook
Advisory Board

Table of Contents

List of Figures

Introduction to
Asian American Genealogical Sourcebook

Asian American Genealogical Sourcebook is the third volume to be published in the *Genealogy Sourcebook Series (GSS)*. This series is designed to be a first-stop guide to researching the genealogy of any person with an Asian, African, Hispanic, or Native American heritage.

Asian American Genealogical Sourcebook is a convenient guide which includes all the information required to begin genealogical research. Part I consists of informative essays prepared by Frederick Brady, Greg Gubler, and others — all experts in the field of Asian American genealogy. Combining historical data and practical genealogical advice, the essays reveal the steps that must be taken to ensure a successful search for information. The essays cover:

● The basic immigration and migration patterns of Asian Americans in the United States.

● Traditions and customs which, when described and explained, will ensure that the information discovered will be interpreted correctly.

● Basic genealogical records, an explanation of the data they contain, and their pertinence to the research of Asian Americans. Although most libraries and archives focus on the Chinese, Japanese, and Koreans (due to their being the earliest and largest Asian groups to immigrate to this country), attention is given herein to other areas of Asia as well, with special emphasis on the records of the Filipinos, in an effort to encourage others to begin the enormous task of inventorying and investigating the records of all Asian immigrant groups.

● Genealogical records particular to Asian Americans — their location and what information they provide. While the focus is on the Chinese, Japanese, and Koreans, similar records may exist for other Asian groups.

● Concrete examples of what may be found in a genealogical record to help in applying the information in the essays to ancestral research.

In addition, a bibliography is provided at the end of each essay as a guide to further information.

Part II lists information resources which can provide just the help needed to overcome obstacles in your research. Hundreds of national, regional, state, and foreign organizations and media are listed including:

● libraries and archives
● genealogical societies
● museums
● newsletters
● databases
● microfilm/microfiche
● periodicals
● guides and directories

These entries were carefully selected from a comprehensive database compiled by Gale Research Inc. Additionally, new information was compiled or updated from telephone research, questionnaires, and key secondary sources to ensure the comprehensiveness and accuracy of the information found in this section of the sourcebook.

Part III provides three indexes. The Author and Title and Organization indexes will allow you to quickly find sources listed in Part II. The Subject index allows you to pinpoint information provided in the essays in Part I concerning a specific topic.

Concept and Scope

While the large scope of the subject area precludes answering every question that may arise, this sourcebook will serve to get you started, showing you where and how any further information you may need can be found.

The basics of genealogical research have been included regardless of ethnic background because depending on how many generations have passed since the lifetime of the ancestor being researched, the basic records can apply to all. The more recently in time the object of your research lived, the more likely this will be true. Libraries, archives, organizations, and media which have a broad focus, non-specific to Asian Americans, are included for the same reason. The experts or material found therein will be able to offer direction to those Asian American genealogical groups, archives, and materials which are available locally. Knowing these basic avenues will also allow you to converse and exchange information with or ask questions of other genealogists or family researchers.

Also included herein are organizations/media specifically concerned with Asian Americans. The farther back your ancestor lived in time, the more imperative information unique to this group becomes.

In order to get the maximum benefit from the information provided in this volume, it is highly recommended that you read the **User's Guide** which directly follows this introduction.

Acknowledgements

Our thanks for the use of the map of the Philippines from the *Atlas of Southeast Asia*. By Richard Ulack and Gyula Pauer. Macmillan Publishing Company, 1989. Copyright © 1989 by Macmillan Publishing Company. All rights reserved. Reprinted with permission of Simon & Schuster, Inc.

We would also like to express our appreciation to the Advisory Board members, Frederick Brady, Greg Gubler, and Basil Yang, for their advice and recommendations concerning the production of this volume.

Additional thanks go to Richard L. Casady and James L. Gardner for their assistance in the preparation of the Chapters One and Two and to Sato Tatsui for his help in the translation of Figures 3.6 and 3.7 in Chapter Three.

Suggestions and Comments are Welcome

We see the *GSS* as an ongoing series, constantly reflecting advancements and changes in the field of genealogical research. As such, we appreciate any suggestions or information you may provide. Further, if we listed an organization or database which is not very helpful or neglected a publication or archive which you consider essential, do not hesitate to let us know about it. All questions, suggestions, and comments may be sent to:

Genealogy Sourcebook Series
Gale Research Inc.
General Biography/Genealogy
835 Penobscot Building
Detroit, MI 48226-4094
Phone: (313)961-2242
Fax: (313)961-6741
Toll-free: (800)347-GALE

User's Guide

Asian American Genealogical Sourcebook consists of three parts: essays on genealogical research; a directory of libraries and archives, private and public organizations, print resources, and other media which aid one in applying the information provided in the essays; and a section of indexes listing the authors, titles and organizations, and subjects covered herein.

Part I. Conducting Genealogical Research

This section consists of three chapters of essays. At the end of each chapter is a bibliography of sources which were either mentioned in the essay or enhance the information provided within that chapter.

Things to Know Before You Begin

A Brief Overview of Asian Immigration. Information as to when Asian Americans immigrated to the United States - how, why, and to what extent it occurred. Outlines the migration patterns of the group throughout the United States. Provides the various aspects of the history of Asian Americans which impact genealogical research of this group.

Possible Problems in Interpreting Data. Discussion of the confusion caused by lack of knowledge about naming practices among Asian Americans, their spoken and written language, changes in calendars and dating styles, traditions regarding marriage and the establishment of a family, and other things which might cause one to misinterpret data.

Basic Genealogy Research Methods and Their Application to Asian Americans

Getting Started. Explains how a family researcher or genealogist can discover a lot of information by searching through records in the home. Examines the structure of Asian genealogies and records. Discusses the organization and records of the Family History Library.

Basic Genealogical Records - U.S. Lists the basic records created in the United States which genealogists seek when conducting research and specifically states the importance of each in the conduction of Asian American research.

Basic Genealogical Records - Asia. Broadly discusses the genealogical records created in the Asian country of origin.

Records Specific to Asian Americans

Overview of Asian American Emigration. Considers the information which must be known before Asian research can begin.

Chinese, Japanese, or Korean Research and Sources. Provides an in-depth analysis of the records which may be available for genealogical research in China, Japan, and Korea, respectively.

Part II. Directory of Genealogical Information

This section consists of four chapters providing information on organizations or media which may prove helpful in conducting genealogical research (**for information as to how to read each entry,** *see* **the section "Reading an Entry" which appears after the description of "Other Media" and precedes the description of Part III**):

Libraries and Archives

This chapter lists federal, state, local, university, and foreign libraries or archives which hold sources valuable to genealogical researchers. Entries are arranged alphabetically by the state where they are located and subarranged alphabetically by name within each state. All fifty states, plus the District of Columbia, are included. Libraries and archives whose name implies a national or regional focus can be found listed in the "National and Regional" section which precedes the listings by state. However, it should be kept in mind that many of the libraries and archives listed by state may also have a national or regional focus. Any archive or library particularly helpful to Asian American research located in a country outside the United States is listed at the end of the states.

Private and Public Organizations

This chapter lists national, regional, state, and local genealogical societies, museums, and other groups which may provide instruction, materials, or referrals. Entries are arranged alphabetically by the state where they are located and subarranged alphabetically by name within each state. All fifty states, plus the District of Columbia, are included. Organizations whose name implies a national or regional focus can be found listed in the "National and Regional" section which precedes the listings by state. However, it should be kept in mind that many of the organizations listed by state may also have a national or regional focus. Any organization helpful to Asian American research located in a country outside the United States is listed at the end of the states.

Print Resources

This chapter lists periodicals, books, atlases, newspapers, and other print material which may help further your research. Again, listings are arranged alphabetically by state, however they are listed not under the state where they are published but under the state which their content covers. For example, *Chinese in Hawaii*, though published in Michigan, would be listed under Hawaii. Any sources covering several states or various regional areas appear under the "National and Regional" section which precedes the state listings. Foreign sources are listed at the end of the section.

Other Media

This chapter covers electronic, video, microfilm, or microfiche sources. Entries are arranged alphabetically by product title.

Reading an Entry

Entries in *Libraries and Archives* and *Private and Public Organizations*. A brief description of the individual components of the fictitious entry shown at the bottom of the next page follows. Each numbered item in the entry is explained in the descriptive paragraph bearing the same number.

[1] **Name of Organization or Library/Archive.** Name of parent organization, society, library, archive or agency that is supportive of genealogical research. *See* item 22 (**AKA**) for those organizations which may be known by two or more distinct names.

[2] **Address.** The permanent address of the library, archive, organization.

[3] **Phone.** Phone, fax, and/or toll-free number(s) of addressee.

[4] **Contact.** Contact person or an officer of the organization, library, or archive listed.

[5] **Staff.** Number of employees.

[6] **Description.** Purpose of organization.

[7] **Founded.** Date archive, organization, or library was founded.

[8] **Subjects.** Subject area(s) covered by the library or archive.

[9] **Members.** Membership of the organization.

[10] **Special collections.** Any special manuscripts, files, materials held by the library or archive.

[11] **Regional groups.** Number of regional groups affiliated with the organization.

[12] **State groups.** Number of state groups affiliated with the organization.

[13] **Local groups.** Number of local groups affiliated with the organization.

[14] **Holdings.** Number of volumes or archival materials held by the library or archive.

[15] **Subscriptions.** Number of serials and magazines subscribed to by the library or archive.

[16] **Services.** Whether library or archive offers interlibrary loan, copying, or any other services to its patrons.

[17] **Computerized services.** Electronic services the

library or archive offers - Internet access, on-line searches, etc.

[18] **Telecommunication services.** Electronic mail address of the organization.

[19] **Special catalogs.** Specialized catalogs that the library or archive has available for patrons' use concerning a specific topic or format.

[20] **Special indexes.** Specialized index that the library or archive has available for patrons' use concerning a specific topic or format.

[21] **Affiliated with.** Name of any organization with which listee is affiliated.

[22] **Also known as.** Any other names by which the library, archive, or organization may be known.

[23] **Formerly.** Any name by which the library, archives, or organization used to be known.

[24] **Remarks.** Additional information on the library, archive, or organization which might be useful.

[25] **Publications.** Name of publication produced by the library, archive, or organization.

Entries in *Print Resources* and *Other Media*. A brief description of the individual components of the fictitious entry shown on the next page follows. Each numbered item is explained in the descriptive paragraph bearing the same number.

[26] **Name of Product.** Name of publication, database, video, or microfiche which provides genealogical information. *See* item 60 (**AKA**) for media which may be known by two or more names.

[27] **Address.** The permanent address of the publisher or vendor which produces or distributes the publication, database, video, or microfiche product.

[28] **Phone.** Phone, fax, and/or toll-free number(s) of addressee.

[29] **Contact.** Author, editor, or contact person for the product listed.

[30] **Subtitle.** Subtitle of print source.

[31] **Covers.** Subject material covered in the print source.

[32] **Publication includes.** Type of information included in the print source.

[33] **Description.** General information describing the source.

---

[1] **Norton Genealogical and Biographical Society**
[2] 101 Oath Street
New York, NY 10013

[3] Phone: (123)123-4567
[4] Willard Q. Tohn, Exec. Dir.

[5] Staff: 11. [6] **Description:** To discover, procure, and perpetuate information and items relating to genealogy, geography, and local history. Maintains research library of 65,000 sources including manuscripts and microforms; publishes compiled data and source material for genealogists and historians. [7] **Founded:** 1869. [8] **Subjects:** Ancestry of Africans, Hispanics, Asians, and Native Americans. [9] **Members:** 1400. [10] **Special Collections:** Gorton Historical Collection on localities surrounding Gorton, NH. [11] **Regional Groups:** 8. [12] **State Groups:** 50. [13] **Local Groups:** 225. [14] **Holdings:** 17,000 volumes and manuscripts. [15] **Subscriptions:** 240 serials. [16] **Services:** Interlibrary loan. [17] **Computerized Services:** Internet access; OPAC. [18] **Telecommunications services:** Electronic mail address, jonesc@cmu.edux. [19] **Special Catalogs:** Union List of Serials for Maryland. [20] **Special Indexes:** Indexes, guides, and bulletins to the proprietary collection. [21] **Affiliated with:** National Association for History. [22] **Also known as:** American Institute for Southern Genealogy. [23] **Formerly:** U.S. Genealogical Institute (1986). [24] **Remarks:** Subscription includes an surname locating service. [25] **Publications:** *Newsletter*, semiannual; *Norton Genealogical and Biographical Record (NYG&B)*, quarterly; offers list of publications.

[34] **Languages.** Indicates the different language versions of the medium available.

[35] **Type.** Indicates the product type - digest, bibliography, microfiche, CD-Rom, etc.

[36] **Entries include.** Describes the information each entry in the print source includes.

[37] **First Published.** Date the print source was first published.

[38] **Arrangement.** How the material in the print source is arranged.

[39] **Indexes.** Whether, and what type of, indexes appear in the print source.

[40] **Pages.** Number of pages in the print source.

[41] **Subjects.** Subjects covered in the print source or other medium.

[42] **Audience.** Intended readership of the print source.

[43] **Frequency.** How often the print source is published.

[44] **Indexed.** If and how often the print source is indexed.

[45] **Publication date.** Date current edition of product was published.

[46] **Circulation.** Number of subscribers to print source.

[47] **Price.** Price of source.

[48] **Subscription.** Cost of periodical subscription.

[49] **Send orders to.** Address to send print source orders to if different from main address.

[50] **U.S. distributor.** U.S. distributors of any publications produced by foreign countries.

---

[26] *A Guide to Research in Brighton, Iowa*

[27] 246 MacElroy Avenue
Suite 246A
Des Moines, IA 36692

[28] Phone: (456)789-1233
Fax: (222)898-7897
[29] Sarah Day-Byner, Author

[30] **Subtitle:** *A Guide to Resources in Your Area.* [31] **Covers:** 200 organizations concerned with genealogy. [32] **Publication includes:** List of newspapers published since 1890. [33] **Description:** To list and decribe organizations which provide resources necessary to conduct genealogical research. [34] **Languages:** Korean, English. [35] **Type:** Directory. [36] **Entries include:** Organization name, address and phone number. [37] **First published:** 1993. [38] **Arrangement:** Classified alphabetically by organization name. [39] **Indexes:** State, subject. [40] **Pages:** 50. [41] **Subjects:** Vital statistics from the tri-state area of Indiana, Ohio, and Kentucky. [42] **Audience:** Genealogists and historians. [43] **Frequency:** Biannual, March. [44] **Indexed:** Biannually in *Genealogy Resource Index (GRI).* [45] **Publication Date:** March 1993. [46] **Circulation:** 17,000. [47] **Price:** $14.95, plus $2.50 shipping; payment with order. [48] **Subscription:** $22.95/yr. [49] **Send orders to:** Acme Publications, Box 22, Dayton, OH 45426. [50] **U.S. Distributor:** Genealogical Publications Co., P.O. Box 97, 204 Malvern St., Phoenix, NM 44238. [51] **ISBN:** 0-8103-7126-3. [52] **ISSN:** 0197-562X. [53] **Geographic coverage:** Northwestern U.S. [54] **Timespan:** Most recent two years. [55] **Updating:** Quarterly. [56] **Also includes:** Glossary, list of special collections. [57] **Online availability:** DIALOG Information Services (file 266). [58] **Also on line as part of:** Genealogical and Historial Abstracts. [59] **Alternate electronic formats:** CD-ROM, General History Index. [60] **Also known as:** *Directory of Regional Facts.* [61] **Former titles:** *Directory of Local History* (1972). [62] **Former database name:** Genealogy Line. [63] **Remarks:** Subscription includes a surname locating service.

51 **ISBN.** ISBN of the print product.

52 **ISSN.** ISSN of the print product.

53 **Geographic coverage.** Describes areas covered by the material in the medium cited.

54 **Timespan.** The timespan covered in the medium.

55 **Updating.** How often the medium is updated.

56 **Also includes.** Additional information included in the print source.

57 **Online availability.** Lists electronic formats from other producers allowing access to the product.

58 **Also online as part of.** Lists electronic formats which include this product as part of their larger database.

59 **Alternate electronic formats.** Availability of the product in electronic formats produced by the same publisher.

60 **Also known as.** Other names by which the product is known.

61 **Former titles.** Former name(s) by which the print source was known.

62 **Former database name.** Former name(s) by which the database was known.

63 **Remarks.** Additional information on the product which might be useful.

Part III. Indexes

This section consists of author, title and organization, and subject indexes which provide the page number(s) wherein the information cited can be located.

Author Index

All appearances of a specific author or editor cited in the "Print Resources" and "Other Media" sections of Part II are listed and the page number(s) on which this information appears are provided.

Title and Organization Index

All appearances of a specific title or organization name listed in Part II are cited and the page number(s) on which the information appears are provided.

Subject Index

Page number(s) wherein a specific topic, term, or location is discussed in the essays located in Part I are cited.

Part I
Conducting Genealogical Research

**Background Material —
Things to Know before You Begin**

**Basic Genealogical Research Methods
& Their Application to Asian Americans**

Records Specific to Asian Americans

Things to Know Before You Begin

Frederick Brady

⌀ Frederick Brady is an Asian Librarian and accredited Japanese genealogist with the Genealogical Society of Utah. A teacher of Asian studies, he also freelances as a writer concentrating on topics related to Japan.

Mr. Brady was ably assisted in the preparation of the first two chapters by Richard L. Casady and James L. Gardner, both catalogers of long-standing at the Family History Library in Salt Lake City. The former contributed much information on Filipino immigration to the United States and the process of locating records at the Family History Library and the National Archives; while the latter supplemented the history, traditions, and basic genealogical records of China, Japan, and Korea which Mr. Brady detailed with the histories, traditions, and basic genealogical records of the other countries of Asia.

A Brief Overview of Asian Immigration

As of the end of the twentieth century, Americans of Asian origin compose a very small minority in the United States, but their numbers are growing impressively. According to census records, as of 1990 less than three percent of the nation's population is Asian, the largest groups being Chinese, Filipino, Japanese, Indian, Korean, and Vietnamese, in that order. The west coast, especially California, is the largest repository of Americans of Asian ancestry, but Hawaii has the largest percentage of Asians in its population.

Chinese and Japanese, entering Hawaii and the west coast in large numbers in the second half of the nineteenth century, became an American concern when the islands became a U.S. possession in 1898. That same year, the Philippine Islands also became a U.S. possession as a result of the Spanish-American War. As a result, Filipinos, as well as Koreans and Indians, began to enter the United States in significant numbers, though these groups did not begin immigrating in earnest until after World War II.

Immigration of Indochinese, especially Vietnamese, effectively began later in the twentieth century. The long involvement of the United States in the war in Vietnam, which spilled over into Cambodia and Laos, accounts for the large numbers of people who immigrated from those countries after the United States pulled out in 1973. As of 1990, 615,000 Vietnamese alone had taken residence in the United States since 1971. (Some of these are actually ethnic Chinese; there are long-established Chinese communities throughout Southeast Asia.) Since the beginning of the 1980s, the Asian population of the Atlantic seaboard states has grown rapidly while declining slightly on the west coast. Most Asian Americans tend to settle in urban areas and surrounding suburbs.

Of added interest is the relative rate of growth of each major Asian group in the United States. According to the U.S. censuses for 1970, 1980, and 1990, the Japanese population growth rate slowed greatly in comparison with earlier decades, while the Chinese and Filipino populations showed very respectable increases in growth. During the same decades, the Indian and Korean populations increased tremendously, as did the Vietnamese population which exploded from nearly zero to a figure comparable with the others. Figure 1.1 summarizes the data. Various economic and political factors have influenced the rate of immigration of each group from time to time and will be explained in later sections.

For general information on the history of Asian peoples' emigration to the United States, the *Harvard Encyclopedia of American Ethnic Groups* (Thernstrom) should be consulted. For very brief but interesting information on Chinese, South Asian, and Japanese emigration, the *Encyclopedia of Asian History* (Embree) is helpful. Two more valuable works, one general in scope and the other focusing specifically on Asians are the *Dictionary of American Immigration History* (Cordasco) and the *Dictionary of Asian American History* (Hyung-

Number of Asians in the United States

| | 1970 | 1980 | 1990 | Percent Increase | | |
		(Thousands)		1970-80	1980-90	1970-90
Chinese	435	806	1,645	85	104	278
Filipino	343	775	1,407	126	82	310
Japanese	591	701	848	19	21	43
Indians	ca. 76	362	815	376	125	972
Koreans	69	355	799	414	125	1058
Vietnamese		262	615		135	

Figure 1.1

chan Kim). Many books have been written about the histories of various Asian groups in America, some of which are listed in the bibliography at the end of this chapter.

As for studies of the types of records which are available and how to obtain access to them, the Genealogical Society of Utah has sponsored two symposia whose proceedings have been published. These include considerable material on Asian records and research and are portions of the 1969 World Conference on Records, published as *Studies in Asian Genealogy* (Spencer J. Palmer) and *Asian and African Family and Local History*. The Family History Library in Salt Lake City, operated by the Genealogical Society of Utah, has a catalog of its Asian holdings which is especially extensive for China and Korea. The library's East Asian card catalog is in the process of being automated.

Chinese Immigration

The Chinese population in the United States will probably pass the two million mark by the end of the twentieth century. This is the largest Chinese community in the world outside of China itself, although it represents only two-tenths of one percent of China's population which numbers over a billion and less than one percent of the population of the United States. The contribution of the Chinese American community cannot be measured by numbers alone. Their history is fascinating, often tragic, and has much to do with the development of civil rights awareness in the United States.

Early Immigration. For centuries, even during long periods of relative seclusion, one of China's major exports has been people. Originally, large communities of "overseas" Chinese, called *hua-chiao*, were established throughout Southeast Asia. The same has now become true in the Americas, Africa, and Europe. The most obvious reason for this is continuing the population growth in the largest country on earth, prompting ambitious and adventurous individuals to seek opportunities abroad.

China has also experienced much civil strife, several foreign invasions, and many natural disasters in the nineteenth and twentieth centuries. This created groups of refugees, forced to seek better lives abroad for themselves and their families. Corrupt and oppressive landlords contributed greatly to the suffering of people all over China during the nineteenth century and many tried to escape. Famine, war, and other disasters caused great economic and social upheavals in the southern regions. In particular, the Opium War (1839–1842), waged by Great Britain in response to China's attempts to curtail opium imports from India, was responsible for much unrest in southern China. Then the Taiping Rebellion (1851–1864) rocked the empire. The Taipings were a militant religious cult whose ideals for social reform eventually attracted over a million disaffected members of Chinese society. The extreme violence of the rebellion and the suppression of the Taipings (between twenty and thirty million dead) provided a greater incentive for survivors in many areas to flee. Long-standing animosities between groups speaking different variants of the Chinese language would also flare into civil strife from time to time, creating more refugees.

Three regions in China, all in southern Guangdong (spelled "Kwangtung" in most older texts) were the places of origin of most of the emigrants of the nineteenth century: the Sam Yap ("Three Districts"), the Sze Yap ("Four Districts"), and Chungshan (or Zhongshan) District. Most emigrants from southern China were speakers of Cantonese although the Hakka and Min languages were also represented in much smaller numbers. It was not until after World War II that speakers of Mandarin, the language of most northern Chinese and the Chinese on Taiwan, began to immigrate to the United States in significant numbers.

Though a few Chinese sailors, merchants, and students had visited the eastern United States in the eighteenth and nineteenth centuries, it was the discovery of gold in California in 1848 which provided the impetus for large-scale immigration, almost all of it to the west coast. There were 4,000 Chinese in the United States in 1850. Though only 500 of them at that time were in California, which became known in China as the ''Golden Mountain'' (*Gum Saan*), in another decade this number had grown to 35,000. The Burlingame Treaty, signed in 1868, attempted to guarantee a steady supply of cheap labor to the United States from China and the treaty had its desired effect. The 1890 census reported 107,488 Chinese, mostly in California, though nearly three times that number had been recorded in immigration records as entering the United States between 1849 and 1882. The huge disparity may be caused by underreporting in the census, deaths, returns home to China, multiple entries for many individuals, and people moving on to other countries. Altogether, during this period, some 2.4 million Chinese left their country seeking opportunities in Southeast Asia, the Pacific islands, and the Americas.

The vast majority of Chinese immigrants in the United States were men: the ratio of males to females in the 1890 census was about twenty-seven to one. Less than four percent of the Chinese in America at that time were female and most of those were prostitutes who had been enslaved and imported to serve the male population. The near non-existence of a stable female population is due to the fact that most of the members of the Chinese community saw themselves as temporary sojourners. They were working to support their faraway families, to whom they eventually hoped to return. Of course, this also prevented the Chinese neighborhoods in the United States from stabilizing until more women arrived to marry and raise families. Yet, even as late as 1940, the ratio of men to women was still three to one.

Besides the gold fields of California, the Chinese later found work in various types of mines in Colorado, Nevada, Utah, and other places throughout the American West as well as in British Columbia. The rapid industrialization taking place in the United States provided many other opportunities for China's surplus labor force as well. Eventually, about 14,000 were employed as laborers by the Central Pacific Railroad. Though they worked hard, the attitude of their bosses seemed to be that they were expendable as there were plenty more Chinese still in China who could be imported. Two thousand Chinese railroad workers unsuccessfully staged a strike in 1867 in an attempt to win the same employment terms as white workers. Significantly, though the Central Pacific was built largely by Chinese hands, no Chinese were present in 1869 at the driving of the golden spike at Promontory, Utah, when the Central Pacific was linked with the Union Pacific Railroad.

The Chinese continued to provide a large portion of the labor on extensions of the railroad system over many years and there remained plenty of work in the mines. Others became farmers, reclaiming supposedly useless land and making it productive; entered into manufacturing and fishing industries; or started small businesses. The scarcity of females made it necessary (or possible) for many men to open businesses in what had until then been traditionally female occupations—operating laundries and restaurants. Some made their way east, where they worked in mills and factories. Others helped to replace slave labor in the surviving plantations of the post war South. By 1890, there were Chinese living in every state of the nation.

Prejudice and Discrimination. From the first, racism was the cause of much suffering on the part of Chinese immigrants. During the gold rush, they were assaulted by other miners. Sometimes they were merely the objects of rough playfulness, at other times they were the targets of serious violence. The Chinese were despised for their strange customs and their willingness to rework seemingly exhausted claims, finding traces of gold which had been overlooked by white miners in their frenzied search for easy riches. Later, in mills and factories, when downturns in the economy caused white laborers to be thrown out of work, the local Chinese community became a convenient outlet for pent-up frustrations. This was especially true when companies used Chinese workers as strikebreakers. In any case, employers' preferences for Chinese labor (they were hardworking, loyal, and could be paid less) caused jealousy among other workers.

Most ''Chinatown'' communities in the western United States were allowed to exist only on the outskirts of towns, well away from white neighborhoods, but close enough to make use of whatever services they had to offer. Their squalor was more a result of circumstance than of choice. It may also have been the result of common wisdom as these Chinese enclaves experienced raids by white men which were attended by violet beatings. Any display of wealth might have caused more jealousy and triggered more raids.

The grossly unfair stereotype of the Chinese as outsiders whose craftiness stole the bread out of the mouths of the children of white men was generally believed. Even some Christian ministers, while professing an interest in the spiritual welfare of the Chinese, helped to perpetuate these prejudices via their condescending attitude toward Chinese culture which proclaimed that it was a Christian's ''duty'' to convert the Chinese to the more ''civilized'' Christianity. In addition, crusading editors and politicians saw opportunities to further their careers by championing the cause of the American worker against the Chinese interloper. All of this resulted in discriminatory laws on the local, state, and federal levels.

A glance through the history of the Chinese in the United States offers many instances of official and unofficial persecution. A few are presented in Figure 1.2.

Such discrimination and persecution had consequences of importance to genealogical researchers. The Chinese from southern China already had a long tradition of distrust for the official administration because of the oppressive and rapacious nature of the Manchu government which had conquered China over two centuries earlier. Defiance and circumvention of the law was applauded in folklore and popular literature such as the historical novel *Shui hu chuan* (variously translated as *The Water Margin, Outlaws of the Marsh,* and *All Men Are Brothers*) whose main characters were seen as champions of the people after the order of Robin Hood. Though few Chinese in America saw themselves as heroes of this magnitude, they continued to distrust authorities in their new country. Arrests of Chinese for minor infractions, or for no good reason at all, occurred frequently. Therefore, if a Chinese man was arrested, he would likely give an alias or nickname rather than his official name. If he were arrested more than once, he might give a different name each time. Even if he did give the same name, different clerks might vary the romanized spelling, further confounding genealogists.

Social Structure of Chinese Communities. Chinatowns sprang up wherever there was a need for inexpensive labor and some of those located in large cities remain today. At first, they were primarily bachelor villages, with few of the comforts and amenities of real homes. Still, they were havens where Chinese men could pretend they were in China, eating their own food and telling stories in their own language. They retained the customs of their homeland, including those which had been forced upon them by their Manchu overlords. Most obvious was the queue (a braid of hair often worn hanging at the back of the head) which was used in China to distinguish Chinese from Manchus, who did not wear it. It became an object of ridicule in America among white co-workers and rowdies looking for sport. The queue was also a symbol to many anti-Chinese of the immigrants' refusal to assimilate.

Chinese religion was a puzzle to Americans, who regarded it as a jumble of heathenish superstitions. In fact, Chinese folk religion, although consisting of a healthy dose of folk beliefs, was created from a group of doctrines taken from Taoism, Confucianism, and Buddhism. Therefore, the average illiterate Chinese laborer was probably no more superstitious than the average illiterate white laborer. Be that as it may, most disputes over beliefs are not a matter of truth versus error, but rather mine versus yours or familiar versus different. For example, a basic tenet of Chinese culture is filial piety (devoutness towards parents) which extends to respect of one's deceased ancestors. This veneration of ancestors becomes a form of worship and family temples are built. This practice was viewed by Christian neighbors with distaste and suspicion.

As the importance of one's ancestors naturally influences one's attitude toward one's living relatives, clan organizations were an important facet of Chinese life. The tendency to bond with men from the same region and of the same surname was pronounced for Chinese Americans. Clan organizations, called *fang*, provided aid and fellowship to men of the same lineage. Many times, several related fang would organize into a larger clan association. A Chinese store often became the locus of an organization, where a man could obtain moral and even financial support from men of his native region. Cooperative ventures could be planned, advice and protection obtained, money borrowed or invested, and business contacts signed. The regional organizations, the first of which were inaugurated in San Francisco as early as 1851, were called *huiguan*, which literally means "meeting hall," and were commonly known in English as benevolent associations. They also provided temporary quarters for recent immigrants, character references for travelers, charitable services, mediation for disputes, and other assistance.

Another type of organization, somewhat in competition with the clan associations and huiguan, was the secret society, known as *tong*. Membership in a tong usually appealed to men who were, for one reason or another, alienated from mainstream Chinese society and could not join a huiguan. Sometimes called the "Chinese Mafia," tongs often displayed similarities with other secret gangster societies. They began as brotherhoods dedicated to mutual aid and protection under harsh governments and had special quasi-religious ceremonies to initiate and promote members, but, in America, they also became involved in various illegal activities such as drug trade, extortion, and prostitution using legitimate business as a front. Unfortunately, the similarities do not end there. "Wars" between rival tongs resulted in assassinations which were played up in the news media, giving the Chinese community at large a bad name. Eventually, as Chinese communities stabilized with the growth of families and a decrease in bachelors who supported the tongs and their activities, the tongs began to disappear. They were greatly diminished by the 1930s, though a criminal minority continues to flourish in the Chinese community which is fed (as in all communities) by alienated youths.

Sampling of Actions Persecuting the Chinese in the United States

Year	Action
1852	California state legislature reenacts an 1850 Foreign Miners' Tax law, applying to the Chinese an older law enacted against the Mexicans wherein a tax was charged before non-whites were allowed to operate or work in a mine.
1867	Unsuccessful strike of Chinese railroad workers.
1871	A Los Angeles riot results in the death of twenty-one Chinese.
1875	Whites dressed as Indians murder sixty-two Chinese miners near the Snake River in Idaho.
1877	California appeals to Congress to limit Chinese immigration.
1879	New California constitution includes anti-Chinese provisions.
1882	By passing the Chinese Exclusion Act, Congress excludes Chinese immigrants from the United States for ten years.
1883	Montana Territorial Supreme Court voids mining claims held by aliens "ineligible for citizenship."
1885	A mob in Rock Springs, Wyoming, kills twenty-eight Chinese and causes five hundred others to flee.
1888	Chinese barred from reentry into the United States unless they are returning to property or family.
1892	Geary Act extends exclusion of the Chinese for another ten years.
1898	On a Hawaiian plantation, a raid by Japanese laborers on Chinese laborers after a fight results in the death of three Chinese, with over twenty injured.
1902	Chinese exclusion is extended for another ten years.
1904	Deficiency Laws extend Chinese exclusion indefinitely in the United States and its possessions.

Figure 1.2

One other movement, small but influential in its own way, was Chinese Christianity. Protestant ministers, out of sincere missionary zeal, were able to convert small numbers of Chinese to Christianity and organize them into churches. The churches began literacy and language programs to help converts learn about American culture and values which aided in creating mutual understanding. They also stood up for civil rights against the efforts of anti-Chinese agitators. However, the condescending ''white man's burden'' attitude (which considered it a duty of all Christians to convert those of foreign birth to the white man's culture) of some of the missionaries did its own share of harm as well. Be that as it may, the altruistic nature of a typical Christian church, coupled with the enthusiasm of recent converts for evangelism, meant that Chinese Christian congregations had an influence for good beyond their relatively small size.

Chinese in Hawaii. Though 195 Chinese workers were in the first group to migrate to Hawaii in 1852, subsequent immigration was only in the hundreds and the Chinese population in Hawaii did not grow very much at first. The opportunities in the ''Golden Mountain'' (California) were much more enticing. This changed in 1876, when the kingdom of Hawaii concluded a reciprocal trade agreement with the United States permitting the import of duty-free Hawaiian sugar to the United States. The increasing demand for cane field labor created a job market for Chinese immigrants.

The Chinese contract laborers in Hawaii were hard, obedient workers, but life on the sugar plantations was brutal. Workers were treated like slaves and living conditions were substandard. Protests were made to officials and some riots were staged, but with little effect. Still, opportunities abounded. The planters were, for the most part, very pleased with the Chinese who continued to immigrate. As early as 1884, about one-fourth of Hawaii's population was Chinese. Most of that number were men—as in the ''Golden Mountain,'' most Chinese in Hawaii were sojourners who hoped to eventually return to China.

The year 1882 was a significant one in the history of Chinese immigration, both to Hawaii and to the United States. In that year, the first of many exclusion acts directed against the Chinese were enacted in the United States. Similar efforts were begun that year in Hawaii by Walter Murray Gibson, a plantation owner who served King Kalakaua as premier and foreign minister. Gibson's government tried unsuccessfully to prevent any more Chinese from entering the kingdom. One reason for growing anti-Chinese feeling was that, as their plantation labor contracts expired, many workers moved to the towns for employment and competed with local residents for customers.

Measures were taken to prevent Chinese sojourners from taking local wives to establish residency and limits were set on the number of farm laborers who could enter from China as well as on the length of time they could stay. At the same time, the government promoted contract immigration from Japan to offset the decrease in the Chinese labor force. These restrictions did play a part in causing the Chinese population in Hawaii to decrease in number from 1884 to 1890, but when the plantations began to feel the bite of a labor shortage, the restrictions were eased, and the Chinese population began to grow rapidly once more.

The Hawaiian monarchy was overthrown in 1893 and a republic was declared. In 1898, the islands were annexed by the United States and the Chinese exclusion laws of the United States, first enacted in 1882, were applied to Hawaii as well. Chinese immigration slowed to a trickle, and the population, which had peaked at about 26,000, began to decrease again. From a low of nearly 22,000 in 1910, the Chinese population of Hawaii did not pass 30,000 until restrictions were lifted after World War II. As Chinese men began to take local wives and start families and bachelors died or returned to China, the community stabilized and the ratio of men to women gradually decreased. From 1898 on, the story of the Chinese in Hawaii is part of the American story.

The Exclusion Era, 1882 to 1943. Perusal of the section on Japanese emigration will show that, though Japanese immigrants had their problems with the governments of Hawaii and the United States, on the whole their experience was quite different from that of the Chinese. To the average local bully, one Asian looked very much like any other, but governments were more discriminating in their policies. The Chinese empire was seen as old and enfeebled, ripe for partition into ''spheres of influence'' by trade-hungry Western powers. Japan, on the other hand, was ruled by a new, vigorous government whose policy of rapid modernization had brought it into competition with the West. The Japanese defeat of the Chinese empire in 1895, followed in 1905 by their defeat of the Russian empire, showed the Western powers that Japan could not be pushed around. Consequently, attempts to exclude or restrict Japanese immigrants had to be conducted much more delicately. Chinese immigrants did not have this slight advantage.

The Chinese communities, not entirely powerless, did not take discrimination passively. Many Chinese American organizations lobbied actively for recognition of their human rights and redress of their grievances, but it was an uphill battle. Sometimes contacts with men of influence in China resulted in demands to the U.S. government for better treatment of Chinese immigrants, but life was still difficult. In addition to the many lesser instances of discrimination committed by the government and the unofficial instances that were ignored, application of the exclusion laws was a major hardship on all Chinese.

Still this discrimination can be seen, in a rather ironic way, as a sort of blessing to the Chinese American community as well. The gradual elimination of the overwhelming bachelor element in the Chinese community, caused in part by discriminatory immigration laws, helped to bring many long-term benefits to the Chinese in the United States. As has been stated, the community of Chinese sojourners had been largely a bachelor community for several decades. Once the exclusion laws made it clear that they were no longer welcome in the United States, large numbers of men returned to China. Others, opting to remain for the rest of their lives, for whatever reasons, eventually died lowering the percentage of males again. Offsetting the decrease in bachelors, some men were able to send for their families, the immigration of whom was provided for in spite of restrictions, while others married local women, often non-whites of other ethnic groups, and began to produce children.

The Chinese community thus settled down and grew naturally, the births of daughters increasing the female population. Family growth brought about the need for more schools, community organizations, social programs, religious activities, and public relations efforts to benefit the children and the community at large. Boys and girls born in America naturally wanted to take part in American life and be equal recipients of its benefits. Struggling for many of those benefits, their victories and setbacks helped establish precedents for future civil rights movements on behalf of other ethnic groups. Also, family men are less likely to be involved in illegal activities, so the tongs and their attendant problems became less of a consideration.

During the exclusion era in the United States, China was in a state of tremendous upheaval. In 1912, after decades of severe unrest, a Chinese republic was declared and the millennia-old empire was swept away. This did not cure the desire of many to emigrate, however. Civil unrest continued, up to and beyond the Japanese invasion at the beginning of World War II, as rival political parties and feuding warlords jockeyed for power.

Loopholes in the exclusion laws allowed thousands of people to leave their troubled native land for the United States during this period. While barring new immigrants from China, the law did allow a man to return to America if he could prove that he had been there before. It also allowed for immigration of immediate family members. These provisions gave rise to practices which are sure to confound genealogists because a man might decide to remain in China and sell his ''slot'' in America,

with his papers, to another. Or, he might return to the United States himself, and bring papers claiming that he had fathered a son while in China. These papers might be sold later to a man who would immigrate, claiming to be the son of the original immigrant, whether or not he was actually related. The true identities and pedigrees of many ''paper sons'' may never be discovered; at least, not through searches of official records. Additionally, the destruction and loss of thousands of vital records in the great San Francisco earthquake and fire of 1906 gave many Chinese the opportunity to claim U.S. citizenship by asserting birth in the United States leaving officials unable to prove otherwise.

The U.S. government made efforts to block the entry of paper sons and slot buyers and these efforts helped make the immigration facility at Angel Island in San Francisco Bay notorious. Most Chinese immigrants were processed at this facility, unofficially known as ''the Ellis Island of the West,'' where to this day, poems carved on the walls describing the frustrations and fears of the immigrants remain. They were confined, sometimes for months or even years, while their stories were checked and rechecked or while they waited for decisions to their appeals of adverse rulings. For some, Angel Island was more a prison than a way station. It did, in fact, become a prisoner of war camp in 1940.

The Chinese American population began to spread out, especially to the eastern and southern areas of the United States. While remaining the state with the largest Chinese population, California saw a significant reduction in the population while New York rose to second place. Movements in large numbers to urban areas and their suburbs brought about the permanent establishment of certain larger, big-city Chinatowns while many smaller Chinatowns disappeared. By 1940, over ninety percent of the Chinese in the United States were urban dwellers. Nearly a quarter of those lived in San Francisco.

Post War Immigration. During World War II, the alliance of China and the United States against Japan made a review of the American policy of discrimination against Chinese immigrants necessary. In 1943, restrictions were lifted to allow 105 Chinese per year to immigrate and citizenship was offered to Chinese already resident in the United States. When the war ended, thousands of women were admitted to the United States as the brides of American servicemen.

Another wave of immigration began as the nationalist Kuomintang party battled the Communist party for supremacy. When the Communists won in 1949 and the nationalists were left in control only of the island of Taiwan, the number of Mandarin-speaking northern Chinese immigrants increased, though the majority of immigrants were still from Hong Kong and the surrounding regions of southern China. Also, the proportion of professional people and students increased. As the United States and mainland China drew apart for political reasons during the Korean War and the ensuing Cold War, movements got underway in Chinatowns across America to show that their communities were loyal to the United States and opposed to communism.

The Lyndon B. Johnson presidential administration, as part of its work to guarantee civil rights to Americans of all ethnic backgrounds, ended the immigration quota system in 1965. The floodgates opened and by 1980 about 300,000 Chinese had immigrated. There was another increase in the proportion of immigrants from Taiwan which, while enjoying great economic prosperity under U.S. patronage, was growing too crowded for some of its citizens. Most of the those emigrating from Taiwan were not native Taiwanese, however, but Mandarin speaking people who had earlier fled from mainland China to escape the communist takeover. Other groups of overseas Chinese came to the United States when their countries of origin, Burma and Indonesia, experienced political upheavals and popular movements against Chinese residents.

As relations with the Communist government in mainland China normalized during the Nixon, Ford, and Carter administrations in the 1970s, mainland Chinese were gradually allowed more freedom of travel. Many students and professional people were able to visit the United States and a large number remained. Nationalist Chinese in Taiwan and America were also able to visit their homeland.

A significant event which is influencing emigration from Hong Kong toward the close of the twentieth century is the agreement between Great Britain and China to return the colony of Hong Kong to Chinese rule in January 1997. When the announcement was made, great numbers of educated professionals began exiting the colony. At the peak of the emigration rush in the mid-1980s, some 25,000 people per year were leaving Hong Kong. Many went to other British possessions or Commonwealth nations with Vancouver, British Columbia, receiving a huge influx. There was a spillover into the United States as well. And though all of these Chinese people tend to be lumped into one group by the surrounding non-Chinese, it is well to remember that there are several subgroups within that community, speaking different languages and enjoying different cultures. They are all Chinese, but a wealth of diversity is encompassed by that single designation.

Japanese Immigration

The history of Japanese immigration, whether to North America or elsewhere, begins comparatively re-

cently. At the time large numbers of Europeans were beginning to colonize North America in the mid-seventeenth century, Japan was closing its ports to international trade and forbidding its people to leave the country for any reason. There had been a trickle of emigration to ports in East and Southeast Asia during the decades before the 1630s, but at that point the newly-established Tokugawa *shogunate* (a feudal, military government) forced the country into more than two centuries of seclusion. The purpose of this policy was to shield the Japanese people from undesirable foreign cultural influences (especially Christianity) and the government from confrontations with powerful potential adversaries such as Spain and England. Japanese citizens who were already abroad when the final seclusion policies were enacted were not allowed to return home. Any who left by accident, such as lost fishermen rescued by foreign ships, also had to remain in exile. At one point, an entire colony of exiled Japanese Christians resided in the Philippines, but they eventually assimilated and had disappeared by the nineteenth century.

After a period of almost total isolation from the rest of the world, from 1639 to 1866, Japanese people were again allowed by their government to travel abroad. Japan was ''reopened'' in 1853–1854 by Commodore Matthew Perry under orders from U.S. President Franklin Pierce. The shogunate was in decline. Ambitious *samurai* (or warrior aristocrats) from western Japan, longtime enemies of the Tokugawa family and its allies, were preparing for an ''imperial restoration'' which would abolish the shogunate and restore the emperor to political prominence with themselves as his key advisors. One of the last acts of the shogunate allowed limited numbers of Japanese to leave their country for officially authorized purposes. Then, late in 1867, the feudal government was swept away, the teenaged emperor was moved from the old capital of Kyoto and installed in the shogun's former capital (renamed Tōkyō), and, in 1868, the Meiji (''Enlightened Rule'') era was proclaimed. That same year, full-fledged emigration began.

Early Immigration. Almost all early emigrants were laborers contracted to work on farms in Hawaii and Guam. Sugar had recently become a major source of income for the kingdom of Hawaii, but local labor was scarce. Chinese immigrants took up some of the slack but were, in many Hawaiians' opinions, becoming too numerous. To offset the Chinese population, a Hawaiian government official named Eugene Van Reed persuaded the Tokugawa government to allow Japanese citizens to work as temporary contract laborers in Hawaii. When the change in governments threatened to annul his plans, Van Reed sneaked the first group out of Japan. The immigrants included two teenaged boys and five women, wives of men in the group. During the journey, one man died and was buried at sea and one of the women gave birth. This group of 148 (some sources say 153) workers arrived in Honolulu in June 1868. All of them were from the Tokyo-Yokohama area and none were farmers. Warmly received by the locals, among whom they caused great curiosity, they are known as *Gannen-mono* (''First-Year People'') because 1868 was the first year of the Meiji era.

The initial optimism of the Gannen-mono was soon shattered when they learned that the owners of the sugar plantations regarded them as little more than slaves. In fact, several plantation owners were former slaveholders from the southern United States. Long hours, brutal lashings, low wages, disregard for illness, deplorable housing, and other cruelties convinced the Japanese that Van Reed had deceived them. Brawls and even suicides among the workers themselves, increased their desire to return home before the three-year contract expired. They complained to the Japanese government which sent agents to investigate in December 1869. Forty people returned to Japan with the officials. Thirteen more followed in 1871 when their contract expired. The ninety or so that remained decided to settle in Hawaii.

Later in 1871, the new Meiji government signed an agreement of amity and commerce with Hawaii, legitimizing the emigration of Japanese to the islands. Emperor Mutsuhito and Kalakaua, who became King of Hawaii in 1874, became friends and held each other in high personal regard. However, despite their friendship, the Japanese government remained leery of exporting its citizens to labor in Hawaii and there was no more organized contract emigration from Japan to Hawaii until 1885. Moreover, Japan needed its citizens to remain in the country in order to recruit colonists for the northernmost island of Hokkaidō, saving it from encroachment by the Russians.

Contract Labor in Hawaii. Still, overpopulation was causing severe economic problems in several districts of Japan, especially in the impoverished, rural areas of the west and south. Finally, out of 28,000 applicants, 945 emigrants were selected by the Japanese government to sail to Hawaii as contract laborers in 1885. They were accompanied by the first Japanese consul to Hawaii, Nakamura Jirō. The group was welcomed personally by King Kalakaua and was initially treated with kindness by the Hawaiian people.

The largest group among these first immigrants of 1885 was from Yamaguchi Prefecture (420). The rest were from the prefectures of Hiroshima (222), Kanagawa (214), Okayama (37), Wakayama (22), Mie (13), Shizuoka (11), and Shiga (5), with a lone man from Miyagi Prefecture. They were followed a few months later by another group of 983 people from Hiroshima

(390), Kumamoto (270), Fukuoka (149), Shiga (74), Niigata (37), Wakayama (33), Kanagawa (12), Gunma (10), and Chiba (8). Incidentally, we should note that there is some disagreement over the exact numbers of immigrants in the early years, caused in some part by the inclusion or omission of officials and others who travelled with the immigrants but were not immigrants themselves or by other people who may have been immigrants but were not contract laborers. There is more agreement on the numbers from 1894 onward.

Unfortunately, some of the old complaints about substandard living quarters and physical abuse arose again and the second 1885 group was accompanied to Hawaii by Special Commissioner Inoue Katsunosuke, who was assigned to investigate matters. The Hawaiian government agreed to several measures to improve the lives of the Japanese, but many abuses on the plantations continued. Nonetheless, by 1894, 29,069 Japanese had immigrated to Hawaii, most of them from southwestern Japan and Okinawa. Not all of them stayed; the total Japanese population of Hawaii in 1896 was estimated to be 24,407. Some men brought their families with them while others sent for their families later or returned to Japan in order to bring them to Hawaii.

Though virtually all of the first Japanese immigrants worked as unskilled laborers on farms and in canneries or in similar venues, the fact is that many of them were not unskilled, uneducated workers. Large numbers were younger sons of landowning families or were merchants or craftsmen who were willing to work at first as laborers in order to save money for more ambitious enterprises. All were more or less literate, able at least to read *kana* script, and many were well-educated or possessed specialized skills. Many students signed on as laborers to gain experience and adventure abroad while saving money for their studies. However, beset by homesickness and seriously demoralized by the treatment they received, many immigrants turned to drinking, gambling, and other intemperate diversions, neglecting to deposit their money in savings accounts for their families back in Japan and embarrassing the Japanese government which took its paternal obligations toward its citizens very seriously.

The Japanese were, on the whole, hard workers, but their native pride revolted against the treatment they received on the plantations. Unlike the Chinese, who bore their afflictions more patiently, some Japanese workers resorted to work stoppages, strikes, and even violence to protest conditions. Some would deliberately make themselves ill by drinking soy sauce in attempts to avoid a day of work and get some badly needed rest. These attempts were usually rewarded by beatings and the men returned to the fields to work. Some of those who were very ill died from being forced to work when they should have received medical attention. Hundreds of laborers tried to desert their plantations, change their names, and make new starts elsewhere in the islands, but, tracked by plantation police, they were flogged and incarcerated if captured. There were a few kind and humane planters who would not allow such brutality, but they seem to have been the exception. Japanese who worked as house servants also tended to receive kind and generous treatment, but most field laborers were treated as slaves.

The Japanese government was so alarmed by the situation, as reported by Special Commissioner Inoue, that Consul Nakamura was recalled in 1886 and replaced by another official, Andō Tarō, whose status was raised to that of diplomatic minister. He was unable to restore order to the Japanese communities in Hawaii until he received assistance from a Japanese Methodist minister from San Francisco, Rev. Miyama Kan'ichi. Andō and Miyama together founded two organizations, the Mutual Aid Association and the Temperance Society, through which they finally began to succeed in promoting order and self-respect among the immigrants. Several similar organizations also attempted to serve the same purpose.

The Hawaiian monarchy was overthrown in 1893 and replaced by a republican government with annexation to the United States as its goal. Still, the abuses on the plantations persisted and the Japanese laborers continued the struggle for their human rights with the new government. In spite of this, immigration accelerated. It has been estimated that some 56,579 Japanese immigrated to Hawaii during the brief republican period which ended in 1900. At that point, contract labor importation came to an end and the period of ''free immigration'' (those seeking work came and went of their own volition) began.

While nearly all of the Japanese immigrants during the nineteenth century were laborers under government-sponsored or private contracts, growing numbers of professional Japanese entered Hawaii as ''free'' immigrants: ministers, merchants, teachers, priests, doctors, businessmen, and other highly-educated immigrants. There were also those engaged in various illegal businesses who were either on the run from Japanese authorities or who simply sought new markets. Many of the businessmen intended to eventually move on to the American mainland, but some changed their plans and remained in Hawaii all of their lives. The opposite was true for many laborers who had originally intended to remain in Hawaii.

In 1898 Hawaii was annexed by the United States. Congress passed the Organic Act in 1900, making the U.S. Constitution applicable to Hawaii and putting a stop to contract immigration. Again, from that time on, all immigration was termed ''free.'' Wages, even for unskilled labor, were far better on the mainland, and tens of

thousands of Japanese immigrants could not resist this lure. Of the 71,281 Japanese free immigrants who travelled to Hawaii between 1900 and 1907, nearly half, as well as large numbers of former contract laborers, continued on to the mainland. Free immigration thus created severe labor shortages in Hawaii which began to offer incentives to Japanese to remain in the islands. Other problems arose on the American mainland.

Early Immigration Restrictions. By 1908, Japan had come to the forefront of world attention because of the tremendous strides made in the modernization of the country during the preceding forty years. Railroads, factories, office buildings, and a telegraph system had been rapidly built; the government and military had been completely overhauled; and a Western-style constitution had been given to the people by their emperor. In 1895 a modernized Japanese army badly trounced the aging Chinese empire. The army and navy went on to impress (and disturb) the Western nations by defeating Russia in 1905.

These events, plus the rapidly increasing Japanese population on the west coast of North America, were alarming to many older residents residing in that area. There was already long-standing prejudice, both official and nonofficial, against the Chinese residents who arrived during the gold rush days of 1850. Japanese immigrants became additional targets of this prejudice, seen by some as merely another type of Chinese. This made it impossible for them to assimilate, however much some may have tried. Matters came to a head in San Francisco in 1906 when the school board tried to force all Japanese children to attend a segregated school in Chinatown. This incident caused a severe strain in diplomatic relations between Japan and the United States.

President Theodore Roosevelt, who had been awarded the Nobel Peace Prize for his role in bringing the war between Japan and Russia to an end, defused the situation. Roosevelt personally persuaded the school board to withdraw its segregation ordinance. He then convinced Congress to grant him the power to forbid the entry of laborers whose passports had been issued for entry into another country which affected all Asians who had immigrated to Hawaii when it was an independent nation.

Roosevelt's next step was development of the notorious ''Gentlemen's Agreement.'' Rather than embarrass the Japanese by allowing Congress to impose immigration restrictions specifically directed against them, Roosevelt exchanged a series of documents with the Japanese government during 1907 and 1908 in which the Japanese were asked to put their own curbs on emigration by not issuing any passports to laborers bound for the United States. The agreement was finalized in 1908 with a con-

Japanese Immigration to Hawaii

Gannen-mono (1868)	148
Government Contracts (1885-1894)	29,069
Private Contracts (1894-1900)	56,579
Free Immigration (1900-1907)	71,281
Yobiyose Jidai (1908-1924)	<u>61,489</u>
Total (1868-1924)	218,566

Figure 1.3

ference between Secretary of State Elihu Root and Japanese Ambassador Plenipotentiary Takahira Kogorō. On its part, the United States agreed to accept laborers who were already in the country, plus their wives and children. While the Gentlemen's Agreement did not end Japanese immigration to the United States because of a provision allowing entry of family members, it did help to allay the fears of many white west coast residents because it was touted as an agreement which limited the entry of Japanese into the United States.

Married immigrants could still send for their families, and they did. This period, which ended in 1924, was called the *yobiyose jidai* ("period of summoning") by the Japanese. Unmarried immigrants even found it possible to obtain wives (and visas for them) through marriage brokers who advertised "picture brides." A man could select his future bride from a set of photographs and marry her by proxy. The new wife could then obtain papers to emigrate to America and meet her husband. All of the legal paperwork was handled by Japan.

In the hands of some entrepreneurs, the picture bride business was no more than a racket either for selling women or for selling passports and passage to women. Not all of the paperwork was handled with proper care,

nor were all of the proxy ceremonies conducted with becoming dignity. When the business came to the attention of members of the American public, it caused considerable negative publicity. Well-intended policies were further abused by those who untruthfully claimed family relations in the attempt to obtain visas. Between 1908 and 1924, 61,489 Japanese family members, including picture brides and reputed relatives, immigrated to the United States.

Before explaining the circumstances of the Immigration Act of 1924, let us summarize Japanese immigration statistics up to that point. Figure 1.3 presents statistics, by period, for Hawaii alone; bear in mind that not all people counted as immigrants remained to be counted later as residents. For comparison, Figure 1.4, based on data taken from the U.S. census, shows statistics for Japanese residents in both Hawaii and the mainland United States, by decade.

It is interesting to note how the Japanese population on the mainland increased in proportion to that in Hawaii and eventually surpassed it. However, these figures can be misleading. There were many who travelled between Japan and Hawaii or the U.S. mainland more than once and therefore, were counted more than once. Further, any

Japanese Residents in Hawaii and the United States Mainland

Year	Mainland	Hawaii	Total
1870	55		55
1880	148	116	264
1890	2,039	12,610	14,649
1900	24,326	61,111	85,437
1910	72,157	79,675	151,832
1920	111,010	109,274	220,284

Figure 1.4

who were bound for mainland stopped in Hawaii enroute and were counted there, too. Also, numbers for years prior to 1900 in the two charts may appear to be contradictive. This is due to the lack of precise records in Hawaii prior to annexation.

A total of 88,927 immigrant births and 29,098 deaths were reported to the Japanese government by 1924. Departures from Hawaii to Japan, the United States, or elsewhere, totaled 152,203. Of the 111,010 Japanese living in the contiguous states in 1920, 93,490 lived on the west coast—71,952 in California alone. By 1924, over half of the Japanese in the United States were American citizens.

About forty-five percent of the Japanese immigrants came from the Chugoku region in the western end of the main island of Honshu. Of these, the majority came from the two prefectures (districts) of Hiroshima and Yamaguchi. The second largest bloc came from the southern island of Kyushu, mainly from the Kumamoto and Fukuoka prefectures. Third in number after the Kyushu natives were immigrants from the island of Okinawa. Regional distinctions have always been important to the Japanese who ascribe different traits and characteristics to people of different prefectures. Dialects also vary sharply from region to region. Okinawans consider themselves an ethnic group apart from the Japanese, with their own language and culture, though the island has always been considered by the Japanese to be part of the Japanese empire. Many of the Japanese social organizations in Hawaii were established along regional lines.

The Immigration Act of 1924. Anti-Japanese sentiment both on the U.S. west coast and in Hawaii peaked in the early 1920s. Because of vigorous protests, the Japanese government had already stopped issuing passports to picture brides bound for the U.S. mainland in 1920, although passports continued to be issued to women bound for Hawaii. Feelings against Japanese in Hawaii were also exacerbated in 1920 by a strike of Japanese and Filipino laborers protesting that their salary of 77 cents for ten hours of work per day was not enough to meet the rising costs of living and asking for a raise to $1.25. While the strike was successful, bringing an improvement in living conditions on the plantations, ill feelings remained and some participants were imprisoned. Additionally, the solidarity of the Japanese communities with their Japanese-language newspapers and schools, was also seen as a threat by non-Japanese in both Hawaii and the U.S. mainland.

Also, by this time, a large and growing second-generation Japanese community had arisen. These *nisei* were of ambiguous citizenship. Born on American soil, they were legally U.S. citizens, but most of them were also registered at birth with the Japanese consulate, making them Japanese citizens as well. Because of the educations they were receiving at the Japanese schools, they were regarded with suspicion by other Americans who considered their loyalties to be equivocal.

Legislation was proposed to establish a quota on Japanese immigration, but a series of misunderstandings (some seemingly deliberate) caused the Japanese to be excluded from immigrating to the United States entirely. At the request of the U.S. President Calvin Coolidge's administration, Japanese Ambassador Hanihara Masanao wrote a letter to the U.S. Congress explaining the views of the Japanese government on immigration quotas. Unfortunately his letter hinted at "grave consequences" if anti-Japanese immigration laws were enacted. This phrase, when taken out of context by anti-Japanese agitators, was viewed as a threat to the United States. As a result, all Japanese or other foreigners of Japanese ancestry were barred from immigrating to the United States in the version of the immigration bill which passed in 1924, though "Japanese" were not specifically named in the bill itself. Deemed "aliens ineligible to citizenship," they remained so until 1952.

The Effects of World War II. By the beginning of World War II, nearly 1.7 million Japanese had emigrated with nearly a quarter-million of them settling in North America and Hawaii. As large as this number is, it is almost insignificant when compared to the huge numbers of Europeans who emigrated to the United States during the same period, especially when seen as a percentage of population increase in the country of origin. Only one percent of the population increase in Japan emigrated and no Japanese population in any major destination (United States, Brazil, Canada, Argentina, Peru) exceeded one percent of the total population. (Nearly all of the more than 1.2 million Japanese who migrated to other Asian countries during this same period were repatriated eventually.)

For Europeans, World War II began in 1939, with Hitler's invasion of Poland. For Americans, it began in December 1941, with the Japanese attack on Pearl Harbor. Actually, the war began in Asia in 1931, when extremists in the Japanese army bombed a railway in Manchuria and used the incident as an excuse to attack nearby Chinese troops. The "Manchurian Incident" was the first of a series of military incidents in East Asia. The Japanese military buildup had been watched with apprehension by the Americans for years and had done nothing to allay anti-Japanese fears among the citizenry. Second- and third-generation citizens felt more American than Japanese, but unlike people of European origin, they still *looked* Japanese and were regarded with increasing suspicion. When Pearl Harbor was attacked, actions concerning the Japanese in America began to snowball.

The action which caused the greatest amount of tragedy for the Japanese community in the United States was the uprooting of 120,313 immigrants and their families (including about 70,000 U.S. citizens) from their homes to relocation camps where they were incarcerated during most of World War II. This occurred on the mainland (but, strangely, not in Hawaii) for purported security reasons, but is considered a hysterical, racist reaction to the assault on Pearl Harbor. No such measures were taken against Americans of German or Italian origin. Property and businesses were expropriated and families were forced to travel to the camps with little preparation. Living conditions in the camps, which were located in desolate areas far from the west coast, were harsh.

Still, 23,000 nisei men and women volunteered to join the U.S. armed forces, with most of the men serving in Italy. It was the greatest of ironies for a man in uniform to bid farewell to his father through the wire fencing of a relocation camp. The Japanese American servicemen and women performed brilliantly, exhibiting bravery and patriotism in defense of the United States and suffering over 9,000 casualties and 600 dead. No act of "subversion" by their interned family members was ever brought to light. A movement for reparations to citizens of Japanese descent was initiated several decades later by the U.S. government, and in 1990, the Ronald Reagan administration began to make reparatory payments to internment camp survivors and their heirs. While accepted as a gesture of good will, the reparations did not make up for the loss of valuable property and the mental anguish suffered by interned Japanese.

The End of Restrictions. During the Allied Occupation of Japan after World War II, Japanese were not permitted to emigrate. In addition to this, over three million military personnel and civilians were repatriated, putting tremendous strain on the resources of a country which had been largely destroyed by war. In 1952, with the Occupation coming to an end, emigration was permitted and encouraged by the Japanese government once again. In that same year, the McCarran-Walter Act re-established a U.S. immigration quota, with exceptions allowed for "non-quota" immigrants such as foreign wives of servicemen and close relatives of U.S. citizens. Thus, with a quota of only 100 immigrants allowed per year for Japan, an average of five times that number actually entered the United States over the next eight years. However, the number of Japanese leaving their country from 1952 to 1969 was still less than ten percent of the number who had left before 1940. Again, they tended to come from southwestern Japan and Okinawa.

The Dwight D. Eisenhower administration, desiring to rebuild Japan as a safeguard against the growing communist threat in China and elsewhere in Asia, lavished economic aid upon the United States' former enemy. The resulting growth created a need for domestic labor in Japan which obviated the need for the labor force to seek employment abroad. By 1969, only 160,921 Japanese had emigrated: 87,122 to North America (nearly all to the United States), 69,792 to South America (mostly to Brazil), and 4,007 to other destinations. As population pressure increases, the Japanese continue to emigrate on a small scale with the majority being from white collar occupations. From the 1970s, many Japanese businesses expanded abroad, taking large numbers of employees with them. Though most employees returned to Japan after a "tour of duty," some remained permanently in their host countries. In the 1980s, immigration to the United States fluctuated between ten and twenty thousand annually. Continual increases in the cost of living in Japan will, no doubt, cause the rate of emigration to accelerate. Though the United States will continue to draw large numbers of immigrants, it is reasonable to expect that other countries will also be recipients.

Korean Immigration

An interesting feature of Korean immigration to the United States is that the great majority of the immigrants have been Christians, mostly Protestants. The story of their immigration, as with the Chinese and Japanese, has a highly political tone. Though thousands of Koreans immigrated (mostly to Hawaii) at the turn of the twentieth century, several factors prevented their immigration in large numbers until the latter third of that century. Therefore the Korean community in the United States, now centered in Los Angeles, is still largely an immigrant community of the first generation. There are divisions within the community, caused as much by social and ideological divisions among those from southern Korea as by the division of Korea, itself into two mutually hostile parts. There is also a gap between more recent arrivals and the thoroughly Americanized descendants of earlier immigrants.

Early Immigration to Hawaii. A few dozen Koreans, most of them diplomats and students and two of them sons of the Emperor Kojong, visited the United States in the late nineteenth century. (Although Korea has never been an empire, its king took the title of emperor in 1897 to show the world that Korea considered itself to be independent and no longer a vassal state of China. The new title expressed the ruler's status as an equal to the emperors of China, Japan, and Russia, all of whom wanted to control his country.) One of the group, a young man, Sŏ Chae-p'il, did not return and became a U.S. citizen, marrying an American woman, and changing his name to Philip Jaisohn. Full-scale immigration, however, began in Hawaii in 1903, shortly after its annexation by the United States. The attraction was, as it had been earlier for the Chinese and Japanese, the work available on the sugar plantations.

Chinese laborers had been brought to Hawaii because the local Hawaiian population and other Pacific Islanders were found to be unsuited to plantation labor and experiments with various European groups had proven to be too expensive. The Chinese worked well, but the locals began to fear their numbers. The Japanese were brought in to offset this situation and eventually similar fears arose concerning them. (Between 1890 and 1900, the Japanese population of Hawaii leaped from 12,000 to 61,000.) The Japanese were also prouder and less tractable than the Chinese, though they too were hard workers. Therefore, the planters became interested in hiring other foreign labor, such as the Koreans, to offset the Japanese influx.

The ancient Korean kingdom, which had been a vassal state (subservient territory) of China for many centuries, was immersed in difficulties at this time. Japan forced the "Hermit Kingdom" out of self-imposed isolation in 1876 and was forcibly attempting to become the country's patron. During the 1890s, China, Japan, and Russia competed for influence in Korea and Manchuria, the vast and rich ancestral homeland of China's ruling dynasty. Japan defeated China in 1895 and Russia in 1905 in contests over ascendancy in these two regions. The Korean people themselves were suffering from the corruption and savagery of a declining, centuries-old, inward-oriented royal dynasty—many were moving into Russian territory to start new lives.

In Hawaii, the monarchy had been abolished and the young republic was annexed by the United States in 1898. This move was favored by the planters because of the market it would provide for their sugar. However, annexation also cleared the way for a mass exodus of Asian laborers in Hawaii who were attracted by higher wages on the mainland. Many who stayed in Hawaii preferred to no longer work in the cane fields. In addition, Congressional legislation in 1882 barring Chinese immigrants now applied to Hawaii as well. Faced with a higher demand for production and a shrinking labor force, the territorial government had to persuade the federal government to approve the import of more Japanese. Wages were raised and working conditions were improved in an attempt to retain the laborers.

In 1897, and again in 1898, the planters tried to obtain Korean labor as well. Since Hawaii would not come entirely under the U.S. Constitution until 1900, the planters wanted to import cheap Asian labor into the islands before contract labor became illegal. However, the plans to import Koreans failed both times as the Korean government did not have an efficient system in place that would allow its citizens to emigrate.

In 1901, the United States changed governments when William McKinley was elected president and the idea of importing Korean labor into Hawaii was revived. Favorable reports of Koreans were circulated stating that they were better workers than either the Chinese or Japanese. To facilitate their immigration, the Hawaiian planters sought aid from the new U.S. Minister to Korea, the influential Horace N. Allen.

Allen had been serving in Korea as a Presbyterian missionary since 1884. He immediately gained the friendship and trust of the king by giving medical assistance to members of the royal family when they were wounded in an abortive coup attempt. Taking an interest in international politics, Allen sought the appointment of the U.S. Minister to Korea. With the help of his friend David Deshler, whose stepfather was a friend of McKinley, Allen finally received his appointment in 1901. Always seeking concessions for Americans in Korea, Allen advocated sending Korean laborers to Hawaii as a means of involving the United States in Korean affairs to the detriment of Japanese interests.

Emperor Kojong was favorable to the idea, especially when he learned that it was possible for Koreans to go where the Chinese could not. There were still several difficulties to overcome—the Hawaiian planters wanted to be sure that Korean workers would not be lured to the mainland by professional recruiters as had been tens of thousands of Japanese workers. As for Korea, the Korean government had long-standing restrictions on emigration, and the possibility of Koreans leaving their country and then returning, perhaps with unorthodox foreign ideas in their heads, troubled many officials. (The 1884 coup attempt had involved some young Koreans who had absorbed Western ideals from Japanese sources. Some of them escaped to America, received further education, and later returned to cause more unrest.) Additionally, as mentioned earlier, the Korean government had no experience with or understanding of emigration regulations and paperwork.

Allen and his associates worked to find a way around the emperor's and planters' concerns as well as the U.S. immigration and contract labor laws. Allen, having been ordered to stay out of Korean internal affairs, deceived both the Hawaiian and the federal government over the nature of the setup and his own deep involvement in it. He persuaded the Korean emperor to set up a Department of Emigration, awarding an emigration franchise to Deshler who was introduced to Kojong as an official of the fictitious "Territorial Bureau of Immigration." To obtain support from other Korean officials, Deshler distributed bribes—a practice which was not unknown to the Korean government.

Prospective emigrants were very poor and federal regulations would not allow their travel to be financed by the planters. Therefore the Deshler East-West Development Company, doubling as the Deshler Bank and using money secretly loaned to it by the planters' association in Hawaii (the planters were also willing to bend laws as necessary), loaned money to the emigrants and put them under an obligation similar to that outlined in a labor contract. Thus, arrangements were finally concluded, with none of the other parties involved having full knowledge of Allen's and Deshler's unethical and illegal preparations. Deshler received $54 for every worker he sent to Hawaii. The Korean Government sold passports to its people for one dollar apiece.

Many Koreans were reluctant to emigrate to a far, unknown place and recruitment was difficult at first. This problem was solved by the actions of American missionaries. They, hoping to have more influence over their flocks in a land already Christianized, painted for their congregations a picture of a rich land of opportunities, both economic and spiritual. As a result, a group of 101 Koreans (a large minority of whom were Christians), arrived in Hawaii in January 1903. Due to on-board proselytizing, almost half of them were converted by the time they landed. Fifteen of the group were denied admission for health reasons, but eighty-six (forty-eight men, sixteen women, and twenty-two children) were allowed to stay.

Most missionaries in Korea enthusiastically encouraged emigration to Hawaii, but a few opposed it because of the detrimental effect it had on the growth of a native church in Korea itself. There were also Korean officials who opposed emigration for several reasons: distress over rumors of ill-treatment and slavery, concern about the spread of western ideas espoused by emigrants returning to Korea—a few may simply have been insufficiently bribed by Deshler. Some were opposed to any kind of tie to the United States. Still, about 600 Koreans had arrived in Hawaii by the end of June 1903. Between 450–500 of these were men who proved to be good workers. In fact, the Koreans worked so well that the planters considered importing fewer Japanese (allowing them to reduce wages).

In June of 1903, however, Korean emigration came to a temporary halt as new U.S. immigration officials became aware of the illegalities of the process. This news strengthened the position of those in Korea who opposed emigration and caused great difficulties for both those prepared to emigrate and for Deshler's company. The Deshler Bank had lent fares and pocket money to the emigrants and needed continuous emigration to keep the money flowing. Also, the emigrants who had sold their homes and goods could not easily return to Korea if turned back in Japan or Hawaii.

In Hawaii, matters were made worse by incidents involving embezzlement of workers' pay, the refusal of some workers to repay their loans, and conflicts between some of the Japanese and Koreans. Then a lawsuit against E. Faxon Bishop, the representative of the sugar planters in Korea, for alleged violations of immigration and contract laws, brought matters to a head. A crisis was averted by a ruling in favor of Bishop. The advantageous ruling was largely due to the strong influence of the planters. Bribery was used by both sides, more skillfully by the planters, and Koreans continued to immigrate. By early 1905, 7,226 Koreans had emigrated to Hawaii: 6,048 men, 637 women, and 541 children. Nearly half of them arrived in 1904.

Emigration under Japanese Rule. War broke out between Japan and Russia in February 1904. Their dispute was mainly over the natural resources and railroad right-of-way in Manchuria, but it also involved the desire of each country to influence Korea's policies. In a sea battle in the Tsushima Straits in May 1905, the Japanese navy destroyed a Russian fleet. The following September, President Theodore Roosevelt persuaded the combatants to sign a peace treaty recognizing Japan's ''paramount interests'' in Korea. In November 1905, Japan established a ''protectorate'' there.

The Korean government had suspended emigration in April 1905, again expressing concerns over poor working conditions and poverty in Hawaii and alleging that Koreans in Mexico were being sold into slavery. A few hundred emigrants already enroute were virtually the last to arrive in Hawaii for several decades. Another blow to Korean emigration was Roosevelt's release of Horace Allen as the U.S. Minister. Allen's popularity had begun to wane after the assassination of McKinley late in 1901 and even the protests of Emperor Kojong did not change the U.S. president's mind.

When the Japanese government established a ''Korean Emigrant Protection Law'' in July 1906, its true purpose was to place tighter restrictions on Korean emigration. Passports were to be issued to Koreans by the Japanese government which resented Korean competition with Japanese labor abroad.

Figure 1.5 compares Japanese and Korean immigration to Hawaii before the Japanese takeover. It illustrates how the Japanese had cause for alarm over the relative growth of the Korean population there. Actually, the percentage of Koreans, as opposed to Japanese, who remained in Hawaii, was even greater. At this time, large numbers of Japanese were moving to California; however, they still comprised between sixty and seventy percent of the plantation laborers in Hawaii.

Japanese and Korean Immigration to Hawaii Prior to Korea's Becoming a Japanese Protectorate

Year	Japanese	Koreans	Ratio
1903	6625	1118	5.9:1
1904	5548	3965	1.4:1
1905 (February)	1070	688	1.6:1
Total:	13243	5771	2.3:1

Figure 1.5

Nearly all of the Korean immigrants up to 1905 were from urban areas, most likely because Deshler's East-West Development Company had offices in large cities and ports. About half of the immigrants were from the area around the capital city of Seoul. This accounts for the high percentage of Christians among the immigrants, since the missionaries first concentrated their efforts on the cities. In *The Korean Frontier in America*, Wayne K. Patterson speculates that many of the emigrants may not have been native to the cities and had already been uprooted by oppressive economic conditions, civil strife, and the Sino-Japanese and Russo-Japanese wars with their attendant disasters. (Christians had been spiritually and psychologically uprooted as well by their change of religion.) Thus, another move to a foreign country was less difficult for them to contemplate than it would have been for those who were still settled near their ancestral tombs.

In the U.S. mainland, rising prejudice against the Japanese was also being applied to the thousand or so Koreans who had moved there from Hawaii. On the government level, now that Korean affairs were being administered by the Japanese, restrictions on Japanese immigration were considered to apply to Koreans as well. In March 1907, the U.S. government passed legislation refusing to admit to the mainland immigrants whose passports had been issued for travel to a U.S. possession or another country. Wives of already resident aliens were still allowed to immigrate, however.

The ''Gentlemen's Agreement'' of 1907–1908 between Japan and the United States also applied to Koreans. This meant that Koreans in Hawaii could remain there or return home after they quit their plantation jobs, but they could not go to the mainland. Korean emigration and movement to the mainland slowed to a trickle and then stopped when Japan annexed Korea in 1910. By then, over 8,000 Koreans had emigrated. The U.S. census reported 4,533 residing in Hawaii and only 461 on the mainland. The rest had gone elsewhere or returned home. The number who returned to Korea decreased to nothing after the Japanese annexation of their homeland.

Korean Post War Politics and Immigration. Because so many of the immigrants were Christians, the church served Korean communities in the United States in many ways. Methodist churches were organized in Hawaii and San Francisco in 1905 and other sects were active at the time as well. In 1918 a Korean Christian Church was organized. These churches served not only as places of spiritual nourishment and comfort, but as social and educational centers, helping the immigrants to learn about and become accustomed to their new environment.

Like the Japanese, the Koreans in Hawaii established schools to pass on their language and culture to the younger generation. Adults also took advantage of after-hours schools, many of which were held in and sponsored by churches. The schools had much to accomplish, considering the high rate of illiteracy among the adults and the declining interest among the young who were becoming Americanized in spite of the prejudices of their neighbors. The schools were hampered by lack of educational materials and the Bible had to serve as a text in many cases. In spite of these disadvantages, most Koreans studied very hard, learning the English language more rapidly than the Chinese or Japanese. They also more readily gave up their native costumes and hair styles in their efforts to assimilate. Of course, such progress meant that the cultural gap widened between the youth and their more conservative elders.

Besides the churches and various secular community organizations, political organizations played an important part in the lives of Korean immigrants. They caused sharp divisions in the community, because conditions at home were so bad politically and economically that it was impossible for Koreans abroad to agree on what should be done. Three political leaders, all American-educated, tried to unite the immigrants and failed because of disagreements among themselves. They were Syngman Rhee (Yi Sŭng-man, 1875–1965) who desired to turn world opinion against the Japanese and thereby force them to relinquish their hold upon Korea; Pak Yong-man (1881–1928) who organized a militia with the aim of liberating Korea by military means; and Ahn Chang-ho (1878–1938) whose solution was to help each of his countrymen strengthen himself spiritually to prepare for independence.

These three men tried to work together for awhile, but their basic differences of philosophy soon drove them and their respective followers apart. Pak split with Rhee and went to China in 1916 where he was assassinated by another Korean in 1928. Rhee's and Ahn's organizations continued to compete with each other, even after Ahn was tortured to death in a Japanese prison in 1938. Rhee went on to win American support for his efforts and became the first president of the Republic of Korea in 1948. Actually he was president of only half of the country as Soviet-trained Korean communists had control by then of the whole northern half of Korea.

During World War II, Koreans in America were in a very strange position. Technically they were Japanese citizens and, as such, were enemy aliens and a threat to national security. In fact, they were staunch anti-Japanese supporters of the Allied cause. One Korean leader in Hawaii even traveled to California to advocate the internment of Japanese. Koreans in Hawaii were considered enemy aliens, though none were interned, while mainland Koreans were declared not to be enemy aliens. In either case, most Koreans began wearing badges stating "I am Korean."

More divisions appeared in the Korean community in the United States after World War II and the Korean War (1950–1953). Korean politics were no less turbulent during this period than before, with riots, military coups, and assassinations occurring frequently. Political disagreements spilled over into emigrant communities as well. Rhee ruled South Korea with an iron hand, and his regime was notoriously corrupt. Many Korean Americans opposed him and he dealt with them by accusing them of being communist sympathizers. When the anticommunist "McCarthy era" was in full swing, such accusations did not have to be true to be deadly. There were also problems between southern Koreans and northern Korean refugees as well as between recent immigrants and the long-established, highly Americanized descendants of early immigrants. War brides of American servicemen were considered second-class Koreans by all the rest and successful Korean Americans of peasant ancestry resented the airs of more recently arrived, impoverished, former gentry.

After violent anti-government demonstrations in which many lives were lost, Rhee was forced to resign the presidency in 1960. General Park Chung-hee, seizing power in 1961, was elected president of the civil government in 1963. In spite of tremendous economic growth, with all of these continuing political troubles, many Koreans were eager to emigrate. On the American side, the 1965 Immigration Act made it much easier for Koreans, along with others throughout the world, to enter the United States. While the Korean population of the United States was a mere 69,130 in 1970 according to the census for that year, by 1980 it had risen to 354,529. The numbers rose again in the mid-1980s after the South Korean government lifted some of the restrictions on its citizens regarding travel abroad. While continuing political troubles are no doubt driving people to seek lives elsewhere, Korea's rapidly expanding economy also contributes to emigration. Many Korean companies are opening offices in the United States, providing opportunities for employees to get a taste of life abroad.

Spread throughout the United States, Koreans reside mainly in urban areas, although the Korean community, centered in Los Angeles, remains a very young community.

South Asian Immigration

Use of the term "Indian" has been a source of confusion in discussions about ethnic groups in the Americas ever since Christopher Columbus mistakenly applied the name to the Arawak tribes he found living in the Caribbean islands. Even after other explorers realized that America was not the "Indies," the name stuck. Now that large numbers of people from the South Asian subcontinent are arriving to live in American countries, more fully descriptive terms such as "East Indian," "Indo-American," or "Asian Indian" are necessary to denote these people. The term "Asian Indian" was first used in the 1980 U.S. census. In library catalogs, including those of the Library of Congress and the Family History Library, the term "East Indians" is used.

It is clear that the term "Indian," even when applied generally to people from India alone, does not do justice to the wealth of cultural, religious, political, and linguistic differences found in that country. Many of these cultures are of great antiquity and are a source of pride to their adherents. The common stereotype of an Indian is that he is a follower of the Hindu religion. While the majority are Hindu, other major South Asian religions are also represented in the Indo-American community: Sikh, Muslim, and Buddhist, for the most part, with a few Jains, Parsees, and Christians. Among the different languages spoken are Hindi, Gujarati, Punjabi, Bengali, and Tamil.

In this text, the term ''South Asian'' will be used because it is understood to apply to inhabitants of the subcontinent in general, and is not limited to describing citizens of India. ''East Indian,'' will be used when appropriate, both to describe people from modern India and early immigrants from all of South Asia because modern national and ethnic distinctions were usually not made before World War II. The great majority of immigrants from South Asia are from modern India, with Pakistan a distant second place, and a few thousand each are from Sri Lanka, Bangladesh, and Nepal. These countries (except for Nepal, which was always independent) were all part of India when it was a colony of the British Empire prior to its independence in 1947/1948. Numbers of people from Sikkim and Bhutan in America are extremely small.

It has been estimated that about forty percent of the South Asians in the United States are Gujaratis from India and another twenty percent are Punjabis from a region which straddles the India-Pakistan border. East Indians form large minorities and even majorities of the populations of several countries far from India: Fiji, Trinidad, Surinam, Mauritius, Guyana, Indonesia, Singapore, etc. Many East Indians have entered the United States from these countries, as well as from several countries in Africa, rather than directly from the subcontinent. A good number of East Indian immigrants never lived in India.

Before the twentieth century, only a handful of East Indians entered the United States. According to records of the Immigration and Naturalization Service, by 1900, only 696 Indians had immigrated. The rate increased considerably after that, but was still less than 17,000 by 1965. Many were laborers, merchants, or students, and large numbers did not remain. The tremendous increases in immigration seen during the 1970s through early 1990s (see Figure 1.1) are due to the relaxing of immigration laws and elimination of quotas by the Lyndon B. Johnson presidential administration in 1965. Records on South Asians who immigrated during the twentieth century are not available at the Family History Library because they are too recently created and nearly all of the people recorded are still living, but they can be obtained from the Immigration and Naturalization Service by those legally entitled. Older records do not deal specifically with South Asians because of their small numbers.

The East Indians who immigrated during the nineteenth and early twentieth centuries ran headfirst into the same prejudices and racist anti-immigration policies experienced by East Asians and Mexicans. Many East Indians entered the United States through Canada, which, like India, has long-standing ties to the British Empire and many returned to Canada in response to the racism.

In 1906, East Indians were declared ineligible for U.S. citizenship on the grounds that they were not white. Their skin color notwithstanding, these people are Caucasians, and on that basis the decision was reversed in 1910. They were again declared ineligible in 1923 by the U.S. Supreme Court and some who had been naturalized had their citizenship revoked before the decision was once more reversed in 1946.

This dizzying performance by the government caused many East Indians to give up and leave the United States. Among the ones who remained, those who were literate and could speak English began to combat discrimination by organizing themselves into support groups and by publishing newspapers in several South Asian languages. One San Francisco paper called the *Ghadar* was the voice of a party of men from Punjab who were also active in efforts to free their homeland from British dominion. In 1918, fourteen members of the Ghadar group were convicted and imprisoned by the U.S. government for violating neutrality laws through their anti-British activities. (Since India's independence in 1947, these men have been held in honor for their part in the movement.)

Immigration from South Asia slowed greatly during the period between the World Wars. Then, in 1946, naturalization rights were restored by the U.S. Congress which removed India from the ''barred immigration'' zone of Asia (the act which established the zone had been passed in 1917). Shortly afterward, India was partitioned into India and Pakistan; the latter country divided again when East Pakistan gained independence in 1971 and became known as Bangladesh. The 1965 Immigration Act made it possible for nearly fifty thousand educated professionals to immigrate from South Asia at a time when they needed employment badly and opportunities were lacking at home. With their families, they have formed the basis of a largely prosperous South Asian community in the United States which tends to live in urban areas and college towns of every state. New York's greater urban area has the highest concentration of South Asians, followed by the San Francisco Bay and Los Angeles areas and Chicago.

Philippines Immigration

There are some striking comparisons and contrasts between the South Asian and Filipino experiences in the United States. Like South Asians, Filipinos did not immigrate in large numbers before the early 1900s (from 1905 to 1914, about 6,000 South Asians immigrated, before they were discouraged by state and federal restrictions; from 1907–1940, about 108,000 Filipinos immigrated). The first substantial numbers of South Asians and Filipinos came as students, then as laborers. Both nationalities suffered under foreign domination: India under the British, the Philippines under Spanish and American rule. The majority of early South Asian and Filipino immigrants came from specific geographic areas: Gujarati-speaking Sikhs from the Punjab, Ilocos-speaking laborers from Luzon. Both groups were politically active: South Asians in the anti-British Ghadar party, Filipinos in labor organizing and campaigning for Filipino independence movements. Both groups, initially finding work in agriculture, suffered discrimination in employment, housing, and social opportunities. Filipinos and South Asians also generally reached the continental United States indirectly: Filipinos via Hawaiian plantations and Indians via Canada, particularly British Columbia.

However, the Filipino experience differs from that of South Asia in three key areas. The Filipino presence in the United States, though limited before the twentieth century, has long-standing historical roots. Spanish galleons brought many Filipino sailors to the New World as far back as the sixteenth century. There is evidence, suggested by Crouchett, Espina, Schurz, and others (see bibliography at the end of this chapter) that Filipino sailors may have settled in Mexican territories during the Spanish colonial period, eventually making their way to what later became the southwestern United States. We do know that Filipino colonies of St. Malo and Manila Village were established in Louisiana near the mouth of the Mississippi in 1833 and 1897, respectively. However, as stated earlier, the first large numbers of Filipinos came in 1903 as students. Called *pensionados*, for the act approved by the Philippine Commission under William Howard Taft, most returned to the Philippines. The first large group to settle in the United States permanently came as laborers to Hawaii.

In 1908, to fill labor shortfalls created by the Gentleman's Agreement with Japan, the Hawaiian Sugar Planters' Association recruited Tagalog and Cebuano-speaking Filipinos from Manila and Cebu City to work on plantations. In 1915, agents recruited mainly Ilocos-speaking workers from Luzon who, because of economic hardships, were more willing to emigrate. According to statistical records, during 1910 to 1919, 29,000 Filipinos entered Hawaii, 4,000 returned home, and 2,000 went on to the mainland. The first wave to the mainland called themselves *Pinays* and *Pinoys* (derived from Fili*pinas* and Fili*pinos*—females and males from the Philippines). In the 1920s, 74,000 went to Hawaii, nearly 26,000 returned, and 13,000 went to the mainland. From 1930 to 1935, 15,000 came, but 31,000 returned home, discouraged by the Great Depression and discriminatory laws. Of the 119,000 who came in those years, there were 9,000 women and 6,000 children. Like South Asians, the Filipino community had a huge ratio of men to women.

Of those planning to stay temporarily, about eighty percent never returned to the Philippines.

The relationship of the United States to the Philippines also affected immigration policy. Since the Philippines was a dependency of the United States, affirmed in the defeat of Aguinaldo's guerrilla forces following the Spanish-American War, it did not fall under the purview of federal immigration laws enacted in 1917 and 1924 and discussed earlier. In addition, the courts had difficulty defining who was Caucasian when confronting the original Aryans of South Asia. Finally, because they, in fact, were entitled to most of the rights of U.S. citizens, anti-Asian legislators could not treat Filipinos like the Chinese, Japanese, and Koreans—although they were barred from full naturalization. (Naturalization had been statutorily restricted, with the exception of ex-slaves, since 1790 to whites only.) In one area, however, state lawmakers did succeed in barring Filipinos, despite their rights as natives of a U.S. dependency: marriage to whites.

In a 1929 survey published at the height of anti-Asian hysteria (*Marriage Laws and Decisions in the United States*), Geoffrey May reveals problems in defining who could marry whom. Most states in the West and South prohibited marriages between people of color and whites. The excluded ethnic groups included African Americans, Native Americans, and ''Mongolians,'' which might be defined as those of Chinese or Japanese ancestry. This applied to marriages in Arizona, California, Georgia, Idaho, Mississippi, Missouri, Nebraska, Oregon, Utah, and Virginia. Georgia, South Dakota, and Wyoming added ''Malayan'' ancestry as a criterion, probably to impact the Filipino population. Though South Asians had dwindled severely in numbers, ''East Indians,'' too, were singled out for exclusion. Louisiana simply prohibited ''persons of color.'' Nevada excluded persons whose skin was ''black, brown, yellow, or red.'' While not targeting all Asians, Montana outlawed intermarriage of whites with anyone who had one-eighth or more Chinese or Japanese blood, which could be applicable to many Filipinos of mixed blood. In Mississippi, one-eighth or more ''Mongolian blood'' was unacceptable; in Oregon one-quarter was the limit. The average penalty in each state was not inconsequential: six months to a year in prison, $300 to $500 in fines. However, nonresidents in most cases bypassed the rules by marrying in a more liberal state. Washington state, surprisingly, though it had a history of anti-Asian violence, had no laws in place against interracial marriage until 1937 when it followed California, Oregon, and Nevada in nullifying marriages between ''Malayans'' and whites.

Anti-immigrant fervor, fueled by the great depression, also affected Filipinos. The Tydings-McDuffie Act of May 1, 1934, limited Filipino immigration to fifty individuals per year and offered paid passage home. As the earlier "Barred Zone" Act of 1917 had with South Asians, Tydings-McDuffie devastated the Filipino community. Real numbers actually declined (although only about twenty percent actually returned to the Philippines) until after World War II, when the Philippines gained its independence and Filipinos were granted U.S. citizenship as the result of several factors.

Prior to World War II, many Filipinos enlisted in the U.S. Merchant Marine and Navy. Though the Merchant Marine Act of 1936 barred non-citizens from service, they had nevertheless earned a measure of respect from the armed forces. The occupation of the Philippines by the Japanese was the final crucible for Filipino valor. Like South Asians, who had shown meritorious service in both the British and American army in two wars, Filipinos showed incontrovertibly their patriotism and their fighting spirit in World War II. Thousands volunteered to fight against an Asian aggressor. Continued discrimination against South Asians, Chinese, and Filipinos was untenable if the United States was to retain their native lands as allies. Consequently, immigration laws were gradually loosened. The Luce-Cellier Act of 1946 raised the quota of Filipinos to 100 and allowed for naturalization. Many Filipino women gained citizenship as war brides. The postwar economic boom brought many back to work in Hawaii. Finally, in 1965, national origins were no longer considered, and many thousands were allowed to emigrate from previously excluded areas of the world. Interestingly, although South Asian communities have proliferated throughout the United States, the highest concentrations of Filipinos are still in Hawaii and California.

Southeast Asia Immigration

Former French Indochinese Countries. Of the more than 600,000 Vietnamese living in the United States in the 1990s, three-fourths entered the country as refugees after 1975. Before that, most Vietnamese immigrants were the families of American servicemen. Though Vietnam and its neighbors, Cambodia and Laos, had long been colonies of French Indochina and most of the educated class spoke French and practiced Catholicism, these people were relocated to the United States because of the sense of responsibility the U.S. government felt toward them. Many had worked for or with the U.S. government and armed forces during America's involvement in the Vietnam War, or were related to people who had. All feared they would be targeted by the victorious communist regime as collaborators.

The Nixon administration negotiated a cease-fire with North Vietnam which took effect in January 1973.

While this did not end the war, it signaled the end of active American involvement. The South Vietnamese government endured until April 1975 when Saigon fell to communist forces. During this two-year period, over 130,000 South Vietnamese were evacuated to the United States. The final phase of the evacuation was rushed and chaotic. In the last week alone, arrangements were made by the U.S. embassy staff there for the departure of 60,000 Vietnamese.

Immigration records these evacuees, five percent of whom were Cambodians, provide much information on them, including age, family size, occupation, education, skills, and religion. The evacuees were flown to Guam to be processed for immigration to the United States. Following that, they were flown to four receiving centers: Camp Pendleton, California; Fort Chaffee, Arkansas; Elgin Air Force Base, Florida; and Fort Indiantown Gap, Pennsylvania. Here they were given alien registration numbers, social security numbers, and medical examinations. They were also screened for a security clearance, a process which included the taking of photographs and fingerprints, and were required to register with voluntary agencies which had contracted with the U.S. government to help ease their entry into American society.

By the end of 1975, nearly all of the evacuees had settled in the United States with a few thousand attempting to return to Vietnam or going on to France and other countries. Papers on these immigrants can be obtained only by those legally entitled, through proper application, as explained in Chapter Two. Due to the rushed nature of the immigrants' departure from Vietnam, they may be the only records of genealogical value which can be found for many. Because they have too recently immigrated and nearly all of the people recorded are still living, the Family History Library has yet to acquire any of these records.

Over ninety percent of the evacuees found employment by 1979, but the majority of their jobs were menial, minimum-wage types of employment. It is to their credit that they worked long hours to improve their situations, but inevitably this caused a conflict with other low-income groups which were displaced by the industrious Vietnamese. The whole situation was an echo of the tensions aroused by low-paid Chinese workers a century earlier.

The evacuees of 1975 are referred to as the "first wave." The "second wave," which began arriving in 1979, was an even more unfortunate group which included the well-known "boat people." These were refugees who had escaped from Vietnam in small boats, many of them unseaworthy and poorly provisioned. A quarter million of these boat people were ethnic Chinese who had been declared an undesirable bourgeois element by the communist regime. They were the prey of corrupt officials on land and pirates at sea. Many were ignored by passing ships as they begged for assistance. Exact figures are unavailable, but some estimates place the death rate among the boat people during their odyssey at fifty percent.

Several Southeast Asian countries refused asylum to the boat people, forcing them to move on. In 1979, an international conference was convened at Geneva, Switzerland, to discuss solutions to the problem. Some countries were persuaded to provide temporary asylum with a promise that other countries would take the refugees off their hands as soon as possible. The number of Indochinese refugees arriving in the United States alone shot from 20,400 in 1978 to 80,700 in 1979; then to 166,700 in 1980; and to 132,500 in 1981. Figures subsequently leveled to about 50,000 refugees per year from Vietnam, Cambodia, and Laos combined, plus about 5,000 more who entered as duly processed immigrants. The huge influx of desperate refugees strained the resources of even the most prosperous host countries.

Also included in the second wave, among the ''land people'' refugees from Cambodia and Laos, were about 50,000 Hmong people from the mountains of all three countries. The second wave was more diverse ethnically and religiously than the first wave had been with proportionately fewer Vietnamese, many more Buddhists, and far fewer Catholics. They tended to be poorer and less educated. Integrating them into American society was more of a challenge. The Refugee Act of 1980 provided eighteen months of domestic resettlement assistance and reimbursements for medical expenses up to three years. Most of these immigrants assimilated quite well, moving off public assistance quickly. Their children tended to excel in school. Others had trouble adjusting and some children became involved in gangs.

As of 1990, immigrants from the three Indochinese nations numbered just over 900,000 with Vietnamese (and ethnic Chinese from Vietnam) making up about two-thirds of that number. Laotian and Cambodian immigrants numbered less than 150,000 each with Hmongs numbering about 85,000. California and Texas are the states with the largest Indochinese populations with the former state far in the lead. Most immigrants tend to prefer California because of relatives and friends who are already established there. However, Vietnamese, Cambodians, Hmong, and Laotians are found in every state.

Aside from the Filipinos and Indochinese discussed above, immigration of other Southeast Asian groups has been in fairly small numbers. As of 1990, most numerous have been Thais at 112,000. Following them are Indonesians and Malaysians, with 44,000 and 28,000, respectively. Burmese have not entered the United States in sufficient numbers. Singaporeans may be listing themselves as Chinese, Malay, or East Indian and thus are undercounted. All of these groups began to immigrate in significant numbers only during the 1970s. Apart from Thais who came as wives of American servicemen, the great majority of adult Thais, Indonesians, Malaysians, and Burmese of both sexes are professional or technical people who work in white collar occupations. All prefer the urban areas of California, New York, and other large states.

Possible Problems in Interpreting Data

For thousands of years, Chinese culture has been the paramount influence in East Asia. In Southeast Asia, Chinese influence has vied with that of India except in Vietnam where Chinese influence was the stronger. Korea and Japan have managed to maintain their own identities, but each has learned much from and owes a great debt to China. In each of the smaller countries it is easy to identify elements of Chinese civilization, but it is also interesting to see how each element has been changed and adapted to suit local needs.

Confucian social and political philosophy, which greatly influences family life and the keeping of genealogical and historical records, has been studied and used to a degree in each of the countries peripheral to China. Buddhist religious philosophy, received from India, modified in China, and passed on, has had its own unique influence. Always pervasive in China is the ancient philosophy of Taoism, which has had much to do with adaptation of Confucianism, Buddhism, and other philosophies to suit contemporary needs in China. The main concern here is the impact these philosophies had on written languages and systems for romanization, calendars, family relationships and adoption practices, naming practices, record keeping practices, changes in political boundaries and the effects on record keeping, and the matters of falsehood and error in records.

The main vehicle of these influences is the Chinese language which had its own standardized writing system many centuries before others existed in East Asia. Indeed, classical Chinese played a role in East Asia similar to that played by Latin in Europe during the same period. Now, just as Europeans no longer communicate in Latin and may have trouble reading records in that language, East Asians do not correspond in classical Chinese and can have problems reading their own records if they are written in that language. The adoption of Chinese characters long ago by the peripheral countries for their written languages, and its influence on the development of local writing systems, dictates a certain level of knowledge of classical Chinese in order to make use of those records.

The Spoken and Written Language

As stated above, language can make genealogical research difficult for Americans of Chinese, Japanese, and Korean descent. Because these languages are written with an entirely different, non-alphabetical script (the language of Japan and Korea is a combination of Chinese characters and native syllabary), most people doing research in these records must find expert help. In addition, other unique aspects of their individual cultures must also be taken into account. Even if one can read the languages, failure to understand a certain custom or method can result in misinformation.

Spoken and Written Language, Chinese. There are several spoken Chinese languages, different enough from one another to be called languages rather than dialects. The differences between some of these spoken languages can be as great as those between English and German. Mandarin, spoken mostly in the north, is the official language of both the People's Republic of China on the mainland and of the Republic of China on the island of Taiwan. It is understood by over ninety percent of the Chinese people and is the first language of about seventy percent of them.

Six other major Chinese languages are Cantonese, spoken in the provinces of south China near Hong Kong; Wu, the language of the Shanghai region; Min, of the Fujian region; Kan and Hsiang, found in the interior; and Hakka, a northern dialect spoken by the descendants of refugees who moved to several areas in south China long ago. The differences in the spoken languages consist mainly of pronunciation and vocal inflections, called tones. Other differences exist in vocabulary, expressions, etc. Each language is further subdivided into its own dialects. There are several other minor Sinitic languages as well, spoken by autonomous tribal groups. Unless otherwise stated, references to spoken Chinese in this text will be to Mandarin.

Written Chinese is much more unified than the spoken languages, so a book printed in one region can be read in any other. In fact, written Chinese is the oldest language still in use in the world and has had much to do with the survival of China itself as a country in spite of regional divisions. It is a difficult language to read and write, requiring much study and a good memory to make even a newspaper intelligible. Because it is non-alphabetic, it stands almost alone among the written languages of the world.

No accurate count exists of the number of Chinese characters known as *hanzi* ("Han letters," after the Han Dynasty of 206 B.C. to 220 A.D.). With variants, simplifications, and obsolete characters included, the number is over 70,000. A good single-volume desktop dictionary will list between 7,000 and 10,000. A character can consist of anywhere from one brush stroke to complex wonders of forty-eight strokes or more; most of the common ones have from ten to fifteen. Chinese is a monosyllabic language, so each character's pronunciation is a single syllable. Words are composed of one or two, and sometimes three, syllables.

Most Chinese surnames are written with one character, but there are names consisting of two or more characters. The latter are sinicized (Chinese influenced) foreign names, usually Mongol or Manchu, whose bearers have assimilated. Of course, in order to do any kind of genealogical research, a person of Chinese ancestry must be able to do more than merely recognize the character representing his surname. While many second-generation Chinese Americans can speak Chinese quite well, reading and writing it are entirely different matters.

Spoken and Written Language, Japanese. Japan is a small country with a homogeneous culture and only one official spoken language. There are regional dialects, of course, but regional differences in Japanese do not prevent understanding to the extent found in China. The aboriginal Ainu language and the language of the Ryūkyū Islands (the latter related to Japanese) are separate languages which are both dying out.

Japanese is as different from Chinese as it is from English, and the adaptation of many thousands of Chinese characters to the needs of the written Japanese language was a long and cumbersome process. There is evidence that Japanese rulers as early as the fifth century were employing Korean scribes educated in the use of Chinese characters called kanji in Japanese. (No records remain from that period, however; the oldest extant Japanese records are land survey records dating from the early eighth century.) The main differences in these languages lay in basic grammar and syntax. Japan used the Chinese language extensively, especially when it was first adopted for official business many centuries ago. Today, only about 2,000 kanji are learned by high school graduation, but an educated person will know over 5,000. Loan words from Chinese make up about five percent of the Japanese vocabulary. Japan has adapted kanji to its own needs and developed a native writing system to supplement it.

Most Japanese surnames are written with two kanji, but there are names consisting of one or three or more characters. As with the Chinese, in order to do any kind of genealogical research, a person of Japanese ancestry must be able to do more than merely recognize the characters representing his or her surname. And, again as with the Chinese, while some second-generation Japanese Americans can speak Japanese to a degree, reading and writing it is an entirely different matter.

Some of the difficulties caused by kanji are due to the fact that many characters will have identical pronunciations and each character has more than one pronunciation. For example, one popular name dictionary lists seven different names all pronounced *Itō*, using four different kanji for *i* and four more for *tō*. These are different names, with different meanings and not just different ways to write one name, as in the case of Smith and Smythe. Actually, Nelson's *The Modern Reader's Japanese-English Character Dictionary* lists 52 characters all pronounced *i* and 196 pronounced *tō*. Each of these characters has at least one other pronunciation which is determined by the context in which it appears. These multiple pronunciations were caused by multiple borrowings of characters over centuries, in different contexts and, perhaps, from different parts of China, and by later applying native Japanese readings, in addition to the Chinese readings, to each one.

An example of the process of adoption and adaptation of kanji in Japan is shown in the character meaning "country." It is pronounced *guo* in Mandarin and *gwok* in Cantonese, the latter being closer to the pronunciation of fifteen hundred years ago. About that time, the character was taken into Japanese as *koku*, and is still pronounced so in certain contexts. However, the native Japanese for "country" is *kuni* and this reading was applied later to the character *koku*, so the character could be pronounced as kuni in other contexts. There are other characters pronounced kuni as well.

Other kanji, with entirely unrelated meanings but pronounced *ku* and *ni*, were used early on to write kuni phonetically before the character koku was used to render it. This was very cumbersome and difficult, especially before standards existed to dictate the use of a particular character for a particular sound.

After a few centuries, the syllabic writing system called *kana* was invented. Cursive kana, called *hiragana*, are simplified versions of the kanji whose pronunciations they represent. These are used today mainly as grammatical particles and word endings, where kanji simply cannot be used. Angular kana, called *katakana*, are pieces taken from kanji whose pronunciations they represent. They are used today mainly to transcribe foreign words. Both kinds of kana, of which there are about fifty each, are found in records, sometimes alongside kanji to give their pronunciations.

With both Chinese and native readings, called *on-yomi* and *kun-yomi* respectively, assigned to characters,

the correct readings of Japanese names can be very difficult to determine. Place names can be looked up in gazetteers and historical dictionaries. Surnames can be looked up as well, but the same name can have varying pronunciations in different regions. For example, the name written with the characters for "deity" and "door" can be pronounced *Kanbe*, *Kamito*, *Kōbe*, or *Jinbe*.

Japanese given names cause a bigger problem as very few standards apply at all. In many cases, the only sure way to learn the pronunciation of the characters in a person's given name is to ask him personally. Determining the reading of a long-deceased ancestor's name so it can be romanized in an American genealogy is nearly impossible and a distant cousin may record it very differently than you do. For this reason, it is very important to include the kanji for names in romanized records, whenever possible, to avoid confusion. Japanese records containing only romanization (or, for that matter, only kana) are nearly worthless to a researcher.

Spoken and Written Language, Korean. The position of the Korean peninsula between the Chinese mainland and the Japanese archipelago makes it a natural route for the spread of Chinese culture to the islands. Of course, the people along that route were profoundly affected and it was the Koreans themselves who passed along the benefits of Chinese civilization to Japan, after they had first absorbed it themselves. In the second century B.C., Chinese outposts were established in northwestern Korea. One of these was later absorbed into the rising Korean kingdoms of Kogury and Paekche. Paekche especially was highly sinicized and from this kingdom Chinese culture strongly influenced the entire Korean peninsula. It was even exported to Paekche's ally, Wa, as Japan was then known. Still later, the kingdom of Silla discovered the advantage of sinicization (Chinese influences) and eventually conquered Paekche and Kogury with Chinese help.

Early in this period, Korean scholars began to be literate in Chinese characters called *hanja* in Korean. Korean, like Japan, is as different from Chinese as it is from English and the adaptation of many thousands of Chinese characters to the needs of the written Korean language was a long and cumbersome process. The main differences in these languages lay in basic grammar and syntax. Originally, Korean scholars simply wrote in Chinese. But after centuries of using hanja as it was, Korean scholars in the mid-fifteenth century were commissioned by their king to invent a native Korean alphabet. They developed an ingenious alphabet called *han'gŭl*, consisting today of fourteen consonants and ten vowels. Scholars and noblemen continued to use Chinese and genealogies are mostly written in that language. Han'gŭl, also called *ŏnmun* (vernacular writing), was left for commoners to use. After Korea divided into two nations, North Korea abolished hanja and began to use han'gŭl exclusively. South Korea, too, uses only a minimum number of hanja, preferring the simplicity of han'gŭl in the majority of its written material. For this reason, it is becoming increasingly difficult for younger Korean people to read the older records.

Korea is a small country with a homogeneous culture and only one spoken language with some regional variations. Loan words from Chinese make up about ten percent of the Korean vocabulary. Korean is much more closely related to Japanese, though those two languages must have separated at least two thousand years ago and are now mutually unintelligible. About 1,800 hanja must be learned by high school graduates in South Korea. A well-educated person will know about 5,000, though characters are not used in Korea nearly to the extent they are in Japan.

As in China, most Korean surnames are written with one character, but there are a few names consisting of two characters. A number of Korean surnames, when written in hanja, are identical to some Chinese surnames. This does not necessarily imply Chinese descent, though there are, of course, a few Korean families of Chinese ancestry. As with the Chinese and Japanese, a person of Korean ancestry must be able to do more than merely recognize the character representing his surname and must realize speaking some Korean is much easier than reading and writing it.

Romanization and Spelling Variations

Chinese. For the Chinese, one of the difficulties caused by hanzi or characters is that many have identical pronunciations in any given Chinese language. For example, one desktop character dictionary lists 123 different hanzi, including at least seven surnames, all pronounced *ji* in Mandarin. These are seven different names, with different meanings, not just different ways to write one name. When tones are considered, the *Ji* surnames are further divided into three groups, but that is irrelevant here because tone marks are not included with romanized spellings in phone books, tax records, diaries, or pedigree charts. Also, though the name is spelled *Ji* according to modern *pinyin* romanization (pinyin is the official romanization standard used in the People's Republic), another older, still common romanization is Wade-Giles, which would render the spelling as *Chi*. The problem is made worse by the fact that there are a couple more surnames pronounced *Chi* and spelled *Ch'i* in Wade-Giles but the diacritic apostrophe is usually omitted by everyone except scholars. Therefore, someone trying to find out which character represents a surname spelled *Chi* has at least nine possibilities to consider.

Varied Spellings of Specific Chinese Cities and Provinces

Post Office	Wade-Giles	Pinyin
Kiangsu	Chiang-su	Jiangsu
Hopeh	Ho-pei	Hebei
Fukien	Fu-chien	Fujian
Peking	Pei-ching	Beijing
Chungking	Chung-ch'ing	Zhongqing

Figure 1.6

Further confusion is caused by a lack of standard romanized spelling when names were recorded over a century ago by Hawaiian and American immigration officials and labor contractors. The name *Ji/Chi* could be spelled as *Jee, Gee, Chee,* etc. And if the bearer of the name spoke Cantonese, Hakka, or any other language or dialect, which was most likely in the nineteenth century, many other spellings based on those pronunciations also come into play. A person who is unable to recognize his own surname in hanzi can hardly get started in genealogical research. In romanized genealogical records, hanzi should be included if at all possible. Chinese records (as well as those in Japanese or Korean) containing only romanization are nearly worthless to a researcher.

It goes without saying that any other Chinese word would present the same problems. To end this section by emphasizing problems caused by romanization, let us look at the common spellings, sometimes called the "post office" spellings, of a few Chinese cities and provinces in Figure 1.6. Their equivalents in Wade-Giles and pinyin are included for comparison. All of these names should be pronounced the same regardless of spelling. This plethora of standard spellings, plus the lack of standards found in many older records, will continue to make research difficult even if all records are someday automated.

Japan. Japanese is quite easy to romanize, but at first there was no system at all. For example, the name Itō was (and sometimes still is) usually romanized without its diacritic over the o (technically making it an entirely different name) or is spelled *Itoh* or *Itou*. Also, three sounds, formerly romanized as *kwa, yi,* and *ye,* have now been merged with *ka, i,* and *e* resulting in names which would now be spelled *Inoue* and *Uemura* but are spelled *Inouye* and *Uyemura* by many of those who bear this name in America.

There are several standard ways to romanize Japanese words. Most popular in foreign countries is the

Hepburn system, but in Japan itself, Hepburn competes with Kunrei which is not well suited to use by foreigners. The problem with Kunrei is that the consonants simply do not reflect actual pronunciation while those in Hepburn do. The surname spelled *Jinbe* according to Hepburn is spelled *Zimbe* in Kunrei; *Fujishima* becomes *Huzisima*.

Korea. As with the hanzi in Chinese, one of the difficulties caused by hanja is that many characters have identical pronunciations. For example, in a dictionary of the 1,800 grade school hanja, there are seven characters, including two surnames, pronounced *sk*, all written with completely different characters. These are different names, not just different ways to write one name. There are several romanization systems differing from one another mainly in their rendering of consonants which are voiced or not voiced according to context. The most widely used romanization system in foreign countries is McCune-Reischauer, though its many rules can be confusing. Because han'gŭl has more vowels than the roman alphabet does, McCune-Reischauer employs diacritic marks to indicate the extra vowels, without which a word's romanized pronunciation is not clearly understood.

Before there were any standard romanization systems, immigration officials and labor recruiters were left to romanize Korean names the best they could. Regional variations in pronunciation came into play, with the result that one well-known surname, usually romanized as *Yi*, can be spelled *Li, I, Yee, Rhee, Lee,* and perhaps a dozen other ways.

Indonesia. On August 17, 1972, Indonesia's Independence Day, then-President Sukarno announced changes in the orthography of. There were changes in spelling: *ch* was to be written as *Kh, dj* as *j, j* as *y, nj* as *ny, sj* as *sy,* and *tj* as *c*. Further, the superscript ''2'' was not to be used to indicate duplication of a word. Thus, ''hati²'' became ''hati-hati.'' These changes are important for the genealogist to note because a person did not have to change his or her name to conform to the new spelling. Also names in records created before the reform will be in the old style.

Naming Practices

China, Japan, and Korea.

In Chinese, Japanese, and Korean, surnames precede given names. However, when written in romanization during dealings with Westerners, surnames are usually written after the given names, in Western style. A surname identifies its bearer as a member of a particular clan, but clan membership and descent from the founding ancestor are not necessarily the same thing, though most people assume they are. China actually has many more surnames than the traditionally listed ''Hundred Surnames'' of antiquity; the count as of 1965 was 1,181. Traditionally, surnames were held by all ethnic Chinese (except slaves) and by any ''barbarians'' who became Chinese through cultural assimilation. It was not the custom in China, as it was in Japan, for branches of a clan to take for themselves unique surnames, though occasionally an emperor would allow a subject to alter the character for his surname as a reward for meritorious service. The altered name was thenceforth a badge of distinction.

Japan has more surnames than any other country in the world. A surname was used to identify its bearer as a member of a particular clan, as in China and Korea, but that is no longer necessarily true. It was the custom in medieval Japan for branches of a clan to distinguish themselves by taking unique surnames. Sometimes each son of a feudal lord would take a new surname of his own. The connection of each new surname to the parent clan was well known. Until 1875, only samurai, about ten percent of the population, bore surnames. However, in that year, all Japanese citizens were required, as part of a new civil registration policy, to take surnames. Many were simply pulled out of the air. Numbers of people adopted the surnames of their former feudal lords without the genealogical right to do so. Other names were derived from residences or local topographical features and a few were assigned in a rather whimsical manner by village clerks. Today, only the imperial family is without a surname.

In contrast to Japan, Korea has fewer surnames than any other country in the world. Not only that, but the three surnames *Kim, Yi,* and *Pak* alone account for about half of the entire population. It was not the custom in Korea, as it was in Japan, for branches of a clan to take for themselves unique surnames. Traditionally, surnames were held by all Koreans except slaves (though it should be kept in mind that the number of slaves was great centuries ago).

Clan genealogies, called *zupu* or *jiapu* in Chinese, have been important in China for ages. Though none are extant from the time of Confucius, their value to the Chinese evidently antedates his era, and his teachings on ancestor veneration were intended merely as codification of a custom which he claimed was already ancient in the fifth century B.C. The Chinese believe that a man must produce male progeny to perpetuate his surname and his descendants must pay him proper homage. Genealogies provide the framework for this custom. Scholars believe that some surnames originated as *xing*, surnames of a matriarchal type taken from ancient totems; and others as *shi*, titles taken by male gentry from the names of fiefs awarded to them. These two types of surname are no longer differentiated.

Since Japanese and Korean clan genealogies were the province of the upper ten percent of traditional society, royalty, court nobility and the samurai class (Japan) and the aristocratic *yangban* class (Korea)—one might think that the other ninety percent of today's population would have trouble linking themselves to a genealogy. However, as these two countries approached the twentieth century, increasing social mobility (both up and down) brought a larger percentage of the population into the genealogies. Still, because several laws have been passed since 1868 to guarantee and protect the civil rights of all Japanese and privacy laws have been enacted to prevent knowledge of ancestry from becoming a social and economic obstacle to descendants of traditional "outcaste" groups, conducting genealogical research can be difficult.

Though we may assume that everyone, ultimately, is descended from the same original groups, records do not exist to prove that assumption. Today, even descendants of slaves have surnames which probably do not indicate their actual ancestry. Destruction of records during wars and other disasters increases the uncertainty, and Korea has suffered great devastation more than once. As a rule, scholars tend to be suspicious of genealogical information claiming to precede the foundation of the Yi Dynasty of Korea.

In China given names are usually in two syllables, written with two Chinese characters. The first character in the names of males of the same generation in a family was determined by a poem composed in the family's honor early in its history. The men of each succeeding generation were named with the character in the poem which corresponded to that generation, plus a second, personal character to complete the name. Thus two distant relatives, meeting for the first time, could ask each other's names and the names of their fathers and determine instantly how they were related. Girls were given names which reflected beauty and feminine virtues. In both cases, however, there were exceptions.

In Japan given names could be as short as "Tsu" or "Ken" or as long as "Jirozaemon" or "Tarokichibei." They were written with Chinese characters, though girls' names were often only in kana. Boys were given names which reflected strength, sincerity, and other virtues, while girls usually received short, meaningless names unless they were well born. In older times, it was often the custom to include numbers in boys' names to denote the order of their birth.

Given names in Korea are usually in two syllables, written with two Chinese characters. A baby boy's name was chosen by his father and grandfather. One of the name characters for males of each generation in a family was predetermined by the rules of the "theory of the five elements" (fire, water, wood, metal, earth). As in China, girls were given names which reflected beauty and feminine virtues.

In all three cultures, royalty and court nobility were usually known by titles or offices, rather than by their personal names. It was customary to address a social superior, even if a member of one's own family, by title as it was considered rude to address him by his given name. Even today some people are addressed as "brother" or "aunt" or some other seemingly familiar title instead of by name, which is deemed too familiar. Because of this, in some records a title may be used in place of a name. A scholar would adopt, besides his own given name, an alias by which he would be known professionally. One responsibility of the clan genealogist was to keep track of everyone's aliases.

The challenges of romanizing Chinese, Japanese, and Korean names were dealt with briefly in the preceding section. Besides spelling, other difficulties are caused by options in capitalization, word separation, diacritical marks, and punctuation which are available in English but not in Chinese, Japanese, or Korean. For instance, in Chinese, a given name might be spelled "Xiaoping" (according to pinyin rules), Hsiao-p'ing (Wade-Giles), or Syao Ping. In Japanese, it might be spelled "Shichirō" (according to Hepburn rules), "Sitiroh," or something else. In Korean, a given name might be spelled "Chnghyn" (according to McCune-Reischauer rules), Chng-hyn, or Jng Hyn. The choice is up to the owner of the name, if he or she is living, but Americans of Asian descent who wish to romanize ancestors' names in family histories should choose a standard and adhere to it.

Countries of South and Southeast Asia.

Every country in these regions of Asia contains a diverse population; many are home to communities of Chinese and various groups from India. These groups usually retain their own traditions in assigning names, unless they are forced to adhere to the traditions of the group which dominates the country in which they live. For example, Chinese in Thailand have found it advantageous to assume a Thai name at various times during the twentieth century. The purpose here is to give an overview of the various naming systems in use among the dominate groups in the countries of South and Southeast Asia. In all areas, the trend is to follow the western pattern of a surname (family name) and a given name, but this is occurring at a different pace in each country. In some places there are still many one-element names or cases where an individual changes his or her name often.

Cambodia. Khmer surnames came into general use circa 1910. The first element of an individual's name is the surname, followed by a one- or two-element given name. An individual is referred to by the given name; some persons may be known only by given names as the surname is not emphasized. In some circumstances the surname appears in the form of an initial as in "J. Gang," where "Gang" is the given name and the first letter of the surname is "J." In some cases, the full surname may not be known. A nickname, sometimes added to the given name, is preceded by the Khmer word *hau* or the French word *dit* (known as). Terms of address are *Lok* (Mr.), *Lok-Srey* (Mrs.), and *Neang* (Miss). Buddhist and royal titles may also be used.

Indonesia. In general, the first part of the name is the given name, followed by the surname. However, Indonesia consists of a large number of different cultures—many of which have their own naming customs. Some of these are fairly simple. The Batak *marga* or clan name is often used as a surname with a given name of either Batak or Christian origin. In some cases a place name may be used as a surname. In some areas, notably Bali, birth order names are given to children, such as Son number one, Son number two, etc. Adult names, distinct from birth order names, childhood nicknames, or childhood aliases, usually consist of a single element. An older usage for the construction of names, which used *anak* (child of), *bin* (son of), *binti* or *binte* (daughter of), and *ibni* (son of, royal form) before the father's name, is seldom used today. *Adat* (law or custom) titles, often preceded by *gelar* (honored as), and titles such as Daeng, Sultan, and Datuk may be used along with many other titles which may indicate royalty, a specific office, a profession, religious honors, religious office, etc. The use of *haji* indicates that the person has completed the pilgrimage to Mecca.

A married woman may take her husband's name with the prefix "Ny." which stands for *Nyonya* (Mrs.) or she may keep her name, using as a surname her husband's family or clan name joined by a hyphen to the surname she received at birth. Hence, the name Reny Siwabessy-Putiray indicates that Siwabessy is the husband's surname while Putiray is Reny's maiden name.

Since a given name may be followed by the father's name, the person's adult name, a clan name, a traditional family name, or a place name, these systems of naming can provide intelligence on various aspects of a person's life. However, the information is limited because of the difficulty of determining the meaning of the surname.

Laos. See Thailand below, as the naming customs of the two countries are similar. Titles indicating a specific position may be used in place of the name of the individual holding the position.

Malaysia and Brunei. Typically, individuals living in these two countries use the first element of a name to indicate the surname, followed by given names. Terms of relationship are featured. A name may refer to the person's father by placing an indicator in front of the father's name. Indicators are: bin (abbreviated as "b."), binte or binti ("bte." or "bt."), and ibni. As with some of the countries listed above, a variety of titles are used.

Union of Myanmar (Burma). Until recently, the Burmese did not use surnames; the practice is still uncommon. A given name may be composed of one to four syllables and the same name may be used by both men and women. Similar to our "Mr.," "Miss," and "Mrs.," honorifics or terms of address may be used to distinguish between the sexes: *U, Ko, Maung,* and *Thakin* are used for men; *Daw, Ma, Mai,* and *Thakinma* for women. Some of these prefixes are also given names and, as such, must be carefully distinguished. Bikhu (masculine) and Bikhuni (feminine) are religious titles. Other titles indicate that the person is not of Burmese ethnicity: *Saw* (masculine) and *Naw* (feminine) indicate that an individual is Shan. Since there are so many similar names, a distinguishing epithet, derived from an individual's profession, place of origin, or some other attribute, may precede the given name. These distinguishing epithets may be altered during an individual's life in response to a change in title or profession or to indicate the performance of an act of merit.

Philippines. Originally, Filipinos had only one name which was often derived from their occupation, a childhood nickname, their tribe, a description, some feature of the place he or she inhabited, etc. After the arrival of the Spanish, natives were encouraged to use Christian names. Surnames were assigned, but emphasized only in the records of the local priest. The result was that many surnames, besides being the same, were taken from the name of a saint or some religious item (for example, De la Cruz means "of the Cross"). Another feature of Philippine names is that the middle name may equate to the maiden name of the mother.

In November 1849, Narciso Claveria, the Spanish Civil Governor-General, decreed that Spanish surnames were to be adopted by all persons in the Philippines. To accomplish this, a list of 60,000 surnames known as the "Catalogo Alfabetico de Apellidos (Alphabetical Catalog of Surnames)" was distributed to the governors of various provinces with instructions that persons were to choose, or have chosen for them, names from the list. Certain families were exempted: the Chinese, those whose names appeared in Spanish records, and those who had used a surname for at least four generations (and were to keep that established surname). How this decree was carried out and to whom it came to be applied, is not precisely known. Some areas took it more seriously than others. Apparently, some pages of the decree were assigned to certain towns, resulting in almost all of the people living there having a surname which begins with the same letter. A civil register or *cabecerias* was to be kept in which the former surname of an individual and the new one were recorded. Most of these records have been lost. For those which still exist, there is the problem as to how many of the people registered reverted to their former surname after the register was completed.

Singapore. Names are based on the ethnic group to which an individual belongs. For example, Malays in Singapore follow Malay naming styles. For the Chinese population, which is a majority in Singapore, non-Chinese elements are sometimes used so that a person will have an English given name which is not a transliteration of the name in Chinese.

Thailand. The use of surnames was mandated in Thailand in 1915. Among the Thai, the first element is usually the given name and it has precedence in identifying persons over the second element which is the surname. The usual form for a general in the Thai army, for example, is the title of general followed by the given name—not the surname, as in the west.

For commoners, the usual terms of address are: *Khun* (masculine, when in the man's presence), *Nai* (masculine, when not in the man's presence), *Nang* (feminine, sometimes married), and *Nangsao* (feminine, unmarried). A complex system of royal titles exists and in described in *Thai Titles and Ranks* (Jones). Until recently, a person's ''name'' might have been his title of office in the government. In some areas a system of nicknames, such as a childhood name given by their parents, was used to identify an individual.

Vietnam. Since there are less than one hundred surnames in Vietnam, individuals are distinguished by their given names and, in many cases, an intercalary word between a given name and surname. A number of religious and royal titles are also used.

Sri Lanka. In early Sinhalese names, the first, and sometimes only, element of the name is a given name. Some given names had a second element which was an epithet indicating a place, profession, or rank. Also, in cases usually involving prominent persons, two styles of names were used. The first style utilized a *wasagama* name which was used with an element indicating a place or profession. The second style utilized a *patabendi* name which was based on a title received in recognition of services provided to royalty. Some of these have been used as surnames. Some surnames are simply western surnames. While others are derived by attaching a western name as a prefix to a Sinhalaese surname. Also a patronymic element may be used in surnames either as the surname itself or in combination with other elements (for example, the suffix ''pal'' is added to the father's personal name). Given names may also be drawn from names of Sinhalese or western origin. They may stand alone, have an honorific final, or be preceded by an initial that stands for a surname. Finally, some individuals follow their given name with a simplified version of their original surname.

India. Indian names are both complex and diverse. Throughout most of India's history, a given name of one or two elements sufficed to distinguish individuals. Only merchants and officers serving the various rulers bore more complex names. By the middle of the nineteenth century, urbanization and the interconnection of villages created conditions in which a more complex naming system was required to distinguish persons who had the same given names. The British style of a given name and surname was selected. But since not all areas of the country were entering a more complex era (and, as such, did not have a need for surnames) and India had a social structure that differed considerably from that of the English, styles of naming have proceeded according to each group's own logic and at its own pace. Indian telephone books for any large city will reveal a number of different systems are at work. This does not mean that there is no pattern to Indian names; rather, it shows the variety of styles available.

With few exceptions, the given name bestowed by parents will be the name that an individual will use throughout life. To this given name may be added other names and titles which are selected and may change over the years. Though India does not have a system of surnames like that of the West, after an added name has been used for a number of generations, it may be treated as a surname; but a person is not required to use it.

The factors used in choosing a given name are important to the genealogist. These factors include gender, caste, religion, locality, and family traditions. With regard to gender, as a general rule, names that end in a short ''a'' or ''i'' are masculine, those that end in a long ''a'' or ''i'' are feminine. Since the distinction between a long or short vowel is not drawn in many transliteration systems, this difference may be lost in the writing of these names in the Roman alphabet. In given names with two elements, one of the elements typically indicates gender. For Sikhs, *Singh* is used only by men and *Kaur* only by women; consequently, Satwant Singh is a masculine name while Satwant Kaur is feminine. The following are other elements that indicate a feminine name: bai or bei (as in Shantabai); behn or ben (as in Jyotsmabehn); dai or dei; Devi (as in Annakura Devi); Di; Kaur (especially among Sikhs); Kumari; Rakhi; lati or lata; wati or vati; and, among Muslims, Banu; Begum; Khatum; and Sahiba.

At least among Christians, Hindus, and Muslims, a person's religious affiliation is often indicated by his given name. This is less so among Jains, one of the oldest religious communities, and new converts to Buddhism. In the past, the differences between Muslim and Hindu names were not sharply observed, but in response to the increased social consciousness of religious differences, given names are being changed accordingly. In the past some Hindu villagers in areas that were influenced by the culture of Muslim rulers might use Muslim given names such as Iqbal, Layaqat, Sultan, or Ulfat. Catholics typically give their children Christian names. Protestants tend to use western given names.

In the traditional Hindu system of social hierarchy, there are four major varna divisions: Brahman (Hindu of the highest caste, usually a priest), Kshatriya (ruler, warrior), Vaishya (merchant), and Shudra (farmer). There are thousands of *jati* or subcastes which are ranked based on local prestige, wealth, and history. Certain names are used by specific castes and subcastes. In South India, varna and jati names are sometimes used as a surname, but the movement against the caste system in the twentieth century has de-emphasized this tradition. Nevertheless, caste elements in names are still important. In some cases, caste elements are manipulated enabling a group to take on the names of persons in a higher caste, so that it might be mistaken as belonging to that caste.

The *gotra* or clan is a group within a jati which claims to be the descendants of a single common ancestor. Consequently they may not marry members of their own gotra or any other gotra that claims descent from that ancestor. These gotra names are sometimes used as surnames among Brahmans in northern India.

Profession, place of birth or ancestral home, parents' hopes for the child, and cultural group are other factors considered in the naming of an individual in India.

Some elements of names are interchangeable and thus, full brothers may have different surnames, understood as being the same by the brothers. For example, since Gupta and Agarwal are interchangeable elements, one brother may be named Jaya Prakash Agarwal and the other, Raj Kumar Gupta.

Calendar Systems and Dates

China, Japan, Korea.

The traditional Chinese lunar calendar, in use for thousands of years in China, was officially adopted in Japan in the early seventh century and has been in use in Korea for at least seventeen centuries. It was also adopted many centuries ago by the countries surrounding China,

so anything said about its use in China will apply with few exceptions to the countries located on the periphery. Some knowledge of astrology and regnal periods is required to understand the calendar. Though replaced by the Gregorian calendar (the solar calendar used in the West) in modern times, it is still used by fortune tellers and to observe ancient holidays.

Years are numbered in cycles of twelve, each year named after an animal of the zodiac (known as the "Twelve Terrestrial Branches"): rat, ox, tiger, hare, dragon, snake, horse, ram, monkey, rooster, dog, or boar. The Twelve Branches are correlated with the "Ten Celestial Stems" (based on the five elements of wood, metal, fire, water, and earth) to create a full cycle of sixty years. Because few emperors (China and Japan) and no kings (Korea) reigned more than sixty years, there is little confusion if a certain regnal year is indicated by its astrological sign instead of given a number, unless the branch name is given without the stem. A chronological chart is necessary to convert the year to a date that coincides with the Gregorian calendar so it can be determined how long ago a specific event occurred.

When a Chinese or Japanese emperor, or a Korean king began his reign, an auspicious name was selected by which that regnal period (and the emperor or king himself) would be known. The year of his accession would be both year one of his own reign and the final year of his predecessor's. In China and Korea, the regnal period kept its name until a change of rulers. In Japan, however, it was common to change the name of the period during an emperor's reign if he was in need of a change in luck. In some Korean cases, the name of the Chinese regnal period was used because of Korea's status as a vassal state.

Months were either twenty-nine or thirty days long and a typical year would be 354 days long. Eventually, of course, such a short year would be completely out of line with equinoxes, solstices, changes of seasons, and such vital functions as planting and harvest. Therefore, from time to time a thirteenth, intercalary month was inserted to rectify the situation. For this reason the Chinese New Year, still celebrated in America according to the traditional calendar, is never on the same day, falling from two to six weeks after the first of January. Also, Japan did not always insert the intercalary month in the same place China did, so the two calendars sometimes do not correspond exactly within a given year.

East Asians indicate months by their numbers: First Month, Second Month, etc. Obviously, if the first month begins some time in February, the twelfth month cannot correspond to December. This is why the simple year conversion charts found in the backs of dictionaries and handbooks on Asian genealogy are inadequate. They do not account for the spillover of a lunar year's last weeks into the first part of the following Gregorian year.

For example, the years Xianfeng (or Hsien-feng) 8 and 9 (in Japan they are cited as the years Ansei 5 and 6; in Korea they are Ch'oljong 9 and 10) will be given as the equivalents of 1858 and 1859 in a simple conversion table. Actually, the first day of the first month of Xianfeng 9 fell upon February 3, 1859, which means that nearly the entire twelfth month of Xianfeng 8 fell in January 1859 and not in 1858 at all. The matter is further complicated by the fact that China began using the Gregorian calendar twice, in 1912 and again in 1949, apparently because internal turmoil prevented it from catching on among the general populace the first time. During that thirty-seven-year period, one does not know for certain whether a recorded date is lunar or solar. (Japan began using the Gregorian Calendar in 1873. Korea adopted this calendar in 1910 when it came under Japanese jurisdiction.) Further, it must be recalled that the Gregorian calendar itself was preceded by the Julian calendar and was not adopted by all Western nations at the same time.

Detailed conversion tables are available, giving day-to-day correspondence between the Chinese lunar and Gregorian calendars, but most people (and most public libraries) in America do not have copies. What does one do, then? From the preceding paragraph the date Xianfeng 8, twelfth month, twenty-fifth day, was shown to correspond to January 28, 1859 (versus December 25, 1858). In a newly prepared genealogical record, it would be best to render this date as it stands, making no attempt at conversion and adding the designation ''lunar'' in parentheses. It can be abbreviated as follows: Xianfeng 8 [1858] 12m 25d (L). This removes the need to convert the date, risking inaccuracy, and informs the reader that you know that this specific Chinese year corresponds mostly (but not entirely) to a specific Gregorian year. Of course, when transcribing a date known to have been recorded according to the Gregorian calendar, it should be transcribed in Western style.

Countries in South and Southeast Asia.

At issue for the genealogist is the types of dating systems that might be encountered. The dating system depends on the type of record and the period in which it was created: if the record was created by an imperial government, then the record will use the dating methods of that government; if it is a church record, then it will use the dating system of the institution that created that record, etc. French records, either civil registration records or religious records, based dates on the Gregorian calendar. British records after 1757 used the same system, as did the Spanish in the Philippines (the Gregorian

calendar was adopted in the sixteenth century by the Catholic countries of Europe). Hence, a researcher in the Philippines need not worry about differences of calendar, nor would a genealogist working with British records in India after 1751. Researchers using local records or records prior to Western imperial expansion are not so lucky. Working out correspondences between indigenous dates and Gregorian calendar dates can be difficult as well as time-consuming.

There are six non-western calendars of such general use with which persons doing research in Asia should be familiar. These are the Indian Saka era calendar, the Vikrama era calendar, the Bengali era calendar, the Buddhist calendar (also called the Great Era calendar), the Islamic calendar, and the Burmese-Arakanese calendar. Each of these dating systems use a complicated method for including intercalculary days in order to make the dates come out right over the years. Each calendar uses a slightly different method to make these adjustments based on local traditions or as a means of a ruler's signaling his independence from another state. The small Thai states now in Northern Thailand based their calendars on local traditions as a way of asserting their independence from each other as well as from Burma, Auythia, and Bangkok. At least one ruler, Akbar, Mogul emperor of India from 1556 to 1605, invented his own calendar and, for a time, imposed it on his empire. In 1582 he outlawed the Islamic calendar, and imposed his own which used February 19, 1556, the date of his ascension to the throne, as its epoch. While most areas stopped using his calendar after his death, it is still is used in other areas of India.

Saka Era Calendar. This solar calendar, used by most of India, was also used at one time or another in most of the countries of South and Southeast Asia. Preceding the Christian era by seventy-eight years, the first day of each year falls in March (or February). This calendar was adopted for use in India along with the Gregorian calendar. The day, March 22, 1957, in the Gregorian calendar corresponds to Chaitra 1, 1879 (1957 minus 78 years equals 1879), on the Saka calendar. A year consists of 365 or 366 days divided into 12 months with Chaitra the first month of the year. The following are the names of the months with the number of days in a specific month in parentheses, followed by the approximate corresponding date on the Gregorian calendar: Chaitra 1 (30 or 31 days depending on whether the year is a leap year) or March 22 (March 21 on a leap year); Vaisaka 1 (31 days) or April 21; Jaisthya 1 (31 days) or May 22; Ashada 1 (31 days) or June 22; Sarvana 1 (31 days) or July 23; Bhadra 1 (31 days) or August 23; Asvina 1 (30 days) or September 23; Kartika 1 (30 days) or October 23; Agrahayana 1 (30 days) or November 23; Pousa 1 (30 days) or December 23; Magha 1 (30 days) or January 21; and Phalguna 1

(30 days) or February 20. Remember, there may be variations in the Saka dates due to the diversity in the ways each locale calculated these dates.

Vikrama Era Calendar. This calendar was created in the Vikrama era, also known as Samvata era, and is widely used, especially in northern India, Rajasthan, and Gujarat. Established in 57 or 58 B.C., all Vikrama era dates are 57 to 58 years ahead of those based on the Gregorian calendar (1957, Vikrama, versus 1900, Gregorian).

Bengali Era Calendar. This calendar is widely used in Bengal, dating from the reign of the emperor Akbar as discussed above. A solar calendar, it begins in February 1556, and Bengali 1307 corresponds to 1900.

Buddhist Calendar (The Great Era). This calendar was used with the saka calendar in Sri Lanka and by natives of the Buddhist countries of Southeast Asia during the period of Western imperialism. Sri Lanka failed in attempts to establish it, rather than the Gregorian calendar, as the official calendar from 1966 to 1971. In Laos and Cambodia, after independence was achieved, the Buddhist calendar was used for local and religious purposes; the Gregorian calendar for purposes of international trade. When the Communists came to power in these countries, the Buddhist calendar was no longer used. In Thailand, which is the only country in this region that was not ruled by a Western power, the Buddhist calendar is generally used in all domestic affairs. This calendar begins with the death of the Buddha in 543 B.C.; hence, the Gregorian year is calculated by subtracting 543 from the Buddhist year (2500, Buddhist, corresponds to 1956 or 1957, Gregorian, depending on the month). The first day of the year falls in April or May.

Islamic Calendar. This calendar is used in countries in which Islam is the official religion: Pakistan, Bangladesh, Malaysia, and Indonesia. But, in all of these countries, the Gregorian calendar is used for international and commercial purposes. This calendar is also used among Islamic communities in India, Sri Lanka, and Thailand. Indonesia uses the Islamic calendar, the Gregorian calendar, and several local calendars (refer to *Indonesian Chronology,* de Casparis). The epoch of this calendar is the Hejira— the flight of Mohammed from Mecca to Medina in July 16, 622 (thus, 1200, Islamic, corresponds to 1822 to 1823, Gregorian). The first day of the year varies considerably in this lunar calendar.

Burmese-Arakanese Calendar. This calendar is used in various regions of Burma; however, the Gregorian is used for international affairs and commerce. A variation of the Buddhist calendar, it begins in 638 A.D. (thus 1162 using this calendar corresponds to 1800 or 1801 on the Gregorian calendar). The first day of the year falls on April 13th.

When dealing with local records, it is crucial to determine the type of the dating system used. Genealogists dealing with local records will need handbooks which provide the corresponding Gregorian dates for local calendar dates. A number of such works are available. (See the bibliography at the end of this chapter.)

Political Boundaries and Ancestral Homelands

China. The Chinese people are the heirs of the oldest living civilization on earth. They claim that the first imperial dynasty, the Xia (or Hsia), was founded about 2000 B.C., though archaeological evidence has only confirmed the existence of the second dynasty, the Shang (1766 to 1122 or 1523 to 1027 B.C.). This is still very impressive antiquity—only slightly younger than Egypt's Middle Kingdom and Hammurabi's Babylon. This early civilization was centered in the North China Plain on the lower Yellow River. It slowly spread, over centuries of conquest and assimilation, to more or less cover the present area of China by the late second century B.C.

Unlike Korea, which was ruled for the thousand years before 1900 by two dynasties, and Japan, which has had only one, China's violent history since the tenth century is dotted with seven dynasties which, at one time or another, ruled all or part of the country. Sometimes competing dynasties ruled different regions simultaneously. Boundaries of provinces (*sheng*) and counties (*xian* or *hsien*) were readjusted each time and again after the takeovers by Republican and Communist governments in the twentieth century. Fortunately, carefully edited historical gazetteers have been compiled to help one sort out the many changes in name and jurisdiction. It is reassuring to note that, though provincial boundaries have moved back and forth, most counties have remained largely intact over the centuries.

Local Chinese officials were charged with the compilation of local histories or *fangzhi* to provide a running account of an area's local history, geography, demography, economy, etc. Of interest to us here is their inclusion of the genealogies and family histories of prominent families. The histories, updated and reissued periodically, are essential to the current production of historical/geographical dictionaries, atlases, and gazetteers.

Clan genealogies are always linked to a locality. The identifying locale is usually the name of a province and county. Many families are so old and numerous that some members, over the centuries, have moved from the original ancestral homeland and established branches of the clan in new locales. It is the responsibility of clan genealogists to maintain records of the links between these branches and the main line. Thus it is possible for a man to know his ancestral homeland and his pedigree going back hundreds of years. The descendants of Confucius (551 to 479 B.C.), for example, are especially proud of their 2,500-year-old line.

Japan. Japan proper consists of four main islands: Honshū, Kyūshū, Shikoku, and Hokkaidō, plus smaller islands which include Sado, Tsushima, and the Ryūkyū chain—all on the extreme eastern edge of Asia. The ancestors of the modern Japanese had gradually spread throughout Kyūshū, Shikoku, and Honshū by about the year 300, pushing back or assimilating older peoples known as Hayato, Emishi, Ezo, and others. Hokkaidō, formerly known as Ezo (after its aboriginal inhabitants), had a small Japanese population because of its location in the cold, snowy north until the late nineteenth century when it was specifically colonized to offset Russian incursions. Okinawa and the other large islands in the Ryūkyūs, though claimed at times by either Japan or China, or both, retained a population of largely Japanese origin.

During its turbulent history, Japan was reorganized administratively many times but the basic delineation of its ancient provinces remained more or less intact. In 824, Japan was organized into sixty-eight provinces (kuni) which endured until 1868, by which time they were administered by 261 feudal domains called *han*. In 1868, the provinces of Mutsu and Dewa were subdivided into six new provinces, but the provinces and domains were abolished when the prefectural system was established in 1871. Even today, with the old provinces broken up or joined together to form the forty-seven modern prefectures (*ken*), the traditional boundaries are still shown on maps and their names are noted in the gazetteers. The old names continue to be used in popular songs as they were used for centuries by poets.

So far as record keeping is concerned, the numerous feudal domains are probably more important than the provincial divisions. Each feudal lord (*daimyō*) was responsible for the records of land, population, and taxes of his own *han*. In modern times the prefectures are subdivided into cities (*shi*) and less urbanized counties (*gun*). Cities and towns (*machi*) or villages (*mura*) are the custodians of the koseki tōhon, an extremely valuable household register which is briefly discussed in Chapter Two. The koseki records for the descendants of many rural people may be a little difficult to locate because Japan's rapidly growing population causes villages to grow into towns. Towns secede from counties and are either absorbed by existing cities or merge with each other to form new cities with new names. Therefore a village and county mentioned in an older record may no longer exist as such. Also, many koseki records in larger

cities were destroyed during World War II bombing raids.

Korea. The ancestors of the Korean people entered the Korean peninsula from Manchuria in prehistoric times. The early northern Korean kingdoms of Kogury, Puy, and Parhae all occupied parts of southern Manchuria for centuries. Although today a few ethnic Koreans still live there, along the northern banks of the Yalu and Tumen rivers, they are the descendants of fairly recent emigrants. During the Kory Dynasty (918 to 1392), the northern border of Korea became fixed at these two rivers.

The Kory Dynasty was followed by the Yi Dynasty (1392 to 1910). In 1413, the new government organized the country into eight *to* or provinces: Kynggi (the capital district), Hwanghae, Kangwn, Ch'ungch'ng, Chlla, Kyngsang, P'yngan, and Hamgyng. The latter five provinces were divided into northern and southern halves in the nineteenth century to create the present-day thirteen provinces; Kynggi and Kangwn are also divided by the demilitarized zone between North and South Korea. Each province is subdivided into local administrative units called *hyn* (variously translated as district, county, or subprefecture).

Again, Chinese influence is apparent in the Koreans' compilation of local histories or *chiji*. As did the Chinese, Koreans also maintained clan genealogies. These genealogies, called *chopko* in Korean, are always linked to a locality. They are said to cover only about ten percent of the population as they were traditionally maintained by families of yangban (royal) status. Still, any Korean, whatever his ancestors' social status or residence, knows the name of his ancestral homeland, going at least a few generations back. This knowledge is actually a necessity in the case of such a huge family as the Kims who will identify themselves as ''Kim of Kwangsan,'' ''Kim of Kyngju,'' etc. The identifying locale is usually a county or city. Other records, to be discussed in a later chapter, are by their nature tied to locations.

Republic of the Philippines. Before the arrival of the Spanish in the 1500s, the Philippines consisted of prosperous settlements which carried on trade with China, Japan, Siam, and India. The Philippines received at least three waves of immigrants during this time period: groups of Negroids from Africa, groups from Vietnam and southern China, and, finally, seafaring people from what is now Borneo, Malaysia, and Indonesia. Each group tended to settle in the coastal areas and push earlier inhabitants back into the rough, mountainous areas at the center of most of the islands which constitute the Philippines. The last wave spoke a number of closely related proto-Malay languages, were believers in Islam, and had strong martial traditions. By the time of the arrival of the Spanish, these peoples were firmly established in the southern part of the Philippines, but less so in the northern part which included the rich farm lands of central Luzon, as these areas were still controlled by local chiefs or *dhatu*.

Spanish interest in the Philippines began with Ferdinand Magellan's arrival in 1521. Landing first in Cebu where he was received by the local dhatu, he then sailed to nearby Mactan Island where he was attacked and killed by its ruler. In 1565, more Spanish ships arrived and the active colonization of the Philippines began. Miguel Lopez de Legazpi attempted to found a capital on Cebu for Spain, but was forced by the resistance of the native population to move to Manila where, after several battles with local dhatus, he finally established a capital. Rapidly, the Spanish founded settlements first in the central part of Luzon, then in the north. When they attempted to move south they were blocked by several Moro sultanates (ruled by Muslim sultans) which, despite having more primitive weaponry than the Spanish, were able to strike suddenly where the Spanish were weak, keeping them off balance.

Spanish colonial policy emphasized the conversion of the inhabitants of the Philippines to Christianity. The Spanish clergy cooperated with the government in maintaining control over the various communities, acting as local representatives of the Spanish government. Consequently the parish records of local churches functioned as public records and the parish priest had considerable power over the administration of government in his parish. For Islamic communities in the Philippines, the prospect of converting to Christianity was the impetus behind their long and fierce resistance. Many fled to Borneo to escape Spanish conquest. [One reason for the success of the American administration of the Philippines in the early 1900s was the amelioration of the hostility of these Islamic groups with a policy of religious freedom.]

These Moro raids were so effective that they resulted in the evacuation of the Spanish from the coastal areas of several islands which they had controlled. However, in the early part of the nineteenth century, the Spanish again took action to strengthen their control of the rugged interior of the islands and expand south against the Moro. This time they were largely successful, though in some places, particularly in the south, Spanish control was tenuous as it often consisted of a small garrison at some strategic point with the surrounding Moro settlements otherwise unaffected.

Success was short-lived, however, as the Philippine Revolution, 1896–1896, precipitated the evacuation of the Spanish from most areas. One of the issues behind the Philippine Revolution was that the leadership positions of the church and government were all dominated by the Spanish. When revolution broke out in most of the provinces of the Philippines, the Spanish clergy left their posts and either went to another country or fled to Manila—local or "secular" clergy often took their places. [During the revolution, Gregorio Aglipay called a conference of sympathetic clergymen to discuss this problem which led to the establishment of a separate church called the "Aglipan" after its organizer.]

The result of the revolution was the concentration of Spanish forces around Manila. It was in this military posture that the American naval squadron commanded by George Dewey found them in 1898 during the Spanish-American War. He crushed the Spanish navy in the battle of Manila Bay on May 1 and then laid siege to Manila allowing the U.S. army to capture it on August 13. The Spanish conquest of the Philippines was over.

During the Spanish-American War, American and Philippine forces worked together to overcome the Spanish. When that war ended, a series of incidents between these two forces gave rise to a conflict lasting from 1899 to 1901. When American troops defeated the Philippine forces, civil government was established in most provinces though some pockets of resistance remained until 1905.

The American period in the history of the Philippines was marked by administrative experimentation and considerable economic development. After the initial takeover, the Philippine Commission attempted to lower the number of administrative personnel and costs by consolidating several provinces and many municipalities into larger units. This practice was abandoned after a few years and areas were returned to the way they were prior to the Spanish-American War. In 1935, the Philippines was made a self-governing commonwealth with full independence to follow in ten years but World War II, and occupation by Japanese forces from 1942 to 1945 made that impossible. Independence was finally granted in 1946 with Manuel Roxas becoming the first president of the Philippines.

At present the Philippines has 75 provinces and metropolitan Manila which are divided into 1,513 municipalities, 21 municipal districts, and 60 chartered cities. These are further subdivided into more than 40,000 *barangays* or villages. During the last one hundred years name changes, shifts in boundaries, and the creation of new administrative units have increased the level of frustration for genealogists—some of which should be alleviated in the section "Basic Genealogical Records—Asia—Republic of the Philippines" in Chapter Two.

Brunei (Negara Brunei Darussalam). In the fifteenth century Brunei was an independent sultanate on the northern coast of Borneo. As the British began to settle on the northern coast of Borneo, one of the strangest episodes of British imperialism occurred—in 1842 James

Brooke, an adventurer, was appointed rajah of Srawak by the Sultan of Brunei. From 1888 until 1983 (when it was given independence), Brunei was a British protectorate. Originally discovered at Seria in 1929, oil is the foundation of Brunei's economy. Brunei consists of four administrative districts.

Cambodia, Kampuchea, or Khmer Republic. The great Angkor kingdom, which at various times dominated Cambodia, Thailand, and Vietnam, was centered at Siamreap in Cambodia. By 1431 Ankor Wat was abandoned, initiating a struggle for control of the area between Thailand and Vietnam. In 1863 Cambodia became a protectorate of France, remaining so until 1949 when it became a state in the French Union. In 1953, full independence was granted. Until 1970, Cambodia, under the leadership of Prince Sihanouk, was a neutral country in regard to the Vietnam War. In that year, General Lon Nol ousted Sihanouk and declared the Khmer Republic—cooperating with American forces against the Vietnamese forces in the area. The Khmer Rouge fought against the government and took Phnom Penh, the capital, in 1975. The new government sought to destroy the westernized infra structure that had been created. Invading in 1978, Vietnam captured Phnom Penh a year later and sponsored Heng Samrin. The country became known as the People's Republic of Kampuchea. Today, Vietnamese troops have evacuated the country, leaving the United Nations to establish a stable government. Cambodia consists of nineteen provinces.

Indonesia. Indonesia was established by the Dutch, the colonial power that dominated the country. Before the Dutch, a number of great empires rose and fell, leaving behind great works of art and architecture. In 1596 the Dutch arrived, took Malacca from the Portuguese, and began a long struggle with the British for control of the area. By the early part of the seventeenth century, the Dutch had established a trading center at Batavia in northern Java and had taken control of Ambon (a key producer of spices). In 1799 the United East Indies Company (V.O.C.), which controlled Dutch interests in Asia from 1602 to 1799, was replaced by a civil government which established the Dutch East Indies. After the turmoil of the Napoleonic period which ended in 1815, the Dutch emerged with their holdings in Batavia and other parts of Indonesia intact, but lost most of the rest of their Asian empire. The late nineteenth and early twentieth centuries saw the Dutch bring all their holdings in Indonesia under their direct control. After the fall of Singapore in World War II, the Japanese quickly overran Indonesia. When they withdrew in 1945, they left behind an army made up of Indonesians that they had trained and armed. Although Indonesian independence was declared in 1945 by Sukarno, because the Dutch attempted to return to the area, it was not actually achieved until 1949.

When Sukarno fell from power in 1965, Suharto became the president of Indonesia, building a government backed by military forces. The capital of Indonesia is Jakarta or Djakarta.

Indonesia, containing a wide range of culturally distinct peoples, consists of twenty-seven provinces (*propinsi*), three special areas (daerah Istimewa Aceh, daerah Istimewa Yogyakarta, daerah Khusus Ibukota Jakarta Raya), fifty-four independent cities (*kotamadya*), five administered cities (*kota administratip*), 247 districts (*kabupaten*), and many sub-districts (*kecamatan*). Genealogical records are created and collected on all these levels.

Laos. The French spread into this area from their empire in Cambodia and Vietnam. By 1893 Laos was a French protectorate with a royal capital in Luang Prabang and an administrative capital at Vientiane. After occupation by the Japanese in World War II, France attempted regain control of Laos, but this proved difficult due to the claims of more important areas on limited French resources. In 1949 Laos became an independent member in the French Union and was granted full independence in 1953. A small Communist party increased its membership and power until, by 1965, it controlled about half of Laos. In 1975, this party, the Pathet Lao or ''Lao Nationalists,'' was able to abolish the monarchy and establish a government of the people.

Laos, its capital at Vientiane, consists of thirteen provinces which are divided into districts further subdivided into villages.

Malaysia. The early history of the area which Malaysia includes consisted of a struggle between western powers interested in controlling the long strait that runs between the Malay Peninsula and Sumatra. The Sultanate of Malacca, founded circa 1400, was claimed by Portugal in 1511 and by the Dutch in 1641. It was ceded by the Dutch to the English in 1824 as part of an exchange in which British claims on Sumatra were relinquished. Earlier the British had acquired Province Wellesley and Panag Island as well as Singapore; the latter had been established as a trading post by Sir Thomas Stamford Raffles in 1819. In 1826 Singapore, Penang, and Malacca formed the Straits Settlement. Singapore became its capital in 1832. In 1896 the Federated Malay States, which consisted of Malay states controlled by the British, was established with its capital in Kuala Lumpur. In 1909, the Unfederated Malay States was established from four states which had been under the influence of Siam. In 1914 these four states annexed Johore. During World War II, the Japanese carried out a rapid campaign that resulted in the defeat of British forces and the capture of Singapore, the site of a huge British naval base. After the Japanese were defeated, the Federation of Malaya was established which consisted of all the Malay States (those once controlled by either Great Britain or Siam) except Singapore. From 1948 to 1960, the British concentrated on suppressing a Communist led insurgency. In 1957 the Federation of Malaya gained independence and the Federation of Malaysia which consisted of Malaya, Sarawak, Sabah, and Singapore was formed in 1963. Singapore withdrew and became an independent state two years later.

Malaysia consists of the federal territory surrounding Kuala Lampur, Kuala Lampur, and eleven peninsular states which are further divided into administrative districts as well as Sabah, with four 4 residencies, and Sarawak, with five divisions (both located on the coast of Borneo).

Union of Myanmar (Burma). The Myanmar, though in the majority, share this area with a number of large groups: the Mon, the Shan, the Karen, and the Kachin. One of the most important tasks of government in this country involves the treatment of these minority groups. In the past, the Myanmar dominated the other groups. At the beginning of the nineteenth century, Myanmar was ruled by its own king. Over the course of three wars, the British took control of the country: the first of the Anglo-Burmese Wars, from 1824 to 1826, gave the British Arakan and Tenasserim; the second (1852) gave them all of lower Myanmar; and the third, from 1885 to 1886, gave them the rest of the country. Shortly after the end of the Japanese occupation during World War II, the Union of Burma gained independence in 1948. However, in 1962, U Win took power in a military coup. A national election on May 27, 1990, resulted in the win of nearly eighty percent of the seats in the Assembly by the National League for Democracy which favored a democratic form of government. However, the military ignored the results of the election and continues to rule this country from the capital of Yangon, formerly known as Rangoon.

Any genealogical researcher should note that on May 27, 1989, the names of many areas were changed. Burma became Myanmar. Arakan State became Rakhine State. Bassein became Pathein. Irrawaddy River became Ayeyarwady River. Pegu became Bago. Prome became Pyay. Rangoon became Yangon. Salween River became Thanlwin. Syriam became Thanlyin. Tenasserim became Tanintharyi. The Union of Burma became the Union of Myanmar, or in Burmese, Myanma Naingngandaw.

Singapore. After Sir Thomas Stamford Raffles discovered a passage which allowed ships coming from the Malacca Straits enroute to China to bypass the many small islands at the tip of the Malay Peninsula, he, in 1819, established a trading post at Singapore. Five years later, Singapore was ceded to the British East India Trading Company. In 1826 the Straits Settlements, which included Singapore, Penang, and Malacca, were organized, eventually becoming a crown colony in 1867. From 1942 to 1945 the Japanese occupied Singapore; after their defeat, Singapore became a crown colony until, in 1963, it became part of the Federation of Malaya. After withdrawing in 1965, it became a separate country.

Thailand. This country was formerly known as Siam. The Thai people (related to the Lao and Shan peoples) founded a series of states in the thirteenth century. They established Ayuthia (1350 to 1767) on the plains of the Chaopaya River in central Thailand as well as Lanna, a league of small states among the hills of northern Thailand which was dominated by Chiangmai. During a disastrous war with Burma, Ayuthia was taken and destroyed in 1767. A new kingdom, established in Thonburi, eventually defeated the Burmese and in 1782 the capital was moved to Bangkok. A series of kings came to the throne of Siam, carrying out reforms of the government, the military, the educational system, and the economy. In 1932 a coup d'etat ended the absolute monarchy. The king remained, but shared his power. In 1939 Siam changed its name to Thailand. Since then there have been several changes in name from Thailand to Siam, back to Thailand. Thailand, the only country in Southeast Asia never to have been ruled by a European country as part of a colonial empire, consists of seventy-four *changwats* (or provinces).

Vietnam. Vietnam's system of writing, religions, early governmental organization, art, and literature show the influence of the Chinese. Wars with China and periods of occupation by China are recurring themes in Vietnamese history. Another is the southern expansion of the Vietnamese from the central area of northern Vietnam—past the part of central Vietnam where the coastal plain narrows and the mountains almost reach the sea, overthrowing the kingdom of Champa, reaching the rich farm lands of the southern portion of Vietnam. The French, by the last quarter of the nineteenth century, extended their control over Vietnam and, in 1887, proclaimed the ''Union Indochinoise'' which included Vietnam and Cambodia. When Japanese occupation of the area ended in 1945, at the end of World War II, the French attempted to reestablish their authority in the area. After a long guerrilla war, the French withdrew in 1954. The country divided in two, with the north conducting a guerrilla war in the south. The United States sent first advisors, then troops beginning in 1961, but signed a treaty to withdraw in 1973. In 1975 Saigon fell to North Vietnam forces and the civil war ended. In 1978 Vietnam invaded Kampuchea, the former Cambodia. In 1979 a border war broke out with China.

Vietnam consists of thirty-six provinces, three cities, and one special zone. Its capital is Hanoi. The former capital of South Vietnam, Saigon, is now known as Ho Chi Minh City.

India. The British, arriving in India in the sixteenth century, expelled the Dutch and the Danish from their holdings, but not the French from their several holdings which were controlled from Pondicherry nor the Portuguese from their center at Goa. British power was exercised through the British East India Company, a trading company, which soon acquired the authority of a state with the power to make treaties, hold court sessions, and raise an army to carry on war. By the early part of the nineteenth century its function as a trading company had been largely eliminated and its major activity became that of government. Because Great Britain was a maritime power based on the navy's control of the sea, British rule in South Asia was centered in three major ports: Bombay Presidency, Bengal Presidency (centered at Calcutta), and Madras Presidency—all enclaves of direct government as well. Some areas were controlled and ruled directly by the British; others were ruled by an Indian prince whose rights were strictly regulated by the British via British residents and political officers located throughout the area and a garrison of British troops or British-trained troops within striking distance. Eventually this system of government gave the British control of the entire area.

This creates problems for the genealogist as whether a given area was under the direct rule of the British or under a local ruler is difficult to determine. One of the reasons for the Sepoy Mutiny in 1857 was to protest the British policy of exerting direct rule over any Indian state in which a ruler died without leaving a direct male heir. (The family did retain the property they owned in that state causing said property to become known as an ''estate'' instead of a ''state.'') This policy caused the map of India to be extremely fluid and subject to considerable change.

In 1857 the British-trained army in northern India rebelled and seized Delhi. Many changes occurred in response after this rebellion was suppressed. The British East India Trading Company was replaced by a viceroy. His government became the British Raj. As a result of nationalist agitation, much of the government of India on provincial and lower levels was overseen by Indians. In return for support against the Japanese in World War II, the British promised the nationalists that independence would be granted after the war. In 1947 India was granted independence, followed by Pakistan (1947) and Ceylon (1948). The result was that large numbers of Muslims in India fled to Pakistan and large numbers of Hindus in Pakistan fled to India amidst riots and fighting. Since independence, India has become one of the major democracies of the world.

Bangladesh. When, in 1947, India and Pakistan gained independence from the British, Pakistan was divided into two parts, separated from one another by India. The capital of the two parts was located in West Pakistan, which now comprises the modern state of Pakistan. In 1971 a civil war broke out between East and West Pakistan and millions of Bengalis fled to India which drew that country into the conflict on the side of East Pakistan. Independence was achieved that same year. East Pakistan changed its name to Bangladesh with its capital located at Dacca. The country consists of nineteen divisions.

Bhutan. This small kingdom, situated in the Himalayas between Tibet and India, is largely Buddhist with a large Hindu minority. In 1865 the British annexed its southern portion to India. In 1949 a treaty between India and Bhutan recognized the right of India to control Bhutan's foreign relations in return for the restoration of the southern portion. In 1969 a constitutional monarchy was established. The capital is located at Thimpu. Bhutan consists of fifteen centers or *dzong*.

Pakistan. Until independence was granted in 1947, the territory that is now Pakistan was part of the British Raj. In 1971 a civil war broke out between Pakistan (then West Pakistan) and East Pakistan in which the latter gained independence and became known as Bangladesh. Pakistan consists of 4 provinces and a Capital Territory around Islamabad, its capital.

Sri Lanka. The history of Sri Lanka (its capital is Columbo) includes a long period of control by various foreign powers as well periods of control by powerful Sinhalese kings. Known as Ceylon until 1972, the Portuguese arrived there in 1505 and found it divided into numerous small kingdoms. The Portuguese were able to establish themselves in the Kotte, the rich plains in the Colombo area, after a number of wars with the kingdom of Kandy which was centered in the rugged mountains in the interior of the island. The Dutch invaded with the support of the King of Kandy, who thought that they would help him drive the Portuguese out in exchange for a trade agreement. The struggle against the Portuguese was long and involved with periods of peace followed by war. By 1644 the Dutch had taken Galle and Negombo; after a six-month siege they finally took Colombo. The British arrived in 1795 during the Napoleonic Wars and quickly overtook the Dutch holdings. In the Treaty of Amiens (1802), British possession was confirmed and Ceylon became a crown colony. The Dutch language continued to be used and Dutch courts continued to function in some areas up to 1822 since many believed that the British would restore Ceylon to the Dutch after Napoleon was defeated. Instead, the able administrator, Frederick North, established a solid British government which incorporated Sinhalese and Dutch practices. In

1803 the British failed to conquer Kandy, but in 1815 Kandy's king was captured and British power was extended into this area despite a number of rebellions. The British established plantations, often worked by Tamils from south India, to export coffee, rubber, and tea (the latter became famous throughout the world). In 1948 the British granted Ceylon independence.

The country consists of nine provinces which are geographic, not administrative, divisions. They have no capitals, bureaucracy, or records. The administrative units are the twenty-two districts.

Nepal. After a period of instability during which tribal divisions made impossible the creation of a centralized government, the Gurkhas, slowly pushed into the region by pressure from the Mogul Empire, conquered this area in 1768 and established a kingdom. In 1815 a British resident was established by treaty at Katmandu, the capital of Nepal, to oversee British interests. During the Sepoy Mutiny, Nepal provided troops to the British and in 1923 the British recognized the independence of Nepal. The fifteen feudal chieftainships that had controlled the government were abolished in 1990 when the king centralized his power. The country consists of eight administrative zones which are divided into districts.

Marriage, Adoption, and Relationships

During the second century B.C., Confucian philosophy became institutionalized in China, not only in government, but throughout society. The same could be said for Korea in the fifteenth century—Korea eventually became the most Confucianized state in Asia. As early as the seventh century, Confucian philosophy began to influence Japanese social and political thinking as well. Though Japan never became as "Confucianized" as Korea, Confucianism and its later hybrid, Neo-Confucianism, strongly influenced the samurai, or warrior ethic, which favored the division of society into stratified castes with the Samurai in charge.

A basic tenet of the Confucian philosophy is the interaction between the "five relationships:" ruler and subject, father and son, husband and wife, older brother and younger brother, and friend and friend. The philosophy is highly patriarchal. Emphasis is placed on the need for the ruler, father, husband, or elder to set a proper example for others, treating them with benevolence. Age is greatly respected. One's conduct is expected to be appropriate to one's station in life and the rules for conduct are explicitly spelled out. Society was divided into rigid castes, according to one's livelihood. Movement between social levels was uncommon in China and Korea and prohibited in Japan.

Confucianism thus had a profound effect on family life. The father ruled the family and led them in displays of respect for his ancestors. The sexes were segregated. A man's wife, selected for him by his elders, owed him her obedience, if not love. Widows were expected to remain faithful to their deceased husbands and not remarry. In China and Korea divorce was considered a disgrace. Women kept their maiden surnames upon marriage, though their children received the father's name. Therefore children were aware of their descent on their mother's paternal side. It is probable that they also knew the line of descent on their father's maternal side but were ignorant of the origins of other female lines. All that really mattered was one's male lineage. In genealogies, there is very little, if any, information on the females in a family although Koreans tend to provide more information on women than do the Chinese.

In Japan, divorce, a simple matter for a man, meant disgrace for his wife who was usually cast off for failing to produce an heir. A woman was taken into her husband's family and took his surname upon marriage. An exception to this rule were cases in which a man with no sons would adopt a younger son of another family as his heir. The young man would marry the man's eldest daughter and take her surname. This kept family property and honors within the family name.

In China and Korea marriage between persons of the same surname was taboo. A man whose wife was unable to produce a male heir could resort to adoption, most often taking a son of a close male relative. This allowed a family to retain its property and honors.

A man could take concubines, and, in China, all of a man's children were considered to be of equal rank. A concubine's children were considered to be the "first lady's" (the man's wife's children). A Korean concubine's children were lower in rank.

False and Erroneous Information

The "Getting Started" section of Chapter Two includes information about inaccuracy in genealogical records, but here we will note some peculiarities of Asian records. Besides the lack of information on females, there is the matter of omission of certain family members. In a society so concerned with propriety, it sometimes occurred that family members would be cast out for misconduct. Not only were they ostracized by the rest of the family; their names were deleted from the clan genealogy or, in Japan, the family register and were not included in subsequent editions. Entire branches may be omitted simply because the genealogy became too large to handle. In Japan, some deletions occurred through adoption out of the family. Reasons for deletions should have been duly noted in general records, so a researcher must look outside of the genealogy for more information unless the omitted branches maintained genealogies of their own.

Also, if a family became impoverished and could not afford to keep a formal record or was inexperienced in keeping a genealogy, data might have been lost or badly recorded.

Though one can make a strong case for the reliability of information found in the average Chinese genealogy, especially after the thirteenth century, and Korean genealogy, problems remain. Forgeries and other unreliable records do exist; we may assume that these originated in the efforts of people to gain respect. There are many instances in Chinese history where men of low rank applied themselves to scholarly studies, passed the civil service examinations, and became both noted officials and honored ancestors of new lines. There are other instances in both Chinese and Korean history where people of low social rank tried to rise in status after fires had destroyed their records. Sometimes Dorean slaves deliberately attempted to destroy the records in order to escape and gain a fresh start in a new locale.

Forgeries and unreliable records exist in Japanese records as well. In fact, the *Shinsen shōjiroku* (*Newly Compiled Record of Surnames*), a ninth century compilation of genealogies, was commissioned by the emperor to correct errors in the records of nobility and prevent the unworthy advancement of people of the wrong blood. As with the Chinese and Koreans, there are instances in Japanese history where people of outcaste rank tried to rise in status after fires had destroyed their records. In other cases, a wealthy merchant (in the lowest social stratum) would lend money to an impoverished samurai in exchange for a promise of intermarriage of the families. Some samurai themselves, having overthrown their former lords and taken their lands, would fabricate impressive genealogies to help legitimize their new status.

Calculated birth dates are another challenge to genealogists. Because of high infant mortality rates in past times, or simply because of a culture's disdain for such details, birth dates were often not recorded. It is frequently necessary to calculate the year of a person's birth by subtracting his age at death from the year of his death. The result is a secondary record of sometimes dubious reliability.

The difficulty originates in the way East Asians count years of a person's age—it is different from the way it is done in the West. While in the West age one is counted as the first anniversary of a baby's birth, in Asia the first year of life is considered age one. Further, the New Year is counted as the starting point, not one's own birth anniversary. Therefore, a baby born in the last couple of days before New Year's Day would technically begin his second year and achieve ''age two'' on that holiday. To put it concretely, a person born in the tenth month of 1851, who died in the summer of 1901, would be listed as age 51 Asian-style, while his actual age in years was still only forty-nine and a few months. Calculating his birth year knowing only the year of death of 1901 and the given age of fifty-one, a genealogist might mistakenly record the birth year as 1850. This is why it is wise to record calculated years in this manner: 1850/51.

Bibliography

Additional information on these sources may be found in Part II.

Alcantara, Ruben R., et al. *The Filipinos in Hawaii: An Annotated Bibliography*. Honolulu: Social Sciences and Linguistics Institute, University of Hawaii, 1977. 152p.

Asian and African Family and Local History. Volume II. Genealogical Society of Utah World Conference on Records. Salt Lake City: The Church of Jesus Christ of Latter-day Saints, 1980.

Asiaweek. Volume 20:43 (October 26, 1994).

Barringer, Herbert R., Robert W. Gardner, and Michael J. Levin. *Asians and Pacific Islanders in the United States*. New York: Russell Sage Foundation, 1993. 371p.

Baxter, Craig, and Syedur Rahman. *Historical Dictionary of Bangladesh*. Asian historical dictionaries; no. 2. Metuchen, NJ: Scarecrow Press, 1989. 144p. Includes bibliography.

Blakely, Patrick D. ''Chinese Surnames.'' Unpublished paper, 1992.

Buku Petunjuk Gereja Katolik Indonesia. Jakarta: Bagian Dokumentasi-Penerangan, Kantor Waligereja Indonesia, 1980–. Directory of Catholic churches in Indonesia.

Burki, Shahid Javed. *Historical Dictionary of Pakistan*. Asian historical dictionaries; no. 3. Metuchen, NJ: Scarecrow Press, 1991. 254p. Includes bibliographic references.

Chan, Sucheng. *Asian Americans: An Interpretive History*. Twayne's Immigrant Heritage of America Series. Boston: Twayne, 1991. 242p.

Chan, Sucheng. *Hmong Means Free: Life in Laos and America*. Asian American History and Culture Series. Philadelphia: Temple University Press, 1994. 267p. Oral histories of five Hmong immigrant families in addition to an extensive historical overview and bibliography.

Chandresekhar, S. ''A Bibliography of Asian Indians in the United States: History of Immigration and Immigrant Communities in the United States.'' In *Population Review*, vol. 25:1–2 (1981), pp. 93–106.

Chandresekhar, S. ''A History of United States Legislation with Respect to Immigration from India.'' In *Population Review*, vol. 25:1–2 (1981), pp. 1–28.

Chandresekhar, S. ''Some Statistics on Asian Indian Immigration to the United States of America.'' In *Population Review*, vol. 25:1–2 (1981), pp. 67–75.

Chieowet, Chaiyamet. *Patitthin 3 phasa, Thai, Sakon, Chin tangtae Pho. 2446 to 2574*. Bangkok, Thailand: Silabankaan, 1978. Provides corresponding dates for the Gregorian, the

Buddhist Era, and the Chinese Calendar for every day of the period of time from 1903 to 2031.

Claveria, Narciso. *Catalogo alfabetico de apellidos* (*Alphabetical Catalog of Surnames*). Transcribase este decreto con el catalogo de apellidos y modelo del pardon a los gefes de las provincias y demas a quien corresponde, Narciso Claveria, Manila, 21 de noviembre de 1849. National archives publication; no. D-3. Manila: National Archives, 1973. 141p.

Cordasco, Francesco. *Dictionary of American Immigration History*. Metuchen, NJ: Scarecrow Press, 1990. 784p. Includes bibliographic references.

Cribb, R[obert] B. *Historical Dictionary of Indonesia*. Asian historical dictionaries; no. 9. Metuchen, NJ: Scarecrow Press, 1992. 633p. Includes maps and bibliographic references. An excellent introduction of Indonesia and one of the most successful of the Asian Historical Dictionaries series.

Crouchett, Lorraine Jacobs. *Filipinos in California: From the Days of the Galleons to the Present*. El Cerrito, CA: Downey Place Publishing House, 1982. 154p.

Cunningham, Alexander. *Book of Indian Eras, with Tables for Calculating Indian Dates*. Varanasi, India: Indological Book House, 1970. 227p. First published in 1883. Includes tables and bibliographic references.

Daftar nama pengarang Melayu Malaysia. Kuala Lumpur: Dewan Bahasa dan Pustaka, Kementerian Pendidikan Malaysia, 1989. 288p. A list of Malaysian names.

Daniels, Roger. *Asian America: Chinese and Japanese in the United States since 1850*. Seattle: University of Washington Press, 1988. 384p. Includes bibliography and index.

Daniels, Roger. *History of Indian Immigration to the United States: An Interpretive Essay*. New York: Asia Society, 1989. 55p. An overview with abundant documentation.

Daniels, Roger. ''The Indian Diaspora in the United States.'' In *Migration: The Asian Experience*, Judith M. Brown and Rosemary Foot, editors. New York: St. Martin's Press, 1994, pp. 83–103.

de Casparis, J.G. *Indonesian Chronology*. Leiden: E.J. Brill, 1978.

DeMonaco, MaryKim. ''Disorderly Departure: An Analysis of the United States Policy Toward Amerasian Immigration.'' In *Brooklyn Journal of International Law*, vol. 15:3 (1989), pp. 641–666. Reprinted in McClain, 1994, pp. 217–285. History of legislation surrounding emigration of mixed race children from Southeast Asia.

Domingo, Benjamin B. *Hawaii's Eminent Filipinos*. Second edition. Manila, Philipines: Foreign Service Institute, 1983. 323p.

Domingo, Benjamin B. *The Philippines and Hawaii*. Second edition. Manila, Philippines: Foreign Service Institute, 1983. 432p.

Eade, J.C. *Southeast Asian Ephemeris: Solar and Planetary Positions, A.D. 638–2000*. Studies on Southeast Asia. Ithaca, NY: Southeast Asia Program, Cornell University, 1989. 175p. Chiefly tables; includes bibliographic references.

Eade, J.C. ''Southeast Asian Intercalation: Variations and Complexities.'' In *Journal of Southeast Asian Studies*, vol. 24, part 2 (September, 1993), pp. 239–250.

Embree, Ainslie T. *Encyclopedia of Asian History*. Prepared under the auspices of the Asia Society. Four volumes. New York: Charles Scribner's Sons, 1988. See especially the article on ''Chinese Emigration,'' by Paul R. Spickard, p. 441. Includes bibliographies and index.

Espina, Marina E. *Filipinos in Louisiana*. New Orleans: A.F. Laborde, 1988. 100p. Traces the early presence of Filipinos in North America back to Spanish colonial times. Some Filipinos established setlements in Louisiana in the 1830s.

Finestone, Jeffrey. *The Royal Family of Thailand*. The descendants of King Chulalongkorn. Bangkok: Phitsanulok Publishing Co., 1989. 688p.

Freeman, James M. *Hearts of Sorrow: Vietnamese-American Lives*. Stanford, CA: Stanford University Press, 1989. 446p.

Freeman-Grenville, G.S.P. *The Muslim and Christian Calendars*. Being tables for the conversion of Muslim and Christian dates from the Hajra to the year A.D. 2000. New York: Oxford University Press, 1963. 87p. Second edition. London: R. Collings, 1977.

Gahlot, Sukhvir Singh, and Ghanshyam Lal Devra. *Indian Calendars, A.D. 1444 to A.D. 1543*. Jodhpur (Rajasthan): Rajasthan Sahitya Mandir, 1980. 201p. Chiefly tables. Includes bibliography.

Golenpaul, Ann. *Information Please Almanac, Atlas and Yearbook*. Planned and supervised by Dan Golenpaul Associates. Boston: Houghton Mifflin Company, 1994. Published annually. Cover title is *Information Please Almanac*.

Gonzales, Juan L., Jr. ''Asian Indian Immigration Patterns: The Origins of the Sikh Community in California.'' In *International Migration Review*, vol. 20 (Spring 1986), pp. 40–53. Explains why eighty-five to ninety percent of East Indian immigrants were of the Sikh religion.

Goonetileke, H.A.I. *A Bibliography of Ceylon*. Two volumes. Bibliotheca Asiatica 5; Bibliotheca Asiatica 14. Zug, Switzerland: Inter Documentation Co., 1973–1976. 865p. Systemic guide to the literature on the land, people, history and culture published in western languages from the sixteenth century to the present day.

Grant, Bruce K. *A Guide to Korean Characters: Reading and Writing Hangŭl and Hanja*. Second revised edition. Elizabeth, NJ: Hollym International, 1982. 367p. Includes bibliography and indexes.

Haines, David W. ''Family and Community Among Vietnamese Refugees.'' In *International Migration Review*, vol. 15 (Spring/Summer 1981), pp. 310–319.

Haines, David W. ''Kinship in Vietnamese Refugee Resettlement.'' In *Journal of Comparative Family Studies*, vol. 1 (1988), pp. 1–17.

Haines, David W. *Refugees as Immigrants: Cambodians, Laotians, and Vietnamese in America*. Totowa, NJ: Rowan & Littlefield, 1989. 198p.

Haines, David W. ''Southeast Asian Refugees in the United States: The Interaction of Kinship and Public Policy.'' In *Anthropological Quarterly*, vol. 3 (1982), pp. 170–181.

Halpern, Joel M., and Lucy Nguyen-Hong-Nhiem. *A Bibliography of Cambodian, Hmong, Lao, and Vietnamese Americans*. Asian Studies Program Special Publication; no. 3. Amherst: University of Massachusetts, 1992. 140p. Broad in scope, including works of an historical, journalistic, sociological, political, and ethnological nature.

Han, Woo-keun. *The History of Korea*. Translated by Lee Kyung-shik. Translation of Hanguk tongsa. Seoul: Eul-yoo Publishing Co., 1970; Honolulu: East-West Center Press, 1971. 551p.

Haroon, Mohammed. *Cataloguing of Indian Muslim Names*. Delhi, India: Indian Bibliographies Bureau, 1984. 72p. Includes index and bibliography.

Hedrick, Basil Calvin, and Anne K. Hedrick. *Historical and Cultural Dictionary of Nepal*. Historical and cultural dictionaries of Asia; no. 2. Metuchen, NJ: Scarecrow Press, 1972. 198p. Includes bibliography.

Hess, Gary R. "The Asian Indian Immigrants in the United States: The Early Phase, 1900–65." In *Population Review*, vol. 25:1–2 (1981), pp. 29–34.

Hess, Gary R. "The Forgotten Asian Americans: The East Indian Community in the United States." In *Pacific Historical Review*, vol. 43 (1974), pp. 577–596.

Hess, Gary R. "The 'Hindu' in America: Immigration and Naturalization Policies and India, 1917–1946." In *Pacific Historical Review*, 38 (1969), pp. 59–79. Reprint in McClain, 1994, pp. 79–99.

Hing, Bill Ong. *Making and Remaking Asian America Through Immigration Policy, 1850–1990*. Stanford, CA: Stanford University Press, 1993. 340p.

Historical Dictionary of Myanmar. Metuchen, NJ: Scarecrow Press, 1995.

A History of Japanese in Hawaii. Honolulu: The United Japanese Society of Hawaii, 1971.

Irwin, A.M.B. *The Burmese and Arakanese Calendars*. Rangoon: 1909.

Jacoby, Harold S. "U.S. Strategies of Asian Indian Immigration Restriction, 1882–1917." In *Population Review*, vol. 25:1–2 (1981), pp. 35–40.

Jensen, Joan M. *Passage from India: Asian Indian Immigration in North America*. New Haven, CT: Yale University Press, 1988. 350p. A more recent work on Asian Indians in America is forthcoming.

Jones, Robert B. *Thai Titles and Ranks*. Including a translation of "Traditions of Royal Linage in Siam" by King Chulalongkorn. Data paper, Cornell University, Southeast Asian Program; no. 81. Ithaca, NY: Southeast Asia Program, Department of Asian Studies, Cornell University, 1971. 147p.

Jones, Russell. *Chinese Names*. Notes on the use of surnames & personal names by the Chinese in Malaysia and Singapore. Petaling Jaya, Selangor, Malaysia: Pelanduk Publications, 1984. 84p. Includes bibliography and index.

Juergensmeyer, Mark. "The Gadar Syndrome: Ethnic Anger and Nationalist Pride." In *Population Review*, vol. 25:1–2 (1982), pp. 48–58. Includes discussion of Sikh nationalism in the Punjab and how it affected immigration.

Karni, Rahadi S. *Bibliography of Malaysia and Singapore*. Kuala Lumpur: Penerbit Universiti Malaya, 1980. 649p.

Kaur, Amarjit. *Historical Dictionary of Malaysia*. Asian historical dictionaries; no. 13. Metuchen, N.J.: Scarecrow Press, 1993. 300p. Includes maps and bibliographic references.

Kelly, Gail P. *From Vietnam to America: A Chronicle of the Vietnamese Immigration to the United States*. Boulder, CO: Westview Press, 1977. 254p.

Khurshid, Anis. *Cataloguing of Pakistani Names*. University of Karachi, Department of Library Science, Occasional Papers. Karachi: Department of Library Science, University of Karachi, 1974. 42p.

Kim, Chin, and Bok Lim C. Kim. "Asian Immigrants in American Law: A Look at the Past and the Challenge Which Remains." In *American University Law Review*, vol. 26 (1977), pp. 373–407. Reprinted in McClain, 1994, pp. 309–407.

Kim, Hyung-chan. *Dictionary of Asian American History*. New York: Greenwood Press, 1986. 627p. Includes short articles on individual topics and events, biographies, surveys, bibliography, chronology, statistical abstract, and index. See especially the entries "Vietnamese," by Sucheng Chen, pp. 734–739 and "Asian Indians," by Raymond B. Williams, pp. 45–48.

Kim, Hyung-chan. *A Legal History of Asian Americans, 1790–1990*. Westport, CT: Greenwood Press. 200p.

Kim, Hyung-chan, and Cynthia C. Mejia. *The Filipinos in America, 1898–1974: A Chronology & Fact Book*. Ethnic Chronology Series; no. 23. Dobbs Ferry, NY: Oceana Publications, 1976. 143p. Includes many news items and an extensive bibliography. Later volumes in the same series update events to 1980.

Kimura, Yukiko. *Issei: Japanese Immigrants in Hawaii*. Honolulu: University of Hawaii Press, 1988. 283p. Includes bibliography and index.

Kitano, Harry H. L., and Roger Daniels. *Asian Americans: Emerging Minorities*. Englewood Cliffs, NJ: Prentice Hall, 1988. 214p. A new edition should publish in 1995.

Knoll, Tricia. *Becoming Americans: Asian Sojourners, Immigrants, and Refugees in the Western United States*. Portland, OR: Coast to Coast Books, 1982. 356p.

Kodansha Encyclopedia of Japan. First edition. Nine volumes. New York: Kodansha, 1983. Also known as *Encyclopedia of Japan*. Includes index. See especially the entries "Emigration," by D. Eleanor Westney, vol. 2, pp. 200–201 and "United States Immigration Acts of 1924, 1952, and 1965," by Roger Daniels, vol. 8, pp. 164–165.

LaBrack, Bruce. "Immigration Law and the Revitalization Process: The Case of the California Sikhs." In *Population Review*, vol. 25:1–2 (1981), pp. 59–66.

LaBrack, Bruce. "The Reconstitution of Sikh Society in Rural California." In *Overseas Indians: A Study in Adaptation*, George Kurian and Ram P. Srivastava, editors. New Delhi: Vikas, 1983, pp. 215–240.

LaBrack, Bruce. *The Sikhs of Northern California: 1904–1986*. Immigrant Communities & Ethnic Minorities in the United States & Canada; no. 22. New York: American Migration Series Press, 1988. 489p.

LaBrack, Bruce, and Karen Isaksen Leonard, "Conflict and Compatibility in Punjabi-Mexican Immigrant Families in Rural California, 1915–1965." In *Journal of Marriage and the Family*, vol. 46:3 (1984), pp. 527–537.

Lasker, Bruno. *Filipino Immigration to Continental United States and to Hawaii*. The American Immigration Collection. New York: Arno Press, 1969. 445p. Reprint of 1931 publication of American Council Institute of Pacific Relations. Supplies a good overview of motivations and problems of Filipino workers in the United States prior to the Tydings-McDuffie Act.

Leba, John Kong, John H. Leba, and Anthony T. Leba. *The Vietnamese Entrepreneurs in the U.S.A.: The First Decade*. Houston, TX: Zieleks, 1985. 259p.

Leonard, Karen Isaken. "Ethnicity Confounded: Punjabi Pioneers in California." In *Sikh History and Religion in the Twentieth Century*, Joseph T. O'Connell et al., editors. South Asian Studies Papers; no. 3. Toronto: University of Toronto Centre for South Asian Studies, 1988, pp. 314–333.

Leonard, Karen Isaken. *Making Ethnic Choices: California's Punjabi Mexican Americans*. Asian American History and

Culture Series. Philadelphia: Temple University Press, 1992. 333p.

Leonard, Karen Isaken. "Marriage and Family Life Among Early Asian Indian Immigrants." In *Population Review*, vol. 25:1–2 (1982), pp. 67–75.

Leonard, Karen Isaken. "Pioneer Voices from California: Reflections on Race, Religion & Ethnicity." In *The Sikh Diaspora: Migration and the Experience Beyond Punjab*, N. Gerald Barrier and Verne A. Dusenbery, editors. Delhi: Chanakya Publications, 1989, pp. 120–140.

Leonard, Karen Isaken. "Punjabi Farmers and California's Alien Land Law." In *Agricultural History*, vol. 59:4 (1985), pp. 549–562.

Leonard, Karen Isaken. *Social History of an Indian Caste: The Kayasths of Hyderabad*. Berkeley, CA: University of California Press, 1978. 353p. Extensive genealogical information and bibliographic apparatus. A model for other works of this nature.

Mangiafico, Luciano. *Contemporary American Immigrants: Patterns of Filipino, Korean, and Chinese Settlement in the United States*. New York: Praeger, 1988. 211p.

Maring, Joel M., and Ester G. Maring. *Historical and Cultural Dictionary of Burma*. Historical and cultural dictionaries of Asia series; no. 4. Metuchen, NJ: Scarecrow Press, 1973. 290p. Includes bibliography.

Mattson, Mark T. *Atlas of the 1990 Census*. New York: Macmillan Publishing Company, 1992. 168p. Includes glossary. Part 1: Population; Part 2: Households; Part 3: Housing; Part 4: Race and Ethnicity; Part 5: Economy; and Part 6: Education.

May, Geoffrey. *Marriage Laws and Decisions in the United States*. A manual. New York: Russell Sage Foundation, 1929. 477p. There are references at the beginning of each state.

McClain, Charles. *Asian Indians, Filipinos, Other Asian Communities and the Law*. Asian Americans and the Law: Historical and Contemporary Perspectives; vol. 4. New York: Garland, 1994. 403p.

Melendy, H. Brett. *Asians in America: Filipinos, Koreans, and East Indians*. Boston: Twayne, 1977. 340p. A social history with abundant documentation.

Melendy, H. Brett. "Filipinos in the United States." In *Pacific Historical Review*, vol. 43 (1974), pp. 520–547. Reprinted in McClain, 1994, pp. 20–47.

Mulliner, Karl, and Lian The-Mulliner. *Historical Dictionary of Singapore*. Metuchen, NJ: Scarecrow Press, 1991. Serves as an introduction to Singapore—its history, culture, and politics.

Muzny, Charles C. *The Vietnamese in Oklahoma City: A Study in Ethnic Change*. Immigrant Communities & Ethnic Minorities in the United States & Canada; no. 37. New York: AMS Press. 200p.

Nelson, Andrew Nathaniel. *The Modern Reader's Japanese-English Character Dictionary*. Second revised edition. Rutland, VT: Charles E. Tuttle Company, 1974. 1109p. Includes bibliographic references.

100-year Calendar, Lanna Thai. Chiang Rai, Thailand: Chiang Rai Teachers' College, 1984.

O'Neill, P.G. *Japanese Names: A Comprehensive Index by Characters and Readings*. First edition. English and Japanese. New York: John Weatherhill, 1972. 359p. Cover title: *Nihon jinmei chimei jiten*.

Palmer, Spencer J. *Studies in Asian Genealogy*. World Conference on Records and Genealogical Seminar at Salt Lake City, Utah, 1969. Provo, Utah: Brigham Young University Press, 1972. 281p. See especially "Chinese Genealogies as a Source for the Study of Chinese Society," by Wolfram Eberhard, p. 28 and "The Korean Chopko as a Historical Source," by Edward W. Wagner, pp. 141–146.

Parise, Frank. *The Book of Calendars*. New York: Facts on File, 1982. 387p. Includes index.

Patterson, Maureen L.P. *South Asian Civilizations*. A bibliographic synthesis. Chicago: University of Chicago Press, 1981. 835p.

Patterson, Wayne. *The Korean Frontier in America: Immigration to Hawaii, 1896–1910*. Honolulu: University of Hawaii Press, 1988. 274p. Includes bibliography and index. Based on PhD dissertation published by the University of Pennsylvania, Philadelphia, 1977.

Rony, A. Kohar. *An Analysis of Indonesian Name Patterns*. Washington, D.C.: 1968.

Rutledge, Paul. *The Vietnamese Experience in America*. Minorities in Modern America. Bloomington: Indiana University Press, 1992. 173p.

Scholberg, Henry. *Bibliography of Goa and the Portugese in India*. New Delhi: Promilla, 1982.

Schurz, William Lytle. *The Manila Galleon*. New York: Dutton, 1959. 453p. An important source on trade routes from the Philippines during the Spanish colonial period (1593–1815) which brought Filipino sailors to the western hemisphere.

Schwartzberg, Joseph E. *A Historical Altas of South Asia*. Revised edition with additional material. Reference series, Association for Asian Studies; no. 2. New York: Oxford University Press, 1992. 376p. A massive work which delineates the geography of the region and the rise and fall of various states. Includes maps.

Shaw, Scott. *Cambodian Refugees in Long Beach, California: The Definitive Study*. Hermosa Beach, CA: Buddha Rose, 1989. 103p.

Shih-chiu, Liang. *A New Practical Chinese-English Dictionary*. Hong Kong: Far East Book Co., 1981. 1355p. Includes four indexes. Other title: *Tsui hsin shih yung Han Ying tz'u tien: A New Practical Chinese-English Dictionary*.

Singh, Jane, et al. *South Asians in North America: An Annotated and Selected Bibliography*. Berkeley, CA: Center for South and Southeast Asia Studies. University of California, 1988. 177p. Includes bibliography of early twentieth century periodicals published by and for South Asian immigrants, mostly in North America.

Singhan, E.V. *Tamil, Hindu, Indian Names*. Singapore: EVS Enterprises, 1982.

Smith, Harold Eugene. *Historical and Cultural Dictionary of Thailand*. Metuchen, NJ: Scarecrow Press, 1976.

Statistical Abstract of the United States. 112th edition. Washington: U.S. Department of Commerce, Economics and Statistics Administrations, Bureau of the Census, 1992. Published annually. An enlarged print edition is published by Bernan Press, Lanham, Maryland. A commercial version is published by Reference Press, Austin, Texas. A computer file of this publication which includes guides is published by the U.S. Department of Commerce, Economics and Statistics Administrations, Bureau of the Census, Data User Services Division (other title: *Statistical Abstract on CD-ROM*; Supplement: *U.S.A. Count-*

ies). A national data book, this title is a statistical reference and guide to over 250 statistical publications and sources from government and private organizations.

Stuart-Fox, Martin, and Mary Kooyman. *Historical Dictionary of Laos*. Asian historical dictionaries; no. 6. Metuchen, NJ: Scarecrow Press, 1992. 258p. Includes extensive bibliography.

Survey Department of Sri Lanka (Minindoru Departamentuva). *The National Atlas of Sri Lanka*. Colombo, Sri Lanka: Survey Department, 1988. 142p. Includes index.

Swamikannu Pillai, L.D. *An Indian Ephemeris, A.D. 700 to A.D. 1799*. Showing the daily solar and lunar reckoning according to the principal systems current in India with their English equivalents; also the ending moments of tithis and nakshatras and the years in the different eras: A.D., Hajra, Saka, Vikrama, Kaliyuga, Kollam, etc. with a perpetual almanac and other auxiliary tables. Seven volumes in eight. Madras: Government Press, 1922. Title of volume one is *General Principles and Tables*. A revised and enlarged edition of Indian chronology, 1911. Volume seven was first published separately in 1915: *An Indian Ephemeris A.D. 700 to A.D. 1999*.

Takaki, Ronald T. *Strangers from a Different Shore: A History of Asian Americans*. Boston: Little, Brown, 1989. 570p. Narrative history which interweaves individual stories of Japanese, Chinese, Korean, Filipino, East Indians, Vietnamese, Cambodian, and Laotian immigrants. Dr. Takaki is also overseeing a fifteen volume historical series, forthcoming from Chelsea House in New York, entitled *The Asian American Experience*. Each volume will discuss a particular nationality.

Tarkalankar, Girish Chandra (Pandit), and (Pandit) Pran Nath Saraswati. *Chronological Tables ... from 1764–1900*. Bhowanipore: Sreenath Bannerjee, 1894.

Thernstrom, Stephan. *Harvard Encyclopedia of American Ethnic Groups*. Cambridge: Belknap Press of Harvard University, 1980. 1076p. Includes bibliographies. See especially the entries "Chinese," by H.M. Lai, pp. 218, 231, 224; "Japanese," by Harry H.L. Kitano, p. 562; "Koreans," by Hyung-chan Kim, p. 602; "Indochinese," by Mary Bowen Wright, pp. 508–510; "East Indians," by Joan M. Jensen, p. 296; "Burmese," p. 290; "Indonesians," p. 513; and "Thai," p. 990.

Thomas, Timothy N. *Indians Overseas: A Guide to Source Materials in the India Office Records for the Study of Indian Emigration, 1830–1950*. London: British Library, 1985. 97p.

Thornton, Edward. *A Gazetteer of the Territories under the Government of the East-India Company and of the Native States on the Continent of India*. Four volumes. London: W. H. Allen, 1857. Much information on the history, ethnography, and political status of various localities.

Ulack, Richard, and Gyula Pauer. *Atlas of Southeast Asia*. New York: Macmillan Publishing Co., 1989. An accessible work on this region, with lots of background material on each country. 171p. Includes index and bibliography.

United States. Central Intelligence Agency. *Arabic Personal Names*. Washington, D.C.: Government Printing Office, 1964.

United States. Central Intelligence Agency. *Burmese Personal Names*. Washington, D.C.: Government Printing Office, 1961.

United States. Central Intelligence Agency. *Gujerati Personal Names*. Washington, D.C.: Government Printing Office, 1965. 44p.

United States. Central Intelligence Agency. *Hindi Personal Names*. Washington, D.C.: Government Printing Office, 1964. 75p.

United States. Central Intelligence Agency. *Nepali Personal Names*. Washington, D.C.: Government Printing Office, 1968. 37p.

United States. Central Intelligence Agency. *Telugu Personal Names*. Washington, D.C.: Government Printing Office, 1964. 50p.

United States. Central Intelligence Agency. *Thai Personal Names*. Washington, D.C.: Government Printing Office, 1964.

United States. Central Intelligence Agency. *Vietnamese Personal Names*. Washington, D.C.: Government Printing Office, 1961.

Vallangca, Caridad Concepcion. *The Second Wave: Pinay & Pinoy (1945–1960)*. San Francisco: Strawberry Hill Press, 1987. 279p. A follow-up to Roberto V. Vallangca, 1977.

Vallangca, Roberto V. *Pinoy, the First Wave, 1898–1941*. San Francisco: Strawberry Hill Press, 1977. 148p. A collection of personal narratives.

The Vietnamese Community in Orange County: An Oral History. Santa Ana, CA: Vietnamese Chamber of Commerce in Orange County, 1991–. An ongoing historical project, four volumes of which have appeared so far.

Ware, Edith W. *Bibliography on Ceylon*. Coral Gabels, FL: University of Miami Press, 1962. 181p.

Who's Who among Asian Americans. Detroit: Gale Research, 1994. Over 6,000 entries with geographic, occupational, and ethnic/cultural heritage indexes.

Basic Genealogy Research Methods and Their Application to Asian Americans

Frederick Brady

Getting Started

Start with yourself. Record everything you know, from both your own memory and any records you possess. Before beginning research on the Asian origins of your family, exhaust all resources relating to your family in America by interviewing all relatives and friends of the family, especially the older ones. You may be surprised at how much data can be recorded. Of course, memories can be faulty. Therefore, names and their spellings, places, dates, and relationships should be verified by obtaining original records (records created to record an event at the time the event takes place) or copies of the original records if at all possible.

When dealing with so many names, dates, and places, it is very easy to make mistakes. Some common errors include misspelling names of persons and places; incorrectly recording dates (writing 1962 or 1826 for 1862); omitting a child from a family, adding one, or attaching the wrong children to the wrong parents; "marrying" a woman to the wrong man; assigning incorrect birth dates so parents are too young to have children or are born after their own children; assigning the wrong sex to a person; or falsifying or omitting information of a sensitive nature, particularly when divorces or illegitimate births occur.

It is often necessary to make assumptions when records are unclear or nonexistent, but such assumptions must be made very carefully and logically. They should also be clearly annotated so a later researcher will know what assumptions were made. As for falsification, every researcher should strive to record information as honestly and accurately as possible. Most family researchers are not professional genealogists. Having a personal stake in the results, they want to be the descendants of "good" people. But those who deliberately falsify data in their genealogy, for whatever reason, should know that some day, someone who cares more about cold facts than family pride will uncover and publish those facts destroying the credibility of that genealogy.

Keep a log of the research process, including notes on where and when the information was found. Record call numbers and microfilm numbers of materials used. (Although be aware that, as libraries grow, materials are often recataloged and reclassified and call numbers and locations change.) Record the full title of the book or manuscript with the name of its author or originating office as well. Cite the sources of information in the notes area of each family group sheet. When necessary, give clear, detailed explanations of apparent discrepancies or other matters which might confuse someone who looks at your material. If you have questions or doubts about something you have written after researching it thoroughly, record those too. Also, keep a log of phone calls annotating the date, the name of the person or place called, and the subject of the call. When letters are sent asking for information, keep copies for your files to ensure that a clear and complete record of correspondence is always available.

Home and Family Sources

Search for old letters; diaries; scrapbooks; photo albums; grade reports from schools; cancelled checks; tax records; purchase receipts; old passports; awards from schools, clubs, and churches; and other materials which may have been stored away in a basement, garage, or attic. Their contents will aid your memory and document or elaborate on the results of interviews, providing dates of events. By observing clothing details, jewelry, background scenes, buildings, cars, and other details in a photo, extra clues as to identities, places, or dates may be discovered. Birth, marriage, and death certificates are primary sources of information and copies can be obtained from city and county offices if they cannot be located in a person's home. If an ancestor was locally prominent, a library or museum may have some of these records.

Most people of Asian ancestry will not have family Bibles, but there may be other religious artifacts on hand such as mortuary tablets or name registers from a family shrine. Military records, household registers, and other documents may be available as well. For Chinese and Koreans, the surname itself is the logical key to use to begin research; while for many Japanese (most of whom did not use surnames until 1875), a copy of a family crest may provide a clue to the family's history and the direction research should take.

Asian Genealogy Systems and Some Asian Records

Record types unique to Asian countries are described in detail in Chapter Three, but some of the major ones will be briefly mentioned here. After emigration, members of Asian communities continued, with some adaptation, to keep their records in the manner with which they were familiar. Most of the adaptations were due to the change in language to English and, to some extent, to the conversion of many community members to Christianity. However, most Asian people tend to be fairly conservative and it should not be surprising to find echoes of old traditions still thriving in America.

Basic differences in philosophy between Asia and Euro-America cause fundamental differences in the genealogical records from these regions. In East Asia, where Confucian philosophy has had a great influence on society for over two thousand years, pedigrees are recorded from the top down, beginning with the honored (and sometimes deified) ancestor. A family genealogical record is patriarchal in nature, giving the descendants of a single man. Occasionally, a few details on the families of certain women who married into the clan will be given, but information on females tends to be sparse. When a clan becomes very large, branches, established in locales other than the ancestral homeland, will keep new genealogies of their own. However, these genealogies are always linked to that of the main line. One's own place in the pedigree is somewhere near the bottom, among numerous brothers and cousins, but one's link with the founding ancestor, regardless of the number of generations in between, is unmistakable.

A Western pedigree chart, on the other hand, begins with oneself and branches out backward in time along both paternal and maternal lines. Western societies are also patriarchal in nature (though not to the extent that Confucian societies are) and while it is possible to find much information on maternal lines, it is usually more difficult. However, while many Western people are able to uncover as much information on some maternal lines as on paternal lines, an Asian may find little or no information.

An East Asian clan genealogy may also double as a family history, complete with biographical entries. A Western-style family history often has single-page pedigree charts and family group sheets (the former shows at a glance how far back the ancestry has been traced on a given individual while the latter shows the individual's parents, spouse, children, and childrens' spouses with dates and places of birth, marriage, death, burial, etc.), followed by brief biographies and stories about branches of the family. One form of Asian genealogy incorporates all of this into the pedigree chart. Beginning at the upper right and proceeding down and left, all information on family members "hangs under" the first ancestor. A single, horizontal line proceeds to the left from his name, with vertical lines going down to his children, who have lines going down from their names to their children's, and so forth. In order to fit everything into book-page format, the descending lines may have to be bent at right angles, going left, up, left again, and finally down again. When biographical information is included after a man's entry, it could be several pages before we come to the entry for his younger brother or son. In such cases, the horizontal pedigree line for that generation keeps going across the tops of the pages until the last son in the next generation is accounted for. The many numbering systems invented by Western genealogists to keep track of descent and generation are not used, so one must be able to follow these lines.

In China and Korea, the most comprehensive and accessible records are clan genealogies, kept by duly appointed clan genealogists. Degree of population coverage is not entirely certain, but it is estimated that in Korea only the wealthier ten percent of the population appears in clan genealogies. In China, the percentage is much higher, but poorer families still tend to be ignored. In addition, many Chinese genealogies were destroyed during the "Cultural Revolution" in China in the 1960s. Members of American branches may or may not be noted in the genealogies kept in China or they may have started new genealogies.

In Japan, genealogies were kept mainly by the upper ten percent of the population which consisted of the court nobility and the samurai class. The rest do appear in carefully kept religious inquisition registers, but individuals can be hard to identify because no one below samurai rank had surnames until 1875. Also, Buddhist temples keep registers of the dead for the purpose of memorial ceremonies (this custom is still observed in Japanese Buddhist temples outside Japan). Because these ceremonies are expensive, the registers of wealthier temple patrons tend to be better kept and preserved. As a result, doing research for a lower-class ancestor in East Asia can be very difficult, if not a near impossibility.

Religion plays a large part in determining the types of records to be obtained and the degree to which they cover the population. Traditionally, in European countries where Christianity predominated, parish priests kept records of births, marriages, deaths, and other events. Coverage was fairly universal. Christian churches in Asia tried to do the same thing, but because their membership was composed of a small minority of people in several countries, population coverage is comparatively minimal. Christian churches with Asian members in America have, of course, kept records of their membership, but rarely in the member's ancestral language and script. If a church was organized specifically for an Asian community, records in the mother tongue may exist for members of the first generation, but later generations will usually be recorded entirely in English.

Besides the Buddhist death records, another type of record exists in Japan which was kept in response to a religion's influence on politics. Anti-Christian policies in the mid-seventeenth century prompted the recording of *shūmon ninbetsuchō* or *shūmon aratamechō*, usually called "examination of religion records" or "religious inquisition records" in English. Periodically, local samurai officials would roust out all inhabitants of a village and force them to prove publicly that they were not secretly Christians. All names of proper Buddhists were then registered. When religious freedom was granted in 1872, this registration system was modified into today's household registration system: the *koseki tōhon*. The koseki system was imposed upon Taiwan and Korea when those countries were under Japanese rule during the first half of the twentieth century. Although modified after liberation from Japan, it continues to be used in both countries.

The Family History Library

After personal records and those of relatives have been thoroughly searched, repositories of genealogical data should be visited or contacted by mail. These include federal, state, and local governments and courthouses; universities and many private organizations; and archives and libraries. One of the most comprehensive repositories is the Family History Library (FHL) of the Genealogical Society of Utah in Salt Lake City. (Other facilities important to genealogical researchers with Asian ancestry are discussed at the end of this chapter.)

The Family History Library offers access to millions of primary and secondary records collected worldwide by the society which also functions as the Family History Department of the Church of Jesus Christ of Latter-day Saints, better known as the Mormons. The Church collects the records in obedience to one of its doctrines—the doctrine which stresses the importance of family ties

even after death. The Society's goal is to collect copies of records it can legally obtain from all over the world.

Concerning records for Asians and Asian Americans, the holdings of the Family History Library contain the largest collection (on microfilm) of Chinese genealogies in the entire world outside of China; the largest collection (on microfilm) of Korean genealogies; microfilm copies of Japanese emigration records, presumably containing the names of all emigrants from 1868 to the 1940s; and microfilm copies of more records on Pacific Coast immigrants than any other single repository. In addition, the Family History Library has published or obtained microfiche and indexes on compact discs (CDs) of tens of millions of names from all over the world which probably include tens of thousands of Asian names.

It has also extracted data from records on tens of millions of deceased individuals and compiled this information into a computer database called the "International Genealogical Index" (IGI). The IGI is available on microfiche and CD as part of the Family History Library's automated *FamilySearch* program. An overwhelming majority of the names listed are European and American. A Japanese edition, produced entirely in Japanese and containing only Japanese names, is available on microfiche at the main library and at the church's service center in Tokyo. Because production of such databases in Asian script is still highly experimental in the 1990s, Chinese and Korean language versions, as well as an updated Japanese language version, may not be available until the turn of the century.

There is also a database called the "Ancestral File," which contains pedigrees and family group records collected from donors over several decades. The Ancestral File is also available on CD through *FamilySearch*. For patrons of European descent, *FamilySearch* can be a real time saver, but because the database relies on information submitted by donors, there is relatively little on Asians as of this writing. Information can also be incorrect, having been submitted mostly by amateur genealogists. Still, it is worth a look, especially if one is part Asian or is a member of a long-established Asian American family. Two advantages of the Ancestral File are that it gives one a good idea of what research has been done (and is yet to be done) and researchers can obtain the names and addresses of those who submitted the data in order to contact them to determine if efforts can be pooled to avoid duplication and increase efficiency.

FamilySearch includes other automated databases such as the military index and Social Security death index. They can be used free of charge at the Family History Library and its branches. (Many libraries with major genealogical collections are also able to access these databases via CD or microfilm/microfiche.) Please note, that, out of respect for privacy, records which are so recent as to contain information on those individuals still living are not collected. With some exceptions, the library will not have records of immigrants after the nineteenth century.

The Granite Mountain Record Vault. Master copies of all microfilms and microfiches owned by the Genealogical Society of Utah and accessed through the Family History Library system are kept near Salt Lake City at the Granite Mountain Record Vault, a massive underground facility which naturally maintains ideal temperature and humidity for film storage. By the end of the twentieth century, nearly three million reels of microfilm will be stored there. The collection includes census records, parish records, genealogies, local histories, court records, emigration and immigration records, military records, newspapers and periodicals, tax records, directories, and many other types of records from all over the world. Acquisition is an ongoing process which occupies about fifty full-time catalogers in the main library. Records are not translated or indexed by the catalogers, but are cataloged in the language in which they are written. All the records are described so that patrons using the library catalog can easily identify those they will want to search.

Family History Centers. To serve patrons unable to travel to Salt Lake City, thousands of branch libraries or family history centers have been established all over the United States and throughout the world. The centers are usually located in local temples of the Church of Jesus Christ of Latter-day Saints. Hours of operation for family history centers vary; call the center in your area to get its schedule. Under the direction of the Family History Library, these centers maintain a core collection of materials on microfilm and microfiche which is intended to supply the general needs of researchers in a particular region. All family history centers provide the Family History Library Catalog and "International Genealogical Index" on microfiche as well as *FamilySearch*. Lists of branch library addresses for the United States and Canada are available free of charge at the main library. However, these addresses are not mailing addresses as the staff at these centers are not able to respond to research requests. All such requests should be directed to the main library in Salt Lake City. See "Libraries and Archives" in Part II under British Columbia, California, Hawaii, Oregon, and Washington for centers in areas important to Asian Americans. One does not have to be a member of the Mormon Church to use the main library or its branches. All microfilms in the collection at the main library are available free of charge, but patrons of the outlying branches must pay a small microfilm copying fee when requesting copies of films that are not already on file at the branch or at its area service center. Lists of genealo-

gists who have been accredited by the Society are also provided. Again, these lists are available from the main library or any of its branches, free of charge.

The Family History Library Catalog. The Family History Library Catalog (FHLC) provides access to all books and microforms in the library's collection except for those under special donor-imposed restrictions. The FHLC, available in both microfiche and CD, is frequently updated. In the main library, hundreds of microfiche readers and computer terminals are provided while the number of fiche readers and computers found in each branch library is determined by the size of the local Mormon population since it's their tithes which maintain the facilities. Staff members are on hand to provide assistance. Research experts at the library have also written dozens of helpful brochures which provide information on all aspects of genealogical research and instruction on how to use the FHLC efficiently. Some of these are free, others can be obtained for a few cents. (In fact, several of the FHL's "Resource Guides" and "Research Outlines" were consulted in the preparation of this chapter).

In the FHLC, access to catalog entries is given by title, author, editor, or other creating agency (if known). However, the most convenient headings to search under are in the Library of Congress Subject Headings section (under headings such as "Koreans—California" or "Chinese Emigration"), the surname catalog (the best place to look for genealogies, family histories, and biographies), and the locality catalog.

The locality catalog is usually the first place to look because most genealogical records are tied to the locality in which a birth, marriage, death, legal transaction, or lawsuit took place. Examples of headings a user can find are "Hawaii—Emigration and Immigration" or "California, Calaveras—Vital Records." City or county records are found under headings beginning with the name of the country and proceeding in descending order to state or province, county, and, finally, city or town. Every country in the world has its own separate set of fiche in the catalog, as does each state in the United States and each province in Canada. See Figure 2.1 for a more detailed example of the way locality headings are arranged. Counties are arranged alphabetically within the state and cities alphabetically within the county, followed by the catalog subdivisions which are also in alphabetical order. From "Utah, Sanpete, Fairview—History" (in Figure 2.1), Utah is the state; Sanpete is the county; Fairview is the city; and History, the catalog subdivision.

Patrons at the Family History Library sometimes miss records which could be very useful because they forget to look on more than one level in the locality section of the catalog. If you cannot find materials from a

----

Detailed Listing from Locality Index

UTAH - ARCHIVES AND LIBRARIES
UTAH - GENEALOGY
UTAH - HISTORY

UTAH, SANPETE - ARCHIVES AND LIBRARIES
UTAH, SANPETE - GENEALOGY
UTAH, SANPETE - HISTORY
UTAH, SANPETE, FAIRVIEW - ARCHIVES AND
 LIBRARIES
UTAH, SANPETE, FAIRVIEW - GENEALOGY
UTAH, SANPETE, FAIRVIEW - HISTORY
UTAH, SANPETE, MANTI - ARCHIVES AND
 LIBRARIES
UTAH, SANPETE, MANTI - GENEALOGY
UTAH, SANPETE, MANTI - HISTORY

UTAH, UINTAH - ARCHIVES AND LIBRARIES
UTAH, UINTAH - GENEALOGY
UTAH, UINTAH - HISTORY

Figure 2.1

certain town when searching on that level, go back to the county level and search there. Towns and cities which have had their records grouped together with records of other towns and cities when they were sent to archives may be found only under the county level. Immigration and census records, often assumed to be located only on the national level, can quite often be found cataloged on the state or county level and, in some cases, even on the city level.

One would want to search most locality headings in Hawaii, key port cities, and agriculture centers in British Columbia, California, Oregon, and Washington to find information on South Asians and Filipinos. This would include the headings of Biography, Business Records and Commerce, Cemeteries, Census, Church Records, Court Records, Directories, Emigration and Immigration, Funeral Homes, Genealogy, Hindu Records, Islamic Records, Land and Property, Medical Records, Merchant Marine, Military Records, Minorities, Naturalization and Citizenship, Newspapers, Obituaries, Probate Records, Public Records, Schools, and Vital Records for key port cities and agricultural centers. South Asians and Filipinos worked and/or settled in the following counties of California: Butte, Fresno, Imperial, Kern, Monterey, Sacramento, San Joaquin, San Luis Obispo, Solano, Sutter,

Tulare, and Yuba. In Washington, they concentrated in the Yakima Valley. In addition, Filipinos and South Asians harvested potatoes in Idaho, beets in Montana, and hops in Oregon. They also canned fish in Alaska.

Some examples of relevant immigration records at the FHL which have been microfilmed include the following from the Immigration and Naturalization Service: Admitted Alien Crew Lists of Vessels Arriving at San Francisco, 1896–1921 (8 reels); Certificate of Head Tax Paid by Aliens Arriving at Seattle from Foreign Contiguous Territory, 1917–1924, 1929 (10 reels); Passenger and Crew Lists of Vessels Arriving at Seattle, Washington, 1890–1921 (58 reels); Index to Passenger Lists of Vessels Arriving at San Francisco, 1893–1934 (28 reels) which includes alphabetical surname indexes to East Indians (1 reel) and Filipinos (6 reels); Passenger Lists of Vessels Arriving at San Francisco from Insular Possessions, 1907–1911 (2 reels) which with Passenger Lists of Vessels Arriving at Seattle and Port Townsend, 1908–1917 (1 reel), would concern primarily passengers from the Orient and Pacific islands; Passenger Lists of Vessels Arriving in San Francisco from Honolulu, 1902–1904 (1 reel); and St. Albans District Manifest Records of Aliens Arriving from Foreign Contiguous Territory: Arrivals at Canadian Border Ports from January 1895 to June 30, 1954 (937 reels) which includes Soundex manifest of non-Canadians crossing the border at St. Albans (as well as at Washington) and the rest of the Canadian border states.

For the Hawaiian Sugar Planters' Association, the FHL has Passenger Manifests of Filipino Contract Laborers, covering the period of 1906 to the 1970s (85 reels). The following separate indexes are included: General File; Free File; Death; Immigration; Varona Agreement; Returned to Manila (Prior to 1946), After 1946, 1946 to the Present; General File 1946 Contracts; Old Timer's File; Free File 1946 Contracts; and Pending File.

For the U.S. District Courts based on the West Coast, there are large collections of naturalization papers. The Washington Western District Naturalization index, for example, has 218 microfilm reels covering the years 1890 to 1953. District Court records from Los Angeles include records to 1979.

There are large vital record indexes for states and many counties on the West Coast and in Hawaii. In surveying these one should keep in mind how anti-miscegenation laws affected Asian Americans. Because of the ban against intermarriage, few South Asian and Filipino women emigrated. Filipinos and South Asians often went to adjoining states or out of the country to marry. South Asians were forced to trade in land through American-born children and spouses because of laws prohibiting alien ownership. (California adopted such a

---

Sampling of Microfilm Records at the Family History Library

Card Index to Chinese Passports, 1884-1898 [Hawaii]
Certificates of Identification of Chinese Immigrants, 1895-1897 [Hawaii]

Certifications of Hawaiian-born Children of Chinese Parentage, 1893-1898
Chinese and Japanese Emigrants into Portland, Oregon

Chinese Arrivals, 1847-1880 [Hawaii]
Chinese Entry Permits, 1888-1898 [Hawaii]

Distribution of Japanese immigrants, 1892-1894
Japanese Emigration Records

Lists of Chinese Passengers Arriving in San Francisco, California, 1882-1914
Registers of Chinese Laborers Arriving at San Francisco, 1882-1888

Ships' Passenger Manifests, 1843-1900
    [Hawaii; includes separate indexes for Chinese and Japanese]

Figure 2.2

---

law in 1913; Washington in 1914; Arizona in 1917; Louisiana in 1921; New Mexico in 1922; Oregon, Idaho, and Montana in 1923; Kansas in 1925; and Utah and Wyoming in 1943.)

Figure 2.2 provides a sampling of specific records on microfilm focusing on the Chinese and Japanese, the two groups which comprised the majority of Asian immigrants before 1900.

One must frequently explore many, or all, of these record types in order to track down an elusive ancestor. Since many South Asian Sikhs and Filipinos, singled out as laborers, were not allowed full participation in American society earlier in the twentieth century, they did not have the opportunity for an education and, consequently, not many have left behind personal accounts of their experiences. Since they were excluded from full citizenship, their names were not recorded by voter registrars or court reporters. Additionally, the census is often criticized for undercounting aliens and ethnic groups in general, though the 1910 and 1920 U.S. Census should certainly be searched.

Catalog records for East Asian materials written in Chinese, Korean, and Japanese are not found in the FHLC fiche or CDs. The reason is that, as of this writing, the cataloging system only accepts the roman alphabet.

During the 1990s, cataloging staff and computer experts have been working on an automated Asian catalog which will allow on-line access to entries in those languages. Until they are finished and all old catalog entries are input, access to entries for records from these three countries (and others, such as Singapore, where ''overseas'' Chinese are a large proportion of the population) is mostly through a card catalog in the main library. Microfilmed copies of that catalog, together with published guides to its use, are available in all branches of the Family History Library system. In regard to records from the Philippines, the library has an extensive collection which is described in the FHLC. Except for Sri Lanka, and a small collection from Indonesia, the amount of materials from the rest of Southeast and South Asia is, unfortunately, quite small.

Basic Genealogical Records—U.S.

Because of their primary importance as the gateways to America for nearly all immigrants from Asia, special emphasis will sometimes be given to the records of

Hawaii and California. However, Oregon, Washington, and British Columbia also played a large part in the admission of Asians to the United States. Using the instructions given in this chapter for searching for records in Hawaii or California, search these other coastal areas as well. Depending when the emigrant settled, it may also be necessary to search for records in states and provinces farther inland.

Before going on to descriptions of the actual record types, it is important to note the difference between primary and secondary records. Primary records, mentioned earlier, are records of first importance. They are created at the time of the event, not later from information in someone's memory. They are also almost exclusively of an official nature, created by people knowledgeable of record-keeping procedures. Examples are birth and death certificates created by a government official or baptism and christening records created by a church official. Primary records can, of course, contain errors (some intentional), but for the most part they are considered to be highly accurate and the best sources to use to provide data or documentation for a genealogy.

Secondary (or "second hand") sources are of less desirability. Still, the information they provide can be accurate despite the fact that they are not created at the time of the event. However, it is this lapse of time and the reliance for detail on fallible human memory (usually that of someone who witnessed the event or someone who was told of the event by a witness) which makes secondary records less desirable as a source of information.

Another type of secondary source may be a publication or article which indexes or prints portions of original records. An example is a book which lists all people naturalized in a certain state over a specific period of time providing the name, age, country of origin, and place of residence for each person listed. Such a source, while not providing all the information in the primary source, often cites exactly where the original record can be located. While mistakes in transcription due to the illegibility of the record or to human error can cause a secondary source of this type to be less than 100 percent accurate, in cases where the original records have been lost due to fire, floods, bad record keeping, etc.; shipped into storage where accessibility is limited; or are maintained by a small staff unable to service requests for records, a secondary source can be of value to a researcher.

Civil Registration/Vital Records

Civil records are, in theory, the most accurate and valuable resource available to genealogists. They are a primary source of information on births, marriages, divorces, and deaths. This is especially true after laws were passed dictating that government officials register all such events. Because the officials were required to issue certificates, every birth, marriage, or death in a given area should have been recorded with a copy on file.

By the time the earliest Asians immigrated to Hawaii, California, and other locations, the bureaucratic machinery was already in place to record those events in the immigrants' lives. In the case of sojourners or others who had not become Hawaiian or American citizens, births, marriages, and deaths were also routinely reported to officials in the native country through consuls or other representatives. Thus, if records from both countries can be obtained, valuable corroboration of the data is possible.

However careful and conscientious local officials and clerks may try to be, some people still slip through the cracks. One peculiarity of Hawaiian records is the "delayed birth" records. Since 1911, a person born in Hawaii whose birth wasn't registered can apply for a delayed birth certificate. The data on these certificates is secondary information and may be slightly inaccurate, but if there is no corroborating information available, whatever is written must be taken at face value.

To search for vital records in the Family History Library Catalog (or any other research center's catalog), look under the heading for the locality plus the subdivision "Vital Records." Some of the record collections have been indexed. Divorce records can be searched for under "Court Records." Be sure to search on all jurisdictional levels: national, state, county, and city (for example: "Hawaii, Maui—Vital Records;" "Hawaii, Maui—Vital Records—Indexes;" and "California, Los Angeles, Los Angeles—Court Records").

Also look in *FamilySearch* for the U.S. Social Security Death Index which lists 39.5 million deceased individuals who had obtained social security numbers. Most of the deaths listed occurred between 1962 and 1988, but a few as early as 1937 can be found. This index may be of help in locating relatives who received death benefits. It may also provide both information on the deceased person's last place of residence and clues to more information available from the Social Security Administration.

The Family History Library has not been able to collect all available vital records from every county in the United States and with few exceptions records from the twentieth century have not been collected, so it may be necessary to contact state offices and archives directly. A useful booklet which lists vital statistics offices in each state is *Where to Write for Vital Records* (see "Print Resources" section in Part II). Several other books on locating vital records are in the reference collection at the Family History Library as well as at many city and county libraries.

Immigration/Naturalization Records

As was related in Chapter One, Chinese contract laborers began to arrive in Hawaii in 1852 when the islands were an independent kingdom, followed by the Japanese in 1868 and 1884. California became a U.S. state in 1850, shortly after the first handful of Chinese gold rushers appeared. By the time the Koreans and Filipinos began to arrive in Hawaii in 1903 and 1906, respectively, Hawaii was a U.S. territory. Because less detailed records on naturalization were kept before 1906, Asian Americans descended from nineteenth-century immigrants will find reconstructing their family history from this record source challenging. Since 1906, the Justice Department has made efforts to maintain all immigration records in a central archive.

Not all of those who arrived to work in Hawaii and the United States stayed, and not all who stayed became citizens. Some immigrants, who intended to stay permanently, applied for citizenship soon after their arrival; others waited many years. Some died without being naturalized. Due to certain policies of the government, it was not possible at times for immigrants from certain countries to apply for citizenship, though their descendants who were born on American soil after 1868 were considered citizens. Since Filipinos and South Asians were not naturalized until much later than most groups, inquiries would be better sent to the Immigration and Naturalization Service (see below). (However, this should not preclude searching archives and courts for older petitions for citizenship, since South Asians had that privilege for a number of years prior to the Singh decision in 1923. Denied petitions also would be recorded.) Therefore searches for immigration and naturalization information cannot be done in the same step.

Naturalization, for most immigrants, was a process requiring several years and much paperwork. First, a "declaration of intent" was submitted by the immigrant any time after his entry into the United States. There was then a wait of two to five years (after 1906, three to seven

years) before a formal petition for citizenship could be filed. Other documents such as affidavits attesting to the applicant's meeting all legal requirements, a signed and dated copy of the U.S. Oath of Allegiance, and the certificate of citizenship itself, complete the record. However, many naturalizations occurred without any paperwork being done at all. For example, all citizens of the former Republic of Hawaii were granted U.S. citizenship en masse in 1898 when Hawaii was annexed by the United States.

Repositories of records relating to applications for naturalization are found in state archives and all levels of courts (of which there are over 5,000). The Family History Library initially targeted larger archives and courts in its acquisition searches and has yet to have obtain records for certain parts of the country. Also, records from the twentieth century have not been collected. See Figure 2.3 for a list of headings from the FHL catalog which should be searched. (These same headings should be searched in the card catalog of any archive or library.)

It may be necessary to search the records of several courts to locate any information on the immigration/naturalization of your ancestor. Copies of immigration records and an index to the records of 1906–1956 are available from the Immigration and Naturalization Service office in one's own state of residence, but the records are closed to all but those legally entitled to access them. The addresses of these offices are available in the federal section of any city telephone directory.

Census Records and the Soundex

Since 1790, the federal government has conducted nationwide censuses every ten years, but because so few Asians lived in the United States before 1850, we will concern ourselves here with censuses from that year on. Each census remains confidential until seventy-two years after the date it is conducted (i.e. until the year 2000, the latest census available is that of 1920). Information in censuses still considered confidential can be released to

---

Headings from the Family History Library Catalog - Immigration/Naturalization Records

UNITED STATES - EMIGRATION AND IMMIGRATION
[STATE] - EMIGRATION AND IMMIGRATION
UNITED STATES or [STATE] - MINORITIES
UNITED STATES - NATURALIZATION AND CITIZENSHIP
[STATE, COUNTY, CITY] - COURT RECORDS
ASIANS - UNITED STATES or [STATE]
[NATIONALITY or ETHNIC GROUP] - UNITED STATES or [STATE]

Figure 2.3

close relatives if the subject is deceased or has given written permission. Form BC-600, ''Application for Search of Census Records,'' can be obtained from the Office of the Census and the Family History Library. A fee is required by the former for a census record search.

The value of census data is obvious: every person living in the country is supposed to be listed. Unfortunately, most of the information recorded in the 1890 census was destroyed in a fire and the records going back further may have been lost or destroyed by a variety of mishaps. Those that weren't (especially the older censuses) contain little information and tend to have been less carefully conducted. Still, any census is considered by most genealogists to be a resource of great importance.

In 1850 the census began to record not only name of the head of the household, as in earlier censuses, but the names of all other residents in a household as well. Age, occupation, and state or country of birth were also listed. The 1870 census noted whether a person's parents were foreign born. From 1880, the census identified family relationships and the state or country of birth of each individual's parents. From 1900, the census began to note the number of years people had been married, the year of immigration, and, for the first time, the full date of birth instead of only the year. The 1920 census reverted to giving only a person's age, without date of birth.

State and local censuses were usually taken in years other than those of the federal censuses. Of particular interest to Chinese Americans is the 1852 California census. All Chinese names in the California censuses of 1852, 1860, 1870, and 1880 have been extracted and listed together in a portion of the Carl T. Smith collection from Hong Kong, microfilms of which are available at the Family History Library. Censuses conducted by some cities in California also should be searched. The Kingdom of Hawaii has census records for 1866, 1878, 1890, and 1896, but some of them do not cover the entire kingdom. From 1900 on, Hawaii is covered by the U.S. censuses.

There are many indexes available to the censuses, but not all have been indexed the same way. Most indexes are statewide, and some cover individual counties and even cities, making it easier to locate someone known to have lived in a particular locale. The indexes, which have been compiled by various organizations, individuals, or the government should be consulted before searching the census itself. However, keep in mind, these indexes are secondary materials. Now that computers are making such tedious tasks as indexing relatively easy to accomplish, efforts are being made to put all census and census index data into automated resource files.

The soundex, first used on the 1880 census, is an index to censuses which lists names by pronunciation rather than spelling. Each surname is given a code consisting of the first letter of the name, plus three numerical digits. Because of the way a code is assigned, names like Johnson, Jenson, and Jansen, or Brown and Braun are listed together. This is an advantage since surname spellings had not yet been standardized by their bearers and, especially in earlier censuses, the census taker spelled names the way he heard family heads pronounce them. In soundex, variations in spelling caused by differences in pronunciation do not divide families in the index. A disadvantage is that unrelated families are found together and must be sorted out. As an example of how the coding system mixes Asian and European names: Chang, Chong, Chung, Camus, Conk, and Cong are all coded as C-520.

The soundex code for a surname is easily determined. There are only four steps involved for most names with a few exceptions for special cases. See Figure 2.4 for a breakdown of how the correct code for a surname is determined.

An example of several of the exceptions listed in Figure 2.4 is the Japanese name Minakuchi. By deleting the *I, A, U, H,* and *I* (leaving Mnkc), we generate the code M-522. But the code for the letter *M* is also 5, so the *N* cannot be used and one of the 2's must also be deleted since the *K* and the *C,* both a ''2,'' appear next to each other because the *U* which separated them was deleted. The correct code, after taking the exceptions to the soundex rules into account and adding zeroes, is M-200 (and not M-522). This will put Minakuchi together with other Japanese names such as Miki, Nishi, Noguchi, the Chinese name Ming, and others—all greatly differing in pronunciation. We see from this example the inadequacies of the soundex. As a result of the tremendous influx of Asian names in the twentieth century which sharply points out its failings and the advancement of computer technology (improving the task of indexing), there may come a time when soundex is totally abandoned.

The primary repositories of census information are state and federal libraries and archives. At the Family History Library, microfilmed copies are available. The catalog entries to search under are ''United States—Census—[Year]'' and ''United States—Census—[Year]—Indexes'' for federal censuses. For state and local censuses, search under ''[State]—Census—[Year];'' ''[State]—Census—[Year]—Indexes;'' ''[State, County]—Census—[Year];'' and ''[State, County]—Census—[Year]—Indexes.'' Some large cities also conducted censuses, so check for those in the catalog as well.

Soundex Coding of Surnames

The basic rules:

1.   Write the surname.

2.   Cross out the vowels (A, E, I, O, U) and the letters W, H, and Y, unless they are the first letter of the name.

3.   Write the first letter of the name.

4.   Write the numbers assigned to the remaining letters from the following table:

$$1 = B, F, P, V$$
$$2 = C, G, J, K, Q, S, X, Z$$
$$3 = D, T$$
$$4 = L$$
$$5 = M, N$$
$$6 = R$$

Thus, the code (C-520) for Chang, Camus, and Cong, etc., is determined as follows:

CHANG	CAMUS	CONG
CHANG	CAMUS	CONG
C 52(0)	C 52(0)	C 52(0)

Exceptions to the basic rules:

1.   Use only the first three digits of codes for long names.

2.   Add zeroes as needed for short names.

3.   If two or more letters side by side have the same soundex code, delete one of them. If the final result is a code of less than three digits, add zeroes as instructed above.

4.   If one or more letters immediately following the first letter have the same code as that letter would have had, delete them.

5.   Names with prefixes such as Van, Le, De (as in Van Buren and LeBaron) should be coded both with and without the prefixes and searched for in both places in the soundex.

6.   If letters with the same number code end up next to each other because a letter between them (such as a vowel) was crossed out, one of the duplicate numerals should be deleted.

Figure 2.4

Church Records

Some churches in the U.S. store their records in central archives, but a great many still hold theirs locally, especially if they are not affiliated with larger organizations or movements. The Family History Library's collection of church records in the United States is very large, but spotty, due to the large number of churches with which it has to negotiate. Many Asian Christians organized congregations consisting wholly of members of their own ethnic group when population numbers supported such an action. Other Asians joined existing local congregations of mostly white membership and determining if such a church had Asian members can be challenging. One advantage of the records of an ethnic congregation is that more records, especially earlier ones, will be in the language of the homeland. While this will make them harder for thoroughly Americanized descendants to read, they will provide better clues to records in the Asian country of origin.

If an ancestor was educated at a Christian school, raised in a Christian orphanage, or married to a Christian, he may have been baptized into the church regardless of whether he considered himself a Christian or even was a member of that church. The record of the ordinance may still exist and could be useful to a genealogist.

Probably the best place to look first for church records is in the section of church listings in the yellow pages of the telephone directory where an ancestor lived. A few major church archives which may be of help are the Diocese of Honolulu, Chancery Office (Roman Catholic); the American Congregational Association—Congregational Library (Congregational); the Presbyterian Church—Department of History—Library (Presbyterian); and the United Methodist Church—General Commission on Archives and History—Library and Archives (Methodist). (See Part II for addresses.)

Buddhists, Sikhs, Hindus, and Muslims are erecting more and more religious buildings in the mainland United States and Hawaii. They, too, depending on when they were established in the United States, will keep or now have records of genealogical value. Of special importance to Japanese Americans are the Buddhist death registers kept in Hawaii by Japanese Buddhist priests at their temples. These are a good example of a cultural practice being transplanted from the ancestral homeland to America.

Religious records can be searched for in the Family History Library Catalog under headings such as "[State, County, City]—Church Records (Christian only)," "[State, County, City]—Buddhist Records," "[State, County, City]—Hindu Records," "[State, County, City]—Islamic Records," and "[State, County, City]—Shinto Records." Be sure to search under all levels: state, county, and especially, city. Other subdivisions which can be used after the locality name are "Church Directories" as well as directories of all of the religions listed above.

Cemetery Records/Tombstone Inscriptions

Although many earlier immigrants who died in America were buried with wooden headstones which soon deteriorated and no longer exist, some do survive. To locate them, churches or temples near your ancestor's home should be contacted since many older American cemeteries are near churches and other religious buildings. A few Chinese clan associations erected ancestral halls (some still in use) in America to serve as their official headquarters. If a hall was built outside a city, members could have been buried on its grounds. Most Asian laborers, considered to be "heathens" (i.e. not Christians), were not allowed burial in Christian cemeteries. Even when an Asian American was a Christian, the Asian, due to discrimination, was buried apart from white Christians.

Cemetery records often give details of a person's life beyond the mere dates of death and burial and location of the grave. But if these records cannot be located, an inscription on a headstone might serve as a substitute source of information for an individual. Funeral homes, formerly known as mortuaries (and before that, undertakers), also have records which should be sought. Look in the Family History Library Catalog under "[State, County, City]—Cemeteries," and "[State, County, City]—Funeral Homes."

Passenger Lists

When ships were the only means of transportation across the Pacific Ocean, all Asian emigrants bound for the Americas in the nineteenth and early twentieth centuries stopped in Hawaii. On the mainland, the most commonly used port was San Francisco. Other important ports were Oakland, Los Angeles, San Diego, Portland, Seattle, and Vancouver. Several collections of passenger lists exist for ships arriving in Hawaii but, unfortunately, few passenger lists for ships arriving on the west coast have been preserved.

The Family History Library has microfilm copies of passenger lists for ships arriving in Honolulu between 1843 and 1900. The original records are available at the Hawaii State Archives. Also included in the copies are separate Chinese and Japanese indexes to the lists. Because Koreans did not begin arriving in Hawaii until 1903, they are not listed. The Library has several different collections of Chinese passenger lists including "Lists of Chinese passengers arriving in San Francisco, California, 1882–1914," "Registers of Chinese laborers arriving in San Francisco, 1882–1888,'' and ''Lists of Chinese passengers arriving Seattle and Port Townsend, 1882–1916.''

The Hawaiian Sugar Planters' Association (HSPA) in Aiea, Hawaii, has passenger lists and indexes of Filipinos from the year 1906. The Family History Library has obtained microfilms of these records. The Hawaii State Archives and the archives of the HSPA should be searched for records on Korean immigrants. If passenger lists are no longer available, other records such as labor permits, passports, work rosters, etc. should be sought. The Family History Library has also obtained microfilm copies of Japanese emigration records. These will be described in Chapter Three.

In addition to the microfilmed records, the Family History Library has many books on Asian immigration, some of which contain personal narratives of individual immigrants. All of these books give valuable historical information on the movements of the immigrants and the challenges they faced. To locate books and microfilms on Asian immigration and passenger lists in the Family History Library, look under ''[State]—Emigration and Immigration,'' ''[State, County]—Emigration and Immigration,'' and ''[State]—Minorities.'' Also look under the specific nationality or ethnic group in the Library of Congress Subject Heading section of the catalog under ''Koreans—Hawaii,'' ''Chinese Americans—Pennsylvania,'' ''Chinese Emigration,'' ''Asians—United States,'' etc.

Passports

If an ancestor was naturalized or born in the United States and applied for a U.S. passport, the document is valuable corroboration of birth and residence information. After 1915 photographs were included. Passport applications dated before 1905 are kept in the National Archives. Copies can be obtained from the Diplomatic Records Branch of the Archives by submitting the passport holder's name, residence, and the approximate date of the passport. Passport applications dated after 1905 are held in the Passport Office at the Department of State, Washington, D.C. Copies can be obtained in a similar manner to that above, except the holder's date of birth is needed instead of residence. There is a small fee for this service.

Foreign passports held by ancestors may have been used in applying for U.S. citizenship. (See the section in this chapter on immigration and naturalization.) It is possible to locate information on foreign passports in the Family History Library collection by searching in the catalog under ''[Country]—Emigration and Immigration.'' More details on this are given in Chapter Three.

Military Records

Tens of thousands of Americans of Asian ancestry have served with distinction in the U.S. military. Especially notable for their sacrifices are the Japanese American men and women who received release from internment camps during World War II to give loyal service to the United States while their families remained behind barbed wire. The National Archives hold records on the Japanese who were interned.

The Family History Library has microfilmed copies of military records up to World War I. Relatively few Asian Americans would have had opportunities to serve in the military until the Spanish American War (1898–1900) and World War I (1914–1918). Military records are also available at the National Archives and other federal offices and state archives. The Family History Library Catalog should be searched under ''United States—Military Records'' and ''[State]—Military Records.''

While the FHL does not have military records for wars in the 1900s, it does have a collection of World War I draft registration cards for 1917 to 1918. They are arranged by state and county for the most part (although larger cities should be searched by street names—fortunately, maps of draft boards have also been preserved). All men between the ages of twenty-one and thirty-one were required to register as of June 5, 1917. Subsequent draft reviews for June 5 and August 24, 1918, listed men who had turned twenty-one since the previous date. The last, on September 12, 1918, included men from the ages eighteen to twenty-on and thirty-one to forty-five. The cards include name; date and place of birth; race; citizenship; personal description; name of employer, dependents, and other family members; marital status; father's place of birth; name and address of nearest relative; and citizenship status. They appear as ''United States Selective Service System, World War I Selective Service System Draft Registration Cards, 1917–1918'' (3680 reels) in the FHL collections.

The FHL also provides, as a part of *FamilySearch*, a military index which lists men and women who died while serving in the U.S. military during the Korean War (1950–1953) and later, up to 1957, plus those who died in Vietnam and neighboring countries from 1957 to 1975.

Court Records

Searching for court records can be as complex and time-consuming as searching for church records due to the number and types of courts in session throughout the United States. Courts exist on the national level, including district and circuit courts, and on the state, county, and city levels. Within these designations there are three kinds of courts: equity, civil, and criminal. The archives of equity courts (also called courts of chancellery, oversaw monetary cases) include estate records, such as wills and inventories of property, and records of other cases where no crime was broken or when the court had been asked to arbitrate as to the fairness of a transaction. Today, this type of court only exists in the United States in Delaware where matters concerning business law are handled. Civil courts, taking over much of the original functions of the equity court, handle lawsuits originating from disputes between individuals such as divorces, citizenship applications, and other non-criminal actions. Criminal courts handle cases where a crime or felony has allegedly been committed.

Any Asian immigrant who applied for citizenship will have a court file. Divorces and deaths which involve the division of property, any kind of lawsuit, or an arrest for any reason will create a court record. Many Asians in the United States in the early days of immigration will have criminal files because they were often arrested from time to time in response to local policies of harassment.

The records of city and county courts in the area in which an individual resided should be considered. Many courthouses still keep their old records on file, though many others are either turning to microfilm or entrusting older records to state archives. Because there are some 5,000 courts throughout the United States, the Family History Library has not yet been able to acquire copies of old records from all of them, though acquisitions continue. To locate microfilms of court records in the Family History Library Catalog, search under all levels of jurisdiction: federal, state, and local (for example "United States—Court Records," "[State, County, City]—Court Records," "[State]—Correctional Institutions," or "[State, County]—Probate Records").

Land Records

Ownership of real estate has always been the basis of taxation and, upon the death of the owner, a part of the work of probate courts. It can also be the cause of lawsuits among heirs and neighbors. When land records are accidentally destroyed, new survey records and deeds are refiled with local courts. As a result, a person who owned land is often much easier to locate in old records than one who did not. He also tended to stay put, a fact which narrows the range of a genealogist's search.

The first Asian immigrants to Hawaii and the United States were nearly all transients: miners, railroad workers, contract plantation laborers, factory hands, etc. They lived and worked on someone else's property and had no intention of staying there permanently. A few changed their minds, however, and the "free immigrants" who followed them often intended to remain in Hawaii or the United States from the start. At certain times and places,

it was not possible for Asians to buy land because of local prejudice. But, when allowed to buy, these people usually purchased small shops or plots of farm land, creating records in local courts or city offices. Aside from a few losses through fire or simple deterioration, these records should still exist, especially because the oldest records concerning Asian Americans are no more than 150 years old.

The first places to look for land records are in the city offices and courthouses of various towns and counties. In the Family History Library Catalog search under the locality ("[State, County, City]"), followed by the subdivision "Land and Property." The Library has films of records from over 1500 courthouses, but the collection is by no means complete. Other subdivisions under which records may be found are "Taxation" and "Public Records."

The researcher should use a little imagination and ingenuity in searching for land records. References in letters, diaries, and personal histories can provide many clues. Old maps can also provide much useful information, as can wills and probate records. Make use of newspapers, periodicals, and local directories or histories which are dealt with in the following three sections of this chapter. Banks and other financial institutions which lent money in mortgage transactions will also have records which can be helpful. To find such records in the Family History Library Catalog, search under "[State, County, City]—Business Records and Commerce." This heading would also be useful in searching for someone known to have owned a business, even if they did not own the property on which it was located.

Newspapers and Periodicals

Most genealogists are well aware of the value of newspapers in research. Besides obituaries; notices of births, betrothals and marriages; and other public notices, some papers in port cities published passenger lists of arriving and departing ships. Advertisements, news, and feature articles can provide information on individuals which may not be found elsewhere. While for some newspapers there are indexes of certain features, such as obituaries, which have been compiled by private individuals, this is not often the case. One drawback of searching old papers, for which an index has not been done, is that microfilm copies must be looked at page by page. If a researcher can supply newspaper staffers with a specific date that an event occurred, they will be able to find and copy it; but when no specific date is known, the researcher should perform the search, himself.

As soon as they were able, immigrant groups, especially the Japanese, began to produce newspapers in America in their native language. Some of these papers are still in publication. Many have added English-language sections as newer readers have come along who are unfamiliar with the ancestral languages, but a handful continue to publish only in the language of the ancestor's country of origin.

FHL does not have many newspapers. Other libraries, such as the Donn Hart Southeast Asia Collection at Northern Illinois University (DeKalb) which has many Filipino newspapers, have extensive special collections. To locate these, one should use sources such as The Library of Congress's *Newspapers in Microform*, a bibliography based upon a nationwide survey of library collections of microfilmed newspapers. It is useful for locating small-town newspapers. However, it does not index by subject. To locate ethnic newspapers and other periodicals, one should consult surveys of specific states. (See the bibliography at the end of this chapter for a list of more sources.)

FHL does, however, have some excellent newspaper indexes. Among these are the following: Index to Births, Marriages, and Deaths in Hawaiian Newspapers Prior to 1950 (6 reels); and San Francisco Newspapers Index, 1904–1949 (703 microfiche taken from index cards at the library of California State University at Sacramento—FHL also has fiche copies of their newspaper indexes for San Diego and Los Angeles).

To locate newspapers, especially those no longer in publication, visit local libraries and the offices of ethnic historical organizations. If a paper has merged with another and is no longer published under its original name, old copies should still be available in the archives of the present-day paper. The catalog of the Family History Library can be searched under "[State, County, City]—Newspapers."

Many established Asian American organizations also issue periodicals. These deal with the history of the ethnic group in America, highlight social and political issues, give news from the country of origin, provide information on genealogical or historical research, advertise local events, lionize celebrities who bring credit to the group, promote ethnic and cultural pride, etc. They can be searched for in the Family History Library Catalog under "[State, County, City]—Periodicals."

Directories

The most familiar kind of directory is the telephone directory, but it is not the only kind. City directories, which existed before telephones were available, give a good picture of the makeup of a town or city in a given year. Besides listing names, addresses, and phone numbers, some directories provide a person's occupation. Directories often include valuable maps (important when boundary changes or the renumbering/renaming of

houses and streets have occurred over the years) and advertisements (which may give additional information on some of the people listed). Businesses, churches, schools, social and professional organizations, many other establishments, and, sometimes, a local ethnic community, will also issue directories.

The Family History Library has a set of over 7,000 microfiches entitled *City Directories of the United States* which include directories for some 250 cities from the late eighteenth century to 1901. These can be located in the Family History Library Catalog under "United States—Directories." The Library also has microfilms of directories for San Francisco, Los Angeles, Honolulu, and other cities, plus a small collection for Hawaii. Search in the catalog under "[State, County, City]—Directories." Local libraries or state archives may also house directories published for the area they service.

Local Histories

Many cities, counties, and organizations of various kinds have produced histories, especially to commemorate anniversaries such as the centennial or jubilee (fiftieth) year. They include names and other data on prominent citizens and their families, often with maps and photographs of people, buildings, businesses, and local scenery. Historical and biographical sections usually give valuable details on the places of origin of founding families. Some local histories may ignore Asian immigrants or treat them as a group without noting details on individuals, but such information can be of use in its own way. A local history by a particular Asian group's mutual support organization will be of most value.

Other Types of Records

Private organizations (Boy Scouts, sororities, fraternities, benevolent societies, ethnic organizations, etc.) produce membership lists, meeting notes, and other materials which can provide information on an individual. They may also maintain archives of older records which can be searched by visitors or staff upon request, sometimes for a fee. Other types of records, many available on microfilm at the Family History Library, include voter registration lists, employment records (such as labor contracts, work rosters, and other records of sugar plantations, railroads, and mining camps), orphanage records, lists of government employees, asylum records, "who's who" type publications, bank records, school records, and oral histories. Reference staff members at the Family History Library and other libraries and archives can provide many useful hints about the types of records available in their collections and how they can be to located. They can also suggest books and handouts to read or recommend a professional genealogist to help research portions of a genealogy.

Basic Genealogical Records—Asia

This section covers genealogical records created in the Asian country of origin. Some records, filmed by the FHL, are listed below under the appropriate country. The section "Private and Public Organizations" in Part II should also be seen for the mailing addresses of the various organizations located in the countries discussed in this section which can provide copies of records of genealogical interest (films of which may or may not be available at the FHL).

Southeast Asia

Asian Americans, with ancestry in Southeast Asia, run into considerable difficulty in tracing lines back into the distant past. Many of the best records were kept by colonial powers, and, as a result, their emphasis was on the colonists rather than those who were of native origin. Other genealogical records have been lost due to wars or natural disasters. The white ant, common throughout the area, which feasts on books is another enemy of the genealogical researcher. The Family History Library (FHL) has a solid collection of records from Indonesia, but very little on the rest of Southeast Asia. A good resource to consult for maps and background material is *The Atlas of Southeast Asia* (Ulack and Pauer, see the bibliography at the end of Chapter One).

Brunei (Negara Brunei Darussalam)

Brunei consists of four administrative districts. Birth and death registration began in 1923; marriage registration began in 1948.

Cambodia, Kampuchea, or Khmer Republic

Cambodia, consisting of nineteen provinces, lacks a centralized system of civil registration.

Indonesia

Civil Registration. Civil registration records begin in 1815 for the Dutch (called "Europeans" in the records) and Chinese. The reason the Chinese were registered with great care is that the Dutch used the Chinese as agents for their government and hence, wanted full information on them. While the name in many of the civil registration records for the Chinese is annotated using the roman alphabet, it is often written in the margin of the records in Chinese characters as well. Hence those doing research on the Chinese in Indonesia may use these records to discover the Chinese characters which made up an ancestor's name.

Later civil registration was extended to some special Indonesian groups, especially Christians. Separate records were kept for each of these groups during the Dutch period, but, after independence, the records were merged together. Not until independence did civil registration cover the entire population. Since 1944 Indonesian, rather than Dutch, is the language in which the records are written. For copies of civil registration records, researchers should write to Kantor Catatan Sipil, [city or town], [division], [province], Indonesia. See also Departemen Kehakiman R.I. and Departemen Agama (both in Jakarta, Indonesia) in "Public and Private Organizations," Part II.

Records microfilmed by the FHL include civil registration records for most localities in Indonesia. This huge collection may be accessed by the name of the locality in Indonesia wherein the ancestor lived.

Church Records. A good source to consult is the directory of the Catholic Church in Indonesia: *Buku Petunjuk Gereja Katolik Indonesia*. This directory lists the Indonesian name of the church, its address, when it was erected, and, in many cases, the name of the local priest. On the basis of this information, a letter of inquiry may be sent.

The FHL has microfilmed many of the parish registers of Roman Catholic churches in Indonesia. This huge collection of records may be accessed by searching under the name of the locality where an ancestor resided. The records of the Dutch Reformed Church have also been microfilmed: Semarang, 1849–1864 (1 reel); Makasar, 1751–1828 (5 reels); Ternaten, 1752–1882 (2 reels); and Jakarata, 1616–1890 (47 reels). The following protestant churches have been microfilmed as well: Gereja Kristen Indonesia (6 churches); Gereja Kristen Jawa (53 churches); Gereja Masehi Injili Minahasa (11 churches); the Batak church, HKBP (which is discussed further in the section "Records of Batak" below); and Armenian Apostolic Church, Jakarta, 1836–1964 (1 reel).

Notarial Records. The FHL has microfilmed records of various notaries in Indonesia. These, accessed via the locality where the notary worked, include contracts, some birth records, adoptions, estates, oaths, etc. There are also documents of sworn evidence for trails of various types of crimes. The localities covered are Situbondo, 1917–1951 (70 reels); Pasuruan, 1939–1949 (3 reels); Surabaya, 1911–1940 (79 reels); Bondowoso, 1920–1950 (56 reels); Banyuwangi, 1925–1950 (62 reels); Kraksaan, 1934–1950 (50 reels); Kediri, 1930–1950 (6 reels); Medan, 1886–1950 (31 reels); Tegal, 1910–1950 (14 reels); Aceh, 1925–1950 (18 reels); Bogor, 1900–1948 (19 reels); Cirebon, 1927–1950 (3 reels);

Indramayu, 1940–1950 (29 reels); and Padang, 1871–1950 (75 reels).

Cemetery Records. The FHL has microfilmed records of various cemeteries located in certain cities in Indonesia. The records, which grant permission to bury, include the name, age (so far as is known), and address of the deceased as well as the name and address of the person who paid for the burial (usually a relative of the deceased). Though most records date from after independence, some go back to the nineteenth century. These records are important since they include many Islamic believers—a group not covered by civil registration prior to independence. The localities covered are: Jakarta, 1813–1989 (324 reels); Surabaya, 1918–1987 (28 reels); Yogyakarta, 1831–1987 (17 reels); Surakarta, 1971–1992 (9 reels); Semarang, 1895–1986 (17 reels); and Ujang Pandang, 1964–1988 (4 reels).

Records of the Batak. The Batak are five or six different minority groups living in northern Sumatra. The FHL has microfilmed the church records of Batak church (83 *ressort* (diocese) and 229 *gereja* (churches) on 90 reels) and oral genealogies of the Toba and Simalung Batak (80 reels). The records of the Huria Kristen Batak Protestan (HKBP) include births, marriages, deaths, baptisms, burials, confirmations, membership lists, transfer of residence documents, membership lists by families, donations, and church minutes or other administrative papers.

Oral Genealogies. In addition to the Batak oral genealogies mentioned above, the FHL has collected oral genealogies for the following groups: Dayaks—Ngaju, Ma'anyan, and Siang from Kalimantan Tengah and Kalimantan Selatan (9 reels); Nias from Nias Island (16 reels); and Toraja from Kabuapten Tanah Toraja (7 reels). There is also an oral genealogical project directed by Benedict Sandin which covers the *Iban* (group of tribes) of Sarawak and Sabah (5 reels).

Manuscripts in Indonesian Palace Libraries. Although the public is not allowed to enter the Indonesian Palace Libraries, the Family History Library has some materials from them. From the court of Surakarta, for instance, the FHL has microfilmed the collections of the Perpustakaan Sonopustoko (Karaton Surakarta), and the Perpustakaan Reksopustoko (Mangkunegaran). The material filmed includes most of the historical and literary manuscripts in the library: *babad* (royal chronicle), *menak* (romantic saga dealing with a royal family), chronicles, genealogies, histories, historical romances, works based on Indian literature (50 reels).

From the court of Yogyakarta, genealogical material microfilmed at the Pakualaman Library includes the genealogies of Pakualam I through VIII; petitions submitted to the court, 1818–1963; and birth registers for the royal

household, 1955–1963 (6 reels). Also from the Library of the Karaton of Yogyakarta, all the genealogies submitted by those wishing to claim descent from Hamengku Buwon IX were microfilmed (42 reels) as well as other material which includes family certificates and other documents (6 reels).

From the court of Cirebon, various manuscripts and published materials have been filmed from the collection of the Karaton Kasepuhan (2 reels).

Laos

Laos does not yet have a modern system of centralized civil registration.

Malaysia

Records begin in the late nineteenth century. A National Registration Department was founded in 1948 in Selangor, Malaysia; however, it does not collect Islamic marriage and divorce records.

Among the holdings of the FHL are parish registers of the Dutch Reformed Church at Malacca, 1642–1825 (6 reels); parish registers of European churches of Penang (also known as Prince of Wales Island), 1805–1929 (2 reels); and parish registers of the Presbyterian Church of Penang, 1894–1926 (1 reel).

Union of Myanmar (Burma)

Civil registration certificates may be obtained through the Ministry of Health in Yangon, Myanmar. Records microfilmed by the FHL include: Burma ecclesiastical returns, registered 1937–1957 (6 reels); Baptism, marriage, and burial transcripts for European churches in Burma from original records held at the India Office in London.

Singapore

Birth and death records date from 1872, marriage records from 1875, and divorce records from 1937. Muslim marriage and divorce records are kept by religious leaders. Records of births and deaths are kept by the Ministry of Home Affairs. Marriage records are kept by the National Registration Department. Divorce records are kept by the Registry at the Supreme Court. Early records may also be found at the Singapore Archives.

Records microfilmed by the FHL include: Telok Ayer Methodist Church records, Marriage records for the Chinese Methodist Church at Telok Ayer, Singapore (1 reel); Armenian Apostolic Church, Surp Krikor Loossavorich, Singapore—births, marriages, and deaths from 1827 to 1976 (text in Armenian and English, part of 1 reel); Church of England, Parish Church of Singapore, 1900 to 1945, includes baptisms, marriages, burials, and confirmations (part of 1 reel); Abstracts of Singapore newspapers and other materials related to Singapore, microfilm of the Carl T. Smith Collection in Hong Kong containing nearly 820 leaves (part of 1 reel).

Thailand

Civil registration began in 1909; family registration began in 1956. Records are held by the Department of Local Administration, Ministry of the Interior, in Bangkok. To request a search of local records, write to the Governor, Civil Registration Department, [name of *changwat* (or province)], Thailand.

Vietnam

A family registration system is used as the basis for the issuance of personal identity cards. To obtain these records, write to the Registrar, Police Station, [Town, Province], Vietnam. Genealogical research is hindered in this country by its isolation after the war. The condition of the French civil registration records and the parish registers of the various churches is not known. A number of records from the pre-French period have survived and various academic institutions in America are attempting to microfilm them. They are reported to include tax records, censuses, and other administrative records. Records at the FHL include: Civil Registration Records for Saigon, 1861 to 1868 (Etat civil); and births, marriages, and deaths for Saigon during the years of French administration (in French, 1 reel).

South Asia

India

Records of the British. Many records exist for the British in India. These include court records, church records, civil registration, military records, cemetery records, and various governmental funds concerned with the British in India. Those microfilmed by the FHL include:

Parish register transcripts from the Presidency of Bengal, 1713 to 1948 (526 reels). These contain baptisms, marriages, and burials taken from Protestant and Catholic churches in Bengal Presidency which included Bengal, Bihar, Orissa, and Bangladesh and, at times, Burma and Malacca. This massive record is indexed and arranged by the year of the act. The majority of entries are for Europeans. The original transcripts are at the India Office in London.

Parish register transcripts from the Presidency of Madras, 1698 to 1948 (136 reels). These contain baptism, marriage, and burial transcripts from European churches in British India. The original transcripts are in the India Office in London. The register covers Madras and the present states of Tamil Nadu and Andhra Pradesh. Indexes make up the first twenty-two reels.

Parish register transcripts from the Presidency of Bombay, 1709 to 1948 (164 reels). They contain baptisms, marriages, and burials for Protestant and Catholic churches in the Presidency of Bombay. Original records are at the India Office in London. Bombay Presidency included Gujarat and Maharashtra states as well as Sind which is now part of Pakistan.

Catholic parish register transcripts for India, 1777 to 1884 (14 reels). The reels contain baptism, marriage, and burial records for Catholic churches in British India including the Presidencies of Bombay, Madras, and Bengal. Original records are at the India Office in London. It includes an index.

Ecclesiastical returns, India and Pakistan, registered 1949 to 1967 (8 reels). European churches are covered.

Records of members of the Church of Jesus Christ of Latter-day Saints of the East Indian Mission, 1852 to 1909 (1 reel). Churches in Bombay, Noonah, and Belgaume as well as Karachi branches of the East Indian or Bombay Mission are covered.

Ecclesiastical returns, Indian States, 1889 to 1950 (3 reels). Parish transcripts of baptisms and burials of European churches in the native states of India. It covers some churches in modern Pakistan and Bangladesh. Original records are in the India Office in London.

Index to marriages, 1852 to 1910, performed by the Office of the Registrar General (part of 1 reel). Civil marriages in the Presidencies of Bengal, Madras, and Bombay.

India navy fund, 1852 to 1864 (2 reels). Contains records of pensions and lists of subscribers.

Indian civil service family pension fund, 1875 to 1956 (4 reels).

Indian military service family pension fund, 1870 to 1956 (16 reels).

Indian military widows and orphans fund, 1915 to 1956 (10 reels).

Lord Clive's pension fund, 1769 to 1882 (13 reels). These reels include entries for Fort Williams, Fort St. George, and other localities in South India.

Miscellaneous pension funds, 1866 to 1921 (2 reels).

Regular and Elders Widow Fund, 1816 to 1900 (4 reels).

Superior service family pension fund of India, 1928 to 1956 (part of 1 reel).

Bengal civil fund, 1772 to 1948 (2 reels).

Bengal family pension fund (2 reels).

Bengal military fund, 1824 to 1892 (6 reels).

Bengal military orphans' society, 1818 to 1873 (4 reels).

Madras civil fund, 1850 to 1886 (part of 1 reel).

Madras military fund, 1815 to 1913 (5 reels).

Madras family pension fund, 1783 to 1921 (2 reels).

Bombay military and civil pension funds, 1829 to 1893 (9 reels).

Bengal wills, 1728 to 1774; Bombay wills, 1728 to 1783; Madras wills, 1753 to 1779; index, 1704 to 1783 (12 reels). Probate records of British subjects filmed from manuscripts in the India Office, London.

India Office list, 1886 to 1940 (484 microfiches). Originally published in fifty-four annual volumes from London.

Civil Registration. The civil registration of India began in the British period, but was are not required for the nation as a whole until 1969. However, in 1886 an act was passed that provided for voluntary registration of important dates and some states and municipalities started birth and death registration prior to this date. In Madras, for example, such records date back to 1867 and have been deposited in Madras' Health Department. Others from 1751 can be found at the Provincial Registers Office. For Europeans, registration dating from the middle of the nineteenth century, covers most of that population. Records may be obtained from the Chief Registrar of Births, Deaths, and Marriages, [Capital City, State], India.

Hindu Pilgrimage Records. These records are of Hindus or Sikhs visiting a specific site. The records have been created by a pundit (a wise or learned man) who writes or invites the pilgrim to write the reasons for the pilgrimage, the name of each person in the party and their castes, the names of the pilgrim's relatives, the location of both his ancestral home and his current home, and other important information. The pundit includes the dates of the pilgrimage on the record and files it. For this service the pilgrim pays a small fee. The pundit uses the information on the record to enable him to discover records of former pilgrimages by other members of a specific family which will establish that he is the pundit for that family. The information on the records tends to be very reliable, includes a large number of ordinary persons as well as the rich and powerful, and can go back in time four or five hundred years.

The pilgrimage records at the FHL include: Hardwar, Uttar Pradesh (over 1000 reels); Mathura, Uttar Pradesh (70 reels); Kurukshetra, Haryana (332 reels); Pahowa, Haryana (326 reels); Chintpurni, Himachal Pradesh (16 reels); and Jawala Mukhi, Himachal Pradesh (35 reels). Since some of these projects are ongoing, the number of reels will increase in time.

Christian Church Records. A good source of addresses for Catholic parishes in India is the *Catholic Directory of India*. Issued every few years, it contains the addresses of the Catholic parishes in India as well as the date each church was erected. Inquiries may be sent directly to each parish requesting a search of its parish registers.

The FHL has microfilmed the church records of the Dutch Reformed Church, St. Francis of Cochin, Kerala, India, 1751 to 1804; the Armenian Apostolic Churches in Tangra (1793 to 1979), Bombay (1917 to 1978), Madras (1829 to 1908), and Calcutta (1793 to 1982); several parishes of the Syrian Orthodox Church, most of them located Kerala, India (6 reels); and the Church of South India which was organized in 1947 as an umbrella organization for various protestant and catholic religious groups in south India (nearly 22 reels).

Islamic Records. Among the holdings of the FHL are the: Family records of the Qadis of Broach, 1846 to 1859—most are records of marriages performed by the Qadis of Broach, which is now in Gujarat, India (1 reel); Muslim marriage records, 1921 to 1955 (2 reels)—originals are housed at the residence of Qazi Mohd,

Mukhtar Musa in Bulandshahr, Uttar Pradesh, India; and Muslim marriage records, 1881 to 1982 (27 reels)—originals are housed at the residence of Qazi Zain-Ul-Abideen in Meerut, Uttar Pradesh, India.

Goa. This former Portuguese possession located on the west coast of India is now part of the territory of Goa, Damaun, and Diu. It was annexed to India in 1961. The microfilm collection of the FHL includes many parish registers of Roman Catholic churches in Goa, including Prodessos de ordenações, 18th to 20th centuries (71 reels) which contains documents listing candidates for appointment to or advancement in the priesthood of the Roman Catholic Church and transcriptions of baptismal certificates and other documents.

Pondicherry. This capital of a centrally administered territory of the same name was a former French possession on the coast of India.

Records at the FHL include those of the Carnatic Mission, 1676 to 1777 (part of 1 reel)—a mission established by French Jesuit missionaries in the seventeenth century which was transferred to the Paris Foreign Mission Society in 1776; civil registration for Pondicherry, 1731 to 1867 (9 reels)—covering Karikal (1731 to 1854), Chandernagor (1817 to 1854), Pondicherry (1817 to 1854), Mahé (1815 to 1854), Yanaon (1817 to 1854), baptisms, marriages, and burials (1791 to 1816), and births, marriages, and deaths (1817 to 1867); civil registration documents for Karikal, 1792 to 1864 (2 reels); and civil registration documents for Mahé, 1826 to 1864 (1 reel). There are also parish registers and other church documents for most of the French Catholic churches in Pondicherry and dependent areas. Churches in the district of South Arcot of Tamil Nadu are part of this collection. One of the French churches covered is the Notre-Dame-des-Anges de Pondicherry, 1587 to 1830 (6 reels) and 1815 to 1990 (2 reels).

Danish Records. Denmark held two trading posts in India during the eighteenth century: Tranquebar, in Tamil Nadu, and Serampore, in West Bengal. The FHL has microfilmed: Civil Documents, 1800 to 1847, Blanketregnskaber (175 reels of which the last reel deals with India)—applications and permissions granted by civil authorities for marriages, divorces, burials, probate, etc.; Census of Serapore, 1840, Foldetælling over Frederiksangor, (1 reel)—lists in English the names of persons of Danish ancestry; Census of Tranquebar, 1834, Optegnelse på folketallet i Tranquebars bye (2 reels)—census of persons of Danish ancestry in Tranquebar.

Bangladesh

Records were kept as early as 1873 when Bangladesh was part of Bengal in the British Raj. Modern registration began in 1960. Marriage and divorce records are filed with the Ministry of Law and Parliamentary Affairs and can be obtained by writing to the Bangladesh Demographic Survey and Vital Registration System in Dhaka, Bangladesh. Other records are deposited at the National Library of Bangladesh which is also at Dhaka.

Bhutan

Civil registration is fairly recent with records housed at the Ministry of Home Affairs in Thimphu, Bhutan.

Pakistan

Civil registration began in 1863. Records can be obtained from the Civil Registration Organization in Islamabad.

Sri Lanka

Records can be obtained from the Ministry of Home Affairs in Colombo, Sri Lanka.

The FHL has microfilmed much of the material at the Department of National Archives in Colombo. The records from the Dutch period include most of the material listed in the two archive inventories that cover these records: M.W. Jurriaanse and S.A.W. Mottau. These include the *thombo* (land survey/census) registers of which there were a series of three (1742 to 1759 cannot be located, but the second and third series, 1760 to 1761 and 1766 to 1771 have survived) during the Dutch period, in addition to those created during the period of Portuguese control. These registers, created for tax purposes, are a kind of land survey carried out by officials who visited the various parts of Ceylon controlled by the Dutch and reported on the land that was owned in each area, who owned it, its quality, and the wealth it generated. Sometimes a map was included for clarification as to what parcel of land was under discussion. A Hoofd Thombo was created prior to the creation of the Land Thombo which registered the name of each head of family that owned land as well as his heirs and other members of the family. There is also a school thombo which is similar to a parish register. Each Dutch Reformed parish included a schoolmaster whose job, in addition to conducting classes, was to register births, marriages, and deaths. Sometimes he would travel to the remote parts of large parishes to accomplish this assignment.

Other records include lists of persons who provided a service to the Dutch in a specific location—washers, food providers, messengers, etc. These groups were often designated as separate castes. There are lists of persons expected to do service in the home militia or to act as bodyguards. Notarial and court records are also included, as are complicated records dealing with the decisions of the three councils (in Colombo, Galle, and Jaffna)

through which the Dutch ruled their holdings in Sri Lanka.

In regard to the British period, most of the civil registration records of Sri Lanka up to independence are to be filmed. Currently, this ongoing project includes almost 20,000 reels. The earliest of these records were created by various Christian churches and typically date from 1822 to 1867 when a civil registration system was introduced by the British. At that time "past births," occurring before 1867, could be registered. In 1897 registration became obligatory. The basic government administrations responsible for registration were the revenue divisions set up for purposes of taxation. Unfortunately, these divisions were extremely susceptible to change. In addition, they were small in size and, today, the location and boundaries of their jurisdiction are unknown. Colombo District, alone, had approximately 87 of these divisions. Marriage registration divisions were larger than birth and death registration divisions. Some birth and death divisions shared the same area of jurisdiction, but were located at different sites. The British attempted to break up a sense of localism by creating multiple points of administration. Hence, a person living in a town could be under the jurisdiction of a police station, a magistrate, a birth and death registration office, and a marriage registration office—all in different locations which are extremely difficult for a family researcher to track. Additionally, the British had as a feature of their registration categories of documents to be used for special purposes. While the Provincial Registrar and the Assistant Provincial Registrar collected records for special communities such as the Muslim fisher communities on the coast, their major responsibility was to register the large Indian communities that came to work on the British owned plantations. Usually registered by the plantation owner, copies were sent to the district registrar's office and to the provincial registrar's office at Colombo. (Since independence, Sri Lankan registration is conducted via voting districts where a researcher runs into similar frustrations.)

Other items which have been filmed include the Journal of the Dutch Burgher Union of Ceylon, Colombo, which covers the genealogy of the Burghers (persons of Dutch ancestry, who at the time of the British control of Ceylon became a separate community) and their families; and the widows and orphans pension fund, 1884 to 1929 (35 reels), a collection of all persons involved in the administration of Sri Lanka under the British which provides names, location and type of employment, salary, names of family members, and dates of birth for the employee and his family.

Nepal

Modern civil registration has covered the population only in the last fifteen years. Marriages and divorces have been kept by the Civil Registration and Vital Statistics Office in Katmandu since 1983 and 1985 respectively.

The large Hindu community in Nepal has many of its religious requirements fulfilled by Maitali Brahmans who came originally from Bihar State in India. The FHL has microfilmed many of the genealogies of this community in India. Because records created by the Maitali Brahmans were often sent to India, these genealogies often include persons from Nepal. Researchers must know the name of their pundit, identifed by family tradition, to locate the appropriate records.

Republic of the Philippines

Church Records

The different parishes of the Catholic Church in the Philippines contain some of the most important records for genealogical research. Most go back to the early period of Spanish involvement with the Philippines. The records cover the general population of Christians, both the Spanish and those native to the islands who converted. At present, about eighty-five percent of the population is Roman Catholic. Thus, for some areas, these records cover most of the general population as well. Care has been exercised in the collection and preservation of these records. The Roman Catholic Church has a long tradition of record-keeping and the parish register is understood to be one of the most important components of an active parish. Readily accessible to research, these records are accurate, detailed, and rich in family information. The names of relatives of the person for whom the record was created are usually included.

Parish registers consist of four basic types of records: baptisms, marriages, confirmations, and burials. Each record type may also contain some other related records. For instance, baptism records may include corrections of earlier records, baptism certificates, etc. Note that these records are arranged according to the date of the event. A baptism record is not a birth record, although it contains the date of birth, and is arranged according to the date of baptism, not the date of birth. Similarly burial records are arranged according to date of burial, not the date of death.

While the FHL in Salt Lake City has microfilmed a large number of parish registers, the microfilm collection is not complete; there is much more information on some provinces than others.

If the collection does not contain the records that the researcher requires, he or she should consult the *Catholic Directory of the Philippines*. In this source, the parishes are arranged by locality. The date of the creation of each parish is indicated and the proper name of the parish church, its address, and the name of the priest in residence is listed. With this information, one can send a letter of inquiry to the appropriate church and request that a search be conducted. If this search is not fruitful, a search of records in adjoining parishes or of the parish registers at the diocese which oversees the parish of an ancestor could be helpful. Letters of inquiry should give specific information on the ancestor including name and date and place of the event. They should also be written in a appropriately polite manner and include a self-addressed stamped envelope.

Large collections of records that have been microfilmed by the FHL are indicated below. In this information, any parish which has had its registers microfilmed is indicated together with years of the register that have been filmed. At the end of each description are the number of reels of microfilm which are involved.

Baptism (*Bautismo*) Records. These records include the name and age of the person who was baptized, the date of baptism, parents' names, residence, the name of the officiator, and, sometimes, the names of the godparents. Copies of some of these records are in the archives of the Archdiocese of Manila. The parish baptismal records from 1932 to 1936 have been indexed. The collection at the FHL includes:

Certificados de Partidos de Bautismos (Certificates of Baptism), 1858–1898 (1 reel).

Partidos de Bautismos (Records of Baptisms) contain documents related to errors in baptism records on the parish level which have been referred to the archdiocesan level for action. They discuss lost records, the legality of a baptism, errors in names on the baptism certificate, the legitimacy of the baptism of a child born out of wedlock, etc. The collection consists of affidavits, depositions, certifications by witnesses, etc. which were created to establish the facts of each case and a statement by the parish priest describing the issue and suggesting possible resolutions. Records are in Spanish, written in long hand, and filed chronologically. Some have been indexed.

Rectificacion de Partidos de Bautismo (Rectification of Records of Baptism) contain records consisting of documents listing corrections made in the baptismal records. They include information on the name, and date and place of birth of the child as well as the names of the parents. These are also in Spanish, written in long hand, and filed chronologically.

Solicitaciones de Chinos sobre Bautismos (Applications of Chinese [Nationals and Immigrants in the Philippines] for Baptism), 1774–1900, contain records from the Archives of the Archdiocese of Manila. (9 reels)

Marriage Records. *Informaciones Matrimoniales* (Information on Marriages) are documents related to marriages including certifications of marriage, affidavits, the parish priest's certificate of eligibility of the candidates to marry, as well as documents providing the background of the marital partners. *Expedientes Matrimoniales* (Marriage Proceedings) contain documents, similar to marriage banns, created in accordance to church procedures before a marriage was officiated. *Casos Matrimoniales* (Marriage Cases) cover cases in which there is some impediment that may lead to the marriage's not being carried out or to its annulment. *Cultos Disparidades* (Disparity of Religions) contain marriages or divorce documents which prove differences of religion or belief between the marital couple. *Dispensas Matrimoniales* (Marriage Dispensations) are marital dispensations allowing the marriage to occur. *Dispensas de Impedimentos* (Dispensation of Impediments) are requests from parish priests to the Archbishop asking permission to marry persons who are closely related. *Dispensas del Impuesto de Afinidad* (Dispensations of Imposition of Affinity) are records granting dispensations to allow for the marriage of persons closely related. *Diligencias Matrimoniales* (Marital Diligence) cover nuptial or matrimonial issues which are considered before the marriage ceremony. *Diligencias sobre Casamientos* (Diligence over Marriages) are records of protests against the granting a marriage dispensation. *Asuntos Esponsales* (Engagement Matters) consist of cases of engagements in which there is some problem; such as, one of the parties to be married is missing, one is a minor, or one is a foreigner necessitating a consular affidavit proving that it is legal for him or her to marry. In other cases the degree of consanguinity (of the same ancestral line) of the parties seeking to marry is under investigation. *Dispensas de Proclamas* (Dispensations of Proclamations of Marriage Banns) contains cases in which a dispensation has been granted which permits persons to marry who have previously wed in a civil ceremony or who have not married, but are living together and have children. Other marriage records include *Dispensas Concepidas* and *Demandas sobre Divorcio* (Petition to Divorce).

Burial Records. *Exhumaciones* cover the exhumation of bodies from a grave due to burial in the wrong location, a change of religion, the desire of relatives to be buried close to each other, changes in cemetery ownership, etc.

Cementerios (cemeteries) contains records relating to the purchase, renovation, or closure of cemeteries. There are also some records related to the exhuming of the dead by priest without the proper authority to do so. Information provided may include the name of the deceased, date and place of death, age at death, place and date of burial, and last residence.

Other Church Records. *Padrón* or *estado de almas* (state of parishoners) contain records of parish enumerations. *Cargo y data* (creditor and debtor) contains the financial statements of a religious order. *Capellanías* (chaplaincy) contain bequests or endowments of property or other income for the support of an ecclesiastical office. *Ordenes* (orders) are ecclesiastical decrees covering religious orders. *Fés de existencia* or *vida* (certificates of life) are certificates of membership in the Catholic church issued to widows and orphans. Santa Visita de las Iglesias (Holy Visits of the Church) contains records of pastoral visitations to various churches by an archbishop or his representative. Visitas Diocesanas (diocesan visitations) contain records of visits to various churches by a bishop or his representative. *Patronatos* (patronships), 1686–1894 (144 reels) and Patronatos II, 1657–1898 (9 reels) contain appointments of clergy and related correspondence of the Archbishop of Manila. Missions of the Jesuits in the Philippines, 1829–1899 contains correspondence and documents concerning the Jesuits (6 reels). There are also microfilms of parishes of the Philippine Independent Church: Cavinti, Nagcarlan, Paete, and Pagsanjan (Laguna); Pila and Santa Cruz (Laguna); San Pablo City (Laguna); Maria Clara Church (Santa Cruz); St. Michael Parish (Bacoor); and St. Michael Parish (Binakayan).

Civil Registration Records

Civil Records of the Spanish Period. Due to the close relationship between the church and state in the Philippines during the Spanish period, civil registration records usually recorded information that was supplied by the church or which dealt with events that transpired because of an individual's relationship with the church. As a result, civil registration records include transcripts of records dealing with baptisms, marriages, and burials much like church records:

Registros civiles (civil registers), 1832–1896, consists of 50 reels which cover mostly Manila and contain some Chinese death records, baptisms, and births as well as matrimonios expedientes and matrimonios ilegal, and a large amount of records which deal with deaths (for which there is an extensive index to defunciones). Civil registers, 1834–1897, contain the same type of information and are arranged by province (3 reels).

Indexes to bautismos, 1706–1898, is a card index to baptism records, arranged by locality (3 reels). Not all provinces are represented.

Defunciones, 1862–1897, contain doctors' certificates of death for Manila (6 reels). Indexes to defunciones, 1800–1898, are incomplete death indexes of arranged by province or locality (8 reels).

Matrimonios, 1805–1895, are marriage records (1 reel). Index to matrimonios (marriages), 1757–1911, is an incomplete index of marriages arranged by province or large city (2 reels).

Civil Records of the American Period. Emphasis is on civil registration and notarials (see the section titled "Court Records" below for the notarial records), since these are easily the most extensive and accurate records which also cover a large portion of the population and, as such, are helpful in tracing persons during this period: Birth registers, 1943–1979, primarily for Manila, (252 reels); Birth certificates, 1945–1988, arranged by province (64 reels); Birth certificates, 1950–1987, arranged by city (55 reels); Birth certificates, 1976–1984, also arranged by city (9 reels); Marriage certificates, 1945–1949, arranged by city (1 reel); and Guardianships, 1923–1964, primarily for Manila (78 reels).

Records Concerning Foreigners in the Philippines

Radicación de extranjeros, 1768–1918, provides residency permits and applications for said permits. Information includes name, age, martial status, birth place, and occupation. (8 reels)

Spanish Records. *Catálogo XX, Títulos de Indias* (Richardo Magdaleno), *Indice de personas nobles y otras de calidad que han estado en Filipinas desde 1521 hasta 1898* (Retana y Gamboa), and *Aspirantes americanos a cargos del Santo Oficio* (Fernández de Recas García) are three sources which can be consulted. They contain names of Spanish citizens living in the Indies, the Philippines, and Spanish America or the Philippines from the sixteenth through the nineteenth centuries. The following records are also important: *Titulos y Nombramientos* or Titles and Appointments of Spanish in the Government of the Philippines, 1778–1898 (43 reels); *Hojas de Servicias* or Personnel Files of Government Employees, 1812–1890 (11 reels); Files (Personal) of Government Employees, 1755–1902 (85 reels); and Pensions (*Pensiones*) of Government Employees, 1796–1898 (5 reels).

Records of Americans. *Estados Unidos* (United States), 1843–1898, contains passports, residency certificates, and permissions allowing U.S. citizens to disembark. Includes some Japanese (3 reels). There is also the Index to Civil Servants in the Philippines, 1898–1950, a card index to civil servants in the Philippines which is arranged by surname (16 reels).

Records of Japanese. *Japón* (Japan), 1870–1898, contains the passports, residences, etc. of Japanese in the Philippines (3 reels). There is also Indexes to Japanese War Crimes Trials Records, 1938–1950, and a Name List of Japanese Emigrants (modern), (1 reel). Japanese

Workers in Philippine Coal Mines, 1903–1905 provides names and places of origin of Japanese works in Philippine coal mines in Bataan run by the Continental Settlement Company (Tairiku Shokumin Gōshi Kaisha) (1 reel).

Chinese Records. Many persons from the Philippines are likely to find that they have some Chinese ancestors since frequent intermarriage occurred—especially in urban areas where Chinese tended to settle. Consequently, records related to Chinese immigrants and residents in the Philippines during period of Spanish control should be consulted. The Spanish allowed Chinese to live in Manila from the early sixteenth century as the Chinese were valued not only for their trade connections (improving trade with China), but also for their industry and social coherence. However, the Chinese rioted and plotted the overthrow of the Spanish at various times during the early period of Spanish control of the Philippines. In 1574 a Chinese revolt, coordinated by the Chinese in the Philippines with those who remained in China, resulted in the attack of the islands by 3,000 men on sixty-two Chinese warships. Although the attempt failed, the Spanish began an effort to control Chinese merchants and residents by keeping careful records of all Chinese in the Philippines. Several locations within the Philippine National Archives house copies of these records, as do archives on the provincial and municipal levels. The most common record type found on the provincial and municipal levels is the *Padrones de Chinos* (Chinese Tax Records) which were registers created for purposes of taxation.

During the American period, the Chinese were not treated as a separate community. Records of Chinese during this period and also the post-independence period will be found filed with those of the general population.

Records at the FHL include:

Chinese Tax Records, 1786–1901 (Padrones de Chinos), is a somewhat complex collection consisting of records from two archives. The first archive covered records from 1786 to 1901; the second, records from 1826 to 1897, though some records (undated) were generated after 1901. All records are from the *Administración de Impuestos* (Administration of Taxes) and list Chinese immigrants, their descriptions, and the taxes paid. These records pertain to the area of and around Manila. (81 reels)

Chinese Tax Records (Padrones de Chinos), 1805–1897, consists of records created by the *Administración de Central de Impuestos* (Central Administration of Taxes) which include those from the following provinces: Albay, Antique, Bataan, Batangas, Bulacan, Cagayan, Camarines Sur, Capiz, Cavite, Cebu, Ilocos, Laguna, Misamis, Negros, Nueva Ecija, Nueva Vizcaya,

Pampanga, Pangasinan, Samar, Surigao del Norte, Tayabas, Zamboanga. The records list Chinese immigrants, their descriptions, and the taxes paid. (4 reels)

Chinos (Chinese), 1501–1901, includes censuses, passports, passenger lists, etc. related to Chinese in Manila and other provinces and municipalities of the Philippines. (130 reels)

Chinese Cemetery at La Loma, Manila, 1875–1985. These are documents created by the Philippines Chinese Charitable Association. (9 reels)

Defunciones de Chinos, 1890–1897, contain death certificates for Chinese in Manila as well as some other areas in the Philippines and provide name, place of birth, age, marital status, profession, address, and various residency certificates. (1 reel)

Indexes to Chinos, 1801–1902, contains an inventory of documents dealing with Chinese in the Philippines, arranged by province. (2 reels)

Chinese Passports (*Pasaportes de Chinos*), 1866–1897, contains passports of Chinese either entering or leaving the Philippines. (2 reels)

Civil Registration Records (Registros civiles), 1832–1898, contains birth, marriage, and death records for Manila. One reel of this fifty reel record contains Chinese deaths from 1886 to 1895.

Baptismal Applications for Chinese Immigrants to the Philippines, 1774–1900 (Solicitaciones de Chinos sobre bautismos), contains applications from the Archives of the Archdiocese of Manila. (9 reels)

School Records

Escuelas y maestros (Schools and teachers), 1810–1898 (42 reels) and Escuelas y maestros, 1858–1898 (5 reels) contain personnel files of teachers and some lists of students.

Tax Records

Tributos (Tributes), 1741–1898, contains tax records. (9 reels)

Prestación personal (Personal tax), 1885–1898 contains tax records giving the names of persons obligated to work on public works projects as well as records of loans and obligations to repay the loans. Name, age, and occupation data is included.

Indexes to *Arbitrios y propios* (Ways and means), 1867–1869, contains an index to land tax records. (1 reel)

Military Records

Calendar of Military Records, 1778–1898 (*Guerra* or War), contains documents of the War Department of the Spanish government of the Philippines. (186 reels)

Guardia Civil (Civil Guard), 1774–1898, contains records of the Civil Guard of the Philippines under the Spanish. These documents include regulations, lists of officers and soldiers, passports, passengers arriving in Manila, etc. (34 reels)

Indexes to Conscription Lists, 1854–1898, *Quintas* (military induction notices), are arranged by province. (1 reel)

Prison Records

Indexes to *Presidios* (Penitentiaries), 1844–1898, contains a card index of prison records. Data includes name of prisoner, age, residence, crime, and number of years of sentence. (13 reels)

Indexes to *Cárceles* (Jails), 1839–1899 consists of a calendar of prison records. (2 reels)

Court Records

These records include: Indexes to various matters (*asuntos*), 1709–1903, consisting of an index to court cases arranged by province (10 reels); *Escrituras de poderes y fianzas* (written power of attorney and bonds), 1804–1908, consisting of powers of attorney and surety bonds arranged by surname (42 reels); Indexes to Court Cases covering guardianships, adoptions, changes of name, etc.; Indexes to Inheritance Records, 1866–1909 (*Declaraciones de herederos* or Declarations of Heirs), primarily covering Manila (1 reel); Testaments, 1711–1905, containing wills, inventories, divisions of property, etc., primarily for Manila (25 reels); Inheritances (*Bienes de difuntos* or Estates of the Deceased), 1743–1917, including a surname index of those primarily from Manila (12 reels); and Inheritances, 1700–1903, primarily covering Manila (151 reels).

From the American period, there are notarial records. These records are some of the most important in genealogical research. They contain extensive information on wills and other legal documents. A will can contain data on members of the family and others who may acquire part of an estate's assets. It may list the location of the property, the full name of the deceased and the names of those in his or her family. Nevertheless, they are difficult records to use since it usually must be known if a will was made and with which notary (and when) the will was registered. However, Notarial Records, Indexes, to Cards and Log Books, 1905–1983 (43 reels), is indexed by the first letter of the surname of person who is deceased making this resource much easier for the researcher to use.

Passports

Passports, 1758–1898, which contains records of both persons leaving the Philippines and those entering it

(5 reels). Lists of Chinese are included. There are also records of passports for 1830–1898 (7 reels).

Provincial Records

Records of the Provinces (*Provincias*), 1525–1904, include municipal and provincial documents covering tax records, conscription, census records, records of the provincial government, etc. which are arranged by province and municipality (562 reels). There is also a Records of Provinces covering 1739–1940 (159 reels).

Civil Registration Records: Provinces and Municipalities

For the researcher, determining a specific locality in the Philippines and its jurisdiction can be a challenge. It is crucial to know the status of a given locality throughout time and that status may have changed several times over the years. Although the Spanish introduced a system of administration to the Philippines based on provinces and municipalities which is still in effect, that system was quite flexible.

Early in the Spanish period, *encomiendas* (estates granted by the king) or *repartimientos* (allotments of land) were instituted. These land grants to notable Spanish settlers gave them the right to collect taxes from other settlers who lived on the land in return for providing for their education and welfare as well as for the defense of the locality and the support of the area's church. The first such grants were made to persons in Cebu in 1570 and spread rapidly through most areas controlled by the Spanish. Within a few years the whole practice was called into question due to the abuse and the resultant loss of power of the central Spanish government to those who received grants. By 1620, the system was completely abolished and replaced by a hierarchy of levels of government and authority. First were the provinces (*alcaldias*) which were composed of towns (*pueblos*), villages (*barrios* or *barangays*), and, sometimes, hamlets (*sitios*). There were also small pioneer settlements (*rancherias*). These towns should not be considered as towns in the American sense—urban centers in contrast to rural areas. Rather they were towns in the sense that the seat of the town would be in an urban center but the rest of it might include a considerable amount of rural land. They were more like small counties which could be expanded, dissolved, annexed to one another, or broken up with various parts used to create new towns or cities.

Spanish administrative units (provinces and sub-provinces), and this is true of the American period and post-independence Philippines as well, were very unstable—subject to change according to the needs of the administration of the region caused by increased Spanish authority, variants in population, or changing levels of economic development. At times, new districts were created in order to give more authority to military commanders so that a particular area could be defended or a newly conquered area could be consolidated. This was particularly true during the nineteenth century when Spanish power in the Philippines greatly expanded. In that century many areas that had largely remained untouched by Spanish government in the interior of many of the islands were brought under effective administrative control. Also with better military organization, new weapons, and the availability of steamships, the Spanish were able to conquer the Islamic areas in the south of the Philippines.

Normally, during the Spanish period, civil registration records of births, marriages, and deaths as well as military, court, notarial, administrative, police, census, and other records were collected on the provincial level. (However, it is important to keep in mind that records which had the status of government documents were also created by the various parishes of the Roman Catholic Church.) During the American and post-independence periods, civil registration records of births, marriages, and deaths were collected by municipalities or cities. But, even during the Spanish period, a city, though often the capital of a specific province, was not under the full control of the province in which it was situated and had status nearly equal to that of a province. Hence, a city was given a wide scope in the generation and collection of records within its boundries. Further, since cities were the sites for provincial archives and provincial records were similar to the those created and collected by the city, itself, the records of the two were sometimes merged with both sets of records housed in the provincial archive.

Each time the administrative status of an area changed, all old records were to be transferred to the replacing administration's provincial archives. But this apparently had a low priority since it often was only partially done or not done at all. Hence, it may be necessary to search all the provincial archives which might at one time have had jurisdiction over an area in addition to the archive which currently oversees that area. (Some indexes are available and these make such work easier.)

Additionally, the name of a province may have changed over time and through the various changes in the geographical composition of the province. The usual Spanish practice was to name the province after its capital city which might also be the name of the island on which it was located, the name of a local group of native people, or the name of a local dialect. For clarity, the reference of the name was usually included: the municipality of Davao, the newly created province of Davao, the island of Panay, the province of Panay, etc. In the American and post-independence periods, Spanish and English terms are both used in the names of provinces: Ilocos Norte, Lanao del Norte, North Cotabato, Eastern Samar, and Misamis Oriental. Sometimes, the same name has been used over time to indicate different areas. For example, Davao was a large, rich province which in 1967 was divided into three provinces: Davao del Norte, Davao del Sur, and Oriental Davao. But in 1972 Davao del Norte changed its name to Davao. Thus, depending on the time frame, Davao can indicate the original, large province or just a segment of that large province.

Municipalities may also cause confusion. Their names also changed over time. They merged, dissolved, and reappeared—especially during the time of American administration. As stated earlier, during the period 1902–1905, some provinces were consolidated, others were deemed sub-provinces which were dependent on another province. Municipalities were also annexed to each other or grouped into municipal districts. [Eventually, most of these changes were reversed.] Finally, growth in population and economy has, over time, resulted in the creation of new provinces and municipalities.

There are several types of records that were created both on the provincial and municipal levels. Birth records give the name and sex of the child, names of parents, whether married, etc. Marriage contracts, not to be confused with marriage banns or dowry contracts, contain essentially the same kind of information as the marriage certificates, but in a slightly different format. Death certificates include the name, age, place of resident, and, if known, the names of parents, spouse, and children. Court records (*protocolos de instrumentos públicos*) created by the Court of First Instance (*Juzgado de Primera Instancia*) include wills, inheritances, contracts, and similar records. Deportations (*deportados*) deal with the internal exile of an undesirable person and include information on his or her family. Land records (*terrenos*) contain the names of land owners petitioning to have their ownership established. Land contracts, bills of sale, and similar land documents are included. Military induction records (*quintas*) contain a list of all males in a village or municipality between the ages of 18 and 25 at a specific point in time, arranged alphabetically by surname. Annotations to entries indicate whether a specific person had some special status (i.e., he was married, he was a student). There is an index of these lists which covers 1854 to 1898. They are called quintas because every fifth person listed would be conscripted. Public records (*cédulas*) consist of a variety of documents including residence certificates, tax certificates, rental fees paid to the government, and the annual budgets of a locality. Records of service and obligation (*prestaciones personales*) are records of persons who owed an obligation for service on public works. Records of lending, and repayment are included. Infor-

mation includes name of person, age, and occupation. School records (*escuelas y maestros*) are records concerning students and teachers which give information on their families and background. Statistical reports (*estadística*) are annual reports on a locality providing such statistical information as the racial composition of the population, their taxes, etc. They are important because they include the names of the persons being enumerated. Tax records (*tributos*) include the name of each person taxed and the amount paid. Considerable information is given concerning those who applied for an exemption to the taxes on their holdings. Census of Chinese (*padrones de chinos*) are listings of the Chinese in a given location with status as to whether the appropriate tax was paid indicated. *Vecindarios* are Spanish census records arranged by locality.

Copies of the records may be obtained by writing the Civil Registrar, City Hall or Municipal Building, [name of city or municipality, name of province], The Philippines (for records held by a city or municipality) or Vital Registry Division, Office of the Civil Registrar-General, National Census and Statistics Office, NEDA, Maysaysay Boulevard, Santa Mesa, Manila, Metropolitan Manila, The Philippines. In making such a request, the name of the person who is being researched, the type of record (birth, marriage, death, etc.), date of record, and the researcher's relationship to the person whose record is being requested should be included as well as an indication of a willingness to pay a small fee for the service.

The following material has been provided as an aid to unravelling the metamorphoses of the various provinces and municipalities of the Philippines (see also figure 2.5). A short administrative history of each province and sub-province is given and the records that have been microfilmed by the FHL are listed. Then a short sketch of the administrative history of each municipality, municipal district, and city within the province or sub-province is provided, including name changes, annexations, date of establishment, etc. A phrase such as ''established 1937 from Butuan'' means that in 1937 the municipality was created from villages formerly in Butuan. The phrase ''separated from'' means that the municipality divided from the municipality from which it was separated, becoming an independent municipality. Any local records and parish registers that have been microfilmed (indicated by ''FHL'') are then listed, followed by local records that have not been microfilmed.

Abra. This province in the northern part of the island of Luzon was formerly part of the old province of Ilocos which was divided into Ilocos Norte and Ilocos Sur in 1818 with the territory that now makes up Abra included in Ilocos Sur. In 1846 Abra, the sub-province of Lepanto,

PROVINCES

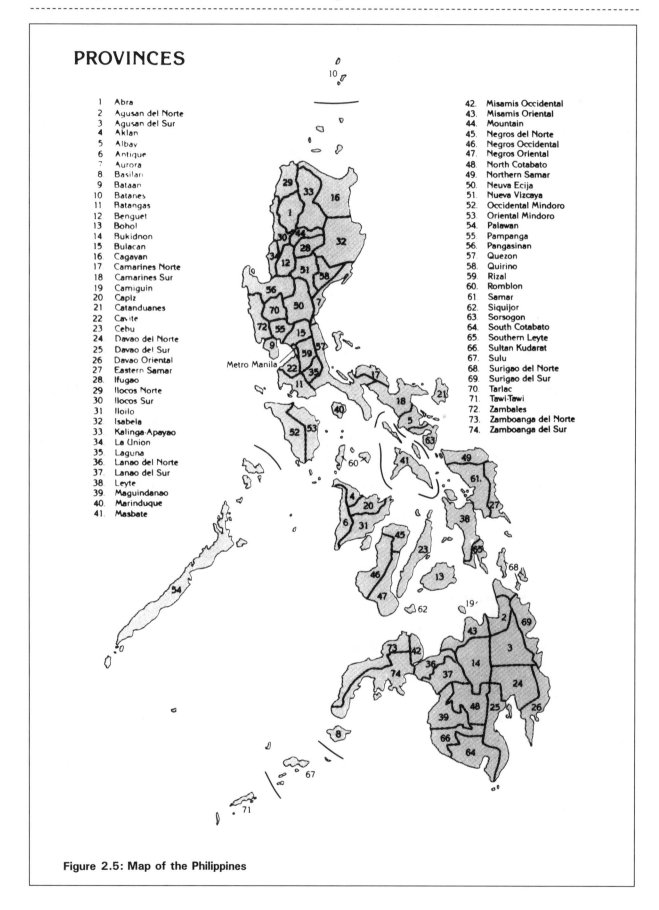

1	Abra
2	Agusan del Norte
3	Agusan del Sur
4	Aklan
5	Albay
6	Antique
7	Aurora
8	Basilan
9	Bataan
10	Batanes
11	Batangas
12	Benguet
13	Bohol
14	Bukidnon
15	Bulacan
16	Cagayan
17	Camarines Norte
18	Camarines Sur
19	Camiguin
20	Capiz
21	Catanduanes
22	Cavite
23	Cebu
24	Davao del Norte
25	Davao del Sur
26	Davao Oriental
27	Eastern Samar
28	Ifugao
29	Ilocos Norte
30	Ilocos Sur
31	Iloilo
32	Isabela
33	Kalinga-Apayao
34	La Union
35	Laguna
36	Lanao del Norte
37	Lanao del Sur
38	Leyte
39	Maguindanao
40	Marinduque
41	Masbate

42	Misamis Occidental
43	Misamis Oriental
44	Mountain
45	Negros del Norte
46	Negros Occidental
47	Negros Oriental
48	North Cotabato
49	Northern Samar
50	Neuva Ecija
51	Nueva Vizcaya
52	Occidental Mindoro
53	Oriental Mindoro
54	Palawan
55	Pampanga
56	Pangasinan
57	Quezon
58	Quirino
59	Rizal
60	Romblon
61	Samar
62	Siquijor
63	Sorsogon
64	South Cotabato
65	Southern Leyte
66	Sultan Kudarat
67	Sulu
68	Surigao del Norte
69	Surigao del Sur
70	Tarlac
71	Tawi-Tawi
72	Zambales
73	Zamboanga del Norte
74	Zamboanga del Sur

Metro Manila

Figure 2.5: Map of the Philippines

and some additional towns were formed into a political-military province called Abra with a capital at Bucay (moved in 1861 to Bangued). In mid-1899 the revolutionary government was displaced by an American military government. In 1901 civil government was established and in 1903 the eleven municipalities of this province were reorganized into five. In 1905 Abra was made a subprovince of Ilocos Sur until 1917 when it was restored as a full province.

> FHL provincial records: civil registration (1897–1898); birth records (1946–1988); marriage contracts (1945–1987); death certificates (1963–1991); court records (1847–1889); deportations (1867–1889); military induction records (1857–1892); public records (1883–1898); records of lending (1859–1898); school records (1848–1911); statistical reports (1896); tax records (1860–1863); and Census of Chinese (1885–1898).

Localities and their records:

> Bangued (city) was made capital of Abra in 1861. Tayum and Pidigan, annexed in 1903, separated again in 1907. FHL records: civil registration, 1922–1928 and notarials, 1916–1928. Local records: civil registration, 1945–.
>
> Boliney (municipal district) was established in 1919. Local records: civil registration, 1960–.
>
> Bucay (municipality), established 1847, was the first provincial capital. Bucay absorbed San José in 1903. FHL records: civil registration, 1922–1931; notarials 1911–; Saint Narcissus parish registers, 1848–1947. Local records: civil registration, 1902.
>
> Danglas (municipality) was established in 1919. FHL records: civil registration, 1922–1928; notarials 1937–. Local records: civil registration, 1914–.
>
> Dolores (municipality), established in 1886, included San Juan in 1903–1928. In 1919 Lagangilang and Tineg separated. Local records: civil registration, 1914–.
>
> Langangilang (municipality) was established in 1919 from Dolores. Local records: civil registration, 1945–.
>
> Langiden (municipality) was established in 1919. Local records: civil registration, 1920–.
>
> La Paz (municipality) was established in 1965. FHL records: civil registration, 1922–1930; notarials, 1911; parish registers, 1911–1949. Local records: civil registration, 1920–.
>
> Licuan (municipality), also known as Basacal or Licuanan, was founded in 1652 and established in 1919. Local records: civil registration, 1968–.
>
> Luba (municipality) was established in 1919. FHL records: civil registration, 1922–1931; notarials, 1921–. Local records: civil registration, 1945–.
>
> Malibcong (municipality) was established in 1919. Local records: civil registration, 1960–.
>
> Manabo (municipality) was established in 1919. FHL records: Civil registration, 1922–1931; notarials, 1920–; Saint Joseph parish registers, 1894–1950. Local records: civil registration, 1957–.
>
> Peñarrubia (municipality), also known as Patoc, Dumayco, and Alfonso XIII prior to 1903, was established in 1919. FHL records: civil registration, 1922–1931; notarials, 1920–. Local records: civil registration, 1945–.
>
> Pidigan (municipality), also known as Pidpideg, was an early Spanish town which was annexed to Bangued in 1903 and separated in 1910. FHL records: civil

> registration, 1922–1931; notarials, 1913–. Local records: civil registration, 1914–.
>
> Pilar (municipality), also known as Baliwag or Balioag, was established in 1884. At various times, it included territory which later became parts of San Isidro and Villavieja. FHL records: civil registration, 1922–1931; notarials, 1911–; Our Lady of the Holy Rosary of Fatima parish registers, 1907–1957. Local records: civil registration, 1948–.
>
> Sal-lapadan (municipality) was established in 1919. FHL records: civil registration, 1922–1931; notarials, 1923–. Local records: civil registration, 1921–.
>
> San Isidro (municipality), also known as Cagutongan, was established in 1950 from a part of Pilar. FHL records: notarials 1934–. Local records: civil registration, 1950–.
>
> San Juan (municipality), also known as Ganagan, was established in 1928 from a part of Dolores. It had been annexed as a village to Dolores in 1903. Local records: civil registration, 1929–.
>
> San Quintin (municipality), also known as Talamey, was established in 1901. FHL records: civil registration, 1922–1931; notarials, 1913–. Local records: civil registration, 1945–.
>
> Tayum (municipality) was established from Bangued in 1907. It had been annexed to Bangued in 1903. FHL records: civil registration, 1922–1931; notarials, 1908–; Saint Catherine of Alexandria parish registers, 1899–1921. Local records: civil registration, 1945–.
>
> Tineg Tineg (municipal district) was established in 1919 from a part of Bangued. Local records: civil registration, 1973–.
>
> Tubo (municipality) was established in 1919 from part of Pilar. It had been a part of the sub-province of Lepanto, annexed to the province of Abra in 1901. Local records: civil registration, 1961.
>
> Villaviciosa (municipality) was established in 1919. FHL records: civil registration, 1922–1930; notarials, 1914–. Local records: civil registration, 1945.
>
> **Bucloc** (municipal district), **Daguioman** (municipal district), **Lacub** (municipality), and **Lagayan** (municipality, from Pingaping and Manaois) were all established in 1919.

Agusan del Norte. This province is in the northeast part of the island of Mindanao, which is located in the southern part of the Philippine Archipelago. Its capital is Butuan. Under the Spanish administration, Agusan formed part of the province of Caraga, which was later known as Surigao. In 1860 it was combined with a number of other provinces to form the East District of Mindanao which, in 1870, was named the District of Surigao. This area was also known as Butuan, or, more popularly, as ''Manobo Country'' after one of the Muslim groups in the area. In 1901 Agusan was made a subprovince of Surigao. In 1907 it was made a separate province. In 1914, the sub-province of Bukidnon was split off. In 1968 it was divided into Agusan del Norte and Agusan del Sur.

> FHL provincial records: birth records (1967–1988); marriage contracts (1949–1987); death certificates (1968–1991); and notarials (1933–1935).

Localities and their records:

Buenavista (municipality) was established in 1937 from Butuan. FHL records: notarials, 1937–. Local records: civil registration, 1937–.

Butuan City (city), also known as Agao or Masao, was chartered in 1950. Buenavista, Nasipit, and Magallanes separated from this city in 1937, 1929, and 1969, respectively. FHL records: birth certificates, 1950–1988; marriage contracts, 1950–1960; death certificates, 1975–1988; civil registration, 1924–1930; notarials, 1920–. Local records: civil registration, 1942–.

Cabadbaran (municipality) was an early Spanish town from which Santiago and Tubay separated in 1903. FHL records: civil registration, 1922–1930; notarials, 1911–. Local records: civil registration, 1911–.

Carmen (municipality) was established in 1949 from Nasipit. FHL records: notarials, 1951–1953. Local records: civil registration, 1949–.

Jabonga (municipality) was established in 1921. Kitcharao separated in 1961. FHL records: civil registration, 1922–1929; notarials, 1922–1939. Local records: civil registration, 1945–.

Kitcharao (municipality) was established in 1961 from Jabonga. Local records: civil registration, 1963–.

Las Nieves (municipality). FHL records: civil registration, 1925–1926. Local records: civil registration, 1955–.

Magallanes (municipality) was established in 1969 from Butuan. Local records: civil registration, 1972–.

Nasipit (municipality) was established in 1929 from Butuan. Carmen separated in 1949. FHL records: civil registration, 1929–1931. Local records: civil registration, 1947–.

Santiago (municipality) was established in 1968 from Cabadbaran.

Tubay (municipality) was established in 1947 from Cabadbaran. It had been annexed to Cabadbaran in 1903. Local records: civil registration, 1947–.

Agusan del Sur. This province was (until 1968) once the southern part of the province of Agusan. See the section on Agusan del Norte above for a brief history of this area. Its capital is Properidad.

FHL provincial records: birth certificates (1967–1988); marriage contracts (1949–1987); death certificates (1967–1991); and notarials (1933–1935).

Localities and their records:

Bayugan (municipality) was established in 1961. Local records: civil registration, 1962–.

Bunawan (municipality), also known as Banawan, was established in 1959. Trento separated in 1968. FHL records: notarials, 1927–. Local records: civil registration, 1969–.

Esperanza (municipality) was established in 1953. San Luis separated in 1968. FHL records: civil registration, 1925–1929. Local records: civil registration, 1945–.

La Paz (municipality) was established in 1965. It had been annexed to Tandag, Surigao del Sur in 1904. At one time, it had been annexed to Talacogon. Local records: civil registration, 1971–.

Loreto (municipality). FHL records: civil registration, 1928–1929; notarials, 1928–1937. Local records: civil registration, 1946–.

Properidad (City) was chartered in 1960. FHL records: civil registration, 1922–1931; notarials, 1927–1932. Local records: civil registration, 1960.

Rosario (municipality) was established in 1969 from San Francisco. Local records: civil registration, 1960–.

San Francisco (municipality) was established in 1959. Rosario separated in 1969. Local records: civil registration, 1960–.

San Luis (municipality) was established in 1968 from Esperanza.

Santa Josefa (municipality) was established in 1965. Local records: civil registration, 1960.

Talacogon (municipality), also known as Linao, was established in 1924. Veruela separated in 1965. FHL records: civil registration, 1922–1931. Local records: civil registration, 1946.

Trento (municipality) was established in 1968 from Bunawan. Local records: civil registration, 1972–.

Veruela (municipality) was established in 1965 from Talacogon to which it had been annexed in 1904. Local records: civil registration, 1960–.

Aklan. This province is located on the northwest part of Panay Island which was conquered by Spanish forces led by Martin de Goiti in 1570. This whole island was made the province of Panay around 1600. In 1716 the province of Capiz was organized from part of the territory of Panay. Aklan was part of Capiz and remained so through the rest of the Spanish period. In 1956, under the American administration, Aklan was separated from Capiz into its own province, one of four provinces that now occupy Panay Island. Its capital is Kalibo.

FHL provincial records: birth certificates (1957–1988); marriage contracts (1956–1987); and death certificates (1964–1991).

Localities and their records:

Altavas (municipality), also known as Jimeno or Laguing Banwa, was established in 1918 from New Washington to which it had been annexed in 1903 under the name "Jimeno." FHL records: civil registration, 1921–1930; notarials, 1924–. Local records: civil registration, 1945–.

Balete (municipality), also known as Balele, was established in 1917 from New Washington. In 1860 this was a part of Batan which was annexed to New Washington in 1903. FHL records: civil registration, 1922–1931; notarials, 1920–. Local records: civil registration, 1946–.

Banga (municipality) was established in 1912 from Kalibo to which it had been annexed in 1903. Libacao separated around 1930. FHL records: civil registration, 1922–1931; notarials, 1910–. Local records: civil registration, 1945.

Batan (municipality), also known as Batang or Bataan, was established in 1931 from New Washington to which it had been annexed in 1903. FHL records: civil registration, 1930–1931; notarials, 1917–; Immaculate Conception parish registers, 1899–1926. Local records: civil registration, 1946–.

Buruanga (municipality), also known as Buswang, Buswanga, and Busuanga, was established in 1911 from Nabas. Malay separated in 1949. FHL records: civil registration, 1922–1931; notarials, 1917–. Local records: civil registration, 1945–.

Ibajay (municipality), also known as Ybajay and Ybahay, was established from Nabas. FHL records: civil registration, 1922–1931; notarials, 1906–; St. Peter the Apostle parish registers, 1882–1931. Local records: civil registration, 1945–.

Kalibo (city), also known as Calibo, Calivo, and Madianos, was established around 1911 from Banga. FHL records: civil registration, 1922–1931; notarials, 1910; St. John the Baptist parish registers, 1787–1941. Local records: civil registration, 1908–.

Lezo (municipality), also known as Guicod and Tierra Alta, was established in 1941 from Numancia to which it had been annexed in 1923. FHL records: notarials, 1913–; St. Isidore parish registers, 1882–1964. Local records: civil registration, 1943–.

Libacao (municipality), also known as Ageangka and Aglanka, was established from Banga. FHL records: civil registration, 1922–1930; notarials, 1911–. Local records: civil registration, 1945–.

Madalag (municipality), also known as Medalag and Madulag, was established in 1948 from Libacao to which it had been annexed in 1903. FHL records: notarials, 1948–. Local records: civil registration, 1948.

Makato (municipality), also known as Taft and Macate, was established in 1948. It had been joined with Tangalan in 1903 to form the municipality of Taft which was renamed Makato in 1917. Tangalan separated in 1948. FHL records: civil registration, 1922–1932; notarials, 1914–; Most Holy Name of Jesus parish registers, 1837–1921. Local records: civil registration, 1945–.

Malay (municipality) was established in 1949 from Buruanga. FHL records: notarials, 1952–. Local records: civil registration, 1950–.

Malinao (municipality) was established in 1796. FHL records: civil registration, 1922–1931; notarials, 1907–; Saint Joseph parish registers, 1796–1958. Local records: civil registration, 1944–.

Nabas (municipality), also known as Alimbo, Navas, and Navis, was established in 1854 from Ibajay. Buruanga separated in 1811. FHL records: civil registration, 1922–1931; notarials, 1912–; St. Isidore parish registers, 1883–1924. Local records: civil registration, 1945–.

New Washington (municipality), also known as Lagantic and Lagantik, was established in 1903 with the consolidation of Batan, Balete, and Jimeno—all of which later separated. FHL records: civil registration, 1922–1932; notarials, 1911–; Our Lady of the Most Holy Rosary parish registers, 1851–1914. Local records: civil registration, 1944–.

Numancia (municipality), also known as Marianos and Madianos, was established in 1923 from Kalibo to which it had been annexed in 1903. Lezo separated in 1941. FHL records: civil registration, 1922–1931; notarials, 1925–. Local records: civil registration, 1947–.

Tangalan (municipality), also known as Tanga-ean, was established in 1948. See history of Makato (municipality) above for more information. FHL records: notarials, 1948–. Local records: civil registration, 1948–.

Albay. This province is situated on the southeastern part of Luzon Island. The area was explored by Luis de Guzman in 1569 and the first settlements established shortly thereafter. The town of Albaybay, under the shorter name of Albay, was established as a pueblo in 1616 and became the capital of the new Partido de Ibalon which was divided in the early 1600s into the provinces of Ibalon and Camarines. In 1836 Ibalon was renamed Albay. Sorsogon was separated from Albay in 1894, becoming its own province. In 1905 Catanduanes, an island that had formerly been an independent province, was made a sub-province of Albay. Then in 1945 Cataduanes was re-established as a separate province. During this period many name changes were made. For example, in 1836, the town of Albay was renamed Legazpi, changing back to Albay in 1908, and then back to Legazpi in 1948 when it became a chartered city. Albay's capital is Legazpi.

> FHL provincial records: civil registration (1864–1895); birth records (1945–1988); marriage contracts (1945–1987); death certificates (1964–1991); court records (1838–1902); deportations (1865–1897); land records (1845–1894); military induction records (1880–1895); notarials (1919–); public records (1884–1889); records of lending (1875–1898); school records (1848–1911); statistical reports or *estadística* (1896); tax records (1853–1962); Census of Chinese (1886–1898).

Localities and their records:

Bacacay (municipality), also known as Bagacay and Bagcay, was an early Spanish town. FHL records: civil registration, 1922–1932; notarials, 1904; St. Rose of Lima parish registers, 1835–1833. Local records: civil registration, 1946–.

Camalig (municipality) was established in 1901. Guinobatan separated in 1901. FHL records: civil registration, 1930–1931; notarials, 1914–; St. John the Baptist parish registers, 1835–1959. Local records: civil registration, 1945–.

Daraga (municipality), also known as Locsin, Cagsawa, and Budiao, was established in 1921 after having been annexed to Albay (Legazpi) in 1908. In 1948, it was annexed once more. In 1954 Cagsawa, again, became an independent municipality. Name changed from Cagsawa to Locsin (in 1959) to Daraga (in 1967).

Guinobatan (municipality), also known as Gubat, Guinabatan, Pinagbunutan, and Bubulusan, was established in 1901 from Camalig. Some of its territory was used to organize the municipality of Pio Duran in 1969. FHL records: civil registration, 1921–1931; notarials, 1904–; Our Lady of the Assumption parish registers, 1863–1927. Local records: civil registration, 1902–.

Jovellar (municipality), known as Quipia prior to 1882, was an early Spanish town. The municipality was established in 1901. FHL records: civil registration, 1922–1931; notarials 1904–; The Decollation of Saint John the Baptist parish registers, 1876–1930. Local records: civil registration, 1955–.

Legazpi (city), also known as Albay, Albaybay, Sawagñan, and Sawangan was an early Spanish town which was combined with Albay and Daraga in 1907. Daraga separated in 1921. The name of Albay was changed to Legazpi in 1925. Chartered in 1948, it included the territory of Daraga and Legazpi. It lost its charter in 1954, when Daraga again separated but was rechartered as a city in 1959. FHL records: civil registration, 1922–1933; notarials, 1904–; birth certificates, 1948–1988; marriage contracts, 1949–1960; death certificates, 1975–

1988; Saint Gregory the Great parish registers, 1868–1950. Local records: civil registration, 1946–.

Libon (municipality), also known as Libong and Villa de Libon, was an early Spanish town. It was established as a municipality in 1901. FHL records: civil registration, 1922–1931; notarials, 1904–; Saint James the Greater parish registers, 1894–1942. Local records: civil registration, 1901–.

Ligao (municipality), also known as Cabasi, was established in 1901 from Oas. Some of its territory was used in organizing the municipality of Pio Duran in 1964. FHL records: civil registration, 1921–1932; notarials, 1904–; Saint Stephen, Protomartyr, parish registers, 1709–1951. Local records: civil registration, 1945–.

Malilipot (municipality), also known as Manlilipot, Manlipot, and Manlilipod was an early Spanish town. It was established as a municipality in 1901. FHL records: civil registration, 1922–1931; notarials, 1914–. Local records: civil registration, 1947–.

Malinao (municipality), also known as Alinao, was established in 1901. Tiwi separated in 1901. FHL records: civil registration, 1922–1932; notarials, 1928–; Saint Anne parish registers, 1782–1949. Local records: civil registration, 1903–.

Manito (municipality), also known as Manitao, was established in 1901. FHL records: civil registration, 1922–1930; notarials, 1917–; Saint Raphael, the Archangel, parish registers, 1899–1973. Local records: civil registration, 1921–.

Oas (municipality), also known as Mahiwas, was established in 1901. FHL records: civil registration, 1922–1932; notarials, 1910–; Saint Michael Archangel parish registers, 1780–1929, and enumeration of members (*padrones de Alma*), 1817–1896. Local records: civil registration, 1901–.

Pio Duran (municipality), also known as Malacbalac, was established in 1964 from parts of the municipalities of Guinobatan, Ligao, and Jovellar. Local records: civil registration, 1964–.

Polangui (municipality), also known as Oyangue and Binanuan, was established in 1901. FHL records: civil registration, 1922–1931; notarials, 1904–; Saints Peter and Paul parish registers, 1823–1948. Local records: civil registration, 1947–.

Rapu-Rapu (municipality) was established in 1901 from the municipality of Bacon in the province of Sorsogon. FHL records: civil registration, 1921–1931; notarials, 1916–; Saint Florentina parish registers, 1891–1936. Local records: civil registration, 1901–.

Santo Domingo (municipality), also known as Libog, Libot, and Madanlog, was established in 1901. The name Libog changed to Santo Domingo in 1959. FHL records: civil registration, 1922–1931; notarials, 1914–; Saint Dominic of Guzman parish registers, 1786–1944. Local records: civil registration, 1945–.

Tabaco (municipality), was established in 1901. FHL records: civil registration, 1921–1932; notarials, 1914–; Saint John the Baptist parish registers, 1852–1934. Local records: civil registration, 1902–.

Tiwi (municipality), also known as Tiui, Tivi, Tigbi, and Tibi, was established in 1901 from Malinao. FHL records: civil registration, 1931–1932: notarials, 1904–; Saint Lawrence parish registers, 1918–1965. Local records: civil registration, 1919–.

Antique. Antique which shares the island of Panay with the provinces of Aklan, Capiz, and Iloilo, occupies the west coast. Originally occupied by Negroids, in the thirteenth century immigrants from Borneo arrived, took the coastal regions, and pushed these early occupiers into the highlands at the center of the island. The three *sakops* or divisions that the people from Borneo established (Hantik, Aklan, and Irong-Irong) are the basis of the modern provinces of Antique, Capiz and Aklan, and Iloilo, respectively. With the arrival of the Spanish, this island became part of the Philippines. By 1580 a settlement had been established at Arevalo in Iloilo, and Panay was grouped with Negros Island to form a province. By 1591 Panay had been divided into many encomiendas including Bugason (Bugasong) and Hantik (Antique) in modern Antique Province. After the suppression of the encomienda system shortly after 1600, the island again became a province with its capital at Arevalo near what is today the City of Iloilo. In 1790 Antique became a province with Hantik (Antique) its capital. Later the capital was moved to Bugasong and for a time the entire province took that name. Finally in 1802 the capital was transferred to San José de Buenavista where it remains today. In 1903 the twenty towns of this province were consolidated into eleven municipalities. These were subdivided again to make the eighteen municipalities of Antique in 1970.

FHL provincial records: civil registration (1868–1896); birth records (1946–1988); marriage contracts (1945–1987); death certificates (1964–1991); court records (1886–1903); deportations (1898); records of lending (1843–1889); school records (1868–1898); statistical reports (1896); tax records (1853–1876); military induction records (1865–1897); Census of Chinese (1869–1898).

Localities and their records:

Anini-y (municipality), also known as Aniy and Aninil, was established in 1949. Originally founded 1828, it was annexed to Dao from 1903 to 1949. FHL records: St. John Nepomucene parish registers, 1855–1939. Local records: Civil registration, 1946–.

Barbaza (municipality), also known as Nalupa and Nalupa Viejo, was established in 1915 from Lawa-an. Listed in 1754 as Nalupa from which (in 1788) Culasi was separated with the remaining part taking the name Nalupa Viejo. In 1859 the town was transferred from Nalupa Viejo to Otñgol and renamed Barbaza. By the time of the American administration, Nalupa Viejo had gone back to another former name, Laua-an. In 1903, Barbaza was reannexed but again separated in 1915. FHL records: civil registration, 1922–1930; notarials, 1903–; St. Anthony of Padua parish registers, 1889–1931. Local records: civil registration, 1946–.

Belison (municipality) was established in 1961 and originally founded in 1743. Local records: civil registration, 1963.

Bugasong (municipality) was founded in 1762, the same year it was separated from Patnoñgon, and the provincial capital was moved to San Jose in 1802. FHL records: civil registration, 1922–1930; notarials, 1909–; The Holy Child parish registers, 1899–1927. Local records: civil registration, 1946.

Caluya (municipality), also known as Palupandan, was separated from Mindoro and annexed to Antique Province in 1917. It includes the island of Sibay, Semirara, and Sibdo. FHL records: civil registration, 1922–1930; notarials, 1915–1918. Local records: civil registration, 1916–.

Culasi (municipality) was established from Nalupa in 1788. See Barbaza (municipality) above. Pandan (1798) and Sebaste (1967) separated. FHL records: civil registration, 1922–1931; notarials, 1904–; Saint Michael Archangel parish registers, 1899–1938. Local records: civil registration, 1914–.

Dao (municipality) was an old Spanish town in 1766. Anini-y was annexed to it in 1903, but then separated in 1949. Local records: civil registration, 1945–.

Hamtic (municipality), also known as Antique, Hamtik, and Hantik, was established in 1954 from San Jose to which it was annexed in 1903. Founded in 1746, it was provincial capital in 1790. Later the capital was transferred to first Bugasong, then San Jose (1802).

Lawa-an (municipality), also known as Nalupa Nuevo and Laua-an. See Barbaza (municipality) for its history. FHL records: civil registration, 1922–1931; notarials, 1906–; Saint Isidore parish registers, 1908–1942. Local records: civil registration, 1947–.

Libertad (municipality), also known as Inyawan and Inaywan, was established in 1949 from Pandan. Local records: civil registration, 1949–.

Pandan (municipality) was an Augustan mission in 1654 which separated from Culasi around 1798. The northern part of Sebaste was annexed in 1903, then separated from Pandan in 1967 to become part of the municipality of Sebaste. FHL records: civil registration, 1922–1933; notarials, 1910–. Local records: civil registration, 1945–.

Patnoñgon (municipality), also known as Patnongan, was established from Bugasong. It was founded in 1762. FHL records: civil registration, 1922–1930; notarials, 1904–; St. Augustine parish registers, 1887–1942. Local records: civil registration, 1943–.

San Jose (city), also known as San Jose de Buenavista and Mala-iba, became a provincial capital in 1802. Antique, Guitas, and part of San Pedro were annexed to it in 1903. Hamtic separated from San Jose in 1954. FHL records: civil registration, 1922–1931; notarials, 1903–; St. Joseph parish registers, 1862–1936. Local records: civil registration, 1945–.

San Remigio (municipality), also known as Hinalinan, Tigbagacay, and Old Town, was established from Sibalom. It was a Spanish town by 1863. Baladjay was annexed in 1903. FHL records: civil registration, 1921–1932; notarials, 1905–. Local records: civil registration, 1952–.

Sebaste (municipality) was established in 1967 out of Culasi and Pandan. The northern part of Sebaste had been annexed to Pandan and the southern part to Culasi in 1903. FHL records: civil registration, 1921–1931; notarials, 1903–; Saint Blaise parish registers, 1897–1953. Local records: civil registration, 1964–.

Sibalom (municipality) was settled in the 1660s. The former town of Egana was annexed in 1903. San Remigio separated from this municipality. FHL records: civil

registration, 1921–1931; notarials 1903–. Local records: civil registration, 1945–.

Tibiao (municipality), also known as Tibyao, was a Spanish town established by 1735. FHL records: civil registration, 1922–1931; notarials, circa 1903–; St. Nicholas of Tolentino parish registers, 1908–1939. Local records: civil registration, 1914–.

Valderrama (municipality) was an old Spanish town. FHL records: civil registration, 1922–1926; St. Luke, the Evangelist, parish registers, 1907–1941. Local records: civil registration, 1945–.

Aurora Sub-province. This sub-province is situated on a thin strip of land along the eastern coast of the island of Luzon. Its proximity to Quezon links much of its history with that province. Under the name Principe, it was brought under the administrative control of the Province of Nueva Ecija in 1818. In the middle part of the nineteenth century it became a *comandancia politico-military* (political military command) with its capital at Baler. In 1902 it was placed under the administration of the province of Tayaba which later became the province of Quezon. In 1951 it became a subprovince of Quezon and was given the name Aurora in honor of the wife of the Philippine president Manuel L. Quezon.

FHL provincial records: birth records (1945–1988); marriage contracts (1945–1987); death certificates (1962–1991); birth certificates (1974–1988); marriage contracts (1980–1987); school records (1867–1897).

Localities and their records:

Baler (city), also known as Valer, was settled in 1609. It was established at its present site in 1735 after destruction of the original city by a tidal wave. Casiguran was annexed in 1906, but separated again in 1907. San Luis (1959) and Dipaculao (1950) also separated. FHL records: civil registration, 1922–1931; notarials, 1913–; San Luis Obispo parish registers, 1892–1943. Local records: civil registration, 1941–.

Casiguran (municipality) was established in 1907 from Baler. Dilasag (1959) and Dinalongan (1966) separated. FHL records: civil registration, 1922–1931; notarials, 1918–; St. Anthony of Padua parish registers, 1906–1941. Local records: civil registration, 1918–.

Dilasag (municipality) was established in 1959 from Casiguran. Local records: civil registration, 1961–.

Dinalongan (municipal district) was established in 1966 from Casiguran.

Dingalan (municipality) was established in 1956. Local records: civil registration, 1956–.

Dipaculao (municipality) was established in 1950 from Baler. Local records: civil registration, 1950–.

Maria Aurora (municipality), also known as Casignan, San Jose and San Jose de Casignan, was established in 1949 and given its present name. Local records: civil registration, 1949–.

San Luis (municipality) was established in 1959 from Baler. Local records: civil registration, 1959–.

Basilan. This province includes the island of Basilan and several adjacent islands which are located south of Mindanao Island in the extreme southwest of the Philippines. In 1637 the Spanish conquered Lamitan which was the strong hold of Sultan Kudarat and established a garrison which was withdrawn in 1663, but restored in 1747. In 1844 fortifications were constructed to guard against Moro raids. At this time the area was placed under the administration of the province of Zamboanga; but in 1863 it was separated from that province and made the Sixth District of the government of Mindanao Island. In 1899 an American military government took control. In 1903, with the restoration of civil government, this area was subordinated to the government of the province of Zamboanga. In 1948 the island became a chartered city independent of Zamboanga; and in 1975 it became a separate province.

> FHL provincial records: birth certificates (1971–1988); death certificates (1974–1991); marriage contracts (1975–1986); deportations (1875–1898); public records (1888–1898); records of lending (1879–1898); and Census of Chinese (1882–1884).

Localities and their records:

Basilan City (city) was established in 1948 from Isabela. The chartered city encompassed the entire island. In 1973 it was dissolved and annexed to Isabela; but subsequently restored. FHL records: birth certificates, 1948–1975, marriage contracts, 1950–1960. Local records: civil registration, 1945–.

Isabela (city), also known as Isabela de Basilan, was established in 1973. FHL records: civil registration, 1882–1898, 1922–1931; notarials, 1911–; school records, 1867–1898; Census of Chinese, 1886–1890.

Lamitan (municipality) was established in 1921. FHL records: civil registration, 1928; notarials, 1928–.

Lantawan (municipality) was established in 1975 from Pilas. **Maluso** (municipality) was established in 1921. **Sumipsip, Tipo-Tipo**, and **Tuburan** (each a municipality) were established in 1975. **Tapiantana** (municipality) was originally part of Sumipsip. **Malamawi** and **Pilas** are other municipalities in this province.

Bataan. The province of Bataan is situated on a long peninsula located on the southwest coast of Luzon, across Manila Bay from the city of Manila. It was probably settled by Juan de Salcedo in 1572 and early colonies were Kamaya, Samal, and Abucay. At one time, it was part of the provinces of Pampanga and Mariveles. When organized as a province in 1754, Balanga became its capital. The new province included the towns of Abucay, Samal, Orani, La Llana-Hermosa, San Juan de Dinalupijan, Pilar, and Orion from the Province of Pampanga and the towns of Mariveles, Cabcaben, Bagac, and Morong from Mariveles. In the Philippine Revolution this was one of the first provinces to revolt. A civil administration was set up on March 2, 1901. In 1903, the twelve municipalities of Bataan were reduced to eight by the consolidation of various towns. At present this province again consists of twelve municipalities.

> FHL provincial records: civil registration (1882–1894); birth records (1945–1988); marriage contracts (1945–

1987); death certificates (1963–1991); court records created by the Court of First Instance (1900–1903); deportations (1865–1895); land records (1787–1896); records of lending (1875–1889); school records (1848–1911); statistical reports (1896); tax records (1815–1877); and Census of Chinese (1866–1896).

Localities and their records:

Abucay (municipality), also known as Abuday, was an early Spanish town. In 1903 it annexed Mabatan. FHL records: civil registration, 1922–1931, 1942–1994; notarials, 1909–. Local records: civil registration, 1943–.

Bagac (municipality) was an early Spanish town. FHL records: civil registration, 1922–1931, 1945–1994; notarials, 1912–. Local records: civil registration, 1945–.

Balanga (City), an early Spanish town, is now the capital of the province. FHL records: civil registration, 1922–1930, 1942–1993; notarials, 1911–. Local records: civil registration, 1942–.

Dinalupihan (municipality), also known as San Juan de Dinalupihan, annexed Hermosa in 1903–1909, separated from it, reannexed it briefly from approximately 1914 to 1918 with the name Bagumbayan. FHL records: civil registration, 1922–1931, 1945–1994; notarials, 1905–. Local records: civil registration, 1929–.

Hermosa (municipality), also known as La Llana Hermosa, was an early Spanish town. See Dinalupihan (municipality) above for its history. FHL records: civil registration, 1922–1932; notarials, circa 1909–. Local records: civil registration, 1929–.

Limay (municipality) was established from Orion in 1917. FHL records: civil registration, 1922–1931, 1945–1994; notarials, circa 1915–. Local records: civil registration, 1945–.

Mariveles (municipality) was an early Spanish town and capital of the province of Mariveles which was reorganized in 1754. FHL records: civil registration, 1922–1932, 1945–1994; notarials, circa 1903–. Local records: civil registration, 1945–.

Morong (municipality), previously known as Moron, underwent a name change to Morong in 1955. FHL records: civil registration, 1922–1931, 1942–1994; notarials, circa 1911–. Local records: civil registration, 1945–.

Orani (municipality) was an early Spanish town. It briefly annexed Samal from 1903–1908. FHL records: civil registration, 1922–1932, 1942–1994; notarials, circa 1915–. Local records: civil registration, 1945–.

Orion (municipality) was an early Spanish town. FHL records: civil registration, 1922–1931, 1942–1946; notarials, circa 1903–. Local records: civil registration, 1943–.

Pilar (municipality) an early Spanish town, was temporarily annexed to Balanga, 1903–1908. FHL records: civil registration, 1922–1931, 1942–1994; notarials, circa 1909–. Local records: civil registration, 1945–.

Samal (municipality), an early Spanish town was annexed to Orani, 1903–1908. FHL records: civil registration, 1922–1931, 1942–1994; notarials, circa 1907–. Local records: civil registration, 1942–.

Batanes. This is the smallest province in the Philippines in both size and population. Made up of ten small islands about 130 miles north of Luzon, the largest of these islands are Itbayat, Batan, and Sabtang; the others are Duquey, Ibuhos, Siayan, Mabudis, Diogo, Northern Island, and Y'Ami. Though the Spanish government did not try to establish its authority in this province until late in the eighteenth century, a number of different Catholic missions (the Dominicans from Cagayian in 1617 and Dominican friars circa 1685) attempted to evangelize the natives on these islands, but it was some time before a major missionary effort finally was able to establish permanent missions. The introduction of the Spanish government was carried out by Jose Basco (the original capital was named after him) in 1791. Five municipalities were established as a district of the province of Cagayan. Apparently between 1852 and 1855, Batanes became an independent province and remained so until 1862 when it became a sub-province of Cagayan. Sometime before 1885 it again became an independent province with its capital at Santo Domingo de Basco. The civil government took control on August 22, 1901, when it was annexed to Cagayan. That same year, the entire group of islands became the single municipality of Basco. In 1907 Batanes again became a sub-province of Cagayan with its capital at Santo Domingo de Basco. In 1918 it became a province.

> FHL provincial records: civil registration (1886–1894); birth records (1952–1987); marriage contracts (1951–1986); death certificates (1969–1980); public records (1885–1898); records of lending (1878–1884); and school records (1818–1898).

Localities and their records:

Basco (city), also known as Santo Domingo de Basco, Santo Domingo, and Basay, was an early Spanish town and the original capital of the province. In 1903 Itbayat, Ivana, Mahatao, and Sabtang were annexed, but later separated and became independent municipalities. FHL records: civil registration, 1922–1932; notarials, 1931–1937. Local records: civil registration, 1946–.

Itbayat (municipality), also known as Isbayat, Ibayat, Maria de Itbayat, and Santa Maria de Mayan, was a Spanish town before 1852. It was annexed to Basco in 1903, but later separated. FHL records: civil registration, 1922–1932. Local records: civil registration, 1909–.

Ivana (municipality), also known as Ibana, Ibanag, San José, and San José de Ibana, was an early Spanish town which was annexed to Basco in 1903, made a municipality sometime before 1967, a municipal district in 1967, and a municipality again in 1969. FHL records: civil registration, 1922–1929; San José parish registers, 1794–1949. Local records: civil registration, 1940–.

Mahatao (municipality), also known as Magatao, Marigatao, San Carlos de Magatao, San Carlos de Magosa, and San Carlos, was an early Spanish town circa 1798 which was annexed to Basco in 1903 and later separated. It was named Mahatao in 1910. FHL records: civil registration, 1928–1930; San Carlos Borromeo parish registers, 1844–1986. Local records: civil registration, 1953–.

Sabtang (municipality), also known as Saptan, San Vicente, San Vicente de Saptang, and San Vicente de Saptan, was established as a town before 1845, annexed to Basco in 1903, and separated out into a municipality before 1967 when it became a municipal district. In 1969 it again became a municipality. FHL records: civil registration, 1922–1931. Local records: civil registration, 1941–.

Uyugan (municipal district) was established in 1909 from Ivana as a municipality, changing into a municipal district in 1967. FHL records: civil registration, 1922–1929. Local records: civil registration, 1946–.

Batangas. This province on the southwestern coast of Luzon Island presently has thirty-two municipalities and two cities, Lipa City and Batangas, the latter of which is the capital. According to the historical traditions of the area, the Batangas region was settled by persons from Borneo beginning in the thirteenth century. By the time of the arrival of the Spanish, native villages were located on the Taal and Pansipit Rivers. In 1581 the province of Bombon was created with a capital at Balayan and territory which included the modern provinces of Batangas, Mindoro, Marinduque, and the southern part of Quezon. At times, the province was also called Balayan, after its capital. In 1732 the capital was transferred to Taal and the whole province took that name. In 1754, the capital was moved to Batangas and the province received its present name. Batangas was one of the first provinces to revolt against the Spanish. On May 2, 1901 the Americans established a civil government.

> FHL provincial records: civil registration (1854–1898); birth records (1945–1988); marriage contracts (1945–1987); death certificates (1964–1991); court records created by the Court of First Instance (1839–1902); deportations (1867–1896); land records (1787–1909); military induction records (1863–1897); public records (1875–1896); records of lending (1854–1878, 1888–1889); school records (1813–1909); statistical reports (1896); tax records (1836–1856); and Census of Chinese (1839–1898).

Localities and their records:

Agoncillo (municipality), also known as Buitna and Pansipit, was established in 1948 from Lemery. The name changed from Pansipit to its present form in 1949. Local records: civil registration, 1911–.

Alitagtag (municipality), also known as Alinagnag and Bauan Sur, was established in 1910 from Bauan. FHL records: civil registration, 1922–1934, 1910–1991; notarials, 1910–; Invencion de la Santa Cruz parish registers, 1913–1944. Local records: civil registration, 1931–.

Balayan (municipality), also known as Kumintang, Balayihan, and Balayang, changed its name from Kunmintang (used since 1578) to Balayihan circa 1590. It was the capital of the province from 1581 to 1732. Calatagan and Tuy were annexed in 1903 but returned to existing as separate municipalities in 1912 and 1911, respectively. FHL records: civil registration, 1921–1931, 1903–1991; notarials, 1903–; Immaculate Conception parish registers, 1757–1943. Local records: civil registration, 1903–.

Balete (municipality), also known as Balite, was established in 1969 from Lipa. FHL records: civil registration, 1945–1992.

Batangas (city), also known as Kumintang and Laurel City, was established as a Spanish town in 1601. Known as Kumintang before that time, it took its present name in 1581. The provincial capital as of 1754, it received its city charter in 1969. In 1832 Ibaan separated from it. FHL records: civil registration, 1922–1932, 1901–1992; birth certificates, 1969–1988; death certificates, 1975–1988; military records, 1858–1897, 1908–1972; notarials, circa 1903–; Immaculate Conception parish registers, 1542–1943. Local records: civil registration, 1900–.

Bauan (municipality), was established as a Spanish town in 1839. The following municipalities were separated from it: Alitagtag (1910), Mabini 1918), San Jose (1767), Tingloy (1955), and San Pascual (1969). FHL records: civil registration, 1922–1932, 1954–1992; military records, 1873–1897, 1945–1992; notarials, 1907–; Immaculate Conception parish registers, 1900–1911. Local records: civil registration, 1945–.

Calaca (municipality) was established in 1839 from Balayan. FHL records: civil registration, 1922–1931, 1902–1991; notarials, 1905–; St. Rafael Archangel parish registers, 1838–1955, and confirmations, 1922–1940. Local records: civil registration, 1948–.

Calatagan (municipality), a Spanish town before 1845, was annexed to Balayan in 1903 and separated in 1912. FHL records: civil registration, 1922–1934, 1911–1991; Santo Domingo de Silas parish registers, 1913–1971. Local records: civil registration, 1912–.

Cuenca (municipality) was a Spanish town before 1885. FHL records: civil registration, 1922–1931, 1945–1991; notarials, 1911–; San Isidro Labrador parish registers, 1879–1966. Local records: civil registration, 1945–.

Ibaan (municipality) was established in 1832 from Batangas. FHL records: civil registration, 1922–1931, 1901–1991; military records, 1870–1897; notarials, circa 1903–; San Santiago parish registers, 1832–1946. Local records: civil registration, 1901–.

Laurel (municipality) was established in 1969 from Talisay. FHL records: civil registration, 1972–1992. Local records: civil registration, 1972–.

Lemery (municipality), also known as Punta and San Geronimo, was an early Spanish town. Originally named San Geronimo, it was annexed to Taal in 1858 and renamed Lemery. It was separated in 1862, reannexed to Taal in 1903, and separated again in 1906. Agoncillo separated from it in 1948. FHL records: civil registration, 1922–1932; notarials, circa 1907–; San Roque parish registers, 1868–1938. Local records: civil registration, 1901–.

Lipa (city), also known as Tagbakin, San Sebastian, and Lipenos, was settled in thirteenth century. It was a Spanish town by 1702 and a chartered city in 1948. The following municipalities separated from it: Malvar (1919), Balete (1969), and Mataasnakahoy (1932). FHL records: civil registration, 1922–1930, 1945–1987; birth certificates, 1945–1988; marriage contracts, 1948–1960; death certificates, 1975–1988; notarials, circa 1903–; San Sebastian parish registers, 1778–1958. Local records: civil registration, 1901–.

Lobo (municipality), also known as Loboo, was established as a Spanish town before 1885. FHL records: civil registration, 1922–1931; notarials, circa 1905–; San Michael Archangel parish registers, 1874–1971. Local records: civil registration, 1901–.

Mabini (municipality) was established in 1918 from Bauan. FHL records: civil registration, 1922–1932; notarials circa 1918–; St. Francis de Paul parish registers, 1918–1967. Local records: civil registration, circa 1918–.

Malvar (municipality), also known as Luta, was established in 1919 from Lipa. FHL records: civil registration, 1922–1931, 1945–1991; notarials, 1918–1925; Immaculate Conception parish registers, 1910–1975. Local records: civil registration, circa 1945–.

Mataasnakahoy (municipality), also known as Mataas-Na-Kahoy, was established in 1932 from Lipa. FHL records: civil registration, 1931–1932, 1945–1991. Local records: civil registration, circa 1945–.

Nasugbu (municipality) was a Spanish town before 1839. Lian was briefly annexed from 1903 to 1915. FHL records: civil registration 1922–1932, 1901–1991; notarials, 1907–; St. Francis Xavier parish registers, 1884–1967. Local records: civil registration, circa 1916–.

Padre Garcia (municipality) was separated from Rosario in 1949. More of Rosario's territory was annexed in 1956. FHL records: civil registration 1949–1992. Local records: civil registration, 1949–.

Rosario (municipality) was a Spanish town before 1839. Taysan was temporarily annexed from 1903 to 1919. Padre Garcia separated in 1949. Part of Rosario's territory was annexed in 1956. FHL records: civil registration, 1922–1932, 1945–1991; notarials, 1903–. Local records: civil registration, 1945–.

San José (municipality), also known as Pook ng Malaking Tubig, San Jose de Malaking Tubig, and San Jose de Malaking, was established in 1767 from Bauan. FHL records: civil registration, 1922–1935, 1945–1992; notarials, 1903–; St. Joseph parish registers, 1765–1935. Local records: civil registration, circa 1945–.

San Juan (municipality), also known as Bolbok, Bocboc, and San Juan de Bocboc, was a Spanish town named San Juan de Bocboc, renamed Bolbok in 1914, and, finally, San Juan in 1933. FHL records: civil registration, 1922–1931, 1901–1992; notarials, 1907–; San Juan Nepomuceno parish registers, 1843–1967. Local records: civil registration, circa 1901–.

San Luis (municipality), also known as Balibago, was a Spanish town before 1862. It was annexed to Taal from 1903–1918. FHL records: civil registration, 1922–1933, 1918–1991. Local records: civil registration, circa 1918–.

San Nicolas (municipality) was established in 1955 from Taal. Local records: civil registration, 1955–.

San Pascual (municipality) was established in 1969 from Bauan. FHL records: civil registration, 1945–1992.

Santa Teresita (municipality) was established in 1961. Local records: civil registration, 1962–.

Santo Tomas (municipality) was an old Spanish town before 1839 with a parish established prior to that in 1666. FHL records: civil registration, 1922–1931; death records, 1952–1992; birth records, 1945–1975; notarials, circa 1907–. Local records: civil registration, 1945–.

Taal (municipality) was the capital of the province Taal 1732–1754, but a parish was erected there prior to that in 1572. Lemery and San Luis were annexed from 1903 to 1906 and 1918, respectively. San Nicolas separated in 1955. FHL records: civil registration, 1922–1932, 1901–1991; military records, 1859–1897; notarials, circa 1903–; Roman Catholic parish registers, 1901–1922. Local records: civil registration, 1901–.

Talisay (municipality), a Spanish town before 1850, was annexed to Tanauan from 1903 to 1906. The villages of Caloocan and Birinayan were annexed in 1956. FHL records: civil registration, 1922–1931, 1945–1990; notarials, 1905–; San Guillermo parish registers, 1899–1964. Local records: civil registration, circa 1945–.

Tanauan (municipality), also known as Tanawan or Tanawaan, was an early Spanish town circa 1583. Annexed Talisay from 1903 to 1906. FHL records: civil registration, 1922–1930, 1945–1991; notarials, 1905–. Local records: civil registration, circa 1945–.

Taysan (municipality), also known as Tiisan, Taisan, and Mercedes was a Spanish town by 1852. It was annexed to Rosario from 1903 to 1919. FHL records: civil registration, 1919–1931, 1918–1992; notarials, 1919–; Our Lady of Mercy parish registers, 1860–1975. Local records: civil registration, circa 1919–.

Tingloy (municipality) was established in 1955 from Bauan. Local records: civil registration, 1955–.

Tuy (municipality), a Spanish town by 1867, was annexed to Balayan from 1903 to 1911. FHL records: civil registration, 1922–1930, 1911–1991; notarials, 1913–1914; St. Vincent Ferrer parish registers, 1866–1949, and Cofradías, 1914–1935. Local records: civil registration, circa 1911–.

Benguet. This province, once part of the original Mountain Province, is situated in the mountains of north-central Luzon. During the Spanish period, the area was so inaccessible that Spanish control was not asserted until just before the Americans became involved in the Philippines. The ''Land of the Igorots'' (inhabitants of this area are largely made up of a tribal population known collectively as Igorots) was visited by Alonso Martin Quirante in 1542 and a Comandancia Politico-General de Igorots was established at Agoo, La Union. The Augustinian friars attempted to evangelize this area from 1654 to 1659, but were unsuccessful. [The few missions that were established over the years failed when the Spanish priests deserted at the end of the Spanish-American War.] Guillermo Galvey led a number of expeditions beginning in 1829 to this area and in 1846 he established a comandancia at La Trinidad where it remained until the end of Spanish rule. On November 23, 1900, civil government was established with the capital at Baguio. Beginning in 1907, missions were reestablished by the Congregation of the Immaculate Heart of Mary. In 1908, the original Mountain Province was divided into seven sub-provinces of which Benguet was one and the others were Bontoc, Ifugao, Amburayan, Lepanto, Kalinga, and Apayao. Baguio was the capital. Rapidly developing into a resort, in 1909 it became a chartered city. In 1920 the boundaries were changed, the sub-provinces of Amburayan and Lepanto were abolished. Bakun, from

Amburayan, and Mankayan, from Lepanto, were annexed to the Benguet sub-province. On June 18, 1966, the former Mountain Province with its various sub-provinces was divided into the four provinces: Mountain Province, Ifugao, Benguet, and Kalinga-Apayao. The division was done roughly along the lines of tribal divisions: the Ibaloi (or Inibaloi) and the Kankanai tribes predominate in Benguet; the Ifugao in Ifugao Province; the Bontoc Igorots in the modern Mountain Province; and the Kalinga, Apayaos, and the Isnegs (Itnegs or Tinguians) in Kalinga-Apayao Province.

> FHL provincial records: civil registration (1893–1894); birth records (1945–1988); marriage contracts (1946–1986); death certificates (1967–1991); court records created by the Court of First Instance (1901–1903); military induction records (1890); public records (1884–1898); records of lending (1880, 1873–1898); statistical reports (1896); tax records (1894); and census of tribe members or *padrones generales de Igorrotes infieles* (1892–1897).

Localities and their records:

Atok (municipality), also known as Atoc, was a Spanish town which was made a municipality in 1963. FHL records: civil registration, 1922–1931. Local records: civil registration, circa 1946–.

Baguio (city), a Spanish town, was the capital of Benguet from 1900 to 1966. It was chartered as a city on September 1, 1909. FHL records: civil registration, 1922–1987; birth certificates, 1946–1988; marriage contracts, 1946–1988; notarials 1911–; medical records from Atok Trail (1961–1990), Atab (1965–1990), Bakakeng Atab (1975–1985), Aurora Hill (1965–1989), Campo Filipino (1962–1989), City Camp (1953–1989), Engineer's Hill (1961–1989), Irisan (1961–1990), Loakan (1961–1990), Middle Quirino Hill (1967–1990), Mines View (1977–1990), New Lucban (1976–1989), Pacdal (1977–1988), Pinsao (1975–1990), Scout Barrio (1961–1989), and Quezon Hill (1970–1990)—all districts of Banguio; Our Lady of Atonement parish registers, 1907–1937. Local records: civil registration, 1945–.

Bakun (municipality), established 1963, was formerly part of the sub-province of Amburayan which was annexed to Benguet Province in 1920. Annexed Ampusuñan in 1936. FHL records: civil registration, 1922–1931; civil registration, 1922–1933 (for Ampusuñan). Local records: civil registration, 1946–.

Bokod (municipality), also known as Bocot, was established in 1963. FHL records: civil registration, 1922–1930; Immaculate Conception of the Blessed Virgin Mary parish registers, 1922–1973. Local records: civil registration, circa 1946–.

Buguias (municipality), also known as Buguias and Bugulas, was established in 1900. FHL records: civil registration, 1922–1931. Local records: civil registration, circa 1947–.

Itogon (municipality) was founded in 1900, established in 1951. FHL records: civil registration, 1922–1933; St. Charles Borromeo parish registers, 1908–1947. Local records: civil registration, circa 1946–.

Kabayan (municipality), also known as Cabayan and Kabagan, was a town by 1900. It was established in

1963. FHL records: civil registration, 1922–1931. Local records: civil registration, circa 1946–.

Kapangan (municipality), also known as Capañgan and Capanga, was a town by 1961. It was established in 1963. FHL records: civil registration, 1922–1931. Local records: civil registration, circa 1946–.

Kibungan (municipality), also known as Cabunga, Cabungan, and Quibuñgan, was established in 1963. FHL records: civil registration, 1922–1935. Local records: civil registration, circa 1948–.

La Trinidad (city), also known as Trinidad, was established in 1950. From 1846 to 1900 and 1966 on, it has been the capital of Benguet Province. FHL records: civil registration, 1925–1931; birth records, 1945–1983; death records, 1945–1988; marriage records, 1960–1989; adoption registers, 1978–1987. Local records: civil registration, circa 1946–.

Mankayan (municipality), formerly a part of the Lepanto sub-province, was annexed to Benguet when that sub-province was dissolved in 1920. It was established in 1955. FHL records: civil registration, 1922–1931; notarials, 1929–. Local records: civil registration, circa 1958–.

Sablan (municipality) was established in 1963. FHL records: civil registration, 1925–1931. Local records: civil registration, circa 1945–.

Tuba (municipality), also known as Twin Peaks, was established in 1963. As Twin Peaks, the town split into Tuba and Pogo in 1912. FHL records: civil registration, 1922–1931; death records, 1945–1989; birth records, 1946–1989; marriage records, 1986–1989. Local records: civil registration, circa 1946–.

Tublay (municipality), a Spanish settlement by 1861, became a township in 1900 and was established in 1963. FHL records: civil registration, 1922–1931. Local records: civil registration, circa 1947–.

Biliran Sub-province. This sub-province of the province of Leyte occupies the island of Biliran just north of the island of Leyte. See the province of Leyte below for the history of this sub-province for the two shared much of that history. Early in Spanish era, the island was known as Panamao. In 1601 the Spanish established a ship building center on the island which used Chinese, African, and Filipino labor overseen by Spanish engineers. In April 1959 the sub-province of Biliran was created from the province of Leyte.

FHL provincial records: see the section on the province of Leyte.

Localities and their records:

Almería (municipality), also known as Bongabong and Solano, was an early Spanish town which was a municipality by 1907 when its seat was moved from the village of Almería to the village of Kawayan and its name was changed to Kawayan. In 1948 a new municipality was created from the consolidation of several villages located in the municipalities of Kawayan and Naval. Since its seat was in the village of Almería, it took the name Almería. FHL local records: notarials, 1905–1908. Local records: civil registration, 1948–.

Biliran (municipality) was an early Spanish town which was annexed to Naval from 1903 to 1910. Annexed Jamoran from Kawayan in 1910. In 1949 Cabucgayan separated.

FHL local records: civil registration, 1922–1931; notarials, 1909–. Local records: civil registration, 1910–.

Cabucgayan (municipality), also known as Cabugayan, was an early Spanish town which was annexed to Caibiran in 1903. In 1949, it separated, along with villages both from Caibiran and Biliran. Local records: civil registration, 1949–.

Caibiran (municipality) was an early Spanish town to which Culaba and Cabucgayan were annexed in 1903, then separated in 1953 and 1949, respectively. FHL local records: civil registration, 1922–1931; notarials, 1905–. Local records: civil registration, 1916–.

Culaba (municipality) was an early Spanish town which was annexed to Caibiran from 1903 to 1953. Local records: civil registration, 1954–.

Kawayan (municipality) was also known as Telegrapo and San Clemente. For the history of this early Spanish town, see the section on Almeria (municipality) above. Maripipi was annexed to this municipality from 1903 to 1914. FHL local records: civil registration, 1922–1931; notarials, 1911–. Local records: civil registration, 1946–.

Maripipi (municipality), also known as Maria-Pepe, was annexed to Kawayan from 1903–1914. FHL local records: civil registration, 1922–1931; notarials, 1915–. Local records: civil registration, 1915–.

Naval (municipality) was an early Spanish town to which Biliran was annexed from 1903 to 1910. Herbay, Villalon, and Villahermosa were annexed by San Isidro in 1903. Jamoran was annexed by Almería in 1948. FHL local records: civil registration, 1922–1935; notarials, 1905–. Local records: civil registration, 1903–.

Bohol Province. This province occupies an oval-shaped island located between the islands of Cebú and Luzon in the south-central part of the Philippine Archipelago. Apparently the Magellan expedition landed near modern Tagbilaran at the village of Bo-ol, after which this province is named. When Miguel Lopez de Legazpi arrived in 1565 and established a blood compact with the local ruler, Datu Sikatuna, Bohol already had trade contacts with China and Portugal. Administratively, Bohol was made a part of the province of Cebú. In 1854 Bohol was separated from Cebú and with Siquijor Island became a separate province. Its capital was at Tagbilaran. After a period of instability, civil government was established there by the Americans on April 1, 1902. On June 4, 1901, Siquijor Island was separated from Bohol and made a sub-province of Negros Oriental.

FHL provincial records: civil registration (1779–1894); birth records (1945–1988); marriage contracts (1945–1987); death certificates (1964–1991); court records created by the Court of First Instance (1860–1903); deportations (1881–1896); military induction records (1889–1893); public records (1881–1898); records of lending (1887–1889); school records (1894–1896); and Census of Chinese (1885–1898).

Localities and their genealogical records:

Albuquerque (municipality), also known as Segundo, New Segundo, Segunto, and Arbol, was a Spanish town circa

1861. Villages of Cornago and Camboac from Loboc were annexed in 1909. In 1918 the villages of Cornago, Abucay, Libjo, Canagong, and Cambdac were separated to form a part of the municipality of Sikatuna. FHL local records: civil registration, 1922–1931, 1913–1992; notarials, 1910–. Local records: civil registration, circa 1913–.

Alicia (municipality), also known as Batuanan, was an early Spanish town annexed to Mabini in 1903. It then was separated and established as a municipality in 1949 with its name changed from Batuanan to Alicia. FHL local records: civil registration, 1950–1992. Local records: civil registration, 1950–.

Anda (municipality) was an early Spanish town. FHL local records: civil registration, 1922–1931, 1941–1993; notarials, 1911–. Local records: civil registration, circa 1941–.

Antequera (municipality), also known as Agad, was established in 1867 from Maribojoc. Villages east of Agutay were annexed in 1903. In 1955 some villages were separated to form part of Catigbian, others were separated (in 1969) to form part of San Isidro. FHL local records: civil registration, 1922–1932, 1902–1992; notarials, 1912–. Local records: civil registrations, circa 1902–.

Baclayon (municipality) was an early Spanish town. Pamilacan Island was placed under its jurisdiction in 1958. FHL local records: civil registration, 1922–1932, 1929–1992; notarials, 1911–. Local records: civil registration, circa 1902–.

Balilihan (municipality), also known as Bilijan and Balilijan, was an early Spanish town, settled before 1839. Villages east of Agutay River in Catigbian were annexed in 1903. Villages of Badiang and Bahaybahay were separated and annexed to Sikatuna in 1918. FHL local records: civil registration, 1922–1931, 1903–1992; notarials, 1911–. Local records: civil registration, circa 1902–.

Batuan (municipality) was established in 1903 from Bilar. FHL local records: civil registration, 1922–1931; notarials, 1913–. Local records: civil registration, circa 1904–.

Bilar (municipality), also known as Bilad, was established from Sevilla. Batuan separated in 1903. FHL local records: civil registration, 1922–1931; notarials, 1912–. Local records: civil registration, circa 1945–.

Buenavista (municipality) was established in 1959 from villages of Buenavista Norte, Buenavista Sur, and Cabul-on (Jetafe municipality); and Daet and Lapacan Sur (Inabanga municipality). There was a minor boundary adjustment in 1961. Local records: civil registration, 1960–.

Calape (municipality) was an early Spanish town. [See descriptions below of San Isidro (municipality) and Tubigon (municipality), both of which separated from Calape.] FHL local records: civil registration, 1922–1931, 1945–1992; notarials, 1911–. Local records: civil registration, circa 1902–.

Candijay (municipality), an early Spanish town, lost Libas to Mabini, but gained Tugas from Guindulman in 1903. FHL local records: civil registration, 1922–1931, 1948–1993; notarials, 1916–. Local records: civil registration, circa 1946–.

Carmen (municipality) was an early Spanish town. FHL local records: civil registration, 1922–1930; notarials,

1912–. Local records: civil registration, 1944– (with a few earlier dates).

Catigbian (municipality), also known as Catigbi-an, San Jacinto, and Jacinto, was a Spanish town before 1848. In 1903 it was broken up with villages west of the Agutay River going to Balilihan, those east going to Antiquera. Its name changed from Jacinto to Catigbian when it was again established (with some loss of territory to Tubigon) as a municipality in 1955. FHL local records: civil registration, 1949–1992. Local records: civil registration, 1949–.

Clarin (municipality), also known as Can-ogong, was established in 1919 from Tubigon. It had been annexed to Tubigon in 1852 from Inabanga (now Inaganga). FHL local records: civil registration, 1922–1930; notarials, circa 1919–. Local records: civil registration, 1919–.

Corella (municipality), also known as Nug-as, was established in 1884 from Baclayon. FHL local records: civil registration, 1922–1932, 1902–1989; notarials, 1911–. Local records: civil registration, 1945–.

Cortes (municipality), also known as Paminuitan, was a Spanish town sometime before 1862. FHL local records: civil registration, 1922–1931; notarials, 1911–. Local records: civil registration, mostly 1945– (with a few earlier).

Dagohoy (municipality) was established 1956. Its boundaries were slightly altered in 1965. Local records: civil registration, 1958–.

Danao (municipality) was established in 1961. Local records: civil registration, 1961–.

Dauis (municipality) was a Spanish town by 1839. FHL local records: civil registration, 1922–1930, 1945–1992; notarials, 1911–. Local records: civil registration, 1945–.

Dimiao (municipality), also known as Damiao and Dimlao, was a Spanish town by 1839. Annexed part of Lila from 1903–1915. FHL local records: civil registration, 1922–1931; notarials, 1911–. Local records: civil registration, 1902–.

Duero (municipality) was a Spanish town by 1885. FHL local records: civil registration, 1922–1931; notarials, 1911–. Local records: civil registration, 1913–.

Garcia-Hernandez (municipality) was a Spanish town by 1864. FHL local records: civil registration, 1922–1931, 1902–1992; notarials, 1911–. Local records: civil registration, 1902–.

Guindulman (municipality), a Spanish town by 1839, lost the village of Tugas to Candijay in 1903. FHL local records: civil registration, 1922–1931, 1942–1992; notarials, circa 1911–. Local records: civil registration, 1945–.

Inaganga (municipality), also known as Inaboñgan, lost the village of Can-ogong to Tubigon (1852), the villages of Daet and Lapacan to Buenavista (1959), and some other territory to Sagbayan (1949). FHL local records: civil registration, 1922–1931, 1945–1992; notarials, 1911–. Local records: civil registration, 1945–.

Jagna (municipality), also known as Hagna and Jatna, was settled before the Spanish period. FHL local records: civil registration, 1922–1930, 1902–1992; notarials, 1912–. Local records: civil registration, 1912–.

Jetafe (municipality), also known as Getafe, was a Spanish town before 1857. See Buenavista (municipality) above for more historical information. FHL local records: civil registration, 1922–1931, 1950–1992; notarials, 1912–. Local records: civil registration, 1949–.

Lila (municipality), an early Spanish town, temporarily lost territory west of the north-south line of Caso de la Población to Damiao and territory east to Loay (1903–1915). FHL local records: civil registration, 1922–1930; notarials 1915–. Local records: civil registration, 1914–.

Loay (municipality), also known as Laoay, was a Spanish town by 1839. Annexed part of Lila from 1903 to 1915 (see Lila above). FHL local records: civil registration, 1922–1932, 1913–1991; notarials, 1912–. Local records: civil registration, 1902–.

Loboc (municipality), a Spanish town by 1839, lost territory to Sevilla when the latter was organized in 1872. FHL local records: civil registration, 1922–1931; notarials, 1911–. Local records: civil registration, 1912–.

Loon (municipality), also known as Laon, was a Spanish town by 1939. FHL local records: civil registration, 1922–1933, 1914–1992; notarials circa 1911–. Local records: civil registration, 1915–.

Mabini (municipality) was established in 1903 by bringing together Batuanan (now Alicia), Cabulao (from Ubay), and Libas (from Candijay). In 1949 Batuanan was separated and established as the municipality of Alicia. FHL local records: civil registration, 1922–1931, 1904–1993; notarials, 1912–. Local records: civil registration, 1904–.

Maribojoc (municipality), also known as Dungguan and Malaboyoc, was an early Spanish town. Antequera separated from it in 1876. FHL local records: civil registration, 1922–1931, 1923–1992; notarials, 1911–. Local records: civil registration, 1939–.

Panglao (municipality), also known as Mapanglao, was a town by 1839. FHL local records: civil registration, 1922–1931, 1945–1992; notarials, 1916–. Local records: civil registration, 1902–.

Pilar (municipality), also known as Vilar and Bilar, was a town by 1945. The municipality was established in 1961. Local records: civil registration, 1962–.

Pitogo (municipality) was established in 1969 from Ubay. Local records: civil registration, 1970–.

Sagbayan (municipality), also known as Borja, Canmaya, and Cambitoon, was established in 1949 from Clarin, Inaganga, Calape, and Tubigon. In 1957 its name was changed from Borja to Sagbayan. Local records: civil registration, 1949–.

San Isidro (municipality) was established in 1969 from the following villages: Caimbang, Cansague, Causwagan Sur, and San Isidro (from the municipality of Catigbian); Abihilan, Banunos, and Cambansag (from the municipality of Antequera); Masonoy and Candungao (from Calape); and Cabanugan (from Tubigon). FHL local records: civil registration, 1970–1992.

San Miguel (municipality) was established in 1961 from Trinidad and Ubay. See these municipalities for the history. Local records: civil registration, 1961–.

Sevilla (municipality), also known as Sebilla, was a town by 1872. FHL local records: civil registration, 1922–1930; notarials, 1911–. Local records: civil registration, 1914–.

Sierra-Bullones (municipality) was established in 1910. FHL local records: civil registration, 1922–1930; notarials, 1912–. Local records: civil registration, 1945–.

Sikatuna (municipality) was established in 1918 from the villages of Carnago, Abucay, Libjo, Canagong, and Camboac (from the municipality of Albuquerque); and Badiang and Bahay-Bahay (from Balilihan). FHL local records: civil registration, 1922–1931; notarials, 1918–. Local records: civil registration, 1918–.

Tagbilaran (city), also known as Tinabilan, was the site of the first mission in 1767. A Spanish village by 1839, it was chartered as a city in 1966. FHL local records: civil registration, 1922–1931; birth records, 1966–1988, 1902–1990; death records, 1976–1988; notarials, 1911–. Local records: civil registration, 1902–.

Talibon (municipality), also known as Talibong, was a town by 1806. In 1903, when the municipality of Ipil was broken up, Talibon annexed the left bank of the Ipil River. Later in 1947 when Trinidad (the former Ipil) was established, the annexed portion was restored to Trinidad. FHL local records: civil registration, 1922–1931, 1945–1992; notarials, 1911–. Local records: civil registration, 1912–.

Trinidad (municipality), also known as Cabizon and Ipil, was temporarily divided between Ubay and Talibon in 1903 (see these municipalities for more information), but the territory was restored when Trinidad was again established in 1947. Local records: civil registration, 1947–.

Tubigon (municipality), also known as Tubigan and Tabagon, was an early Spanish town. In 1852 the village of Can-ogong was annexed from Inagonga (Inaganga). Part of Catigbian was annexed in 1955. FHL local records: civil registration, 1922–1931, 1947–1992; notarials, 1912–. Local records: civil registration, 1932–.

Ubay (municipality), a Spanish town by 1840, lost the village of Cabulao when the latter was annexed to Mabini in 1903. FHL local records: civil registration, 1922–1931; notarials, 1911–. Local records: civil registration, 1935–.

Valencia (municipality) was an early town. FHL local records: civil registration, 1922–1931, 1903–1992; notarials, 1911–. Local records: civil registration, 1913–.

Bukidnon. This land-locked province, its capital at Malaybalay, occupies the north central part of the island of Mindanao. It is named for the Bukidnon or "mountain people," who fled the coming the Spanish, ending up in this remote and isolated area. As late as 1908 a major part of this province remained unexplored. The surrounding provinces claim jurisdiction over various parts of the area, but only the province of Misamis appears to exercise some kind of control. In 1849 the Spanish government began its attempt to settle the area. In 1860 Bukidnon was attached to the province of Misamis to form the "Northern District" of the newly established government of Mindanao. With the establishment of civil government in May, 1901, Bukidnon became a sub-province of Misamis. In 1903 the southern half of this area was annexed to the Cotabato District of the Moro Province. In 1909 Bukidnon became a sub-province of the province of Agusan. In 1914 it became a province in the Department of Mindanao and Sulu.

FHL provincial records: birth records (1946–1988); marriage contracts (1945–1987); and death certificates (1965–1991).

Localities and their genealogical records:

Baungon (municipality). Local records: civil registration, 1949–.

Damulog (municipality) was established in 1971. Local records: civil registration, 1972–.

Dangcagan (municipality) was established in 1961. Pulangi (1965), Quezon (1966), and Kitaotao (1966) were separated. Local records: civil registration, 1961–.

Don Carlos (municipality) was established in 1966 from Maramag. Local records: civil registration, 1968–.

Impasugong (municipality), also known as Impasungong, was an early Spanish town. FHL local records: civil registration, 1923–1924. Local records: civil registration, circa 1944–.

Kadingilan (municipality) was established in 1971 from Kibawe. Local records: civil registration, 1972–.

Kaliangan (municipality) was established in 1966 from Pangantokan. Local records: civil registration, 1968–.

Kibawe (municipality), also known as Guibawe, was established in 1931 from Maramag. Kadingilan separated in 1971. Local records: civil registration, 1950–.

Kitaotao (municipality) was established in 1966 from Maramag and Dangcagan. Local records: civil registration, 1971–.

Lantapan (municipality) was established in 1966 from Malaybalay. Local records: civil registration, 1968–.

Libona (municipality) was established in 1957. FHL local records: civil registration, 1923–1924. Local records: civil registration, circa 1947–.

Malaybalay (city), also known as Oroquieta, was an early Spanish town. Lantapan and San Fernando separated in 1966, and 1965, respectively. FHL local records: civil registration, 1922–1925; San Isidro Labrador parish registers, 1890–1932. Local records: civil registration, circa 1946–.

Malitbog (municipality), an early Spanish town, was established in 1963 from Manolo Fortich. Local records: civil registration, 1947–.

Manolo Fortich (municipality), also known as Maluko, was an early Spanish town. Former name of Maluko was changed to Manolo Fortich in 1957. Malitbog separated in 1963. Local records: civil registration, 1947–.

Maramag (municipality) was established circa 1957 after being separated from Don Carlos, Kibawe, Kitaotao, Pulangi, Quezon, and San Fernando. FHL local records: civil registration, 1922–1926. Local records: civil registration, circa 1941–.

Pangantocan (municipality) was established in 1963. Kalilangan separated in 1966. Local records: civil registration, 1964–.

Pulangi (municipality), also known as Pulanggi and Pulangui, was established in 1965 from Maramag, Valencia, and Dangcagan. Local records: civil registration, 1968–.

Quezon (municipality) was established in 1966 from Maramag and Dangcagan. Local records: civil registration, 1968–.

San Fernando (municipality) was established in 1959 from Malaybalay and Maramag. Local records: civil registration, 1968–.

Sumilao (municipality) was an early Spanish town. FHL local records: Christ the King (village of Kisolon) parish registers, 1908–1939. Local records: civil registration, 1946–.

Talakag (municipality) was an early Spanish town. Former name of Kabalangasan was changed to Talakag in 1870. Local records: civil registration, 1948–.

Valencia (municipality) was established in 1959. Pulangi separated in 1965. Local records: civil registration, 1961–.

Bulacan. This province occupies the part of central Luzon bounded by Manila Bay on the northwest, the provinces of Pampanga and Rizal to the west and south respectively, Nueva Ecija to the north, and Quezon to the east. Settled long before the arrival of the Spanish, it was known as Ma-yi. The Spanish organized the settlements into towns early in their administration and joined this area to the province of Manila. In 1591, Bulacan became a district in the province of Pampanga and its own independent province soon thereafter. Since the capital of the province was at Meycauayan, the newly formed province was known by that name. In 1848 its boundaries were expanded to include town of San Miguel de Mayuma and some adjacent territory from the province of Pampanga. During the Philippine Revolution, this province was a center of revolutionary activity against the Spanish. It was here that the constitution was signed and the Philippine Republic proclaimed. In February 1901 the Americans established civil government in this province with the capital at Malolos. In 1903 its twenty-five municipalities were consolidated into thirteen; however, most of these have since been re-established in response to the growth in population in the area.

FHL provincial records: civil registration (1853–1898); birth records (1945–1988); marriage contracts (1945–1987); death certificates (1964–1991); court records created by the Court of First Instance (1902–1903); deportations (1867–1897); land records (1756–1902); military induction records (1848–1898); public records (1876–1898); records of lending (1855–1898); school records (1863–1899); statistical reports (1754–1755); and tax records (1849–1894).

Localities and their genealogical records:

Angat (municipality) was an early Spanish town. Norzagaray was annexed from 1903 to 1908. Some territory was contributed to Dona Remedios Trinidad which became a municipality in 1977. FHL local records: civil registration, 1922–1932, 1945–1989; military induction records, 1889–1892; notarials, 1911–; Saint Monica parish registers, 1896–1931. Local records: civil registration, 1945–.

Balagtas (municipality), also known as Bigaa prior to 1966, was established in 1912 from Bocaue to which it had been annexed in 1903. Pandi separated in 1946. FHL local records: civil registration, 1931; notarials, 1911–; Saint Laurence Martyr parish registers, 1732–1897. Local records: civil registration, 1912–.

Baliuag (municipality), also known as Baliwag, was an early Spanish town separated from Plaridel in 1732.

Bustos and San Rafael were annexed from 1903 to 1917 and 1908, respectively. FHL local records: civil registration, 1922–1931, 1904–1954; notarials, 1913–; Saint Augustine parish registers, 1733–1939. Local records: civil registration, 1904–.

Bocaue (municipality), also known as Bukawe, was an early Spanish town. Balagtas was annexed from 1903 to 1912. FHL local records: civil registration, 1922–1932, 1916–1947; notarials, 1913–; Saint Martin parish registers, 1762–1961. Local records: civil registration, 1916–.

Bulacan (municipality) was an early Spanish town. Guiguinto was annexed from 1903 to 1915. FHL local records: civil registration, 1922–1924, 1916–1947; notarials, 1912–; Assumption of Our Lady parish registers, 1672–1941. Local records: civil registration, 1945–.

Bustos (municipality) was an early Spanish town. It was annexed to Baliuag from 1903 to 1917. FHL local records: civil registration, 1922–1932, 1917–1994; notarials, 1912–; Infant Jesus parish registers, 1872–1939. Local records: civil registration, 1917–.

Calumpit (municipality), also known as Calompit, was an early Spanish town. Annexed Hagonoy from 1903 until the latter became its own municipality. FHL local records: civil registration, 1922–1931, 1967–1961; notarials, 1905–; Saint John the Baptist parish registers, 1672–1969. Local records: civil registration, 1901–.

Doña Remedios Trinidad (municipality) was established in 1977 from parts of Angat, Norzagaray, and San Miguel.

Guiguinto (municipality), also known as Hihinto, was an early Spanish town annexed to Bulacan from 1903 to 1915. FHL local records: civil registration, 1923–1932, 1915–1992; notarials, 1918–; Saint Ildefonsus, Archbishop of Toledo, parish registers, 1905–1950. Local records: civil registration, 1915–.

Hagonoy (municipality), also known as Agonoy, was established from Calumpit to which it had been annexed in 1903. FHL local records: civil registration, 1922–1935, 1928–1982; notarials, 1911–; Saint Anne parish registers, 1731–1942. Local records: civil registration, 1901–.

Malolos (city), also known as Malulos, was an early Spanish town and capital of this province from 1898. Santa Isabel and Barasoain temporarily separated from 1854 to 1903. FHL local records: civil registration, 1922–1932; notarials, 1911–; birth registers, 1901–1937; marriage contracts 1923–1951; death records, 1910–1915; Immaculate Conception parish registers, 1697–1932; St. Elizabeth, Queen of Hungary (located in Santa Isabel, an early Spanish town which is now part of Malolos) parish registers, 1900–1935; Our Lady of Carmel (located in Barasoain, also an early Spanish town which is now part of Malolos) parish registers, 1859–1955. Local records: civil registration, 1901–.

Marilao (municipality), also known as Marilaw and Madilaw, was established in 1915 from Meycauyan to which it had been annexed in 1903. FHL local records: civil registration, 1922–1931, 1915–1989; notarials, 1911–; Saint Michael Archangel parish registers, 1900–1953, and church documents, 1901–1959. Local records: civil registration, 1915–.

Meycauayan (municipality), also known as Mecabayan, was an early Spanish town. Annexed Marilao from 1903 to 1915. FHL local records: civil registration, 1922–1933; notarials, 1905–; birth registers, 1901–1987; birth certificates, 1906–1948; marriage registers, 1936–1948; medical documents, 1914–1986; death certificates, 1916–1949; death records, 1914–1988; military induction records, 1873–1894; Saint Francis of Assisi parish registers, 1845–1943. Local records: civil registration, 1914–.

Norzagaray (municipality), also known as Norsagaray and Casay, was an early Spanish town. It was annexed to Angat from 1903 to 1908. In 1977 some territory was separated and used to create to Dona Remedios Trinidad. FHL local records: civil registration, 1922–1932, 1959–1991; notarials, 1903–; military induction records, 1873–1894; Saint Andrew, the Apostle, parish registers, 1899–1951. Local records: civil registration, 1959–.

Obando (municipality), also known as Ubando and Catangalan, was annexed to Polo (now Valenzuela) from 1903 to 1907. FHL local records: civil registration, 1922–1931, 1908–1991; notarials, 1903–; Saint Paschal Baylon parish registers, 1754–1951. Local records: civil registration, 1908–.

Pandi (municipality) was an early Spanish town—annexed to Balagtas from 1903 to 1946. FHL local records: civil registration, 1946–1989; notarials, 1929–; Immaculate Conception parish registers, 1911–1976. Local records: civil registration, 1946–.

Paombong (municipality), also known as Paombon, was an early Spanish town. FHL local records: civil registration, 1922–1932, 1946–1992; notarials, 1906–; Saint James, the Apostle, parish registers, 1775–1962. Local records: civil registration, 1910–.

Plaridel (municipality), also known as Quingwa, Quiñgua, and Kingwa, was an early Spanish town. Annexed Pulilan from 1903 to 1909. Its name was changed from Quingua to Plaridel in 1936.

Pulilan (municipality) was an early Spanish town annexed to Plaridel from 1903 to 1909. FHL local records: civil registration, 1922–1931; notarials, 1903–; Saint Isidore parish registers, 1855–1961. Local records: civil registration, 1913–.

San Ildefonso (municipality), also known as Bulak, was an early Spanish town which was annexed to San Miguel from 1903 to 1909. FHL local records: civil registration, 1922–1931, 1974–1993; notarials, 1911–; Saint Ildefonsus parish registers, 1886–1935. Local records: civil registration, 1945–.

San José del Monte (municipality), also known as San José, was an early Spanish town which had been part of Meycauayan. It was annexed to Santa Maria from 1903 to 1918. FHL local records: civil registration, 1922–1932; notarials, 1903–. Local records: civil registration, 1950–.

San Miguel (municipality), also known as San Miguel de Mayumo and Mayumo, was an early Spanish town which had been transferred from Pampanga province to Balacan province in 1848. Annexed San Ildefonso from 1903 to 1909. FHL local records: notarials, 1919–; Saint Michael, the Archangel, parish registers, 1821–1941. Local records: civil registration, 1916–.

San Rafael (municipality), also known as Buenavista, was an early Spanish town which was annexed to Baliuag from 1903 to 1908. FHL local records: civil registration, 1922–1932, 1950–1994; notarials, 1911–; Saint John of God parish registers, 1897–1953. Local records: civil registration, 1950–.

Santa Maria (municipality), also known as Santa Maria de Pandi, was an early Spanish town to which San Jose del Monte was annexed from 1903 to 1918. FHL local records: civil registration, 1922–1931, 1916–1991; notarials, 1917–; Immaculate Conception parish registers, 1806–1927. Local records: civil registration, 1917–.

Valenzuela, also known as Polo, was transferred to metropolitan Manila.

Cagayan. This province is situated on northern part of Luzon Island. It is bordered on the west by the provinces of Ilocos Norte and Kalinga-Apayao, on the south by Isabela province, and on the east and north by the Philippine Sea and the Babuyan Channel. It includes the islands of Camiguin, Calayan, Babuyan, Fuga, and Dalupiri with their small dependent islands. An expedition by Juan P. Carreon in 1581 defeated the Japanese pirate Tayfusa and established a fort at Nueva Segovia (now called Lal-lo). By 1583 Cagayan (or Nueva Segovia as it was then called, after its capital) was a recognized administrative unit which included much of northern Luzon Island. In 1839 Nueva Vizcaya separated and became an independent province; the capital of Cagayan was moved from Nueva Segovia to Tuguegerao. In 1856 the province of Isabela was formed from the provinces of Nueva Segovia and Cagayan. Batanes was made a sub-province of Cagayan (1862), and a full province in 1885. Kalinga and Apayao were organized as a comandancia, a kind of district, in 1889 and 1890, respectively. Following the suppression of the forces of the Philippine Revolution in this area, a civil government was established in August 1901. In 1903 the thirty-three municipalities of Cagayan were condensed into twenty-two. Batanes and Apayao were made sub-provinces and Kalinga was made a sub-province of the newly created province of Lepanto-Bontoc. Later Apayao was annexed to Lepanto-Bontoc which eventually became part of the Mountain Province. Batanes was separated from Cagayan to form a "special" province in 1909, becoming a "regular" province in 1918.

> FHL provincial records: civil registration (1875–1895); birth records (1945–1988); marriage contracts (1945–1987); death certificates (1964–1991); court records created by the Court of First Instance (1851–1906); deportations (1867–1893); land records (1826–1900); military induction records (1882–1887); public records (1884–1898); records of lending (1860–1898); school records (1865–1898); statistical reports (1754–1755, 1896); tax records (1790–1861); Census of Chinese (1884–1897).

Localities and their genealogical records:

Abulug (municipality), also known as Abulog and Tulug, was an early Spanish town. The village of Mabuttal separated and was annexed to Ballesteros in 1914. FHL local records: civil registration, 1928–1930; notarials, 1905–; Saint Thomas Aquinas parish registers, 1870–1937. Local records: civil registration, 1945–.

Alcalá (municipality), also known as Fula and Fulay, was an early Spanish town. The name Fula was changed to Alcala circa 1850. Baggao was organized from some of its territory circa 1898. FHL local records: civil registration, 1928–1933; notarials, 1905–. Local records: civil registration, 1945–.

Allacapan (municipality) was established in 1945 with some territory going to Ballesteros. FHL local records: civil registration, 1928–1931; notarials, 1911–. Local records: civil registration, 1952–.

Amulung (municipality) was an early Spanish town. Annexed the town of Córdoba in 1903. FHL local records: civil registration, 1922–1931; notarials, 1908–. Local records: civil registration, 1945–.

Aparri (municipality) was an early Spanish town. Annexed Babuyan Island in 1903 and parts of Buguey town from 1903 until 1915 when the latter became a separate municipality. Lost some villages to Balesteros in 1914. Annexed Calayan from 1912 to 1920. FHL local records: civil registration, 1922–1933; notarials, 1904–. Local records: civil registration, 1914–.

Baggao (municipality), a Spanish town, separated circa 1898 from Alcalá. FHL local records: civil registration, 1922–1930; notarials, 1911–. Local records: civil registration, 1954–.

Ballesteros (municipality) was established in 1911 from Aparri and Abulug. Annexed villages from Aparri in 1914 and from Allacapan in 1945. FHL local records: civil registration, 1922–1932; notarials, 1911–. Local records: civil registration, 1911–.

Buguey (municipality) had portions annexed to Aparri and Camalaniugan from 1903 to 1915. Gonzaga separated in 1917 as did Santa Teresita in 1963. FHL local records: civil registration, 1922–1931; notarials, 1911–; Roman Catholic parish registers, 1887–1914. Local records: civil registration, 1945–.

Calayan (municipality), also known as Catulayan, was an early Spanish town on Calayan Island to which were annexed the islands of Camiguin, Dalupiri, and Claro Babuyan in 1903. It was annexed to Aparri as a village from 1912 until 1920 when it was established as a separate municipality. FHL local records: civil registration, 1922–1931; notarials, 1925–. Local records: civil registration, 1960–.

Camalaniugan (municipality) was an early Spanish town to which a portion of Buguey was annexed from 1903 to 1915. FHL local records: civil registration, 1922–1930; notarials, 1925–; Saint Hyacinth parish registers, 1859–1914. Local records: civil registration, 1945–.

Claveria (municipality) was an early Spanish town. FHL local records: civil registration, 1922–1931; notarials, 1907–; Saint Joseph parish registers, 1879–1933. Local records: civil registration, 1901–.

Enrile (municipality), also known as Cabugag and Cabug, was organized as a Spanish town in 1849 from Tuguegarao. FHL local records: civil registration, 1922–1933; notarials, 1911–; Our Lady of Snows parish registers, 1944–1939. Local records: civil registration, 1948–.

Gattaran (municipality), also known as Dummun, Gattac, and Cattaran, was an early Spanish town to which was annexed part of the former municipality of Nassiping on the east side of Cagayan River in 1903. Lasam separated in 1950. FHL local records: civil registration, 1922–

1931; notarials, 1911–. Local records: civil registration, 1945–.

Gonzaga (municipality), also known as Gampao, Wangag, and Rumangay, was formerly part of Camalaniugan—going with Buguey when it separated in 1915. Separated from Buguey in 1917. Santa Ana separated in 1950. FHL local records: civil registration, 1927–1931; notarials, 1918–. Local records: civil registration, 1945–.

Iguig (municipality) was an early Spanish town. FHL local records: civil registration, 1922–1933; notarials, 1911–; Saint James parish registers, 1861–1933. Local records: civil registration, 1945–.

Lal-lo (municipality), also known as Nueva Segovia, was an early Spanish town and the provincial capital from 1581–1839. FHL local records: civil registration, 1922–1931; notarials, 1912–. Local records: civil registration, 1945–.

Lasam (municipality) was established in 1950 from Gattaran. FHL local records: notarials, 1951–. Local records: civil registration, 1951–.

Pamplona (municipality) was an early Spanish town. FHL local records: civil registration, 1922–1933; notarials, 1911–; Roman Catholic parish registers, 1810–1943. Local records: civil registration, 1948–.

Peñablanca (municipality), also known as Bubug and Alimannao, was an early Spanish town organized in 1892 from Tuguegarao. FHL local records: civil registration, 1922–1932; notarials, 1911–. Local records: civil registration, 1945–.

Piat (municipality), also known as Pia and Pias, was an early Spanish town. FHL local records: civil registration, 1922–1931; notarials, 1912–; Saint Dominic parish registers, 1780–1932. Local records: civil registration, 1906–.

Rizal (municipality), also known as Manawan, Malaueg, and Malaneg, was an early Spanish town which was consolidated with Mauanan in 1903 under the name Manawan (which was changed to Rizal in 1914). FHL local records: civil registration, 1922–1931; notarials, 1914–; Roman Catholic parish registers, 1900–1941. Local records: civil registration, 1914–.

Sanchez-Mira (municipality) was an early Spanish town. FHL local records: civil registration, 1922–1932; notarials, 1905–; Saint Rock parish registers, 1895–1907. Local records: civil registration, 1915–.

Santa Ana (municipality), also known as Palawig, was established in 1950 from Gonzaga. FHL local records: notarials, 1950–. Local records: civil registration, 1950–.

Santa Praxedes (municipality), also known as Langañgan prior to 1964, was established in 1969. FHL local records: civil registration, 1922–1931; notarials, 1923–. Local records: civil registration, 1923–.

Santa Teresita (municipality) was established in 1963 from Buguey. Local records: civil registration, 1963–.

Santo Niño (municipality), also known as Faire, Lobo, Tabang, and Kabarungan, was an early Spanish town. Lobo and Tabang became parishes in 1598 and 1631, respectively. In 1903 this municipality annexed the portion of the former municipality of Nassiping located on the western side of the Capayan River. The name of Santo Niño was replaced by Faire from 1914 to 1969. FHL local records: civil registration, 1922–1932; notarials, 1911–; Santo Niño parish registers, 1899–

1947. Local records: civil registration, 1917– (with gaps).

Solana (municipality), also known as Marague, was an early Spanish town by 1852. FHL local records: civil registration, 1922–1931; notarials, 1911–; Saint Vincent Ferrer parish registers, 1852–1961. Local records: civil registration, 1906–.

Tuao (municipality) was an early Spanish town. FHL local records: civil registration, 1922–1931; notarials, 1911–; Guardian Angels parish registers, 1778–1949. Local records: civil registration, 1902–.

Tuguegarao (city), an early Spanish town, has been the provincial capital from 1839. FHL local records: civil registration, 1923–1933; notarials, 1911–. Local records: civil registration, 1945–.

Camarines Norte. This province occupies the northern part of the Bicol Peninsula in southern Luzon. Until 1919 it formed, together with Camarines Sur, the province of Camarines. By the time the Spanish arrived in 1571, there were already a number of settlements involved in trade in this area as well as some working gold mines. Soon after the arrival of the Spanish, Christian missions were established first by the Augustinians and then (in 1578) by the Franciscans. From 1573 until the early seventeenth century, Camarines was a single province that included the entire Bicol Peninsula with its dependent islands. Its capital was at Caceres which is now the city of Naga in Camarines Sur. In the early seventeenth century the southern part of the peninsula was separated to form Partido de Ibalon which is now the province of Albay. In 1829 Camarines was divided into Camarines Norte and Camarines Sur, but after some boundary adjustments, the two areas were reunited in 1854. They were temporarily divided again from 1857 to 1893. When civil government was established in this area in April 1901, it oversaw "Ambos Camarines" or "both Camarines." In March 1919, division reoccurred with Camarines Norte made up of nine towns and the islands along its coast, its capital at Daet.

FHL provincial records: civil registration (1857–1906); birth records (1945–1988); marriage contracts (1945–1987); death certificates (1964–1991); court records created by the Court of First Instance (1888–1898); deportations (1872–1877); land records (1839–1918); military induction records (1860–1901); public records (1879–1897); records of lending (1878–1893); school records (1866–1898); tax records (1856–1857); Census of Chinese (1884–1889, 1894–1896); court cases on land transactions or *información posesoria* (1839–1907); and documents concerning the municipal and provincial government in Ambos Camarines (1758–1918) [284 reels].

Localities and their genealogical records:

Basud (municipality), also known as Basod and Basud-Basud, was an early Spanish town. It was annexed to Daet from 1903 to 1909. Imelda separated in 1970. FHL local records: civil registration, 1922–1931; notarials, 1910–. Local records: civil registration, 1945–.

Capalonga (municipality), also known as Capalungan and Capalongan, was an early Spanish town. Santa Elena separated in 1969. FHL local records: civil registration, 1922–1930; notarials from 1911. Local records: civil registration from 1911.

Daet (city), an early Spanish town, annexed Calasgasan in 1902. Basud, Imelda, and Mercedes separated in 1909, 1970, and 1948, respectively. FHL local records: civil registration, 1925–1932; notarials, 1901–; Saint John the Baptist parish registers, 1849–1958. Local records: civil registration, 1945–.

Imelda (municipality) was established in 1970 from Basud and Daet.

Jose Panganiban (municipality), also known as Mambulao and Mambulawan, was an early Spanish town. The name changed from Mambulao to Jose Panganiban in 1934. FHL local records: civil registration, 1922–1931; notarials, 1911–. Local records: civil registration, 1942–.

Labo (municipality), also known as Lobo and Busog-on, was an early Spanish town. FHL local records: civil registration, 1923–1930; notarials, 1906–; Saint John Lateran parish registers, 1883–1954. Local records: civil registration, 1945–.

Mercedes (municipality), also known as Barra, was established in 1948 from Daet. Local records: civil registration, 1948–.

Paracale (municipality), also known as Paracali, was an early Spanish town. FHL local records: civil registration, 1922–1923; notarials, 1908–; Purification of the Blessed Virgin Mary parish registers, 1799–1958. Local records: civil registration, 1901–.

San Vicente (municipality) was an early Spanish town. FHL local records: civil registration, 1922–1930; notarials, 1911–; Saint Vincent Ferrer parish registers, 1878–1974. Local records: civil registration, 1949–.

Santa Elena (municipality) was established in 1969 from Capalonga. Local records: civil registration, 1972–.

Talisay (municipality), also known as Tarisay, was an early Spanish town which was annexed to Vinzons from 1903 to 1909. FHL local records: civil registration, 1922–1932; notarials, 1911–; Saint Francis of Assisi parish registers, 1920–1965. Local records: civil registration, 1947–.

Vinzons (municipality), also known as Indán and Hamindang, was an early Spanish town to which Talisay was annexed from 1903 to 1909. The name Indan was changed to Vinzons in 1945. FHL local records: civil registration, 1922–1933; notarials, 1910–; Saints Peter and Paul parish registers, 1862–1972. Local records: civil registration, 1903–.

Camarines Sur. The province occupies, roughly, the center of the Bicol Peninsula in southern Luzon. Until 1919 it was part of Camarines or Ambos Camarines province. See the section on Camarines Norte above for a sketch history of the province to 1919. Its capital was transferred from Naga to Pili in 1948.

FHL provincial records [In addition to those listed in Camarines Norte above, the following records, pertaining only to Camarines Sur, also apply]: indexes to land records (1841–1910); and census (1873–1899).

Localities and their genealogical records:

Baao (municipality), also known as Bao, was an early Spanish town. FHL local records: civil registration, 1922–1931; notarials, 1904–. Local records: civil registration, 1945–.

Balatan (municipality) was established in 1949 from Nabua. FHL local records: notarials, 1952–. Local records: civil registration, 1952–.

Bato (municipality), also known as Kalilingo, was an early Spanish town. FHL local records: civil registration, 1922–1931; notarials, 1906–; Most Blessed Trinity parish registers, 1790–1932. Local records: civil registration, 1946–.

Bombon (municipality) was established in 1949 from Magarao. FHL local records: notarials, 1950–; Our Lady of the Holy Rosary parish registers, 1824–1941. Local records: civil registration, 1949–.

Buhi (municipality), also known as Buy, was an early Spanish town. FHL local records: civil registration, 1922–1931; notarials, 1911–; Saint Francis of Assisi parish registers, 1776–1936, and census of members, 1848–1897. Local records: civil registration, 1905–.

Bula (municipality) was an early Spanish town. FHL local records: civil registration, 1922–1930; notarials, 1912–; Saint Mary Magdalene parish registers, 1865–1968. Local records: civil registration, 1945–.

Cabusao (municipality) was established in 1911 from Libmanan. FHL local records: civil registration, 1922–1930; notarials, 1911–. Local records: civil registration, 1951–.

Calabanga (municipality) was also known as Caravanga, Calabañgan, and Calabagñan. FHL local records: civil registration, 1922–1930; notarials, 1911–; Nativity of the Blessed Virgin Mary parish registers, 1776–1929; Immaculate Conception (Quipayo) parish registers, 1818–1964. Local records: civil registration, 1957–.

Camaligan (municipality), an early Spanish town, was established in 1909 from Naga to which it had been annexed in 1903. FHL local records: civil registration, 1922–1925; notarials, 1911–; Saint Anthony of Padua parish registers, 1827–1957. Local records: civil registration, 1914–.

Canaman (municipality), also known as Poro, was an early Spanish town which was established in 1909 from Naga to which it had been annexed in 1909. FHL local records: civil registration, 1922–1931; notarials, 1901–; Assumption of the Blessed Virgin Mary parish registers, 1824–1977. Local records: civil registration, 1914–.

Caramoan (municipality), an early Spanish town, was in the province of Albay until 1846. Garchitorena separated in 1949. FHL local records: civil registration, 1922–1930; notarials, 1910–. Local records: civil registration, 1945–.

Del Gallego (municipality) was an early Spanish town. FHL local records: notarials, 1937–1944. Local records: civil registration, 1946–.

Gainza (municipality) was an early Spanish town. FHL local records: civil registration, 1925–1926; notarials, 1911–; Saint Dominic Guzmán parish registers, 1821–1943. Local records: civil registration, 1948–.

Garchitorena (municipality), also known as Pigbanua, San Miguel, and Andreson, was established in 1949 from Caramoan. That same year, the name was changed from Andreson to Garchitorena. FHL local records: notarials, 1948–1959. Local records: civil registration, 1966–.

Goa (municipality) was an early Spanish town. FHL local records: civil registration, 1922–1930; notarials, 1901–; Saint John the Baptist parish registers, 1874–1945. Local records: civil registration, 1903–.

Iriga (city), also known as Iraga and Yragga, was an early Spanish town. FHL local records: civil registration, 1922–1931; birth certificates, 1968–1988; death certificates, 1976–1988; notarials, 1904–; Saint Anthony of Padua parish registers, 1837–1940. Local records: civil registration, 1948–.

Lagonoy (municipality), also known as Lagunoy, was an early Spanish town in the province of Albay until 1846. The village of Panicuan was separated and annexed to Presentación from 1961 to 1969. FHL local records: civil registration, 1922–1930; notarials, 1911–; Saints Philip and James parish registers, 1771–1947, and church censuses, 1855–1897. Local records: civil registration, 1945–.

Libmanan (municipality), also known as Libangñan and Libabanan, was an early Spanish town from which Cabusao separated in 1911. The villages of Palong and San Rafael were annexed to the municipality of Pamploma circa 1914. FHL local records: civil registration, 1922–1930; notarials, 1904–; Saint James the Apostle parish registers, 1730–1934, and church censuses, 1822–1895. Local records: civil registration, 1904–.

Lupi (municipality), also known as Tapi, Lupi Viejo, and Lupi Nuevo, was an early Spanish town which was part of Camarines Norte until 1846. FHL local records: notarials, 1911–. Local records: civil registration, 1945–.

Magarao (municipality) was an early Spanish town. Some villages were separated to form the municipality of Canaman in 1909. Annexed the village of Bombon from Calabanga from 1913 to 1949. FHL local records: notarials, 1911–; Saint Anne parish registers, 1835–1971. Local records: civil registration, 1917–.

Milaor (municipality) was an early Spanish town from which San Fernando separated in 1813. FHL local records: notarials, 1911–; Saint Joseph parish registers, 1716–1969, and church census records, 1822–1895. Local records: civil registration, 1918–.

Minalabac (municipality), also known as Manalabac, Minalava, and Minalabag, was an early Spanish town. FHL local records: civil registration, 1922–1930; notarials, 1911–; Roman Catholic parish registers, 1877–1940. Local records: civil registration, 1917–.

Nabua (municipality), also known as Bua, was an early Spanish town from which Balatan separated in 1949. FHL local records: civil registration, 1925–1930; notarials, 1911–; Finding the Holy Cross parish registers, 1834–1929. Local records: civil registration, 1914–.

Naga (city), also known as Nueva Caceres and Caceres, was an early Spanish town and provincial capital from 1575 to 1948. It was downgraded to a municipality in 1901 and chartered a city in 1948. Annexed Canaman and Camaligan from 1903 to 1909. The name Nueva Caceres was changed to Naga in 1914. FHL local records: civil registration, 1922–1931; notarials, 1901–; birth certificates, 1955–1988; marriage contracts, 1955–1960; death certificates, 1976–1988; Saint John, the Evangelist, parish registers, 1746–1931; Saint Francis of

Assisi parish registers, 1860–1915. Local records: civil registration, 1945–.

Ocampo (municipality), also known as Tinablanan and Mabatobato, was an early Spanish town which was annexed to Pili from 1903 to 1949. Subsequently, the name was changed from Mabatobato to Ocampo. FHL local records: notarials, 1944–1958. Local records: civil registration, 1949–.

Pamplona (municipality) was an early Spanish town to which were annexed the villages of Palong and San Rafael from Libmanan in 1914. FHL local records: notarials, 1911–. Local records: civil registration, 1945–.

Pasacao (municipality) was an early Spanish town. Annexed the villages of Palong and San Rafael from Libmanan circa 1914. FHL local records: civil registration, 1922–1924; notarials, 1904–; Saint Rose of Lima parish registers, 1900–1962. Local records: civil registration, 1945–.

Pili (city), an early Spanish town, was the provincial capital from 1955. Annexed Ocampo from 1903 to 1949. FHL local records: civil registration, 1922–1933; notarials, 1911–. Local records: civil registration, 1943–.

Presentación (municipality), also known as Parubcan prior to 1969, was established in 1961 from Lagonoy. Local records: civil registration, 1964–.

Ragay (municipality), also known as Hagay, was an early Spanish town which from 1829 to 1846 was in the province of Camarines Norte. FHL local records: civil registration, 1922–1931; notarials, 1908–. Local records: civil registration, 1914–.

Sagñay (municipality), also known as Sagnay, was an early Spanish town which separated from Buhi in 1860. FHL local records: civil registration, 1922–1931; notarials, 1911–; Saint Andrew parish registers, 1856–1942. Local records: civil registration, 1945–.

San Fernando (municipality), also known as Boboran, was an early Spanish town. FHL local records: civil registration, 1929–1931; notarials, 1911–. Local records: civil registration, 1916–.

San José (municipality) was an early Spanish town. FHL local records: civil registration, 1922–1933; notarials, 1911–; Roman Catholic parish registers, 1819–1947. Local records: civil registration, 1902–.

Sipocot (municipality) was an early Spanish town which was part of the province of Camarines Norte from 1824 to 1846. FHL local records: civil registration, 1922–1931; notarials, 1911–; Saint John the Baptist parish registers, 1851–1943. Local records: civil registration, 1945–.

Siruma (municipality), also known as Boboan and Baugon, was an early Spanish town. Established as a municipality in 1901, it moved to its present site in 1913. FHL local records: civil registration, 1922–1931; notarials, 1912–. Local records: civil registration, 1944–.

Tigaon (municipality) was an early Spanish town. FHL local records: civil registration, 1922–1930; notarials, 1911–; Saint Clare parish registers, 1790–1941. Local records: civil registration, 1945–.

Tinambac (municipality), also known as Himoragat, was an early Spanish town. FHL local records: civil registration, 1922–1931; notarials, 1907–. Local records: civil registration, 1914–.

Camiguin. This island province lays at the northern tip of the province of Misamis Oriental with which its history is closely related. When the Spanish arrived in the late sixteenth century, it was part of the province of Cebu. Evangelization of the island was carried out by the Augustan Recollects (beginning in 1622), the Jesuits (from 1624), and the Columbian Fathers (since 1952). In 1818 the province of Cebu was dissolved and reorganized as the province of Misamis. When that province was divided in 1929, Camiguin became part of Misamis Oriental. During much of the American period, the administration of the island was consolidated into one municipality; namely, Mambajao. In June 1955 the island was made a sub-province of Misamis Oriental. Then in June 1966 it was made a separate province with its capital at Mambajao.

> FHL provincial records: birth certificates (1968–1988); marriage contracts (1968–1986); and death certificates (1968–1991).

Localities and their genealogical records:

Catarman (municipality), also known as Bonbon and Guiab, was an early Spanish town annexed to Mambajao from 1903 to 1912. FHL local records: civil registration, 1922–1931; notarials, 1912–; San Roque parish registers, 1842–1977. Local records: civil registration, 1912–.

Guinsiliban (municipality), also known as Guinsilitan, was an early Spanish town which was annexed to Mambajao from 1903 to 1950. Local records: civil registration, 1950–.

Mahinog (municipality) was annexed to Mambajao from 1903 to 1948. FHL local records: San Michael parish registers, 1860–1984. Local records: civil registration, 1948–.

Mambajao (city), also known as Mamajao, Mambuhao, and Mambukao, was an early Spanish town to which all the other localities were temporarily annexed in 1903 and separated again at various times. FHL local records: civil registration, 1922–1932; notarials, 1918–. Local records: civil registration, 1945–.

Sagay (municipality) was an early Spanish town which was annexed temporarily to Mambajao in 1903. FHL local records: civil registration, 1922–1932; notarials, 1911–; Our Lady of the Rosary parish registers, 1848–1967. Local records: civil registration, 1910–.

Capiz. This province is situated on the island of Panay with the provinces of Ilolo, Antique, and Aklan. In 1591 the island of Panay was organized as a separate province with its capital at Arevalo, now in the province of Iloilo. About that same time, the evangelization of the island began with the Augustinian Recollects who established centers at Panay, 1580 (in modern Capiz); Kalibo, 1581; and Ibajay, 1596 (the latter two are both now in modern Aklan). In 1716 Capiz was separated from Panay Province to form its own province. Then in 1853 the islands that comprise modern Romblon Province were grouped into a separate comandancia, under the jurisdiction of Capiz. In 1898 the Spanish evacuated Panay and the province was ruled by the revolutionary government until it was taken over by American forces. A civil government was established in April 1901. A short time earlier, the modern Romblon Province islands were separated from Capiz and made a separate province. A sub-province of Capiz beginning in 1907, they again became a separate province in 1917. Aklan was also separated from Capiz and made a province.

> FHL provincial records: civil registration (1866–1896); birth records (1945–1988); marriage contracts (1945–1987); death certificates (1964–1991); court records created by the Court of First Instance (1844–1903); deportations (1894–1896); land records (1869–1892); public records (1880–1898); records of lending (1871–1898); school records (1867–1898); statistical reports (1896); and Census of Chinese (1886–1898).

Localities and their genealogical records:

Cuartero (municipality), also known as Binudhi-an, Punda and Mapanag, was an early Spanish town which was annexed to Dao from 1903 to 1938. FHL local records: notarials, 1978–; Saint Anthony of Padua parish registers, 1918–1930. Local records: civil registration, 1953–.

Dao (municipality) was an early Spanish town to which Cuartero was annexed from 1903 to 1938. FHL local records: civil registration, 1921–1933; notarials, 1911–; Saint Thomas of Villanueva parish registers, 1900–1928. Local records: civil registration, 1968–.

Dumalag (municipality), also known as Dumalig, was an early Spanish town. Local records: civil registration, 1945–.

Dumarao (municipality) was an early Spanish town. FHL local records: civil registration, 1922–1931; notarials, 1911–. Local records: civil registration, 1945–.

Ivisan (municipality), also known as Iuisan and Ibisan, was an early Spanish town. FHL local records: civil registration, 1922–1931; notarials, 1919–. Local records: civil registration, 1945–.

Jamindan (municipality), also known as Hamindang, was an early Spanish town to which was annexed Jagnaya in 1903. FHL local records: civil registration, 1922–1929; notarials, 1912–. Local records: civil registration, 1945–.

Ma-ayon (municipality) was an early Spanish town which was annexed to Pontevedra from 1903 to 1955. Local records: civil registration, 1955–.

Mambusao (municipality), also known as Tipi and Tipic, was an early Spanish town. FHL local records: civil registration, 1922–1931; notarials, 1909–; Saint Catherine of Alexandria parish registers, 1897–1925. Local records: civil registration, 1945–.

Panay (municipality) was an early Spanish town from 1581. FHL local records: civil registration, 1922–1931; notarials, 1910–; census, 1884–1885; Saint Monica parish registers, 1898–1925. Local records: civil registration, 1945–.

Panitan (municipality), also known as Cabacol, was an early Spanish town. FHL local records: civil registration, 1922–1932; notarials, 1911–. Local records: civil registration, 1945–.

Pilar (municipality), also known as Sibala, was an early Spanish town to which was annexed Casanayan in 1903.

President Roxas separated in 1949. FHL local records: civil registration, 1922–1931; notarials, 1910–; The Blessed Trinity parish registers, 1918–1949. Local records: civil registration, 1953–.

Pontevedra (municipality), also known as Kaguyoman, was an early Spanish town to which was annexed Ma-ayon from 1903 to 1955. FHL local records: civil registration, 1921–1931; notarials, 1909–; census, 1884–1885. Local records: civil registration, 1945–.

President Roxas, also known as Latud-Latud, was established in 1949 from Pilar. Local records: civil registration, 1949–.

Roxas (city), also known as Capiz and Cadiz, was an early Spanish town. It became the capital of the province of Cadiz in 1746. Loctugan was annexed in 1903. The city was chartered in May, 1951. FHL local records: civil registration, 1922–1931; notarials, 1908–; birth certificates, 1951–1988; marriage contracts, 1950–1960; death certificates, 1975–1988; military inductions, 1877–1884; Saint Therese (located at Loctugan in Roxas) parish registers, 1886–1957. Local records: civil registration, 1945–.

Sapi-an (municipality) was an early Spanish town. FHL local records: civil registration, 1922–1931; notarials, 1911–. Local records: civil registration, 1945–.

Sigma (municipality) was an early Spanish town. FHL local records: civil registration, 1922–1931; Saint John the Baptist parish registers, 1883–1930. Local records: civil registration, 1945–.

Tapaz (municipality) was an early Spanish town. FHL local records: civil registration, 1922–1933; notarials, 1906–. Local records: civil registration, 1946–.

Catánduanes. This province occupies the island of the same name just off the tip of Camarines Sur on the Bicol Peninsula of Luzon Island. Known also as Catanduan and Catandognan, the name is thought to derive from the tando trees that flourish on the island. The early history of the island is closely related to the history of the province of Bicol Peninsula. In 1591 it was a part of the province of Vicor and Camarines which was ruled from Nueva Caceres (now Naga of Camarines Sur province). When the former province of Bicol was divided, the island was brought under the jurisdiction of Ibalon province (now Albay) and ruled from the provincial capital of Albay (now Legazpi). The Franciscans from the nearby mainland arrived and established centers on the island throughout the seventeenth century. The parish at Virac, erected in 1755, eventually became the diocesan seat for the province. In 1755 the Moros raided the island, burned several towns, and destroyed many records. It was only in 1898 that Catánduanes became a separate province. In 1901 its municipalities were annexed to Albay, but in 1905 Catánduanes was organized as a sub-province of Albay until March 1946 when it became a separate province.

FHL provincial records: birth records (1945–1988); marriage contracts (1945–1987); death certificates (1964–1991); and Census of Chinese (1895–1898).

Localities and their genealogical records:

Bagamanoc (municipality) was an early Spanish town which was annexed to Viga in 1906. It remained a part of Panganiban when the latter separated to become established as a municipality in 1921. In 1950 it separated from Panganiban. FHL local records: Saint Anthony of Padua parish registers, 1889–1972. Local records: civil registration, 1950–.

Baras (municipality) was an early Spanish town which was annexed to Bato from 1906 to 1912. In 1951 some villages separated to form the municipality of Gigmoto. FHL local records: civil registration, 1922–1931; notarials, 1904–; Saint Laurence parish registers, 1897–1961. Local records: civil registration, 1948–.

Bato (municipality) was an early Spanish town to which was annexed Baras from 1906 to 1912. FHL local records: civil registration, 1921–1931; notarials, 1916–; Saint Anthony of Padua parish registers, 1912–1968. Local records: civil registration, 1915–.

Caramoran (municipality), also known as Sabangan, was an early Spanish town which was annexed to Pandan from 1906 to 1948. FHL local records: Saint John the Baptist parish registers, 1889–1895. Local records: civil registration, 1961–.

Gigmoto (municipality) was established in 1951 from Viga and Baras. Local records: civil registration, 1951–.

Pandan (municipality) was an early Spanish town to which was annexed Caramoran from 1906 to 1948. FHL local records: civil registration, 1922–1932; notarials, 1904–; Roman Catholic parish registers, 1822–1927. Local records: civil registration, 1947–.

Panganiban (municipality), also known as Jose Panganiban (prior to 1957) and Payo (from 1957 to 1959), was an early Spanish town which was annexed to Viga until 1921. Bagamanoc separated in 1950. FHL local records: civil registration, 1922–1932; notarials, 1921–; Saint James the Greater parish registers, 1905–1972. Local records: civil registration, 1947–.

San Andres (municipality), also known as Calolbong, Calolbon, and Caragnag, was an early Spanish town. The name Calolbon was changed to San Andres in 1964. FHL local records: civil registration, 1921–1931; notarials, 1906–; Saint Andrew parish registers, 1811–1934. Local records: civil registration, 1922–.

San Miguel (municipality), also known as Aguas, was established in 1952 from Bato. Local records: civil registration, 1953–.

Viga (municipality), also known as Biga, Mala-biga, and Ca-bigas, was an early Spanish town. See Bagamanoc (municipality) and Panganiban (municipality) above for more information. FHL local records: civil registration, 1922–1931; notarials, 1917–. Local records: civil registration, 1901–.

Virac (city), also known as Vidak, was an early Spanish town. Annexed village of Cabugao from Bato in 1906. FHL local records: civil registration, 1922–1932; departations, 1896; notarials, 1904–; Our Lady of the Immaculate Conception parish registers, 1756–1937, and church census records, 1817–1866; Saint John the Baptist (Cabugao) parish registers, 1851–1922. Local records: civil registration, 1915–.

Cavite. This province occupies the southwest corner of Luzon Island and is situated just south of Manila Bay. The area, settled before the arrival of the Spanish, quickly became a province encompassing Cavite City, the site of a Spanish naval base and ship yard where many Spanish ships, including the Manila galleons, were constructed or fitted out. There was conflict between the Spanish and the local population over land rights and the strict discipline imposed by the friars of the large church-controlled haciendas. In 1872 the first military mutiny was quickly put down by the Spanish authorities. In the Philippine Revolution, Cavite sided with the revolutionaries. Although the Spanish finally succeeded in sweeping them from the province, their defeat by the Americans gave the revolutionaries a new foothold on Cavite. American civil government began in June 1901. The Lubang Islands formerly of Mindoro were annexed to Cavite in 1901, but in 1902 they were annexed, along with most of Mindoro, to Marinduque. The provincial capital was moved from municipality of Cavite to Trece Martires (1954) and, finally, Imus (1977).

> FHL provincial records: civil registration (1869–1895); birth records (1945–1988); marriage contracts (1945–1987); death certificates (1964–1991); court records created by the Court of First Instance (1900–1902); deportations (1854–1897); land records (1797–1900); military induction records (1860–1897); public records (1880–1898); records of lending (1877–1898); school records (1862–1898); statistical reports (1894); tax records (1779–1897); Census of Chinese (1859–1898); index to various provincial and municipal documents for Cavite (1786–1901); and a calendar of records dealing with the opium (*anfión*) trade in the provinces of Cavite and Pampanga (1814–1893).

Localities and their genealogical records:

Alfonso (municipality), also known as Alfonso XIII and Alas-as, was an early Spanish village to which was annexed General Aguinaldo (then Bailen) and Mendez-Nuñez from 1903 to 1915. FHL local records: civil registration, 1923–1921, 1921–1991; notarials, 1905–; Saint John Nepomucene parish registers, 1861–1948. Local records: civil registration, 1920–.

Amadeo (municipality), also known as Masilao, was an early Spanish town which was annexed to Silang from 1903 to 1915. FHL local records: civil registration, 1922–1930; notarials, 1917–; Saint Mary Magdalene parish registers, 1910–1952. Local records: civil registration, 1905–.

Bacoor (municipality) was an early Spanish town annexed to Imus from 1903 to 1907. FHL local records: civil registration, 1922–1931, 1933–1951; notarials, 1903–; birth certificates, 1933–1951; birth registers, 1940–1984; marriage contracts, 1931–1987; marriage registers, 1940–1989; death certificates, 1938–1953; death registers, 1926–1898; Saint Michael Archangel parish registers, 1793–1952; Philippine Independent Church, Saint Michael's Parish, parish records, 1903–1948. Local records: civil registration, 1912–.

Carmona (municipality) was an early Spanish town which was annexed to Silang from 1903 to circa 1909. FHL local records: civil registration, 1922–1930, 1901–1991; notarials, 1903–; Saint Joseph parish registers, 1863–1958. Local records: civil registration, 1901–.

Cavite City (city) was an early Spanish town which, before it became independent, was a part of Kawit municipality. In 1903 it was consolidated with Puerto de Cavite, San Roque, and La Caridad. Isla de Corregidor was annexed in 1909. FHL local records: civil registration, 1904–1989; notarials, 1903–; birth certificates, 1945–1988, 1915–1951; birth registers, 1904–1989; marriage contracts, 1914–1950; marriage records, 1912–1989; death certificates, 1909–1957; San Roque parish registers, 1900–1957. Local records: civil registration, 1902–.

Corregidor Island, known by the Spanish administration as San José and the American administration as Isla de Corregidor, was annexed to Cavite City in 1909. A municipality from 1913–1931; it is now an almost uninhabited national preserve memorializing the dead of World War II. FHL local records: notarials, 1903–; deportations, 1875–1898. Local records: civil registration, 1913–1931.

Dasmariñas (municipality), also known as Pérez Dasmarinas, was established in 1917 from Imus to which it had been annexed in 1903. FHL local records: civil registration, 1922–1930, 1917–1988; notarials, 1917–; Immaculate Conception parish registers, 1867–1958. Local records: civil registration, 1917–.

General Emilio Aguinaldo (municipality), also known as Bailen (1858–1965) and Batasan (prior to 1858), was an early Spanish town which was annexed to the municipality of Alfonso from 1903 to 1915. FHL local records: civil registration, 1922–1930, 1915–1991; notarials, 1939–; Saint Joseph parish registers, 1897–1963. Local records: civil registration, 1915–.

General Trías (municipality), also known as San Francisco de Malabon (prior to 1914) and Malabon (1914–1920), was an early Spanish town to which was annexed Tanza (formerly Santa Cruz de Malabon) from 1903 to 1909. FHL local records: civil registration, 1922–1930, 1916–1991; notarials, 1905–; Saint Francis of Assisi parish registers, 1771–1970. Local records: civil registration, 1914–.

Imus (city) was an early Spanish town to which were annexed Bacoor and Dasmariñas from 1903 until 1907 and 1917, respectively. It has been the capital of province of Cavite since 1977. FHL local records: civil registration, 1922–1933, 1901–1988; notarials, 1903–; Our Lady of the Pillar parish registers, 1795–1940. Local records: civil registration, 1901–.

Indang (municipality), also known as Idang, was an early Spanish town from which Alfonso separated in 1859. FHL local records: civil registration, 1921–1933, 1918–1991; notarials, 1905–; Saint Gregory the Great parish registers, 1710–1948. Local records: civil registration, 1903–.

Kawit (municipality), also known as Cavite Viejo, was an early Spanish town which was annexed to municipality of Noveleta from 1903 to 1907. It annexed the village of San Juan from Noveleta in 1915. FHL local records: civil registration, 1922–1931, 1911–1989; notarials, 1905–; Saint Mary Magdalene parish registers, 1826–1971. Local records: civil registration, 1911–.

Magallanes (municipality) was an early Spanish town which was annexed to the municipality of Maragondon from 1903 to circa 1915. FHL local records: civil registration, 1916–1989; notarials, 1916–. Local records: civil registration, 1916–.

Maragondon (municipality), also known as Maragondong and Marigondon, was an early Spanish town to which was annexed Magallanes from 1903 to circa 1915. FHL local records: civil registration, 1922–1928, 1911–1991; notarials, 1905–; Assumption of Our Lady parish registers, 1802–1975. Local records: civil registration, 1912–.

Mendez-Nuñez (municipality) was an early Spanish town annexed to Alfonso from 1903 to 1915. FHL local records: civil registration, 1922–1931, 1915–1991; notarials, 1915–; Saint Augustine parish registers, 1881–1953. Local records: civil registration, 1915–.

Naic (municipality) was an early Spanish town to which Ternate was annexed from 1903 to 1914. FHL local records: civil registration, 1921–1932; notarials, 1903–; birth certificates, 1988; marriage contracts, 1945–1949; marriage records, 1912–1988; death certificates, 1940–1988; Immaculate Conception parish registers, 1820–1939. Local records: civil registration, 1912–.

Noveleta (municipality), also known as Tierra Alta, was an early Spanish town to which Kawit and Rosario were annexed from 1903 to 1907 and 1911, respectively. FHL local records: civil registration, 1921–1931, 1922–1989; notarials, 1907–. Local records: civil registration, 1917–.

Rosario (municipality), also known as Tejero and Salinas Marcella, was an early Spanish town which was annexed to Noveleta from 1903 to 1911. FHL local records: civil registration, 1922–1931, 1957–1991; notarials, 1905–; Our Lady of the Most Holy Rosary parish registers, 1897–1938. Local records: civil registration, 1957–.

Silang (municipality) was an early Spanish town from which Carmona separated. Annexed Amadeo from 1903 to 1915. FHL local records: civil registration, 1922–1931, 1948–1978; notarials, 1903–; Purification of Our Lady parish registers, 1898–1944. Local records: civil registration, 1903–.

Tagaytay (city) was chartered in 1938, reduced to a municipality by the Japanese, and restored as a city in 1946. FHL local records: civil registration, 1943–1989; birth certificates, 1960–1988. Local records: civil registration, 1942–.

Tanza (municipality), also known as Santa Cruz de Malabon (prior to 1914), was an early Spanish town which was annexed to the municipality of General Trías (then San Francisco de Malabon) from 1903 to 1910. Amaya was separated from 1953 to 1954. FHL local records: civil registration, 1923–1928, 1943–1991; notarials, 1911–; Holy Cross parish registers, 1774–1952. Local records: civil registration, 1915–.

Ternate (municipality), also known as Ternato, was an early Spanish town which was annexed to Naic from 1903 to 1914. FHL local records: civil registration, 1922–1931, 1895–1991; notarials, 1946–. Local records: civil registration, 1945–.

Trece Martires (city), chartered as a city in 1955, was the provincial capital from 1955 to 1977. FHL local records: civil registration, 1950–1991; birth certificates, 1968–1988; death certificates, 1975–1988. Local records: civil registration, 1956–.

Cebu. This province encompasses the island of the same name as well as the 167 dependent islands which surround it. Cebu island is about 200 kilometers long and 40 kilometers wide. It was on this island that Magellan landed in April 1521 and was killed by the local warriors.

In 1565 Legazpi also landed here, but was forced to move on to Panay Island in 1569 and then to Manila in 1571 due to the opposition of the Portuguese. As an important center of Spanish administration in this area of the Philippines, Cebu's jurisdiction included what are now the modern provinces of Cebu, Bohol, Samar, and Leyte, as well as the eastern half of Negros and the northern half of Mindanao Island. In 1734 Negros Island became a separate district. A year later, Leyte and Samar were separated as a single unit and, in 1738, they were further separated into two individual units. Then in 1854 Bohol became an independent province. At one time, Davao, Surigao, Agusan, Misamis, Lanao and Zamboanga, all the current provinces of Mindanao, had administrative ties with Cebu. [See each province for more details.] The evangelization of the province was carried out by the Augustinians who established early religious centers at Bantayan in 1580, Cebu in 1598, Carcar in 1599, Boljoon in 1606, Barili in 1614, and Mandaue in 1738. At first Cebu did not join the revolution against Spain, but in 1898 when the Spanish evacuated, revolutionary forces took over for three months until they were replaced by American forces. In April 1901 a civil government was established, but continuing resistance made necessary the reimposition of a military government. With order restored, a civil government was again established on January 1, 1902. In 1903 the consolidating of municipalities began, but as was the case in the other provinces, many of the annexed municipalities eventually separated and regained their status as independent and separate municipalities.

> FHL provincial records: civil registration (1784–1897); birth records (1945–1988); marriage contracts (1945–1987); death certificates (1959–1991); court records created by the Court of First Instance (1818–1902); deportations (1876–1895); land records (1848–1897); military induction records (1857–1897); public records (1881–1897); records of lending (1873–1898); school records (1849–1898); statistical reports (1896–1897); tax records (1846–1852); and Census of Chinese (1869–1897).

Localities and their genealogical records:

Alcántara (municipality), also known as Kugtong, was an early Spanish town which was annexed to Moalboal from 1903 to 1914. FHL local records: civil registration, 1922–1928; notarials, 1901–. Local records: civil registration, 1945–.

Alcoy (municipality), also known as Mamboje and Mambaje, was an early Spanish town which changed its name from Mamboje to Alcoy in 1869. It was annexed to Dalaguete from 1903 to 1917. FHL local records: civil registration, 1922–1931, 1917–1994; notarials, 1917–; Saint Rose of Lima parish registers, 1890–1931. Local records: civil registration, 1917–.

Alegría (municipality), also known as Tubod, was an early Spanish town. FHL local records: civil registration, 1922–1931; notarials, 1911–; Saint Francis Xavier

parish registers, 1857–1938. Local records: civil
registration, 1902–.

Aloguínsan (municipality), also known as Olokinsan, was
an early Spanish town which was separated from
Pinamungajan in 1821. FHL local records: civil
registration, 1922–1931, 1947–1993; notarials, 1907–;
Saint Raphael the Archangel parish registers, 1912–
1926. Local records: civil registration, 1945–.

Argao (municipality), also known as Sali-Argao, was an
early Spanish town. FHL local records: civil registration,
1921–1934, 1943–1994; notarials, 1911–; San Miguel
Arcángel parish registers, 1842–1939. Local records:
civil registration, 1940–.

Asturias (municipality), also known as Naghalin, was an
early Spanish town. FHL local records: civil registration,
1921–1930; notarials, 1911–; San Roque parish
registers, 1885–1948. Local records: civil registration,
1917–.

Badían (municipality), also known as Badiang and
Badyang, was an early Spanish town. FHL local records:
civil registration, 1922–1932, 1918–1993; notarials,
1911–; Santiago Apóstol parish registers, 1843–1960.
Local records: civil registration, 1945–.

Balambán (municipality), also known as Balambang, was an
early Spanish town. FHL local records: civil registration,
1923–1932; notarials, 1911–; Saint Francis of Assisi
parish registers, 1875–1939. Local records: civil
registration, 1911–.

Bantayan (municipality) was an early Spanish town to
which Santa Fe and Madridejos had been annexed in
1903, then separated in 1917 and 1910, respectively.
FHL local records: civil registration, 1922–1932, 1901–
1994; notarials, 1906–. Local records: civil registration,
1901–.

Barili (municipality) was an early Spanish town. FHL local
records: civil registration, 1923–1932; notarials, 1908–;
Saint Anne, Our Lady's Mother, parish registers, 1809–
1937. Local records: civil registration, 1945–.

Bogo (municipality) was an early Spanish town. FHL local
records: civil registration, 1920–1930, 1901–1994;
notarials, 1910–. Local records: civil registration,
1913–.

Boljoón (municipality), also known as Boljo, was an early
Spanish town. FHL local records: civil registration,
1922–1931; notarials, 1911–; Patronage of Saint Joseph
parish registers, 1793–1970. Local records: civil
registration, 1902–.

Borbón (municipality), also known as Silmogue, was an
early Spanish town. FHL local records: civil registration,
1922–1933; notarials, 1911–. Local records: civil
registration, 1945–.

Carcar (municipality), also known as Sialo, Valladolid,
Kabkab, Kabkaban, and Kabkad, was an early Spanish
town. FHL local records: civil registration, 1929–1933,
1946–1994; notarials, 1907–; Saint Catherine of
Alexandria parish registers, 1759–1935. Local records:
civil registration, 1945–.

Carmen (municipality) was an early Spanish town. FHL
local records: civil registration, 1922–1933, 1946–1993;
notarials, 1911–; Saint Augustine parish registers, 1851–
1964. Local records: civil registration, 1946–.

Catmón (municipality), also known as Cadmon, was an
early Spanish town to which Sogod was annexed from
1903 to circa 1921. FHL local records: civil registration,
1922–1933, 1902–1993; notarials, 1911–; San

Guillermo parish registers, 1847–1948. Local records:
civil registration, 1902–.

Cebu (city), also known as Cubu, Sugbu, Sebu, Zebu,
Zebut, and San Miguel, was an early Spanish town. It
became a municipality during the term of American civil
government and was chartered a city in November 1936.
The former municipalities of El Pardo and Talamban
(formerly Mabolo) were annexed in 1903. FHL local
records: civil registration, 1922–1934; notarials, 1911–;
marriage contracts, 1945–1960; birth certificates, 1945–
1988; death certificates, 1975–1988; San Tomás de
Villanueva (at El Prado in Cebú City) parish registers,
1866–1951; Patronato de San José (at Mabolo in Cebú
City) parish registers, 1770–1927. Local records: civil
registration, 1923–.

Compostela (municipality) was an early Spanish town
which was annexed to Liloan from 1903 to 1919. FHL
local records: civil registration, 1922–1931, 1919–1993;
notarials, 1932–; Santiago Apóstol parish registers,
1883–1929. Local records: civil registration, 1919–.

Consolación (municipality) was an early Spanish town
which was annexed to Mandaue from 1903 to circa
1919. FHL local records: civil registration, 1922–1933,
1945–1993; notarials, 1922–. Local records: civil
registration, 1945–.

Córdoba (municipality), also known as Cordova and Day-
as, was an early Spanish town which was annexed to
Lapu-Lapu (Opon) from 1903 to 1913. FHL local
records: civil registration, 1922–1932, 1945–1993;
notarials, 1913–; San Roque parish registers, 1864–
1954. Local records: civil registration, 1945–.

Daánbantayan (municipality) was an early Spanish town.
FHL local records: civil registration, 1922–1931, 1917–
1993; notarials, 1911–; Saint Rose of Lima parish
registers, 1810–1926. Local records: civil registration,
1914–.

Dalaguete (municipality), also known as Daraquette,
Dalakit, and Unab, was an early Spanish town to which
Alcoy was annexed from 1903 to 1917. Local records:
civil registration, 1902–.

Danao (city) was chartered as a city in June 1961. FHL
local records: civil registration, 1922–1931, 1902–1993;
notarials, 1902–; birth certificates, 1957–1988; death
certificates, 1976–1988. Local records: civil registration,
1902–.

Dumanjug (municipality), also known as Dumanhug, was
an early Spanish town to which Ronda was annexed
from 1903 to 1913. FHL local records: civil registration,
1922–1931, 1946–1994; notarials, 1901–; Saint Francis
of Assisi parish registers, 1854–1948. Local records:
civil registration, 1945–.

Ginatilan (municipality), also known as Guinatilan,
Hinatdan, Hinatlan, and Hinatilan, was an early Spanish
town. FHL local records: civil registration, 1922–1928,
1946–1993; notarials, 1932–; Saint Gregory the Great
parish registers, 1848–1953. Local records: civil
registration, 1945–.

Lapu-Lapu (city), also known as Opon, Opong, and Mactan,
was an early Spanish town to which, in 1903, Córdoba
and Santa Rosa were annexed. Córdoba separated in
1913. FHL local records: civil registration, 1922–1932,
1945–1993; notarials, 1915–; birth certificates, 1961–
1988; death certificates, 1975–1988; Nuestra Señora de
la Virgen de Regla parish registers, 1724–1927. Local
records: civil registration, 1946–.

Liloan (municipality) was an early Spanish town to which Compostela was annexed from 1903 to 1919. FHL local records: civil registration, 1922–1931, 1945–1993; notarials, 1904–; San Fernando parish registers, 1845–1931. Local records: civil registration, 1945–.

Madridejos (municipality), also known as Lawis, was an early Spanish town which was annexed to Bantayan from 1903 to 1910. FHL local records: civil registration, 1922–1930, 1917–1993; notarials, 1917–. Local records: civil registration, 1917–.

Malabuyoc (municipality), also known as Malaboyoc, was an early Spanish town. FHL local records: civil registration, 1962–1993. Local records: civil registration, 1901–.

Mandaue City (city), also known as Mandawe, was an early Spanish town to which Consolacion was annexed from 1903 to circa 1919. FHL local records: civil registration, 1922–1934, 1902–1993; notarials, 1902–; birth certificates, 1969–1988; death certificates, 1976–1988. Local records: civil registration, 1902–.

Medellín (municipality), also known as Buenavista, Medelin, and Tawagan, was an early Spanish town. FHL local records: civil registration, 1922–1931, 1915–1993; notarials, 1912–. Local records: civil registration, 1915–.

Minganilla (municipality) was an early Spanish town. FHL local records: civil registration, 1922–1930, 1944–1994; notarials, 1911–; Immaculate Heart of Mary parish registers, 1856–1952. Local records: civil registration, 1945–.

Moalboal (municipality), also known as Moalbual and Mualbual, was an early Spanish town to which Alcántara was annexed from 1903 to 1914. FHL local records: civil registration, 1922–1933, 1944–1993; notarials, 1911–; Saint John Nepomucene parish registers, 1850–1952. Local records: civil registration, 1945–.

Naga (municipality) was an early Spanish town. FHL local records: civil registration, 1922–1931; notarials, 1903–; Roman Catholic parish registers, 1832–1928. Local records: civil registration, 1914–.

Oslob (municipality), also known as Lawis, was an early Spanish town to which Nueva Caceres and Santander were annexed from 1903 to 1917. FHL local records: civil registration, 1922–1931, 1945–1994; notarials, 1903–; Saint Joseph the Carpenter (at Nueva Caceres) parish registers, 1882–1977. Local records: civil registration, 1945–.

Pilar (municipality), also known as Pusong and Lilang, was an early Spanish town. FHL local records: notarials, 1911–. Local records: civil registration, 1945–.

Pinamungajan (municipality). FHL local records: civil registration, 1922–1932, 1963–1993; notarials, 1911–; Saint Monica parish registers, 1850–1947. Local records: civil registration, 1945–.

Poro (municipality), also known as Polo, was an early Spanish town which was annexed to Tudela from 1903 to 1909. FHL local records: civil registration, 1922–1932, 1913–1994; notarials, 1914–. Local records: civil registration, 1945–.

Ronda (municipality), also known as Pungtud and Joloyaw, was an early Spanish town which was annexed to Dumanjug from 1903 to 1913. FHL local records: civil registration, 1922–1931; notarials, 1914–; Our Lady of

Sorrow parish registers, 1890–1938. Local records: civil registration, 1913–.

Samboan (municipality), also known as Sambuan, Samboang, and Sambowang, was an early Spanish town to which, in 1903, San Sabastian was annexed. FHL local records: civil registration, 1922–1932, 1917–1993; notarials, 1910–; Saint Michael the Archangel parish registers, 1842–1935; San Sebastián (at Bato) parish registers, 1910–1949. Local records: civil registration, 1902–.

San Fernando (municipality) was an early Spanish town. FHL local records: civil registration, 1922–1931, 1917–1993; notarials, 1903–; San Isidro Labrador parish registers, 1895–1935. Local records: civil registration, 1902–.

San Francisco (municipality) was an early Spanish town. FHL local records: civil registration, 1922–1932; notarials, 1907–. Local records: civil registration, 1917–.

San Remigio (municipality), also known as Punta, Punta Isabel, and Kanghagas, was an early Spanish town. FHL local records: civil registration, 1922–1931, 1924–1978; notarials, 1912–; Saint John Nepomucene parish registers, 1864–1952. Local records: civil registration, 1902–.

Santa Fé (municipality), also known as Utong, was an early Spanish town which was annexed to Bantayan from 1903 to 1917. FHL local records: civil registration, 1922–1932, 1937–1994; notarials, 1912–. Local records: civil registration, 1937–.

Santander (municipality) was an early Spanish town which was annexed to Oslob from 1903 to 1917. FHL local records: civil registration, 1926–1931, 1918–1993; notarials, 1920–; Saint Gabriel the Archangel parish registers, 1898–1957. Local records: civil registration, 1918–.

Sibonga (municipality) was an early Spanish town. FHL local records: civil registration, 1922–1932, 1934–1994; notarials, 1911–; Our Lady of the Pillar parish registers, 1827–1957. Local records: civil registration, 1934–.

Sogod (municipality) was an early Spanish town which was annexed to Catmon from 1903 to circa 1921. FHL local records: civil registration, 1922–1928, 1920–1993; notarials, 1921–; San Santiago Apóstol parish registers, 1844–1940. Local records: civil registration, 1921–.

Tabogon (municipality), also known as Tabagan, was an early Spanish town. FHL local records: civil registration, 1922–1932, 1945–1993; notarials, 1906–. Local records: civil registration, 1945–.

Tabuelan (municipality) was established in 1953. FHL local records: civil registration, 1953–1993; notarials, 1953–. Local records: civil registration, 1953–.

Talisay (municipality) was an early Spanish town. FHL local records: civil registration, 1922–1933, 1945–1994; notarials, 1911–. Local records: civil registration, 1945–.

Toledo (city), also known as Hinolawan and Hinawan, was chartered in June 1960. FHL local records: civil registration, 1922–1932, 1946–1993; notarials, 1907–; birth certificates, 1957–1988; marriage contracts, 1952–1960; death certificates, 1976–1988; Saint John of Sahagun parish registers, 1864–1930. Local records: civil registration, 1946–.

Tuburan (municipality), also known as Daligdigan, was an early Spanish town. FHL local records: civil registration,

1922–1931, 1914–1993; notarials, 1903–; Saint Anthony of Padua parish registers, 1857–1941. Local records: civil registration, 1913–.

Tudela (municipality), also known as Tag-Anitao, was an early Spanish town to which Poro was annexed from 1903 to 1909. FHL local records: civil registration, 1922–1931, 1938–1994; notarials, 1912–. Local records: civil registration, 1938–.

Davao. This province occupies, roughly, the southeastern portion of the island of Mindanao. By the end of the sixteenth century the Spanish had set up a number of towns around the gulf of Davao, but the area further south remained under the control of the Sultan of Mindanao. The administration of the island of Mindanao was under the control of Cebu. The district of Caraga (now Surigao) was transferred from Cebu to Zamboanga. In 1844 the Spanish governor of Zamboanga persuaded the Sultan of Mindanao to transfer control over the Davao region to the Spanish government. In 1847 Davao town was established by Don José Oyanguren, who in 1849 was made the governor of the new of province of Nueva Guipuzcoa (named after his home province in Spain) with its capital at Davao town which was renamed Vergara (after his home town). In 1855 the province was divided into the comandancia of Bislig and the comandancia of Davao. In 1860 the government of Mindanao was reorganized with the creation of the six districts. The comandancia of Bislig was made a part of Surigao in the Third or East District and Davao remained in the Fourth or Southeastern District. In June 1903 civil government was established and Davao became one of the five districts of the Moro Province. In 1914 these five district became seven provinces under the Department of Mindanao and Sulu. In 1920 this department was dissolved and its duties were taken over by the Bureau of Non-Christian Tribes. In 1922 Davao became a separate province. In May 1967 the province was divided into Davao del Sur, Davao Oriental, and Davao del Norte, the latter changing its name to Davao in 1972.

FHL provincial records: civil registration (1869–1895); birth records (1945–1988); marriage contracts (1946–1987); death certificates (1960–1991); deportations (1887–1898); military induction records (1882–1896); public records (1884–1898); records of lending (1855–1871); school records (1866–1898); statistical reports (1896); and Census of Chinese (1884–1891).

Localities and their records:

Asunción (municipality), also known as Saug (prior to 1957), and New Leyte, was an early Spanish town from which New Corella separated in 1964.

Babak (municipality) was established in 1953. Local records: civil registration, 1960–.

Carmen (municipality) was established in 1965 from Panabo. Local records: civil registration, 1968–.

Compostela (municipality), also known as Campo de Castila, was established in 1921. The following were separated to become additional municipalities: Monkayo (1954), Nabunturan (1957), New Bataan (1965), and

Montevista (1966). Local records: civil registration, 1946–.

Kapalong (municipality) was established in 1921 from Tagum. FHL local records: civil registration, 1929; notarials, 1936–1941. Local records: civil registration, 1946–.

Kaputian (municipality) was established in 1965 from Samal. Local records: civil registration, 1968–.

Mabini (municipality), also known as Doña Alicia prior to 1954, was established in 1953. In 1967 Maco separated. Local records: civil registration, 1953–.

Maco (municipality) was established in 1967 from Mabini. Local records: civil registration, 1968–.

Mawab (municipality) was established in 1959. Local records: civil registration, 1960–.

Monkayo (municipality), also known as Moncayo, was established in 1954 from Compostela. FHL local records: civil registration, 1922–1931; notarials, 1929–. Local records: civil registration, 1954–.

Montevista (municipality) was established in 1966 from portions of Nabunturan, Compostela, Monkayo, Asuncion, and New Corella. Local records: civil registration, 1968–.

Nabunturan (municipality) was established in 1957 from Compostela. Local records: civil registration, 1957–.

New Bataan (municipality) was established in 1965 from Compostela. Local records: civil registration, 1968–.

New Corella (municipality) was established in 1964 from Asuncion. Local records: civil registration, 1968–.

Panabo (municipality) was established in 1949 from Tagum. Carmen separated in 1965. Local records: civil registration, 1949–.

Pantukan (municipality) was established in 1937. Local records: civil registration, 1945–.

Samal (municipality) was established in 1948. Kaputian separated in 1965. FHL local records: civil registration, 1922–1936; notarials, 1937–. Local records: civil registration, 1942–.

Santo Tomás (municipality) was established in 1959. Local records: civil registration, 1960–.

Tagum (city), was an early Spanish town, from which Panabo and Kapalong separated in 1949 and 1921, respectively. FHL local records: civil registration, 1928–1929; notarials, 1928–. Local records: civil registration, 1946–.

Davao del Sur. This province occupies the southern part of the island of Mindanao. In 1967 the former province of Davao was divided three provinces: Davao del Norte, Davao del Sur, and Davao Oriental. For more information on the history of Davao del Sur, see the section on Davao above.

FHL provincial records: See section above on the province of Davao.

Localities and their genealogical records:

Bansalan (municipality) was established in 1952 from Digos. Magsaysay separated in 1967; Mantanao in 1957. Local records: civil registration, 1958–.

Davao City (city), also known as Vergara, was an early Spanish town and capital of Nueva Guipuzcoa Province, 1849–1858. Annexed Guianga when it became a city in March 1937. Local records: civil registration, 1945–.

Digos (city) was established in 1949. Bansalan separated in 1952. Local records: civil registration, 1949–.

Hagonoy (municipality) was established in 1953 from Padada. Local records: civil registration, 1953–.

José Abad Santos (municipality), also known as Trinidad prior to 1955, was established in 1948 by a consolidation of the municipal districts of Batulake and Caburan. Local records: civil registration, 1950–.

Kiblawan (municipality) was established in 1966 from Sulop. Local records: civil registration, 1968–.

Magsaysay (municipality) was established in 1967 from Bansalan. Local records: civil registration, 1965–.

Malalag (municipality) was established in 1953. Santa María separated in 1966. FHL local records: notarials, 1917–1919. Local records: civil registration, 1953–.

Malita (municipality) was established in 1937. FHL local records: civil registration, 1922–1931; notarials, 1917–. Local records: civil registration, 1945–.

Matanao (municipality) was established in 1957 from Bansalan. Local records: civil registration, 1965–.

Padada (municipality) was established in 1949. Hagonoy separated in 1953. Local records: civil registration, 1949–.

Santa Cruz (municipality) was an early Spanish town. FHL local records: civil registration, 1922–1931; notarials, 1914–. Local records: civil registration, 1949–.

Santa María (municipality) was established in 1966 from Malalag. Local records: civil registration, 1968–.

Sulop (municipality) was established in 1959. Kiblawan separated in 1966.

Davao Oriental. This province occupies the southeast coast of the island of Mindanao. In 1967 the former province of Davao was divided into three provinces: Davao del Norte (modern Davao), Davao del Sur, and Davao Oriental. Since these three provinces shared the same history until that year, they have been treated together in the section on Davao above.

FHL provincial records: See the section on Davao above.

Localities and their genealogical records:

Baganga (municipality), also known as Ba-ñga-ñga, was an early Spanish town. FHL local records: civil registration, 1922–1924; notarials, 1911–. Local records: civil registration, 1946–.

Banay-Banay (municipality) was established in 1969 from Lupon.

Boston (municipality) was established in 1969 from Cateel. Local records: civil registration, 1972–.

Caraga (municipality) was an early Spanish town. FHL local records: civil registration, 1922–1933; notarials, 1922–. Local records: civil registration, 1915–.

Cateel (municipality), also known as Cateel Nuevo, was an early Spanish town from which Boston separated in 1969. FHL local records: civil registration, 1922–1933; notarials, 1912–. Local records: civil registration, 1945–.

Governor Generoso (municipality) was established in 1948. San Isidro separated in 1966. FHL local records: civil registration, 1922–1931. Local records: civil registration, 1948–.

Lupon (municipality), also known as Sumlog, was established in 1948. Banay-Banay separated in 1969. FHL local records: civil registration, 1922–1931; notarials, 1922–. Local records: civil registration, 1920–.

Manay (municipality) was established in 1914. Tarragona separated in 1966. FHL local records: civil registration, 1922–1931; notarials, 1922–. Local records: civil registration, 1948–.

Mati (city), also known as Matti and Ma-ati, was an early Spanish town from which part of Tarragona separated in 1966. FHL local records: civil registration, 1922–1931; notarials, 1903–. Local records: civil registration, 1915–.

San Isidore (municipality) was established in 1966 from Governor Generoso. FHL local records: civil registration, 1922–1931; notarials, 1933–. Local records: civil registration, 1968–.

Tarragona (municipality) was established in 1966 from Mati and Manay. Local records: civil registration, 1968–.

Eastern Samar. This province occupies the eastern portion of the island of Samar. In June 1965 the former province of Samar was divided into three provinces: Northern Samar, Eastern Samar, and Western Samar (the modern Samar). For the administrative history of these three provinces, see the section on Samar below.

FHL provincial records: See section below on the province of Samar.

Localities and their genealogical records:

Arteche (municipality), also known as San Ramón, was established in 1951 from Oras. Local records: civil registration, 1951–.

Balangiga (municipality), also known as Balanguingui, was an early Spanish town that separated from Guiuan in 1768. Quinapundan was annexed from 1903 to 1946. Giporlos separated in 1949; Lawa-an in 1959. FHL local records: civil registration, 1921–1931; notarials, 1911–; Saint Lawrence parish registers, 1854–1952. Local records: civil registration, 1931–.

Balangkayan (municipality) was established in 1959 from Maydolong and Llorente. Local records: civil registration, 1959–.

Borongan (city) was an early Spanish town from which Maydolong separated in 1951. FHL local records: civil registration, 1921–1931; notarials, 1919–; Our Lady of the Nativity parish registers, 1842–1952. Local records: civil registration, 1915–.

Can-avid (municipality) was established in 1948 from Dolores. Local records: civil registration, 1948–.

Dolores (municipality), also known as Paric and Bakud, was an early Spanish town which was annexed to Taft in 1903, then separated in 1909 and renamed Dolores. Can-avid separated in 1948. FHL local records: civil registration, 1922–1931; notarials, 1919–; Roman Catholic parish registers, 1903–1951. Local records: civil registration, 1948–.

General MacArthur (municipality), also known as Togas, Pambujan, Pambujan Sur, and New Hernani, was an early Spanish town established in 1947 from Hernani. Local records: civil registration, 1947–.

Giporlos (municipality) was established in 1949 from Balangiga. Local records: civil registration, 1949–.

Guiuan (municipality), also known as Guibang, Quiuan, and Guioan, was an early Spanish town to which Mercedes and Salcedo were annexed in 1903, then separated from in 1948 and 1909, respectively. Balangiga separated in 1768. FHL local records: civil registration, 1922;

notarials, 1926–. Local records: civil registration, 1952–.

Hernani (municipality), also known as Nag-as, was an early Spanish town which was annexed to Llorente from 1903 to 1913. General MacArthur separated in 1947. FHL local records: civil registration, 1922–1931; notarials, 1932–; Our Lady of the Seven Dolors parish registers, 1943–1972. Local records: civil registration, 1913–.

Jipapad (municipality) was established in 1964. FHL local records: civil registration, 1922–1931. Local records: civil registration, 1965–.

Lawa-an (municipality) was established in 1959 from Balangiga. Local records: civil registration, 1965–.

Llorente (municipality), also known as Llanang, Lupok, Lanang, and Tanang, took the name Llorente when it was established as a municipality in 1903 by the consolidation of Lanag and Hernani. Hernani separated in 1913. FHL local records: civil registration, 1922–1931; notarials, 1911–; Saint Anthony of Padua parish registers, 1811–1969. Local records: civil registration, 1903–.

Maslog (municipality) was established in 1919 as a municipal district. FHL local records: civil registration, 1928–1930. Local records: civil registration, 1960–.

Maydolong (municipality) was established in 1951 from Borongan. Part separated and went to Balangkayan in 1960. Local records: civil registration, 1951–.

Mercedes (municipality) was an early Spanish town which was annexed to Guiuan from 1903 to 1948. Local records: civil registration, 1948–.

Oras (municipality) was an early Spanish town from which San Policarpio (1948), Arteche (1951), and Lapinig (in North Samar) separated. FHL local records: civil registration, 1921–1932; notarials, 1911–; Roman Catholic parish registers, 1905–1943. Local records: civil registration, 1920–.

Quinapundan (municipality), also known as Quinapondan, was an early Spanish town which was annexed to Balangiga from 1903 to 1946. Local records: civil registration, 1947–.

Salcedo (municipality), also known as Cabak, was an early Spanish town which was annexed to Guiuan from 1903 to circa 1909. FHL local records: civil registration, 1922–1932; notarials, 1911–. Local records: civil registration, 1935–.

San Julian (municipality), also known as Nonok, was an early Spanish town annexed to Taft from 1903 to 1906. FHL local records: civil registration, 1922–1925; notarials, 1911–; Our Lady of the Seven Dolors parish registers for 1892–1943. Local records: civil registration, 1937–.

San Policarpio (municipality), also known as Bunga, was established from Oras in 1948. Local records: civil registration, 1949–.

Sulat (municipality), also known as Panulatsulat, Suslatan, and Sinulat, was an early Spanish town which was annexed to Taft from 1903 to 1906. FHL local records: civil registration, 1922–1931; notarials, 1911–. Local records: civil registration, 1950–.

Taft (municipality), also known as Tubig, was an early Spanish town. In 1903 the municipalities of Tubig, Paric, Sulat, and San Julián were consolidated to create the new municipality of Taft—the latter three separated again in 1906 with Paric renamed Dolores. FHL local records: civil registration, 1922–1932; notarials, 1919–;

Santiago Apóstol parish registers, 1904–1959. Local records: civil registration, 1944–.

Guimaras Sub-province. This province occupies the island of Guimaras as well as several nearby islands located between the islands of Panay and Negros. In 1591 it was part of Oton province (later called Arevalo and, eventually, Iloilo). It remained a part of Iloilo through both the Spanish and American periods of Philippine history. In June 1966 it became a sub-province of Iloilo. See the section on the province of Iloilo below for additional information.

> FHL provincial records: See the section on the province of Iloilo below.

Localities and their genealogical records:

Buenavista (municipality) was an early Spanish town to which was annexed Jordan (then Nagaba), Nabalas, and Nueva Valencia in 1903. Jordan separated in 1918 and Nueva Valencia in 1941. It has been the capital of Guimaras since 1969. FHL local records: civil registration, 1922–1932; notarials, 1910–. Local records: civil registration, 1945–.

Jordán (municipality), also known as Nagaba, was an early Spanish town which was annexed to Buenavista from 1903 to 1918. It was the capital of the sub-province from 1966–1969. FHL local records: civil registration, 1922–1932; notarials, 1910–. Local records: civil registration, 1945–.

Nueva Valencia (municipality) was an early Spanish town which was annexed to Buenavista from 1903 to 1941. Local records: civil registration, 1965–.

Ifugao. This province lays in the mountains of northern Luzon in territory so remote that it was not penetrated by the agents of the Spanish government until the nineteenth century. Ifugao became part of the province of Nueva Vizcaya when it was created in 1839. Evangelization began in 1849, after more than a century of failures, with the work of the missionaries of the Immaculate Heart of Mary. By 1880 some towns and centers of Spanish power had been established. Although Ifugao did not take part in the Philippine Revolution, during the period of struggle between American and revolutionary forces, it did play a role. It was through Ifugao that the troops of revolutionary General Aguinaldo retreated enroute to Palanan in the province of Isabela to surrender. During the American period, Ifugao was detached from the province of Nueva Vizcaya and made a sub-province of the newly created Mountain Province. In June 1966 the former Mountain Province was broken up to create the provinces of Ifugao, Benguet, Kalinga-Apayao, and Bontoc (the latter was subsequently renamed the Mountain Province). [The records of all of these provinces should examined when doing research on any one of the provinces listed.]

> FHL provincial records: birth records (1945–1988); birth certificates (1967–1988); marriage contracts (1967–1986); death certificates (1967–1986); and statistical reports (1896).

Localities and their genealogical records:

Banaue (municipality) was established in 1963. FHL local records: civil registration, 1921–1931. Local records: civil registration, 1945–.

Hungduan (municipality) was established in 1963. FHL local records: civil registration, 1922–1929. Local records: civil registration, 1947–.

Kiangan (municipality), also known as Quingan or Quiangan, was established in 1963. FHL local records: civil registration, 1923–1924; notarials, 1946–. Local records: civil registration, 1945–.

Lagawe (city), also known as Burnay and Lagaui, was established in 1963. The name was changed from Burnay to Lagawe in 1961. It has been the capital of the province since 1966. FHL local records: civil registration, 1922–1931. Local records: civil registration, 1946–.

Lamut (municipality) was created a municipal district in 1959 from Kiangan. Local records: civil registration, 1959–.

Mayaoyao (municipality), also known as Mayoyao, was established in 1963. FHL local records: civil registration, 1922–1931. Local records: civil registration, 1943–.

Potia (municipality) became a municipal district in 1955; a municipality in 1963. Local records: civil registration, 1956–.

Ilocos Norte. This province occupies the northwest part of the island of Luzon in northern Philippines. In February 1818 the former province of Ilocos was divided into Ilocos Norte and Ilocos Sur. [For a discussion of the administration of Ilocos before it was divided, see the section below on Ilocos Sur.] Occupied only briefly by forces of the Philippine Revolution, in August 1901 civil government was established by the Americans. The province was the center of a split in the Roman Catholic Church. Earlier this area had been evangelized by the Augustinians, but local antagonisms with Spanish clergy during the time of rising Philippine nationalism resulted in an immediate acceptance of the Philippine Independent Church founded by Gregorio Aglipay, a native of Ilocos Norte. In 1904 the Aglipayan Church began to be a major force in the area.

FHL provincial records: civil registration (1797–1897); birth records (1945–1988); marriage contracts (1945–1987); death certificates (1957–1991); court records created by the Court of First Instance (1855–1903); deportations (1877–1897); land records (1734–1896); military induction records (1865–1897); public records (1884–1898); records of lending (1876–1898); school records (1862–1898); statistical reports (1896); tax records (1828–1853); Census of Chinese (1886–1897); and notarials (1926–1932).

Localities and their genealogical records:

Adams (municipal district) was established in 1919. FHL local records: civil registration, 1922–1931.

Bacarra (municipality) was an early Spanish town to which Vintar was annexed from 1903 to 1909. FHL local records: civil registration, 1922–1931; notarials, 1909–; Saint Andrew, the Apostle, parish registers for 1702–1979. Local records: civil registration, 1902–.

Badoc (municipality) was an early Spanish town. FHL local records: civil registration, 1922–1931. Local records: civil registration, 1927–.

Bangui (municipality), also known as Bangi and Ba'ngi, was an early Spanish town from which Burgos (1913), Dumalneg (1919), and Pagudpud (1960) were separated. FHL local records: civil registration, 1922–1931; notarials, 1911–; Saint Lawrence parish registers, 1837–1977. Local records: civil registration, 1945–.

Batac (municipality), an early Spanish town, was established in 1913. Espiritu (then Banna) was annexed from 1903 to 1913. Pinili was separated in 1920. Some villages were separated and annexed to the new municipality of Currimao in 1921. FHL local records: civil registration, 1922–1932; notarials, 1910–; Our Lady of the Immaculate Conception parish registers, 1785–1966. Local records: civil registration, 1901–.

Burgos (municipality), also known as Nagpartian prior to 1914, was established in 1913 from Bangui. FHL local records: civil registration, 1922–1931; notarials, 1928–; Saint John of Sahagun parish registers, 1851–1971. Local records: civil registration, 1945–.

Carasi (municipal district), also known as Nagpapalcan, was established in 1919. FHL local records: civil registration, 1929–1930. Local records: civil registration, 1962–.

Currimao (municipality), also known as Corremao and Corrimao, was established in 1921 from Paoay. FHL local records: civil registration, 1922–1931; notarials, 1931–. Local records: civil registration, 1945–.

Dingras (municipality), also known as Dineras, was an early Spanish town to which Solsona was annexed from 1903 to 1910. Marcos separated in 1963. FHL local records: civil registration, 1922–1932; notarials, 1907–; Saint Joseph parish registers, 1847–1969. Local records: civil registration, 1903–.

Dumalneg (municipal district), also known as Banbanag, was established as a municipal district in 1919 from Bangui. FHL local records: civil registration, 1924–1931; notarials, 1954–. Local records: civil registration, 1946–.

Espiritu (municipality), also known as Banna prior to 1964, was an early Spanish town which was annexed to Batac from 1903 to 1913. FHL local records: civil registration, 1922–1929; notarials, 1913–. Local records: civil registration, 1913–.

Laoag City (city) was an early Spanish town to which San Nicolás was annexed from 1903 to 1909. It was granted a city charter in January 1966. FHL local records: civil registration, 1922–1931; notarials, 1905–; birth certificates, 1965–1988; death certificates, 1975–1988; Saint William the Hermit parish registers for 1748–1979. Local records: civil registration, 1902–.

Marcos (municipality) was established in 1963 from Dingras. Local records: civil registration, 1963–.

Nueva Era (municipality) was established in 1919. FHL local records: civil registration, 1922–1931; notarials, 1931–. Local records: civil registration, 1922–.

Pagudpud (municipality) was established in 1960 from Bangui. (It was originally created in 1954, then dissolved in 1957.) Local records: civil registration, 1954–.

Paoay (municipality) was an early Spanish town. Currimao separated in 1921. FHL local records: civil registration, 1922–1931; notarials, 1908–; The Conversion of Saint

Augustine of Hippo parish registers, 1759–1979. Local records: civil registration, 1902–.

Pasuquin (municipality) was an early Spanish town. FHL local records: civil registration, 1922–1930; notarials, 1928–; Saint James the Greater parish registers, 1790–1967. Local records: civil registration, 1943–.

Piddig (municipality), also known as Piddipid, was an early Spanish town. FHL local records: civil registration, 1922–1931; notarials, 1908–. Local records: civil registration, 1945–.

Pinili (municipality) was an early Spanish town established in 1919 from Batac. FHL local records: civil registration, 1922–1931; notarials, 1927–. Local records: civil registration, 1920–.

San Nicolás (municipality) was an early Spanish town which was annexed to Laoag from 1903 to 1909. FHL local records: civil registration, 1922–1933; notarials, 1907–; Saint Nicholas of Tolentino parish registers for 1854–1967. Local records: civil registration, 1902–.

Sarrat (municipality), also known as San Miguel and Cabayugan, was an early Spanish town. The name San Miguel was changed to Sarrat in 1914. FHL local records: civil registration, 1922–1932; notarials, 1945–; Saint Monica parish registers, 1828–1967. Local records: civil registration, 1898–.

Solsona (municipality), also known as Santiago, was an early Spanish town which was annexed to Dingras from 1903 to 1910. FHL local records: civil registration, 1922–1932; notarials, 1910–. Local records: civil registration, 1904–.

Vintar (municipality), also known as Bintar and Baguinsusu, was an early Spanish town which was annexed to Bacarra from 1903 to 1909. FHL local records: civil registration, 1922–1933; notarials, 1910–; Saint Nicolas of Tolentino parish registers, 1830–1980. Local records: civil registration, 1902–.

Ilocos Sur. This province, situated on the northwest coast of the island of Luzon, consisted of thriving trading communities prior to the arrival of the Spanish. Beginning in 1572 Juan de Salcedo lead many expeditions to the area and, despite considerable native opposition, was able to establish several towns. One of these "Villa Fernandina," at the site of the native town of Vigan, was made the capital of the new province of Ilocos or Ylocos. This province included modern Ilocos Norte, Ilocos Sur, and modern Abra as well as portions of both La Union and the Mountain Provinces. Evangelization began as soon as Spanish power was established. The Augustinians and Dominicans did much of the early missionary work. They were joined later by the Jesuits, Vincentians, and other orders. The first diocese was established in 1595 at Nueva Segovia (across the river from Lal-lo in what is, today, Cagayan province), but due to flooding was moved, retaining the name Nueva Segovia, to Vigan (modern Ilocos). In 1611 Ilocos lost a part of what is now modern La Union to the newly created province of Pangasinan. After that, the boundaries of the province remained fixed until February 1818 when Ilocos was divided into Ilocos Norte (capital at Laoag) and Ilocos Sur (Vigan retained as its capital). In addition to the territory of modern Ilocos Sur, that of modern Abra, and the northeast corner of modern La Union was included. In 1854, Abra separated and was established as a separate province. That same year, La Union province was formed from the union of territory from Ilocos Sur and Pangasinan. Civil government was established in Ilocos in October 1903. Many of the municipalities of the Spanish period were consolidated with one another as part of administrative reform. The province of Abra was made a sub-province of Ilocos Sur from April 1905 to March 1917 when it again became a province. In December 1941 Japanese forces invaded Ilocos Sur and many important records were lost when local government buildings were burned.

FHL provincial records: civil registration (1883–1897); birth records (1945–1988); marriage contracts (1952–1987); death certificates (1957–1991); court records created by the Court of First Instance (1840–1903); deportations (1885–1889); land records (1734–1896); military induction records (1868–1897); public records (1884–1896); records of lending (1878–1898); school records (1858–1898); statistical reports (1896); tax records (1736–1897); and Census of Chinese (1852–1897).

Localities and their records:

Alilem (municipality) was an early Spanish town established as a municipality in 1963. It was a part of the former Amburayan sub-province in the province of Lepanto-Bontoc from 1902 to 1908 and a part of the Mountain Province from 1908 to 1920. FHL local records: civil registration, 1922–1924. Local records: civil registration, 1946–.

Banayoyo (municipality). FHL local records: civil registration, 1922–1931; notarials, 1919–. Local records: civil registration, 1945–.

Bantay (municipality) was an early Spanish town which was annexed to Vigan from 1903 to 1911. FHL local records: civil registration, 1922–1932; notarials, 1911–; Conversion of Saint Augustine of Hippo parish registers, 1737–1947. Local records: civil registration, 1903–.

Burgos (municipality), also known as Bato, was an early Spanish town formed by the consolidation of village of Bato with Nueva Coveta in 1878. FHL local records: civil registration, 1922–1931; notarials, 1924–. Local records: civil registration, 1945–.

Cabugao (municipality) was an early Spanish town. FHL local records: civil registration, 1927–1931; notarials, 1906–; Saint Mark the Evangelist parish registers, 1871–1979. Local records: civil registration, 1902–.

Candón (municipality) was an early Spanish town. FHL local records: civil registration, 1922–1931; notarials, 1906–; Saint John of Sahagun parish registers, 1903–1977. Local records: civil registration, 1946–.

Caoayan (municipality), also known as Kawayan and Cauayan, was an early Spanish town annexed to Vigan from 1903 to 1911. FHL local records: notarials, 1911–; Patronage of the Blessed Virgin Mary parish registers, 1825–1978. Local records: civil registration, 1902–.

Cervantes (municipality), an early Spanish town, was the capital of the former province of Lepanto-Bontoc and the sub-province of Lepanto from 1902 to 1908 when

Lepanto was abolished and annexed to Ilocos Sur. FHL local records: civil registration, 1922–1931; notarials, 1919–. Local records: civil registration, 1946–.

Galimuyod (municipality), also known as Cabisilan, was established circa 1916. FHL local records: civil registration, 1922–1931; notarials, 1919–. Local records: civil registration, 1945–.

Gregorio del Pilar (municipality), also known as Concepción and Led-ag, was part of the Lepanto sub-province (Lepanto-Bontoc province) from 1902 to 1908 and a part of Mountain province from 1908 to 1920. The name Concepcion was changed to Gregorio del Pilar in 1955. FHL local records: civil registration, 1922–1931; notarials, 1929–. Local records: civil registration, 1945–.

Lidlidda (municipality) was established in 1919. FHL local records: civil registration, 1922–1931; notarials, 1919–. Local records: civil registration, 1949–.

Magsiñgal (municipality) was an early Spanish town organized in 1676 from the villages of Malungon, Bangay, Masingal, Quinnuang, and Cabanayan. FHL local records: civil registration, 1922–1931; notarials, 1909–; Saint William the Hermit parish registers, 1728–1954. Local records: civil registration, 1903–.

Nagbukel (municipality) was established in 1919. FHL local records: civil registration, 1929; notarials, 1928–. Local records: civil registration, 1945–.

Narvacan (municipality) was an early Spanish town. FHL local records: civil registration, 1922–1933; notarials, 1908–; Saint Lucy parish registers, 1738–1975. Local records: civil registration, 1945–.

Quirino (municipality), also known as Angaki and Angaqui was established in 1963. It was part of Lepanto sub-province (Lepanto-Bontoc province) from 1902 to 1908 and a part of Mountain province from 1908 to 1920. The name Angaki was changed to Quirino in 1964. FHL local records: civil registration, 1922–1930. Local records: civil registration, 1946–.

Salcedo (municipality), also known as Baugen and Bauguen, was an early Spanish town annexed to Santa Lucia from 1903 to 1917. The name Baugen was changed to Salcedo in 1957. FHL local records: civil registration, 1922–1930; notarials, 1926–. Local records: civil registration, 1945–.

San Emilio (municipality), also known as Dey-agan, was established in 1963. It was part of Lepanto sub-province (Lepanto-Bontoc province) from 1902 to 1908 and a part of Mountain province from 1908 to 1920. FHL local records: civil registration, 1922–1931. Local records: civil registration, 1916–.

San Esteban (municipality), an early Spanish town, was established in 1911 from Santiago to which it had been annexed in 1903. FHL local records: civil registration, 1922–1931; notarials, 1911–; Saint Stephen Protomartyr parish registers, 1845–1972. Local records: civil registration, 1914–.

San Ildefonso (municipality) was an early Spanish town, annexed to Santo Domingo in 1903 and then separated. FHL local records: civil registration, 1922–1931; notarials, 1911–; San Ildefonso parish registers, 1803–1976.

San Juan (municipality), also known as Lapog and Lapo, was an early Spanish town. The name Lapog was changed to San Juan in 1961. FHL local records: civil

registration, 1922–1931; notarials, 1908–. Local records: civil registration, 1945–.

San Vicente (municipality), an early Spanish town, was annexed to Vigan from 1903 to 1911. FHL local records: civil registration, 1922–1931; notarials, 1911–; Saint Vincent Ferrer parish registers, 1800–1977. Local records: civil registration, 1919–.

Santa (municipality), also known as Santa Catalina and Nagpanaoan, was an early Spanish town. FHL local records: civil registration, 1922–1932; notarials, 1911–; Saint Catherine of Alexandria parish registers, 1724–1976. Local records: civil registration, 1902–.

Santa Catalina (municipality), an early Spanish town, was annexed to Vigan from 1903 to 1907. FHL local records: civil registration, 1922–1931; notarials, 1908–; Saint Catherine of Alexandria parish registers, 1834–1978. Local records: civil registration, 1945–.

Santa Cruz (municipality), also known as Tariphong, Tarinong, Napiñget, and Naiñget, was an early Spanish town. FHL local records: civil registration, 1922–1932; notarials, 1908–; Immaculate Conception parish registers, 1759–1967. Local records: civil registration, 1904–.

Santa Lucía (municipality), an early Spanish town, annexed Salcedo from 1903 to 1917. FHL local records: civil registration, 1922–1931; notarials, 1911–; Saint Lucy parish registers, 1769–1971. Local records: civil registration, 1902–.

Santa María (municipality), also known as Purok and Bukaneg, was an early Spanish town. FHL local records: civil registration, 1922–1931; notarials, 1910–; Assumption of the Blessed Virgin Mary parish registers, 1767–1977. Local records: civil registration, 1945–.

Santiago (municipality), an early Spanish town, annexed San Esteban from 1903 to 1911. FHL local records: civil registration, 1922–1931; notarials, 1911–. Local records: civil registration, 1946–.

Santo Domingo (municipality) was an early Spanish town to which San Ildefonso was annexed in 1903, then separated. FHL local records: civil registration, 1928–1931; notarials, 1907–; Saint Dominic of Guzmán parish registers, 1772–1962. Local records: civil registration, 1902–.

Sigay (municipality), also known as Coscosnong, Tangadan, Sigcay, and San Ramon, was an early Spanish town which from 1902 to 1908 was part of the Amburayan sub-province (province of Lepanto-Bontoc) and, from 1908 to 1920, part of the Mountain Province. FHL local records: civil registration, 1922–1931; notarials, 1925–.

Sinait (municipality), also known as Sin-nait, was an early Spanish town. FHL local records: civil registration, 1922–1932; notarials, 1907–; Saint Nicholas of Tolentino parish registers, 1844–1979. Local records: civil registration, 1901–.

Sugpon (municipality) was an early Spanish town which from 1902 to 1908 was part of the Amburayan sub-province (province of Lepanto-Bontoc) and, from 1908 to 1920, part of the Mountain Province. Local records: civil registration, 1945–.

Suyó (municipality) was an early Spanish town which from 1902 to 1908 was part of the Amburayan sub-province (province of Lepanto-Bontoc) and, from 1908 to 1920, part of the Mountain Province. It was established in 1963. FHL local records: civil registration, 1929–1930;

notarials, 1925–. Local records: civil registration, 1945–.

Tagudin (municipality), an early Spanish town, was annexed from May 1907 to August 1908 as the capital of the Amburayan sub-province (province of Lepanto-Bontoc). It was part of the Mountain Province from 1908 to 1920. FHL local records: civil registration, 1922–1931; notarials, 1906–; Conversion of Saint Augustine of Hippo parish registers, 1760–1978. Local records: civil registration, 1917–.

Vigan (city), also known as Bigan and Villa Fernandina, was an early Spanish town to which were annexed Santa Catalina (separated 1907), Bantay (separated 1911), Caoayan (separated 1911), and San Vicente (separated 1911). FHL local records: civil registration, 1922–1932; notarials, 1905–; Conversion of Saint Paul the Apostle parish registers, 1713–1939. Local records: civil registration, 1913–.

Iloilo. This province is situated on the southeast portion of the island of Panay in the central Philippines. It includes several dependent islands, the largest of which, Guimaras, forms (since 1966) a sub-province of Iloilo. Panay Island also is the site of three other provinces, Aklan, Antique, and Capiz, which like Iloilo were originally inhabited by Negrito tribes, followed by invaders from Borneo in the thirteenth century, and by the Spanish in the middle of the sixteenth century. In 1565 Miguel Lopez de Legazpi attempted to establish a Spanish center of power on Cebu, but due to Portuguese and native opposition, he moved the settlement to Panay Island and, eventually, to Manila (1571). Circa 1583 Spanish influence in the area made it possible for the province of Panay to be organized. The province included Panay Island, part of Negros, and all of Guimaras with a capital at Arevalo. When the capital was transferred to the town of Iloilo in 1688, the province also became known as Iloilo. At this time the Augustinians were active in evangelizing the area. By the end of the sixteenth century they had established centers in Oton, Dumangas, Janiuay, Tigbauan, and Passi. In the eighteenth century, a period of increases in economics and population, the Spanish divided the province of Panay (Iloilo), creating Capiz as a separate district in 1716. Then the western half of Negros Island was separated from Iloilo and the eastern half from Cebu, with the two recombined to form a separate district in 1734. In 1790 territory from the provinces of Iloilo and Capiz was used to create the district of Antique. In 1798, Antique and Negros Island became provinces. The district of Concepción was created in the nineteenth century from part of the province of Iloilo, but was dissolved and returned to Iloilo by the American government in 1901. Suppression of the forces of the Philippine Revolution by American forces took two years in Iloilo. In April 1901, following the surrender of Philippine forces in February, the Americans established a civil government in the province. In 1903 the fifty-one municipalities were consoli-

dated into seventeen and Iloilo, the city, was reduced to a municipality.

FHL provincial records: civil registration (1850–1897); birth records (1945–1987); death certificates (1957–1991); court records created by the Court of First Instance (1884–1903); deportations (1849–1898); land records (1705–1909); military induction records (1866–1898); public records (1879–1898); records of lending (1870–1898); school records (1852–1901); statistical reports (1896); tax records (1827–1857); Census of Chinese (1886–1898); and census (1876–1877).

Localities and their records:

Ajuy (municipality), also known as Ajui and Ahui, was an early Spanish town which was annexed to Sara from 1903 to 1917. FHL local records: civil registration, 1922–1932; notarials, 1918–. Local records: civil registration, 1945–.

Alimodian (municipality) was an early Spanish town which was annexed to Leon from 1903 to 1919. FHL local records: civil registration, 1922–1931, 1945–1994; notarials, 1903–. Local records: civil registration, 1945–.

Anilao (municipality) was an early Spanish town which was annexed to Banate from 1903 to 1939. Local records: civil registration, 1947–.

Badiangan (municipality) was established in 1967 from Janiuay. Local records: civil registration, 1968–.

Balasan (municipality) was an early Spanish town to which were annexed Batad, Carles, and Estancia in 1903; then separated in 1949, circa 1920, and 1919, respectively. FHL local records: civil registration, 1924–1931; notarials, 1906–. Local records: civil registration, 1915–.

Banate (municipality) was an early Spanish town to which were annexed Anilao and Barotac Viejo from 1903 to 1939 and 1918, respectively. FHL local records: civil registration, 1922–1931, 1938–1989; notarials, 1904–. Local records: civil registration, 1945–.

Barotac Nuevo (municipality) was an early Spanish town. Annexed Dumangas from 1903 to 1911. FHL local records: civil registration, 1922–1931, 1914–1994; notarials, 1904–. Local records: civil registration, 1914–.

Barotac Viejo (municipality), an early Spanish town, was annexed to Banate from 1903 to 1918. San Rafael separated in 1969. FHL local records: civil registration, 1922–1931, 1895–1993; notarials, 1905–. Local records: civil registration, 1945–.

Batad (municipality) was an early Spanish town which was annexed to Balasan from 1903 to 1949. Local records: civil registration, 1950–.

Bingawan (municipality) was established in 1969 from Calinog. Local records: civil registration, 1970–.

Buenavista (municipality) was an early Spanish town to which in 1903 were annexed Jordán (separated 1918), Nabalas, and Nueva Valencia (separated 1941). It was made the capital of the sub-province in 1969. FHL local records: civil registration, 1922–1932; notarials, 1910–. Local records: civil registration, 1945–.

Cabatuan (municipality), an early Spanish town, annexed Maasin from 1903 to 1918. FHL local records: civil registration, 1922–1931, 1945–1994; notarials, 1905–. Local records: civil registration, 1945–.

Calinog (municipality), an early Spanish town, was annexed to Passi from 1903 to 1921. Bingawan separated in 1969. FHL local records: civil registration, 1922–1931, 1948–1994. Local records: civil registration, 1945–.

Carles (municipality), an early Spanish town, was annexed to Balasan from 1903 to circa 1929. FHL local records: civil registration, 1922–1931; notarials, 1920–. Local records: civil registration, 1921–.

Concepción (municipality), an early Spanish town was annexed to Sara from 1903 to 1921. FHL local records: civil registration, 1922–1932, 1921–1994; notarials, 1921–. Local records: civil registration, 1921–.

Dingle (municipality), an early Spanish town, was annexed to Pototan from 1903 to 1909. FHL local records: civil registration, 1922–1931; notarials, 1909–. Local records: civil registration, 1945–.

Dueñas (municipality), an early Spanish town, was annexed to Passi from 1903 to circa 1911. FHL local records: civil registration, 1922–1931, 1945–1994; notarials, 1912–. Local records: civil registration, 1945–.

Dumangas (municipality), an early Spanish town, was annexed to Barotac Nuevoto in 1911. FHL local records: civil registration, 1922–1931, 1947–1992; notarials, 1911–. Local records: civil registration, 1945–.

Estancia (municipality), an early Spanish town, was annexed to Balasan until 1919. FHL local records: civil registration, 1922–1931; notarials, 1921–. Local records: civil registration, 1948–.

Guimbal (municipality), an early Spanish town, annexed Igbaras and Tubuñgan from 1903 to 1919 and 1938, respectively. FHL local records: civil registration, 1922–1932, 1947–1994; notarials, 1903–. Local records: civil registration, 1945–.

Igbaras (municipality), an early Spanish town, was annexed to Guimbal until 1919. FHL local records: civil registration, 1925–1932, 1947–1994; notarials, 1919–. Local records: civil registration, 1946–.

Iloilo City (city), also known as Hilo, Ilo, Ilong-Ilong, Iloylo, Yloilo, Ylong-Ylong, and Ylo-Ylo, dates from 1583 as a Spanish settlement. Became capital of the province in 1688. It was chartered as a city in 1893, became a municipality in 1903, and again reverted to a city in 1936 with Iloilo, Arévalo, and LePaz. Jaro was annexed in 1903, consolidated with Pavia in 1907 (and later separated), and annexed again by Iloilo City in 1940. FHL local records: civil registration, 1924–1931; notarials, 1908–; birth certificates, 1947–1988; marriage contracts, 1949–1960; death certificates, 1975–1988; Arévalo (district of Iloilo City) civil registration, 1922–1932, and notarials, 1912–; Jaro (district of Iloilo City) civil registration, 1928–1932, and notarials, 1912–; La Paz (district of Iloilo City) civil registration, 1928–1932, and notarials, 1920–; Malo (district of Iloilo City) notarials, 1921–1924. Local records: civil registration, 1945–.

Janiuay (municipality), also known as Jaiuay, Janinay, and Magat-ob, was an early Spanish town to which Lambunao was annexed from 1903 to 1912. Badiangan separated in 1967. FHL local records: civil registration, 1922–1931; notarials, 1907–. Local records: civil registration, 1945–.

Jordán (municipality), also known as Nagaba, was an early Spanish town which was annexed to Buenavistato from 1903 to 1918. It was the capital of Guimaras sub-province from 1966 to 1969. FHL local records: civil

registration, 1922–1933; notarials, 1910–. Local records: civil registration, 1945–.

Lambunao (municipality), also known as Lambanao, was an early Spanish town which was annexed to Janiuay from 1903 to 1912. FHL local records: civil registration, 1922–1930, 1945–1994; notarials, 1912–. Local records: civil registration, 1945–.

Lawigan (municipality) was established in 1961. Local records: civil registration, 1961–.

Leganes (municipality), an early Spanish town, was annexed to Santa Barbara in 1903. It was later annexed to Jaro, but separated in 1940. FHL local records: civil registration, 1945–1994. Local records: civil registration, 1945–.

Lemery (municipality), an early Spanish town, was annexed to Sara, but later separated in 1948. Local records: civil registration, 1948–.

León (municipality), also known as Comando, was an early Spanish town to which were annexed, in 1903, San Miguel (separated circa 1916) and Alimodian (separated in 1919). FHL local records: civil registration, 1922–1932, 1902–1994; notarials, 1910–. Local records: civil registration, 1901–.

Maasin (municipality), an early Spanish town, was annexed to Cabatuan until 1918. FHL local records: civil registration, 1922–1930; notarials, 1918–. Local records: civil registration, 1944–.

Miagao (municipality) was an early Spanish town to which San Joaquin was annexed from 1903 to 1911. FHL local records: civil registration, 1922–1930, 1945–1994; notarials, 1911–. Local records: civil registration, 1960–.

Mina (municipality), an early Spanish town, was annexed to Pototan until 1968. Local records: civil registration, 1970–.

New Lucena (municipality), also known as Lucena prior to 1955, was established in 1946 from Santa Barbara. FHL local records: civil registration, 1947–1994. Local records: civil registration, 1947–.

Nueva Valencia (municipality), an early Spanish town, was annexed to Buenavistato in 1918. Local records: civil registration, 1964–.

Otón (municipality) was an early Spanish town. FHL local records: civil registration, 1922–1930, 1947–1991; notarials, 1909–. Local records: civil registration, 1944–.

Passi (municipality), also known as Pasi, was an early Spanish town to which were annexed, in 1903, Calinog (separated 1921), Duenas (separated circa 1911), and San Enrique (separated 1957). FHL local records: civil registration, 1922–1931; notarials, 1909–. Local records: civil registration, 1945–.

Pavia (municipality), an early Spanish town, was annexed to Santa Barbara, separated and annexed to Iloilo City in 1905, and separated and annexed to Jaro from 1907 to circa 1919. FHL local records: civil registration, 1922–1931; notarials, 1903–. Local records: civil registration, 1945–.

Pototan (municipality) was an early Spanish town. Annexed Dingle and Mina from 1903 to 1909 and 1968, respectively. FHL local records: civil registration, 1922–1931; notarials, 1903–. Local records: civil registration, 1945–.

San Dionisio (municipality) , an early Spanish town, was annexed to Sara until 1921. FHL local records: civil registration, 1922–1931, 1945–1994; notarials, 1921–. Local records: civil registration, 1946–.

San Enrique (municipality), an early Spanish town, was annexed to Passi until 1957. FHL local records: civil registration, 1957–1994. Local records: civil registration, 1957–.

San Joaquin (municipality), also known as Talisayan, was an early Spanish town annexed to Miagaoto from 1903 to 1911. FHL local records: civil registration, 1922–1933, 1946–1982; notarials, 1911–. Local records: civil registration, 1945–.

San Miguel (municipality), also known as Angoy, was an early Spanish town annexed to Leonto from 1903 to circa 1916. FHL local records: civil registration, 1922–1932, 1945–1994; notarials, 1916–. Local records: civil registration, 1945–.

San Rafael (municipality) was established in 1969 from Barotac Viejo. Local records: civil registration, 1972–.

Santa Barbara (municipality) was an early Spanish town to which in 1903 were annexed Leganes (later became part of the district of Jaro in Iloilo City), New Lucena (separated 1946), Zarraga (separated 1941), and Pavia (separated 1905, became part of Iloilo City, and was annexed to Jaro in 1905). FHL local records: civil registration, 1922–1931, 1945–1994; notarials, 1905–. Local records: civil registration, 1946–.

Sara (municipality) was an early Spanish town to which in 1903 were annexed Ajuy (separated 1917), Concepción (separated 1921), Lemery (separated 1948), and San Dionisio (separated 1921). FHL local records: civil registration, 1922–1933, 1939–1994; notarials, 1903–. Local records: civil registration, 1912–.

Tigbuan (municipality), also known as Figbauan, Cordova, and Cordoba, was an early Spanish town which annexed Cordova in 1903. FHL local records: civil registration, 1922–1931, 1945–1994; notarials, 1905–. Local records: civil registration, 1945–.

Tubuñgan (municipality), an early Spanish town, was annexed to Guimbal until 1938. FHL local records: civil registration, 1945–1994. Local records: civil registration, 1945–.

Zarraga (municipality), an early Spanish town, was annexed to Santa Barbara from 1903 to 1941. FHL local records: civil registration, 1945–1994; notarials, 1903–. Local records: civil registration, 1945–.

Isabela. This province is situated, roughly, in the center of the island of Luzon in the northern Philippines. Its eastern shore fronts on the Pacific Ocean. Chinese and Japanese traders knew this area before the coming of the Spanish. From the beginning of the extension of Spanish power in this area, the Dominican missionaries from Cagayan to the north began evangelization of the area. Opposition to them and to Spanish rule in general came from the Gaddanes and the Mayoyaos, as well as other communities of natives until a Spanish expedition in the middle of the nineteenth century brought these peoples under full Spanish control. Because this area was also designated a Spanish penal colony for political prisoners, native captives, and those who had managed to escape the death penalty, the area exhibited an atmosphere of general lawlessness and provided havens for outlaws in the outlying areas to which full Spanish authority had not yet extended. In May 1856 Isabela, named in honor of Queen Isabela II of Spain, was organized as a separate province from territory formerly under the jurisdiction of the provinces of Cagayan and Neuva Vizcaya. Although, the Philippine Revolution swept away Spanish power in this province, it was here, in Palanan, that General Emilio Aguinaldo, the President of the Philippine Republic, was captured by American forces. With the onset of the Philippine Revolution, the Dominicans had left and were replaced by the local clergy, aided by the Missionaries of the Immaculate Heart (from 1910 to 1948) and the Missionaries of Our Lady of La Salette (1948–). In August 1901 civil government was established. In 1903 and, again, in 1905 the American administration attempted to cut administrative costs by consolidating municipalities. Many of these have subsequently been restored.

FHL provincial records: birth records (1945–1988); marriage contracts (1945–1987); death certificates (1957–1991); court records created by the Court of First Instance (1857–1903); deportations (1865–1897); military induction records (1870–1897); public records (1884–1898); school records (1867–1898); statistical reports (1896); and Census of Chinese (1880–1898).

Localities and their important records:

Alicia (municipality) was established in 1949 from Angadanan. Local records: civil registration, 1950–.

Angadanan (municipality), also known as Angaduan, Tagle, and Tagel, was established in 1905 under the name Tagel. The name was changed to Angadanan in 1911. Parts of this municipality were used to create the municipality of San Guillermo in 1967. FHL local records: civil registration, 1922–1931; notarials, 1911–. Local records: civil registration, 1951–.

Aurora (municipality), also known as Dalig prior to 1940, was established in 1948. Burgos separated in 1967. FHL local records: civil registration, 1928–1932; notarials, 1926–. Local records: civil registration, 1945–.

Benito Soliven (municipality) was established in 1967 of territory from the municipalities of San Mariano, Ilagan, and Naguilian. Local records: civil registration, 1968–.

Burgos (municipality) was established in 1967 from Aurora and Gamu. Local records: civil registration, 1968–.

Cabagán (municipality), also known as Cabagán Nuevo, was an early Spanish town to which Cabagán Viejo and Santo Tomás were annexed in 1905. Santo Tomas separated in 1949. FHL local records: civil registration, 1922–1933; notarials, 1910–. Local records: civil registration, 1913–.

Cabatuan (municipality) was established in 1949 from Cauayan. Local records: civil registration, 1950–.

Cauayan (municipality) was an early Spanish town to which Reina Mercedes was annexed from 1903 to 1913. FHL local records: civil registration, 1922–1931; notarials, 1911–. Local records: civil registration, 1945–.

Cordon (municipality), also known as Estela, was an early Spanish town which was annexed to Echague from 1903 to 1910 and to Santiago from 1910 to 1939 when it was finally established as an independent municipality. Local records: civil registration, 1945–.

Dinapigui (municipal district) was established in 1969.

Divilican (municipal district) was established in 1969. Local records: civil registration, 1972–.

Echague (municipality) was an early Spanish town to which Santiago and Cordon were annexed from 1903 to 1910. Jones (in 1921), San Isidro (in 1967), and Ramon (in 1960) also separated. FHL local records: civil registration, 1922–1932; notarials, 1911–; Saint Joseph parish registers, 1887–1927. Local records: civil registration, 1945–.

Gamú (municipality), also known as Bamu, was an early Spanish town from which separated Burgos (1967), Quirino (1967), and Roxas (1948). FHL local records: civil registration, 1922–1931; notarials, 1911–; Saint Rose of Lima parish registers, 1738–1938. Local records: civil registration, 1912–.

Ilagan (city), also known as Baculud, was an early Spanish town to which was annexed Palanan from 1903 to 1906. FHL local records: civil registration, 1922–1931; notarials, 1907–; Saint Ferdinand parish registers, 1763–1964. Local records: civil registration, 1945–.

Jones (municipality) was established in 1921 from Echague. San Agustín separated in 1949. FHL local records: civil registration, 1922–1931; notarials, 1913–. Local records: civil registration, 1921–.

Luna (municipality), also known as Antatet prior to 1951, was established in 1949 from Cauayan. FHL local records: civil registration, 1928–1931; notarials, 1926–. Local records: civil registration, 1945–.

Maconacon (municipal district) was established in 1969. Local records: civil registration, 1972–.

Magsaysay (municipality) was established in 1957 from Tumauini. Local records: civil registration, 1957–.

Mallig (municipality) was established in 1952 from various villages in the municipalities of Ilagan, Roxas, Tumauini, and Santo Tomas. Quezon separated in 1959. Local records: civil registration, 1953–.

Naguilian (municipality) was an early Spanish town. FHL local records: civil registration, 1922–1931; notarials, 1911–; Saint Joseph parish registers, 1898–1948. Local records: civil registration, 1945–.

Palanan (municipality) was an early Spanish town that was annexed to Ilagan from 1903 to 1906. FHL local records: civil registration, 1923; notarials, 1911–. Local records: civil registration, 1962–.

Quezon (municipality) was established in 1959 from Mallig. Local records: civil registration, 1960–.

Quirino (municipality) was established in 1967 from portions of the municipalities of Ilagan, Roxas, and Gamú. Local records: civil registration, 1968–.

Ramon (municipality) was established in 1960 from portions of the municipalities of Santiago, San Mateo, and Echague. Local records: civil registration, 1964–.

Reina Mercedes (municipality) was an early Spanish town annexed to Cauayan from 1903 to 1913. FHL local records: civil registration, 1922–1932; notarials, 1913–; Saint Anthony of Padua parish registers, 1887–1954. Local records: civil registration, 1946–.

Roxas (municipality), also known as Vira, was established in 1948 from Gamú. San Manuel separated in 1957. In addition, portions were taken to form Mallig in 1952 and Quirino in 1967. Local records: civil registration, 1948–.

San Agustín (municipality) was established in 1949 from Jones. Local records: civil registration, 1950–.

San Guillermo (municipality) was established from Echague and Angadanan in 1967. Local records: civil registration, 1968–.

San Isidro (municipality) was established in 1967 from Echague. Local records: civil registration, 1968–.

San Manuel (municipality), also known as Callang, was established in 1957 from Roxas. Local records: civil registration, 1957–.

San Mariano (municipality) was established in 1927. Portions were taken to create the municipality of Benito Soliven in 1967. FHL local records: civil registration, 1923–1931; notarials, 1928–. Local records: civil registration, 1942–.

San Mateo (municipality) was established in 1946 from Santiago. Local records: civil registration, 1946–.

San Pablo (municipality) was an early Spanish town. FHL local records: civil registration, 1923–1931; notarials, 1912–. Local records: civil registration, 1945–.

Santa Maria (municipality) was an early Spanish town. FHL local records: civil registration, 1922–1931; notarials, 1913–. Local records: civil registration, 1943–.

Santiago (municipality), also known as Carig, was established in 1910 from Echague. FHL local records: civil registration, 1923; notarials, 1910–. Local records: civil registration, 1950–.

Santo Tomás (municipality). Created as a town in 1902. Annexed to Cabagan Neuvo from 1905 to 1949. Some of its territory was used to create the municipality of Mallig in 1952. Local records: civil registration, 1950–.

Tumauini (municipality) was an early Spanish town from which Magsaysay separated in 1957. Some portions were used to create the municipality of Mallig in 1952. FHL local records: civil registration, 1922–1931; notarials, 1907–; Saint Matthias parish registers, 1842–1973. Local records: civil registration, 1945–.

Kalinga-Apayao. This province, situated in the interior of the northern part of the island of Luzon, is so remote that it received little attention from the Spanish authorities. It formed part of the former Spanish province of Nueva Segovia (later called Cagayan) which included most of northeastern Luzon. In 1839 most of what is now Kalinga was made part of the newly created province of Nueva Vizcaya while Apayao was retained by the province of Cagaya. In 1880 the Spanish attempted to extend their authority into the mountainous interior of Luzon. A military district was established in Kalinga with the name Itaves. In 1890 another was established in Apayao and called Apayos. Both the Augustinians and the Dominicans had a long, but largely unsuccessful, presence in this area. With the evacuation of Spanish during the Philippine Revolution, their missions were vacated until 1907 when the missionaries of the Immaculate Heart of Mary arrived. A civil government was established in February 1901 with Kalinga and Apayao made part of the province of Cagayan. In 1907 Kalinga became a sub-province of Lepanto-Bontoc and Apayao became a sub-province of Cagayan. In 1908 both were made sub-provinces of the newly created Mountain Province. They were separated from the Mountain Province and united to form the new province of Kalinga-Apayao, named for the two tribes which inhabit it, in June 1966. Since Kalinga and Apayao roughly correspond to the territory occupied by the two large tribes, the division between them is important. Kalinga includes the municipal districts and municipalities of Balbalan, Lubuagan, Pinukpuk, Tabuk (provincial capital), Tanudan, Tinglayan, Quirino, and Liwan. Apayao is composed of the municipal districts and municipalities of Luna, Flora, Kabugao, Pudtol, Conner, and Bayag.

> FHL provincial records: birth records (1945–1988); birth certificates (1968–1988); marriage contracts (1946–1987); death certificates (1967–1990); and statistical reports (1896).

Localities and their records:

Balbalan (municipality) was established in 1963. FHL local records: civil registration, 1922–1933; notarials, 1941–. Local records: civil registration, 1945–.

Calanasan (municipality), also known as Bayag prior to 1967) was established in 1963. FHL local records: civil registration, 1922–1931; notarials, 1922–. Local records: civil registration, 1943–.

Conner (municipality) was established in 1963. FHL local records: civil registration, 1922–1931. Local records: civil registration, 1951–.

Flora (municipality) was established in 1963 from Pudtol. Local records: civil registration, 1963–.

Kabugao (municipality) was established in 1963. FHL local records: notarials, 1946–1957. Local records: civil registration, 1943–.

Lubuagan (municipality) was established in 1963. FHL local records: civil registration, 1922–1924; notarials, 1941–. Local records: civil registration, 1916–.

Luna (municipality) was established in 1963. FHL local records: civil registration, 1930; notarials, 1946–. Local records: civil registration, 1947–.

Pasil (municipality) was established in 1966. Local records: civil registration, 1968–.

Pinukpuk (municipality) was established in 1963. FHL local records: civil registration, 1922–1931. Local records: civil registration, 1945–.

Pudtol (municipality), also known as Futtul, was established in 1959. Flora separated in 1963. Local records: civil registration, 1945–.

Quirino (municipality).

Rizal (municipality), also known as Liwan prior to 1971, was established in 1965. Local records: civil registration, 1965–.

Santa Marcela (municipality) was established in 1967. Local records: civil registration, 1967–.

Tabuk (municipality), also known as Tabuc, was established in 1950. It was the capital of the sub-province Kalinga from 1901 to 1966. Since 1966, it has been the capital of province Kalinga-Apayao. FHL local records: civil registration, 1922–1931; notarials, 1945–. Local records: civil registration, 1916–.

Tanudan (municipality) was established in 1963. Local records: civil registration, 1941–.

Tinglayan (municipality) was established in 1963. FHL local records: civil registration, 1922–1929. Local records: civil registration, 1964–.

Laguna. This province occupies the south-central portion of the island of Luzon. Laguna had large settlements of both Chinese and Malay before the coming of the Spanish. After the establishment of a seat of government at Manila in 1571, Spanish forces conducted a sweep through areas along the coasts of western Luzon, destroying centers that might have competed with the military or economic dominance of the Spanish settlement at Manila. Soon after the extension of Spanish power, the missionaries arrived: the Augustinians in 1572 and the Franciscans in 1577. Within a few years mission centers had been set up along the coast of this area. Originally Laguna was a part of the Manila Province, but soon it was given the status of an independent province. Since the capital and largest town was Bay, the province was often called by that name. In 1688 the capital was moved to Pagsanjan and, in 1858, to Santa Cruz where it remains. In 1853 the newly created province of Morong (later named Rizal) took a lot of territory from Laguna, some of which was returned as a result of boundary adjustments in later years. Laguna was a center of revolutionary activity against the Spanish. In this province the Philippine Revolution easily swept away Spanish power. But, in July 1902 American forces established a civil government there. In 1903 municipalities were temporarily consolidated.

> FHL provincial records: civil registration (1846–1898); birth records (1945–1988); marriage contracts (1945–1987); death certificates (1899–1893, 1957–1991); court records created by the Court of First Instance (1861–1882); deportations (1875–1897); land records (1836–1921); military induction records (1733–1896); public records (1875–1898); records of lending (1820–1890); school records (1781–1899); statistical reports (1894); tax records (1802–1878); and Census of Chinese (1859–1897).

Localities and their records:

Alaminos (municipality), also known as Threchera and Trenchera prior to 1833, was an early Spanish town annexed to San Pablo from 1903 to 1907. FHL local records: civil registration, 1922–1932; notarials, 1909–; Our Lady of the Pillar parish registers, 1895–1962. Local records: civil registration, 1945–.

Bay (municipality), an early Spanish town, was the capital of the province Laguna until 1688. It was annexed to Los Baños from 1903 to 1909. FHL local records: civil registration, 1926–1931, 1945–1991; notarials, 1909–; Saint Augustine parish registers, 1906–1968. Local records: civil registration, 1945–.

Biñan (municipality), also known as Biñang, was an early Spanish town to which San Pedro was annexed from 1903 to 1907. Annexed Muntinlupa of Rizal which was transferred back to Rizal and then annexed to Taguin. FHL local records: civil registration, 1926–1931, 1903–1990; notarials, 1908–; Saint Isidro Labrador parish registers, 1845–1944. Local records: civil registration, 1913–.

Cabuyao (municipality), also known as Tabuko and Kabuyao, was an early Spanish town from which Calamba separated circa 1909. FHL local records: civil registration, 1921–1929, 1962–1989; notarials, 1907–;

San Policarpio parish registers, 1803–1968. Local records: civil registration, 1962–.

Calamba (municipality) was established in circa 1909 from Cabuyao. FHL local records: civil registration, 1922–1933, 1945–1989; notarials, 1904–; Saint John the Baptist parish registers, 1812–1947. Local records: civil registration, 1945–.

Calauan (municipality), also known as Calauang and Kalawang, was an early Spanish town which was burned in 1901 during the Philippine Revolution and rebuilt in 1902. FHL local records: civil registration, 1922–1931, 1945–1991; notarials, 1903–; San Isidro Labrador parish registers, 1812–1847. Local records: civil registration, 1945–.

Cavinti (municipality) was an early Spanish town annexed to Luisiana from 1903 to 1907. FHL local records: civil registration, 1922–1931, 1932–1991; notarials, 1904–; Transfiguration of Our Lord parish registers, 1852–1974. Local records: civil registration, 1902–.

Famy (municipality) was an early Spanish town annexed to Siniloan from 1903 to 1910. FHL local records: civil registration, 1923–1931, 1930–1988; notarials, 1911–. Local records: civil registration, 1945–.

Kalayaan (municipality), also known as Loñgos and Tabing Dagat, was an early Spanish town annexed to Paete in 1903, consolidated with town of San Antonio (also in Paete), and separated in 1909. The name of Loñgos was changed to Kalayaan in 1956. FHL local records: civil registration, 1922–1931, 1945–1991; notarials, 1911–. Local records: civil registration, 1945–.

Liliw (municipality), also known as Lilio prior to 1965, was an early Spanish town. FHL local records: civil registration, 1922–1931, 1903–1991; notarials, 1911–; Saint John the Baptist parish registers, 1801–1962. Local records: civil registration, 1903–.

Los Baños (municipality), also known as Baños, Mainit, and College, was an early Spanish town to which Bay was annexed from 1903 to 1904. FHL local records: civil registration, 1922–1933, 1912–1990; notarials, 1905–; Our Lady of the Immaculate Conception parish registers, 1832–1967. Local records: civil registration, 1911–.

Luisiana (municipality), also known as Nasunog and Ibanag Nasunog, was an early Spanish town to which Cavinti was annexed from 1903 to 1907. FHL local records: civil registration, 1922–1931, 1942–1991; notarials, 1907–; Our Lady of the Holy Rosary parish registers, 1873–1975. Local records: civil registration, 1945–.

Lumban (municipality), also known as Lumbang, was an early Spanish town. FHL local records: civil registration, 1922–1930, 1951–1991; notarials, 1903–; Saint Sebastian parish registers, 1867–1974. Local records: civil registration, 1904–.

Mabitac (municipality) was an early Spanish town to which Santa María was annexed from 1903 to 1910. FHL local records: civil registration, 1922–1931, 1945–1991; notarials, 1911–. Local records: civil registration, 1945–.

Magdalena (municipality), also known as Amiling, was an early Spanish town that separated from Majayjay in 1821. FHL local records: civil registration, 1922–1931, 1902–1991; notarials, 1905–; Mary Magdalene parish registers, 1821–1908. Local records: civil registration, 1902–.

Majayjay (municipality), also known as Majaijay and Majaijai, was an early Spanish town. FHL local records: civil registration, 1922–1931, 1903–1991; notarials, 1907–; Saint Gregory the Great parish registers, 1748–1961. Local records: civil registration, 1903–.

Nagcarlan (municipality) was an early Spanish town. FHL local records: civil registration, 1922–1932, 1904–1991; notarials, 1905–; San Bartolomé Apóstol parish registers, 1796–1968; Philippine Independent Church parish registers, 1917–1983. Local records: civil registration, 1903–.

Paete (municipality), also known as San Lorenzo, was an early Spanish town to which Kalayaan (then called Loñgos) and San Antonio were annexed in 1903. Kalayaan and San Antonio were consolidated in 1909 under the name Kalayaan. FHL local records: civil registration, 1922–1931, 1903–1991; notarials, 1904–; San Santiago Apóstol parish registers, 1796–1968; Philippine Independent Church parish registers, 1918–1951. Local records: civil registration, 1950–.

Pagsanjan (municipality), also known as Pagsanhan and Pinagsanjan, was an early Spanish town. FHL local records: civil registration, 1921–1932, 1945–1991; notarials, 1909–; Our Lady of Guadalupe parish registers, 1828–1959; Philippine Independent Church parish registers, 1918–1983. Local records: civil registration, 1945–.

Pakil (municipality), also known as Paquil, was an early Spanish town annexed to Pangil from 1903 to 1927. FHL local records: San Pedro de Alcántara parish registers, 1701–1968. Local records: civil registration, 1931–.

Pañgil (municipality) was an early Spanish town to which Pakil was annexed from 1903 to 1927. FHL local records: civil registration, 1927–1930, 1904–1991. Local records: civil registration, 1945–.

Pila (municipality), also known as Pagalanan, was an early Spanish town. FHL local records: civil registration, 1922–1932, 1948–1957; notarials, 1907–; Saint Anthony of Padua parish registers, 1725–1966; Philippine Independent Church parish registers, 1935–1951. Local records: civil registration, 1901–.

Rizal (municipality) was established in 1919 from Nagcarlan. FHL local records: civil registration, 1925–1931, 1945–1991; notarials, 1919–; Saint Michael the Archangel parish registers, 1918–1973. Local records: civil registration, 1945–.

San Pablo City (city), an early Spanish town, was chartered as a city in May 1940. Annexed Alaminos from 1903 to 1907. FHL local records: civil registration, 1923–1931, 1918–1991; notarials, 1906–; birth certificates, 1945–1988; marriage contracts, 1945–1958; death certificates, 1975–1988; Saint Paul, the Hermit, parish registers, 1672–1965 (67 reels, this church was a mission church devoted to the Chinese); Philippine Independent Church parish registers, 1936–1947. Local records: civil registration, 1901–.

San Pedro (municipality), also known as San Pedro de Tunasan prior to 1914, was an early Spanish town annexed to Biñan from 1903 to 1907. FHL local records: civil registration, 1922–1932, 1907–1991; notarials, 1916–; Saint Peter the Apostle parish registers, 1800–1963. Local records: civil registration, 1907–.

Santa Cruz (city), an early Spanish town, has been the capital of the province since 1858. FHL local records:

civil registration, 1922–1931, 1940–1991; notarials, 1905–; Philippine Independent Church parish registers, 1903–1956. Local records: civil registration, 1912–.

Santa María (municipality) was an early Spanish town annexed to Mabitac from 1903 to 1910. FHL local records: civil registration, 1923–1924, 1980–1991; notarials, 1903–. Local records: civil registration, 1945–.

Santa Rosa (municipality) was an early Spanish town. FHL local records: civil registration, 1922–1924, 1915–1991; notarials, 1904–; Saint Rose of Lima parish registers, 1792–1963. Local records: civil registration, 1903–.

Siniloan (municipality), also known as Guiling-Guiling and Sinluluang, was an early Spanish town to which Famy was annexed from 1903 to 1910. FHL local records: civil registration, 1922–1932, 1945–1989; notarials, 1907–. Local records: civil registration, 1944–.

Victoria (municipality) was established in 1949 from Pila. FHL local records: civil registration, 1949–1991. Local records: civil registration, 1949–.

Lanao del Norte. This province occupies the portion of the island of Mindanao where it meets the Zamboanga Peninsula. In May 1959 the former province of Lanao was divided into the provinces of Lanao del Norte and Lanao del Sur. Lanao was the only province in the Philippines where the Spanish were never firmly in control. They did try to exert power over this area through a series of expeditions against the ruling sultans. In 1637 one such expedition was able to take the Muslim stronghold at Lancitan on the Lanao coast. Two years later an expedition overtook the interior of Lanao. These expeditions, though successful, did not lead to further efforts by the Spanish since Spanish resources were limited and a series of campaigns was not possible. The result was that the Maranaos, an Islamic tribe of fierce warriors and part of the Moros, who migrated to this area in the thirteenth century from what is now Malaysia, were left largely alone. The Jesuits established a mission at Iligan and, in the next century, at several other settlements in Lanao. These establishments were probably not the result of a successful conversion of the Maranaos, but, rather, were due to the number of immigrants from Christianized areas arriving in the Visayas. In 1768 the Jesuits were expelled from the Philippines and their work was taken over by the Recollects until their return in 1921. In 1948 the Columbian Fathers succeeded the Jesuits. In the late nineteenth century the Spanish again attempted to subjugate this area. In the last decade of the nineteenth century a series of campaigns brought the coast of Lanao under control. Later expeditions pushed inland and, finally, the Islamic capital and stronghold at Marawi was captured in 1894. In October of 1895, Lanao became the seventh district in the new province of Minadanao and Sulu. By 1896 the Philippine Revolution had broken out and the Spanish withdrew from this region in order to concentrate their forces in Luzon. In 1900 the Americans landed at Iligan and established a government which mainly ad-

ministered the areas that had been Christianized by the Spanish. In 1903 Lanao became one of the five districts of the new Moro Province which located its capital at Zamboanga. A series of bloody encounters between American forces initially under the command of General John J. Pershing and the Moros continued until American control was firmly established in 1913. In 1914 Lanao became one of the seven provinces under the Deportionment of Mindanao and Sulu which had succeeded the Moro Province. In May 1959 in response to the immigration of Christian Cebuano-speakers to the northern coast of Lanao which had changed the composition of that area, the province was divided into Lanao del Norte with its capital at Iligan City and Lanao del Sur with its capital at Marawi City.

FHL provincial records: birth records (1947–1988); marriage contracts (1945–1987); and death certificates (1959–1991).

Localities and their records:

Bacolod (municipality) was established in 1956 from Kolambugan. Local records: civil registration, 1956–.

Balo-i (municipality), also known as Momuñgan, Pantar, and Balut, was established in 1948 from the consolidation of the municipal districts of Pantar, Balut, and Momungan. Tagoloan separated in 1956. FHL local records: civil registration, 1922–1930; notarial, 1941–. Local records: civil registration, 1946–.

Baroy (municipality) was established in 1949 from the consolidation of portions of the municipalities of Tubod and Kolambugan. Local records: civil registration, 1949–.

Iligan City (city), chartered in June 1950, has been the capital of Lanao del Norte since 1959. Kauswagan separated in 1948. FHL local records: civil registration, 1922–1933; notarial, 1910–; birth certificates, 1951–1988; death certificates, 1975–1988; deportations, 1891–1898. Local records: civil registration, 1941–.

Kapatagan (municipality) was established in 1949. Sapad separated in 1967. Local records: civil registration, 1946–.

Karomatan (municipality) was established in 1953. Local records: civil registration, 1953–.

Kauswagan (municipality) was established in 1948 from Iligan City. Local records: civil registration, 1948–.

Kolambugan (municipality) was an early Spanish town from which separated Bacolod (1956), Tubod (1946), Tangcal (1956), and Baroy (1949). FHL local records: notarial, 1930–. Local records: civil registration, 1966–.

Lala (municipality) was established in 1949 from Tubod. FHL local records: notarial, 1930–. Local records: civil registration, 1949–.

Linamon (municipality) was established in 1960. Local records: civil registration, 1960–.

Magsaysay (municipality) was established in 1965. Local records: civil registration, 1960–.

Maigo (municipality) was established in 1969. Local records: civil registration, 1959–.

Matuñgao (municipality) was established in 1949. In 1969 Pantao Ragat separated; Poona-Piagapo separated in 1976. Local records: civil registration, 1949–.

Munai (municipal district).

Nunuñgan (municipality) and **Pantao Ragat** (municipality) were established in 1969.

Poona-Piagapo (municipality) was established in 1976 from Matungao and Pantao Ragat.

Salvador (municipality) was established in 1960. Local records: civil registration, 1960–.

Sapad (municipality) was established in 1967 from Kapatagan. Local records: civil registration, 1972–.

Tagoloan (municipality) was established in 1969 from Baloi.

Tangcal (municipal district) was established in 1956 from Kolambugan. Local records: civil registration, 1963–.

Tubod (municipality) was established in 1946 from Kolambugan. Lala and Baroy separated in 1949. Local records: civil registration, 1947–.

Lanao del Sur. This land-locked province is located in the northwestern portion of the island of Mindanao, surrounding Lake Lanao. In this province reside large numbers of the Maranaos, an Islamic tribe that migrated from Malaysian in the thirteenth century. In 1959 the former province of Lanao was divided into Lanao del Norte and Lanao del Sur with the northern province containing large numbers of Christians, the southern portion a large majority of Muslims. (For a short historical sketch of the administration of the province of Lanao prior to its division, see the section on Lanao del Norte above.)

FHL provincial records: birth records (1947–1988); marriage contracts (1945–1959, 1965–1986); and death certificates (1959–1973).

Localities and their records:

Bacolod Grande (municipality) was established in 1963.

Balabagan (municipality) was established in 1960 from the consolidation of territory from Malabang and Dianaton. Local records: civil registration, 1974–.

Balindong (municipality), also known as Watu prior to 1956, was established in 1963.

Bayang (municipality) and **Binidayan** (municipality) were established in 1963.

Buadiposo-Buntog (municipality) was established in 1977.

Bubong (municipality) was established in 1963.

Butig (municipality) was established in 1963. Dianaton separated in 1966.

Calanogas (municipality) was established in 1977.

Dianaton (municipality) was established in 1966 of territory from Butig and Balabangan.

Ganassi (municipality) was established in 1961.

Kapai (municipality) was established in 1967.

Lumbat-a-Bayabao (municipality), also known as Maguing prior to 1956, was established circa 1977. Wao separated in 1956.

Lumbayanague (municipality) was established in 1977.

Lumbatan (municipality) was established in 1963. FHL local records: notarial, 1928–1934. Local records: civil registration, 1959–.

Madlum (municipality) was established in 1967.

Madamba (municipality) was established in 1963.

Malabang (municipality) was established circa 1966. Balabagan separated in 1960. FHL local records: civil registration, 1922–1930; notarial, 1919–. Local records: civil registration, 1966–.

Marantao (municipality) was established in 1963.

Marawi City (city), also known as Dansalan City prior to 1956, was chartered in September 1950. It was an early capital of the Moro Sultanate. FHL local records: civil registration, 1922–1927; notarial, 1911–; birth records, 1949–1988; death certificates, 1975–1988. Local records: civil registration, 1930–.

Morogong (municipality) was established in 1977.

Masiu (municipality) and **Molundo** (municipality) were established in 1963.

Pagayawan (municipality), also known as Tatarikan prior to 1963, was established in 1963.

Piagapo (municipality) was established in 1961 from Saguiaran.

Poon-a-Bayabao (municipality), also known as Gata prior to 1956, was established in 1963 as were **Pualas** (municipality) and **Ramain** (municipality), also known as Ramain-Ditsaan.

Saguiaran (municipality) was established in 1963. Piagapo separated in 1961.

Sultan Gumander (municipality) was established in 1977.

Tamparan (municipality) was established in 1960.

Taraka (municipality), **Tubaran** (municipality), and **Tugaya** (municipality) were established in 1963.

Wao (municipality) was established as a municipal district in 1956 from Lumba-a-Bayabao and as a municipality in 1961.

La Union. This province is situated on the western coast of the island of Luzon, between the provinces of Ilocos Sur (to the north) and Pangasinan (to the south). Before the Spanish arrived, the area contained flourishing trading settlements: Purao (now Balaoan), Bauang, and Agoo. Augustinian missionaries were attracted to these towns where they established the first mission centers in the late sixteenth century. The province of La Union was created in April 1854 from "the Union" of the southern portion of Ilocos Sur and the northern portion of Pangasinan. During the Philippine Revolution, Spanish power in this area was soon swept away. While the American and revolutionary forces clashed, the Americans occupied the province after winning the battle of Aringay River. In August 1901 civil government was established. In 1902 the area consisting of the municipalities of Sudipen, Santol, and San Gabriel was annexed to the sub-province of Amburayan, province of Lepanto-Bontoc. When that province was abolished this territory remained in the same sub-province under the jurisdiction of the Mountain Province. In February 1920 Amburayan was abolished and the three municipalities returned to La Union.

FHL provincial records: civil registration (1783–1898); birth records (1946–1988); marriage contracts (1945–1987); death certificates (1957–1991); court records created by the Court of First Instance (1901–1903); deportations (1872–1896); land records (1882–1889); military induction records (1883–1898); public records (1884–1898); records of lending (1854); school records (1865–1898); statistical reports (1894–1896); and Census of Chinese (1866–1896).

Localities and their records:

Agoo (municipality) was an early Spanish town. FHL local records: civil registration, 1922–1931, 1898–1991; notarial, 1907–; Saint Monica parish registers, 1867–1955. Local records: civil registration, 1898–.

Aringay (municipality) was an early Spanish town to which Galiano and Caba were annexed in 1903. Caba separated in 1907. FHL local records: civil registration, 1922–1932, 1945–1992; notarial, 1904–; Saint Lucy parish registers, 1739–1944. Local records: civil registration, 1945–.

Bacnotan (municipality), also known as Bagnotan, was an early Spanish town. FHL local records: civil registration, 1922–1932, 1902–1992; notarial, 1905–; Saint Michael the Archangel parish registers, 1835–1957. Local records: civil registration, 1902–.

Bagulin (municipality) was established in 1963. FHL local records: civil registration, 1922–1932. Local records: civil registration, 1945–.

Balaoan (municipality), also known as Purao and Balaoang, was an early Spanish town. FHL local records: civil registration, 1922–1933, 1945–1992; notarial, 1906–; Saint Nicholas of Tolentino parish registers, 1798–1977. Local records: civil registration, 1945–.

Bangar (municipality) was an early Spanish town. FHL local records: civil registration, 1922–1930; notarial, 1907–; Saint Christopher parish registers, 1848–1935. Local records: civil registration, 1945–.

Bauang (municipality), also known as Baoang, was an early Spanish town. FHL local records: civil registration, 1922–1931, 1903–1991; notarial, 1901–; Saint Peter's Chair parish registers, 1870–1941. Local records: civil registration, 1904–.

Burgos (municipality) was established in 1963 from Naguilian. FHL local records: civil registration, 1922–1931; notarial, 1927–. Local records: civil registration, 1945–.

Caba (municipality) was an early Spanish town annexed to Aringay from 1903 to 1907. FHL local records: civil registration, 1922–1932, 1945–1991; notarial, 1909–. Local records: civil registration, 1910–.

Luna (municipality), also known as Namacpacan, Namacpalcan, and Namagpacan, was an early Spanish town. The name Namacpacan was changed to Luna in 1906. FHL local records: civil registration, 1922–1931; notarial, 1906–; Saint Catherine of Alexandria parish registers, 1790–1952. Local records: civil registration, 1902–.

Naguilian (municipality) was an early Spanish town from which Burgos separated in 1963. FHL local records: civil registration, 1922–1932, 1902–1992; notarial, 1908–. Local records: civil registration, 1902–.

Pugo (municipality) was established in 1947. FHL local records: civil registration, 1922–1931; notarial, 1933–. Local records: civil registration, 1945–.

Rosario (municipality), an early Spanish town, was annexed to Santo Tomas from 1903 to circa 1907. FHL local records: civil registration, 1922–1931; notarial, 1908–; Immaculate Conception parish registers, 1910–1963. Local records: civil registration, 1945–.

San Fernando (city), also known as Pindagan, has been the capital of La Union province since 1854. FHL local records: civil registration, 1922–1931; notarial, 1905–; Saint William the Hermit parish registers, 1712–1937. Local records: civil registration, 1945–.

San Gabriel (municipality) was an early Spanish town annexed in 1905 to Amburayan, sub-province of the province of Lepanto-Bontoc, until the province was dissolved in 1908. It remained with Amburayan which was subordinated to the newly created Mountain Province. In 1920, this municipality was returned to La Union. FHL local records: civil registration, 1922–1931; notarial, 1920–. Local records: civil registration, 1945–.

San Juan (municipality) was an early Spanish town. FHL local records: civil registration, 1922–1932; notarial, 1905–; Saint John the Baptist parish registers, 1889–1917. Local records: civil registration, 1945–.

Santo Tomás (municipality) was an early Spanish town to which Rosario was annexed from 1903 to circa 1907. FHL local records: civil registration, 1922–1931, 1913–1992; notarial, 1906–. Local records: civil registration, 1914–.

Santol (municipality), an early Spanish town, was annexed in 1905 to Amburayan, a sub-province of the province of Lepanto-Bontoc, until that province was dissolved in 1908. Amburayan was then subordinated to the newly created Mountain Province. In 1920, Santol was returned to La Union. It was established as a municipality in 1949. FHL local records: civil registration, 1922–1931; notarial, 1921–. Local records: civil registration, 1918–.

Sudipen (municipality), also known as Sudipan, was an early Spanish town which was annexed in 1905 to Amburayan, a sub-province of the province of Lepanto-Bontoc, until that province was dissolved in 1908. Amburayan was then subordinated to the newly created Mountain Province. In 1920, Sudipen was returned to La Union. It was established as a municipality in 1947. FHL local records: civil registration, 1922–1931; notarial, 1919–. Local records: civil registration, 1945–.

Tubao (municipality) was an early Spanish town. FHL local records: civil registration, 1922–1933, 1945–1992; notarial, 1905–; Saint Isidore the Farmer parish registers, 1896–1952. Local records: civil registration, 1945–.

Leyte. This province and the province of Southern Leyte encompass the island of Leyte and nearby islands. When the Spanish arrived, they found this island contained several settlements based on trade and manufacture. Early in the Spanish period, Leyte (then called Tandaya) and Samar (then called Ibabao) were placed under the jurisdiction of Cebu. In 1735 Leyte, which included Samar at that time, was made a separate province. In 1768, Samar was separated as an independent province. In May 1959 Leyte province was divided into two provinces: Leyte and Southern Leyte. The sub-province of Biliran, subordinate to the province of Leyte, had been organized a month earlier. Leyte has had several capitals, beginning with Carigara, then Palo, Tanawan, and, finally, Tacloban which remains the capital. The Americans established a civil government in April 1901, after suppressing the revolutionary forces which had taken control after the Spanish evacuated the island. In 1942 the Japanese Imperial Army landed at Tacloban in their drive to conquer the Philippines. In 1944 American forces under General MacArthur landed and, after heavy fighting, overcame the Japanese forces. One of the consequences of the incursion by the Japanese was the destruction of records.

> FHL provincial records: civil registration (1867–1897); birth records (1945–1988); marriage contracts (1945–1987); death certificates (1964–1991); court records created by the Court of First Instance (1854–1903); deportations (1872–1897); land records (1882); military induction records (1874–1898); public records (1871–1897); records of lending (1857–1889); school records (1809–1898); tax records (1852–1855); and Census of Chinese (1884–1898).

Localities and their records:

Abuyog (municipality), also known as Abuyo, was an early Spanish town. FHL local records: civil registration, 1922–1931; notarial, 1911–. Local records: civil registration, 1947–.

Alangalang (municipality) was an early Spanish town to which San Miguel was annexed from 1903 to circa 1910. FHL local records: civil registration, 1922–1930; notarial, 1913–. Local records: civil registration, 1909–.

Albuera (municipality), also known as Sibuhay and Herera, was an early Spanish town which was annexed to Ormoc from 1903 to 1918. FHL local records: civil registration, 1922–1931; notarial, 1911–. Local records: civil registration, 1918–.

Almeria (municipality). See the Biliran Sub-province above.

Babatñgon (municipality), also known as Babatoñgan, was an early Spanish town to which Malibago was annexed in 1903. FHL local records: civil registration, 1923–1931; notarial, 1911–. Local records: civil registration, 1942–.

Barugo (municipality) was an early Spanish town. FHL local records: civil registration, 1921–1929; notarial, 1905–. Local records: civil registration, 1945–.

Bato (municipality) was an early Spanish town. FHL local records: civil registration, 1922–1931; notarial, 1911–; Holy Name of Jesus parish registers, 1881–1940. Local records: civil registration, 1911–.

Baybay (municipality) was an early Spanish town. FHL local records: civil registration, 1922–1931; notarial, 1905–; Immaculate Conception parish registers, 1813–1928. Local records: civil registration, 1902–.

Biliran (municipality). See the Biliran Sub-province above.

Burauen (municipality), also known as Buranen, Armasin, Malabca, Lagiwan, Burabod, Bura-on, and Burawon, was an early Spanish town from which Julita separated in 1949. FHL local records: civil registration, 1921–1931; notarial, 1911–. Local records: civil registration, 1944–.

Cabucgayan (municipality) and **Caibiran** (municipality). See the Biliran Sub-province above.

Calubian (municipality). FHL local records: civil registration, 1922–1930; notarial, 1911–. Local records: civil registration, 1919–.

Capoocan (municipality) was an early Spanish town annexed to Carigara from 1903 to 1918. FHL local records: civil registration, 1922–1930; notarial, 1925–. Local records: civil registration, 1957–.

Carigara (municipality), also known as Kangara, Kalgara, Kandaya, Tandaya, and Kandarag, was an early Spanish town to which Capoocan was annexed from 1903 to

1918. FHL local records: civil registration, 1926–1930; notarial, 1911–. Local records: civil registration, 1944–.

Culaba (municipality). See the Biliran Sub-province above.

Dagami (municipality) was an early Spanish town to which were annexed Pastrana and Tabontabon which separated in 1912 and 1953, respectively. FHL local records: civil registration, 1924; notarial, 1905–. Local records: civil registration, 1945–.

Dulag (municipality) was an early Spanish town from which Mayorga separated in 1955. FHL local records: civil registration, 1925–1930; notarial, 1909–. Local records: civil registration, 1944–.

Hilongos (municipality), also known as Ilongos, was an early Spanish town. FHL local records: civil registration, 1922–1931; notarial, 1913–; Immaculate Conception parish registers, 1864–1928. Local records: civil registration, 1911–.

Hindang (municipality) was a Spanish town. FHL local records: civil registration, 1923–1931; notarial, 1911–; Saint Michael the Archangel parish registers, 1843–1965. Local records: civil registration, 1976–.

Inopacan (municipality), also known as Inopakan, was an early Spanish town. FHL local records: civil registration, 1922–1931; notarial, 1905–; Saint Isidore parish registers, 1904–1982. Local records: civil registration, 1915–.

Isabel (municipality), also known as Quiot and Dupong, was an early Spanish town to which Merida was annexed from 1903 to 1948. Local records: civil registration, 1948–.

Jaro (municipality), also known as Salug, was an early Spanish town. FHL local records: civil registration, 1922–1931; notarial, 1905–. Local records: civil registration, 1945–.

Javier (municipality), also known as Bugho prior to 1965, was established in 1961. Local records: civil registration, 1964–.

Julita (municipality) was established in 1949 from Burauen. Local records: civil registration, 1950–.

Kananga (municipality) was established in 1950 from Ormoc. Local records: civil registration, 1950–.

Kawayan (municipality). See the Biliran Sub-province above.

La Paz (municipality) was established in 1918, probably from Burauen. FHL local records: civil registration, 1922–1930; notarial, 1918–. Local records: civil registration, 1918–.

Leyte (municipality), also known as Leite, was an early Spanish town. FHL local records: civil registration, 1921–1931; notarial, 1904–. Local records: civil registration, 1945–.

MacArthur (municipality), also known as Bagacay and Tarragona, had its name changed to MacArthur from Bagacay in 1950. Local records: civil registration, 1950–.

Mahaplag (municipality) was established in 1958. Local records: civil registration, 1958–.

Maripipi (municipality). See the Biliran Sub-province above.

Matag-ob (municipality) was established in 1957 from Palompon. Local records: civil registration, 1957–.

Matalom (municipality) was an early Spanish town to which Cajaguaan was annexed in 1903. FHL local records: civil registration, 1922–1931; notarial, 1911–;

Saint Joseph parish registers, 1843–1940. Local records: civil registration, 1902–.

Mayorga (municipality) was established in 1955 from Dulag. FHL local records: notarial, 1903–1906. Local records: civil registration, 1955–.

Merida (municipality), also known as Siapon, was an early Spanish town to which Isabel (formerly Quiot) was annexed from 1903 to 1948. FHL local records: civil registration, 1922–1931; notarial, 1911–. Local records: civil registration, 1941–.

Naval (municipality). See the Biliran Sub-province above.

Ormoc City (city), also known as Ugmok, Ugmuk, and Ogmuc, was an early Spanish town to which Albuera was annexed from 1903 to 1918. It was chartered as a city in October 1947. FHL local records: civil registration, 1922–1931; notarial, 1907–; birth certificates, 1947–1988; marriage contracts, 1947–1960; death certificates, 1976–1988. Local records: civil registration, 1945–.

Palo (municipality) was an early Spanish town. Santa Fe separated in 1949. FHL local records: civil registration, 1922–1923; notarial, 1912–. Local records: civil registration, 1915–.

Palompon (municipality), also known as Pamplona, Hinablayan, Paung-Pung, and Paung-Pong, was an early Spanish town from which Matag-ob separated in 1957. FHL local records: civil registration, 1922–1931; notarial, 1911–. Local records: civil registration, 1918–.

Pastrana (municipality) was an early Spanish town which was annexed to Dagami from 1903 to 1912. FHL local records: civil registration, 1921–1931; notarial, 1903–. Local records: civil registration, 1945–.

San Isidro (municipality), also known as San Isidro de Campo and Punong, was an early Spanish town to which Villaba was annexed from 1903 to 1910. Tabango separated in 1949. FHL local records: civil registration, 1922–1932; notarial, 1909–. Local records: civil registration, 1912–.

San Miguel (municipality) was an early Spanish town which was annexed to Alangalang from 1903 to circa 1910. FHL local records: civil registration, 1923–1924; notarial, 1911–. Local records: civil registration, 1945–.

Santa Fé (municipality), also known as Esquala and Maslog, was established in 1949 from Palo. Local records: civil registration, 1949–.

Tabango (municipality), also known as Tabañgo and María Cristina, was an early Spanish town which was annexed to San Isidro in 1903, then separated in 1949. At the time of the separation, it acquired some territory from Leyte. Local records: civil registration, 1950–.

Tabontabon (municipality) was an early Spanish town annexed to Dagami from 1903 to 1953. Local records: civil registration, 1955–.

Tacloban City (city), an early Spanish town, was chartered as a city in June 1952. FHL local records: civil registration, 1921–1933; notarial, 1912–; birth certificates, 1955–1988; marriage contracts, 1956–1960; death certificates, 1975–1988. Local records: civil registration, 1901–.

Tanauan (municipality) was an early Spanish town. FHL local records: civil registration, 1922–1933; notarial, 1911–. Local records: civil registration, 1944–.

Tolosa (municipality) was an early Spanish town. FHL local records: civil registration, 1922–1933; notarial, 1911–. Local records: civil registration, 1902–.

Tunga (municipality), also known as Tuñga, was established in 1949. Local records: civil registration, 1949–.

Villaba (municipality), also known as Hamindangon, Nueva Galicia, Villa Alba, and Villava, was an early Spanish town annexed to San Isidro from 1903 to 1910. FHL local records: civil registration, 1922–1932; notarial, 1911–. Local records: civil registration, 1945–.

Maguindanao. This province occupies the southwest coast of the island of Mindanao in the southern Philippines. Until 1966 it was a portion of the former province of Cotabato as were the modern provinces of North Cotabato and Sultan Kudarat. This area was a major center for commerce. Approximately three hundred years before the arrival of the Spanish, waves of immigrants from present-day Malaysia settled on the coast bringing with them Islam and traditions of local independencies. By the end of the fourteenth century, the Sultanate of Maguindanao was established by Sharif Mohammed Kabungsuwan. Throughout the sixteenth and seventeenth centuries the Spanish made attempts to subjugate this area. The last attempt was the construction of a post at Buhayon in 1639, but within a year it had to be abandoned. The Moros of Cotabato were left to themselves until 1851 when the Spanish established a naval base on the coast of Cotabato and in the next two decades carried out military expeditions, built forts, and positioned garrisons on the coast and in the interior. In 1862 the town of Cotabato was founded and made the capital of the district of Cotabato which was under the jurisdiction of Cebu. In 1898 Cotabato was made the fifth district of Mindanao. After Spain ceded the Philippines to the United States and until the arrival of American forces, a local government was established for the Christian towns and another for the Moro settlements. In June 1903 civil government was established by the Americans and Cotabato was made one of the five districts of the newly created Moro Province. In 1914 this province was dissolved and each of its districts became independent provinces under the general supervision of the Deportionment of Mindanao and Sulu. In 1939, in response to the newly passed Land Settlement Act, large numbers of immigrants from other parts of the Philippines moved to this area. During World War II, there was much small scale fighting between resistance forces and the Japanese Army. As a result, the region was never fully controlled by the Japanese even though entire towns were burned along with their records. With liberation and then independence in 1947, this area remained underdeveloped. In 1966, in an attempt to make government more effective, the province was divided into Cotabato and South Cotabato. Cotabato was divided again in November 1973 into the provinces of Maguindanao and Sultan Kudarat.

FHL provincial records: civil registration (1867–1897); birth records (1969–1987); marriage contracts (1974–1986); death certificates (1975–1991); deportations (1865–1898); military induction records (1869–1896);

public records (1894–1897); records of lending (1878–1898); school records (1871–1898); and Census of Chinese (1878–1898).

Localities and their records:

Ampatuan (municipality) was established in 1959 from Datu Piang. Local records: civil registration, 1959–.

Barira (municipality) was established in 1977 from Buldon.

Buldon (municipality) was established in 1961 from Parang. Barira separated in 1977. Local records: civil registration, 1962–.

Buluan (municipality) was established in 1947. FHL local records: civil registration, 1929–1931. Local records: civil registration, 1946–.

Cotabato City (city), also known as Mindanao and Maguindanao, was the capital of the province from 1872 to 1973. Kabuntalan separated in 1949. It was chartered in June 1959. FHL local records: birth certificates, 1956–1988; marriage contracts, 1951–1960; death certificates, 1975–1988; notarial, 1911–. Local records: civil registration, 1967–.

Datu Paglas (municipality) was established in 1973 from Columbio of the province of Sultan Kudarat.

Datu Piang (municipality), also known as Dulawan prior to 1954, was established in 1936. Talayan separated in 1976. FHL local records: civil registration, 1932–1934. Local records: civil registration, 1945–.

Dinaig (municipality) was established in 1947. Salaman was annexed in 1947, but later separated. FHL local records: civil registration, 1923–1930. Local records: civil registration, 1945–.

Kabuntalan (municipality), also known as Tumbao prior to 1976, was established in 1949 from Cotabato. Local records: civil registration, 1967–.

Maganoy (municipality), established in 1963, was once the capital of the province. FHL local records: civil registration, 1924–1931. Local records: civil registration, 1967–.

Matanog (municipality) was established in 1975 from Parang.

Pagalungan (municipality) was established in 1947. FHL local records: notarial, 1931–1936. Local records: civil registration, 1945–.

Parang (municipality), also known as Pollok and Polloc, was established early, dissolved circa 1945, and reestablished in 1947. Buldon (1967) and Matanog (1975) separated. FHL local records: civil registration, 1925–1926; notarial, 1937–1938. Local records: civil registration, 1945–.

South Upi (municipality) was established in 1976 from Upi.

Sultan Kudarat (city), also known as Nuling prior to 1969, was established in 1947. It has been the provincial capital since July 1977. FHL local records: notarial, 1927–1936. Local records: civil registration, 1945–.

Sultan sa Barongis (municipality), also known as Lambayong, was established in 1952. Local records: civil registration, 1952–.

Talayan (municipality) was established in 1976 with the consolidation of villages from Dinaig and Datu Paing.

Upi (municipality) was established in 1955 from Dinaig. South Upi separated in 1976. Local records: civil registration, 1955–.

Manila and Metropolitan Manila. The coming of the Spanish gave Manila its central place in the history of the Philippines. In 1570 after Governor-General Legazpi had been driven from Cebu and Panay by Portuguese pirates and native forces, he organized a series of expeditions to the Manila area. By 1571 he was able to move his government there after overcoming considerable local opposition. In 1574 another enemy soon materialized in the person of Chinese pirate Limahong who was hired by Chinese traders who resented Spanish attempts to control and tax them. Although Limahongform's forces were defeated by the Spanish (with difficulty), throughout the seventeenth century, Chinese riots were a threat to Spanish control of Manila. Manila was the capital of Philippines as well as the capital of the province of Manila which early in its history included most of the island of Luzon. From this huge province, called Tondo throughout most of the Spanish period, the provinces of Pampanga, Bulacan, Rizal, Laguna, Batangas, Quezon, Mindoro, Masbate, and Marinduque eventually separated. During the Seven Years War, the British occupied Manila from 1762 to 1764 and retreating Spanish forces burned many valuable records. British troops, sacking the city, destroyed and looted still more. Circa 1853 the District of the San Mateo Mountains was established by combining towns from the provinces of Tondo and Laguna. It was renamed Morong District and Tondo was given the name of Manila circa 1859. Beginning in 1892 the revolutionary movement grew in Manila and its suburbs. By 1896 it had broken out into open rebellion. With the advent of the Spanish-American War in 1898, Spanish power was swept aside by American and Philippine forces. Spain, however, ceded the Philippines only to the United States causing Filipino and American forces to engage in the "Mock Battle" of Manila in August 1898. After a three-year struggle, General Emilio Aguinaldo surrendered to American troops at Palanan in the province of Isabela in March 1901. By July of that year a civil government was established by the Americans in Manila. Via administrative reforms carried out early in the American period, the province of Manila was dissolved—its towns combined with those of the District of Morong to form the new province of Rizal. After a year of adjustment, the towns and districts of Manila were defined in essentially the same configuration as they are at present. With the coming of World War II in 1942, the towns and municipalities of Quezon City, Caloocan, San Juan del Monte, Mandaluyong, Makati, Pasay, and Parañaque were joined with Manila City to form "Greater Manila" and simplify administration during the war. Captured by the Japanese, Manila was liberated after a long hard campaign in which most of the city was destroyed. Shortly after the war "Greater Manila" was dissolved, and in 1948, the capital was transferred to Quezon City. In 1976 it was returned to Manila and Metropolitan Manila, properly the "National Capital Region," was created. One of the major innovations in government after independence was the development of a system of administration for the area around Manila, a city which is highly urbanized and contains many of the essential institutions of Philippine society: the national government, the center of the Roman Catholic Church in the Philippines, major universities and research centers, and industry and transportation. A ''mega city'' was created which has four cities and thirteen municipalities from surrounding provinces overseen by a governor, but partially remaining under their previous provincial jurisdictions.

FHL provincial records: See the records described in the section concerning national records.

Localities and their records:

Caloocan (city), also known as Aromahan, Espina, and Libis Espina, was an early Spanish town to which Novaliches was annexed from 1903 to 1949. FHL local records: civil registration, 1850–1897, 1922–1932; notarial, 1911–; birth certificates, 1949–1988; death certificates, 1975–1988; death records, 1886–1895; land records, 1881–1896; military induction records, 1868–1895; San Roque parish registers, 1901–1956. Local records: civil registration, 1916–.

Las Piñas (municipality) was an early Spanish town which was annexed to Parañaque from 1903 to 1907. FHL local records: civil registration, 1797–1896, 1922–1932; birth certificates, 1972–1988; death certificates, 1977–1988; military induction records, 1868–1898; public records, 1884–1898; census, 1871–1894; Saint Joseph parish registers, 1777–1953. Local records: civil registration, 1908–.

Makati (municipality), also known as San Pedro, Macati, and San Pedro Makati, was an early Spanish town. Its name changed from San Pedro Makati to Makati in 1914. FHL local records: civil registration, 1850–1855, 1921–1931; notarial, 1911–; birth certificates, 1977–1988; death certificates, 1977–1988; military induction records, 1874–1897; public records, 1888–1898; census, 1874–1895; Saint Peter parish registers, 1809–1855. Local records: civil registration, 1939–.

Malabon (municipality), also known as Tambobong, was an early Spanish town to which Navotas was annexed from 1903 to 1906. FHL local records: civil registration, 1836–1898, 1928–1932; notarial, 1914–; birth certificates, 1977–1988; death certificates, 1977–1988; land records, 1847–1887; Immaculate Concepción (located in village of Concepción) parish registers, 1907–1949; San Bartolomé (village of San Bartolomé) parish registers, 1673–1928. Local records: civil registration, 1903–.

Mandaluyong (municipality), also known as San Felipe, San Felipe Neri, and Mandaluyon, was an early Spanish town to which San Juan del Monte was annexed and separated from in 1907. It changed its name from San Felipe Neri to Mandaluyong in 1931. FHL local records: civil registration, 1866–1893, 1923–1924; notarial, 1903–; birth certificates, 1977–1988; death certificates, 1977–1988; military induction records, 1868–1896; census, 1877–1896; Immaculate Conception parish registers, 1863–1943. Local records: civil registration, 1914–.

Manila (city) was also known as Maynilad, Manilad, and Mainila. It includes the municipalities of Binondo (early Spanish town also known as Prensa and San Nicholas), Ermita (early Spanish town also known as La Hermita and Hermita), Intramuros, Malate (also known as Maalat, Mahalat, and Malatte), Paco (also known as Dilao, San Fernando de Dilao, and Bagundiwa), Pandacan (also known as Pandanan), Quiapo (also known as Kiapo), Sampaloc (also known as Santa Mesa, Sampalok, and Camachilihan), San Miguel, Santa Ana (also known as San Andres, Bukid, Namayan, and Santa Ana de Sapa), Santa Cruz, Santa Mesa, Tondo (also known as Tongdo and Tundo), and Marikina (also known as Mariquina and Jesus de la Peña). FHL local records: Binondo—civil registration 1814–1899, notarial 1919–, death certificates 1875–1899, military induction records 1861–1897, public records 1882–1898, census 1871–1898, Our Lady of the Most Holy Rosary parish registers 1894–1956; Ermita—civil registration 1863–1900, death certificates 1885–1895, military induction records 1868–1898, public records 1885–1898, census 1875–1898, Saint Vincent de Paul parish registers 1909–1956; Malate—civil registration 1817–1897, military induction records 1868–1897, public records 1884–1898, census 1871–1898, records of lending 1875–1895; Paco—civil registration 1888–1894 and 1945–1961, military induction records 1868–1897, public records 1884–1898, records of lending 1859–1898, census 1881–1895, Holy Sepulcher parish registers 1945–1961; Pandacan—civil registration 1870–1895, military induction records 1868–1897, public records 1884–1898, census 1877–1896, records of lending 1870–1898, Holy Infant Jesus parish registers 1778–1934, Santo Niño parish registers 1831–1952; Quiapo—civil registration 1842–1898, military induction records 1868–1897, public records 1884–1898, census 1877–1896, records of lending 1860–1890, Saint John the Baptist parish registers 1856–1938, San Miguel parish registers 1831–1952; Sampaloc—civil registration 1858–1898, military induction records 1860–1897, public records 1885–1898, census 1870–1898, Our Lady of Loreto parish registers 1945–1947, Most Holy Trinity (village of Balic-Balic) parish registers 1931–1951, military induction records (village of Dapitan) 1891–1897; San Miguel—civil registration 1853–1895, military induction records 1868–1897, public records 1885–1898, census 1844–1898, records of lending 1885–1898, Saint Michael the Archangel parish registers 1642–1969; Santa Ana—civil registration 1872–1897, military induction records 1868–1898, public records 1890–1898, census 1871–1898, Our Lady of the Abandoned parish registers 1693–1951; Santa Cruz—civil registration 1885–1897, tax records 1856–1857, public records 1885–1898, census 1868–1898, Our Lady of the Pilar parish registers 1687–1972, Espíritu Santo parish registers 1923–1947; San Jose de Trozo (village in Santa Cruz)—civil registration 1882–1890, public records 1885–1898, records of lending 1865–1890; Santa Mesa—Sacred Heart of Jesus parish registers 1904–1964; Tondo—civil registration 1849–1875 and 1886–1895, military induction records 1854–1898, public records 1882–1898, records of lending 1870–1898, census 1875–1898; Marikina—civil registration 1851–1894 and 1922–1931, notarial 1906–, birth certificates

1977–1988, death certificates 1977–1993, military induction records 1868–1896, public records 1884–1898, census 1875–1898, Our Lady of the Abandoned parish registers 1899–1945. Local records: Marikina—civil registration, 1919–.

Muntinglupa (municipality), also known as Muntinlupa, was an early Spanish town which was annexed to Taguig from 1905 to 1917. FHL local records: civil registration, 1870–1891; birth certificates, 1977–1988; death certificates, 1977–1988; military induction records, 1868–1896; public records, 1884–1898; records of lending, 1863–1892; census, 1881–1894. Local records: civil registration, 1918–.

Navotas (municipality), also known as Tambobong and Nabotas, was an early Spanish town which was annexed to Malabon from 1903 to 1906. FHL local records: civil registration, 1870–1895, 1836–1898, 1922–1931, 1915–1986; notarial, 1904–; birth certificates, 1977–1988; death certificates, 1977–1988; military induction records, 1868–1897; public records, 1884–1897; census, 1866–1898; Saint Joseph parish registers, 1906–1958. Local records: civil registration, 1916–.

Parañaque (municipality), also known as Palañac, was an early Spanish town to which Las Piñas was annexed from 1903 to 1907. FHL local records: civil registration, 1870–1895, 1922–1933; notarial, 1912–; birth certificates, 1977–1988; death certificates, 1977–1988; birth records, 1903–1986, 1874–1893; marriage records, 1915–1946; death records, 1916–1986; land records, 1781–1897; military induction records, 1868–1897; public records, 1888–1898; census, 1858–1898; Saint Andrew, the Apostle, parish registers, 1682–1952. Local records: civil registration, 1903–.

Pasay City (city), also known as Pineda (prior to 1901), Pasay (1901–circa 1945), and Rizal City (circa 1945–1950), was chartered in June 1947. FHL local records: civil registration, 1870–1895, 1922–1931; notarial, 1908–; birth certificates, 1950–1988; death certificates, 1975–1988; land records, 1866–1868; military induction records, 1868–1897; public records, 1884–1898; census, 1875–1897; records of lending, 1856–1897; village of Malibay—notarial 1929–, public records 1884–1898; Saint Clare of Montefalco parish registers, 1864–1932; Our Lady of Sorrows parish registers, 1941–1964; Santa Clara parish registers, 1926–1947; Santa Rita (village of Baclaran) parish registers, 1906–1955. Local records: civil registration, 1901–.

Pasig (city), an early Spanish town, has been the capital of the province of Rizal since 1901. FHL local records: civil registration, 1815–1895, 1922–1932, 1913–1975; notarial, 1903–; birth certificates, 1977–1988; death certificates, 1977–1988; land records, 1789–1898; military induction records, 1874–1894; public records, 1894–1898; census, 1857–1898; Immaculate Conception parish registers, 1899–1955. Local records: civil registration, 1901–.

Pateros (municipality), also known as Agoho, was an early Spanish town which was annexed to Taguig from 1903 to 1909. FHL local records: civil registration, 1851–1892, 1922–1924; notarial, 1905–; birth certificates, 1977–1988; death certificates, 1977–1988; land records, 1801–1850; military induction records, 1862–1897; census, 1857–1898; records of lending, 1875–1898; San Roque parish registers, 1946–1958. Local records: civil registration, 1942–.

Quezon City (city) was chartered in October 1939. Annexed Novaliches in 1949. Novaliches (municipality), also known as Tala, was an early Spanish town which previously was annexed to Caloocan City (in 1903). FHL local records: birth certificates 1948–1987, death certificates 1947–1988, marriage contracts 1948–1960, notarial 1929–; Novaliches—civil registration 1870–1896, notarial 1912–, military induction records 1868–1898, public records 1884–1898, census 1879–1898, Our Lady of Mercy parish registers 1930–1972; San Pedro Bautista (in San Francisco del Monte) parish registers 1931–1969. Local records: civil registration, 1945–.

San Juan del Monte (municipality), also known as San Juan, was an early Spanish town which was annexed to Mandaluyong from 1903 to 1907. FHL local records: civil registration, 1847–1892, 1883–1894, 1922–1932; notarial, 1911–; birth certificates, 1977–1988; death certificates, 1977–1988; military induction records, 1861–1898; census, 1878–1898; Saint John the Baptist parish registers, 1894–1954. Local records: civil registration, 1910–.

San Vincente de Paul (municipality). FHL local records: Saint Vincent de Paul parish registers, 1909–1965.

Singalong (municipality). FHL local records: Saint Anthony of Padua parish registers, 1905–1929.

Taguig (municipality), also known as Tagig, was an early Spanish town to which Pateros and Muntinglupa were annexed in 1905, then separated in 1909 and 1917, respectively. FHL local records: civil registration, 1848–1897, 1921–1924; notarial, 1909–; birth certificates, 1977–1988; death certificates, 1977–1988; military induction records, 1868–1898; public records, 1880–1898; census, 1878–1892. Local records: civil registration, 1942–.

Trozo (municipality). FHL local records: civil registration, 1879–1892.

Valenzuela (municipality). FHL local records: notarial, 1960–; birth certificates, 1977–1988; death certificates, 1977–1988.

Marinduque. This province occupies the island of the same name just south of Luzon Island in the central Philippines. It was explored by the Spanish circa 1570 with settlements within a decade. In 1581 it was incorporated into the new province of Balayan (modern Batangas), but in the early seventeenth century it was separated and made portion of the province of Mindoro. In May 1901 American civil government was established in the region. At some point during this time Marinduque became a province, capital at Boac, which, in June 1902, annexed the former province of Mindoro and the islands of Lubang. In November of that year, the province of Marinduque was dissolved and annexed to the province of Tayabas (now Quezon). In August 1907, Marinduque was made a sub-province of Tayabas and, in February 1920, it was made an independent province.

FHL provincial records: birth records (1945–1988); marriage contracts (1947–1987); death certificates (1969–1988); and court records created by the Court of First Instance (1901–1903).

Localities and their records:

Boac (city), also known as Biac-na-Bayan, was an early Spanish town which annexed Mogpog from 1904 to circa 1918. FHL local records: notarial, 1903–; Immaculate Conception parish registers, 1807–1966. Local records: civil registration, 1901–.

Buenavista (municipality) was established in 1918 by the consolidation of villages from Gasan and Torrijos. FHL local records: civil registration, 1922–1931; notarial, 1921–. Local records: civil registration, 1915–.

Gasan (municipality) was an early Spanish town from which Buenavista separated in 1918. FHL local records: civil registration, 1922–1931; notarial, 1906–; Roman Catholic parish registers, 1839–1979. Local records: civil registration, 1902–.

Mogpog (municipality) was an early Spanish town which was annexed to Boac from 1904 to circa 1918. FHL local records: civil registration, 1922–1932; notarial, 1903–; Saint Isidore Labrador parish registers, 1884–1931. Local records: civil registration, 1945–.

Santa Cruz (municipality) was an early Spanish town. FHL local records: civil registration, 1922–1932; notarial, 1909–; Holy Cross parish registers, 1834–1934. Local records: civil registration, 1902–.

Torrijos (municipality), also known as Torrijo, was an early Spanish town. FHL local records: civil registration, 1929–1931; notarial, 1907–; Saint Ignatius Loyola parish registers, 1889–1900. Local records: civil registration, 1945–.

Masbate. This island province is located just south of the Bicol Peninsula on Luzon Island. It consists of the large island of Masbate, the smaller islands of Burias and Ticao, and fourteen still smaller islands. By 1569 the Spanish had explored these islands, but left them largely undeveloped. All were supposed to be part of the early province of Ibalon which developed into the modern province of Albay, but Cebu also had some interest in the islands. The seat of the government of the islands shifted from one small settlement to another until it was fixed in Masbate town which later became a city. The government records were kept in Cagay which was inland and, thus, not as vulnerable to Moro raids as the coastal settlements. In response to the gold strike of 1837 at Aroroy and the large growth in population, the government was reorganized with the islands of Masbate and Ticao forming a district (capital at San Jacinto) and the island of Burias forming another district (capital at San Pascual). These islands did not take part in the Philippine Revolution nor in the resistance to American forces. With the establishment of civil government in March 1901, the islands of Masbate, Ticao, and Burias were formed into a separate province; but in January 1906, they were made a sub-province of the province of Sorsogon. In February 1921, they again became a separate province.

FHL provincial records: civil registration (1857–1897); birth records (1945–1988); marriage contracts (1945–1987); death certificates (1955–1991); court records created by the Court of First Instance (1901–1903); military induction records (1875–1895); public records (1881–1898); school records (1859–1897); statistical reports (1896–1897); and Census of Chinese (1885–1894).

Localities and their records:

Aroroy (municipality), also known as Al-oro and Al-oroy, was an early Spanish town to which Baleno and San Agustin were annexed in 1903. Baleno separated in 1939. FHL local records: civil registration, 1922–1931; notarial, 1911–. Local records: civil registration, 1945–.

Baleno (municipality), also known as Daan-Lungsod, was an early Spanish town which was annexed to Aroroy from 1903 to 1949; Our Lady of the Pillar parish registers, 1858–1935. Local records: civil registration, 1949–.

Balud (municipality) was established in 1949 from Milagros. Local records: civil registration, 1949–.

Batuan (municipality), also known as Zaragoza, was established in 1951 from San Fernando. Local records: civil registration, 1952–.

Cataiñgan (municipality) was an early Spanish town from which Pio V. Corpuz and Placer separated in 1951 and 1949, respectively. FHL local records: civil registration, 1921–1931; notarial, 1911–; Saint Vincent Ferrer parish registers, 1892–1952. Local records: civil registration, 1948–.

Cawayan (municipality), also known as Caruca-wa-yan, was established in 1949 from Milagros. Local records: civil registration, 1949–.

Claveria (municipality) was an early Spanish town which was annexed to San Pascual from 1903 to 1959. Local records: civil registration, 1959–.

Dismasalang (municipality) was established in 1901. Annexed Palanas from 1903 to 1951. Uson separated in 1949. FHL local records: civil registration, 1921–1931; notarial, 1911–. Local records: civil registration, 1917–.

Esperanza (municipality) was established in 1959. Local records: civil registration, 1959–.

Mandaon (municipality) was an early Spanish town annexed to Milagros from 1911 to 1949. Local records: civil registration, 1949–.

Masbate (city), also known as Palanog and Wa-ay-ngaran, was an early Spanish town which annexed Magdalena in 1903 and Mobo in 1910. Mobo separated in 1949. It was the capital from 1901 to 1905, becoming the capital again in 1920. FHL local records: civil registration, 1923–1931; notarial, 1915–. Local records: civil registration, 1947–.

Milagros (municipality), also known as Asid and Acid, was an early Spanish town which annexed Malbug in 1903. Balud and Mandaon separated in 1949. FHL local records: civil registration, 1922–1930; notarial, 1912–; Saint Joseph parish registers, 1874–1944. Local records: civil registration, 1904–.

Mobo (municipality) was an early Spanish town which was annexed to Masbate from 1910 to 1949. FHL local records: notarial, 1911–; Saint Nicholas of Tolentino parish registers, 1898–1974. Local records: civil registration, 1949–.

Monreal (municipality) was established in 1957 from San Jacinto. Local records: civil registration, 1958–.

Palanas (municipality) was an early Spanish town which was annexed to Dimasalang from 1903 to 1951. FHL local records: Holy Name of Jesus parish registers, 1911–1942. Local records: civil registration, 1951–.

Pio V. Corpuz (municipality), also known as Limbuhan and Consolación, was established in 1951 from Cataingan. The name Limbuhan was changed to Pio V. Corpuz in 1954. Local records: civil registration, 1951–.

Placer (municipality), also known as Naocondacu, was established in 1907 from Palanas. Annexed to Cataiñgan, but separated in 1949.

San Fernando (municipality), also known as Tabunan, was an early Spanish town from which Batuan separated in 1951. FHL local records: civil registration, 1922–1931; notarial, 1911–. Local records: civil registration, 1932–.

San Jacinto (municipality) was an early Spanish town from which Monreal separated in 1957. Local records: civil registration, 1912–.

San Pascual (municipality) was an early Spanish town which annexed Claveria from 1903 to 1959. FHL local records: civil registration, 1922–1931; notarial, 1912–; Finding the Holy Cross parish registers, 1897–1956. Local records: civil registration, 1946–.

Uson (municipality), also known as Kulase, was an early Spanish town which was annexed to Dimasalang from 1912 to 1949. FHL local records: notarial, 1919–1920; Saints Peter and Paul parish registers, 1849–1948. Local records: civil registration, 1950–.

Misamis Occidental. This province occupies the eastern section of the Zamboanga Peninsula of the island of Mindanao in the southern portion of the Philippines. When the Spanish arrived in this area it was already populated with several coastal settlements. The Jesuits arrived in 1596, but left after encountering the hostility of the natives. The Augustinian Recollects reached this area in 1622. Their enlistment of the support of a local native leader Datu Salanpang precipitated a civil war with his overlord, Sultan Kudarat, ruler of Mindanao and Sulu. Spanish forces intervened, establishing control in the area. The Jesuits returned in 1624 and founded some mission centers. They were expelled in 1768 and succeeded by the Augustinian Recollects until their return in 1860. During the Philippine Revolution, they again evacuated the area and were replaced in 1921 by American Jesuits, who, in turn, were replaced by the Columbian Fathers in 1938. The Spanish government in this area focused on the Christian coastal communities, administering them from Cebu. In 1818 they were formed into a district. In 1850 the district became one of the four divisions of the Christian settlements in Mindanao which included the entire northern coast of that island. After the Philippine Revolution, American forces arrived in Misamis in 1899, but were unable to establish a civil government until May 1901. In June 1903 the new Moro Province was organized and the boundaries were revised again. The newly created district of Lanao included territory which split Misamis into two portions. In 1903, the province was reorganized, several municipalities consolidated, and a system of government of non-Christian groups introduced to include the Moros. In 1907 the northern half of modern Bukidnon province, which is inhabited by non-Christians, was separated and made the sub-province of Bukidnon under Agusan Province. Finally in November 1929, Misamis was divided into the provinces of Misamis Occidental and Misamis Oriental. In June 1957 the island of Camiguin separated from Misamis Oriental as a sub-province until, in June 1966, it became an independent province.

> FHL provincial records: civil registration (1864–1897), birth records (1946–1988), marriage contracts (1945–1987), death certificates (1960–1991), court records created by the Court of First Instance (1901–1903), deportations (1880–1891), military induction records (1877–1890), public records (1884–1898), records of lending (1876–1898), school records (1869–1898), statistical reports (1896), tax records (1843–1858), and Census of Chinese (1884–1895).

Localities and their records:

Aloran (municipality), also known as Anoran, was an early Spanish town which was annexed to Oroquieta at end of the Spanish period, then separated in 1917. Concepcion separated in 1956. FHL local records: civil registration, 1922–1932; notarial, 1925–. Local records: civil registration, 1918–.

Baliangao (municipality), also known as Baling-langaw, was an early Spanish town annexed to Plaridel (then named Langaran) in late nineteenth century and separated in 1910. FHL local records: civil registration, 1922–1931; notarial, 1911–. Local records: civil registration, 1913–.

Bonifacio (municipality), also known as Ligson and Digson, was established in 1940 from Tangub. Local records: civil registration, 1940–.

Calamba (municipality), also known as Suloman, was established in 1947 from Plaridel. Local records: civil registration, 1948–.

Clarin (municipality), also known as Locolan and Locoland, was established in 1921 from Ozamiz. FHL local records: civil registration, 1922–1931; notarial, 1925–. Local records: civil registration, 1921–.

Concepción (municipality) was established as a municipality (1956) from Aloran. It was made a municipal district (1967), but became a municipality again a year later. Local records: civil registration, 1957–.

Jiménez (municipality), also known as Palilan, Polilan, and Geminez, was an early Spanish town from which Panaon (1966) and Sinacaban (1949) separated. FHL local records: civil registration, 1922–1931; notarial, 1909–. Local records: civil registration, 1902–.

Lopez-Jaena (municipality), also known as Baisong, Manella, and Daisug, was established in 1929 from Plaridel. FHL local records: civil registration, 1929–1933; notarial, 1929–. Local records: civil registration, 1950–.

Oroquieta City (city), also known as Jiménez, Layanan, and Layawan, was an early Spanish town from which Aloran separated in 1917. It was chartered in January 1970 and has been the capital of the province since January 1930. FHL local records: civil registration, 1921–1932; notarial, 1911–; birth certificates, 1969–1988; death certificates, 1975–1988. Local records: civil registration, 1907–.

Ozamiz City (city), also known as Misamis and Misamiz, was an early Spanish town and, during the Spanish period, was a provincial capital. Annexed Tudela from

1903 to 1921. Tangub (1930) and Clarin (1921) separated. It was chartered as a city in July 1949. FHL local records: civil registration, 1922–1931; notarial, 1911–; birth certificates, 1950–1988; marriage contracts, 1950–1960; death certificates, 1975–1988. Local records: civil registration, 1937–.

Panaon (municipality) was established in 1966 from Jiménez. Local records: civil registration, 1968–.

Plaridel (municipality), also known as Langaran prior to 1914, was an early Spanish town. Lopez-Jaena (1929) and Baliangao (1910) separated. FHL local records: civil registration, 1922–1931; notarial, 1911–. Local records: civil registration, 1913–.

Sapang Dalaga (municipality) was established in 1957. Local records: civil registration, 1957–.

Sinacaban (municipality) was established in 1949 from Jiménez. Local records: civil registration, 1949–.

Tangub City (city), also known as Bawang and Regidor, was established in 1930 from Ozamiz and chartered in February 1968. Bonifacio separated in 1940. FHL local records: civil registration, 1930–1931; notarial, 1928–; birth certificates, 1968–1987; death certificates, 1977–1988. Local records: civil registration, 1948–.

Tudela (municipality), also known as Loculan and Lucso-on, was an early Spanish town annexed to Ozamiz from 1903 to 1921. Local records: civil registration, 1921–.

Misamis Oriental. This province occupies a portion of the northern coast of the island of Minadanao. In November 1929 the former province of Misamis was divided into Misamis Occidental and Misamis Oriental. For a brief administrative history of Misamis see the section on Misamis Occidental above. In June 1957 Camiguin was made a sub-province of Misamis Oriental and in June 1966 it became a full province.

FHL provincial records: See the section on Misamis Occidental above.

Localities and their records:

Alubijid (municipality) was an early Spanish town annexed to Cagayan de Oro from 1903 to 1940. Laguindingan separated in 1963. Local records: civil registration, 1940–.

Balingasag (municipality) was an early Spanish town to which the following municipalities were annexed in 1903, then separated: Jasaan (1948), Langonglong (1949), and Salay (circa 1918). FHL local records: civil registration, 1924–1930; notarial, 1911–. Local records: civil registration, 1913–.

Balingoan (municipality) was established in 1952 from Talisayan. FHL local records: notarial, 1939–1940. Local records: civil registration, 1952–.

Binuangan (municipality) was established in 1968 from Salay. Local records: civil registration, 1972–.

Cagayan de Oro (city), also known as Kalambaguhan, Cagayan, Cagayhaan, and Cagayan de Misamis was an early Spanish town to which were annexed in 1903, then separated: Alubijid (1940), Opol (1950), and El Salvador (1948). It was chartered in June 1950. FHL local records: civil registration, 1922–1932; notarial, 1910–; birth certificates, 1950–1980; marriage contracts, 1950–1960; death certificates, 1975–1988. Local records: civil registration, 1945–.

Claveria (municipality), also known as Ticala, was established in 1950. It was annexed to Misamis Oriental from Bukidnon province in 1921 and was a municipal district until 1950. Local records: civil registration, 1943–.

El Salvador (municipality), also known as Salvador, was an early Spanish town annexed to Cagayan de Oro from 1903 to 1948. FHL local records: notarial, 1911–; Saint Our Lady of Snows parish registers, 1866–1930. Local records: civil registration, 1948–.

Ginoog (city), also known as Gingood, Hingooc, Hingoog, and Pingoog, was an early Spanish town that was annexed to Talisayan from 1903 to 1907. Magsaysay separated in 1948. It was chartered in 1960. FHL local records: civil registration, 1928; notarial, 1911–; birth certificates, 1954–1988; death certificates, 1976–1988; Our Lady of the Snows parish registers, 1866–1930. Local records: civil registration, 1909–.

Gitagum (municipality) was established in 1961. Local records: civil registration, 1961–.

Initao (municipality) was an early Spanish town, a portion of which was annexed to the province of Lanao. Naawan and Libertad separated in 1957 and 1963, respectively. FHL local records: civil registration, 1922–1931; notarial, 1910–. Local records: civil registration, 1921–.

Jasaan (municipality) was an early Spanish town which was annexed to Balingasag from 1903 to 1948. FHL local records: Immaculate Conception parish registers, 1820–1944. Local records: civil registration, 1948–.

Kinogitan (municipality), also known as Quinoguitan, was established in 1929 from Talisayan. FHL local records: civil registration, 1929–1931; notarial, 1915–. Local records: civil registration, 1946–.

Lagonglong (municipality), also known as Lagoniong, was established in 1949 from Balingasag. Local records: civil registration, 1949–.

Laguindingan (municipality) was established in 1963 from Alubijid. Local records: civil registration, 1963–.

Libertad (municipality) was annexed to Initao from 1954 to 1963. Local records: civil registration, 1963–.

Lugait (municipality) was established in 1961. Local records: civil registration, 1961–.

Magsaysay (municipality), also known as Linugos, was established in 1948 from Gingoog. Local records: civil registration, 1948–.

Manticao (municipality) was established in 1949. Local records: civil registration, 1949–.

Medina (municipality). Local records: civil registration, 1948–.

Naawan (municipality), also known as Naauan, was established in 1957 from Initao. Local records: civil registration, 1957–.

Opol (municipality) was an early Spanish town annexed to Cagayan de Oro from 1903 to 1950. Local records: civil registration, 1950–.

Salay (municipality) was an early Spanish town annexed to Balingasag from 1903 to circa 1918. Binuangan separated in 1968. FHL local records: civil registration, 1922–1930; notarial, 1920–. Local records: civil registration, 1919–.

Subongcogon (municipality) was established in 1963. Local records: civil registration, 1963–.

Tagoloan (municipality), also known as Kabuñgahan and Manaol, annexed the former municipalities of Agusan and Santa Ana in 1903. Villanueva separated in 1962. Local records: civil registration, 1945–.

Talisayan (municipality) was an early Spanish town to which Gingoo was annexed from 1903 to 1907. Kinogitan (1929) and Baliñgoan (1952) separated. FHL local records: civil registration, 1928–1932; notarial, 1911–. Local records: civil registration, 1945–.

Villanueva (municipality) was established in 1962 from Tagoloan. Local records: civil registration, 1962–.

Mountain Province.

This inland province occupies the interior of the northern portion of the island of Luzon in the northern Philippines. It comprises the high mountain ranges of Luzon which are the source of many of the island's rivers. Though an occasional military expedition was sent to area and a few mission centers were established, this area was one of the least accessible and hospitable parts of the Philippines. In 1829 an expedition led by Guillermo Galvey went to the District of Benguet. He was impressed with the possibilities of development there, returning several times and founding various settlements. The provinces developed around the districts that he and those who followed after him established. Lepanto became a province in 1952, Bontoc in 1859. In 1889 a military district was established in modern Kalinga; followed the next year by one in modern Cayapa and Cabugaoan. For more information, see the sections on the other portions of provinces that were part of the Mountain Province during the Spanish period: Kalinga-Apayao, Ifugao, and Benguet. In May 1902, the new province of Lepanto-Bontoc was formed containing the three sub-provinces of Lepanto, Bontoc, and Amburayan. In May 1907 Kalinga was separated from Cagayan and became a sub-province of Lepanto-Bontoc. When, in August 1908, that province was abolished, its four sub-provinces were combined with the three sub-provinces of Apayao (Apayao, Ifugao, and Benguet) to form the Mountain Province. In February 1920 the sub-provinces of Amburayan and Lepanto were dissolved, a portion going to Benguet and a portion to La Union. Finally in June 1966 the Mountain Province was abolished and the provinces of Benguet, Ifugao, Kalinga-Apayao, and Bontoc were formed. Later Bontoc changed its name to the Mountain Province although its territory included only one of the seven sub-provinces that had been part of the Mountain Province in 1908.

> FHL provincial records: birth records (1945–1988), marriage contracts (1946–1986), death certificates (1961–1991), records of lending (1873–1898), school records (1871–1898), statistical reports (1896), and Census of Chinese (1886).

Localities and their records:

Barlig (municipality) was established in 1963. FHL local records: civil registration, 1930. Local records: civil registration, 1946–.

Bauko (municipality) was an early Spanish town, established as a municipality in 1963, which was a portion of Lepanto Sub-province from 1902 to 1920.

FHL local records: civil registration, 1922–1931; notarial, 1950–; Our Blessed Lady of Lourdes parish registers, 1908–1971. Local records: civil registration, 1946–.

Besao (municipality) was an early Spanish town which was portion of Lepanto Sub-province until 1920. It was established as a municipality in 1963. FHL local records: civil registration, 1922–1934. Local records: civil registration, 1945–.

Bontoc (city) was an early Spanish town which was established in 1963. FHL local records: civil registration, 1921–1931; notarial, 1902–; civil registration (village of Talubin), 1922–1931; Santa Rita parish registers, 1893–1973. Local records: civil registration, 1955–.

Calao (municipality) was in the sub-province of Ifugao. FHL local records: civil registration, 1922–1924.

Natonin (municipality) was established in 1963. Paracelis separated in 1966. FHL local records: civil registration, 1922–1931. Local records: civil registration, 1947–.

Paracelis (municipality), also known as Paracales, was established in 1966 from Natonin. Local records: civil registration, 1962–.

Sabangan (municipality) was established in 1963. FHL local records: civil registration, 1922–1931. Local records: civil registration, 1916–.

Sadanga (municipality), also known as Saddanga and Sadañga, was established in 1963. FHL local records: civil registration, 1922–1931. Local records: civil registration, 1945–.

Tadian (municipality), also known as Kayan and Cayan, was an early Spanish town. The name Kayan was changed to Tadian in 1959. FHL local records: civil registration, 1922–1931; civil registration (village of Banaao), 1925–1931. Local records: civil registration, 1946–.

Negros del Norte.

This province separated from Negros Occidental in 1986. See the section on Negros Occidental below for its history.

> FHL provincial records: See the section on Negros Occidental below.

Localities and their records:

Bago City (city) was an early Spanish town, a portion of which was annexed to Pulupandan during the Philippine Revolution, but returned in 1903. It was chartered in January 1966. FHL local records: civil registration, 1922–1932, 1945–1990; notarial, 1906–; birth certificates, 1965–1987; death certificates, 1975–1988; Saint John the Baptist parish registers, 1848–1968. Local records: civil registration, 1945–.

Cadiz City (city), also known as Hitalon, Valdevieso, and Cadiz Nuevo, was an early Spanish town. It was chartered in June 1967. FHL local records: civil registration, 1921–1931; notarial, 1904–; birth certificates, 1968–1988; death certificates, 1977–1988. Local records: civil registration, 1946–.

Calatrava (municipality) was an early Spanish town which was annexed to San Carlos from 1903 to circa 1919. FHL local records: civil registration, 1924–1932, 1954–1978; notarial, 1923–; Saints Peter and Paul parish registers, 1922–1940. Local records: civil registration, 1945–.

Enrique B. Magalona (municipality), also known as Saravia, Sarabia, and Tukgawan, was an early Spanish town. Its name changed from Saravia to Enrique B. Magalona in 1967. FHL local records: civil registration, 1923–1932, 1946–1989; notarial, 1905–. Local records: civil registration, 1943–.

Escalante (municipality) was an early Spanish town. FHL local records: civil registration, 1921–1931, 1943–1990; notarial, 1911–; Saint Francis of Assisi parish registers, 1860–1931. Local records: civil registration, 1947–.

Manapla (municipality) was an early Spanish town. FHL local records: civil registration, 1922–1930; notarial, 1903–. Local records: civil registration, 1945–.

Sagay (municipality) was an early Spanish town. FHL local records: civil registration, 1922–1931, 1945–1990; notarial, 1910–. Local records: civil registration, 1945–.

Toboso (municipality). FHL local records: notarial, 1950–1953. Local records: civil registration, 1948–.

Victorias (municipality) was also known as Victoria and Malijao. FHL local records: civil registration, 1922–1927, 1942–1989; notarial, 1903–; Our Lady of Victory parish registers, 1918–1947. Local records: civil registration, 1945–.

Negros Occidental. This province occupies the southwestern portion of the island of Negros. It shares the island with the provinces of Negros Oriental and Negros del Norte. When the Spanish first arrived, they called it Buglas, but changed it to Negros in response to the Negrito settlements found there. Since the western side was close to the province of Iloilo, it was governed from Iloilo, while the eastern portion came under the jurisdiction of Cebu. In 1768 the two portions of the island were combined into one district. In 1856 this district was made a province as a mark of its growing importance to a newly developed sugar industry and the population growth it had undergone as it absorbed migrants coming to the area from Panay Island to work. In 1890 the province was split into Negros Oriental and Negros Occidental. When the Spanish were forced to evacuate the island during the Philippine Revolution in 1898, the revolutionary government united the two portions into the Estado Cantonal de Negros and an election was held for representatives to a provincial legislature. When American forces arrived, countered all resistance, and established a civil government in April 1901, the province was redivided.

FHL provincial records: civil registration (1886–1908), birth records (1945–1988), marriage contracts (1945–1987), death certificates (1960–1991), court records created by the Court of First Instance (1885–1902), land records (1850–1889), military induction records (1870–1897), public records (1887–1898), records of lending (1867–1898), school records (1860–1898), tax records (1814–1840), and Census of Chinese (1889–1897).

Localities and their records:

Bacolod City (city), also known as Bacolot, was an early Spanish town which was the capital of Negros from 1849 to 1890. It has been the capital of Negros Occidental since 1890. Annexed a portion of Sum-ag in 1903. The city was chartered in June 1938. FHL local records: civil registration, 1922–1931, 1945–1988; notarial, 1911–; birth certificates, 1945–1988; marriage contracts, 1946–1955; death certificates, 1975–1988; cemetery records of Rolling Hills Memorial, 1982–1990; Saint Sebastian parish registers, 1755–1976; Saint John Nepomuceno (located at Sum-ag) parish registers, 1855–1949. Local records: civil registration, 1901–.

Binalbagan (municipality) was an early Spanish town to which village of Soledad was annexed in 1903. FHL local records: civil registration, 1922–1932, 1945–1990; notarial, 1911–. Local records: civil registration, 1945–.

Candoni (municipality) was established in 1958. FHL local records: civil registration, 1961–1990. Local records: civil registration, 1961–.

Cauayan (municipality) was established in 1903 from consolidation of the former municipalities of Isin and Guijulngan (province of Negros Oriental); the latter separated in 1914. FHL local records: civil registration, 1922–1932, 1946–1990; notarial, 1909–. Local records: civil registration, 1946–.

Himamaylan (municipality), also known as Jimamailan, Simamailan, and Himaucaylan, was early Spanish town and capital of province of Negros until 1849. FHL local records: civil registration, 1922–1930; notarial, 1910–. Local records: civil registration, 1948–.

Hinigaran (municipality), also known as Jinigaran, Guinigaran, and Ginigaran, was an early Spanish town. FHL local records: civil registration, 1922–1931, 1912–1990; notarial, 1911–; Saint Mary Magdalene parish registers, 1866–1948. Local records: civil registration, 1912–.

Hinoba-an (municipality), also known as Asia prior to 1959, was established in 1948. Local records: civil registration, 1949–.

Ilog (municipality), also known as San Juan de Ilog, was an early Spanish town which annexed Kabankalan from 1903 to 1907. FHL local records: civil registration, 1922–1931, 1946–1989; notarial, 1911–. Local records: civil registration, 1945–.

Isabela (municipality) was an early Spanish town from which Moises Padilla separated in 1957. FHL local records: civil registration, 1922–1931, 1946–1990; notarial, 1911–. Local records: civil registration, 1946–.

Kabankalan (municipality), also known as Cauancalan, Cabangalan, and Cabancalan was an early Spanish town which was annexed to Ilog from 1903 to 1907. FHL local records: civil registration, 1922–1931, 1943–1990; notarial, 1911–. Local records: civil registration, 1908–.

La Carlota (city), also known as Carlota, was an early Spanish town which annexed San Enrique from 1903 to 1918. It was chartered in January 1966. FHL local records: civil registration, 1922–1935, 1947–1990; notarial, 1911–; birth certificates, 1966–1987; death certificates, 1976–1988; Our Lady of Peace parish registers, 1873–1952. Local records: civil registration, 1947–.

La Castellana (municipality) was an early Spanish town which was annexed to Pontevedra from 1903 to 1918. FHL local records: civil registration, 1922–1935, 1935–1990; notarial, 1928–. Local records: civil registration, 1935–.

Moises Padilla (municipality), also known as Magallon prior to 1957, was established in 1951 from Isabela. Local records: civil registration, 1951–.

Murcia (municipality) was an early Spanish town to which portion of Sum-ag was annexed in 1903. FHL local records: civil registration, 1922–1931, 1945–1990;

----

notarial, 1905–; Immaculate Conception parish registers, 1861–1952. Local records: civil registration, 1945–.

Pontevedra (municipality), also known as Marayo and Ponte Piedra, was an early Spanish town which annexed La Castellana from 1903 to 1918. FHL local records: civil registration, 1922–1932, 1946–1990; notarial, 1911–. Local records: civil registration, 1946–.

Pulupandan (municipality) was an early Spanish town to which a portion of Bago was annexed during the Philippine Revolution, but separated in 1903. Annexed Valladolid from 1903 to 1917. FHL local records: civil registration, 1922–1933, 1944–1990; notarial, 1915–. Local records: civil registration, 1945–.

San Carlos (city), also known as Nabingkalan, was an early Spanish town to which Calatrava (now in Negros del Norte) was annexed from 1903 to circa 1919. FHL local records: civil registration, 1921–1933, 1937–1990; notarial, 1903–; birth certificates, 1950–1988; marriage contracts, 1949–1960; death certificates, 1976–1988; Saint Charles Borromeo parish registers, 1892–1949; medical records, 1920–1930; medical records for a specific *barangay* or district of San Carlos City (the name of the barangay is in parentheses): 1977–1990 (San Juan), 1977–1989 (Ermita), 1968–1977 (Bulwangan), 1987 (Rizal), 1969–1989 (Quezon Proper), 1987–1989 (Maglunod), 1986–1989 (Cabugan), no dates (Palampas and Guadalupe), 1977–1989 (Punao). Local records: civil registration, 1945–.

San Enrique (municipality) was an early Spanish town which was annexed to La Carlota from 1903 to 1918. FHL local records: civil registration, 1922–1930, 1946–1990; notarial, 1904–; death records, 1946–1988; marriage contracts, 1949–1960; Purification of Our Lady parish registers, 1935–1946. Local records: civil registration, 1945–.

Silay (city), an early Spanish town, was chartered as a city in June 1957. FHL local records: civil registration, 1922–1933, 1911–1989; notarial, 1905–; birth certificates, 1949–1988; marriage contracts, 1949–1960; death certificates, 1976–1988. Local records: civil registration, 1911–.

Sipalay (municipality) was established in 1948. FHL local records: notarial, 1951–. Local records: civil registration, 1949–.

Talisay (municipality), also known as Minuluan, was an early Spanish town. FHL local records: civil registration, 1921–1933, 1943–1989; notarial, 1925–; Saint Nicholas of Tolentino parish registers, 1825–1947. Local records: civil registration, 1943–.

Valladolid (municipality) was an early Spanish town to which was annexed Pulupandan from 1903 to 1917. FHL local records: civil registration, 1922–1931; notarial, 1905–. Local records: civil registration, 1945–.

Negros Oriental. This province occupies the southeastern part of Negros Island. As it has been closely affiliated with the other provinces on this island, Negros del Norte and Negros Occidental, see the section on Negros Occidental above for a brief discussion of its administrative history. In 1971 the sub-province Siquijor was separated from Negros Oriental and made a full province.

FHL provincial records: See the section on Negros Occidental above.

Localities and their records:

Amlan (municipality), also known as Ayuquitan, Amblan, and Ayuquitan Nuevo, was an early Spanish town which was annexed to Ayuquitan in 1903. In 1950 it changed its name from Ayuquitan to Amlan. San José separated in 1955. FHL local records: civil registration, 1930–1931; notarials, 1920–; Saint Andrew, the Apostle, parish registers, 1863–1929. Local records: civil registration, 1944–.

Ayuñgon (municipality), also known as Ayungan and Ayongon, was established in 1924 from Tayasan. FHL local records: civil registration, 1921–1931; notarials, 1931–.

Bacong (municipality), also known as Bacon and Bocong, was an early Spanish town. FHL local records: civil registration, 1922–1931; notarials, 1907–; Saint Augustine of Hippo parish registers, 1871–1945. Local records: civil registration, 1912–.

Bais (city) was an early Spanish town to which Manjuyod was annexed from 1903 to 1909. Mabinay separated in 1960. It was chartered as a city in September, 1968. FHL local records: civil registration, 1922–1931, 1901–1990; notarials, 1907–; birth certificates, 1968–1988; death certificates, 1982–1988; Saint Nicholas of Tolentino parish registers, 1873–1949. Local records: civil registration, 1909–.

Basay (municipality, was established in 1968 from Bayawan.

Bayawan (municipality), also known as Bayauan, Tolon, Tolong, and Tolong Nuevo, was an early Spanish town which was annexed to Tolong in 1903. Santa Catalina separated in 1947. In 1952 the name was changed from Tolong Nuevo to Bayawan. FHL local records: civil registration, 1922–1929, 1949–1991; notarials, 1911–. Local records: civil registration, 1945–.

Bindoy (municipality), also known as Payabon, was established in 1949 from Manjuyod. FHL local records: civil registration, 1949–1990. Local records: civil registration, 1949–.

Canlaon (city), also known as Mabigo, was established in 1947 from Vallehermoso and chartered in April 1967. FHL local records: birth certificates, 1969–1988; death certificates, 1976–1988; notarials, 1950–. Local records: civil registration, 1947–.

Dauin (municipality), also known as Dauen and Danin, was an early Spanish town to which Zamboanguita was annexed from 1903 to 1909. FHL local records: civil registration, 1922–1931, 1945–1990; notarials, 1924–; Saint Nicholas of Tolentino parish registers, 1884–1906. Local records: civil registration, 1942–.

Dumaguete (city), also known as Dumaquette, Managuet, and Dananguet, was an early Spanish town to which Sibulan was annexed from 1903 to 1911. It was chartered in June 1948. Once the capital of the province from 1890 to 1898, it became the capital again in 1901. FHL local records: civil registration, 1922–1931, 1901–1990; notarials, 1904–; birth certificates, 1946–1988; marriage contracts, 1948–1960; death certificates, 1976–1988; Saint Catherine of Alexandria parish registers, 1869–1965. Local records: civil registration, 1901–.

Guihulngan (municipality), also known as Guihulugan, was an early Spanish town which was annexed to Cauayan, in the province of Negros Occidental, until 1914. Vallehermoso separated in 1914. FHL local records: civil registration, 1928–1931, 1902–1990; notarials,

1907–; Our Lady of Good Success parish registers, 1914–1964. Local records: civil registration, 1946–.

Jimalalud (municipality), also known as Jimalalot and Simalalub, was an early Spanish town to which Tayasan was annexed from 1903 to 1913. La Libertad separated in 1919. FHL local records: civil registration, 1914–1932; notarials, 1903–; Holy Child parish registers, 1914–1964. Local records: civil registration, 1957–.

La Libertad (municipality), also known as Libertad and Jinoba-an, was an early Spanish town which was annexed to Tayasan when it was annexed to Jimamalud in 1903. When Tayasan separated in 1913, La Libertad remained with Jimamalud, eventually separating in 1919. FHL local records: civil registration, 1922–1932, 1945–1990; notarials, 1920–; Saint Sebastian parish registers, 1924–1959. Local records: civil registration, 1945–.

Mabinay (municipality) was established in 1960 from Bais. Local records: civil registration, 1960–.

Manjuyod (municipality), also known as Manjuyud, was an early Spanish town which was annexed to Bais from 1903 to 1909. Bindoy separated in 1949. FHL local records: civil registration, 1922–1933, 1945–1990; notarials, 1930–; Saint Francis of Assisi parish registers, 1925–1987. Local records: civil registration, 1946–.

Pamplona (municipality), also known as Tampa, was established in 1950 from Tanjay. Local records: civil registration, 1950–.

San José (municipality) was established circa 1955 from Amlan. FHL local records: civil registration, 1955–1990. Local records: civil registration, 1955–.

Santa Catalina (municipality), also known as Teleng, Telong, Tolong, Old Tolong, and Tolong Viejo, was established in 1947 from Bayawan. The name of Tolong Viejo was changed to Santa Catalina in 1947. FHL local records: civil registration, 1943–1991. Local records: civil registration, 1948–.

Siaton (municipality) was an early Spanish town. FHL local records: civil registration, 1922–1931, 1947–1990; notarials, 1911–; Saint Nicholas de Bari parish registers, 1848–1948. Local records: civil registration, 1947–.

Sibulan (municipality) was an early Spanish town annexed to Dumaguete from 1903 to 1911. FHL local records: civil registration, 1922–1931, 1945–1991; notarials, 1911–; Saint Anthony of Padua parish registers, 1944–1957. Local records: civil registration, 1945–.

Tanjay (municipality), also known as Tanhay, was an early Spanish town and former capital of Negros Province. Pamplona separated in 1950. FHL local records: civil registration, 1922–1934, 1945–1990; notarials, 1911–; Saint James the Greater parish registers, 1800–1987. Local records: civil registration, 1945–.

Tayasan (municipality), also known as Tiyasan and Cabadiangan, was an early Spanish town to which Jimamalud and La Libertad were annexed in 1903, then separated in 1913 and 1919, respectively. Ayuñgon separated in 1924. FHL local records: civil registration, 1922–1932, 1954–1990; notarials, 1911–; Saint Anthony of Padua parish registers, 1932–1974. Local records: civil registration, 1937–.

Valencia (municipality), also known as Nueva Valencia, Ermita, and Luzuriaga, was an early Spanish town. The name Nueva Valencia was changed to Luzuriaga in 1905 and to Valencia in 1948. FHL local records: civil registration, 1922–1931, 1916–1990; Our Lady of the

Abandoned parish registers, 1855–1952. Local records: civil registration, 1916–.

Vallehermoso (municipality), also known as Kanlambat, was established in 1913 from Guihulngan. Canlaon separated 1946. FHL local records: civil registration, 1922–1931, 1945–1990; notarials, 1913–; Saint Isidore the Farmer parish registers, 1895–1954. Local records: civil registration, 1924–.

Zamboanguita (municipality) was an early Spanish town which was annexed to Dauin from 1903 to 1909. FHL local records: civil registration, 1911–1931, 1947–1990; notarials, 1953–; Saint Isidore the Farmer parish registers, 1861–1971. Local records: civil registration, 1947–.

North Cotabato.

North Cotabato. This inland province is located in the interior of Mindanao Island. In November 1973 the former province of Cotabato was divided into three provinces: Maguindanao, Sultan Kudarat, and North Cotabato. See the section on Maguindanao above for a history of the area.

FHL provincial records: civil registration (1862–1897), birth records (1967–1988), marriage contracts (1974–1987), death certificates (1974–1991), deportations (1865–1898), military induction records (1869–1896), public records (1894–1897), records of lending (1878–1898), school records (1871–1898), and Census of Chinese (1878–1898).

Localities and their records:

Alamada (municipality) was established in 1969 from Libungan. Local records: civil registration, 1970–.

Carmen (municipality) was established in 1956. Local records: civil registration, 1957–.

Kabacan (municipality) was established in 1947. Local records: civil registration, 1948–.

Kidapawan (city) was established in 1947. The following municipalities separated: Magpet (1963), Makilala (1954), and President Roxas (1967). Local records: civil registration, 1948–.

Libungan (municipality) was established in 1961. Alamada separated in 1969. Local records: civil registration, 1961–.

Magpet (municipality) was established in 1963 from Kidapawan. Local records: civil registration, 1963–.

Makilala (municipality) was established in 1954 from Kidapawan. Local records: civil registration, 1954–.

Matalam (municipality) was established in 1961. Local records: civil registration, 1966–.

Midsayap (municipality) was established in 1936. Kabuntalan, now in Maguindanao Province, separated. Local records: civil registration, 1945–.

M'lang (municipality) was established in 1951. Local records: civil registration, 1951–.

Pigkawayan (municipality) was established in 1953. Local records: civil registration, 1953–.

Pikit (municipality) was established in 1949 from Pagalungan of Maguindanao Province. Local records: civil registration, 1950–.

President Roxas (municipality) was established in 1967 from Kidapawan. Local records: civil registration, 1968–.

Tulunan (municipality) was established in 1961. Local records: civil registration, 1964–.

Northern Samar. This province occupies the northern portion of the island of Samar. On June 1965 the former province of Samar, which included the entire island, was divided into three provinces: Northern Samar, Eastern Samar, and Western Samar. Later Western Samar changed its name to Samar. For a discussion of the administrative history of Samar before its division, see the section on Samar below.

> FHL provincial records: civil registration (1808–1897), birth certificates (1967–1987), birth records (1945–1988), marriage contracts (1948–1987), death certificates (1966–1991), court records created by the Court of First Instance (1902–1903), deportations (1881–1898), land records (1894–1895), military induction records (1886–1887), notarials (1911–), records of lending (1872–1898), school records (1858–1898), statistical reports (1896), tax records (1832–1889), and Census of Chinese (1880–1898).

Localities and their records:

Allen (municipality), also known as La Granja, was established in 1903 from the consolidation of the former municipalities of La Granja and San Antonio. The following municipalities separated: San Antonio (1906), San Isidro (1954), and Victoria (1968). FHL local records: civil registration, 1922–1931; notarials, 1906–. Local records: civil registration, 1945–.

Biri (municipality) was established from Bobon in 1969. Local records: civil registration, 1970–.

Bobon (municipality) was an early Spanish town that was annexed to Catarman from 1903 to 1906. FHL local records: civil registration, 1923–1930; notarials, 1914–. Local records: civil registration, 1907–.

Capul (municipality), also known as Abak and Abac, was an early Spanish town from which San Vicente separated in 1966. FHL local records: civil registration, 1922–1931; notarials, 1905–. Local records: civil registration, 1945–.

Catarman (city) was an early Spanish town to which Bobon and Mondragon were annexed from 1903 to 1906. FHL local records: civil registration, 1921–1931; notarials, 1911–. Local records: civil registration, 1945–.

Catubig (municipality), also known as Kagninipa, was an early Spanish town. FHL local records: civil registration, 1920–1931; notarials, 1911–. Local records: civil registration, 1913–.

Gamay (municipality), an early Spanish town, was established in 1947 from Palapag. Lapinig separated in 1956. Local records: civil registration, 1947–.

Laoang (municipality), also known as Lawag and Lagwan, was an early Spanish town. FHL local records: civil registration, 1922–1926; notarials, 1911–. Local records: civil registration, 1945–.

Lapinig (municipality), a municipality from 1946 to 1950, was reestablished in 1956 with the consolidation of some territory from Gamay, Oras (Eastern Samar), and Jipapad (Eastern Samar). Local records: civil registration, 1956–.

Las Navas (municipality), also known as Bongto, Bongo-de, Binongto-an, and De Las Navas, was an early Spanish town annexed to Catubig from 1885 to 1948. Local records: civil registration, 1949–.

Lavezares (municipality), also known as Labezares and Pinonayan, was an early Spanish town. FHL local records: notarials, 1913–. Local records: civil registration, 1958–.

Mapanas (municipality) was established in 1966 from Gamay. Local records: civil registration, 1968–.

Mondragon (municipality), also known as Kinay, was an early Spanish town which was annexed to Catarman from 1903 to 1906. FHL local records: civil registration, 1922–1931; notarials, 1912–. Local records: civil registration, 1925–.

Palapag (municipality), also known as Palpag, was an early Spanish town from which Gamay separated in 1947. FHL local records: civil registration, 1922–1931; notarials, 1913–. Local records: civil registration, 1941–.

Pambujan (municipality) was an early Spanish town from which separated Silvino Lobos (1967) and San Roque (1960). FHL local records: civil registration, 1921–1931; notarials, 1911–. Local records: civil registration, 1945–.

Rosario (municipality) was established in 1969 from San Jose.

San Antonio (municipality), also known as Manoglaya, Sugodsugod, and Matabia, was an early Spanish town annexed to Allen from 1903 to 1906. FHL local records: civil registration, 1922–1931; notarials, 1913–. Local records: civil registration, 1914–.

San Isidro (municipality) was established in 1954 from Allen. Victoria separated in 1968. Local records: civil registration, 1954–.

San José (municipality) was established in 1919. Rosario separated in 1969. Local records: civil registration, 1947–.

San Roque (municipality) was established in 1960 from Pambujan. Local records: civil registration, 1969–.

San Vincente (municipality) was established in 1966 from Capul. Local records: civil registration, 1968–.

Silvino Lobos (municipality) was established in 1967 from the consolidation of territory from Pambujan and the municipal district of Matuginao. Local records: civil registration, 1968–.

Tagapul-an (municipality).

Victoria (municipality) was established in 1968 from San Isidro and Allen. Local records: civil registration, 1968–.

Nueva Ecija. This rich agricultural province lies in the central part of Luzon Island. The Augustinian missionaries were among the first to explore and establish settlements. They pushed up the Rio Grande de la Pampanga and organized towns and missions centers along its banks, some of which were later given to the Franciscans (1728). Because it was part of Pampanga until 1701 when Nueva Ecija was separated, see the section on that province for the administrative history prior to the eighteenth century. During the first half of the nineteenth century, Nueva Ecija grew by annexing territory from surrounding provinces. In 1853 a major portion of the province was lost when Principe District annexed the part of Nueva Ecija facing the Pacific Ocean. In 1856 Isabela province was organized from territory in Nueva Ecija as well as from the provinces of Nueva Vizcaya and Cagayan. In

1858 Infanta (the former Binangonan de Lampon) and the Polillo Islands were organized as the new district of Infanta which was placed under the jurisdiction of Laguna province. Nueva Ecija joined the Philippine Revolution against Spain in 1896 and, by 1898, had overthrown the regional government, establishing a provincial government which was soon dissolved by the arrival of American forces. By June 1901 a civil government was in place. In 1903 the American policy of cutting down on the size of government resulted in the temporary consolidation of many municipalities. The capital of the province was located at Cabanatuan until the town was destroyed by a fire in 1816. At that point, the capital was moved to San Isidro. It was transferred back to Cabanatuan from 1912 to 1965 when it was transferred to its current location in Palayan City.

> FHL provincial records: civil registration (1888–1897), birth records (1945–1988), marriage contracts (1945–1987), death certificates (1975–1988), death records (1888–1897), land records (1882–1897), inheritances (1842–1897), military induction records (1868–1897), public records (1884–1898), notarials (1911–), records of lending (1840–1898), school records (1824–1898), statistical reports (1896), tax records (1847–1877), and Census of Chinese (1824–1896).

Localities and their records:

Aliaga (municipality), also known as Alinga, was an early Spanish town to which Zaragosa was annexed from 1903 to 1907. FHL local records: civil registration, 1922–1931, 1971–1994; notarials, 1903–; Our Lady of Solera parish registers, 1871–1952. Local records: civil registration, 1910–.

Bongabon (municipality) was an early Spanish town from which separated Rizal (1913) and Laur (1917). FHL local records: civil registration, 1922–1931; notarials, 1907–. Local records: civil registration, 1913–.

Cabanatuan City (city), also known as Cabanatum and Kabanatuwaan, was an early Spanish town to which Santa Rosa was annexed from 1903 to 1907. General Mamerto Natividad separated in 1957. FHL local records: civil registration, 1923–1932; notarials, 1905–; birth certificates, 1948–1988; marriage contracts, 1947–1960; death certificates, 1975–1988; Saint Nicholas of Tolentino parish registers, 1860–1936. Local records: civil registration, 1945–.

Cabiao (municipality), also known as Cabia, Kabyaw, Kabyawan, and Batong Kabyawan was an early Spanish town which was annexed to San Isidro from 1903 to 1907. FHL local records: civil registration, 1922–1931; notarials, 1911–; Saint John Nepomuceno parish registers, 1847–1961. Local records: civil registration, 1945–.

Carranglan (municipality), also known as Dangla, Kadanglaan, and Carrancalan, was an early Spanish town. FHL local records: civil registration, 1922–1931; notarials, 1916–. Local records: civil registration, 1945–.

Cuyapo (municipality) was an early Spanish town to which Nampicuan was annexed from 1903 to 1907. Some villages were also separated to create the municipality of Talugtug in 1948. FHL local records: civil registration,

1921–1932; notarials, 1905–; Saint Roch parish registers, 1873–1944. Local records: civil registration, 1902–.

Gabaldon (municipality), also known as Bitulok (prior to 1953) and Sabani (1953 to 1955), was established in 1950 from Laur. Local records: civil registration, 1950–.

Gapan (municipality), also known as Gapang, was an early Spanish town. FHL local records: civil registration, 1921–1932; notarials, 1908–; Three Kings parish registers, 1721–1944. Local records: civil registration, 1902–.

General Mamerto Natividad (municipality) was established in 1957 from Cabanatuan. Local records: civil registration, 1957–.

General Tinio (municipality), also known as Papaya and Payapa, was established in 1921 from Penaranda. Its name was changed from Papaya to General Tinio in 1957. FHL local records: civil registration, 1920–1930; notarials, 1921–. Local records: civil registration, 1921–.

Guimba (municipality), also known as San Juan de Guimba prior to 1914, was an early Spanish town. It contributed territory to the formation of Talugtug in 1948. FHL local records: civil registration, 1922–1931, 1944–1994; notarials, 1903–. Local records: civil registration, 1914–.

Jaen (municipality) was an early Spanish town annexed to San Antonio from 1903 to 1907. FHL local records: civil registration, 1922–1931, 1961–1994; notarials, 1905–; Saint Augustine parish registers, 1871–1954. Local records: civil registration, 1961–.

Laur (municipality), also known as San Esteban, was established in 1917 from Bongabon. Gabaldon separated in 1950. FHL local records: civil registration, 1922–1932; notarials, 1918–. Local records: civil registration, 1950–.

Licab (municipality) was an early Spanish town. FHL local records: civil registration, 1922–1931; notarials, 1905–. Local records: civil registration, 1921–.

Llanera (municipality) was established in 1955 from territory from San José, Talavera, and Rizal. Local records: civil registration, 1955–.

Lupao (municipality) was an early Spanish town which was annexed to San José from 1903 to 1913. It contributed territory to the new municipality of Talugtug in 1948. FHL local records: civil registration, 1922–1931; notarials, 1911–. Local records: civil registration, 1913–.

Muñoz (municipality), also known as Lumang and Bayan, was established in 1913. FHL local records: civil registration, 1922–1931; notarials, 1911–. Local records: civil registration, 1945–.

Nampicuan (municipality), also known as Nampican, was an early Spanish town which was annexed to Cuyapo from 1903 to 1907. FHL local records: civil registration, 1922–1931; notarials, 1963–. Local records: civil registration, 1917–.

Palayan City (city), an early Spanish town, was chartered as a city in June 1965. It has been the provincial capital since 1969. FHL local records: birth certificates, 1968–1987. Local records: civil registration, 1969–.

Pantabañgan (municipality) was an early Spanish town. FHL local records: civil registration, 1926–1931; notarials, 1911–. Local records: civil registration, 1919–.

Peñaranda (municipality), also known as Mapisong, was an early Spanish town to which San Leonardo was annexed from 1903 to 1907. General Tinio separated in 1921. FHL local records: civil registration, 1922–1931; notarials, 1911–; Immaculate Conception parish registers, 1891–1950. Local records: civil registration, 1941–.

Quezon (municipality) was an early Spanish town. FHL local records: civil registration, 1922–1932; notarials, 1916–. Local records: civil registration, 1916–.

Rizal (municipality) was established in 1913 from Bongabon. FHL local records: notarials, 1915–. Local records: civil registration, 1917–.

San Antonio (municipality) was an early Spanish town which was part of the province of Pampanga until 1848. Annexed Jaen from 1903 to 1907. FHL local records: civil registration, 1922–1931, 1942–1994; notarials, 1911–; Saint Anthony, Abbot, parish registers, 1843–1943. Local records: civil registration, 1945–.

San Isidro (municipality), also known as Factoria, was an early Spanish town which was the provincial capital from 1852 to 1912. Annexed Cabiao from 1903 to 1907. FHL local records: civil registration, 1922–1932; notarials, 1911–; Saint Isidore Farmer parish registers. Local records: civil registration, 1942–.

San José (city), also known as Kabaritan, was an early Spanish town to which Lupao was annexed from 1903 to 1913. It was chartered in August 1969. FHL local records: civil registration, 1922–1931; notarials, 1909–; birth certificates, 1970–1988; death certificates, 1976–1988. Local records: civil registration, 1945–.

San Leonardo (municipality) was an early Spanish town to which Peñaranda was annexed from 1903 to 1907. FHL local records: civil registration, 1923–1930, 1913–1994; notarials, 1903–; Saint Bartholomew parish registers, 1896–1950. Local records: civil registration, 1912–.

Santa Rosa (municipality) was an early Spanish town which was annexed to Cabanatuan from 1903 to 1907. FHL local records: civil registration, 1922–1932, 1945–1994; notarials, 1908–; Saint Rose parish registers, 1910–1947. Local records: civil registration, 1912–.

Santo Domingo (municipality), also known as Pulong-Bule and Pulong-Buli, was an early Spanish town which was annexed to Talavera from 1903 to 1907. FHL local records: civil registration, 1922–1932; notarials, 1903–. Local records: civil registration, 1902–.

Talavera (municipality) was an early Spanish town to which Santo Domingo was annexed from 1903 to 1907. Lost some territory to the new municipality of Llanera in 1955. FHL local records: civil registration, 1922–1934; notarials, 1904; Saint Isidore Labrador parish registers, 1911–1950. Local records: civil registration, 1912–.

Talugtug (municipality), also known as Talugtug Balita, was established in 1948 of territory from the municipalities of Guimba, Munoz, Cuyapo, and Lupao. Local records: civil registration, 1948–.

Zaragosa (municipality), also known as Zaragoza, was an early Spanish town which was annexed to Aliaga from 1903 to 1907. FHL local records: civil registration, 1922–1931; notarials, 1903–. Local records: civil registration, 1916–.

Nueva Vizcaya. This inland province occupies the north portion of central Luzon. The Spanish explorers found it inhabited by a number of tribes including the Igorots,

Ifugaos, Ilongots, Aetas, Gaddanes, and Malaats. The first Spanish, Dominicans interested in evangelization, came from Cagayan to the north. Because primitive living conditions and native hostility made missionary work difficult and dangerous, the first missions were ultimately abandoned. In the first half of the nineteenth century, the Spanish government undertook a series of military expeditions meant to subdue the natives and project Spanish power into the region. By May 1839 Nueva Vizcaya had become a province with the newly created sub-province of Ifugao under its jurisdiction. Its territory included the modern provinces of Nueva Vizcaya, Quirino, and Ifugao as well as a portion of Isabela. When Isabela was formed into a province in 1856, a large amount of territory from Nueva Vizcaya went into it. Retained were Ifugao (now a district) and the towns of Aritao, Bagabag, Bambang, Bayombong, Dupax, and Solano. The capital was at Bayombong. The Philippine Revolution, overcoming the Spanish, was itself pushed aside by American forces. In January 1902 a civil government was established. The Americans experimented with a new form of administration in this area. Since the province was not rich or populous enough for it to support a regular provincial administration, a simplified form of local administration was introduced which would meet the needs of the tribal areas in which Spanish authority had not been firmly established. The province was placed under the administrative jurisdiction of the province of the Bureau of Non-Christian Tribes. This pattern of government was extended to several other areas in the Philippines. In 1908 Ifugao was annexed as a sub-province to the newly created Mountain Province and the former district of Binatangan (or the Ilongot District), high in the mountains of Luzon, was transferred to Nueva Vizcaya. The boundary disputes arising from this transfer were not settled until 1950. From June 1966 to September 1971, when it was established as a province, Quirino existed as a sub-province.

FHL provincial records: civil registration (1888–1893), birth records (1946–1988), marriage contracts (1945–1987), death certificates (1960–1991), death records (1888–1893), court records created by the Court of First Instance (1873–1884), deportations (1865–1898), land records (1850–1890), military induction records (1888–1891), public records (1884–1898), records of lending (1869–1898), school records (1824–1908), statistical reports (1896), tax records (1848), and Census of Chinese (1885–1892).

Localities and their records:

Ambaguio (municipal district), an early Spanish town, was established as a municipal district in 1966 from Bayombong.

Aritao (municipality), also known as Mabato, Buhay, Ajanas, Burbur, and Burubur, was an early Spanish town which was annexed to Dupax (modern Dupax del Norte) in 1903 and separated in 1920 as municipal district. It was established as a municipality in 1950. FHL local records: civil registration, 1922–1931; notarials, 1920–; civil registration (suburb of Pingkian), 1925–1929; Saint Catherine of Alexandria parish registers, 1844–1958. Local records: civil registration, 1945–.

Bagabag (municipality), also known as Nagconventuan and Dalla, became a town in 1902 and a municipality in 1950. In 1967 Diadi separated. FHL local records: civil registration, 1922–1931; notarials, 1922–. Local records: civil registration, 1945–.

Bambang (municipality), also known as Bangbang and Santa Maria de Abiang, became a town in 1902 and a municipality in 1950. FHL local records: civil registration, 1922–1931; notarials, 1933–; Roman Catholic parish registers, 1851–1938. Local records: civil registration, 1949–.

Bayombong (city), also known as Buyumbung and Buymbung, became a town in 1902 and a municipality in 1950. Ambaguio separated in 1966. It is the capital of the province. FHL local records: civil registration, 1922–1931; notarials, 1923–; Saint Dominic parish registers, 1848–1950. Local records: civil registration, 1945–.

Diadi (municipality) became a municipal district in 1967 from Bagabag.

Dupax del Norte (municipality), an early Spanish town, was made town in 1902 and municipality in 1950. Aritao was annexed from 1903 to 1920. It was split into Dupax del Norte and Dupax del Sur in 1971. FHL local records: civil registration, 1922–1931; notarials from 1920. Local records: civil registration from 1950; Saint Vincent Ferrer parish registers, 1767–1978.

Dupax del Sur (municipality) was established from the division of Dupax into Dupax del Norte and Dupax del Sur. FHL local records: civil registration, 1922–1931; notarials, 1920–.

Kasibu (municipality) was established in 1960 from Bambang. Local records: civil registration, 1960–.

Kayapa (municipality), also known as Cayapa, was an early Spanish town. Part of Benguet in the Mountain Province from 1901 to 1905, it was transferred to Nueva Vizcaya and made a part of the municipal district of Pingkian (now in the Aritao municipality). It became a town in 1913, a municipal district in 1938, and a municipality in 1950. FHL local records: civil registration, 1922–1929; notarials, 1925–1933. Local records: civil registration, 1946–.

Quezon (municipality) was established in 1963 from Solano. Local records: civil registration, 1964–.

Santa Fé (municipality), also known as Imugan prior to 1959, was established in that year from Aritao. FHL local records: civil registration, 1921–1927; notarials, 1925–. Local records: civil registration, 1959–.

Solano (municipality), also known as Lumabang, Binatuan, and Lungabang, became a town in 1902 and a municipality in 1950. Villa Verde (then called Ibung) was annexed from 1902 to 1957. FHL local records: civil registration, 1923; notarials, 1921–; Saint Louis parish registers, 1875–1932. Local records: civil registration, 1946–.

Villa Verde (municipality), also known as Ibung prior to 1959, was annexed to Solano from 1902 to 1957. Local records: civil registration, 1957–.

Occidental Mindoro. This province occupies the western portion of the island of Mindoro, an island just to the south of Luzon Island. When the first Spanish arrived in 1570, they found the island settled by Tagalogs on the coast and Mangayans in the interior. These prosperous trading settlements are reflected in the name; originally Mait, it was changed to Mindoro—a corruption of Mina de Oro or "gold mine." When the province of Balayan (now Batangas) was established in 1581, Mindoro was placed under its jurisdiction. In the seventeenth century it was separated and made a district with Puerto Galera as its capital until 1837 when Calapan became the capital. By 1839 Mindoro had become a province. During the seventeenth and eighteenth centuries, Moro pirates were a threat to the inhabitants of the island. Pirate strongholds, set up at Mamburao and Balete, resulted in the depopulation of the coastal areas. In 1778 Don Jose Gomez lead an expedition which took the Moro stronghold at Mamburao and stopped the Moro raids. When the Americans established a civil government in June 1902, Mindoro was annexed to Marinduque province. But in November 1902 it was separated and was, once again, an independent province. In September 1905 it was made a "special" province and its municipalities were reduced to the status of towns and settlements. In 1919 the municipalities and municipal districts were restored and, in February 1921, Mindoro again became a "regular" province. Mindoro was divided into the two provinces of Occidental Mindoro and Oriental Mindoro in June 1950.

FHL provincial records: civil registration (1885–1895), birth records (1951–1988), marriage contracts (1951–1988), death certificates (1960–1991), court records created by the Court of First Instance (1902), deportations (1867–1898), land records (1850–1890), military induction records (1875–1898), public records (1884–1898), notarials (1909–), records of lending (1858–1898), school records (1790–1898), statistical reports (1896–1897), and Census of Chinese (1881–1897).

Localities and their records:

Abra de Ilog (municipality), also known as Abra de Ylog, was an early Spanish town which was annexed to Mamburao from 1905 to 1910. FHL local records: civil registration, 1922–1931; notarials, 1913–. Local records: civil registration, 1948–.

Calintaan (municipality) was established in 1966 from Sablayan. Local records: civil registration, 1968–.

Looc (municipality) was an early Spanish town annexed to Lubang from 1905 to 1917. FHL local records: civil registration, 1922–1931; notarials, 1907–. Local records: civil registration, 1917–.

Lubang (municipality), also known as Luban, was annexed to Mindoro in November 1902. Annexed Looc from 1905 to 1917. FHL local records: civil registration, 1922–1931; notarials, 1907–. Local records: civil registration, 1916–.

Magsaysay (municipality) was established in 1969 from San José. Local records: civil registration, 1970–.

Mamburao (city) was an early Spanish town to which Abra de Ilog and Paluan were annexed from 1905 to 1910. Santa Cruz (1949) and Magsaysay separated (1969). FHL local records: civil registration, 1922–1926. Local records: civil registration, 1915–.

Paluan (municipality), also known as Palauan and Lipa, was an early Spanish town annexed to Mamburao from 1905 to 1910. FHL local records: civil registration, 1922–1927; notarials, 1909–. Local records: civil registration, 1916–.

Rizal (municipality) was established in 1969 from San José.

Sablayan (municipality) was an early Spanish town from which Calintaan separated in 1966. FHL local records: civil registration, 1922–1931. Local records: civil registration, 1918–.

San José (municipality), also known as Pandurucan, was established in 1910. Magsaysay and Rizal separated in 1969. FHL local records: civil registration, 1922–1931; Saint Joseph parish registers, 1912–1915. Local records: civil registration, 1934–.

Santa Cruz (municipality) was established in 1949 from Mamburao. Local records: civil registration, 1949–.

Oriental Mindoro. This province occupies the eastern portion of the island of Mindoro. Until 1950 this province and Occidental Mindoro formed the province of Mindoro. For a short administrative history of the former province of Mindoro, see the section on Mindoro Occidental above.

FHL provincial records: See the section on Occidental Mindoro above.

Localities and their records:

Baco (municipality), also known as Bako, New Bako, and Calabugao, was established in 1921 from Calapan. Annexed San Teodoro from 1921 to 1928. FHL local records: civil registration, 1922–1931. Local records: civil registration, 1921–.

Bansud (municipality) was established in 1959 from Bongabong. Local records: civil registration, 1959–.

Bongabong (municipality), also known as Bongabon, Bangabon, Sucol, Sumilang, and Anilao, was an early Spanish town which was annexed to Pinamalayan in 1904, made a municipal district in 1920, and established as a municipality in 1927. Bansud separated in 1959. FHL local records: civil registration, 1922–1931. Local records: civil registration, 1948–.

Bulalakao (municipality), also known as San Pedro, Bulalacao, and Caburayan, was an early Spanish town to which Mansalay was annexed from 1905 to 1928. The name Bulalakao was changed to San Pedro in 1960, then back to Bulalakao in 1969. FHL local records: civil registration, 1922–1930. Local records: civil registration, 1945–.

Calapan (city), also known as Calap, was an early Spanish town to which Puerto Galera was annexed from 1905 to 1927. Baco separated in 1921. The capital of the former province of Mindoro from 1837 to 1902 and, again, from 1905 to 1950, it has been the capital of Oriental Mindoro since 1950. FHL local records: civil registration, 1922–1931; notarials, 1911–; Holy Infant parish registers, 1881–1945. Local records: civil registration, 1905–.

Gloria (municipality) was established in 1964 from Pinamalayan. Local records: civil registration, 1968–.

Mansalay (municipality) was an early Spanish town which was annexed to Bulalakao from 1905 to 1928. FHL local records: civil registration, 1929–1931. Local records: civil registration, 1949–.

Naujan (municipality) was an early Spanish town from which Victoria separated in 1953. FHL local records: civil registration, 1922–1931; notarials, 1903–; Saint Nicholas of Tolentino parish registers, 1807–1937. Local records: civil registration, 1917–.

Pinamalayan (municipality) was an early Spanish town to which Bongabon (1904 to 1920) and Pola (1905 to 1912) were annexed. Gloria separated in 1964. FHL local records: civil registration, 1922–1931; notarials, 1905–; Saint Augustine parish registers, 1895–1916. Local records: civil registration, 1945–.

Pola (municipality) was an early Spanish town which was annexed to Pinamalayan from 1905 to 1912. Socorro separated in 1963. FHL local records: civil registration, 1922–1932; notarials, 1905–; Saint John the Baptist parish registers, 1905–1943. Local records: civil registration, 1916–.

Puerto Galera (municipality) was an early Spanish town which was annexed to Calapan from 1905 to 1927. It was the provincial capital from the seventeenth century to 1837 and from 1902 to 1905. FHL local records: civil registration, 1922–1931. Local records: civil registration, 1942–.

Roxas (municipality), also known as Paclasan, Palasan, and Paglasan, was established in 1948 from Mansalay. It had been a part of Bulalakao until 1929 when it was annexed to Mansalay. Local records: civil registration, 1948–.

San Teodoro (municipality), also known as Subaan and Lumangbayan, was burned by American forces in 1902. It was annexed to Baco from 1921 to 1928. FHL local records: civil registration, 1929–1931. Local records: civil registration, 1929–.

Socorro (municipality) was established in 1969 from Pola. Local records: civil registration, 1963–.

Victoria (municipality) was established in 1953 from Naujan. Local records: civil registration, 1953–.

Palawan. This province is composed of 1,769 islands, most very small, to the west and south of the main Philippine islands. Palawan Island is the largest of the islands; others of importance are Busuanga, Culion, Linapacan, Cuyo, Dumaran, Balabac, and the Cagayanes group. When the Spanish arrived at Palawan Island, they found it under the control of the Moros and the Sultanate of Borneo. As a result, early Spanish settlements were established on the smaller islands to the north of Palawan Island. During the seventeenth century, the Augustinians attempted to evangelize some of the smaller northern islands, but were driven out. Only when a Christian settlement was located next to a Spanish fort, did it have a chance to survive. The Spanish, in the early eighteenth century, entered the island of Palawan and directly challenged Moro authority by building a strong fort at the town of Taytay. After successive attempts to force the Spanish out, the Sultanate ceded all of the island of Palawan to the Spanish. Large scale immigration to the island failed due to disease. Nevertheless, by 1818

Palawan had become a province under the name Calamianes with a capital at Taytay. In 1858 Calamianes was divided into two provinces: Castilla, which included the Calamianes Island group and the northern portion of Palawan with a capital at Taytay, and Asturias, which included southern Palawan Island with a capital at Puerto Princesa. After failing to increase Palawan's population by encouraging immigration from Ilocos Norte and Ilocos Sur, the Spanish government established penal colonies on Palawan (then called Paragua). At the end of Spanish rule, the government in this area was reorganized into three provinces: Calamianes, which included northern Palan and the islands north of it; Paragua, which included the southern portion of Palawan Island; and Balabac, which included the island of the same name. In June 1902 American forces established a civil government in the province and, in May 1903, the province of Paragua was created out of the three provinces that the Spanish had established. In June 1905 the name was changed to Palawan and, later the same year, the area was deemed a "special" province. Culion Island was separated in 1906 to form a leper colony.

> FHL provincial records: birth records (1945–1988), marriage contracts (1945–1987), death certificates (1960–1991), military induction records (1876–1896), public records (1885–1898), records of lending (1889–1898), statistical reports (1896), and Census of Chinese (1889–1898).

Localities and their records:

Aborlan (municipality), also known as Abraham, was established as a municipal district in 1910 and a municipality in 1949. Narra and Quezon separated in 1969 and 1951, respectively. FHL local records: civil registration, 1928–1929. Local records: civil registration, 1954–.

Agutaya (municipality), also known as Agustaya and Agutayan, was established in 1916. FHL local records: civil registration, 1926–1931; Saint John the Baptist parish registers, 1912–1984. Local records: civil registration, 1903–.

Araceli (municipality), also known as Dumaran prior to 1954, was annexed to Puerto Princesa from 1905 to circa 1909. FHL local records: civil registration, 1927–1929. Local records: civil registration, 1909–.

Balabac (municipality), also known as Malbog and Balabag, was established in 1957. The capital of Balabac District in 1858, it later became the capital of the province of Balabac until 1902 (consequently, there are records in Balabac that are usually found only in a city). FHL local records: public records, 1883–1898; records of lending, 1898; census of Chinese, 1889–1894; deportations, 1867–1898; tax records, 1881–1896. Local records: civil registration, 1929–.

Batarasa (municipality) was established in 1961 from Brooke's Point. Local records: civil registration, 1964–.

Brooke's Point (municipality), also known as Bonbon, was an early Spanish town and the capital of the subprovince of Paragua Sur in late nineteenth century. It was established as a municipality in 1949. Batarasa (1961) and Quezon (1951) separated. FHL local records:

civil registration, 1922–1931. Local records: civil registration, 1916–.

Busuanga (municipality), also known as Busuangan, was established in 1950 from Coron. Local records: civil registration, 1950–.

Cagayancillo (municipality) was an early Spanish town on Cagayan Island. FHL local records: civil registration, 1928–1930; Saint Nicholas of Tolentino parish registers, 1887–1895. Local records: civil registration, 1928–.

Calamianes Island Group (includes some records relating to the Spanish period). FHL local records: civil registration, 1892–1897; tax records, 1856–1859; public records, 1881–1898; Census of Chinese, 1855–1895; school records, 1857–1898.

Coron (municipality), also known as Peñon de Coron, Corong, and Bacuang, was an early Spanish town from which separated Busuanga (1950) and Linapacan (1954). Its name was changed from Bucuang to Coron in 1902. FHL local records: civil registration, 1922–1932. Local records: civil registration, 1945–.

Culion Reservation was an early Spanish settlement which was detached from Palawan to create a leper colony under the jurisdiction of the Deportionment of the Interior in 1906.

Cuyo (municipality) was an early Spanish town from which Magsaysay separated in 1961. It was the capital of Calamianes until 1902 and the capital of the province of Paragua from 1902 to 1903. FHL local records: civil registration, 1922–1932; Saint Augustine of Hippo parish registers, 1894–1989. Local records: civil registration, 1900–.

Dumaran (municipality) was established in 1963 from the villages of the municipalities of Araceli, Roxas, and Taytay. FHL local records: civil registration, 1922–1932.

El Nido (municipality), also known as Bacuit and Talindak, was established in 1916 from Taytay. Its name was changed from Bacuit to El Nido in 1954. FHL local records: civil registration, 1922–1931. Local records: civil registration, 1942–.

Linapacan (municipality) was established in 1954 from Coron. Local records: civil registration, 1956–.

Magsaysay (municipality) was established in 1963 from Cuyo. Local records: civil registration, 1964–.

Narra (municipality) was established in 1969 from Aborlan. Local records: civil registration, 1970–.

Puerto Princesa (city), also known as Puerto Yguahit, Asuncion, and Puerto de la Asuncion, was an early Spanish town. Its name of Puerto Yguahit was changed to Puerto de la Asuncion in 1882 in honor of the daughter of Queen Isabela II of Spain. At the death of Princess Asuncion, its name was changed to Puerto Princesa. Once the capital of Asturias (also called Paragua during this period of time) from 1858 to 1902, it has been the capital of the province of Palawan since 1905. Temporarily annexed San Vincente (1960 to 1969), and Ariceli (1905 to circa 1909). It was chartered as a city in January 1970. FHL local records: civil registration, 1922–1932; birth certificates, 1969–1988; death certificates, 1976–1988; deportations, 1873–1898; Immaculate Conception parish registers, 1872–1940. Local records: civil registration, 1925–.

Quezon (municipality) was established in 1951 by the consolidation of villages from the municipalities of

Aborlan and Brooke's Point. Local records: civil registration, 1952–.

Roxas (municipality) was established in 1951 from Puerto Princesa. San Vincente, then a village, was annexed to Puerto Princesa from Roxas in 1960. Local records: civil registration, 1951–.

San Vicente (municipality) was annexed as a village to Puerto Princesa from Roxas in 1960. It separated in 1969 with some territory from Taytay. Local records: civil registration, 1972–.

Taytay (municipality), also known as Taitay, was an early Spanish town from which some villages separated to create Dumaran in 1961. More villages were lost when the municipality of San Vincente was formed in 1969. FHL local records: civil registration, 1922–1930. Local records: civil registration, 1951–.

Pampanga. This province is located in the southern portion of central Luzon on a broad, rich plain. When the Spanish established their capital in Manila in 1571, they established contact with this area which included large thriving settlements that produced much of the material used in trade with China, Japan, and India. Attempts to get the inhabitants to accept Spanish rule were unsuccessful. A war followed and, despite formidable resistance and several set-backs, Spanish arms and experience prevailed. Within a few years this area became a province which included modern Pampanga, Bataan, Nueva Ecija, and Bulacan. By 1591 it was a semi-autonomous district of Pampanga. Augustinian missionaries made a major effort in this area and soon established a number of mission centers in the region. In 1754 Bataan became an independent province as did Nueva Ecija (1848) and Tarlac (1873). The people of Pampanga strongly supported the Philippine Revolution in 1896 and finally overcame the Spanish. In the summer of 1899 American forces arrived and were able to establish civil government in the province in February 1901. The usual consolidation of municipalities began and, as in other provinces, was reversed as the population of the area expanded. Clark Air Force Base was established by the United States near Angeles City, the provincial capital. This is also the area where the Hukbalahap, an underground movement which resisted the Japanese and then sought to overthrow the regular government of the Philippines, developed.

FHL provincial records: civil registration (1885–1895), birth records (1945–1988), marriage contracts (1945–1987), death certificates (1962–1991), notarials (1911–), court records created by the Court of First Instance (1828–1933), deportations (1867–1894), land records (1755–1898), military induction records (1870–1898), public records (1880–1898), records of lending (1873), school records (1884–1894), statistical reports (1884–1894), tax records (1835–1873), and Census of Chinese (1891–1896).

Localities and their records:

Angeles City (city) was an early Spanish town. It was chartered in January 1963. FHL local records: civil registration, 1922–1933, 1913–1993; notarials, 1908–;

birth certificates, 1963–1988; death certificates, 1975–1988; Our Lady of the Holy Rosary parish registers, 1814–1948. Local records: civil registration, 1901–.

Apalit (municipality), also known as Apali, was an early Spanish town. FHL local records: civil registration, 1922–1931, 1904–1993; notarials, 1903–; Saints Peter and Paul parish registers, 1881–1937. Local records: civil registration, 1943–.

Arayat (municipality) was an early Spanish town to which Santa Ana was annexed from 1903 to 1913. FHL local records: civil registration, 1922–1931, 1970–1993; notarials, 1907–; Saint Catherine parish registers, 1758–1948. Local records: civil registration, 1970–.

Bacolor (municipality), an early Spanish town, was the capital of Pampanga until 1904. FHL local records: civil registration, 1922–1932, 1902–1993; notarials, 1907–; Our Lady of the Holy Rosary parish registers, 1680–1962; Saint James the Apostle (located in the village of Betis) parish registers, 1905–1937. Local records: civil registration, 1902–.

Candaba (municipality), also known as Candava, was an early Spanish town. FHL local records: civil registration, 1922–1932, 1913–1992; notarials, 1903–; Saint Andrew parish registers, 1672–1965. Local records: civil registration, 1913–.

Floridablanca (municipality) was an early Spanish town. FHL local records: civil registration, 1922–1931, 1947–1993; notarials, 1908–; Saint Joseph parish registers, 1823–1937. Local records: civil registration, 1903–.

Guagua (municipality) was an early Spanish town to which Sexmoan was annexed from 1903 to 1909. FHL local records: civil registration, 1922–1932, 1940–1993; notarials, 1907–; Immaculate Conception parish registers, 1823–1935. Local records: civil registration, 1909–.

Lubao (municipality) was an early Spanish town. FHL local records: civil registration, 1922–1930, 1947–1993; notarials, 1907–; Saint Augustine parish registers, 1621–1930. Local records: civil registration, 1947–.

Mabalacat (municipality), also known as Mabalacad, was an early Spanish town. FHL local records: civil registration, 1922–1933, 1946–1993; notarials, 1907–; Purification of Our Lady parish registers, 1872–1950. Local records: civil registration, 1945–.

Macabebe (municipality) was an early Spanish town to which San Miguel (now Masantol) was annexed from 1903 to 1907. FHL local records: civil registration, 1922–1931, 1916–1993; notarials, 1905–; Saint Nicholas of Tolentino parish registers, 1899–1950. Local records: civil registration, 1913–.

Magalang (municipality), also known as Magalan and San Pedro de Magalang, was an early Spanish town. FHL local records: civil registration, 1928–1931, 1913–1993; notarials, 1905–. Local records: civil registration, 1903–.

Masantol (municipality), also known as San Miguel prior to 1907, was an early Spanish town which was annexed to Macabebe from 1903 to 1907. FHL local records: civil registration, 1922–1926, 1914–1993; notarials, 1913–; Saint Michael the Archangel parish registers, 1894–1937. Local records: civil registration, 1914–.

México (municipality) was an early Spanish town. FHL local records: civil registration, 1922–1926, 1938–1993; notarials, 1913–; Saint Monica parish registers, 1672–1943. Local records: civil registration, 1913–.

Minalin (municipality), also known as Minalis and Santa María, was an early Spanish town which in 1903 was annexed to Santo Tomás, which, in 1904, was annexed to San Fernando, from which Minalin separated in 1907. FHL local records: civil registration, 1922–1933, 1909–1993; notarials, 1912–; Saint Monica parish registers, 1774–1953. Local records: civil registration, 1909–.

Porac (municipality) was an early Spanish town. FHL local records: civil registration, 1922–1932, 1951–1990; notarials, 1912–; Saint Catherine parish registers, 1897–1921. Local records: civil registration, 1951–.

San Fernando (city), also known as Culiat, was an early Spanish town to which Santo Tomás was annexed from 1904 to 1952. It was chartered in June 1963. FHL local records: civil registration, 1922–1932, 1945–1993; notarials, 1911–; The Assumption parish registers, 1883–1947; Saint Vincent Ferrer (located in the village of Calucut) parish registers, 1901–1940. Local records: civil registration, 1942–.

San Luis (municipality), also known as Cabagsac and San Nicolas de Cabagsac, was an early Spanish town to which San Simon was annexed from 1903 to 1907. FHL local records: civil registration, 1922–1931, 1933–1993; notarials, 1911–; Saint Aloysius Gonzaga parish registers, 1770–1951. Local records: civil registration, 1901–.

San Simon (municipality) was an early Spanish town which was annexed to San Luis from 1903 to 1907. FHL local records: civil registration, 1922–1931, 1913–1993; notarials, 1911–; Saint Simon the Apostle parish registers, 1772–1936. Local records: civil registration, 1903–.

Santa Ana (municipality), also known as Pinpin, was an early Spanish town which was annexed to Arayat from 1903 to 1913. FHL local records: civil registration, 1922–1931, 1988–1992; notarials, 1913–; Saint Anne parish registers, 1779–1936. Local records: civil registration, 1951–.

Santa Rita (municipality), also known as Gasac, was an early Spanish town. FHL local records: civil registration, 1922–1931, 1951–1993; notarials, 1913–; Saint Rita parish registers, 1671–1944. Local records: civil registration, 1903–.

Santo Tomás (municipality), also known as Baliwag, Baliuag, and Maliwag, was an early Spanish town to which Minalin was annexed in 1903. Annexed to San Fernando from 1904 to 1952. FHL local records: Saint Thomas parish registers, 1952–1993. Local records: civil registration, 1952–.

Sexmoan (municipality), also known as Sesmoan, was an early Spanish town which was annexed to Guagua from 1903 to 1909. FHL local records: civil registration, 1922–1931, 1946–1993; notarials, 1913–; Saint Lucy parish registers, 1669–1962. Local records: civil registration, 1945–.

Pangasinan. This province occupies a portion of the central plains of Luzon Island. The province's name before the Spanish came was Layug na Caboloan, but seeing the production of salt (*asin*) as one of the important occupations in this area, they renamed it Pangasinan. In 1572 Martin de Goiti successfully carried out a vigorous campaign to subdue the natives of central Luzon, crushing resistance and bringing the area under Spanish control. When the Chinese pirate Limahong was repulsed by the Spanish in his attack on Manila, he turned to Pangasinan and was, again, turned back. By 1580 Pangasinan became a district and, by 1611, a province. In 1854 the province of La Union was formed out of its territory. When the Americans established a civil government in February 1901, the province underwent some minor boundary adjustments and consolidations of municipalities, the latter of which were later restored.

FHL provincial records: civil registration (1886–1895), birth records (1945–1988), marriage contracts (1945–1987), death certificates (1961–1991), court records created by the Court of First Instance (1896–1919), deportations (1875–1897), land records (1850–1890), military induction records (1869–1897), public records (1882–1890), records of lending (1869–1898), school records (1852–1898), statistical reports (1894–1896), tax records (1853–1855), and Census of Chinese (1833–1896).

Localities and their records:

Agno (municipality) was an early Spanish town which was part of the province of Zambales until it was annexed to Pangasinan in 1903. FHL local records: civil registration, 1922–1932; notarials, 1911–; Saint Catherine of Alexandria parish registers, 1831–1978. Local records: civil registration, 1914–.

Aguilar (municipality) was an early Spanish town which was annexed to Bugallon from 1903 to 1907. FHL local records: civil registration, 1922–1931; notarials, 1911–; Saint Joseph the Patriarch parish registers, 1813–1943. Local records: civil registration, 1950–.

Alaminos (municipality) was an early Spanish town annexed from Zambales. FHL local records: civil registration, 1922–1931; notarials, 1906–; Saint Joseph the Portioniarch parish registers, 1847–1964. Local records: civil registration, 1937–.

Alcalá (municipality), also known as Dangla, was an early Spanish town to which Santo Tomás was annexed from 1903 to 1908. FHL local records: civil registration, 1922–1932; notarials, 1903–; Holy Cross parish registers, 1908–1964. Local records: civil registration, 1902–.

Anda (municipality), also known as Sorongan Baca, was an early Spanish town annexed from Zambales. FHL local records: civil registration, 1922–1931; notarials, 1905–. Local records: civil registration, 1916–.

Asingan (municipality), also known as Asingang, was an early Spanish town to which San Manuel was annexed from 1903 to 1907. FHL local records: civil registration, 1922–1931; notarials, 1904–; Saint Louis Beltran parish registers, 1787–1954. Local records: civil registration, 1942–.

Balungao (municipality) was an early Spanish town annexed from province of Nueva Ecija in 1901. Annexed to Rosales from 1903 to 1907. FHL local records: civil registration, 1922–1932, 1949–1989; notarials, 1908–. Local records: civil registration, 1949–.

Bani (municipality), also known as San Simon, was an early Spanish town annexed from province of Zambales in 1903. FHL local records: civil registration, 1922–1933; notarials, 1910–; Our Lady of the Immaculate

Conception parish registers, 1900–1977. Local records: civil registration, 1904–.

Basista (municipality) was established in 1961. Local records: civil registration, 1961–.

Bautista (municipality) was an early Spanish town. FHL local records: civil registration, 1922–1932; notarials, 1911–; Saint John the Baptist parish registers, 1923–1942. Local records: civil registration, 1901–.

Bayambang (municipality) was an early Spanish town. FHL local records: civil registration, 1922–1931; notarials, 1911–; Saint John Ferrer parish registers, 1898–1943. Local records: civil registration, 1902–.

Binalonan (municipality) was an early Spanish town. FHL local records: civil registration, 1922–1932; notarials, 1908–; Holy Child, Jesus, parish registers, 1845–1935. Local records: civil registration, 1902–.

Binmaley (municipality) was an early Spanish town. FHL local records: civil registration, 1922–1933, 1917–1988; notarials, 1910–; Our Lady of Purification parish registers, 1615–1946. Local records: civil registration, 1916–.

Bolinao (municipality) was an early Spanish town annexed from Zambales in 1903. FHL local records: civil registration, 1922–1931; notarials, 1912–; Saint James the Great parish registers, 1655–1942. Local records: civil registration, 1902–.

Bugallon (municipality) was an early Spanish town to which Aguilar was annexed from 1903 to 1907. FHL local records: civil registration, 1922–1934; notarials, 1908–; Saint Andrew parish registers, 1733–1977. Local records: civil registration, 1902–.

Burgos (municipality), also known as San Isidro Potot, San Isidro, and San Isidro Putot, was an early Spanish town annexed from the province of Zambales in 1903. Mabini (1908) and Dasol (1911) separated. FHL local records: civil registration, 1922–1931; notarials, 1912–. Local records: civil registration, 1917–.

Calasiao (municipality) was an early Spanish town to which Santa Barbara was annexed from 1903 to 1907. FHL local records: civil registration, 1922–1932; notarials, 1905–; Saints Peter and Paul parish registers, 1844–1932. Local records: civil registration, 1917–.

Dagupan (city), also known as Bacnotan, Bagnotan, and Nandaragupan, was an early Spanish town. It was chartered in June, 1947. FHL local records: civil registration, 1922–1931; notarials, 1903–; birth certificates, 1945–1988; birth records, 1936–1967; death certificates, 1975–1988; death records, 1956–1986; marriage records, 1942–1985; marriage contracts, 1945–1960; deportations, 1891–1893. Local records: civil registration, 1902–.

Dasol (municipality), also known as Dazol, was an early Spanish town annexed from province of Nueva Ecija in 1901. It was established in 1911 from Burgos. FHL local records: civil registration, 1922–1930; notarials, 1911–. Local records: civil registration, 1950–.

Infanta (municipality), an early Spanish town, was annexed from province of Zambales in 1903. FHL local records: civil registration, 1922–1932; notarials, 1913–. Local records: civil registration, 1951–.

Labrador (municipality), also known as San Isidro Labrador and San Isidro, was an early Spanish town which was annexed to Sual from 1903 to 1908. FHL local records: notarials, 1911; Saint Isidore, the Farmer, parish

registers, 1816–1977. Local records: civil registration, 1950–.

Lingayen (city), an early Spanish town, has been the capital of Pangasinan since the beginning of the Spanish period. FHL local records: civil registration, 1922–1933; notarials, 1901–; Three Kings parish registers, 1860–1930. Local records: civil registration, 1901–.

Mabini (municipality), also known as Balincaguin prior to 1929, was annexed from the province of Zambales in 1903 as portion of municipality of San Isidro Potot (now Burgos). Separated from Burgos in 1908. FHL local records: civil registration, 1922–1931; notarials, 1912–; Holy Child Jesus parish registers, 1902–1942. Local records: civil registration, 1912–.

Malasiqui (municipality) was an early Spanish town. FHL local records: civil registration, 1922–1931; notarials, 1908–; Saint Ildephonse of Saville parish registers, 1820–1950. Local records: civil registration, 1930–.

Manaoag (municipality), also known as Manawag, was an early Spanish town to which San Jacinto was annexed from 1903 to 1907. FHL local records: civil registration, 1922–1932; notarials, 1906–; Our Lady of the Most Holy Rosary parish registers, 1731–1949. Local records: civil registration, 1901–.

Mañgaldan (municipality) was an early Spanish town to which Mapandan was annexed from 1903 to 1908. FHL local records: civil registration, 1922–1931; notarials, 1906–; Saint Thomas Aquinas parish registers, 1720–1944. Local records: civil registration, 1902–.

Mañgatarem (municipality), also known as Mangataren, was an early Spanish town to which Urbiztondo was annexed from 1903 to 1907. FHL local records: civil registration, 1922–1932; notarials, 1904–; Saint Raymond parish registers, 1834–1956. Local records: civil registration, 1950–.

Mapandan (municipality) was an early Spanish town which was annexed to Mangaldan from 1903 to 1908. FHL local records: civil registration, 1922–1931; notarials, 1911–; Saint Joseph the Patriarch parish registers, 1905–1961. Local records: civil registration, 1902–.

Natividad (municipality), also known as Cabaguan, was an early Spanish town which was annexed to San Nicolas from 1903 to 1907. FHL local records: civil registration, 1922–1931; notarials, 1903–. Local records: civil registration, 1918–.

Pozorrubio (municipality), also known as Cabaguan, was an early Spanish town. FHL local records: civil registration, 1922–1931; notarials, 1903–. Local records: civil registration, 1945–.

Rosales (municipality) was an early Spanish town, annexed from province of Nueva Ecija in 1901. Annexed Balungao from 1903 to 1907. FHL local records: civil registration, 1922–1931, 1902–1989; notarials, 1905–; Saint Anthony of Padua parish registers, 1915–1966. Local records: civil registration, 1902–.

San Carlos (city), also known as Sapan Palapar and Binalatongan, was chartered in January 1966. FHL local records: civil registration, 1922–1932; notarials, 1903–; birth certificates, 1964–1988; death certificates, 1875–1988; Saint Dominic parish registers, 1731–1929. Local records: civil registration, 1943–.

San Fabian (municipality) was an early Spanish town to which Sison was annexed from 1903 to 1907. FHL local records: civil registration, 1922–1931; notarials, 1906–;

Saint Fabian parish registers, 1718–1930. Local records: civil registration, 1945–.

San Jacinto (municipality) was an early Spanish town which was annexed to Manaoag from 1903 to 1907. FHL local records: civil registration, 1922–1931; notarials, 1911–; Saint Hyacinth parish registers, 1898–1977. Local records: civil registration, 1902–.

San Manuel (municipality), also known as Guiset, was an early Spanish town which was annexed to Asingan from 1903 to 1907. FHL local records: civil registration, 1922–1931; notarials, 1911–. Local records: civil registration, 1945–.

San Nicolas (municipality) was an early Spanish town to which Natividad was annexed from 1903 to 1907. FHL local records: civil registration, 1922–1931; notarials, 1906–. Local records: civil registration, 1940–.

San Quintin (municipality), an early Spanish town, was annexed from province of Nueva Ecija in 1901. FHL local records: civil registration, 1922–1931; notarials, 1905–; Saint Paschal Baylon parish registers, 1908–1944. Local records: civil registration, 1902–.

Santa Barbara (municipality) was an early Spanish town which was annexed to Calasiao from 1903 to 1907. FHL local records: civil registration, 1922–1931; notarials, 1903–; Holy Family parish registers, 1742–1949. Local records: civil registration, 1919–.

Santa María (municipality) was an early Spanish town which was annexed to Tayug from 1903 to 1907. FHL local records: civil registration, 1922–1929; notarials, 1911–; Our Lady of the Pillar parish registers, 1898–1977. Local records: civil registration, 1950–.

Santo Tomás (municipality) was an early Spanish town which was annexed to Acala from 1903 to 1908. FHL local records: civil registration, 1922–1931; notarials, 1911–. Local records: civil registration, 1945–.

Sison (municipality), also known as Alava, was an early Spanish town which, when called Alava, was annexed to San Fabian from 1903 to 1907. Alava and Sison were consolidated in 1918 under the name Sison. FHL local records: civil registration, 1922–1931; notarials, 1911–; Our Lady of Mount Carmel parish registers, 1910–1944. Local records: civil registration, 1945–.

Sual (municipality) was an early Spanish town to which Labrador (then called San Isidro) was annexed from 1903 to 1908. FHL local records: civil registration, 1929–1931; notarials, 1903–; Saint Peter Martyr parish registers, 1818–1971. Local records: civil registration, 1905–.

Tayug (municipality), also known as Tayub, Tayup, and Tayog, was an early Spanish town to which Santa María was annexed from 1903 to 1907. Some of its villages were used to create new municipality of Natividad in 1907. FHL local records: civil registration, 1922–1931, 1945–1989; notarials, 1906–. Local records: civil registration, 1945–.

Umingan (municipality), also known as Humingan, was an early Spanish town which was annexed from the province of Nueva Ecija in 1901. FHL local records: civil registration, 1922–1931; notarials, 1903–; birth records, 1923–1989; marriage contracts, 1918–1989; death records, 1901–1989; Our Lady of the Immaculate Conception parish registers, 1916–1972. Local records: civil registration, 1917–.

Urbiztondo (municipality) was an early Spanish town which was annexed to Mangatarem from 1903 to 1907. FHL

local records: civil registration, 1922–1931; notarials, 1906–. Local records: civil registration, 1952–.

Urdaneta (municipality) was an early Spanish town. FHL local records: civil registration, 1922–1932; notarials, 1906–; Our Lady of the Immaculate Conception parish registers, 1860–1929. Local records: civil registration, 1918–.

Villasis (municipality), also known as Panduyucan, was an early Spanish town. FHL local records: civil registration, 1922–1933; notarials, 1908–; Saint Anthony, Abbot, parish registers, 1902–1961. Local records: civil registration, 1904–.

Quezon. This province, formerly called Tayabas, occupies a strip of land between the east coast of Luzon Island and the mountains situated in the interior of the island. Its northern border begins at the southern end of the Isabela Province and the southern border extends past the neck of land that joins Luzon to Camarines Norte and other provinces in the southern portion of the island. The province also includes the Polilio Island just off the coast of Quezon as well as the sub-province of Aurora which occupies, roughly, the northern quarter of the province. (See the section on the sub-province of Aurora.) Early in the Spanish period this area was administered by the provinces on the west side of the island of Luzon, but the mountains at the center of Luzon made travel from one side of the island to the other difficult. In 1591 the province of Kalilaya, named after its capital (the modern Unisan), was created in roughly the same territory as Quezon now occupies. Circa 1750 the provincial capital was moved to Tayabas and the name of the province also became known as Tayabas. In 1818 the northern portion of the province was annexed to Nueva Ecija. In 1853 the central portion of the territory taken for Nueva Ecija, including the Polillo Islands, was annexed to Laguna Province. In the 1880s the Spanish attempted to extend their power to the interior of Luzon. To that end they created military districts which were dependent on the established provinces. The district of Infanta was dependent on the province of Laguna, Principe on Nueva Ecija. When civil government was established by the Americans in this area in March 1901, the capital was moved from Tayabas to Lucena. In June 1902 the districts of Principe and Infanta, including the Polillo Islands, were dissolved and annexed to Tayabas as was, in November 1902, the former province of Marinduque. In May 1907 Marinduque became a sub-province of Tayabas and was restored as a province in February 1921. In September 1946 the name of the province was changed to Quezon in honor of Manuel L. Quezon, the first president of the Philippines, former governor of Tayabas. The sub-province of Aurora was organized with, roughly, the same territory that the former district of Principe occupied in June 1951.

FHL provincial records: civil registration (1859–1896),
birth records (1945–1988), marriage contracts (1945–

1987), death certificates (1962–1991), land records (1770–1879), military induction records (1891–1897), public records (1880–1897), records of lending (1843–1892), school records (1859–1898), statistical reports (1754–1755, 1896), and Census of Chinese (1885–1897).

Localities and their records:

Agdañgan (municipality) was established in 1939 from Unisan. FHL local records: notarials, 1946–1948. Local records: civil registration, 1939–.

Alabat (municipality) was an early Spanish town from which Quezon separated in 1914. Perez separated in 1929. FHL local records: civil registration, 1922–1931; notarials, 1911–. Local records: civil registration, 1901–.

Atimonan (municipality), also known as Antimonan, was an early Spanish town from which Padre Burgos (1917) and Plaridel (1962) separated. FHL local records: civil registration, 1922–1931; notarials, 1913–. Local records: civil registration, 1964–.

Baler. See Aurora Sub-province.

Buenavista (municipality), also known as Peri, Piris, Peris, and Perez, became a municipality during the Japanese occupation in 1942, but was dissolved after World War II. It, again, became municipality in 1950 from Guinayangan; its name was changed from Piris to Buenavista. Local records: civil registration, 1950–.

Burdeos (municipality) was established in 1948 from Polillo. Patnanungan separated in 1961. Local records: civil registration, 1948–.

Calauag (municipality), also known as Caluag, was an early Spanish town. FHL local records: civil registration, 1922–1933; notarials, 1903–; Saint Peter the Apostle parish registers, 1853–1946. Local records: civil registration, 1901–.

Candelaria (municipality) was an early Spanish town which was annexed to Sariaya from 1902 to 1907. FHL local records: civil registration, 1925–1931; notarials, 1911–; Saint John the Baptist parish registers. Local records: civil registration, 1945–.

Casiguran. See Aurora Sub-province.

Catanauan (municipality) was an early Spanish town. FHL local records: civil registration, 1922–1932; notarials, 1904–. Local records: civil registration, 1901–.

Dilasag, **Dinalongan**, **Dingalan**, and **Dipaculao**. See Aurora Sub-province.

Dolores (municipality), also known as Nuestra Señora de los Dolores, was an early Spanish town which was annexed to Tiaong from 1902 to 1910. FHL local records: civil registration, 1922–1931; notarials, 1911–; Our Lady of Sorrows parish registers, 1902–1976. Local records: civil registration, 1911–.

General Luna (municipality), also known as Hingoso and Hinguso, was established in 1929 from Macalelon; the name was changed from Hingoso to General Luna. FHL local records: civil registration, 1929–1931; notarials, 1929–. Local records: civil registration, 1931–.

General Neker (municipality) was established in 1949. Local records: civil registration, 1949–.

Guinayangan (municipality) was an early Spanish town from which Buenavista separated in 1950. FHL local records: civil registration, 1922–1931; notarials, 1914–; Saint Louis Gonzaga parish registers, 1845–1941. Local records: civil registration, 1946–.

Gumaca (municipality) was an early Spanish town from which Lopez (the former Talolong) separated in 1860. FHL local records: civil registration, 1922–1931; notarials, 1913–; Saint Didacus of Alcala parish registers, 1829–1949. Local records: civil registration, 1902–.

Infanta (municipality), also known as Binangonan de Lampon prior to 1902, was an early Spanish town. FHL local records: civil registration, 1922–1931; notarials, 1904–; military induction records, 1868–1898; civil registration (village of Laguimanoc), 1922–1927; Infant Jesus of Prague and Saint Mark, the Evangelist, parish registers, 1862–1944. Local records: civil registration, 1916–.

Jumalig (municipality) was established in 1961 from Polillo. Local records: civil registration, 1962–.

Lopez (municipality), also known as Talolong, was an early Spanish town. FHL local records: civil registration, 1922–1931; notarials, 1910–. Local records: civil registration, 1968–.

Lucban (municipality) was an early Spanish town. FHL local records: civil registration, 1922–1933; notarials, 1907–. Local records: civil registration, 1946–.

Lucena (city), also known as Buenavista, Oroquieta, and Cotta, has been the provincial capital since 1901. It was chartered in June 1961. FHL local records: civil registration, 1922–1931; notarials, 1901–; birth certificates, 1950–1988; death certificates, 1975–1988; Saint Ferdinand, the King, parish registers, 1881–1953. Local records: civil registration, 1974–.

Macalelon (municipality) was an early Spanish town which was annexed to Pitogo from 1903 to 1912. General Luna separated in 1929. FHL local records: civil registration, 1922–1931; notarials, 1913–; Immaculate Conception parish registers, 1875–1965. Local records: civil registration, 1904–.

Maria Aurora. See Aurora Sub-province.

Mauban (municipality) was an early Spanish town. FHL local records: civil registration, 1922–1930; notarials, 1908–; Saint Bonaventure parish registers, 1848–1958. Local records: civil registration, 1905–.

Mulanay (municipality), also known as Malunay, was an early Spanish town to which San Narciso was annexed from 1903 to 1913. FHL local records: civil registration, 1922–1931; notarials, 1913–; Saint Peter the Apostle parish registers, 1846–1943. Local records: civil registration, 1917–.

Padre Burgos (municipality), also known as Laguimanoc, Lawin-Manok, and Laguingmonk, was established in 1917 from Atimonan. Its name was changed from Laguimanoc to Padre Burgos in 1927. FHL local records: civil registration, 1928–1931; notarials, 1933–. Local records: civil registration, 1947–.

Pagbilao (municipality) was an early Spanish town. FHL local records: civil registration, 1922–1932; notarials, 1907–; Saint Catherine of Alexandria parish registers, 1794–1937. Local records: civil registration, 1911–.

Panukulan (municipality) was established in 1959 from Polillo. Local records: civil registration, 1959–.

Patnanungan (municipality) was established in 1961 from Burdeos. Local records: civil registration, 1962–.

Perez (municipality), also known as Sangirin prior to 1929, was established in 1929 from Alabat. FHL local records: civil registration, 1929–1931; notarials, 1930–. Local records: civil registration, 1950–.

Pitogo (municipality), also known as Mayuboc, was an early Spanish town to which was annexed Macalelon from 1903 to 1912. Annexed Unisan from 1903 to 1909. FHL local records: civil registration, 1922–1931; notarials, 1910–; Conversion of Saint Paul parish registers, 1841–1976. Local records: civil registration, 1955–.

Plaridel (municipality) was established in 1962 from Atimonan. Local records: civil registration, 1962–.

Polillo (municipality), also known as Pulo, was an early Spanish town on the island of Polillo from which separated Burdeos (1948), Panululan (1959), and Jumalig (1961). FHL local records: civil registration, 1922–1931; notarials, 1913–; Saint Joseph parish registers, 1850–1950. Local records: civil registration, 1905–.

Quezon (municipality) was established in 1914 from Alabat. FHL local records: civil registration, 1922–1932; notarials, 1925–. Local records: civil registration, 1941–.

Real (municipality) was established as a municipal district in 1960 and as a municipality in 1963. Local records: civil registration, 1961–.

Sampaloc (municipality), also known as Dingin no. 77 (prior to 1892) and Alfonso XIII (1892 to 1902), was formerly village number 77 (Dingin no. 77) in Lucban. FHL local records: civil registration, 1922–1931; notarials, 1911–; Saint Vincent Ferrer parish registers, 1914–1935. Local records: civil registration, 1944–.

San Andres (municipality) was established as a municipal district in 1959 and as a municipality in 1965. Local records: civil registration, 1966–.

San Antonio (municipality) was established in 1957. Local records: civil registration, 1957–.

San Francisco (municipality), also known as Aurora (1940 to 1967) and Bondo (1938 to 1940), was established in 1938 from Mulanay under the name Bondo. FHL local records: notarials, 1939–1947. Local records: civil registration, 1938–.

San Luis. See Aurora Sub-province.

San Narciso (municipality) was an early Spanish town which was annexed to Mulanay from 1903 to 1913. FHL local records: civil registration, 1922–1931; notarials, 1912–. Local records: civil registration, 1913–.

Sariaya (municipality), also known as Sadyaya, Saryaya, and Sarjaya, was an early Spanish town which annexed Candelaria from 1902 to 1907. FHL local records: civil registration, 1921–1933; notarials, 1911–; Saint Francis of Assisi parish registers, 1776–1941. Local records: civil registration, 1902–.

Tagkawayan (municipality), also known as Tagkawayang and Bato, was established in 1941. FHL local records: notarials, 1934–1953. Local records: civil registration, 1945–.

Tayabas (municipality) was an early Spanish town which was the provincial capital until 1901. FHL local records: civil registration, 1922–1931; notarials, 1903–; deportations, 1867–1897; military induction records, 1886–1895; Saint Michael the Archangel parish registers, 1838–1945. Local records: civil registration, 1945–.

Tiaong (municipality), also known as Tiaon, Nayum, Tiyaran, and Tia Ong, was an early Spanish town which annexed Dolores from 1902 to 1910. FHL local records:

civil registration, 1922–1931; notarials, 1909–; Saint John the Baptist parish registers, 1856–1948. Local records: civil registration, 1909–.

Unisan (municipality), also known as Kalilaya and Kalilayan, was an early Spanish town which was annexed to Pitogo from 1903 to 1909. FHL local records: civil registration, 1922–1931; notarials, 1913–; Saint John the Baptist parish registers, 1875–1966. Local records: civil registration, 1909–.

Quirino. This inland province occupies an eastern section of central Luzon Island. The high mountains in the interior of the island of Luzon made it difficult for communication with the nearby provinces. Consequently, Quirino, which had been a part of Nueva Vizcaya, was made a sub-province of Nueva Vizcaya in June 1966 and an independent province in September 1971.

FHL provincial records: birth records (1946–1988), birth certificates (1971–1988), marriage contracts (1945–1987), and death certificates (1971–1988). See also the provincial records for the province of Nueva Vizcaya.

Localities and their records:

Aglipay (municipality) was annexed from the province of Isabela in 1948 and established as a municipality in 1950. Some of its territory was annexed to create Saguday (1959) and Cabarroquis (1969). Local records: civil registration, 1951–.

Cabarroquis (city) was established in 1969 from Diffun and Aglipay. Local records: civil registration, 1972–.

Diffun (municipality) was annexed from the province of Isabela in 1948 and established as a municipality in 1950. Some of its territory was annexed to create Saguday (1959) and Cabarroquis (1969). Local records: civil registration, 1952–.

Maddela (municipality) also known as Pinappagan, was established in 1950. FHL local records: civil registration, 1929–1931; notarials, 1936–1938. Local records: civil registration, 1946–.

Saguday (municipality) was established in 1959 from Diffun and Aglipay. Local records: civil registration, 1963–.

Rizal. This province is located in the southern portion of central Luzon. Bordering Metropolitan Manila, Rizal contributed many of the districts and cities used in its formation. See the section on Metropolitan Manila above for an early history of the area. In 1859 Tondo Province was renamed Manila Province; at the same time, the District of the Mountains of San Mateo was renamed Morong District. Early on, this area was a center for the Philippine Revolution. The Americans arrived in 1898, spent 1899 fighting the Philippine revolutionary forces, and established a civil government in the area by June 1901. Rizal Province was created by uniting the former District of Morong with all of Manila Province less the city of Manila. During World War II, President Quezon sought to simplify the administration of the area by creating Greater Manila which consolidated the towns surrounding Manila with the government of Manila. At the end of Japanese occupation, Greater Manila was dissolved. In May 1976 Metropolitan Manila was created.

FHL provincial records: (Several jurisdictions may be covered by the records—the District of Morong, Metro Manila, etc.) civil registration (1820–1876), birth records (1945–1988), marriage contracts (1945–1987), death certificates (1899–1993), court records created by the Court of First Instance (1901–1902), land records (1811–1919), military induction records (1972–1897), records of lending (1840–1898), school records (1781–1899), and Census of Chinese (1960–1897).

Localities and their records:

Angono (municipality) was an early Spanish town which was annexed both to Taytay and, later, Binangonan in 1903, then separated in 1938. FHL local records: civil registration, 1938–1992; notarials, 1932–; land records, 1850–1890. Local records: civil registration, 1939–.

Antipolo (municipality) was an early Spanish town to which Teresa was annexed from 1903 to 1919. FHL local records: civil registration, 1922–1933; notarials, 1908–. Local records: civil registration, 1908–.

Baras (municipality), also known as Santiago, was an early Spanish town which was annexed to Morong (1903) and Tanay (1906) and separated in 1921. FHL local records: civil registration, 1922–1930, 1924–1988; notarials, 1921–; Saint Joseph parish registers, 1840–1963. Local records: civil registration, 1941–.

Binangonan (municipality) was an early Spanish town which was briefly annexed to Morong for a few months in 1903. When it was separated, Angono separated also as part of Binangonan. Angono separated in 1938. FHL local records: civil registration, 1922–1931; notarials, 1911–; Saint Ursule parish registers, 1798–1932. Local records: civil registration, 1904–.

Cainta (municipality), an early Spanish town, was annexed to Taytay from 1903 to 1914. FHL local records: civil registration, 1922–1932; notarials, 1911–; Our Lady of the Light parish registers, 1900–1972. Local records: civil registration, 1914–.

Caloocan. See Metropolitan Manila above.

Cardona (municipality), also known as Sapao, was an early Spanish town which was annexed to Morong from 1903 to 1914. FHL local records: civil registration, 1922–1931, 1978–1990; notarials, 1914–; Our Lady of the Most Holy Rosary parish registers, 1900–1972. Local records: civil registration, 1945–.

Jalajala (municipality), also known as Pila, was an early Spanish town which was annexed to Pililla from 1903 to 1907. FHL local records: civil registration, 1922–1931, 1914–1988; notarials, 1911–; Saint Michael the Archangel parish registers, 1881–1921. Local records: civil registration, 1914–.

Las Piñas, **Makati**, **Malabon**, **Mandaluyong**, and **Marikina**. See Metropolitan Manila above.

Montalban (municipality), also known as Montalvan, was an early Spanish town which was annexed to San Mateo from 1903 to 1908. FHL local records: civil registration, 1885–1894, 1922–1931, 1945–1992; notarials, 1911–; death records, 1894; land records, 1761–1892; military induction records, 1884–1898; records of lending, 1871–1893; public records, 1886–1898; census, 1879–1891. Local records: civil registration, 1945–.

Morong (municipality) was an early Spanish town which was the capital of Morong Province from 1853 to 1901 when the province was dissolved. It was annexed to the newly created Rizal Province in 1901. The following municipalities were annexed in 1903: Binangonan (separated in 1903), Baras (reannexed to Taytay in 1906), and Cardona (separated in 1914). FHL local records: civil registration, 1820–1898, 1922–1931, 1912–1989; notarials, 1912–; deportations, 1867–1885; land records, 1850–1890; military induction records, 1865–1898; public records, 1873–1898; records of lending, 1877–1892; statistical reports, 1896; Saint Jerome parish registers, 1896–1941. Local records: civil registration, 1901–.

Muntinglupa, **Navotas**, **Novaliches**, **Parañaque**, **Pasay** (city), **Pasig** (city), and **Pateros**. See Metropolitan Manila above.

Pililla (municipality), also known as Pilang-Morong, was an early Spanish town to which Jalajala was annexed from 1903 to 1907. FHL local records: civil registration, 1921–1931, 1946–1989; notarials, 1911–; Saint Mary Magdalene parish registers, 1851–1977. Local records: civil registration, 1945–.

Quezon City (city) and **San Juan del Monte**. See Metropolitan Manila above.

San Mateo (municipality) was an early Spanish town to which Montalban was annexed from 1903 to 1908. FHL local records: civil registration, 1872–1896, 1922–1931, 1901–1991; notarials, 1903–; death certificates, 1977–1988; military induction records, 1868–1897; public records, 1884–1898; records of lending, 1877–1896, census, 1884, 1886. Local records: civil registration, 1901–.

Tagig. See Metropolitan Manila above.

Tanay (municipality), also known as Tan-ay and Monte Tan-ay, was an early Spanish town to which Baras was annexed from 1906 to 1921. FHL local records: civil registration, 1922–1934, 1945–1988; notarials, 1903–; Saint Ildephonsus parish registers, 1620–1971. Local records: civil registration, 1945–.

Taytay (municipality) was an early Spanish town to which were annexed the municipalities of Angono and Canta in 1903; Angono separated that same year, Cainta separated in 1914. FHL local records: civil registration, 1922–1932; notarials, 1905–; Saint John the Baptist parish registers, 1835–1949. Local records: civil registration, 1945–.

Teresa (municipality) was an early Spanish town which was annexed to Antipolo from 1903 to 1919. FHL local records: civil registration, 1922–1932, 1950–1992; notarials, 1917–. Local records: civil registration, 1950–.

Romblon. This island province is comprised of a group of islands just off the center of Luzon. The major islands are Romblon, Tablas, Sibuyan, Banton, Simara, Carabao, Alad, Logbon, and Cobrador. The Spanish, by the end of the sixteenth century, had established their authority and administered the area from Arevalo (now the province of Iloilo). The evangelization of the island was slow and uncertain until Spanish forts were built at Christian mission sites as protection against Moro raids. In 1716 the islands were separated from Iloilo and attached to the newly created province of Capiz. They were formed into a district, dependent on Capiz, in 1953. When American civil government was established in March 1901, Romblon became a province. As tax revenues were not sufficient to support the province, it became a sub-province of Capiz until February 1918. At that point, it again became a province. From 1940 to 1946, all the municipalities in Romblon were temporarily consolidated into four special municipalities: Banton, Sibuyan, Maghali, and Tablas.

> FHL provincial records: civil registration (1876–1896), birth records (1947–1988), marriage contracts (1945–1986), death certificates (1962–1991), court records created by the Court of First Instance (1901–1902), deportations (1888–1889), military induction records (1868–1897), public records (1885–1898), records of lending (1877–1898), school records (1866–1897), statistical reports (1896), and Census of Chinese (1889–1898).

Localities and their records:

Alcantara (municipality) was established in 1961. Local records: civil registration, 1961–.

Banton (municipality), also known as Jones (1918 to 1959), was an early Spanish town which was annexed to Romblon from 1903 to 1918. It was the seat of the special municipality of Maghali to which Concepcion and Corcuera were annexed in 1940. In 1946 Maghali was dissolved. FHL local records: civil registration, 1922–1931. Local records: civil registration, 1918–.

Cajidiocan (municipality), also known as Sibuyan, was an early Spanish town to which Magdiwang (formerly Magallanes) was annexed from 1903 to 1933. Annexing Magdiwang and San Fernando, it was the seat of the special municipality of Sibuyan from 1940–1946. FHL local records: civil registration, 1922–1931; Saint Barbara parish registers, 1779–1951. Local records: civil registration, 1921–.

Calatrava (municipal district) was established in 1968 from San Agustin.

Concepción (municipality), also known as Sibale, was an early Spanish town which was annexed to Mindoro Province in 1907, to Romblon Province in 1918, and back to Mindoro Province in 1924. Annexed to the special municipality of Maghali in Romblon Province from 1940 to 1946. FHL local records: civil registration, 1922–1931. Local records: civil registration, 1916–.

Corcuera (municipality) was an early Spanish town annexed to Romblon in 1903, to Banton from 1918 to 1931, and to the special municipality of Maghali from 1940 to 1946. FHL local records: civil registration, 1931. Local records: civil registration, 1931–.

Looc (municipality) was an early Spanish town to which Santa Fe was annexed in 1903. It was annexed to the special municipality of Odioñgan from 1940 to 1946. FHL local records: civil registration, 1922–1930; Saint Joseph parish registers, 1884–1898. Local records: civil registration, 1914–.

Magdiwang (municipality), also known as Magallanes, Magyanes, and Na-ilog, was an early Spanish town which was annexed to Cajidiocan from 1903 to 1933 (when its name was changed from Magallanes to Magdiwang). It was annexed to the special municipality of Sibuyan from 1940 to 1946. FHL local records: Our

Lady of the Most Holy Rosary parish registers, 1871–1935. Local records: civil registration, 1947–.

Odioñgan (municipality), also known as Indiongan and Tablas, was an early Spanish town to which San Andres (then known as Despujols) was annexed from 1903 to 1946. It was the seat of the special municipality of Tablas (1940 to 1946). FHL local records: civil registration, 1922–1931. Local records: civil registration, 1906–.

Romblon (city), also known as Domblon, was an early Spanish town to which Banton and Corcuera were annexed from 1903 to 1918. FHL local records: civil registration, 1922–1931; Saint Joseph, Spouse of the Blessed Virgin Mary, parish registers, 1879–1965. Local records: civil registration, 1925–.

San Agustin (municipality), also known as Badajoz and Guintigui-an, was an early Spanish town which was annexed to the special municipality of Tablas (1940 to 1946). Its name was changed from Badajoz to San Agustin in 1957. FHL local records: civil registration, 1928–1930; Saint Augustine parish registers, 1855–1953. Local records: civil registration, 1915–.

San Andres (municipality), also known as Despujols, Salado, and Parpaguha, was an early Spanish town which was annexed to Odiongan from 1903 to 1920 and to the special municipality of Tablas (1940 to 1946). FHL local records: civil registration, 1928–1930. Local records: civil registration, 1922–.

San Fernando (municipality), also known as Pag-Alad and Aeagra, was an early Spanish town annexed to the special municipality of Sibuyan (1940 to 1946). FHL local records: civil registration, 1922–1931; notarials, 1907–; Immaculate Conception parish registers, 1881–1956. Local records: civil registration, 1947–.

San José (municipality), also known as Carabao Island prior to 1965, became a municipal district in 1961 and a municipality in 1969. Local records: civil registration, 1968–.

Santa Fé (municipality) was an early Spanish town annexed to Looc from 1903 to 1948. Local records: civil registration, 1940–.

Samar. This province occupies the southwest portion of the island of Samar. Under the early Spanish government, this island was governed from Cebu. Later it became a separate province or district, but in 1735 Samar (then named Ibabao) and Leyte (then named Tandaya) were joined into one province with its capital at Carigara, Leyte. In 1768, Samar separated and became a province with its capital at Catbalogan. With the revision of governments in the lower Philippines in 1860, Samar became a politico-military province and it remained so until a civil government was declared by the Americans in June 1902. In June 1965 it was divided into Eastern Samar, Northern Samar, and Western Samar. The latter changed its name to Samar in June 1969.

> FHL provincial records: civil registration (1808–1897, 1961–1982), birth records (1945–1988), marriage contracts (1948–1987), death certificates (1962–1991), court records created by the Court of First Instance (1902–1903), deportations (1881–1898), military induction records (1886–1887), public records (1885–1898), records of lending (1872–1898), school records

(1858–1898), statistical reports (1896), tax records (1832–1889), and Census of Chinese (1888–1898).

Localities and their records:

Almagro (municipality), also known as Alimagro, was an early Spanish town from which Tagapul-an separated in 1970. FHL local records: civil registration, 1922–1930; notarials, 1911–. Local records: civil registration, 1914–.

Basey (municipality), also known as Baysay, was an early Spanish town which annexed the territory of Santa Rita on the left side of the Silanga River from 1903 to 1906. Marabut separated in 1949. FHL local records: civil registration, 1922–1931; notarials, 1911–; Saint Michael the Archangel parish registers, 1853–1912. Local records: civil registration, 1945–.

Calbayog City (city), also known as Caybago and Anislag, was an early Spanish town to which Santa Margarita and Weyler were annexed in 1903. Santa Margarita separated in 1909. When it was chartered as a city in June 1948, the municipalities of Oquendo and Tinambacan, located within the city, were annexed and made into districts. Oquendo District was an early Spanish town that was also known as Bato, Yndivel, Relles, and Oquendo Viejo. Tinambacan District, also known as Tinambadan, Weyler, Bayler, and Mabini, was an early Spanish town which had been annexed to Calbayog earlier (from 1903 to 1910). FHL local records: civil registration, 1921–1931; notarials, 1911–; birth certificates, 1949–1988; marriage contracts, 1950–1956; death certificates, 1976–1988; civil registration (Calbayog District), 1949–; Oquendo District—civil registration 1922–1931, notarials 1926–; Tinambacan District—civil registration 1922–1930, notarials 1912–. Local records: civil registration, 1913–; civil registration (Oquendo District), 1946–; civil registration (Tinambacan District), 1956–.

Calbiga (municipality) was an early Spanish town to which Pinabacdao was annexed from 1903 to circa 1947. FHL local records: civil registration, 1922–1931; notarials, 1911–; Annunciation of Our Lady parish registers, 1845–1974. Local records: civil registration, 1945–.

Catbalogan (city), also known as Catbala-ogan, was an early Spanish town which annexed Jiabong and part of Tarangnan in 1903; they separated in 1948 and 1906, respectively. FHL local records: civil registration, 1928; notarials, 1912–; Saint Bartholomew parish registers, 1795–1932. Local records: civil registration, 1902–.

Daram (municipality), also known as Benongto-an and Binongtuan, was established in 1949 from Zumarranga. Local records: civil registration, 1949–.

Gandara (municipality), also known as Bangahon and Dumalo-ong, was an early Spanish town to which part of Tarangnan was annexed from 1903 to 1906. FHL local records: notarials, 1912–. Local records: civil registration, 1950–.

Hinabangan (municipality), also known as Nahi-abangan, was an early Spanish town which was established as a municipal district in 1919 and consolidated with the municipal district of Concord to form a municipality in 1948. FHL local records: civil registration, 1928–1930; civil registration (Concord), 1926–1928. Local records: civil registration, 1945–.

Jiabong (municipality), also known as Hiabong, was an early Spanish town which was annexed to Catbalogan

from 1903 to 1948. FHL local records: Saint Pascual Baylon parish registers, 1891–1938. Local records: civil registration, 1948–.

Marabut (municipality), also known as Lipata and Santo Niño, was established in 1948 from Basey. Local records: civil registration, 1949–.

Matuguinao (municipality) was established in 1919. FHL local records: civil registration, 1928–1931; notarials, 1922–. Local records: civil registration, 1945–.

Motiong (municipality) was an early Spanish town annexed to Wright from 1903 to 1948. Local records: civil registration, 1948–.

Pinabacdao (municipality) was an early Spanish town annexed to Calbiga from 1903 to circa 1947. Local records: civil registration, 1946–.

San Jose de Buan (municipality) was established in 1969 as a municipality, having been a municipal district. FHL local records: civil registration, 1930–1931. Local records: civil registration, 1960–.

San Sebastian (municipality), also known as Balogo, was an early Spanish town annexed to Wright from 1903 to 1950. Local records: civil registration, 1950–.

Santa Margarita (municipality), also known as Magsohong and Margarita, was an early Spanish town annexed to Calbayog from 1903 to 1909. FHL local records: civil registration, 1922–1931; notarials, 1911–. Local records: civil registration, 1947–.

Santa Rita (municipality) was an early Spanish town which in 1903 had territory on the left bank of the Silanga River annexed to Basey and territory on the right bank annexed to Villareal. Both portions separated and reunited in 1906. FHL local records: civil registration, 1922–1931; notarials, 1911–. Local records: civil registration, 1958–.

Santo Niño (municipality), also known as Lubancauayan, Limbang, and Kawayan, was an early Spanish town. FHL local records: civil registration, 1922–1930; notarials, 1911–. Local records: civil registration, 1945–.

Tagapul-an (municipality) was established in 1970 from Almagro.

Talalora (municipality), also known as Lukban, was established in 1947 from Villareal. Local records: civil registration, 1965–.

Tarangnan (municipality), also known as Taraguan and Tinagub, was an early Spanish town. From 1903 to 1906 part of it was annexed to Catbalogan and part to Gandara. FHL local records: civil registration, 1921–1930; notarials, 1911–. Local records: civil registration, 1902–.

Villareal (municipality), also known as Omawas, was an early Spanish town which annexed the portion of Santa Rita located on the right bank of the Silanga River from 1903 to 1906. FHL local records: civil registration, 1921–1930; notarials, 1910–; Saint Rose of Lima parish registers, 1762–1948. Local records: civil registration, 1945–.

Wright (municipality), also known as Paranas, Ranas, Palanas, and Para-ranas, was established, under the name Wright, from the consolidation of the municipalities of Paranas, Motiong, and San Sebastian in 1903. Motiong (1948) and San Sebastian (1950) separated. FHL local records: civil registration, 1922–1930; notarials, 1911–; Saints Peter and Paul parish registers, 1902–1967. Local records: civil registration, 1945–.

Zumarraga (municipality), also known as Cawayan, was an early Spanish town from which separated Daram in 1949. FHL local records: civil registration, 1922–1932; notarials, 1911–. Local records: civil registration, 1902–.

Siquijor. This island province lies east of the province of Negros Oriental. It has been known by a number of names, including Katugasan and Isla de Fuego. Before 1854 Siquijor was administered from Cebu, but in that year, Bohol annexed the island of Siquijor and separated from Cebu. Made a sub-province of Negros Oriental in October 1907, Siquijor became an independent province in September 1917. Approximately one year later, its capital was transferred from Larena to Siquijor.

> FHL provincial records: birth certificates (1970–1988), death certificates (1972–1991), and marriage contracts (1972–1986).

Localities and their records:

Enrique Villanueva (municipality), also known as Talingting prior to 1931, was established in 1925 from Larena. FHL local records: civil registration, 1925–1931, 1925–1991; notarials, 1926–1936. Local records: civil registration, 1925–.

Larena (municipality), also known as Canoan and Kananan, was an early Spanish town which annexed Canoan in 1903. Enrique Villanueva separated in 1925. FHL local records: civil registration, 1922–1933, 1944–1990; notarials, 1909–. Local records: civil registration, 1945–.

Lazi (municipality), also known as Lacy, Tigbawan, and Tigbauan, was an early Spanish town which annexed Maria from 1903 to 1910. FHL local records: civil registration, 1922–1929, 1944–1991; notarials, 1918–; Saint Isidore, the Farmer, parish registers, 1857–1953. Local records: civil registration, 1944–.

María (municipality), also known as Canmeniac, Kangmenia, and Kangmenya, was an early Spanish town which was annexed to Lazi from 1903 to 1910. FHL local records: civil registration, 1922–1931, 1916–1991; notarials, 1917–1925; Our Lady of Divine Providence parish registers, 1880–1973. Local records: civil registration, 1916–.

San Juan (municipality), also known as Calipay and Kapilay, was an early Spanish town annexed to Siquijor from 1903 to 1912. FHL local records: civil registration, 1922–1930, 1947–1991; notarials, 1912–; Saint Augustine of Hippo parish registers, 1889–1969. Local records: civil registration, 1944–.

Siquijor (city), also known as Katugasan, Sikohod, and Sikiho, was an early Spanish town which annexed San Juan from 1903 to 1912. FHL local records: civil registration, 1902–1931, 1937–1991; notarials, 1911–; Saint Francis of Assisi parish registers, 1835–1948.

Sorsogon. This province is located on the tip of the Bicol Peninsula of Luzon Island. The early history of the area is obscure, but it appears to have been visited by a number of Spanish explorers. Its first Spanish settlements (missions) were established by Catholic missionaries at Casiguran (1600), Bulusan (1630), Bacon (1617), Sorsogon (1628), and Donsol (1681). This province was

the source of the Spanish galleons which were built in the ship yard at Bagatao. Originally, Sorsogon was a part of the former province of Ibalon (later named Albay). In 1864 it became a military district dependent on Albay; in October 1894 it became a full province. The Philippine Revolution of 1896 resulted in the evacuation of all Spanish from the area. In April 1901 American forces established a civil government. The province of Masbate was annexed to Sorsogon as a sub-province from 1906 to 1921.

> FHL provincial records: birth records (1946–1988), marriage contracts (1947–1987), death certificates (1962–1991), court records created by the Court of First Instance (1901), deportations (1896), land records (1850–1890), public records (1884–1898), Census of Chinese (1895–1897), and notarials (1908–1949).

Localities and their records:

Bacon (municipality) was an early Spanish town. A portion of Prieto Díaz separated in 1903. FHL local records: civil registration, 1921–1931; notarials, circa 1911–; Our Lady of the Annunciation parish registers, 1779–1932. Local records: civil registration, 1951–.

Barcelona (municipality) was an early Spanish town. FHL local records: civil registration, 1922–1931; notarials, circa 1905–; Saint Joseph parish registers, 1868–1939. Local records: civil registration, 1946–.

Bulan (municipality) was an early Spanish town. FHL local records: civil registration, 1927–1931; notarials, circa 1911–; Our Lady of the Immaculate Conception parish registers, 1839–1898 and 1801–1951. Local records: civil registration, 1947–.

Bulusan (municipality) was an early Spanish town. FHL local records: civil registration, 1922–1926; notarials, circa 1911–; Saint James, the Greater, parish registers, 1756–1936 and 1800–1898. Local records: civil registration, 1901–.

Casiguran (municipality) was an early Spanish town. FHL local records: notarials, 1911–; Saint Anthony parish registers, 1840–1935. Local records: civil registration, 1945–.

Castilla (municipality) was an early Spanish town. FHL local records: notarials, 1921–; Saint John, the Baptist, parish registers, 1876–1931, and church census, 1833–1918. Local records: civil registration, 1966–.

Donsol (municipality) was an early Spanish town. FHL local records: civil registration, 1921–1930; notarials, 1903–; Saint Joseph parish registers, 1890–1938. Local records: civil registration, 1918–.

Gubat (municipality) was an early Spanish town. Prieto Díaz separated in 1903. FHL local records: civil registration, 1921–1931; notarials, 1912–; Saint Anthony of Padua parish registers, 1758–1936. Local records: civil registration, 1945– (a few earlier).

Irosin (municipality), also known as Iricon and Irocin, was an early Spanish town. FHL local records: civil registration, 1922–1931; notarials, 1911–; Saint Michael the Archangel parish registers, 1876–1929. Local records: civil registration, 1945–.

Juban (municipality), also known as Tuban, was an early Spanish town. FHL local records: civil registration, 1922–28; notarials, 1904–; Saint Anthony of Padua parish registers, 1848–1931. Local records: civil registration, 1946–.

Magallanes (municipality) was an early Spanish town. FHL local records: civil registration, 1921–1932; notarials, circa 1911–; Our Lady of Mount Carmel parish registers, 1864–1929. Local records: civil registration, 1949– (a few earlier).

Matnog (municipality), also known as Magnoc, was an early Spanish town. FHL local records: civil registration, 1928–1931; notarials, 1912–; Holy Infant Jesus parish registers, 1913–1941. Local records: civil registration, 1948–.

Pilar (municipality) was an early Spanish town. FHL local records: civil registration, 1928–1929; notarials, 1908–; Our Lady of the Pilar parish registers, 1901–1928. Local records: civil registration, 1953–.

Prieto Diáz (municipality) was established in 1903 though the consolidation of the villages of Manlabong and Mantufar from the municipality of Bacon, and the village of Calas from the municipality of Gubat. FHL local records: civil registration, 1922–1930; notarials, 1911–; Saint Lawrence parish registers, 1878–1951. Local records: civil registration, 1948–.

Santa Magdalena (municipality) was an early Spanish town. FHL local records: civil registration, 1922–1930; Our Lady of Magdalene parish registers, 1890–1947. Local records: civil registration, 1967–.

Sorsogon (city), an early Spanish town, has been the capital of the province since 1894. FHL local records: civil registration, 1930–1931; notarials, 1902–; Saints Peter and Paul parish registers, 1754–1933. Local records: civil registration, 1901–.

South Cotabato. This province, situated on the southern coast of the island of Mindanao, originated when the former province of Cotabato was divided into the provinces of Sultan Kudarat, Maguindanao, North Catabato, and South Cotabato in July 1966. See section on the province of Maguindanao above for the administrative history.

FHL provincial records: civil registration (1862–1897), birth records (1967–1988), marriage contracts (1968–1987), death certificates (1967–1991), deportations (1865–1898), military induction records (1869–1896), public records (1894–1898), records of lending (1878–1898), school records (1871–1898), and Census of Chinese (1878–1898).

Localities and their records:

Alabel (municipality) was established in 1971 from General Santos.

Banga (municipality) was established in 1953. Surallah and T'boli separated in 1961 and 1974, respectively. Local records: civil registration, 1953–.

General Santos (city), also known as Dadiangas, Rajah Buayan, and Buayan, was established as a municipality in 1947. Its name was changed from Buayan to General Santos in 1954. It was chartered as a city in 1968. Malungon separated in 1969. FHL local records: birth certificates, 1968–1988; death certificates, 1976–1988. Local records: civil registration, 1948–.

Glan (municipality) was established in 1949 from Buayan (now General Santos). Malapatan separated in 1969. FHL local records: civil registration, 1930–1931;

notarials, circa 1917–. Local records: civil registration, 1947–.

Kiamba (municipality) was established in 1948 from Lebak, province of Sultan Kudarat, to which it had been annexed earlier. FHL local records: civil registration, 1928–1931; notarials, circa 1923–. Local records: civil registration, 1944–.

Koronadal (municipality) was established in 1947. Local records: civil registration, 1963–.

Maasim (municipality) was established in 1964. T'boli separated in 1974. Local records: civil registration, 1965–.

Maitum (municipality) was established in 1964 from Kiamba. T'boli separated in 1974. Local records: civil registration, 1959–.

Malapatan (municipality) was established in 1969 from Glan.

Malungon (municipality) was established in 1969 from General Santos.

Norala (municipality) was established in 1953. Local records: civil registration, 1953–.

Polomolok (municipality) was established in 1957. T'boli separated in 1974. Local records: civil registration, 1957–.

Surallah (municipality) was established in 1963 from Banga. T'boli separated in 1974. Local records: civil registration, 1963–.

Tampakan (municipality) was established in 1969 from Tupi.

Tantangan (municipality) was established in 1961. Local records: civil registration, 1961–.

T'boli (municipality) was established in 1974, in the interior of the province, from territory formerly held by Surallah, Banga, Tupi, Polomolok, Maasim, Kiamba, and Maitum.

Tupi (municipality) was established in 1953. T'boli and Tampakan separated in 1974 and 1969, respectively. Local records: civil registration, 1962–.

Southern Leyte. This province occupies the southeastern portion of Leyte Island. It also includes the islands of Panaoan and Limasawa. In July 1960 this province was divided from Leyte Province. See the section on Leyte Province above for the administrative history.

FHL provincial records: civil registration (1891–1898), birth records (1946–1988), marriage contracts (1945–1987), death certificates (1963–1991), court records created by the Court of First Instance (1847–1903), deportations (1867–1889), military induction records (1857–1898), public records (1883–1893), records of lending (1859–1898), and school records (1848–1911).

Localities and their records:

Anahawan (municipality), also known as Delgado, was established in 1930 from Hinundayan. FHL local records: civil registration, 1931; notarials, 1931–1936. Local records: civil registration, 1940–.

Bontoc (municipality) was established in 1950 from Sogod. Local records: civil registration, 1950–.

Hinunangan (municipality), also known as Honoñganan, was an early Spanish town which annexed Hinundayan from 1903 to 1910. FHL local records: civil registration, 1922–1932; notarials, circa 1912–; Saints Peter and Paul parish registers, 1851–1934. Local records: civil registration, 1951–.

Hinundayan (municipality) was established in 1910 from Hinunangan to which it had been annexed in 1903. Anahawan separated in 1930. FHL local records: civil registration, 1922–1931; notarials, circa 1911–; Saint Joseph parish registers, 1885–1981. Local records: civil registration, 1915–.

Libagon (municipality), also known as Sogod Norte, was established in 1913 from Sogod to which it had been annexed in 1903. In 1913 its name was changed to Libagon. FHL local records: civil registration, 1921–1929; notarials, 1914–; Immaculate Conception parish registers, 1869–1949. Local records: civil registration, 1916–.

Liloan (municipality), also known as Panaon, was an early Spanish town. FHL local records: civil registration, 1922–1931; notarials, 1912–; Saint Ignatius Loyola parish registers, 1907–1952. Local records: civil registration, 1945–.

Maasin (city), an early Spanish town, annexed Macrohon (except for San Roque) from 1903 to 1908. FHL local records: civil registration, 1922–1932; notarials, 1911–; Our Lady's Assumption parish registers, 1796–1945. Local records: civil registration, 1945–.

Macrohon (municipality), also known as MacCrohon, was an early Spanish town established in 1908 from Maasin to which it had been annexed in 1903. FHL local records: civil registration, 1922–1931; notarials, 1911–; Saint Michael the Archangel parish registers, 1862–1944. Local records: civil registration, 1909–.

Malitbog (municipality) was an early Spanish town. Tomas Oppus separated in 1969. FHL local records: civil registration, 1922–1930; notarials, 1911–; Holy Name of Jesus parish registers, 1850–1945. Local records: civil registration, 1916–.

Padre Burgos (municipality) was established in 1957. Local records: civil registration, 1957–.

Pintuyan (municipality), an early Spanish town, was formerly a village in municipality of San Ricardo. In 1907 when the municipality seat was transferred from San Ricardo to Pintuyan, the entire municipality took the name Pintuyan. San Ricardo separated in 1971. FHL local records: civil registration, 1922–1931; notarials, 1913–. Local records: civil registration, 1957–.

Saint Bernard (municipality) was established in 1954. Local records: civil registration, 1955–.

San Francisco (municipality) was established in 1949. Local records: civil registration, 1951–.

San Juan (municipality), also known as Cabalian, Tunga, Kabulihan, and Cabilian, was an early Spanish town. Its name was changed from Cabalian to San Juan in 1961. FHL local records: civil registration, 1922–1931; notarials, 1928–; Saint John the Baptist parish registers, 1861–1973. Local records: civil registration, 1902–.

San Ricardo (municipality) was established in 1971 from Pintuyan. It had been a municipality earlier, but when the municipality seat was transferred from San Richardo to Pintuyan in 1907, the entire municipality took the name Pintuyan.

Silago (municipality), also known as Morcelago, was an early Spanish town established in 1950 from Hinunangan. Local records: civil registration, 1951–.

Sogod (municipality), also known as Sogod Sur, was an early Spanish town. Annexed Sogod Norte (now Libagon) from 1903 to 1913. FHL local records: civil registration, 1922–1930; notarials, 1911–; Holy Name of Jesus parish registers, 1850–1945. Local records: civil registration, 1916–.

Tomas Oppus (municipality) was established in 1969 from Malitbog. Local records: civil registration, 1972–.

Sultan Kudarat. This province occupies the southwest coast of the island of Mindanao. It was formed in 1973 when the former province of Cotabato was divided into Sultan Kudarat, Maguindao, and North Cotabato. See the administrative history of Cotabato Province in the section on Maguindanao above.

FHL provincial records: civil registration (1867–1897), birth records (1969–1988), marriage contracts (1974–1987), death certificates (1974–1991), deportations (1865–1898), land records (1865–1898), military induction records (1869–1896), public records (1894–1897), records of lending (1878–1898), school records (1871–1898), and Census of Chinese (1878–1898).

Localities and their records:

Bagumbayan (municipality) was established in 1969 from Isulan.

Columbio (municipality) was established in 1961 from Buluan of Maguindanao Province. Datu Paglas separated and became part of Maguindanao. Local records: civil registration, 1961–.

Esperanza (municipality) was established in 1973 from Ampatuan of Maguindanao Province.

Isulan (city), also known as Insulan, was established in 1957. Bagumbayan separated in 1969. Local records: civil registration, 1960–.

Kalamansig (municipality) was established in 1961 from Lebak and Palimbang. Local records: civil registration, 1962–.

Lebak (municipality) was established in 1948 from Kiamba of South Cotabato Province to which it had been annexed in 1947. FHL local records: civil registration, 1923–1930; notarials, 1923–1930. Local records: civil registration, 1919–.

Lutayan (municipality) was established in 1967 from Buluan of Maguindanao Province. Local records: civil registration, 1968–.

Mariano Marcos (municipality) was established in 1973 from Sultan Sa Barongis of Maguindanao Province.

Palimbang (municipality) was established in 1959. Kalamansig separated in 1961. Local records: civil registration, 1959–.

President Quirino (municipality) was established in 1973 from Buluan of Maguindanao Province.

Tacurong (municipality) was established in 1951 from Buluan of Maguindanao Province. Local records: civil registration, 1953–.

Sulu. The province of Sulu is composed of some 2,000 islands that extend from Zamboanga Peninsula in a southwest direction to the Island of Borneo. Jolo, its capital, was a center of international trade before the arrival of the Spanish as well as the site of an Islamic sultanate. One ruler, Abu Bakr, ascended the throne in 1450 and carried out social and administrative reforms that included the establishment and reform of Islam, the division of his state into four administrative areas, and the establishment of a legal system based on Islamic law.

During the sixteenth and seventeenth centuries, the Spanish government attempted to establish control via a series of mostly unsuccessful military expeditions, although one did result in the evacuation of Jolo by the Sulu forces. The Moro raids that were a constant annoyance to the Spanish in the southern Philippines originated in this area. Early in the nineteenth century the British also failed in their attempts to extend their control from Borneo into Sulu. In the middle of the nineteenth century the Spanish were finally successful in suppressing Sulu. Governor-General Urbiztondo's steam ships proved to be superior to native war ships. The victory allowed the Spanish to incorporate Sulu into the lands controlled by the Spanish crown and to establish a small Spanish fort and trading post at Jolo. Another expedition in 1876 meant the Spanish were able to establish a large garrison at Jolo. In 1884 a civil war broke out between three Moro factions—each of which put forward a claimant to the throne of the Sultanate of Sulu. Spanish intervention complicated the situation, delaying its resolution until 1894. Though Sulu did not take part in the Philippine Revolution, all Spanish were evacuated from Sulu during that time. General John C. Bates of the United States arrived to negotiate a treaty with the Sultan of Sulu. The Bates Treaty, or the Treaty of Sulu (1899), recognized the sovereignty of the Sultan, guaranteeing free exercise of the Islamic religion and respect for Islamic traditions. In June 1903, Sulu became one of the five districts of the Province of Moro with its provincial capital at Zamboanga and district capital at Jolo. In 1914, the Moro Province was replaced by the Department of Mindanao and Sulu with Sulu becoming a full province. In 1915 the Sultan of Sulu gave up his traditional political rights, but remained the head of the Islamic religion in Sulu. Finally in 1944 the Sultanate was abolished and Sulu became part of the Philippine Commonwealth. In 1947 the Philippine government acquired the islands of Taganak, Bakkungan, Bayuna, Sibaung, and Lihiman which had been leased by the Sultan to the British North Borneo Company. In 1973 these islands together with a few others were detached from the province of Sulu to form the province of Tawi-Tawi.

> FHL provincial records: birth records (1947–1988), marriage contracts (1949–1986), death certificates (1966–1991), land records (1876–1898), and school records (1880–1898). There are also the provincial and district administrative papers of the Spanish government in this area (Mindanao y Sulu). This vast collection includes 147 reels of microfilm.

Localities and their records:

Indanan (municipality) was established in 1959.

Jolo (city) was the capital of the Sultanate of Sulu and the site of a Spanish fort from 1638 to 1646. FHL local records: civil registration, 1883–1898, 1922–1932; deportations, 1876–1898, military induction records, 1876–1895; public records, 1884–1897; census of

Chinese, 1887–1898; notarials, 1910–; Roman Catholic parish records, 1877 to 1984. Local records: civil registration, 1974–.

Kalingalan Caluang (municipality) was established in 1975 from Luuk.

Luuk (municipality) was established in 1959. Kalingal Caluang separated in 1975. Local records: civil registration, 1949–.

Maimbung (municipality) was established in 1959. Local records: civil registration, 1973–.

Marunggas (municipal district).

Pananaw (municipality), also known as Panamao, was established in 1959.

Pangutaran (municipality) was established in 1959. Local records: civil registration, 1950–.

Parang (municipality) was established in 1959. FHL local records: notarials, 1911–.

Pata (municipality) was established in 1959.

Patikul (municipality) was established in 1959. Local records: civil registration, 1974–.

Siasi (municipality) was established in 1959. FHL local records: civil registration, 1890–1898. Local records: civil registration, 1950–.

Talipaw (municipality), also known as Talipao, was established in 1959. Local records: civil registration, 1950–.

Tapul (municipality) was established in 1959.

Tungkil (municipality) was established in 1959. Local records: civil registration, 1955–.

Surigao del Norte. This province is located on the northern tip of the island of Mindanao. It also includes the islands of Dinagat, Siargao, and Bucas Grande. The former Surigao province, which was divided in 1960 into Surigao del Norte and Surigao del Sur, has a rather complex administrative history. In the early sixteenth century, it was visited by a number of Portuguese and Spanish explorers, one of whom, Ruy Lopez de Villalobos, named it Cesarea Caroli, in honor of King Charles V of Spain. It soon came to be known by the Spanish as Caraga, since most of the native population belonged to the Caraga tribe. In 1597, the Jesuits began attempts to evangelize the inhabitants of Butuan (modern Agusan) and Caraga (modern Surigao), but with limited success. In 1609 Juan de Vega led a military expedition to this area, defeated the local forces, established a fort at Tandag which became the center of Spanish authority in this region, and founded the province of Caraga. It comprised more or less the northern half of the island of Mindanao: the modern provinces of Surigao del Norte, Surigao del Sur, Agusan del Norte, and Agusan del Sur; the northern part of Cavao Oriental; and the eastern portion of Misamis Oriental. In 1622 the Augustinian Recollects established missions and founded parishes in Caraga (1622) and Bislig (1642). They remained until 1875 when the secular clergy and Benedictine monks (1893 to 1908) took over. In 1818, Misamis separated and became a district. In 1849, a new province, Nueva Guipuzcoa (later called Davao) was created. Its territory included the modern provinces of Davao, Davao del Norte, Davao Oriental, Surigao del Sur, and, roughly, the southern half of Surigao del Norte. Since Tandag, the capital of the former province of Caraga, had been annexed to Davao, Surigao became the provincial capital of Nueva Guipuzcoa. The province was divided in 1855 into Bislig and Davao. In 1860 the government of Mindanao was reorganized into a District of Mindanao with six districts, one of which was Surigao (with Bislig annexed). By 1898, the territory of the two modern provinces of Agusan del Norte and Agusan del Sur had been organized into Butuan which was under Surigao. The Philippines Revolution did not have a strong following in this area and American forces quickly organized a military government. In May 1901 a civil government was established and Butuan became a sub-province of Surigao until 1907 when it became the separate province of Agusan. In 1903 the Moro Province was created. This province consisted of five districts— one of which, the district of Davao, absorbed the towns of the former district of Bislig. These towns are now located mainly in Davao Oriental. In that same year, the thirty-four municipalities of Surigao were consolidated into twenty-nine and, a year later, into only twelve. As stated earlier, in 1960 Surigao was divided into Surigao del Norte and Surigao del Sur. At present two orders are established in this area: the Sacred Heart Missionaries (1908–) and the Divine World Missionaries (1973–).

> FHL provincial records: civil registration (1869–1897), birth records (1960–1988), marriage contracts (1946– 1987), death certificates (1962–1991), court records created by the Court of First Instance (1901), deportations (1872–1898), land records (1873), military induction records (1879–1895), public records (1884– 1898), records of lending (1887–1889), school records (1856–1898), statistical reports (1896), tax records (1840–1897), Census of Chinese (1895), and notarials (1910).

Localities and their records:

Alegria (municipality) was established in 1968 from Mainit. Local records: civil registration, 1969–.

Bacuag (municipality) was established in 1919 after having been annexed to Gigaguitin in 1904. FHL local records: civil registration, 1921–1931; notarials, 1919–. Local records: civil registration, 1919–.

Basilisa (municipality), also known as Rizal, was established in 1969 from Dinagat.

Burgos (municipality) was established in 1967 from Sapao (now known as Santa Monica).

Cagdianao (municipality) was established in 1960. Local records: civil registration, 1964–.

Claver (municipality) was established in 1955 from Gigaquit to which it had been annexed in 1904. Local records: civil registration, 1955–.

Dapa (municipality) was an early Spanish town. In 1904 it annexed Numancia (now Del Carmen, separated circa 1929), Cabuntog (now General Luna, separated 1929), and Sapao (now Santa Monica, separated 1953). FHL local records: civil registration, 1922–1930; notarials, 1914–. Local records: civil registration, 1926–.

Del Carmen (municipality), also known as Numancia and Cucub, was established circa 1929 from Dapa to which it had been annexed in 1904. San Benito separated in 1971. Its name was changed from Numancia to Del Carman in 1966. FHL local records: civil registration, 1917–1930; notarials, 1911–.

Dinagat (municipality), an early Spanish town, annexed Loreto from 1904 to 1919. Rizal (now Basilisa) separated in 1969. FHL local records: civil registration, 1922–1931; notarials, 1911–. Local records: civil registration, 1950–.

General Luna (municipality), also known as Cabuntog prior to 1929, was established in 1929 from Dapa to which it had been annexed in 1904. FHL local records: civil registration, 1929–1931. Local records: civil registration, 1945–.

Gigaquit (municipality), an early Spanish town, annexed Bacuag (separated 1919) and Claver (separated in 1955) in 1904. FHL local records: civil registration, 1922– 1933; notarials, 1912–. Local records: civil registration, 1951–.

Libjo (municipality), also known as Albor prior to 1967, was established in 1960. Local records: civil registration, 1960–.

Loreto (municipality), also known as Mabua, was an early Spanish town that was established in 1919 from Dinagat to which it had been annexed in 1904. Tubajon separated in 1969. FHL local records: civil registration, 1922–1932; notarials, 1919–. Local records: civil registration, 1960–.

Mainit (municipality), also known as Maynit, was established circa 1919 from Placer to which it had been annexed in 1904. Alegria separated in 1968. FHL local records: notarials, 1935–. Local records: civil registration, 1945–.

Malimono (municipality) was established in 1956.

Pilar (municipality) was established in 1953.

Placer (municipality), also known as Villa Franca and Villa Francia, was an early Spanish town to which Tagana-an and Mainit were annexed in 1904 and separated in 1947 and 1944, respectively. FHL local records: civil registration, 1924–1930; notarials, 1910–. Local records: civil registration, 1954–.

San Benito (municipality) was established in 1971 from Del Carmen and Santa Monica.

San Francisco (municipality), also known as Anao-aon prior to 1971, was established in 1957 from Surigao to which it had been annexed in 1903. Local records: civil registration, 1957–.

San Isidro (municipality) was established in 1960. Local records: civil registration, 1960–.

Santa Monica (municipality), also known as Sapao prior to 1967, was established in 1953 from Dapa to which it had been annexed in 1904. It includes all the Siargao Islands. Local records: civil registration, 1953–.

Sison (municipality) was established in 1960. Local records: civil registration, 1960–.

Socorro (municipality) was established in 1961. Local records: civil registration, 1965–.

Surigao (city), a Spanish town by 1655 and provincial capital by 1848, annexed Anao-aon (now San Francisco) in 1903 (separated in 1957) and Nonoc in 1904. It was chartered as a city in August 1970. FHL local records: civil registration, 1930; notarials, 1909–; birth records,

1969–1988; death certificates, 1975–1988. Local records: civil registration, 1944–.

Tagana-an (municipality), also known as Tagoanan, was established in 1947 from Placer to which it had been annexed in 1904. Local records: civil registration, 1947–.

Tubajon (municipality) was established in 1969 from Loreto.

Tubod (municipality) was established in 1957. Local records: civil registration, 1958–.

Surigao del Sur. The province of Surigao del Sur is situated on the eastern coast of Mindanao Island. In 1960 the former province of Surigao was divided into Surigao del Norte and Surigao del Sur. See the section on Surigao del Norte above for an administrative history of Surigao.

FHL provincial records: civil registration (1869–1897), birth records (1960–1988), marriage contracts (1946–1987), death certificates (1962–1991), court records created by the Court of First Instance (1901), deportations (1872–1898), land records (1873), military induction records (1879–1895), public records (1884–1898), records of lending (1887–1889), school records (1856–1898), statistical reports (1896), tax records (1840–1897), Census of Chinese (1895), and notarials (1910).

Localities and their records:

Barobo (municipality) was established in 1960. Local records: civil registration, 1961–.

Bayabas (municipality) was established in 1961. Local records: civil registration, 1962–.

Bislig (municipality), an early Spanish town, was established in 1921 from Hinatuan to which it had been annexed in 1904. Annexed the former municipal districts of Coleto and Hinatuan in 1959. FHL local records: civil registration, 1921–1931; notarials, 1913–. Local records: civil registration, 1921–.

Cagwait (municipality) was established in 1953 from Tago. Local records: civil registration, 1953–.

Cantilan (municipality), also known as Cantilang and Gantilang was an early Spanish town to which were annexed the villages of Carrascal and Lanuza—both of which separated in 1919. Annexed the former municipal district of Cabangahan in 1959. FHL local records: civil registration, 1929–1933; notarials, 1911–. Local records: civil registration, 1964–.

Carmen (municipality) was established in 1971 from Lanuza.

Carrascal (municipality) was established in 1919 from Cantilan to which it had been annexed in 1904. FHL local records: civil registration, 1922–1932; notarials, 1927–1932. Local records: civil registration, 1945–.

Cortes (municipality) was established in 1953 from Tandag to which it had been annexed in 1904. Local records: civil registration, 1953–.

Hinatuan (municipality), also known as Jinatuan, was an early Spanish town to which Bislig was annexed from 1904 to 1921. Lingig separated in 1921, as did Tagbina in 1969. FHL local records: civil registration, 1922–1932; notarials, 1916–. Local records: civil registration, 1947–.

Lanuza (municipality), an early Spanish town, was annexed to Cantilan until 1919. FHL local records: civil registration, 1922–1931. Local records: civil registration, 1916–.

Lianga (municipality), an early Spanish town, annexed the former municipal district of Soriano in 1959. FHL local records: notarials, 1911–. Local records: civil registration, 1950–.

Lingig (municipality), also known as Linguig, was established in 1921 from Hinatuan. It was annexed to Bislig in 1903; Bislig was annexed to Hinatuan in 1904. It received a number of small villages from the province of Davao Oriental. FHL local records: civil registration, 1922–1930. Local records: civil registration, 1951–.

Madrid (municipality) was established in 1953. Local records: civil registration, 1953–.

Marihatag (municipality), also known as Oteiza and Oteyza, was established in 1951. FHL local records: notarials, 1933–1940. Local records: civil registration, 1951–.

San Agustin (municipality) was established in 1962 from Marihatag. Local records: civil registration, 1962–.

San Miguel (municipality) was established in 1962 from Tago. Local records: civil registration, 1962–.

Tagbina (municipality) was established in 1969 from Hinatuan.

Tago (municipality) was established in 1919 from Tandag to which it had been annexed in 1904. Cagwait (1953) and San Miguel (1962) separated. FHL local records: civil registration, 1922–1931; notarials, 1919–. Local records: civil registration, 1919–.

Tandag (municipality), also known as Tandang, Tandagan, and Tanda, was an early Spanish town to which in 1904 were annexed the following villages of the province of Agusan del Sur: Cortés, Tago, Marihatag, and La Paz of which the first three separated in 1953, 1919, and 1951, respectively. FHL local records: notarials, circa 1911–. Local records: civil registration, 1950–.

Province of Tarlac. This province is located in the center of Luzon Island in the northern part of the Philippines. Due to its remote location in the mountainous interior of central Luzon, it was one of the last provinces to be established by the Spanish. Originally inhabited by tribes of Negroids, its central location has attracted settlers from the various coastal provinces of Luzon; hence it has been called the melting pot of Luzon. Settlers from nearby provinces founded Tarlac (1686), Bamban (1710), Capas (1712), and Paniqui (1754). The Augustinian Recollect missionaries were the first to found missions and parishes in this area: Tarlac (1720), Bamban (1710), Capas (1712), and Capas (1776), and later, Concepción, Victoria, and La Paz. The northern portion of the province was evangelized by both the Augustinians and the Dominicans. In 1860 it became a comandancia which annexed additional territory from the province of Pampanga. In 1873 it became a full province, annexing the following towns from Pamanga: Bamban, Capas, Concepción, Victoria, and Tarlac; and three towns from the newly created province of Pangasinan: Camaling, Gerona, and Panique. During the Philippine Revolution of 1896, the province was a center of anti-Spanish agitation. During this same time, the city of Paniqui was chosen by Gregorio Aglipay to host the conference of Filipino clergy which established the Philippine Independent Church, now called the Aglipayan Church. In late 1899 American forces established a military government, replacing it with a civil government in February 1901.

FHL provincial records: civil registration (1879–1891), birth records (1945–1988), marriage contracts (1945–1987), death certificates (1962–1991), court records created by the Court of First Instance (1901–1903), deportations (1883–1898), land records (1850–1908), military induction records (1896–1897), public records (1885–1898), records of lending (1880–1898), school records (1865–1898), statistical reports (1894), Census of Chinese (1890–1898), and notarials (1903–).

Localities and their records:

Anao (municipality), established in 1908, was annexed as village to Paniqui from 1903 to 1908. It was organized by the consolidation of villages from two municipalities: Anao and San Francisco from Paníqui, and San Ramón from Moncada. FHL local records: civil registration, 1922–1931; notarials, circa 1909–; Saint Nicholas parish registers, 1900–1957. Local records: civil registration, 1970–.

Bamban (municipality) was an early Spanish town. FHL local records: civil registration, 1922–1932; notarials, 1911–; The Infant Jesus parish registers, 1903–1972. Local records: civil registration, 1901–.

Camiling (municipality), also known as San Miguel de Camiling, was an early Spanish town which in 1903 annexed Santa Ignacia (separated in 1914) and San Clemente (separated in 1915). Mayantoc separated in 1917. The village of San Vicente was annexed by Santa Ignacia in 1920. FHL local records: civil registration, 1921–1932; notarials, circa 1903–; Saint Michael parish registers, 1834–1949. Local records: civil registration, 1918–.

Capas (municipality), also known as Capaz, was a town founded by the Spanish in 1712. It annexed the town of O'Donnell, and the villages of Calynicuan and San Agustin (from the former municipality of Murcia) in 1903. FHL local records: civil registration, 1922–1932, 1981–1993; notarials, 1903–. Local records: civil registration, 1901–.

Concepción (municipality), also known as Conception, was an early Spanish town. In 1903, it annexed the village of Kaut from municipality of La Paz along with the villages of Santa Rosa, San Juan, and San Agustin from the former municipality of Murcia. The villages of Bantug and Kaut separated and were annexed to La Paz in 1906 and 1907, respectively. FHL local records: civil registration, 1923–1931, 1945–1992; notarials, circa 1906–; Immaculate Conception parish registers, 1866–1929. Local records: civil registration, 1945–.

Gerona (municipality), also known as Barug, was established in 1907 from Pura to which it had been annexed in 1903. FHL local records: civil registration, 1922–1932, 1912–1993; notarials, 1910–; Saint Catherine of Alexandria parish registers, 1854–1954. Local records: civil registration, 1912–.

La Paz (municipality) was established in 1906 from Tarlac to which it had been annexed (minus the village of Kaut which was annexed to Concepción) in 1903. The villages of Bantug and Kaut were annexed to La Paz in 1906 and 1907, respectively. FHL local records: civil

registration, 1922–1931; notarials, 1911–; Our Lady of Peace parish registers, 1925–1976. Local records: civil registration, 1901–.

Mayantoc (municipality), also known as San Francisco de Mayantoc, was established in 1917 from Camiling. A town organized by the Revolutionary government in 1898 and named San Francisco de Mayantoc was abolished by the Americans. FHL local records: civil registration, 1922–1931; notarials, 1917–. Local records: civil registration, 1917–.

Moncada (municipality), an early Spanish town, annexed the villages of San Ramón, Legazpi, San Agustin, and Salcedo from Paniqui in 1907. Anao and San Manuel separated in 1908. FHL local records: civil registration, 1922–1945; notarials, 1907–; Saint Raymund Nonatus parish registers, 1882–1933. Local records: civil registration, 1942–.

Paniqui (municipality), also known as Manggan and Marikit, was an early Spanish town, formerly part of Guimba of Nueva Ecija. It annexed Anao from 1903 to 1908. The villages of San Roman, Legazpi, San Agustin, and Salcedo separated and were annexed by Moncada in 1907. Ramos separated in 1921. FHL local records: civil registration, 1929–1931; notarials, 1907–; Roman Catholic parish registers, 1792–1938. Local records: civil registration, 1958–.

Pura (municipality) was established in 1907 from Gerona to which it had been annexed in 1903. FHL local records: civil registration, 1922–1932, 1908–1992; notarials, 1908–; Saint Anthony parish registers, 1906–1955. Local records: civil registration, 1908–.

Ramos (municipality), also known as Bani, was established in 1921 from Paniqui. FHL local records: civil registration, 1922–1932; notarials, 1921–. Local records: civil registration, 1942–.

San Clemente (municipality), also known as Mambog, was established in 1915 from Camiling to which it had been annexed in 1903. FHL local records: civil registration, 1922–1931; notarials, 1915–. Local records: civil registration, 1917–.

San Manuel (municipality), also known as Lanat and San José, was established in 1908 from Moncada. FHL local records: civil registration, 1922–1931; notarials, circa 1911–. Local records: civil registration, 1909–.

Santa Ignacia (municipality), also known as Binaca, was established in 1914 from Camiling to which it had been annexed in 1903. Annexed the village of San Vicente from Camiling in 1920. FHL local records: civil registration, 1922–1931; notarials, 1914–. Local records: civil registration, 1951–.

Tarlac (city) was an early Spanish town founded in 1686 which annexed the municipalities of Moriones and La Paz, and the villages of San Miguel, San Carlos, and Burut (from the former municipality of Murcia) in 1903. La Paz separated in 1906. FHL local records: civil registration, 1922–1931; notarials, 1914–; San Sebastián parish registers, 1740–1941. Local records: civil registration, 1901–.

Victoria (municipality), also known as Canarum and San Vincente de Canarum, was an early Spanish town. FHL local records: civil registration, 1921–1931; notarials, 1903–; Immaculate Conception parish registers, 1868–1939. Local records: civil registration, 1901–.

Tawi-Tawi. This province, a collection of islands between the Sulu Archipelago and the island of Borneo, is the southernmost province in the Philippines. It includes the Cagayan de Sulu Islands, the Sulu Islands, the Turtle Islands, and the Tawi-Tawi Islands. Until formed into a separate province in 1973, these islands were part of Sulu Province. British, German, and Spanish interests struggled for control of this area. In 1885, Spain assumed control of the region as part of the Philippines. For an administrative history, see the section on the province of Sulu above.

> FHL provincial records: birth records (1975–1988), marriage contracts (1947–1986), and death certificates (1974–1981).

Localities and their records:

Balimbing (municipality) was established in 1959. Local records: civil registration, 1958–.

Bonggaw (municipality), also known as Bongaw and Bongao, was established in 1959. Ceded territory to Languyan when that municipality was established in 1977. Local records: civil registration, 1971–.

Cagayan de Tawi-Tawi (municipality), also known as Cagayan de Sulu prior to 1975, was established in 1959. Local records: civil registration, 1950–.

Languyan (municipality) was established in 1977 from the consolidation of portions of Bonggaw, Tandu Bas, and South Ubian.

Sapa-Sapa (municipality) was established in 1977 from Tandu Bas.

Simunul (municipality) was established in 1959. Local records: civil registration, 1957–.

Sitangkay (municipality), also known as Sitangkai and Sibutu, was established in 1959. Local records: civil registration, 1949–.

South Ubian (municipality), established in 1959, lost territory to Lanhuyan when that municipality was established in 1977.

Tandu Bas (municipality), also known as Tandubas, was established in 1959. Ceded territory to Sapa-Sapa and Languyan when they were both established in 1977. Local records: civil registration, 1967–.

Turtle Islands Taganak (municipality) was established in 1959. Local records: civil registration, 1957–.

Zambales. This province is situated on the long, irregular, western coast of central Luzon, facing the South China Sea. The name is derived from the name of the major tribe in this area, the Zambals. Legend states that one of the tribe's chiefs was rescued from Chinese pirates by Juan de Salcedo of Spain, who then used the good will generated from this act to establish Spanish sovereignty over the area. Consequently, Zambales became one of the earliest provinces organized by the Spanish in the Philippines. Early towns included Masinloc (1607), Iba (1611), Santa Cruz (1612), and Botolan (1736). Masinloc was the first capital, though it was later moved to Iba. The Augustinian Recollect Order began the evangelization of this area in 1607 with a center at Subi. Centers at Iba (1681), Masinloc (1607), Santa Cruz (1612), and Botolan (1736)

followed. When the Recollects were forced to leave during the Philippine Revolution in 1898, the centers were overseen by secular clergy until the arrival of the Divine World Fathers in 1928 and the Columban Fathers in 1951. After the collapse of the forces of the Philippine Revolution in this province, the Americans established a civil government in August 1901. In late 1903 the boundaries of the province were adjusted with the northern portion, which included the towns of Alaminos, Bolinao, San Isidro, Potot (later Burgos), Infanta, Bani, Anda and Agno, annexed to the province of Pangasinan.

> FHL provincial records: civil registration (1858–1896), birth records (1945–1988), marriage contracts (1945–1987), death certificates (1962–1991), court records created by the Court of First Instance (1901–1903), deportations (1871–1897), military induction records (1876–1897), public records (1879–1898), records of lending (1876–1898), school records (1863–1897), statistical reports (1896), tax records (1832–1861), Census of Chinese (1886–1897), and notarials (1903–).

Localities and their records:

Botolan (municipality), also known as Babayan, was established in 1736 as the town of Babayan, but was moved and renamed Botolan in 1819. Cabangan was annexed in 1903. It was established as a municipality circa 1949. FHL local records: civil registration, 1922–1931, 1951–1992; notarials, 1905–; Saint Monica parish registers, 1829–1897. Local records: civil registration, 1951–.

Cabangan (municipality), also known as Cabangaan, was established circa 1949 from Botolan to which it had been annexed in 1903. FHL local records: civil registration, 1922–1930; notarials, 1903–; Saint Rose parish registers, 1890–1891. Local records: civil registration, 1950–.

Candelaria (municipality), also known as San Vicente, was established in 1910 from Masinloc to which it had been annexed in 1903. FHL local records: civil registration, 1922–1931, 1910–1994; notarials, 1911–; Saint Vincent Ferrer parish registers, 1894–1952. Local records: civil registration, 1910–.

Castillejos (municipality), also known as Ugit and Besita, was established in 1910 from San Mascelino to which it had been annexed in 1903. The village of Balaybay was annexed from Subic in 1939. FHL local records: civil registration, 1922–1931, 1931–1993; notarials, 1908–; Saint Nicholas parish registers, 1900–1957. Local records: civil registration, 1912–.

Iba (city), founded in 1611 as a Spanish town, is the capital of the province. Palauig was annexed from 1903 to 1910. FHL local records: civil registration, 1921–1933, 1914–1980; notarials, 1911–; Saint Augustine parish registers, 1877–1938. Local records: civil registration, 1913–.

Masinloc (municipality), an early Spanish town founded in 1607, was the provincial capital in the Spanish period. Candelaria was annexed from 1903 to 1910. FHL local records: civil registration, 1922–1931, 1900–1994; notarials, 1905–; Saint Andrew parish registers, 1849–1952. Local records: civil registration, 1900–.

Olongapo (city), an early Spanish town formerly in Subic, was established as a municipality in 1959 and chartered as a city in 1966. FHL local records: civil registration, 1922–1931, 1945–1992; birth certificates, 1966–1988; death certificates, 1975–1988; notarials, 1911–. Local records: civil registration, 1945–.

Palauig (municipality), also known as Palauag, was organized as a town in Masinloc by the Spanish in 1870. It was annexed to Iba from 1903 to 1910. FHL local records: civil registration, 1922–1930; notarials, 1911–. Local records: civil registration, 1951–.

San Antonio (municipality), also known as Pamalisaracan (or some variant), was a Spanish village in Castillejos in 1836. It was annexed to San Narciso in 1846 and became a town in 1849. Annexed by San Marinloc in 1903, it was established as a municipality in 1908. FHL local records: civil registration, 1922–1931; notarials, 1911–. Local records: civil registration, 1912–.

San Felipe (municipality), a Spanish town by 1853, was annexed to San Narciso from 1903 until its separation and establishment as a municipality in 1908. FHL local records: civil registration, 1922–1931, 1908–1993; notarials, 1908–. Local records: civil registration, 1908–.

San Marcelino (municipality), also known as Vega, was an early Spanish town which annexed Castillejos and San Antonio from 1903 to 1910 and 1908, respectively. FHL local records: civil registration, 1922–1931, 1941–1993; notarials, 1908–. Local records: civil registration, 1901–.

San Narciso (municipality), also known as Alusiis and Claveria, was a Spanish town in Cangan, then Castillejos. San Felipe was annexed from 1903 to 1908. FHL local records: civil registration, 1922–1931, 1939–1992; notarials, 1911–; Saint Sebastion parish registers, 1849–1950. Local records: civil registration, 1911–.

Santa Cruz (municipality), also known as Sigayan, was founded as a town in 1612 by the Spanish. FHL local records: civil registration, 1921–1931, 1902–1994; notarials, 1910–; Saint Michael, the Archangel, parish registers, 1838–1939. Local records: civil registration, 1902–.

Subic (municipality), also known as Hubic and Subik, was a settlement before the arrival of the Spanish. Ceded the village of Balaybay to Castillejos in 1939. It was formerly the site of an American naval base (established in 1901). FHL local records: civil registration, 1922–1931, 1901–1992; notarials, 1911–; Saint James parish registers, 1929–1966. Local records: civil registration, 1901–.

Zamboanga del Norte. This province is situated on the northern half of the Zamboanga Peninsula and is part of what was the province of Zamboanga. All during the Spanish period, Zamboanga (known variously as Sibugay, Sibuguey, and Sibuguei) was a major source of difficulty. The Islamic Moros refused to be governed by the Spanish and rejected conversion to Christianity—one of the major objectives of Spanish government. From their center in the fortified town of Dapitan, the Spanish sent expeditions to subjugate the Moros until 1622 when forces were withdrawn to concentrate on pushing back the those of Ko T'sen, a Chinese pirate, which were threatening Manila and Spain's entire presence in the Philippines. The threat was diminished in 1636 with the victory of the Spanish fleet over ships led by the brother of the Sultan of Mindanao. By 1719 the Spanish were again attempting to establish communities in Zamboanga. However, the Moros still were not contained. When the Spanish found the costs of suppressing them prohibitive, they began, in 1832, to recruit local Filipinos to supplement forces under the command of Spanish officers. This practice proved advantageous. By 1837 Zamboanga had grown enough to become a province. In 1860 it became one of the six districts of Mindanao and Sulu. For most of this period, Zamboanga was the capital of Spanish government in Mindanao (from 1872 to 1875 Cotabato was the capital). This area was also a center of revolutionary activity against the Spanish which ultimately resulted in the defeat and withdrawal of Spanish forces. On June 1, 1903 civil government was established by the Americans and Moro Province was created with Zamboanga as one of its five component districts. Dapitan became a subdistrict of Zamboanga until 1905 when it was abolished as a subdistrict and annexed to Zamboanga as an integral part. In September 1914 Moro Province was dissolved and the Department of Mindanao and Sulu was established with Zamboanga a province. In 1920 the department was dissolved and replaced by the Bureau of Non-Christian Tribes under the Department of the Interior of the central government. Shortly after World War II, the capital was moved from Zamboanga City to Dipolog, to the new town of Molave (1948), and to Pagadian (1953). Basilan, a part of Zamboanga Province until 1937, became a part of Zamboanga City until 1948 when it was detached to form a separate province. In 1952 Zamboanga was divided into Zamboanga del Norte and Zamboanga del Sur.

FHL provincial records: civil registration (1851–1897), birth records (1945–1988), marriage contracts (1946–1987), census records (1851–1898), death certificates (1965–1991), deportations (1850–1890), land records (1820–1890), notarials (1912–1914), public records (1882–1898), school records (1849–1898), statistical reports (1896), tax records (1854–1864), and Census of Chinese (1881–1898).

Localities and their records:

Dapitan (city), also known as Dapite, Dapito, and Dapyte, was originally settled by migrants from Bohol. It was chartered as a city on November 8, 1963. Dipolog separated in 1913. FHL local records: civil registration, 1922–1931; birth certificates, 1966–1988; death certificates, 1976–1988; notarials, 1903–; Saint James, the Greater, parish registers, 1802–1951. Local records: civil registration, 1940–.

Dipolog (city), also known as Dipoloc, Dipag, Dipolo, Dipaag, Siripolo, and Dipulog, was part of the Spanish province of Misamis until the end of Spanish rule in 1898. Annexed in 1903 to the Dapitan District of Zamboanga, it was established as a municipality in 1913 from Dapitan and chartered as a city in 1970. Katipunan (1915) and Polanco (1951) were separated. FHL local records: civil registration, 1921–1931; birth certificates, 1968–1988; death certificates, 1976–1988; notarials, circa 1911–; Our Lady of the Holy Rosary parish registers, 1896–1941. Local records: civil registration, 1946–.

Katipunan (municipality), also known as Lubungan and Dicayo, was annexed to Dipolog from 1913 to 1915. Its name was changed from Lubungan to Katipunan in 1931. FHL local records: Saint Francis Xavier parish registers, 1796–1964. Local records: civil registration, 1916–.

Labason (municipality), also known as Rabasa, was established in 1948 from Sindangan. Local records: civil registration, 1948–.

La Libertad (municipality) was established in 1959 from Rizal. Local records: civil registration, 1959–.

Liloy (municipality) was established in 1951. In 1959 Salug was separated. Local records: civil registration, 1952–.

Manukan (municipality), also known as Banukan, was established in 1951 from Katipunan to which it had been annexed in 1918. Local records: civil registration, 1951–.

Mutia (municipality) was established in 1960. Local records: civil registration, 1960–.

Piñan (municipality), also known as New Piñan prior to 1960, was established in 1951 from Dipolog. Sergio Osmeña separated in 1963. Local records: civil registration, 1951–.

Polanco (municipality), also known as Tilyatid, was established in 1951 from Dipolog. It was annexed from Dapitan to Dipolog in 1914. Local records: civil registration, 1951–.

President Manuel A. Roxas (municipality), also known as Roxas, was established in 1967 from Katipunan. Local records: civil registration, 1968–.

Rizal (municipality) was established in 1950 from La Libertad. Local records: civil registration, 1951–.

Salug (municipality) was established in 1959 from Liloy. Local records: civil registration, 1959–.

Sergio Osmeña (municipality) was established in 1963 from Piñan. Local records: civil registration, 1963–.

Siayan (municipality) was established in 1967 from Sindangan. Local records: civil registration, 1968–.

Sibuco (municipality) was established in 1959 from Siocon. Local records: civil registration, 1959–.

Sibutad (municipality) was established in 1959 from Sibuco. Local records: civil registration, 1959–.

Sindañgan (municipality) was established in 1937 from the consolidation of the municipal districts of Sindangan and Panganuran. Siayan was separated (1967), as was Labason (1948). FHL local records: civil registration, 1921–1925; notarials, 1921–. Local records: civil registration, 1939–.

Siocon (municipality), also known as Sicogon, was established in 1937 from the consolidation of the municipal districts of Sibuko (separated in 1959) and Siraway (separated in 1968). Local records: civil registration, 1941–.

Siraway (municipality) was established in 1968 from Siocon.

Zamboanga del Sur. This province is located on the southern half of the Zamboanga Peninsula. In 1952 the province of Zamboanga was divided into this province and Zamboanga del Norte. For the administrative history of Zamboanga, see the section on Zamboanga del Norte above.

FHL provincial records: civil registration (1851–1897), birth records (1945–1988), marriage contracts (1945–1987), death certificates (1962–1991), deportations (1850–1890), land records (1820–1890), public records (1882–1898), school records (1849–1898), statistical reports (1896), tax records (1854–1864), and Census of Chinese (1881–1898).

Localities and their records:

Alicia (municipality) was established in 1951 from Margosatubig. Local records: civil registration, 1952–.

Aurora (municipality) was established in 1942 from Pagadian. Local records: civil registration, 1942–.

Bayog (municipality) was established in 1967 from Buug. Local records: civil registration, 1968–.

Buug (municipality) was established in 1960. Bayog separated in 1967. Local records: civil registration, 1960–.

Dimataling (municipality) was established in 1950 from villages in the city of Pagadian and the municipality of Margosatubig. In 1950 Dinas was separated and three more villages were annexed from Margosatubig. Local records: civil registration, 1971–.

Dinas (municipality) was established in 1950 from Dimataling. Local records: civil registration, 1950–.

Dumalinao (municipality) was established in 1956 from Pagadian. Local records: civil registration, 1956–.

Dumingag (municipality) was established in 1957. Midsalip was separated in 1967. Local records: civil registration, 1958–.

Ipil (municipality) was established in 1949 from Kabasalan. Local records: civil registration, 1949–.

Kabasalan (municipality) was established in 1937 from consolidation of the municipal districts of Kabasalan and Bangaan. Naga (1867) and Ipil (1949) were separated. FHL local records: civil registration, 1925–1928; notarials, 1934–. Local records: civil registration, 1925–.

Kumalarang (municipality) was established in 1959. Local records: civil registration, 1971–.

Labanga (municipality) was established in 1949 from Pagadian. FHL local records: civil registration, 1921–1931; notarials, 1911–. Local records: civil registration, 1963–.

Lapuyan (municipality) was established in 1957.

Mabuhay (municipality) was established in 1967 from Olutanga. Local records: civil registration, 1968–.

Mahayag (municipality) was established in 1960. Local records: civil registration, 1960–.

Malangas (municipality) was established in 1951 from Margosatubig. Local records: civil registration, 1951–.

Margosatubig (municipality) was established in 1937 by the consolidation of the municipal districts of Margosatub and Malangas. In 1951 some villages were separated and annexed to Dimataling. Malangas was also separated in that year. FHL local records: civil registration, 1922–1929; notarials, 1928–. Local records: civil registration, 1948–.

Midsalip (municipality) was established in 1967 from villages in municipalities of Dumingag and Ramon Magsaysay. Local records: civil registration, 1968–.

Molave (municipality) was established in 1948. Local records: civil registration, 1949–.

Naga (municipality) was established in 1967 from Kabasalan. Local records: civil registration, 1968–.

Nilo (municipality). Local records: civil registration, 1964–.

Olutanga (municipality) was established in 1957. Mabuhay was separated in 1967. Local records: civil registration, 1958–.

Pagadian (city) was established in 1937 from the consolidation of the municipal districts of Labangan and Dinas. The following municipalities were separated: Labangan (1949), Aurora (1942), Dimataling (1950), and Dumalinao (1956). Chartered as a city in 1969, it has been the capital of the province since 1952. FHL local records: birth certificates, 1969–1988; death certificates, 1976–1988. Local records: civil registration, 1946–.

Ramón Magsaysay (municipality), also known as Liargao prior to 1960, was established in 1956 from Midsalip. Local records: civil registration, 1958–.

San Miguel (municipality) was established in 1960. Local records: civil registration, 1960–.

San Pablo (municipality) was established in 1957. Local records: civil registration, 1958–.

Siay (municipality) was established in 1956. Local records: civil registration, 1958–.

Tabina (municipality) was established in 1961. Local records: civil registration, 1961–.

Tambulig (municipality) was established in 1957. Local records: civil registration, 1958–.

Titay (municipality) was established in 1960. Local records: civil registration, 1960–.

Tukuran (municipality) was established in 1958. Local records: civil registration, 1959–.

Tungawan (municipality) was established in 1960. Local records: civil registration, 1960–.

Zamboanga (city), settled by the Spanish in 1635, was a Spanish town in 1636. In 1901, the village of Tetuan was annexed. Under the Spanish, it was the capital of the local comandancia and, through 1913, the capital of the Zamboanga District. Chartered as a city in 1911, it reverted to a municipality in 1914 and then to a city in 1937 with territory that included the municipalities of Zamboanga and Bolong, the municipal district of Taluksangay, and the whole of the island of Basilan. Later Basilan was separated as an independent province. FHL local records: birth certificates, 1945–1988; marriage contracts, 1945–1960; death certificates, 1975–1988; civil registration, 1914–1933; notarials, 1911–; subdivision of Bolong—civil registration 1929–1931, notarials, 1930–; notarials (subdivision of San Ramon), 1932–1937; notarials (subdivision of Taluksangay), 1930–1934. Local records: civil registration, 1942–.

Organizations and Repositories

Part II will list many archives, libraries, genealogical societies, and historical associations to which the researcher can turn for assistance. Here, we will focus on a few which are particularly well known. However, no repository or organization should be neglected in your research. Often the most useful information on an elusive individual can be found tucked away in a place which other researchers have overlooked. Further, organizations sometimes disband or move to new addresses and new organizations arise from time to time. Check telephone directories for current addresses and phone numbers and watch newspapers for announcements of conferences, meetings, and cultural events which may provide information.

When asking for assistance, it is best to have specific questions ready on particular problems that have been encountered. A researcher can receive help much more quickly and easily if he or she asks questions such as "How can I find immigration records for San Francisco?," "Do you have any records of Chinese cemeteries in Hawaii?," or "My grandmother died in Tacoma in 1903 or 1904. How can I get a copy of her death certificate?" rather than "What do I do next?" or "I need to know how my grandfather got here."

National Archives. Long known to scholars as a rich historical repository, as with most archives, the more recent records for living persons are not always available to the public, due to their confidential nature. The Archives arranges its documents by Record Group number (RG) and government entity. There are also Field Branches, located throughout the United States, which service their respective regions and contain some records not found in Washington, D.C. Since early South Asian and Filipino immigrants settled mainly on the West Coast and in Hawaii, one would focus on the San Francisco, Seattle, and Los Angeles branches for inquiries. (See "Libraries and Archives" in Part II for locations of all the branches.) While the Archives does not perform genealogical research for patrons, or keep files on particular families, it can respond to requests by mail when exact information is specified. This may include requests for service records, pension file applications, bounty land warrant application files, and census pages. Key subjects for genealogical research in the archives include passenger lists, military service records, and naturalization records. As an example, some key Record Groups to search for the Philippines are RG 41, Bureau of Marine Inspection and Navigation for merchant seamen lists; RG 338, 391, 395, and U.S. Army Pacific, Mobile Units, and Overseas Operations and Commands, for reports involving troops in the Philippines, Filipino scouts, and guerrillas during the Japanese occupation; RG 24, Bureau of Naval Personnel, for service records of Filipino sailors; RG 153, Office of Judge Advocate General (Army), Insular Affairs Section, for cases involving the Philippines, 1915 to 1933; RG 85, Immigration and Naturalization Service; and RG 21, U.S. District Courts, for naturalization petitions. Recent service and pension information can be requested from the National Personnel Records Center (see ''Libraries and Archives,'' Part II).

Immigration and Naturalization Service (INS). The INS is the main repository for all records of immigrants. Requests for records on one's own family should be directed to the INS office in one's own state of residence.

Hawaii State Archives. Because virtually all travelers, sojourners, and immigrants bound from Asian ports for the American Pacific Coast passed through Hawaii and Hawaii was the final destination for so many thousands of Asians, the Hawaii State Archives is the best place to look for records on these people. Records date from the earliest days of the bureaucracy established by the Kingdom of Hawaii. They include passenger lists, vital records, immigration records to 1900, and court records.

Bishop Museum Library. This library's collection is especially strong in Japanese materials including Japanese-language newspapers and immigrant records.

Hawaii Chinese History Center. The collection, which is available to members, includes records on Chinese immigrant societies in Hawaii. It also includes transcriptions of Chinese tombstones, oral histories on tape, and newspaper clippings.

Hawaiian Sugar Planters' Association. The collection includes records of immigrants, mostly Filipino, who worked for sugar plantations from 1906 to 1941. Some Japanese and Chinese records are also included.

California State Archives. The collection includes many records on early settlers and immigrants including census records.

University of California at Los Angeles. The university library has one of the major Asian collections in the United States and also has a large amount of Asian American materials. While the main focus is on the Japanese—Chinese, Koreans, and Filipinos are also well represented. Ethnic newspapers, diaries, taped interviews with immigrants, a comprehensive book collection, and microfilmed materials on Japanese emigrants obtained from the Japanese Foreign Ministry are among its holdings.

Chinese Historical Society of America. This society maintains a library and museum, collects oral histories and publications relating to Chinese Americans, and holds periodic seminars.

Japanese American Citizen's League. This organization has branches in major cities all over the United States and holds periodic conferences at which issues relating to Japanese Americans are discussed. Older members are growing increasingly concerned about the preservation of records concerning immigrants and the transmission of their contents to later generations.

Korean National Association. This organization has branches in major cities throughout the United States, wherever large groups of Koreans reside. Among other activities, this association works to promote research into the history of Koreans in the United States.

Chinatown Cultural Center. The collection focuses on materials concerning the Chinese in New York.

Bibliography

Additional information on these sources may be found in Part II.

Anderson, Gerald H. *Studies in Philippine Church History.* Ithaca, NY: Cornell University Press, 1969. 421p. A standard source for tracing the record-keeping practices of Philippine churches.

Asian Americans Information Directory. Second edition. Detroit: Gale Research, 1995. Arranged by nationality and subject. Includes substantial bibliographic information on Asian-oriented books, periodicals, and databases, as well as names, addresses and telephone numbers of historical and cultural societies, public and private agencies, foundations, community resources, and support groups.

Beard, Timothy Field, with Denise Demong. *How to Find Your Family Roots.* New York: McGraw-Hill Book Company, 1977. 1007p. Includes index.

The Bengal Obituary. Or, a record to perpetuate the memory of the departed worth, being a compilation of tablets & monumental inscriptions from various parts of the Bengal & Agra presidencies, to which is added biographical sketches & memories in the history of British India since the formation of the European settlement to the present time. Also known as *Record to Perpetuate the Memory of the Departed Worth.* Two volumes. Calcutta: Homes and Co., 1848. Reprint. Bibhash Gupta, 1987. 426p.

Bogardus, Emory S. ''The Filipino Press in the United States.'' In *Sociology and Social Research,* vol. 18 (July-August 1934), pp. 582–585.

Bro-Jorgensen, J.O. *Asiatiske, vestindiske og guineiske handelskompagnier.* København: Rigsarkivet, 1969. Inventories of the records of various Danish trading companies in, among other places, India.

Burma, Register of European Deaths and Burials. London: British Association for Cemeteries in South Asia, 1983. 190p. Includes index and bibliography.

Catholic Directory of India. New Delhi: The Catholic Bishops' Conference of India Centre, 1984?–. 203p. Issued every few years, it contains the addresses of the Catholic parishes in India, and includes their addresses as well as the date when they were erected. Also includes an index.

Catholic Directory of the Philippines. Manila: Catholic Trade, 1981.

Cotton, Julian James. *List of Inscriptions on Tombs or Monuments in Madras Possessing Historical or Archaeological Interest.* Three volumes. Madras: Government Press, 1945–1946. Includes cemeteries in South India, a few in Sumatra.

Crofton, O.S. *List of Inscriptions on Tombs or Monuments in the Central Provinces and Berar with Biographical Notes.* Nagpur: Government Printing, 1932. Covers cemeteries in the states of Maharastra, Madhya Pradesh, and Rajasthan.

Davies, Vincent. *British Cemeteries of Patna & Dinapore.* London: British Association for Cemeteries in South Asia, 1989.

Diehl, Katherine S. "Christians in India and How to Trace Their Family Histories." In *World Conference on Records: Preserving Our Heritage.* Volume 11. Asian and African Family and Local History. Salt Lake City: Corporation of the President of the Church of Jesus Christ of Latter-day Saints, 1980.

Directory of the Archdiocese of Goa and Daman. S.l.: The Archdiocese, 1971.

Elwood, Douglas J. *Churches amd Sects in the Philippines.* A descriptive study of contemporary religious group movements. Silliman University monograph, series A: Religious Studies; no. 1. Dumaguete City, Philippines: Silliman University, 1968. 213p. Includes bibliographic references.

Farrington, Susan Maria. *Peshawar Cemetery: North West Frontier Province, Pakistan.* London: British Association for Cemeteries in South Asia, 1992.

Farrington, Susan Maria. *Quetta, Monuments and Inscriptions: Baluchistan, Pakistan.* London: British Association for Cemeteries in South Asia, 1992.

Fernàndez de Recas, Guillermo Sergio. *Aspirantes americanos a cargos del Santo Oficio; sus genealogías ascendentes (Americans Who Aspire to the Responsibilites of Holy Office).* Mexico, D.F.: Librería de Manuel Porrúa, 1956. 253p. Includes genealogical sketches for the 1,208 persons who applied for position with the Inquisition during the period from the sixteenth to the nineteenth centuries in Spanish America and the Philippines.

Flores-Meiser, Enya P. "The Filipino American Press." In *The Ethnic Press in America: A Historical Analysis and Handbook,* Sally M. Miller. New York: Greenwood Press, 1987, pp. 85–99. Contains a good overview of Filipino American magazines and newspapers published since the early 1900s.

Goswamy, B.N. "Pilgrimage Records of India: A Rich Source of Genealogy and Family History." In *World Conference on Records, Aug. 12 to 15, 1980.* Salt Lake City: 1980.

Harfield, Alan [G]. *Christian Cemeteries and Memorials in Malacca.* London: British Association for Cemeteries in South Asia, 1984. Also includes a list of deaths at Malacca from 1813 to 1843.

Harfield, A[lan] G. *Christian Cemeteries of Penang & Perak.* London?: British Association for Cemeteries in South Asia, 1987. 195p. Includes index.

Harfield, Alan [G]. *Early Cemeteries in Singapore.* London: British Association for Cemeteries in South Asia, 1988.

Hart, Donn V. "The Filipino American Press in the United States: A Neglected Resource." In *Journalism Quarterly,* vol. 54 (Spring 1977), pp. 135–139.

Hodson, Vernon Charles Paget. *List of the Officers of the Bengal Army, 1758–1834.* Alphabetically arranged and annotated with biographical and genealogical notices. Also known as: *Officers of the Bengal Army, 1758–1834* or *List of the Officers of the Bengal Army.* Four volumes. London: Constable (Phillimore is listed on volumes 3 and 4), 1927–1947. Volume 1: A–C; volume 2: D–K; volume 3: L–R; volume 4: S–Z.

Huen, P. Lim Pui. *Newspapers Published in the Malaysian Area, with a Union List of Local Holdings.* 19–?

Indonesia. Kantor Bibliografi Nasional. *Authority file: nama-nama pengarang Indonesia (Authority File: Names of Indonesian authors).* Jakarta: Kantor Bibliografi Nasional, Lembaga Perpustakaan, Departemen P & K, 1975. 175p.

Johnson, Richard. *How to Locate Anyone Who Is or Has Been in the Military: Armed Forces Locator Directory.* Fifth edition, revised. San Antonio, TX: Military Information Enterprises, 1993. 247p.

Jurriaanse, Maria Wilhelmina. *Catalogue of the Archives of the Dutch Central Government of Coastal Ceylon, 1640–1796.* Colombo: Ceylon Government Press, 1943. 354p. The Hague: General State Archives, 1975. Inventory of the Archives of the Dutch Government in the Divisions of Galle (Matara) and Jaffnapatnam.

Keeth, Kent H. *A Directory of Libraries in Malaysia.* Kuala Lumpur: University of Malay Library, 1965. 163p.

Kim, Hyung-chan. *Asian American Studies: An Annotated Bibliography and Research Guide.* Bibliographies and Indexes in American History; no. 11. New York: Greenwood Press, 1989. 504p. Includes extensive indexes, though Asian ethnic groups do not receive separate treatment in the arrangement of topics in the text.

Labouchardiers, Basil. *French Cemetery, Park Street, Calcutta.* London: British Association for Cemeteries in South Asia, 1983.

Lewis, John Perry. *List of Inscriptions on Tombstones and Monuments in Ceylon, of Historical or Local Interest, with an Obituary of Persons Uncommemorated.* Colombo: H.C. Cottle, Government Printers, 1913.

Llewellyn-Jones, Rosie. *Tenth Anniversary Souvenir Chowkidar.* London: British Association for Cemeteries in South Asia, 1986. Includes short essays on British cemeteries in south and southeast Asia.

Magdaleno, Richardo. *Catálogo XX del Archivo General de Simancas: Títulas de Indias (Catalog 20 of the General Archive of Simancas, Names of the Indies).* Valladolid: 1954. 980p.

Malaysian Church Directory. Singapore: Singapore Every Home Crusade, 1980. In Chinese and English.

Marikar, A.I.L. *Genealogical Tables of Sri Lanka Moors, Malays, and other Muslims.* Colombo: Moors' Islamic Cultural Home, 1981. 400p.

Meerman, Archilles. *The Chapter List of the Madre de Deus Province in India, 1569–1790.* Bangalore: 1959. Deals with the Franciscans in India.

Neagles, James C. *U.S. Military Records.* A guide to federal and state sources, colonial America to the present. Salt Lake City: Ancestry, 1994. 441p.

Newspapers in Microform, United States, 1948–1983. Two volumes: A-0, P-Z. Library of Congress Catalogs. Washington, D.C.: Library of Congress, 1983. Includes title index.

Norell, Irene P. *Literature of the Filipino-American in the United States: A Selective and Annotated Bibliography.* San Francisco, CA: R and E Research Associates, 1976. 84p.

Palmer, Stephen J. *Studies in Asian Genealogy.* Provo, Utah: Brigham Young University Press, 1972. 281p.

Retana, W[esceslao] E[milio]. *Indice de personas nobles y otras de calidad que han estado en Filipinas desde 1521 hasta 1898. (Index of Noble Persons and Others of Quality Who Have Remained in the Philippines from 1521 to 1898).* Madrid:

Librería de Victoriano Suarez, 1921. 84p. This is an index of nobles who lived in the Philippines from 1521 to 1898.

Saito, Shiro. *Philippine Newspapers in Selected American Libraries: A Union List*. Occasional Paper; no. 6. Honolulu: East-West Center Library, University of Hawaii, 1966. 46p.

Scholberg, Henry. *South Asia Biographical Dictionary Index.* Two volumes. Zug, Switzerland: Inter Documention Company, 1987. 1008p. An index of names of persons who appear in various biographical dictionaries.

The South Park Street Cemetery, Calcutta. Calcutta?: Association for the Preservation of Historical Cemeteries in India, 1986. 20p. A study of the architecture of tombs and mausolea and biographical details of members of the British community in Bengal buried in the cemetery during the period 1767–1850.

The Status Report of Civil Registry Records. Manila: Philippines Government, 1972. Lists local records which have not been microfilmed.

Szucs, Loretto Dennis, and Sandra Hargreaves Luebking. *The Archives: A Guide to the National Archives Field Branches.* Salt Lake City: Ancestry, 1988. 340p. Focuses on the collections of genealogical value of the particular branches. It is arranged alphabetically by record group, supplies detailed historical background, and is well-indexed.

United States. National Archives and Records Administration. *Guide to the National Archives of the United States.* Washington, D.C.: National Archives, 1987. 896p. Much more detailed than *Guide to Genealogical Research in the National Archives.* The index is less subject-specific. Arrangement is by government entity.

United States. National Archives and Records Service. *Guide to Genealogical Research in the National Archives.* Washington, D.C.: National Archives, 1985. 304p. Colorful, amply illustrated guide to records of genealogical value. Arrangement is by subject.

Van Niel, Robert. *A Survey of Historical Source Materials in Java and Manila.* Asian studies at Hawaii; no. 5. Honolulu: University of Hawaii Press, 1970. 255p.

Vance, Lee W[endell] and Violeta C. Canon. *Tracing Your Philippine Ancestors.* Provo, UT: Stevenson's Genealogical Center, 1980. 771p. Comprehensive guide to genealogical research overseas. Includes maps, forms, and index.

Vierow, Duain, and Jack M. Shelby. *Malaysia Christian Handbook.* Petaling Jaya, Selangor: Glad Sounds, 1979.

Von Oeyen, Robert R., Jr. *Philippine Evangelical Protestant and Independent Catholic Churches.* A historical bibliography of church records, publications, and source material located in the Greater Manila Area. University of the Philippines Asia Center bibliographic series; no. 1. Quzon City, Philippines: Asia Center, University of the Philippines, 1970.

Who's Who in Malaysia and Singapore. Kuala Lumpur: Who's Who Publications, 1956–. A serial that presents the profiles of important persons. Some slight variations in title over the years.

Wilson, C.R. *List of Inscriptions on Tombs or Monuments in Bengal Possessing Historical or Archaelogical Interest.* Calcutta: Superintendent of Government Printing, 1896. Includes cemeteries from Calcutta, Bengal, Sikkim, and Orissa.

Wright, Gillian. *Shri Lanka.* Lincolnwood, Illinois: Passport Books, 1994. A recent guidebook, that will give some background on localities mentioned in various records.

Zia, Helen, and Susan B. Gall. *Notable Asian Americans.* Detroit: Gale Research, 1995. 468p. Includes occupation, ethnicity, and subject indexes.

Records Specific to Asian Americans

Greg Gubler

Ⓞ *Greg Gubler holds a joint appointment as Associate Professor of History and University Archivist at the Hawaii Campus of Brigham Young University. He was formerly the Senior Research Specialist for East Asia (1976–1982) at the Genealogical Society of Utah (now the Family History Department) in Salt Lake City. Receiving his Ph.D. in East Asian history from Florida State University in 1975, he also served on the faculty of the University of Florida (1972–1974), was a Fulbright Scholar to Nanyang University in Singapore (1968–1970), and resided in Japan as a Marine and missionary for the Church of Jesus Christ of Latter-day Saints. He has traveled and researched extensively in East Asia, lectured at international conferences, and authored many articles and monographs. Presently he is completing a definitive study of the Japanese diplomat Satō Naotake.*

Overview of Asian American Emigration

The sporadic nature of emigration from Asia to America and the diversity of the groups involved poses special problems for the researcher. Those doing research may encounter immigrants as early as the 1850s or as recent as the past decade. Among the Asian immigrants, the Chinese were the pioneers but were thwarted by the passing of the Chinese Exclusion Act in 1882. Japanese emigration, ironically, mushroomed in the 1880s only to flounder with the Gentleman's Agreement in 1908 and again when they were barred as a group due to 1924 U.S. congressional legislation. Korean immigration occurred briefly after the turn of the century until Japan annexed the country in 1910. Immigrants from the Philippines arrived during the years between World Wars I and II when the country was a U.S. colony and sugar interests prevailed. However, it was not until after World War II and the passing of the Walter-McCarran Act in 1952 that Asians were able to gain full status and quotas for the various Asian groups began to increase dramatically. There is now a whole generation of diverse immigrants from Asia. Since most of these ethnic groups have continued to organize and maintain ties with the country of origin, it is imperative to know something about the ethnic organizations that have been created as well as the records which can be found abroad.

This chapter addresses some of the mechanisms of immigration as well as the organizations involved in facilitating the transition. The key, of course, is to find the immigrant ancestor and to be able to tap into overseas records. As one encounters the records of the East or Asia, a new landscape is apparent, at least initially. Though we can describe the basic record types and content, there is considerable work left before there are complete inventories available of the records of the various Asian countries. This chapter merely introduces the range of records which were created and some research possibilities.

Making Genealogical Connections

In order to make the proper genealogical connections, several pieces of information are essential. First, one must determine the place of origin of the ancestor. This can be an Asian village, town, or city. There may still be some ties to the so-called native area, but unfortunately these ties gradually vanish as people move about and older generations pass on. While many of the younger generation have only vague ideas of family origins, some of the older members of the ethnic community may know considerably more. Whenever possible, they should be approached for information or clues about past addresses and specific information on localities abroad. The sources cited in this volume, especially those focusing on the United States and Hawaii, may also provide clues or valuable information. It is helpful, too, if one can find the proper characters, or at least the proper spelling, of the names of various geographic jurisdictions.

It is also crucial to know the name (and characters) of the immigrant or immigrant ancestor if that person immigrated several generations ago. That name may also appear in records abroad, though sometimes in a slightly different form. By making this connection, one may be able to proceed to other lines and extend the genealogy and the scope of the family history. It is helpful to have some idea of various dates (i.e. birth, emigration), the more specific the better. This will make it easier to locate the proper record abroad.

This general introduction may at least suggest some of the major sources and approaches to research abroad. Currently, there are no complete surveys on the quantity of Asian records available though there are research papers on the record types and who they cover for Hong Kong, Taiwan and Japan (see Bibliography at the end of this chapter). The search for record sources in Asia is not easy, particularly in light of language difficulties. However, with the assistance of native speakers and a little luck, a number of Asian Americans have encountered surprising success. One must proceed like a detective, first plotting research strategies and scanning sources. By making the proper connections in a methodic manner, the puzzle begins to unfold.

Chinese Research and Sources

The resilience of Chinese culture and institutions is of considerable importance to Chinese Americans researching their families. Reverence for their elders and ancestors is considered one of the outstanding virtues of Chinese culture. This trait is evidenced in their record-keeping traditions and clan (extended families) practices of ancestor veneration fostered by centuries of Confucianism. Even today, Chinese families pay their respect to ancestors in a prescribed sequence for several weeks at Ching Ming in the early spring. In Cantonese, the common saying, ''Yum sai see yuen,'' or literally, ''when drinking water, remember the source,'' is an admonition to remember one's ancestors. The worst of sins in old China was to neglect one's ancestral duties. These duties and the individual's position in the family were spelled out in genealogical records so there never was a question of where one fit in. Chinese families still have a strong sense of their origins and traditions although this sense is less strong in regard to the younger generations. It is only through becoming closer to the elders that the importance of these connections to origin begin to be realized.

As discussed in Chapter Two, from clues in home, family, and public sources, one may be able to discover the immigrant ancestor. Chinese associations and clan groups may also provide records that could be helpful. Knowing the Chinese characters for an ancestor's name and place of origin can also smooth the path to information. However, even if these characters are known, it does not automatically mean that an ancestor's native village can be found among the thousands of villages in a particular province. It does help though, as do detailed maps and consultation with people of expertise.

Chinese Association Records

As the Chinese migrated overseas, they continued to affiliate with traditional associations and groups. Because of persecution and isolation in America, Chinatowns became places of refuge for many Chinese. Wherever they settled, ethnic organizations provided assistance as benevolent associations providing material aid and protection for immigrants in a strange new land. Many of the associations had halls or meeting places but these are hard to find as few organizations are still in existence. Records and membership files, when they exist or if they were kept, have either been transferred to local archives or have ended up in private hands. Unfortunately, there are no comprehensive lists of what records were kept and what repositories are involved. However, the Chinese Historical Society of America (San Francisco) and Hawaii Chinese History Center (Honolulu) may be able to help in this regard.

Many Chinese who migrated abroad became affiliated with clan associations, or family or kinship organizations. These organizations were more inclusive outside of Asia, frequently becoming surname organizations. People were not necessarily related but a relationship was assumed for those with the same surname. Some of the more common Chinese surnames had large followings. For example, there were around 35,000 Lees in the national association. The Wong and Chin associations were also very large. According to *Your Chinese Roots*, there were about fifty such organizations in the San Francisco area some ten years ago (Tan 1986).

Most Chinese were also affiliated with district associations or *hui-kuan* as they were called in Cantonese. These associations were usually organized into a district which encompassed a group of villages of origin. Most common among the Cantonese were certain villages and areas near the Pearl River estuary between Canton and Hong Kong such as Zhongshan (or Chungshan), Sam Yap, and Sze Yap. These associations continued to maintain close ties with the native villages and provided assistance back home to villagers as well as to new immigrants. Like a perpetual bank fund, the associations' funds were replenished and increased as immigrants gained wealth.

Some groups stayed together based on the dialects spoken in the community. Cantonese-speakers were the most common among the early immigrants. In recent years, however, Mandarin-speaking immigrants from Taiwan have become more numerous and have forged their own communities and groups, particularly in southern California.

Acting as larger ethnic community organizations representing the Chinese in general are groups like the Chinese Benevolent Association in San Francisco, New York, and Chicago. This association in San Francisco is known as the "Six Companies" (Tan 1986, 137) as it represents six of the most prominent district associations. The passing of the Chinese Exclusion Act in 1882 brought the various organizations closer together in order to protect Chinese rights and interests. The Chinese Historical Society of America, for instance, has a considerable amount of information on Chinese groups in America.

Tongs (fraternal organizations) also existed in cities where Chinese settled. The Chinese Tong has existed since the late nineteenth century. Often single males not affiliated with clan or district associations would join these groups. Some were involved in protective services for illegal activities gaining a bad reputation as they spawned gangs and became involved in criminal rackets. Interestingly, other Asian groups, including Vietnamese and Filipinos, are now involved in similar organizations.

Arthur Yu (1971) studied Chinese associations in Hawaii and noted that the first community organization, the Liu Yee Wui, was started in 1854 to help establish a cemetery. Other organizations were created to counter anti-Chinese sentiment which intensified in the 1870s and 1880s. By 1884 the United Chinese Society was formed to represent Chinese in Hawaii. In all, Yu identifies 23 surname organizations, 12 district or subdistrict organizations, and 12 associations or clubs at the village level.

In addition, there were political, fraternal, and economic organizations, including at least a dozen guilds representing specific occupations. There were also women's clubs and educational and recreational groups. The Hamilton Library at the University of Hawaii-Manoa has an excellent collection of sources on the Chinese in Hawaii. The Hawaii Chinese History Center has an excellent collection of maps of the various villages in China, photos, oral histories of prominent Chinese in Hawaii, and genealogies.

Records of the Segregated Chinese

Prior to 1882 there were few immigration laws or restrictions on entry into the United States and millions of immigrants, including the Chinese, came to seek economic opportunity. After the Chinese Exclusion Act of that year, the Secretary of the Treasury was charged with administering immigration laws aimed mainly at the Chinese. By 1891 an Office of Immigration was created within the Treasury Department. By 1895 this became the Immigration Bureau. In 1906 the Immigration and Naturalization Service (INS) was created, administered by the Department of Commerce and Labor. The Department of Labor split off in 1913 and the functions were separated until 1933 when Immigration and Naturalization came again under the same bureau. Finally, in 1940 the INS came under the jurisdiction of the Department of Justice, where it remains.

It was not until 1943 that the act excluding Chinese was repealed. Exclusion was aimed against Chinese laborers; certified people from professional occupations were allowed to enter the country after scrutiny. Those who had arrived prior to 1882 were allowed to stay if they had the proper documentation. As a result, these exclusionary laws resulted in a large amount of paperwork as claims were investigated and authenticated. These records, though created under these earlier offices and bureaus, are now under the control of the INS. In the past few decades, the records have been moved to the National Archives and regional centers. These records are now being processed and made available for research. Many of the records from the Washington D.C. archives have been moved to the huge facility in College Park, Maryland.

The collection at the National Archives includes Chinese immigration records covering 1882–1925. A paper on the holdings was presented by Robert L. Worden of the Library of Congress at the Mid-Atlantic Regional Conference for the Association for Asian Studies. He reported that the records were in varying states of preservation. The largest group contains some 215 document boxes of general correspondence (1898–1908), organized by file numbers and date. In addition, there is a card index of file numbers though incomplete (same dates) and large files of letters registered and sent during this period to the authorities by Chinese. Other files include special cases: customs, smuggling, deportation, and those arrested, each as separate categories. There are also chronological- and numerical-based records relating to Chinese "certificates of residence" as well as miscellaneous records.

In order to use these records one needs to know the name of the immigrant at the time the papers were filed and some basic dates. There is no question that the search can be daunting. Nevertheless, there are many valuable pieces of information within these files including dates and places of birth, maps of villages, and even items on parentage in China.

Most of the Chinese exclusionary records for Chinese from Hawaii and San Francisco, about 1500 cubic feet of them in 25,000 files, are located at the National

Archives—Pacific Sierra Region in San Bruno, CA. Many of the records were created by the INS and its predecessors in Hawaii from 1898 to 1943. There are many certificates of registration and considerable correspondence similar to that found in the National Archives files, but the focus is on records generated by local offices; these records are presently being inventoried.

The National Archives—Pacific Northwest Region in Seattle has records from the Pacific Northwest while the records center near Los Angeles, National Archives—Pacific Southwest, has records for Chinese in Southern California which were turned over by the INS. These smaller collections also contain correspondence, reports, and transcripts of testimony and interrogations. As the Chinese were required to report all travel in order to be considered for permanent residence, a large number of documents were generated. These immigration records are all part of National Archives Record Group 85.

Pre-1900 Records of Chinese in Hawaii

Hawaii was a separate kingdom until 1893 when it became a republic. In 1900 as a territory of the United States, it came under the jurisdiction of the U.S. government. Records prior to annexation are in the Hawaii State Archives in Honolulu. Most of these have been filmed and are available through the Family History Library (FHL) in Salt Lake City and its branches. Interestingly, restrictions and legislation in the Kingdom of Hawaii, similar to that in the United States, also resulted in a separate group of Chinese records. Many of these files came under the control of the Chinese Bureau of the Board of Immigration in 1887. Collectively, they are valuable sources on the early Chinese in Hawaii. As many Chinese in Hawaii moved on to the West Coast after annexation, these records can be helpful to those Asian Americans on the mainland as well as those in Hawaii for tracing immigrants back to China.

A few Chinese arrived individually on ships in Hawaii as early as the 1780s, but it was not until the 1850s that large numbers began to arrive to work in the sugar plantations. Chinese appear more frequently in passenger lists from this time on. A special index of Chinese arrivals in ships and passenger manifests, available at the archives and filmed by the FHL, covers 1842–1900. There is some question as to the percentage of Chinese included. The biggest problem in deciphering the index is in the romanization of Chinese names. Many of the names are personal names prefaced with the honorific, "Ah," which makes it difficult to determine the original Chinese surname.

The Kingdom of Hawaii established a Board of Immigration in 1864 in order to regulate the procurement process for laborers working on the plantations. The board's correspondence and letters of procurement for Chinese laborers (from 1864–1900), placed under the Minister of Interior, are in the Interior Department File at the Hawaii State Archives. Most of the Chinese came to Hawaii from Chungshan and its surrounding districts in Kwangtung Province and were funneled through Hong Kong. The noted British shipping and trade company, Jordine-Matheson, acted as the commercial agent and later as consular agent. Correspondence between Minister of Foreign Affairs of the kingdom and the Hong Kong agent is also available in the Hawaii State Archives under "Foreign Affairs."

In 1887 the Hawaiian law was revised extensively to curtail the immigration of Chinese laborers into Hawaii. The influence of attitudes in the United States and the fear of being overwhelmed by Chinese immigrants played a large part in this exclusion policy. Chinese were required to have special permits to enter and stay in the Kingdom of Hawaii. To obtain these "Chinese Permits," the law required two photographs (one full view and one profile view) and a receipt for payment of taxes. The creation of the Chinese Bureau resulted in a plethora of records. A card index to Chinese passports (1884–1898) at the Hawaii State Archives provides access.

All kinds of documents and permissions were granted by the Chinese Bureau, including entry permits, work permits, records of naturalizations (1842–1892), registers of those who returned to China, registers of Hawaiian-born children of Chinese parentage (1893–1898), labor permits of those who died in Hawaii, and certificates of identification. In addition, there are special categories of data such as a register of Chinese women (1893–1898), permits for Chinese clergy, permits for Chinese teachers, permits for doctors and herbal practitioners, and even permits for children. Those employing Chinese were expected by the Chinese Bureau to pay a bond. An index of these sureties lists the employer named in the register of sureties, the individual arriving, and the ship used for transport. The registers themselves note the execution of the bonds either for workers or for merchants and travelers. Many of these records reveal the general place of origin. Transcriptions of the names is tricky and may require additional research in order to make connections to records in China.

Also of value in the Hawaii State Archives are account books from the Bureau of Labor identifying laborers by plantation. Many Chinese are listed on the records of the plantations.

The Archives at the Bishop Museum in Honolulu has about 90,000 photographs in the On Char Collection, mostly Chinese, from the late nineteenth century to the 1970s. The Bishop Museum organizes the collection by individuals and subject.

The Exodus Abroad and Ties to the Homeland

The eighteenth century in China was a period of great chaos and population growth. Chinese in impoverished provinces and districts were looking for opportunities abroad where quick fortunes could be made. As "temporary sojourners" abroad, many had the dream of getting rich and returning to China with more esteem and enough wealth to provide their family with security, but because conditions there were so bad during this tumultuous period, many never returned. Most, however, continued to have a strong sentimental attachment to their homeland and the land of their ancestors. As stated earlier, this was in large part due to the strong Confucian emphasis on piety toward the fathers, the related beliefs in ancestor veneration and lineage continuity, and traditional Chinese feelings toward the soil and the native village.

To recap and supplement the history of twentieth-century China presented in Chapter One, the Ch'ing dynasty collapsed in 1912, followed by the disruptive warlord period (1916–1927). This, in turn, was followed by a depression and deepening conflicts with Japan. The nations of the world sympathized with the Chinese plight but were unable to help due to the economic and political problems they were experiencing.

The Japanese invasion of China and the subsequent destructive war which continued from 1937 to 1945 resulted in a tremendous displacement of the Chinese population. As a result, many Chinese sought refuge elsewhere. One of the most momentous events in Asian (if not in world) history was the Communist takeover of China in the late 1940s. Friction grew between the United States and China due to both U.S. involvement in the Korean War (1950–1953) and its support of the expatriate Nationalist government in Taiwan. This friction continued unabated for two decades until reconciliation with the People's Republic began in the early 1970s.

Each major political episode in China seems to result in new waves of emigration. The Tiananmen Incident in 1989, wherein students staged a protest which ended when the Chinese government sent tanks and soldiers into Tiananmen Square, resulted in legislation allowing Chinese students to remain in the United States as many feared persecution were they to return. The pending Chinese takeover of the British Crown Colony of Hong Kong in 1997 has made Chinese there nervous, though Canada and Australia have been more sympathetic than the United States to this situation in terms of their immigration policy.

Although they have left China, the Chinese abroad are still considered *huajiao* (overseas Chinese) by the Peking government and efforts have been made to win their support or, at least, sympathy. The People's Republic generally has allowed correspondence to continue between relatives under specific conditions and these contacts and, more recently, visits to the ancestral village are encouraged. The government recognizes the obvious economic benefits, including much-needed foreign exchange. A structured itinerary and a guide or attendant are normally prerequisites for visitors. Someone must assume responsibility for the visitor, and no one is free to roam as he or she pleases. As a result of these policies, official attitudes toward genealogical research vary considerably. There is a degree of arbitrariness which, when coupled with the somewhat uncertain state of record preservation, can produce a variety of results. Some visitors are more successful in their research than others.

This can also be true for those who correspond with relatives in China asking for genealogical information. Some have managed to get complete genealogies, albeit a portion at a time, while others have relatives who either avoid the issue or seem unwilling or unable to conduct a search.

Frank Ching, whose *Ancestors: 900 Years in the Life of a Chinese Family* became a publishing milestone, was able to unravel over twenty generations of ancestry. He not only found genealogies but researched many other records as well to breathe life into his family history. For example, he reported that on his second journey he was able to find a tombstone in an "overgrown area" (1988, 30) which contained information on an ancestor buried back in the 11th century. This ancestor was apparently the founder of the Chin (Shanghai dialect for Ching) clan in Wuxi; he located the burial site from a notation in the clan genealogy.

Family Registers and Vital Records

Taiwan. The past few decades have seen a large influx of Chinese from Taiwan (Republic of China), particularly to California but also to major U.S. urban centers. In Taiwan, those Chinese who came over from China because the Civil War (1947–1950), are called "Mainlanders." Both this group and the native Taiwanese have kept up their genealogies—portions of which have been copied from the original genealogy begun in China. Chen's *Catalog of Chinese Genealogies in Taiwan* is a good source to consult.

While Taiwan maintains the traditions of pre-communist China, the fifty-year occupation by Japan has had some impact. For instance, as in Japan, changes in the status of members of the family are noted by a household in a family register (*hukou mingpu*) using a registration system called *huji dengji*. (Although Chinese traditions are apparent in the small changes which were made in the system.) The change in status can be the result of a birth, marriage, death, etc. The information is reported to a district office where the data is recorded in one multi-page file for each specific family. This system makes it easy to follow a family back to 1896 (and earlier, when the parents of the first family to be registered are listed) when this system started in Taiwan.

Hong Kong. While not originally from Hong Kong, many Chinese have used Hong Kong as a temporary home until they were able to find a place abroad. Though largely Chinese in population, Hong Kong developed as a colonial outpost under British rule (except for the brief occupation by the Japanese during World War II). In 1997 the colony is slated to come under the control of the People's Republic of China amid promises of semi-autonomy. No one can predict the shape or form of this arrangement at this point.

The British influence is reflected in Hong Kong's vital records which are maintained in the Registrar General's Department. As in the West, birth and death records (1873–) and marriage records (1946–) are on file there. The information on the records usually reflects the same information found on these records in the United States with the exception that many include Chinese characters in addition to English spellings. A good source to consult is *Major Genealogical Record Sources in Hong Kong.*

People's Republic of China. While there were records kept during the Nationalist era (1926–1948) on the mainland, few remain due to the ensuing chaos. The People's Republic initiated a comprehensive census in 1953 and began requiring reports on change of status because of births, marriages, deaths, and employment. These records are located at the town and village level of government but the availability is always a political question given the nature of the regime. (The regime has also tried to direct family planning and decision making by assigning party and community leaders responsibilities and powers formerly held by clans and families.)

An adequate survey does not yet exist as to the quantity and availability of the vital records of the People's Republic. Reviewing these records and visiting an ancestral town or village may provide data on three or four generations, but it is to traditional genealogies, gravestones, and other sources that one must turn to find information for several generations. The Genealogical Society of Utah is continually filming records held by archives and libraries on the mainland, making these sources available through the Family History Library and its Family History Centers. In just the past two decades, over ten thousand records have been acquired. This is an impressive start, but, as China is so large, it is only a beginning. As these records and those of Chinese Americans are shared, however, the impact can increase exponen-

tially, greatly facilitating research into Chinese sources and expanding our understanding of Chinese lineages.

Clan and Family Genealogies

Those of Chinese lineage should ask about the existence of a family book or genealogy (*Ka Poo* in Cantonese). These appear in manuscript or published form and contain the genealogy of a family, subclan, or clan or consist of inclusive surname genealogies covering many clans. Because of their scope and the length of time they might cover (the compilation of genealogies originated 2,000 to 3,000 years ago; compilation of clan genealogies began nearly 1,000 years ago), determining if one exists for your ancestral line should be your first priority. Starting with the founder of the clan, Chinese genealogies include the patrilineal line from that original ancestor. Women are usually listed only as wives under their family names (''wife from Zhou family'').

Most genealogies cover a clan with all its branches residing in a specific district in a particular province of China. That is why knowing your ancestor's surname and native village is important. While many Chinese Americans may know the native village, if they have not kept in touch with relatives still in China over the generations, they will not be aware of jurisdictional changes which have occurred since the advent of Communism. Many former villages have been reorganized into communes or new districts or towns. Knowing relatives who never immigrated will make the translation of the native village into its current designation less painful.

The Chinese genealogy consists mainly of pedigree charts (skeletal representations of a lineage) and tables but there are also notes which include details on the origin and history of the clan, lineage rules, ancestral rites, clan property, specific family members, gravesites, etc. The tables reveal the most detailed information. The style most used (Ou Yangxiu, A.D. 1007–1072) lists five generations listed vertically on a page with branches (each brother is a separate branch) extending to the left of the first son of each generation. Information listed can range from providing the male's name and stating that he had a wife and sons (giving none of their names) to listing a male's name, other names he was known by, his wife's name, his rank among civil officials, the date and time of birth and death, his place of burial, the ancestors by whom he was buried, the date and time of birth and death of his wife, her place of burial, the names of their sons, the order of the sons' births, and the various locations in which they resided. A male may use several names depending on his stage in life ending with that given to him posthumously. Most genealogies, by either including detailed information on an ancestor or using generational names (*paiming*), help a researcher to identify each individual listed. For information on transcribing the language and dates listed, refer to the "Problems in Interpreting Data" section of Chapter One.

Chinese Local Histories

Chinese local histories or gazetteers (*fangzhi* or *difangzhi*) are a very important and often neglected record category. As histories, they go beyond the usual historical summary common to histories in the West. Since there is usually substantial geographic information in the record, they are also referred to as gazetteers. At the provincial (*sheng*), prefectural (*fu*), sub-prefectural (*zhou*), and district (*xian*) levels of government, detailed records were traditionally kept by local mandarins or officials. The writing of local histories on an empire-wide basis was prescribed during the Tang dynasty (618–906 A.D.) and continued during the Sung dynasty (960–1260). The compilation and rewriting of these records was particularly common during the Manchu Qing dynasty (1644–1912). The practice disappeared after the collapse of imperial China in 1912.

In Chinese, local histories are called *fang-chih* or *difang-chih*. The great majority of these records are at the district or *hsien* level and thus provide a detailed glimpse of certain topics of local interest. Besides an overview of local geographic and topographical features, information on ancestral burial sites, clan halls, and shrines is frequently included. Particularly unique to this source is the influence of Confucian morality. There are often biographies and lists of filial sons, virtuous women and chaste widows (unlike Chinese genealogies, local histories do not ignore the "second" sex), and noteworthy officials. Because a local history includes so many short biographies, it has been referred to as a "vast Who's Who" (*Chinese Local Histories as a Service For the Genealogist* 1974, 10). Some local histories even include genealogical tables of prominent families similar to those found in Chinese clan genealogies.

The Family History Library is continually acquiring local histories, especially those covering the areas from which Chinese emigrated. These records are listed by locality in romanized form in the catalog of the Family History Department and in character form in the Asian catalog. Local histories are also found in larger university libraries with strong Asian collections, both in the United States and in East Asia. Libraries and archives in Mainland China, Hong Kong, and Taiwan also usually have a selection of local histories.

Ancestral Tablets

Another traditional source with genealogical information is the ancestral tablet (*shenju* or *shenwei*), usually simple wooden tablets with ancestral names inscribed on the face. Birth and/or death dates are commonly included. These tablets were traditionally kept on household altars, in clan temples, or at grave sites. A shorter version was usually handed down from generation to generation in the family. While they are increasingly difficult to find, they should be sought, particularly for those in Chinese communities. Ancestral tablets for the wealthy may be highly ornate and in recent years many of them include pictures of the deceased. Also, many contain interior compartments with additional information inside. In poorer families, however, information may be written on slips of paper or strips of wood instead. The researcher desiring to investigate this source should always approach the family with discretion as the tablets are considered to be sacred.

Ancestral Graves

As is true in researching an ancestor of any ethnic group, the inscriptions on tombstones (*mubei* or *mubiao*) can reveal genealogical information. Normally located near the ancestor's native village or in clan burial areas, they provide name, burial date, and place of origin among other data. While many of these suffer from neglect and may require thorough searching to find in the People's Republic of China, inscriptions on tombstones can provide the clues needed to locate more records.

Examination Rosters

A number of people have lines where an ancestor was an official or a successful candidate in the traditional Chinese civil service exam. Those who aspired to office had to pass these exams, which were given at intervals at the district, prefectural, provincial, and metropolitan levels. Rosters (*dengkelu, kemubiao,* or *xuanjubiao*) often listed considerable information on each of the successful candidates including name, the type of exam and degree received, the date of the exam, official position and title, and the name of the father and other relatives of note— sometimes listing up to ten generations of ancestry as well. Although these exams began as early as the 7th century, they are generally not available until the Ming period (1368–1644). The system continued until the Boxer Rebellion in 1900 when exams were canceled. They are a valuable source for genealogical information but are limited to the elite and may be difficult to locate. The FHL has a growing collection, though the majority that exist are still among the holdings of libraries and archives in China.

Other Chinese Sources

Chinese often wrote eulogies about ancestors, created biographies, and kept records of important events. Land records included names of people involved in the transactions described, sometimes names of parents, as well as information on the location and size of the property. Chinese Christians may also be recorded in Christian church records covering christenings, marriages, deaths, burials, and memberships. There may also be personal records in the family such as journals, diaries, and guest records. Although there is a wealth of records in China in spite of the neglect occurring during the past century, one must keep in mind that writing was mainly the province of scholars in traditional China as it required considerable study and practice. Thus, the richer areas and families in China are heavily recorded while poorer families and areas generally have few records.

Japanese Research and Sources

Being able to locate the *shusshin* (native village or "where one comes from") is the key to unraveling family history in Japan. This is relatively easy for recent Japanese immigrants but for those of the fourth and fifth generation, the search can be challenging. Japanese Americans bring with them many of the traditions and institutions of their native country. Most maintain close ties with fellow Japanese and become affiliated with organizations sharing their common interests. Many communities also published newspapers in Japanese or both Japanese and English as the *nisei* (second generation of children of immigrants) became more numerous. These ethnic organizations and newspapers published directories and information on individuals, usually including their occupations and prefectural origins. Japanese Buddhist temples and Shinto shrines were erected in the larger communities. A few ethnic Christian churches were also established. All of these are worth investigating.

Although the past century has witnessed considerable mobility and emigration, prior to the 1870s Japanese were often forbidden to go abroad, could not change their occupations, and had to have special permission just to leave their native village. All comings and goings to and from the village were recorded and residents were expected to be affiliated with neighborhood associations, temples, or shrines. Marriages were arranged and were limited to someone in the same village or to one nearby. Many of the more isolated villages in Japan experienced a high rate of intermarriage among relatives in the same village. Society was essentially "frozen" in an extremely hierarchical multi-layered structure (samurai on top; peasants comprising the great majority of the population on the bottom; and artisans and merchants located mainly in the towns). Everyone was expected to act according to his or her station in what was a strongly male-dominated, feudal society. Thus, the history of most Japanese families is intertwined with the native village or town.

Although Japan went through a social revolution with the Meiji Revolution (1868) and the subsequent end of feudalism, the new Meiji government continued to monitor any changes in the status of households or individuals through a comprehensive household registration system introduced in 1872. The native town or village became the *honseki-chi* (permanent domicile) as individuals were required to be entered on a household register (*koseki*) under the name of the head of house (*koshu*). Notifications of any changes were sent to the "permanent domicile" regardless of whether Japanese were "temporarily abroad" (*dekasegi*) or working in another locale. In the latter instance, a register of temporary residence had to be filed for tax and employment purposes.

As a result of this system, those who went abroad, if Japanese born, often stayed on the register for years. This applied to their children as well. The registers were continually updated via the required reports which were submitted to the nearest consulate. The immigrant generation, referred to as the *issei*, were considered sojourners or temporary residents abroad. As record entries, they were only struck from the register upon death, the renunciation of citizenship, or upon being moved to another register as the family branched out.

Research Problems in Using or Locating Japanese Records

In addition to problems in research delineated in Chapter One, others arise when researching Japanese records other than the koseki. While this household register is fairly uniform since it is based on points of law and procedures which are spelled out, this is not the case with most of the other records of Japan. During the Tokugawa period (1603–1867), the records of the over 250 feudal domains show considerable variation in style and content as do those of the over 80,000 Buddhist temples in Japan. The general disorganization, diversity, and scattered nature of materials make research of records created prior to 1868 difficult.

A cursory survey of materials relating to a small town in Chiba Prefecture illustrates the problem. Over 20,000 items still exist providing information on the town and its inhabitants during the Tokugawa era but they are found in over 80 separate locations, in both private and public collections. Although this may be an extreme case, it nonetheless illustrates several points: the copious amount of paperwork produced during this bureaucratic era, the often vexing problem of locating and identifying Japanese sources, and the necessity of knowing the locale and the traditions.

A further roadblock to research is that most commoners were not allowed surnames until the 1870s. Before that time, given names were often passed down from generation to generation. As explained in "Naming Practices," in Chapter One, when surnames were allowed, they reflected preferences more than tradition. This certainly contributed to the explosion in surnames. The sheer number of surnames in Japan can be a blessing or curse in research. Some names are extremely rare and are found only in a specific locale. Others like Sato or Suzuki number over two million each. There are over 70,000 names that differ phonetically and an estimated 110,000 that differ by character combinations. No country on earth with a homogenous population like Japan can compare to this. The Japanese, as a result, have a great interest in the origins and images represented (whether they come from place names, landscape features, plants, animals, or combinations of the above, etc.) in each other's surnames. Therefore, a considerable number of books written in Japanese have been published on Japanese surnames, especially those discussing the more common surnames or those surnames of a particular locale.

Equally vexing is the use of multiple given names and the problem of multiple readings where a character can be interpreted several ways. The names of many children were given personal or unique readings. (See "Spoken and Written Language, Japanese," Chapter One, for additional information on given names.) Japanese genealogies may list changes in names at various stages in a person's life. Even in the modern period, one can be confused as to whether a given name is really a title.

The frequent use of cursive and variant characters (*hentaiji*), depending on the area where the record was created, can make it difficult to read the older records. This makes knowledge of the history of an area essential. In addition, styles of handwriting, changing over the centuries, make it difficult for all researchers, regardless of ethnic ancestry, to read records created in eras other than their own.

Japanese Emigration Records and Papers

Over 30,000 contract laborers came to Hawaii from 1885 to the end of 1894 to work on sugar plantations. The first emigrants were from areas hard hit by famine and a depressed economy, particularly from Hiroshima, Yamaguchi, Kumamoto, and Fukuoka prefectures in the south and Fukushima and Niigata prefectures further north. Each emigrant, needing an exit permit with the seal of the prefectural governor, was entered in a temporary register (*kiryubo*, part of the registration system from 1886) and given a local permit or identification paper. The emigrant then used the exit permit and a signed copy of the labor agreement, which listed terms of employment and guarantees, to apply for a passport.

From 1894 to 1908, Japanese emigration companies (*imingaisha*) served as brokers for contract laborers bound for Hawaii and West Coast venues. Besides recruiting laborers, these companies helped facilitate a smooth transition abroad and guaranteed return passage to Japanese citizens after the completion of their contracts. The companies also assisted in the transmittal of the funds and paperwork for what the Japanese called *dekasegi* (those temporarily abroad).

Category 3 records in the Japanese Diplomatic Records Office (Nihon Gaikō Shiryō-kan) deal extensively with emigration overseas, including those enroute to Hawaii and the West Coast. These records, though in Japanese, are available at the Family History Library. In order to access them, one must know the name of the emigrant, his native prefecture and village, and the approximate date on which he emigrated.

Among the wide range of these records are those of the emigration companies, papers on Japanese who died abroad, permits for overseas immigration, prefectural government reports on immigration, and paperwork on immigrants from the various consulates in the United States. However, because these sources are in *kyt' kanji* (old-style characters) and are so highly diverse, their effective use will depend on locating finding aids and in-depth inventories.

Records Possessed by Emigrant

In order to leave Japan and work abroad, it was necessary to present the proper papers both in Japan and at the final destination. Each individual would need a labor emigration or exit permit authorized by the prefectural governor; a card or paper of identification issued by the leading official of his village, town, or city; a passport issued by the Minister of Foreign Affairs, Foreign Office; and a labor contract issued by the representatives of the immigration bureau and the future employers. The labor emigration permit often cited the name of the emigrant, his address of origin, and the date of departure. The names of the emigrant and the head of his household, the Japanese address of his registered domicile, and a picture and description of the emigrant were normally provided in the identification papers. Among the data listed in his passport were his name, passport number and date of issue, Japanese address, age or date of birth, date of admittance, name of sailing ship, and the name of the head of his household. The labor contract, in both Japanese and English, provided the emigrant's name, the name of his employer, the period of employment, the wages to be paid, and other conditions and guarantees of employment. The data on these documents and the num-

Japanese Research and Sources *∅* Asian American Genealogical Sourcebook

ber and types of documents required could vary depending on the circumstances prompting the emigration and the period of time involved. For example, an exit permit issued in the early twentieth-century listed the date of approval; destination; name of emigrant; and the emigrant's place of origin, height, date and order of birth, name of father, and occupation.

These papers, in the personal possession of the immigrant, were either handed down or discarded, though some duplicate copies were made and retained by the issuing agencies. In certain instances, Japanese travel agencies and mortuaries ended up with some of these papers.

Prefectural Association Records

Associations were organized in the United States and Hawaii to assist immigrants in the transition. The *kenjinkai* or *kenkai* normally included people originating from the same prefecture (similar to, but smaller than a state). Members of associations traded with each other, helped each other out financially, celebrated holidays and special occasions together, and encouraged feelings of mutual obligation. The associations produced membership lists and directories, and newsletters. There was a regular written correspondence among the members. The bonds were strong as members shared a common dialect, heri-

tage, and local affinity. In addition, many were related and often worked in the same occupations.

In Hawaii, which had the largest number of immigrants, there were strong prefectural associations for Hiroshima, Yamaguchi, Kumamoto, Okinawa, Niigata, Fukushima, and Fukuoka. There were still "19 active kenjinkai in the L.A. phone book" (Kitano 1969, 94) in 1964. Seattle had active associations from the Hiroshima, Okayama, Yamaguchi, Fukuoka, Kumamoto, Wakayama, Shige, and Ehime prefectures at one time.

In recent years, many of these organizations have disappeared or no longer have offices. (Records ended up in private hands or were donated to local repositories.) However, in Hawaii, the United Okinawan Association and several groups, such as one for Hiroshima and Yamaguchi, are still active. Local branches of the Japanese American Citizen's League and older residents may be able to help in locating these organizations.

Japanese Associations

Japanese associations, both national and regional, were founded in the United States to protect the interest of Japanese Americans and to coordinate various activities within their respective communities. Since the immigrants were "aliens ineligible for citizenship," they continued to observe Japanese customs and traditions and

---

Japanese Associations

Japanese American Citizen's League
Founded: 1930, in Seattle.   Goal: To represent the interests of American-born Japanese.
Publishes: The Pacific Citizen. Comment: Still oversees many local branches.

United Japanese Society
Formerly: The Hawaiian Japanese Civic Association. Comment: Affiliated associations located in the towns and plantations of the Hawaiian islands.

Japanese Association of America
Founded: 1901, in San Francisco. Comment: By 1920 there were forty local affiliates and 16,000 members in northern California, Utah, Nevada, and Colorado.

Central Japanese Association.
Comment: Strong in southern California. By 1920 there were twenty local associations and about 8,000 members. Other chapters were located in Texas, New York and Illinois.

Northwest American Japanese Association.
Comment: Fourteen local chapters, principally in the Seattle and Tacoma, Washington, areas.

Japanese American Association of Oregon.
Comment: Though based mainly in the Portland, Oregon, there were five chapters in Idaho.

Figure 3.1

maintained close ties with nearby Japanese consulates. In the 1920s there were nearly one hundred associations, most of which were affiliated with the major groups listed in Figure 3.1 (some of these groups dissolved with the outbreak of World War II).

Most local chapters printed membership lists, directories, newsletters, and bulletins. Many of these materials were mimeographed or hand-written in Japanese, though English was used more often as time progressed. Information of genealogical value may include the full name, prefecture of origin, address, and occupation. In the larger directories, business advertisements and pictures were common. Though a number of these records were likely destroyed at the onset of World War II, libraries with major collections on Japanese Americans such as the University of California—Los Angeles, the University of Washington, the University of California—Berkeley, and the University of Hawaii-Manoa do have some of these materials among their holdings. Older residents of a community may also be helpful.

Household and Family Registrations

The household or family register (koseki) is an excellent genealogical source, often called the "trump card" of Japanese genealogy. These registers were first introduced in Japan as part of the Taika Reforms (645 A.D.) but soon disappeared. With the restoration of the emperor in 1868 and policies aimed at modernizing the country, a thorough household registration system was instituted. Serving as a kind of census, it allowed the government to keep track of the members of each household.

Essentially a register of important events from the cradle to the grave for each individual listed, members of a specific household were listed under the name of the head of house. Japanese immigrants, for sometime unable to become American citizens, continued to supply information for the koseki to the nearest Japanese consulate for transmittal to Japan. All information is listed in a prescribed sequence as specified in directions provided by the Japanese government. Though the basic format has been modified five times since the first registers in 1872, the information is still recorded on double-folded rice paper with an individual crossed out when he dies or leaves the household covered by a particular register. In 1948 the head of the house became the head of the family. Since that time, the size of registers has been reduced as the emphasis is now on a husband and his wife and children (the conjugal family) rather than the much larger household of the prewar period.

The basic format lists the registered locality or honseki (prefecture, town, or village and address); the name of "first one entered" (hittosha) or, in earlier registers, head of house (koshu); the reason and date

koseki was established or if honseki was changed, the date of and reason for the change and the previous honseki; the father's name, sex, and relationship; the mother's name, sex, and relationship; the name of husband or head of house; the dates of birth of the above; and the reason for entry of new data to a particular koseki. For new entries, the name and relationship of the applicant is provided. If there was a birth, the date and place of birth and date of notice is listed. In marriage, the date of acceptance of marriage notification and the name of spouse will be provided. For adopted children, the names of the adopted parents and their relationship will be mentioned. Other items fixed by the Household Registration Law may also be included. Changes were usually submitted within seven to ten days after the event which necessitated the change took place.

The name of the head of the family and his address in Japan must be known in order to locate copies of the koseki. Knowing the latter will allow the researcher to contact the local office overseeing the record. As in other countries, changes in boundaries and jurisdiction can have an impact on an ancestor's home address. If the researcher knows Japanese, the sources *Zenkoku shichō-son yōran* and *Dai Nippon bunken chizu narabi ni chimei sōran* should be consulted. The former is an annual directory of Japanese cities, towns, and villages. The latter is an annual containing maps grouped by prefecture with a list of current place names and the addresses of government offices.

Once the local office is known, a request for copies of records can be sent. The request, written in simple English, should include a statement delineating the reason the copies are needed (the assistance of older relatives who are more closely related to the ancestor is helpful); the name and address of the ancestor with any other data which would be of help in finding the correct register; and the inclusion of an international money order, purchased from the researcher's local post office.

It should be kept in mind that an office can remove registers dated from 1886 from circulation after retaining them for at least eighty years. These withdrawn registers are called *joseki* records. The ultimate disposition of the joseki records depends on each individual office. They could be stored elsewhere, retained, or destroyed. Additionally, all records prior to 1886 are closed as the format used allowed the recording of private and class information.

Records of the Japanese Consulate in Honolulu

Closely related to the koseki and of considerable value to the residents of Hawaii are the records of the Japanese Consulate General in Honolulu. The availability

Translation of Portion of Index Card of Japanese Consulate in Honolulu

[surname] KIMURA		[registered locality or Honseki] Yamaguchi-ken, --Óshima-chó-- [address]			
[given name]	[relation-ship]	[occupa-tion]	[date of birth]	[present address]	[notes]
Konroku	father Genkichi	farming	11-5-99 12-5-10 2nd time	Kauai, K---	died on 1-1-35
Fusa	wife of Konroku	"	11-6-13	K---	died on 3-25-34
Ichiró	eldest son	succeeded as head of house on 1-10-35 11-6-13 ¦ 6-29-11		K---	married ABE K- 9-4-33
Jiró	second son	born in Hawaii	5-5-15	Óshima-chó, Y---	left Hawaii 2-5-33
Harue	eldest daughter	born in Hawaii	4-4-20	Honolulu	married NAKA-- 2-14-38

Figure 3.2

of these files, however, is subject to the directives of the Japanese Ministry of Foreign Affairs in Tokyo. Access is limited to family members and descendants only.

Among the most frequently reviewed items are over 50,000 index cards providing information on a good portion of the Japanese living in Hawaii from 1885 to the present. The honseki (registered domicile in Japan), temporary Hawaiian address, pertinent dates (birth, death, marriage, and adoptions), and notes on entry and departure from households are among the data found on these cards. A partial translation of an index card can be found in Figure 3.2 (it is illegal to produce an exact facsimile).

Figure 3.3 contains a list of the other records known to be among the consulate's holdings. However, perusal is not allowed and staff limitations may preclude access to some of the records listed.

There are also some records of contract immigrants (1885–1910) and immigrants (1901–1910) in addition to a number of personal records (1868–1910).

Japanese Consulate General (Honolulu): Sampling of Holdings

Record	Coverage	Content	Volumes
Honseki-chi chóbo	circa 1900	Lists permanent domiciles in Japan	8
Seishi Todoke-gaki	1891-1893	Contains notifications of births and deaths	30
Nyukoku chóbo	1885-1910	Registers of entry into Hawaii	19
Shutsugoku chóbo	1909-1941	Registers of departures	30
Shibo kiroku	1890-1913	Death records	5
Shusshó kiroku	1898-1913	Birth records (includes parents' names)	6

Figure 3.3

Buddhist Death Registers

An entry in a Buddhist death register, or *kakochō*, begins with the name of the individual whose death is being recorded. However the name recorded is the Buddhist posthumous, or vow, name which consists of a series of characters reflecting hopes for the other-world or virtues and the sex and status of the deceased. Few researchers probably know the posthumous name of their ancestor so whether or not a register is helpful depends in large part on the detail of that register (or on the depth of the historical knowledge of the area of the local priest). If the birth name of the listee or one of his relatives is provided, then a link to an ancestor can be established and the researcher may also find the ancestor's exact date of death, names of others and their relationship to the ancestor, or the age at which the ancestor died.

The Buddhist custom of assigning a posthumous name was common in Japan by 1700. Today, a review of the nearly 80,000 Buddhist temples in Japan would reveal that most have kakochō among their records. The temple with which the ancestor was affiliated (either in Japan or the United States) must be known in order to locate the applicable death register. Once known, the address can be located by looking in telephone books or directories.

One of the most comprehensive directories is *Zenkoku jiin meikan* or *Nationwide Directory of Buddhist Temples* (Zenkoku Jiin Meikan Kankukai 1973), in which the temples are indexed by locality. Volume four contains a listing of Buddhist temples in the United States. The Hongwanji and the Jōdō Sect headquarters temples are both located in Honolulu. The Shingon, Sōtō Zen, and Ōtani sects are also well represented in Hawaii. The headquarters of the Buddhist Churches of America is located in San Francisco. Headquarters temples for the Shingon, Nichiren, Ōtani, Jōdō, and Sōtō Zen sects are located in the Los Angeles area.

There are essentially three types of kakochō, classified by the way they are arranged: 1) Chronological or *nendobetsu* kakochō which is arranged in general chronological sequence by calendar year. 2) Ritual or *higuribetsu* kakochō (also called *hibi* or *nichi-nichi*) created by the priest as a guide to days of deaths. Following the old lunar cycle of 29 or 30 days per month, there are normally 30 divisions in the register. Observances can thus be made collectively for everyone who died on the seventh day of any month. This allows for the frequent memorialization of the deceased. It also reminds the priest of specific anniversaries in which the family may want to become involved. A few registers are indexed on a monthly calendar (*tsukibetsu*) basis. This format allows easy recognition of those who have a death anniversary during the first month, for example, so they can be memo-

---

Basic Structure of a Buddhist Death Register

	Posthumous name		
		(Arranged by day of month, month of year, or in general chronological order)	Name of temple, sect, and faction (often on cover of death register)
Margin notes (seldom present)	Death or anniversary date (standard entry, a few are incomplete)		
Age at death (commonly found in more recent entries)	Relationship (included in most of the earlier entries)	Common name (either self, relative, feudal sponser, or supporter)	Dates of the record

Figure 3.4

rialized any time during that month. 3) The family or household type (*iebetsu* kakochō) is essentially a copy of a death register either recorded for patron families by the temple or made by the families themselves. Some are found in temples but the majority are in the houses of the older living descendants of the deceased. This record can be valuable in reconstructing families because of the arrangement of the data by family unit. Figure 3.4 provides the basic structure of the record.

Mortuary Tablets

Buddhist ihai or mortuary tablets can be of value in researching deceased relatives and noteworthy ancestors (see Figure 3.5). The posthumous name is prominent on the front face along with the date of death. The reverse side usually bears the person's name in life and, in some cases, a brief account of that life. An age at death is also found on many of the more recent ihai.

While the practice of creating ihai and placing them on the family *butsudan* (altar) or in a special room or alcove in the temple became popular during the Tokugawa period (1600–1867), the actual origins of the system began much earlier. These types of memorial tablets, first used in Sung China (960–1260), were introduced to Japan around the thirteenth century. The practice of creating ihai in Japan differs from that in China,

though both are of result of the tradition of ancestor veneration.

Since many of the older tablets have been discarded after many generations and people have moved from place to place, individual family collections are generally not as complete as some of those in temples—though they are more personal. Occasionally, especially in rural areas (less affected by change than are cities), an ihai will be located that dates from the feudal period. An older tablet may also be located for a person of importance. Some of the older ones are hard to read because of the effects of time and incense smoke. Others have been created with ornate, lacquered frames and gold-lettered characters to replace the older tablets created with India ink on natural wood. Today strips of paper or cards called *Kuri-ihai* are gaining acceptance as inexpensive replacements for ihai.

The Grave Site and Tombstone Inscriptions

The ancestral grave site or *ō-haka* can be an important place for a researcher to visit. Before the coming of Buddhism, stone rooms and earthen mounds were used to memorialize the wealthy and powerful in Japan. (With the advent of Buddhism and the belief that the deceased went to Paradise, less attention was paid to the corpse.) Some of these were very large and are still identifiable today. Stone monuments were erected over the remains of the deceased or special memorials were built. Several types of monuments were popular by the eleventh century. These included the *gorintō* (five-ring monument or tower), the *itabi* (plate or stone slab type), and layered or piled monuments or towers. Sanskrit inscriptions were used as were characters. Most of these sites and inscriptions have weathered to the point of being unreadable and require considerable expertise to interpret the type of monument and the identity of the person honored.

With the forced affiliation of the populace to Buddhism in the latter half of the seventeenth century, the inscriptions (*bohimei*) took on a Buddhist flavor. Many of the markers were located adjacent to Buddhist temples. Posthumous names became the prominent entry along with the date of death. Some also included the deceased's common name, the age at death, and the family *mon* (crest) engraved in the stone.

Because of the cost of an appropriate marker, it was common to erect a collective gravestone for the deceased ''from generation to generation'' of a specific family. On the other hand, those of influence often had their life's achievements and highlights inscribed on the tombstone or on one of the faces. The poor generally used wooden markers, most of which have long since decomposed.

Figure 3.5: Mortuary Tablet

The practice of honoring the dead spread as Japanese moved abroad. Japanese cemeteries located near plantations in Hawaii were common. At first, in the larger communities, Japanese were buried in scattered graves, but by 1900, Japanese cemeteries (*Nihon bochi*) were appearing in the areas with Japanese community organizations. Most of the inscriptions are in Japanese, though English is also used.

Among Japanese in larger cities throughout the world, cremations are common, especially among Buddhists. Cremations increased as mortuaries became available which catered mainly to Japanese, such as the Hosoi and DoDo Mortuaries in Honolulu. These mortuaries, which have branches throughout the islands, have maintained records of the cremations.

One can discover a number of clues in the history of a family if they were prominent and of long standing in the community. This is particularly so in a rural environment, rather than in a city, since outlying areas were normally less disturbed by the great changes that have occurred throughout the centuries. The monument might include clues as to a person's rank, status, or wealth and the location of the family home (unless the markers were moved).

Biographical information may also be recorded as may eulogies. While it is possible to decipher those inscribed with deep, large letters sometimes to an age of over 400 years, those with smaller letters (but deeply engraved) may be legible for only 200–300 years. The majority, however, even if well cared for, become illegible after 100–200 years depending on the quality of the stone. Using special rubbing techniques (use of black chalk) or other methods (for example, copying over wet paper in candlelight), can enable one to read many that have weathered badly.

Japanese Genealogies

Some Japanese Americans may be able to tie into Japanese compiled genealogies (*keizu* or *kafu*) if ancestors were samurai or aristocrats. Not many peasants had genealogies, though as the merchant class emerged, it showed interest in compiling them. Most Japanese genealogies were created during Japan's feudal years. While similar to the Chinese counterpart, particularly the focus on male succession, there are some differences based on the Japanese preference for the feudal group and lineage relationships to the emperor rather than the clan and founding ancestor as in China. Genealogies in Japan range from the simple, handwritten, family variety to the more elaborate genealogies of feudal lords (*daimyō*) and aristocrats.

In theory all Japanese lines run into the Imperial line and the genealogies illustrate the divine origins of the race. The earliest Japanese writings, the *Kojiki* (Record of Ancient Matters) and *Nihonji* (Chronicles of Japan), compiled in the eighth century, include the genealogies and mythical traditions of the Imperial line. According to myth, a divine brother and sister gave birth to the islands of Japan and other gods, including Amaterasu, the Sun Goddess. From this line came the first emperor Jimmu (circa 660 B.C.), followed by a long line of emperors and empresses. From the beginning, these records were written to enhance the prestige of the ruling family.

Confined to the Imperial Family and nobility at first, genealogies were adopted by the feudal lords and samurai in the thirteenth century to justify their newfound status. The beginning of the feudal age was the start of a period of great social and political change. The Minamoto sought to claim legitimacy as *shōgun* (military dictators) during the Kamakura Period (1185–1333) as did the Ashikaga and many of their retainers. Unfortunately, many of the genealogies and records of Japan created were destroyed during the chaotic hundred year period (1460–1569) which began with the Onin Rebellion and ended with the reunification of the country.

As Japan was reunified, genealogies became critical in justifying one's aristocratic or *samurai* status, particularly after the ascendancy of the powerful Tokugawa family in 1600 as masters of Japan. It was common to graft into a genealogy of a clan or family close to the Imperial family which explains the preference for Fujiwara and Minamoto lineages. In the seventeenth century, there were some famous professional genealogists who made a good living at this business (*keizu-kai*). They had considerable knowledge of old genealogies and were able to work with individuals to create a suitable pedigree. These genealogies must be treated with suspicion since they are of a genre referred to as *nise keizu* or false genealogies.

Ota Ryō, a pioneer advocate of *keifugaku* (the study and comparison of genealogies), has written several volumes discussing this problem and outlining the various lineages and branches. He suggests that genealogies, including Imperial connections developed prior to the mid-sixteenth century, should be approached with caution. One should not accept these early lineages without checking the logic and context of the record and verifying the data with other sources. For more information, refer to Ota's *Shinhen seishi kakei dai-jiten*.

Genealogies were regulated from the mid-seventeenth century. In the early days of the nineteenth century, the Tokugawa government created an official genealogy, *Kansei chōshu shokafu* (Kansei collection of the genealogies of retainers), covering the principal feudal lords and higher ranked retainers. Each of the various domains also published genealogies of the lords and higher-ranked samurai. Lower-ranked samurai and *ashigari* (foot soldiers) were usually covered in *samurai kafu* (samurai genealogies) or *samurai-chō* (samurai rosters).

The most comprehensive inventory of Japanese genealogies is Maruyama Koichi's *Keizu bunken shiryōs ran* (a comprehensive survey of Japanese genealogical materials). This detailed reference work is indexed by prefecture and repository as well as by collection and type of source. Many specialized dictionaries relating to biographies and place names, both at the national and local level, are listed.

The Family History Library has copies of genealogies from many prefectural and local libraries in Japan, including Yamaguchi and Fukuoka prefectures (the source of many emigrants). Although, most of these are in classical Japanese and can be difficult to decipher.

The detail of some of these genealogies can best be illustrated by a translation of a portion of a lineage chart of the Iwamuro family. See Figure 3.6.

Unlike Chinese genealogies, Japanese genealogical lines tend to shift back and forth with adoptions and the granting of feudal privileges. Biographical entries, where they occur for important people, can be extremely detailed. Figure 3.7 shows an example of a biographical entry from the Genealogy of the Lords of Takamatsu (in Shikoku).

The many names and titles in Figure 3.7 illustrate the feudal nature of these records and the complexity of dealing with Japanese historical sources. Further, dates up to the 1870s are based on the lunar calendar. Though these genealogies represent only the upper levels of society and, thus, a small portion of all Japanese, they can provide valuable information for those descendants with the proper lines.

Japanese Crests

Japanese families did have family crests (*kamon* or *iemon*). Although a crest may have been slightly modified to denote a specific branch of a family, if the basic design was highly unique, it can serve to identify the various branches of that family. However, if a crest was a common one, used by several families, such an identification should be made with caution.

Some feudal records, such as *bukan* (heraldry records), will show the crests of feudal lords and samurai. The most definitive work on the subject is Numata Raisuke's *Nihon monshō-gaku* which discusses in depth the origin and typology of family crests.

Crests usually do not represent surnames, but are more often linked with family branches located in certain areas. For example, many prominent samurai families

used variations of "feathers of the hawk," while the powerful Mori family from Yamaguchi prefecture used "three stars over a one," the famous Tokugawa family used "three leaf hollyhock," and "16-petal chrysanthemum" was restricted to the Japanese imperial family.

Surveillance Records of the Tokugawa Era

It takes considerable time, a great deal of skill, and some luck to sort through and make connections with the diverse feudal sources of the Tokugawa period (1600–1867). While a tremendous amount of paperwork was created during this highly regimented era, much of it is only of peripheral value to family history research. Nonetheless, it should be considered since putting the family history puzzle together may require every piece and clue that can be found. This is no easy task, especially when one is dealing with a society and record keeping system so different than the one to which one is accustomed.

The source you seek will depend largely on the class origins or feudal status of the ancestor for whom you are searching. In addition, the name given the source can vary considerably among the over 250 domains of the realm as it was then structured. And the individual domain itself underwent constant changes in the organization and size due to changing relationships with the ruling shogunate and internal politics.

One of the most reliable of the sources of the period was the so-called "Examination of Religion Register" (*shōmon aratamechō*). This source originated during a time when Christianity was under suspicion and foreigners were mistrusted. The Tokugawa Shogunate developed the register during an inquisition which identified Christians when the general population was forced to affiliate with local Buddhist temples, or, in some cases, Shintō shrines. This affiliation was certified by priests and confirmed by local civil authorities in a periodic census of each family unit in a town or village. By 1665, the inquisition census became mandatory throughout Japan.

The title and content of this record usually varied by domain but the title *ninbetsuchō* (census register) was commonly used. From 1721 the record became the basis of a national census of the masses (samurai, officials, and certain other groups were exempt). The ninbetsuchō usually included information which was valuable in understanding the family's religious composition, its religious affiliation, each member's age at the time of the census, and their relationship to one another. These registers were continued until the Meiji Restoration when the Jinshin Koseki (household register of 1872) was instituted.

Though these censuses were usually conducted at three year intervals, rarely are complete censuses available today. Among the exceptions is the collection from

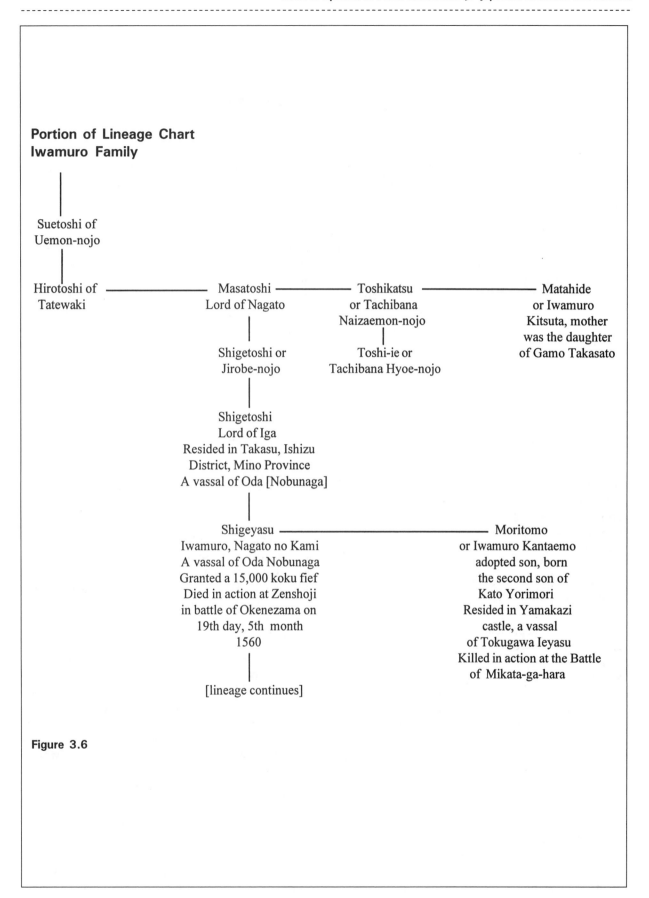

**Portion of Lineage Chart
Iwamuro Family**

Suetoshi of
Uemon-nojo

Hirotoshi of ——————————— Masatoshi ——————— Toshikatsu ————————————— Matahide
Tatewaki   Lord of Nagato   or Tachibana   or Iwamuro
                                                                      Naizaemon-nojo   Kitsuta, mother
                                                                                                           was the daughter
                                              Shigetoshi or   Toshi-ie or   of Gamo Takasato
                                              Jirobe-nojo   Tachibana Hyoe-nojo

                                              Shigetoshi
                                              Lord of Iga
                                              Resided in Takasu, Ishizu
                                              District, Mino Province
                                              A vassal of Oda [Nobunaga]

                                              Shigeyasu ——————————————————————— Moritomo
                                              Iwamuro, Nagato no Kami   or Iwamuro Kantaemo
                                              A vassal of Oda Nobunaga   adopted son, born
                                              Granted a 15,000 koku fief   the second son of
                                              Died in action at Zenshoji   Kato Yorimori
                                              in battle of Okenezama on   Resided in Yamakazi
                                              19th day, 5th month   castle, a vassal
                                              1560   of Tokugawa Ieyasu
                                                                                          Killed in action at the Battle
                                                                                          of Mikata-ga-hara
                                              [lineage continues]

Figure 3.6

Biographical Entry from the Genealogy of the Lords of Takamatsu

Yoritan

Also known as Shunmin, and by the pen name Hoko. Was also known as Sanuki no Kami. Takemaru was his childhood name, and he was also known as Kunitarō and Sadagorō. Had the titles Kunai-taifu and Ukyō-taifu. Was the son of Minamoto Noboru, the brother of Jirō, having the same mother. Was born at the mansion in the Ōgawa district [of Edo or present-day Tokyo] on 22nd day of the 12th month in 1810. He participated in the ceremony of hair dressing on the 27th day of the 9th month of 1811. His name was changed to Kunitarō on the 28th day of the 12th month in 1812. His name was changed to Sadagorō on the 1st day of the 2nd month in 1813. He participated in the ceremony of putting on the *hakama* on the 11th day of the 11th month in 1814. He was moved to the family mansion in Yanokura [a section of Edo] on the 5th day of the 11th month in 1817. A petition was made for him to become an adopted son on the 24th day of the 12th month in 1817. [The record continues for several pages until his death many years later.]

Figure 3.7

Suwa (Nagano Prefecture) where 144 of the original 201 annual censuses (1701–1871) have survived. The longest period without records is four years. For a twenty-year period (1693–1712) the month of birth is listed in addition to the data listed above. When located, these records have great potential as villagers intermarried and remained in the village (at the same occupations) from generation to generation.

There are a large number of records of peripheral value that can provide clues about the history of villages and families. These include *mura meisaichō* (particulars of villages) which periodically listed the activities and composition of the village, but more in survey terms than genealogical. There were *nayosechō* (registers of cultivated land) and *kenchichō* (land registers) that mention the names and holdings of land owners. Villages also had rosters (*gōchō*) created for civil authorities mainly for tax purposes.

Another unique record of the feudal period was the *gonin-gumichō* or literally, "five men-in-a-group register." It was essentially a neighborhood-type association in which each head of household certified that his household was cooperating with government edicts and policies. The information, however, is limited and is mainly

useful in identifying family heads in a locale at a particular time.

There are also a number of regulatory-type records that kept track of the movements of the population and of specific groups. These include *okurijō* (records of transfer), records of entrance and exit, and reports of widows and widowers. They all have some genealogical information but are limited in their coverage. Other items, kept by individuals, are personal correspondence, diaries, guest lists, and personal notes and records. These must also be considered in research.

For those of samurai ancestry, there were a large number of distinctive records created for this privileged group: rosters (*samuraichō*) and corresponding status reports (*bugenchō*), service records (*hōkōgaki* or *yuishogaki*), lists of fiefs (*bugenchō*), heraldic records (*bukan*) and samurai genealogies (*samurai kafu*). Most of these records, focusing on legitimizing the retainers and defining their stipends and positions, contain some biographical information as well.

There are other important groups, such as feudal lords, court nobles, and those of the Imperial Household, that are listed in a considerable inventory of records and documents applicable to family history research. A comprehensive survey of Japanese genealogical sources at the various prefectural and local archives is found in Maruyama's *Keizu bunken shiryō soran.*

Other Japanese Sources

There are many other records that include information on Japanese both in America and Japan. The records of travel agencies, Japanese mortuaries, ethnic Christian and Buddhist churches, and Japanese schools can provide valuable information as can wills (*yiugonjō*), land records, military records, pension records (*onkyō juryōsha kiroku*), and lists of repatriates (*fukuin jōsensha meibo*). *Major Genealogical Record Sources in Japan* is a good source of information on these records.

Korean Research and Sources

The first significant Korean immigration did not occur until the first decade of this century. The greatest number, about 7,000, arrived in Hawaii between 1903 to 1905, most of whom were initially employed on the sugar plantations. This early era is covered in depth in Wayne Patterson's study on the early pioneers, *The Korean Frontier in Hawaii.* Korean emigration was stopped after Korea was annexed into the Japanese empire in 1910.

The various Korean groups in the United States organized the Korean National Association (*Kook Min Hoe*) in 1909, an organization that still exists in Los Angeles. A weekly newspaper (*Sinhan minpo*) was published in San Francisco for many years. Political groups promoting Korean independence from Japan flourished for the next decade but eventually faded as those behind the movement gradually lost hope. In 1930, there were only 6,000 Koreans living in Hawaii and a few thousand in California. The relatively small size and closeness of the early Korean community are advantages to the researcher.

Most of the Koreans in the United States have arrived since racial quotas were lifted on immigrants in 1965. By the year 2000, it is estimated that the number of Koreans in the United States could pass the one million mark.

Los Angeles has the largest percentage of Koreans with a large "Koreatown," serving as the gateway for many immigrants. San Francisco, Honolulu, New York, Chicago, and Washington, D.C. are also popular destinations. More recently, Atlanta, Houston, and Seattle have proven attractive.

Although the Korean National Association still exists, Korean ethnic churches, particularly Protestant, have become religious and social centers to many Koreans in recent years. In areas with larger Korean populations, Korean schools for children of immigrants have been established. Though more prominent Koreans may be found in histories and directories, finding the ethnic church and groups with which a family was affiliated should provide information helpful in shedding more light on the family history.

Except for the pioneer generation, which is now into the fourth and fifth generation in the United States, the great majority of Koreans are very recent arrivals. Most researchers should be able to trace their families through household or family registers and, if so, may be able to tie in with traditional records. This, of course, depends considerably on the availability of assistance from abroad and whether the lineage the researcher encounters has some prominence.

Korean Records and Traditional Society

Korean Americans have an intense pride in their homeland and ethnic identity. Most have maintained close ties with family members back home and continue to use the Korean language in business and family situations. Like their Chinese "cousins," they have respect for their elders and ancestors. In recent years, however, these traditions have given way to economic concerns. Nonetheless, to families with more illustrious lineages, it can be a great source of pride.

Most Korean Americans can stay abreast of developments in Korea and communicate with family abroad as *han'gŭl*, the simplified Korean written phonetic system, is easy to learn and remember. However, as most traditional records are in the classical language in Chinese characters, even Koreans in Korea are becoming increasingly less capable of reading historical records.

Korea is recognized as having an exceptionally rich record-keeping tradition as well as a high rate of literacy. Traditional records reflect a strong Chinese influence, particularly those records of the long Confucian-dominated Yi dynasty (1392–1910). During this period the basic political division into provinces (twenty-one) and districts or counties was fixed. With Japanese annexation and rule from 1910 to the end of World War II, Japanese-style registers were imposed. After the war, Korea was divided into north and south. North Korea's failed attempt to conquer the south (1950–1953) accomplished the destruction of much of the country.

Though many records were destroyed, because of the abundance of records and the multiple copies of genealogies, there are still many which survive. A survey of record types and content was made by Korean specialist, Mark Peterson, for the Genealogical Society of Utah in 1980, but the paper was not published. Nonetheless, his pioneering survey and papers delivered at the 1969 and

1989 World Conference on records are very helpful in providing an overview of Korean research and sources. *Anata kara anata e no senzo* is also useful. (The English-language version is titled *From You to Your Ancestors*.) One's success in Korean research will depend on from where the family originated (North Korea is a closed country), his connections and contacts with family still in Korea, the lines being researched, and the element of chance.

Like China, the clan in Korea (*ssijoki*) was the unit of family organization sharing the same surname (*song*) and clan seat (*pon'gwan*). A person's standing depended greatly on the status of the clan. Most of the great clans descended from those who held government offices in previous dynasties according to June-ho Song in his paper on Korean *chopko* (clan genealogy).

Prior to the Confucian-dominated Yi dynasty when clans were not as firmly established in Korean society, women were treated more equally and were included in the records. The influence of Buddhism was stronger and families more diverse. During the Yi dynasty, especially from the 1600s, Korean society reflecting the domination by men and various divisions in status, became highly stratified with Confucian scholar-officials (*yangban*) at the top level. The yangban were found at the dynastic seat (Seoul), city and town (*si* and *myun*), county or district (*gun*), and village (*li*) levels. Because of their status, they and their families are the best-recorded group, by far. As traditions loosened their hold in the twentieth century, nearly twenty-five percent of all Koreans can, through intermarriage or direct line, tie into these records. The largest group of Koreans, however, descend from commoners for whom there are considerably less records available. This is also true for those descended from slaves. (In Korea, the term "slave" had two different meanings: a slave was either owned by a master or worked in an occupation which provided no social standing to its holder.)

Korean Household Registers

One record that does cover the general population is the *hojuk*, a census instituted by the Yi dynasty which was in effect from early 1600 to 1910. Normally, a census was conducted every three years with one copy retained by the family and two copies held by the government. Besides the household under the master or head of the house, these census records also listed the *sajo* or "four ancestors" (through the great grandfather and including the mother's father). The status of the individual (aristocratic yangban, commoner, or slave) was also listed, along with the age or year of birth for every person in the family. Though many of these records no longer exist, those that do are of considerable value because they include the families of commoners and slaves. The latter may be listed incidentally under yangban families, organized by "groups of five" (neighborhood associations consisting of the heads of household of five families). Though it is unlikely many families still have copies of this traditional source, there are collections at some libraries and archives (particularly the Kyujangguk in South Korea). The Family History Library also has a small collection of these census records.

When the Japanese colonial administration began to rule Korea after 1910, a system similar to that used in Japan, the koseki (household register), was instituted. Preprinted forms, used for a more comprehensive census which listed information under the name of the head of house, were called the *hojuk-tungpon*. Unlike the earlier census, these records were updated through mandated reports as changes in family status occurred. When families divided (for example, the marriage of a younger son), a new register was created for the new head of household (the son who married). When the Japanese departed in 1945, the Republic of Korea kept this system of registration with certain modifications.

The natural place to begin one's research in South Korea, therefore, is at the government office where the ancestor's family is registered. These offices are found at the *ku* (ward) level in larger cities or in *myon* offices in rural areas. One must ascertain the ancestor's place of origin and the name of the head of the house in order to locate the right government office and file. The information which can be found includes data on births, marriages, deaths, and other changes in family status—all on one record.

Korean Genealogies

Many South Koreans still maintain clan genealogies (*chopko*). Manuscripts of family histories (*kasung*) are incorporated into the more recently published genealogies. Although chopko are written in classical Chinese, they are read in Korean.

To locate the correct genealogy, the ancestor's surname and clan seat or *pon'gwan* (a county-level administrative district) must be known. This is because twenty-two percent of the Korean population is surnamed "Kim" and fifteen percent is known by "Yi" (Lee). Knowing the clan seat (Kim of Kyongji) will insure that the right genealogy for a surname has been obtained.

Most Korean genealogies use the Chinese tabular format developed by Ou-yang Xiu, containing much the same information discussed in the section on Chinese "Clan and Family Genealogies." The level of accuracy is best for the twenty most recent generations.

The genealogies include, among other things, information on gravesites. See Figure 3.8 for a drawing of how

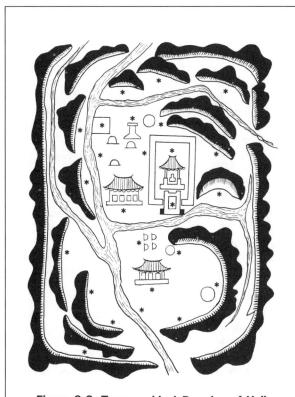

Figure 3.8: Topographical Drawing of Hall

an ancestral hall and gravesite might be laid out topographically in a genealogy.

Printed genealogies are published by clan organizations, many of which have offices in Seoul or the home provinces. As multiple copies and editions were usually printed, clan members, local libraries, and major repositories such as the National Central Library would likely have copies. The Family History Library has the largest collection found in one place. Since these genealogies focus on the male line, it is necessary to trace the maternal line using the genealogy of the wife's father.

Korean chopko are considered a mirror of life as they comprehensively cover the hereditary ruling yangban class of the Yi period and their extensive families. The focus is on the descent group as it fans out from the original, or found ancestry (*sijo*), into many branches. Numerous Koreans can tie into a genealogy as they move back through the generations. Though prominent local families still keep genealogies today, a certain amount of wealth and tradition are prerequisites. Genealogies for commoners are rare. When they do exist, most are relatively plain and in manuscript form.

Korean Local Histories

Korean local histories or gazetteers (*jibang-ji*), though very similar to their Chinese counterpart, are of more recent origin—from the 1500s to the end of the Yi dynasty. There are fewer administrative units and a much smaller area is involved. Most local histories are on the county level but cities and towns also have these kinds of histories and some even exist for provinces.

Besides the usual geographic and topographical overview, these so-called "histories" also include important events and the biographies of noteworthy people in the area. Like the Chinese histories, the Korean histories also have sections covering the economic and educational aspects of the area. While they cover categories similar to those of the Chinese (merit subjects, filial sons, virtuous women, chaste widows, etc.), they differ in that they glorify military heroes and list a military examination.

Korean Examination Rosters

Those who passed the government examination in Korea were listed in the *pangmok* (examination rosters). The large bureaucracy created by the Yi dynasty was staffed primarily through the examination system. The dynasty used Confucian civil service exams similar to those of the Chinese, though in Korea there were also military examinations (*mukwa*) and examinations for specialists (those with expertise in medicine, foreign languages, scientific-technical areas, etc.). In addition to including the name and examination data of the successful candidate, these rosters listed the father's name and titles, the clan seat or native place, and the names of any brothers along with the posts and offices they occupied. Some more comprehensive rosters listed up to eight generations of ancestry beyond the candidate's father. Examination rosters are of particular value for those with yangban ancestry. This source is available in libraries and archives (particularly the National Central Library, Seoul) in Korea. Many have been filmed and are available in the collection of the Family History Library. One must, however, know the pertinent names and dates to locate the roster. Clan and family genealogies can be of great help in this regard.

Other Korean Sources

There are many other records in Korea containing genealogical information. A few of them are detailed in this section. However, there are many other records of potential genealogical value that remain to be surveyed.

One traditional source valued by researchers is the *tongseng hwahui mun'gi*, a type of inheritance document. Koreans divided property equally among siblings who conferred in the decision. Women were gradually excluded as Confucianism prevailed in the 17th century and slaves were generally listed as property. These records also included some children and relationships not listed in clan genealogies.

Records of adoptions were also kept by the Yi dynasty bureaucrats. These listed the names of both fathers (natural and adopted) as well as that of the adopted son and the date of adoption. Many of these are found in the Kyujanggguk collection at the Seoul National University.

Royal family records of the Yi dynasty are at the Changsogak (the Royal Family Library) in Seoul. Dynastic records and genealogies are also located at the Seoul National University Library and the National Central Library (also in Seoul). Many of these have been filmed and are part of the collection of the Family History Library.

The collected writings (*munjip*) of prominent individuals from the 1300s to the present are also an excellent source as several obituaries and eulogies are included. Many, written as tributes to descendants, are very factual. Biographies in chronological form as well as memorials to the throne (often mentioning individual family members) were also part of this tradition. Munjip are scattered in various public and private collections. Some have been filmed by the Family History Library.

Christianity made significant inroads after its introduction in Korea in the 1860s. Approximately 15 percent of the population of South Korea is Christian. Christian records include christenings, marriages, deaths, burials, and memberships. See Chapter Two for more information.

Newspapers should also be reviewed. Korean newspapers (*shin-mun*) include information on prominent individuals. Again, see Chapter Two for more information on the value of newspapers.

Bibliography

Additional information on these sources may be found in Part II.

Akira, Hayami. ''Shumon aratamecho of tsujite mita Shindhu Yokouchi-mura no choki jinko tokei.'' In *The Demographic Aspects of a Rural Village in Tokugawa, Japan, 1671–1871*. Management and Labor Series, no. 202. Tokyo: Keio University, 1967–68. Pp. 69–105.

Anata kara anata e no senzō. The Church of Jesus Christ of Latter-day Saints. Tokyo: Tokyo Distribution Center, 1979. Japanese version of genealogy class manual *From You to Your Ancestors*.

Association of Hawaiian Archivists. *Directory of Historical Records Repositories in Hawaii*. Honolulu: Association of Hawaiian Archivists, 1994.

Char, Wai Jane, and Francis H. Woo. *Geography of Kwangtung Province for Hawaii Residents*. Honolulu: Hawaii Chinese History Center, 1981.

Chen, Mei Kuei. *Catalog of Chinese Genealogies in Taiwan (T'ai-wan ch'u tsu p'u mu lu)*. Taipei: Ch'eng Publishing Co., 1987. 1000p.

Chinese Local Histories as a Source for the Genealogist. Genealogical Research Papers. Series J, no. 3. Salt Lake City: Family History Department of the Church of Jesus Christ of Latter-day Saints, 1974.

Ching, Frank. *Ancestors: 900 Years in the Life of a Chinese Family (Ch'in shih ch'ien tsai shih)*. First edition. New York: Wm. Morrow & Co., 1988. 528p.

Choy, Bong-Youn. *Koreans in America*. Chicago: Nelson-Hall, 1979. 371p. Includes oral histories of early Koreans, index, and bibliography.

Conroy, Hilary, and T. Scott Miyakawa. *East Across the Pacific*. Historical and sociological studies of Japanese immigration and assimilation. Santa Barbara, CA: ABC-Clio Press, 1972. 322p.

Dai Nippon bunken chizu narabi ni chimei sōran. Tokyo: Kokusai Chigaku Kyokai. Japanese maps grouped by prefecture with a comprehensive list of present-day place names and addresses of government offices.

Ferguson, Anthony W., and Warrick H. Chin. ''A Treasury from the East: What We Can Learn from Chinese Genealogy.'' In *Ensign* (October 1988), pp. 17–19.

Freedman, Maurice. *Family and Kinship in Modern China*. Stanford, CA: Stanford University Press, 1980.

Gardner, Arthur L. *The Koreans in Hawaii*. An annotated bibliography. Honolulu: Social Science Research Institute, University of Hawaii, 1970. 83p.

Gardner, Charles S. *Chinese Traditional Historiography*. Harvard historical monographs; v. 11. Cambridge, MA: Harvard University Press, 1938. Revised edition with additions and corrections, 1961. 124p. Includes bibliographical footnotes and index.

Gubler, Greg. ''Characters and Ancestors: The Case of China and Korea.'' In *Genealogy Digest*, vol. 9–4 (Winter 1978), pp. 5–11. Reprinted in vol. 13-1 (January 1982).

Gubler, Greg. ''Characters and Ancestors: And Then There is Japan.'' In *Genealogy Digest*, vol. 10-1 (January 1979), pp. 40–43.

Gubler, Greg. ''Chinese Clan Genealogies: An Interim Report.'' Manuscript. Salt Lake City: Family History Department, 1981.

Gubler, Greg. ''Family History for Japanese Americans.'' In *Proceedings of the World Conference on Records, 1980*. Volume 11:805. Salt Lake City: 1980.

Gubler, Greg. ''Looking East: The Realities of Genealogical Research In Japan.'' In *Genealogical Journal*, vol 8:2 (May-June 1979), pp. 43–50.

Gubler, Greg. ''Nike Amerika-jin no tame no kashi.'' [''Family History of Japanese Americans.''] Two Parts. In *Seishi to kakei* [*Surnames and Lineages*], no. 40 (1984), pp. 56–64; no. 41 (1985), pp. 55–61.

Hayes, James. ''Chinese Genealogies as Local and Family History.'' In *Proceedings of the World Conference on Records, 1980*. Volume 11:824. Salt Lake City: 1980.

Hirata, Kin-itsu and Greg Gubler. ''Breaking the Impasse: Sources and Options in Japanese Family History Research.''

In *Proceedings of the World Conference on Records, 1980.* Volume 11: 818b. Salt Lake City: 1980.

Kimura, Motoi. *Bunken shiryō chosa no jitsumu.* [*Surveying Japanese Documentary Materials*]. Chihoshi manyuaru; 2. Tokyo: Kashiwa Shobo, 1974. 359p.

Kitano, Harry H.L. *Japanese Americans: The Evolution of a Subculture.* Englewood Cliffs, NJ: Prentice-Hall, 1969. 186p. Includes bibliography. Second edition, 1976. 231p. Includes index and bibliography.

Kobayashi, Naoki Chris. Assisted by Tsumura Matazaburo. *Catalog of Historical Records of Japanese Nationals Traveling Abroad and Foreign Nationals Arriving In Japan.* Manuscript. May 1989.

Lai, Kum Pui, and Violet Lau Lai. *Researching One's Chinese Roots: Proceedings of the 1985 Genealogy Conference in Hawaii.* Honolulu: Hawaii Chinese History Center, 1988.

Lau, Chau-Mun. *The Chinese in Hawaii: A Checklist of Chinese Materials in the Asia and Hawaiian Collections of the University of Hawaii Library.* Honolulu: University of Hawaii Library, 1975. 55p.

Lin, Tien-Wei. "Chinese Clan Genealogies and Family Histories: Clan Genealogies as They Relate to Local History." In *Proceedings of the World Conference on Records, 1980.* Volume 11:824c. Salt Lake City: 1980.

Lo, Hsiang-lin. *A Study of Chinese Genealogies (Chung-kuo tsu p'u yen chiu).* Hong Kong: Institute of Chinese Culture, 1971. 324p. Includes bibliographic references.

Major Genealogical Record Sources in Hong Kong. The Church of Jesus Christ of Latter-day Saints, Genealogical Society, Research Department, Series J; no. 4. Revised edition. Salt Lake City: Genealogical Society of the Church of Jesus Christ of Latter-day Saints, 1976. 14p.

Major Genealogical Record Sources in Japan. The Church of Jesus Christ of Latter-day Saints, Genealogical Society, Research Department, Series J; no. 1. Revised edition. Salt Lake City: Genealogical Society of the Church of Jesus Christ of Latter-day Saints, 1974. 18p.

Major Genealogical Record Sources in Taiwan. The Church of Jesus Christ of Latter-day Saints, Genealogical Society, Research Department, Series J; no. 2. Revised edition. Salt Lake City: Genealogical Department of the Church of Jesus Christ of Latter-day Saints, 1976. Chiefly tables; includes bibliography.

Maruyama, Koichi. *Keizu bunken shiryōs ran.* [*A Comprehensive Survey of Japanese Genealogical Materials*]. Tokyo: Ryokuin Shobo, 1979, 714p., includes index; 1992, 916p., includes indexes.

Matsuda, Mitsugu. *The Japanese in Hawaii: An Annotated Bibliography of Japanese Americans.* Revised by Dennis M. Ogawa with Jerry Y. Fujioka. Hawaii series; no. 5. Honolulu: Social Sciences and Linguistics Institute, University of Hawaii, 1975. 304p. Distributed by the University Press of Hawaii. Includes index.

Moriyama, Alan Takeo. *Imingaisha: Japanese Emigration Companies and Hawaii, 1894–1908.* Honolulu: University of Hawaii Press, 1985. 206p. Includes index and bibliography.

Naquin, Susan, and Evelyn S. Rawski. *Chinese Society in the Eighteenth Century.* New Haven, CT: Yale University Press, 1987. 270p. Includes index and bibliography.

Nihon no koseki. [*The Japanese Household Register.*] Series J, no. 5. Tokyo: Family History Department of the Church of Jesus Christ of Latter-day Saints, Tokyo Distribution Center, 1978.

Ohai, Jean. "Family History for Chinese Americans," In *Proceedings of the World Conference on Records, 1980.* Volume 11:807. Salt Lake City: 1980.

Okinawa Club of America. *History of Okinawans in North America.* [*Hokubei Okinawajin Shi.*] Translated by Ben Kobashigawa. Los Angeles: Okinawa Club of America and the Asian American Studies Center, University of California, Los Angeles, 1988. 608p. Includes bibliographical references and indexes.

Ota, Akira. *Seishi to kakei.* [*Surnames and lineages.*] Tokyo: Sogensha, 1942. 1366p.

Ota, Ryō. *Shinhen seishi kakei daijiten.* [*Newly revised comprehensive dictionary of surnames and lineages.*] Revised by Niwa Motoji. Tokyo: Akita Shoten, 1974.

Palmer, Spencer J. *Studies in Asian Genealogy.* Provo, Utah: Brigham Young University Press, 1972. 281p. Papers of the 1969 World Conference on Records dealing with Asia.

Patterson, Wayne. *The Korean Frontier in America: Immigration to Hawaii, 1896–1910.* Honolulu: University of Hawaii Press, 1988. 274p. Includes index and bibliography.

Peterson, Mark. *Records of Genealogical Value in Korea.* Manuscript. Salt Lake City: Genealogical Society of Utah, 1980.

Peterson, Mark. "Women and Traditional Sources: Sources for Genealogies for Women in Korea." In *Proceedings of the World Conference on Records, 1980.* Volume 11:831b. Salt Lake City: 1980.

Raisuke, Numata. *Nihon monshogaku.* [*The Study of Family Crests.*] Published in 1926, 1937. 10430p.

Song, June-ho. "An Interpretive History of Yangban Family Records." In *Proceedings on the World Conference of Records, 1980.* Volume 11:816. Salt Lake City: 1980.

Suzuki, Kenji. "East Asian Family History Sources: The Genealogical Society of Utah Collection, Japan." In *Proceedings of the World Conference on Records, 1980.* Volume 11:814c. Salt Lake City: 1980.

Taga, Akigorō. *Sōfu no kenkyu.* [*A Study of Chinese Genealogies.*] Tokyo: Toyo Bunko, 1960. Analytical study of Chinese genealogical books. Volume one includes union lists of Chinese genealogies.

Tan, Thomas Tsu-wee. *Your Chinese Roots: The Overseas Chinese Story.* Singapore: Times Books International, 1986.

Telford, Ted A. "East Asian Family History Sources: The Genealogical Society of Utah Collection, China." In *Proceedings of the World Conference on Records, 1980.* Volume 11:814. Salt Lake City: 1980.

Telford, Ted A. "Women and Traditional Sources—Chinese Clan Genealogies: Tracing the Female Line." In *Proceedings of the World Conference on Records, 1980.* Volume 11:831c. Salt Lake City: 1980.

Telford, Ted A., Melvin Thatcher, and Basil P. N. Yang. *An Annotated Bibliography of Chinese Clan Genealogies.* Taipei, Taiwan: Cheng Wen Publishing Co., 1981.

Thatcher, Melvin. "Local History Sources for China at the Genealogical Society of Utah." In *Chinese Studies (Chung-kuo yen-chiu),* vol. 3:2 (December 1985), pp. 419–459.

Wang, Shih-ching. "Chinese Clan Genealogies and Family Histories: Historiography of Chinese Genealogies—Taiwan." In

Proceedings of the World Conference on Records, 1980. Volume 11:824c. Salt Lake City: 1980.

Wolf, Arthur P. *Religion and Ritual in Chinese Society.* Stanford, CA: Stanford University Press, 1974. 377p. Consists chiefly of papers presented at a conference sponsered by the Subcommittee on Research on Chinese Society of the Joint Committee on Contemporary China held at Asilomar Conference Grounds, Pacific Grove, California, October 11–15, 1971.

Worden, Robert L. ''The Segregated Chinese Files of the I.N.S. at the National Archives.'' Paper presented at the Mid-Atlantic Regional Conference of the Association for Asian Studies, Washington, D.C., October 28–29, 1978.

Yang, Basil. ''East Asian Family Sources: The Genealogical Society of Utah Collection, Korea.'' In *Proceedings of the World Conference on Records, 1980.* Volume 11:814a. Salt Lake City: 1980.

Young, Nancy Foon. *The Chinese in Hawaii: An Annotated Bibliography.* Hawaii Series; no. 4. Honolulu: Social Science Research Institute, University of Hawaii, 1973. 149p. Distributed by University Press of Hawaii.

Yu, Arthur Yun-Chao. ''A Study of Chinese Organizations in Hawaii with Special Reference to Assimilative Trends.'' In *Working Papers of the East-West Center Learning Institute.* Honolulu: East-West Center, May 1971.

Zenkoku Jiin Meikan Kankokai. *Zenkoku jiin meikan.* [*Nationwide Directory of Buddhist Temples.*] Four volumes. Tokyo: Zenkoku Jiin Meikan Kankokai, 1973.

Zenkoku shichoson yoran. Annual directory of Japanese cities, towns, and villages. Tokyo: Daiichi Hoki Shuppan, 1963–.

Part II
Directory of Genealogical Information

Libraries & Archives

Private & Public Organizations

Print Resources

Other Media

Libraries and Archives

‑‑‑

⌀ This chapter lists libraries, archives, and repositories both within and outside the United States which hold materials relevant to genealogists whether their focus is on genealogy in general or on a specific ethnic group. A description of special collections and services available to users may be provided for each institution. Federal institutions and those private and public institutions whose name implies a national focus appear first, followed by state institutions with a regional focus which may also have a national focus. Institutions which either have an international focus or are located outside of the United States, if present, appear at the end of the chapter. All institutions are listed alphabetically within each category.

National and Regional

‑‑

American Baptist Historical Society Archives

Box 851   Phone: (215)768-2378
Valley Forge, PA 19482-0851   Beverly Carson,
Administrator/Archivist

Special collections: Historical records of Board of National Ministries, Board of International Ministries, Board of Educational Ministries, Ministers and Missionary Benefit Board, Office of General Secretary.

American Congregational Association Congregational Library

14 Beacon St.   Phone: (617)523-0470
Boston, MA 02108   Fax: (617)523-0491
Rev. Dr. Harold F. Worthley,
Librarian

Staff: Prof 2; Other 3. **Description:** Contains town histories, local church histories, and church records. **Founded:** 1853. **Holdings:** 125,000 books; 100,000 pamphlets and periodicals. **Subscriptions:** 80 journals and other serials. **Services:** Interlibrary loan; copying; direct mail service available to individuals in the U.S.; library open to the public.

American Family Records Association Library

PO Box 15505   Phone: (816)252-0950
Kansas City, MO 64106   Fax: (816)252-0950

Founded: 1985. **Subjects:** Genealogy, history, adoptive relationships. **Special collections:** Genealogy circulating collection. **Holdings:** 3000 volumes. **Services:** Interlibrary loan; library open to the public. **Remarks:** Association promotes preservation of and access to public and private genealogical records. Collection is located in the North Independence Branch of Mid-Continent Public Library, Independence, MO. **Publications:** *Genealogy from the Heartland*, 1992.

Chinese Historical Society of America Archives

650 Commercial St.   Phone: (415)391-1188
San Francisco, CA 94111

Subjects: Chinese in America, late 19th century to present. **Special collections:** Records of the Chinatown Factfinding Committee; archives of the Chinese Constitutionalist Party. **Holdings:** Newspaper clippings; photographs; manuscripts. **Remarks:** Archives are located in the Asian American Studies Library, 101 Wheeler Hall, University of California, Berkeley. **Publications:** Monthly newsletter, 10/year; *Chinese America: History and Perspectives*, annual.

Church of Jesus Christ of Latter-day Saints Family History Library

35 N. West Temple   Phone: (801)240-2331
Salt Lake City, UT 84150   Fax: (801)240-5551
Stephen Kendall, Director

Staff: Professional 120; Other 98. **Founded:** 1894. **Subjects:** Genealogy, family history, church and civil records, local history. **Special collections:** Family Group Records Collection (8 million family reconstitution forms from the U.S. and other countries); oral genealogy tapes; international collection of manuscripts identifying individuals in historic populations (microfilm); military rosters; baptismal records; wills; civil registration records; notarial collections; International Genealogical Index (over 200 million names; microfiche, CD-ROM); U.S. census from 1790–1920. **Holdings:** 240,000 volumes; 3000 bound periodical volumes; 1.8 million reels of microfilm; 350,000 microfiche. **Subscriptions:** 135 journals and other serials. **Services:** Copying; orientation film; research classes; center open to the public. **Computerized services:** Produces Family Search CD-ROM. **Special catalogs:**

Family History Catalog (COM & CD-ROM); Catálogo de Pasajeros a Indias (microfilm). **Remarks:** Branch family history centers (over 2000 in 60 countries) having access to most films are added to the system on a continuing basis. Largest collection of Hispanic genealogical materials in the world. **Publications:** *Genealogical Research Papers*, irregular; *News of the Family History Library*—to genealogical societies; Personal Ancestral File (genealogical software); see also Ancestral File, International Genealogical Index, Social Security Death Index and Military Index, Family History Library Catalog, and Family Search in "Other Media."

Department of the Army
U.S. Army Military History Institute

Carlisle Barracks
Carlisle, PA 17013-5008

Remarks: Accepts and provides information on nearly all military units involved in the history of the United States.

Japanese American National Library

1619 Sutter St.	Phone: (415)567-5006
PO Box 590598	Karl K. Matsushita, Director
San Francisco, CA 94159	

Staff: 3. **Founded:** 1969. **Subjects:** Japanese in United States and Canada. **Special collections:** National Repository of Japanese American Redress (50 boxes); Japanese American vernacular newspapers (27). **Holdings:** 15,000 books, 46 bound periodical volumes; 30 nonbook items. **Subscriptions:** 21 journals and other serials; 27 newspapers. **Services:** Copying; library open to the public for references use only; phone inquiries accepted. **Special indexes:** Abstract-Index of Japanese American Vernacular Newspapers, quarterly. **Remarks:** Library is said to collect all published materials relating to the Japanese in the U.S. and Canada, particularly in the fields of history, literature, art, social sciences, mental health, interracial marriage, medicine, and current events.

Library of Congress
American Folklife Center

Thomas Jefferson Bldg.	Phone: (202)707-6590
Washington, DC 20540-8100	Alan Jabbour, Director

Staff: Prof. 13; Other 5. **Founded:** 1976. **Subjects:** American folklife with emphasis on research, public programs, and technical assistance; folksong; folk music; folklife; ethnomusicology; oral history. **Special collections:** Archive of Folk Culture. **Holdings:** 4000 books; 1300 serial titles; 40,000 hours of unpublished field recordings; manuscript collection (600,000 pages); results of current research projects including fieldnotes, sound recordings, photographs, and videotapes; 200,000 ephemera; 170,000 photographs. **Services:** Copying (limited); reading room open to the public; listening by appointment; correspondence and telephone inquiries. **Computerized services:** Computerized public access catalog, internal databases. **Special catalogs:** Catalog of issued LPs/cassettes (pamphlet); catalog of recorded collections (card); catalog of individual titles on some recordings (card); catalog of manuscript and microform collections (card). **Remarks:** Publishes *Folklife Center News,* quarterly; mailing list composed of folklife organizations, institutions, and individuals—additions made upon request; *Folklife Sourcebook: A Directory of Folklife and Fieldwork* (English and Spanish editions); *American Folk Music and Folklore Recordings: A Selected List;* LC recordings of folk music and lore; 200 reference and finding aids—available

upon request; Federal Cyclinder Project Catalogs; list of publications—available upon request.

Library of Congress
Asian Division

John Adams Bldg., LA 130	Phone: (202)707-5426
Washington, DC 20540	Hisao Matsumoto, Acting Chief

Holdings: Asian Division contains 1.6 million volumes in Asian languages. Chinese: 570,000 volumes, with emphasis on local histories, rare books, and materials of the Ch'ing period, 1644–1911, and post-1949 periodical publications. Japanese: 716,000 volumes, with emphasis on social sciences and modern history. Korean: 95,000 volumes, with emphasis on historical works and current publications. Southern Asia: 216,000 volumes of research literature from Pakistan to Philippines, especially Bengali, Punjabi, Gujarati, Marathi, Hindi, Tamil, Telugu, Malayalam, Oriya, Kannada, Urdu, Sindhi, Nepali, Newari, Assamese, Indonesian, Vietnamese, Thai, Malaysian, and Burmese; 29,300 reels of microfilm; 144,000 microfiche.

Library of Congress
Humanities and Social Sciences Division
Local History and Genealogy Section

Thomas Jefferson Bldg., Rm. G20	Phone: (202)707-5537
Washington, DC 20540-5554	Judith P. Austin, Head

Staff: 9. **Remarks:** The Library of Congress has more than 400,000 volumes of U.S. and European genealogy, heraldry, and U.S. local history, including compiled genealogies, city directories, and published vital statistics, military records, and church registers. The Local History and Genealogy Room has a 10,000 volume reference collection, 40 current periodicals, and several card catalogs, including a 200,000 entry index to biographical histories from 50 states. The section offers its services to persons over high school age. Researchers may be referred to other divisions.

Library of Congress
Humanities and Social Sciences Division
Microform Reading Room Section

Thomas Jefferson Bldg.—LJ-107	Phone: (202)707-5522
Washington, DC 20540-5550	Fax: (202)707-1957
	Robert Costenbader, Head

Staff: 7. **Subjects:** Areas include early state records; early English and American periodicals; American and British black journals; underground newspapers; oral histories; U.S. nondepository documents; copyright records of the U.S. District Courts, 1790–1870; Barbour Collection of Connecticut vital records; State labor reports, 1865–1900; American labor union constitutions and proceedings; English books to 1700; Western Americana; pre-1900 Canadiana; manuscripts of American interest filmed by the American Council of Learned Societies; archives of the Japanese Ministry of the Foreign Affairs and other ministries, 1868–1945; translations from Mainland China, Japan, Indonesia; Schomburg clipping file on black history; Spanish Civil War pamphlets. **Holdings:** 5.5 million reels and strips of microfilm, microfiche, and micro-opaques. **Services:** Reading room is open to persons above high school age. **Remarks:** A guide to selected microform sets is available on request; see the *Guide to the American Indian Doc-*

toral Dissertations and *Inventory to the National Indian Collection of Indian Manuscripts.*

Library of Congress
Manuscript Division

James Madison Memorial   Phone: (202)707-5383
  Bldg., LM 101-102   James H. Hutson, Chief
101 Independence Ave., SE
Washington, DC 20540

Subjects: Collections of the papers of most of the presidents, from George Washington through Calvin Coolidge, other political, military, scientific, and literary leaders, and records of numerous enterprises and institutions, totaling more than 45 million pieces. Among them: National Association for the Advancement of Colored People, American Colonization Society, National American Woman Suffrage Association, National Urban League, Kraus Collection (Latin America), Harkness Collection (Mexico and Peru), WPA collection (Federal Writer's Project and Historical Records Survey, which includes transcripts of laws relating to slaves, notices and records of slave sales, newspaper advertisements of slave auctions and runaways, tax enumerations on slaves, and records of slave transfer and manumission). **Services:** Reading room is open to adults and high school students with a letter of introduction from faculty advisors.

Library of Congress
Prints & Photographs Division

James Madison Memorial   Phone: (202)707-5836
  Bldg., LM 339   Fax: (202)707-5844
Washington, DC 20540   Stephen Edward Ostrow, Chief

Staff: Prof. 22; Other 8. **Founded:** 1897. **Subjects:** Architecture, design, engineering, popular and applied graphic art, documentary photographs, fine prints, master photographs, postures. **Special collections:** Civil War drawings by Edwin Forbes, A.R. Waud, and others (originals); Mathew B. Brady and the Brady-Handy Collection (Civil War, portraits, the American scene); the Carnegie Survey of the Architecture of the South, Archive of Hispanic Culture (photographs of Latin American art and architecture); Detroit Publishing Company archives, 1898–1914; collection of slave photographs. **Holdings:** 190,000 prints and drawings; 80,000 posters, 12 million photographic prints and negatives, daguerreotypes, slides; 1.8 million architectural drawings and related materials; 50,000 images on video disc. **Services:** Photoduplication; open to the public. **Computerized services:** Multiple Use MARC System (MUMS), SCORPIO. **Remarks:** The division houses 15 million images other than painting and sculpture.

National Archives
National Archives and Records
Administration

8th & Constitution Ave. NW   Phone: (202)501-5400
Washington, DC 20408   Fax: (202)501-5005
     Dr. Trudy Huskamp Peterson,
     Acting Archv.

Staff: 625. **Founded:** 1934. **Subjects:** United States history, archives and manuscripts, genealogical research, government publications, U.S. politics and government. **Special collections:** Printed Archives of the Federal Government (GPO Collection); Gift Collection; Polar Archives. **Holdings:** 1.64 million cubic feet of textual cartographic, audiovisual, and machine readable records, 1774 to present; 4 billion documents; 235,000 reels of

microfilm; 170,000 reels of motion picture film; 180,000 sound recordings; 7 million still pictures; 2 million maps and charts; 9 million aerial photographs; 6000 magnetic computer electronic data sets. **Subscriptions:** 700 journals and other serials. **Services:** Copying; archives open to public. **Special indexes:** List of special indexes available on request. **Publications:** List of publications available on request.

National Archives—Alaska Region
National Archives and Records
Administration

654 W 3rd Ave.   Phone: (907)271-2441
Rm. 012   (907)271-2443
Anchorage, AK 99501   Fax: (907)271-2443
     Thomas E. Wiltsey, Director

Staff: Prof 4. **Founded:** 1991. **Subjects:** U.S. District Courts, Bureau of Indian Affairs, Alaska Road Commission, Bureau of Land Management, U.S. Customs Service, Military. **Special collections:** Records of federal agencies in Alaska. **Holdings:** 9000 cubic feet of archival items; 5000 sheets of microfiche; 65,000 reels of microfilm. **Subscriptions:** 6 journals and other serials. **Services:** Copying; library open to public. **Publications:** Finding aids, inventories, guides to records and film holdings.

National Archives and Records
Administration
General Reference Branch

7th and Pennsylvania Ave NW   Phone: (202)501-5170
Washington, DC 20408

Description: Maintains pension application files, based on Federal service before World War I; bounty-land warrant application files based on Federal service before 1856; and military service records based on service in the United States Army (officers who served before June 30, 1917, enlisted men who served before October 31, 1912), Navy (officers serving before 1903, enlisted men serving before 1886), Marine Corps (officers serving before 1896 and enlisted men serving before 1905), and Confederate Armed Forces (1861–1865) as well as persons who served in regular forces raised by the federal government, volunteers fighting in various wars from the Revolutionary War through the Philippine Insurrection (1775–1902). **Services:** Upon receipt of a National Archives Trust Fund Form (NATF) 80, Order for Copies of Veterans Records, will copy complete compiled military service or bounty-land application files or any documents in the pension files containing genealogical information. Pension application files contain the most complete information regarding a military career and should be requested first. **Remarks:** Once file is located, notice of fee charged for copying is sent.

National Archives and Records
Administration
Washington National Records Center

4205 Suitland Rd., Rm. 121   Phone: (301)763-7000
Suitland, MD 20746   Ferris E. Stovel, Director

Staff: Professional 125. **Founded:** 1968. **Subjects:** Records of U.S. Government agencies in the District of Columbia, Maryland, Virginia, West Virginia; records of the United States Army, Air Force, and Navy worldwide. **Holdings:** 3.2 million cubic feet of records. **Subscriptions:** 15 journals and other serials. **Services:** Access to information is obtained by contacting the Federal agency that created the records. **Computerized services:** Internal databases. Performs searches free of charge. Contact Person: Andrew Jones.

National Archives—Central Plains Region
National Archives and Records Administration

2312 E Bannister Rd.   Phone: (816)926-6272
Kansas City, MO 64131   Fax: (816)926-6982
                                        Diana L. Duff, Director
                                        Mark A. Corriston, Assistant
                                        Director

Staff: Prof 5; Other 7. **Founded:** 1968. **Subjects:** Noncurrent administrative and program records of historical and informational value accessioned from Federal Agencies in the states of Iowa, Nebraska, Kansas, Missouri, and North and South Dakota. **Special collections:** Pre-1900 records from the Bureau of Customs, Geological Survey, Internal Revenue Service, Forest Service, U.S. Coast Guard, U.S. Attorneys and Marshals, Weather Bureau, U.S. Army Engineers, Bureau of Indian Affairs Reservations (located in the present states of North and South Dakota, Minnesota, Nebraska, and Kansas, 1850–1965), U.S. District and Territorial Courts, 1824–1965. **Holdings:** 30,000 cubic feet of records. **Services:** Copying, reference service; reading and research rooms open to the public. **Computerized services:** Archival Information Service (internal database). **Special catalogs:** In-house archives inventories and shelf lists. **Publications:** *Guide to Research in the Central Plains Region,* book.

National Archives—Great Lakes Region
National Archives and Records Administration

7358 S Pulaski Rd.   Phone: (312)581-7816
Chicago, IL 60629   Peter W. Bunce, Director

Staff: Prof 4; Other 6. **Founded:** 1969. **Subjects:** Federal Government records for Illinois, Wisconsin, Michigan, Indiana, Ohio, and Minnesota. **Special collections:** Judicial Branch records—U.S. Circuit and District Courts, 1870–1974; U.S. Circuit Court of Appeals, 6th and 7th Circuits, 1891–1965; Executive Branch records of various civilian and military agencies, 1800–1987. **Holdings:** 60,140 cubic feet of records, 50,000 reels of microfilm. **Services:** Copying; genealogy workshops; professional workshops; exhibit program; archives open to public with restrictions. **Computerized services:** NARS A-1 (internal database). **Publications:** *Guide to Records in the National Archives—Great Lakes Region, Microfilm Publications in the National Archives—Great Lakes Region.*

National Archives—Mid-Atlantic Region
National Archives and Records Administration

9th & Market Sts., Rm. 1350   Phone: (215)597-3000
Philadelphia, PA 19107   Fax: (215)597-2303
                                        Robert J. Plowman, Director
                                        Joseph J. Sheehan, Assistant
                                        Director

Staff: Prof 7. **Founded:** 1969. **Subjects:** Archives and records of federal agencies located in Pennsylvania, Delaware, Maryland, Virginia, and West Virginia. **Special collections:** Records of U.S. District Court, U.S. Court of Appeals for 3rd and 4th Circuit, U.S. Corps of Engineers, Bureau of Census, National Park Service, Bureau of Mines, U.S. Attorneys and Marshals, Bureau of Cus-

toms. **Holdings:** 42,000 cubic feet of federal government archives; 27,500 reels of microfilm. **Subscriptions:** 25 journals and other serials. **Services:** Copying; branch open to public with restrictions, dependent on agency regulations. **Special catalogs:** List of microfilm holdings; list of textual record holdings. **Publications:** *Branch News,* biennial.

National Archives—New England Region
National Archives and Records Administration

380 Trapelo Rd.   Phone: (617)647-8100
Waltham, MA 02154   James K. Owens, Director

Staff: Prof 3; Other 3. **Founded:** 1969. **Subjects:** Noncurrent permanent federal government records for agencies located in Connecticut, Maine, Massachusetts, New Hampshire, Rhode Island, and Vermont. **Holdings:** 23,000 cubic feet of records of federal agencies in New England, 1789–1977: U.S. District and Circuit Courts, U.S. Court of Appeals, customs and Coast Guard activities, Life Saving Service Stations Logs, Naval Shore Establishments including Boston and Portsmouth, NH naval shipyards, Bureau of Public Roads, U.S. Army Corps of Engineers, War Manpower Commission (World War II); Office of Scientific Research and Development (Harvard/MIT Labs); 65,000 reels of microfilm of National Archives publications; U.S. Census reports, 1790–1910 on microfilm. **Subscriptions:** 12 journals and other serials. **Services:** Copying; branch open to the public. **Computerized services:** National Archives—Archival Information System (internal database). **Publications:** *Guide to Records in the National Archives—New England Region, Microfilm Publications in the National Archives—New England Region,* and *Sources for Family History in the National Archives—New England Region,* (leaflet).

National Archives—Northeast Region
National Archives and Records Administration

201 Varick St.   Phone: (212)337-1300
New York, NY 10014   Fax: (212)337-1306
                                        Robert C. Morris, Director

Staff: Professional 5; Other 5. **Founded:** 1970. **Subjects:** Permanently valuable records of federal agencies in New York State, New Jersey, Puerto Rico, and the Virgin Islands, 1790–1978. **Holdings:** 62,000 cubic feet of archival materials; 42,000 reels of National Archives microfilm. **Services:** Copying; branch open to the public for research. **Computerized services:** NARS-5, NARS-A1 (internal databases).

National Archives—Pacific Northwest Region
National Archives and Records Administration

6125 Sand Point Way NE   Phone: (206)526-6507
Seattle, WA 98115   (206)526-6347
                                        Phillip E. Lothyan, Director

Staff: 7. **Founded:** 1969. **Subjects:** Historical records of federal agencies for Montana, Idaho, Oregon, and Washington; Bureau of Customs; Bureau of Land Management; Bureau of Indian Affairs; U.S. Army Corps of Engineers; U.S. District Courts; Bonneville Power Administration. **Special collections:** Census records for all states and territories, 1790–1920. **Holdings:** 30,000 cubic feet of records; 60,000 reels of microfilm. **Services:** Copying; branch open to public with restrictions. **Computerized services:** InterNet (electronic mail service). **Remarks:** Electronic Mail address: YGO@CU.NIH.GOV (InterNet). **Publications:** Guide, 1988; Preliminary Inventories; Special Lists; Research Opportunities at the National Archives—Seattle Branch, 1985.

National Archives—Pacific Sierra Region
National Archives and Records Administration

1000 Commodore Dr.　　　Phone: (415)876-9009
San Bruno, CA 94066　　　Fax: (415)876-9233
　　　　　　　　　　　Waverly B. Lowell, Director

Staff: Professional 5; Other 6. **Founded:** 1969. **Subjects:** Archival records of the Federal Government in Nevada (except Clark County), Northern California, Hawaii, the Pacific Ocean areas. **Special collections:** Records of the Government of American Samoa; records of the Bureau of Indian Affairs, California and Nevada; Chinese immigration records; records of Federal district courts in Northern California, Hawaii, and Nevada, and of the U.S. Courts of Appeals for the Ninth Circuit; records relating to migratory labor. **Holdings:** 41,000 cubic feet of original records; 31,000 reels of microfilm. **Subscriptions:** 6 journals and other serials. **Services:** Copying; branch open to the public. **Computerized services:** Chinese Immigration to Hawaii, 1898–1947 (internal database). **Special indexes:** Admiralty case files of the U.S. District Court for the Northern District California, 1850–1990 (microfilm). **Publications:** *Guide to Records in the National Archives, Pacific Sierra Region*; *Microfilm Publications Concerning Spanish Private Land Grant Claims*; reference information papers on Federal records relating to ethnic groups; reference information paper on records of Federal district and appellate courts.

National Archives—Pacific Southwest Region
National Archives and Records Administration

24000 Avila Rd.　　　　　Phone: (714)643-4241
Box 6719　　　　　　　　　(714)643-4242
Laguna Niguel, CA　　　　Fax: (714)643-4832
　92607-6719　　　　Diane S. Nixon, Regional
　　　　　　　　　　　　　　　Director

Staff: Prof 4; Other 6. **Founded:** 1969. **Subjects:** Inactive and noncurrent Federal Government records for Arizona, southern California, and Clark County, Nevada. **Special collections:** National Archives microfilm publications of national significance; records of Bureau of Indian Affairs, Bureau of Customs, U.S. Navy, U.S. District Court. **Holdings:** 22,000 cubic feet of original records. **Services:** Copying; branch open to public with restrictions. **Publications:** *Guide to the National Archives—Pacific Southwest Region.*

National Archives—Rocky Mountain Region
National Archives and Records Administration

Denver Federal Center　　Phone: (303)236-0817
Bldg. 48　　　　　　　　Fax: (303)236-9354
Denver, CO 80225　　　Joel Barker, Director

Staff: Prof 3; Other 4. **Founded:** 1969. **Subjects:** Archival records of the federal government for Colorado, Montana, Arizona, New Mexico, North and South Dakota, Utah, and Wyoming.

Special collections: Records of 60 federal agencies, including the U.S. District Courts, Bureau of Indian Affairs. **Holdings:** 23,000 cubic feet of archives; 60,000 reels of microfilm; census on microfilm. **Services:** Copying; reference service to researchers; branch open to public.

National Archives—Southeast Region
National Archives and Records Administration

1557 St. Joseph Ave.　　Phone: (404)763-7477
East Point, GA 30344　　Fax: (404)763-7815
　　　　　　　　　　　Gayle P. Peters, Director

Staff: Prof 4; Other 9. **Founded:** 1969. **Subjects:** Historically valuable records, 1716–1978, of the Federal Government from field offices and courts in Alabama, Georgia, Florida, Kentucky, Tennessee, Mississippi, and North and South Carolina. **Special collections:** Selective Service System for the entire United States. **Holdings:** 45,000 cubic feet of records; 46,000 reels of microfilm. **Services:** Copying; branch open to the public. **Computerized services:** National Archives A-1 (internal database). **Special catalogs:** Catalog of Federal Court records; shelf list finding aids on material in regional archives and in Records Center. **Publications:** Research Opportunities and list of microfilm available, biennial.

National Archives—Southwest Region
National Archives and Records Administration

Ft. Worth Federal Ctr., Bldg.　　Phone: (817)334-5525
　1　　　　　　　　　Kent Carter, Director,
Box 6216　　　　　　　　Archives Branch
Fort Worth, TX 76115

Staff: Professional 3; Other 5. **Founded:** 1969. **Subjects:** Inactive records of U.S. government agencies in Texas, Oklahoma, Arkansas, New Mexico, Louisiana. **Special collections:** U.S. census reports, 1790–1920; index to some Civil War service records; passenger records from various ports; Bureau of Indian Affairs records from the state of Oklahoma. **Holdings:** 65,000 cubic feet of records; 70,000 reels of microfilm. **Services:** Copying; archives open to the public except for restricted records.

National Genealogical Society Library

4527 17th St. N.　　　　Phone: (703)525-0050
Arlington, VA 22207-2399　Fax: (703)525-0052
　　　　　　　　　　　Dereka Smith, Librarian

Staff: Professional 1; Other 8. **Description:** Individuals are members; libraries and societies are subscribers. Promotes genealogical research; stimulates and fosters preservation and publication of records of genealogical interest including national, state, county, township, city, town, church, cemetery, Bible, and family records. Members list with the society the families in which they are working and on which they can exchange data with one another. **Founded:** 1903. **Subjects:** Genealogy, local history, bibliography, biography. **Special collections:** Manuscript collections of former members. **Holdings:** 23,000 books; 5000 bound periodical volumes; 300 boxes of manuscript materials; 40 VF drawers of documents, clippings, pamphlets; microfilm; microfiche. **Subscriptions:** 20 journals and other serials. **Services:** Copying; library open to the public. Operates speakers bureau and National Genealogy Hall of Fame; bestows awards. **Computer-**

ized services: OCLC. **Publications:** *National Genealogical Society Quarterly*; *National Genealogical Society Newsletter*, bimonthly; 109 special publications, book list revised 1988 with supplements, 1989.

National Personnel Records Center (Military Records)
National Archives and Records Administration

9700 Page Ave.
St. Louis, MO 63132-5100

Phone: (314)538-4201
David L. Petree, Director

Staff: 500. **Founded:** 1952. **Subjects:** Service and medical records of persons who have served in the Armed Forces, noncurrent records of organizations which have been a part of the military establishment, personnel and medical records of former federal civilian employees. **Holdings:** 1.8 milion cubic feet of military and personnel records (MPR) and organizational records; 1.9 million cubic feet of civilian personnel records (CPR) and agency organizational records. **Services:** Library not open to the public. Answers written requests for information (Standard Form 180: Request Pertaining to Military Records); for a fee, provides copies. **Remarks:** Maintains and services the records of separated military personnel of the Army (1912 to present), Navy (1885 to present), Air Force (1947 to present), Marine Corps (1905 to present), Coast Guard (1906 to present). The National Personnel Records Center (CPR) maintains and services the personnel and medical records of former civilian employees and is located at 111 Winnebago St., St. Louis, 63118-4199.

National Society, Daughters of the American Revolution
Library

1776 D St. NW
Washington, DC 20006-5392

Phone: (202)879-3229
Fax: (202)879-3252
Eric G. Grundset, Library Director

Staff: Professional 6; Other 12. **Founded:** 1896. **Subjects:** Genealogy, U.S. local history, U.S. history, American Indian history, American women's history. **Special collections:** Genealogies; United States, state, county, local histories; published rosters of Revolutionary War soldiers; published vital records; cemetery inscriptions; Bible records; transcripts of various county records (such as wills), compiled by the Genealogical Records Committees of DAR; published archives of some of the thirteen original states; abstracts of some Revolutionary War pension files; American Indian history, genealogy, culture; U.S. City Directory Collection, 20th century. **Holdings:** 120,000 books; 12,000 bound periodical volumes; 250,000 files of manuscript material, genealogical records, pamphlets. **Subscriptions:** 650 journals and other serials. **Services:** Copying; library open to the public on a fee basis. **Special catalogs:** DAR Library Catalog, volume 1: Family Histories and Genealogies, 1982; supplement to volume 1, 1984; volume 2: State and Local Histories and Records, 1986; volume 3: Acquisitions 1985–1991, 1991. **Publications:** *Continental Columns* (newsletter).

Presbyterian Church
Department of History
Library

425 Lombard St.
Philadelphia, PA 19147

Phone: (215)627-1852
Fax: (215)627-0509
Frederick J. Heyser Jr., Director

Staff: Prof 10; Other 10. **Description:** Contains church records and histories. **Founded:** 1852. **Subjects:** American Presbyterian history. **Special collections:** American Indian Missionary Correspondence and Papers (manuscripts and microfilm); American Sunday School Union (manuscripts); Archives of Presbyterian Church and Predecessor Denominations; Board of Foreign Missions (manuscripts and microfilm); Early American and European Imprints, before 1800; Sheldon Jackson Collections, Alaska; Missions; National Council of Church Archives. **Holdings:** 250,000 books; 1875 reels of microfilm; 9000 pictures of churches and ministers; 5000 communion tokens; 21 million arranged archival materials. **Subscriptions:** 407 journals and other serials. **Services:** Copying; library open to the public. **Formerly:** Presbyterian Historical Society—Library.

United Methodist Church
General Commission on Archives and History
Libraries and Archives

36 Madison Ave.
Box 127
Madison, NJ 07940

Phone: (201)822-2787
Fax: (201)408-3909
Kenneth E. Rowe, Librarian

Staff: Prof 3; Other 3. **Founded:** 1866. **Subjects:** Church records of Methodist Episcopal Church, Methodist Episcopal Church (South), Methodist Protestant Church, Methodist Church, Evangelical United Brethren Church, United Brethren in Christ Church, Evangelical Church, Evangelical Association, United Evangelical Church; United Methodist Church. **Special collections:** Board of Mission correspondence from missionaries and overseas conference journals; private papers of Methodist leaders and bishops. **Holdings:** 70,000 books; 1600 bound periodical volumes; 4 million archival items; 100,000 feet of microfilm; 100 tubes of blueprints. **Subscriptions:** 600 journals and other serials. **Services:** Interlibrary loan; copying; library open to the public with restrictions. **Computerized services:** OCLC, RLIN, DIALOG Information Services. **Remarks:** Includes the holdings of the Association of Methodist Historical Societies and the former E.U.B. Historical Society.

Alabama

Alabama A & M University
J.F. Drake Memorial Learning Resources Center

Box 489
Normal, AL 35762

Phone: (205)851-5760
Fax: (205)851-5768
Dr. Birdie O. Weir, Director

Staff: Professional 10; Other 14. **Founded:** 1904. **Subjects:** Education, business and economics, agriculture, the sciences, computer science, literature. **Special collections:** Black Collection (3551 items); Archival Collection (3004 items); Schomburg Collection; Carnegie-Mydral Collection. **Holdings:** 231,304 books; 21,140 bound periodical volumes; 4008 AV programs; 16,452 periodicals on microfilm; 769 college catalogs; 661 telephone directories; 10,951 vertical files; 497,806 ERIC microfiche; 136,532 government documents; Wall Street Journal on microfiche (11,015); NewsBank on microfiche (21,566); Business NewsBank on microfiche (2735). **Subscriptions:** 1580 journals and other serials; 93 newspapers; 652 microfilm subscriptions. **Services:** Interlibrary loan; copying; videotaping; center open to the public; courtesy card must be purchased for check out of materials by persons not enrolled at the university or at one of the cooperating institutions. **Computerized services:** DIALOG Information Services; Internet (electronic mail service). Performs searches on fee basis. Contact Person: Prudence W. Bryant, Supervisor, Reference & Information Services. **Publications:** *Mixed Media* (newsletter), annual; *In the News* (newsletter)—for internal distribution only; *LRC Fast Facts*; *LRC Handbook of Programs and Services*; brochures.

Alabama (State) Department of Archives and History
Reference Room

PO Box 300
100n Ave.
Montgomery, AL 36130-0100

Phone: (205)242-4435
Debbie Pendleton, Head,
Public Services Division

Staff: Professional 4; Other 2. **Founded:** 1901. **Subjects:** Alabama—history, politics and government, economic conditions, family history, social life and customs. **Special collections:** Federal records include mortality schedules 1850–1880, population schedules 1820–1880, 1860 slave schedules. **Holdings:** State and local government records; state publications; private records; maps; photographs; newspapers. **Subscriptions:** 90 journals and other serials. **Services:** Interlibrary loan (limited); copying; room open to the public with restrictions (registration required). **Computerized services:** OCLC, RLIN; RLG (electronic mail service).

Mobile Public Library
Local History and Genealogy Division

704 Government St.
Mobile, AL 36602-1499

Phone: (205)434-7093
Fax: (205)434-5866
George H. Schroeter, Head

Staff: Professional 1; Other 3. **Founded:** 1961. **Subjects:** Genealogy, Mobile history. **Special collections:** Panton-Leslie colonial trade papers, 1770–1840; Hunley Civil War papers. **Holdings:** 15,112 books; 1700 bound periodical volumes; 1814 reels of microfilm of Mobile newspapers; 6900 reels of microfilm of federal census records; 56 reels of microfilm of French and Spanish colonial records; 206 reels of microfilm on miscellaneous subjects including Indian Rolls (1832–1905). **Subscriptions:** 41 journals and other serials; 7 newspapers. **Services:** Copying; library open to the public for reference use only. **Special indexes:** Vertical file index (card); map index (card); index to Mobile Register Obituaries, 1986 to present (book).

Samford University
Harwell Goodwin Davis Library
Special Collections

800 Lakeshore Dr.
Birmingham, AL 35229

Phone: (205)870-2749
Fax: (205)870-2642
Elizabeth C. Wells, Special
Collections Librarian

Staff: Professional 1; Other 3. **Founded:** 1957. **Subjects:** Alabama history, literature, and imprints; Early Southeast—Indians, travel, law; genealogical source records; Southern Reconstruction; Irish history and genealogy. **Special collections:** William H. Brantley Collection (books; 19th and 20th century manuscripts; 18th and 19th century maps); Douglas C. McMurtrie Collection; John Ruskin Collection; John Masefield Collection; Alfred Tennyson Collection; Lafcadio Hearn Collection. **Holdings:** 25,653 books; 2562 bound periodical volumes; 806 microcards; 349 phonograph records; 2725 maps; 1477 linear feet of manuscripts; 7739 reels of microfilm; 7828 prints and photographs; 3113 microfiche; 150 oral histories; 37 atlases; 1 globe; 60 relief models. **Subscriptions:** 330 journals and other serials. **Services:** Interlibrary loan; copying; collections open to the public. **Computerized services:** DIALOG Information Services. **Special catalogs:** Map Catalog; Catalog of the Casey Collection of Irish History and Genealogy. **Special indexes:** Analytical Information Index; index to *The Alabama Baptist* (newspaper).

Alaska

Alaska (State) Department of Education
Division of Libraries, Archives and Museums
Archives & Records Management Services (ARMS)

141 Willoughby Ave.
Juneau, AK 99801-1720

Phone: (907)465-2275
Fax: (907)465-2465
Virginia A. Newton Ph.D.,
State Archivist

Staff: Professional 6; Other 7. **Founded:** 1971. **Subjects:** Alaska territorial and state government. **Holdings:** 6,000 cubic feet of territorial and state government records. **Services:** Copying; archives open to the public. **Computerized services:** WLN; internal database. **Special catalogs:** Finding aids to records. **Special indexes:** Microfilm index (card); index to noncurrent foreign and domestic corporation records (online); Alaska State Government Records Management Manual; Alaska Local Government General Records Retention Schedules; Alaska School District General Retention Schedules; Records Management Resources for Local Governments in Alaska. **Remarks:** The archives are the official repository for all permanently valuable records of the executive, legislative, and judicial branches of Alaska's state government. **Publications:** *Alaska State Archives: A Guide*.

Alaska State Library
Alaska Historical Collections

PO Box 110571
Juneau, AK 99811-0571

Phone: (907)465-2925
Fax: (907)465-2990
Kathryn H. Shelton, Head,
Historical Collections

Staff: Professional 3; Other 4. **Founded:** 1900. **Subjects:** Alaska, Yukon, Arctic; Russian, especially Siberian, culture. **Special collections:** Alaska government publications; James Wickersham Collection; Snow Family Papers; L.H. Bayers Maritime Collection; Winter and Pond photograph collection; John Granger Alaska postcard collection. **Holdings:** 35,000 volumes, manuscripts, tapes, video cassettes, maps; 110,000 photographs; microfilm. **Services:** Mail or telephone reference and copying services; noncirculating collection open to the public for research. **Computerized services:** DIALOG Information Services, OCLC. **Formerly:** Alaska (State) Department of Education, Division of Libraries, Archives and Museums—Historical Library Section. **Publications:** *Some Books About Alaska Received*, annual; *Polar Libraries Bulletin*, biannual; historical monograph series, guides, and bibliographies.

Arizona

Arizona (State) Department of Library, Archives & Public Records

State Capitol, Rm. 200
1700 W. Washington
Phoenix, AZ 85007

Phone: (602)542-5630
Fax: (602)542-4400
Sharon G. Womack, Director

Staff: Professional 44; Other 72. **Founded:** 1864. **Subjects:** Arizona and southwestern history, law, genealogy. **Special collections:** State Archives. **Holdings:** 1.1 million volumes; federal document depository; state document center; state reference center (Arizona public libraries only). **Subscriptions:** 1700 journals and other serials; 130 newspapers. **Services:** Interlibrary loan; library open to the public for reference use only. **Computerized services:** DIALOG Information Services. Performs searches on fee basis.

Church of Jesus Christ of Latter-day Saints Genealogical Society Branch Library

1536 E. Cherokee Ln.
Safford, AZ 85546

Phone: (602)428-3194
Leven B. Ferrin

Staff: 50. **Founded:** 1939. **Subjects:** Genealogy. **Special collections:** Indian Tribes (pamphlets); World Conference, 1969 (18 volumes); World Conference, 1981 (13 volumes); Genealogical Society Series (12 volumes). **Holdings:** 5000 books; 1087 bound periodical volumes; 3000 films; microfiche for genealogical research. **Subscriptions:** 21 journals and other serials. **Services:** Interlibrary loan; copying; center open to the public. **Computerized services:** Ancestral Search, Computers, Personal Ancestral File (internal databases).

Phoenix Public Library
Arizona Room

12 E. McDowell Rd.
Phoenix, AZ 85004

Phone: (602)262-4636

Staff: Professional 1; Other 1. **Subjects:** Phoenix and Arizona history, Southwestern Indians, Southwestern water and land use, Mexican Americans, Southwestern art. **Special collections:** James Harvey McClintock papers, 1864–1934. **Holdings:** 20,000 books; 225 bound periodical volumes; Phoenix municipal records. **Subscriptions:** 45 journals and other serials. **Services:** Copying; room open to the public.

Arkansas

Arkansas State Library

One Capitol Mall
Little Rock, AR 72201

Phone: (501)682-1527
Fax: (501)682-1529
Jack C. Mulkey, Associate Director

Staff: Professional 12; Other 35. **Founded:** 1935. **Special collections:** Arkansas. **Holdings:** 144,278 volumes; 24 VF drawers. **Subscriptions:** 285 journals and other serials. **Services:** Library open to the public. **Computerized services:** OCLC. **Remarks:** Electronic mail address: ALA 0967 (ALANET).

Southwest Arkansas Regional Archives

Box 134
Washington, AR 71862

Phone: (501)983-2633

Staff: Professional 1. **Founded:** 1978. **Subjects:** History of Southwest Arkansas, Caddo Indians. **Special collections:** Rare books collection on Southwest Arkansas and Texas; census and court records for twelve southwest Arkansas counties; newspapers of southwest Arkansas; index and service records for Civil War soldiers who served in Arkansas units. **Holdings:** 1500 books; 3000 reels of microfilm; original court records of Hempstead County, 1819–1910; pictures; manuscripts; family histories; theses; sheet music; newspapers; maps; pamphlets; journals; genealogical records. **Services:** Copying; archives open to the public for reference use only. **Publications:** *SARA Newsletter*, quarterly.

California

California State Archives

201 N. Sunrise Ave.
Roseville, CA 95661

Phone: (916)773-3000
Fax: (916)773-8249
John F. Burns, Chief of Archives

Staff: Professional 7; Other 11. **Founded:** 1850. **Subjects:** California government and politics. **Special collections:** Spanish land grants (19 volumes); State government Oral History Program transcripts (100 volumes). **Holdings:** 60,000 cubic feet of documents, photographs, microforms, maps, audiotapes, films, videotapes, computer materials, and artifacts. **Subscriptions:** 20 journals and other serials. **Services:** Copying; archives open to the public. **Computerized services:** RLIN. **Remarks:** Maintained by California State Secretary of State. **Publications:** *California Originals* (newsletter), quarterly available upon request.

California State Library

Library & Courts Bldg.   Phone: (916)654-0183
914 Capitol Mall   Fax: (916)654-0064
Box 942837   Gary E. Strong, State
Sacramento, CA 94237-0001   Librarian

Staff: Professional 86; Other 102. **Founded:** 1850. **Subjects:** General research collection in support of state government, Californiana, law, genealogy (holdings compiled by D.A.R. containing cemetery records, the 1852 State Census, etc; pre-statehood newspapers on microfilm are some of the items concerning genealogy), population, public administration, statistics. **Holdings:** 708,542 volumes; 780,449 documents; 2.6 million microforms; 74,700 maps and charts; 11 16mm films; 165 video recordings; 310,231 audio recordings; federal and state government document depository. **Subscriptions:** 7006 journals, serials, and newspapers. **Services:** Interlibrary loan; copying; consultant service for public libraries; library open to the public. **Computerized services:** DIALOG Information Services, InfoPro Technologies, ORBIT Search Service, Mead Data Central; OnTyme Electronic Message Network Service, Internet (electronic mail services). **Special indexes:** California State Publications, monthly (hardcopy; cumulations on COM). **Remarks:** Electronic mail addresses: CSLILL (OnTyme Electronic Message Network Service); csl__ill@library.ca.gov (Internet). Includes the holdings of the State Law Library. **Publications:** List of publications— available on request.

California State Library
Sutro Library

480 Winston Dr.   Phone: (415)557-0421
San Francisco, CA 94132   Fax: (415)557-9325
                                          Clyde Janes, Supervising
                                          Librarian

Staff: Professional 2; Other 5. **Founded:** 1917. **Subjects:** American genealogy and local history, English history, history of science and technology, Americana, bibliography, voyages and travels, Mexican history, valuable collection of printed works containing Hispanic material, Hebraica, natural history. **Special collections:** Papers of Sir Joseph Banks, 1760–1820; the Mexican Pamphlet Collection. **Holdings:** 150,000 volumes; 20,000 manuscripts. **Subscriptions:** 87 journals and other serials. **Services:** Interlibrary loan; copying; library open to the public. **Remarks:** Library specializes in works published prior to 1900. **Publications:** *Anatomy of a Library* (brochure on the collection); *New Arrivals in American Local History and Genealogy*, quarterly— free upon request.

Compton Library

240 West Compton Blvd.
Compton, CA 90220

Family History Center, Los Angeles

10741 Santa Monica Blvd.   Phone: (310)474-2202
Los Angeles, CA 90025

Description: Branch of the Family History Library of the Church of Jesus Christ of Latter-day Saints. **Subjects:** Genealogy, family

history, church and civil records, local history. **Remarks:** Access to main library microfilm.

Family History Center, Oakland

4780 Lincoln Ave.   Phone: (510)531-3905
Oakland, CA 94602

Description: Branch of the Family History Library of the Church of Jesus Christ of Latter-day Saints. **Subjects:** Genealogy, family history, church and civil records, local history. **Remarks:** Access to main library microfilm.

Family History Center, Pasadena

770 N. Sierra Madre Villa   Phone: (818)351-8517
Pasadena, CA 91107

Description: Branch of the Family History Library of the Church of Jesus Christ of Latter-day Saints. **Subjects:** Genealogy, family history, church and civil records, local history. **Remarks:** Access to main library microfilm.

Family History Center, Sacramento

2745 Eastern Ave.   Phone: (916)621-2090
Sacramento, CA 95821

Description: Branch of the Family History Library of the Church of Jesus Christ of Latter-day Saints. **Subjects:** Genealogy, family history, church and civil records, local history. **Remarks:** Access to main library microfilm.

Family History Center, San Diego

15750 Bernardo Heights   Phone: (619)487-2304
San Diego, CA 92128

Description: Branch of the Family History Library of the Church of Jesus Christ of Latter-day Saints. **Subjects:** Genealogy, family history, church and civil records, local history. **Remarks:** Access to main library microfilm.

Family History Center, San Diego

3705 10th Ave.   Phone: (619)295-9808
San Diego, CA 92103

Description: Branch of the Family History Library of the Church of Jesus Christ of Latter-day Saints. **Subjects:** Genealogy, family history, church and civil records, local history. **Remarks:** Access to main library microfilm.

Family History Center, San Francisco

730 Sharp Park Rd.   Phone: (415)355-4986
Pacifica, CA 94044

Description: Branch of the Family History Library of the Church of Jesus Christ of Latter-day Saints. **Subjects:** Genealogy, family history, church and civil records, local history. **Remarks:** Access to main library microfilm.

Family History Center, San Jose

2175 Santiago St.   Phone: (408)274-8592
San Jose, CA 95122

Description: Branch of the Family History Library of the Church of Jesus Christ of Latter-day Saints. **Subjects:** Genealogy, family history, church and civil records, local history. **Remarks:** Access to main library microfilm.

Fresno County Free Library
Special Collections

2420 Mariposa St. Phone: (209)488-3195
Fresno, CA 93721 Fax: (209)488-1971
John K. Kallenberg, Librarian

Founded: 1910. **Subjects:** Fresno County—local history, architecture; American Indians—Mono, Miwok, Yokut. **Special collections:** Local History Collection (15 linear feet of oral history manuscripts, vertical files of ephemera, biographical sketches, broadsides, maps, pamphlets); Ta-Kwa-Teu-Nee-Ya-Y Collection (200 books); South East Asian Acculturation Collection (300 books). **Holdings:** 122 bound periodical volumes; 15 linear feet of archival materials; 15,000 microfiche; Fresno newspapers on microfilm (1860 to present). **Subscriptions:** 4 journals and other serials; 5 newspapers. **Services:** Copying; library open to the public. **Computerized services:** VU/TEXT Information Services; internal database. Performs searches. Contact Person: Linda Sitterding, Local History Librarian. **Special indexes:** Historical Landmarks and Records Commission Index; Fresno papers index (1851 to present); Photograph Index; Oral History Index. **Publications:** *Ta-Kwa-Teu-Nee-Ya-Y Bibliography*; *South East Asian Cultural Materials Bibliography*.

Gardena Library
Los Angeles County Public Library

1731 West Gardena Boulevard
Gardena, CA 90247

Held-Poage Memorial Home & Research Library

603 W. Perkins St. Phone: (707)462-6969
Ukiah, CA 95482-4726 Lila J. Lee, Librarian

Staff: 2. **Founded:** 1970. **Subjects:** History—Mendocino County, California, U.S., Civil War; Pomo and other Indians. **Special collections:** Writings of Edith Van Allen Murphey, Dr. John Whiz Hudson, Helen Carpenter. **Holdings:** 5000 books; 16,000 negatives; photographs; maps; bound county records; clippings; genealogies. **Subscriptions:** 13 journals and other serials. **Services:** Interlibrary loan; copying; library open to the public on a limited schedule for reference use only, by appointment. **Remarks:** Maintained by Mendocino County Historical Society.

Los Angeles Public Library
History and Genealogy Department

630 W. 5th St. Phone: (213)228-7400
Los Angeles, CA 90071 Fax: (213)228-7409
Jane Nowak, Department Manager

Staff: Professional 8; Other 13.5. **Subjects:** History, travel, biography, Californiana, genealogy, local history, heraldry, newspapers. **Special collections:** Genealogy (38,000 volumes); Californiana (20,000 items); maps and atlases; American Indians; Security Pacific Bank historic photograph collection; Herald Examiner Newspaper and Photograph Morgues. **Holdings:** 290,000 volumes; 91,000 maps; 2.7 million photographs; 800 historical specimen newspapers; 25,000 reels of microfilm of newspapers; 4 CD-ROMs; U.S. city directories; census records. **Subscriptions:** 1300 journals and other serials; 65 newspapers. **Services:** Interlibrary loan; copying (limited). **Computerized services:** DIALOG Information Services, EasyNet; internal databases; Internet (electronic mail service). Performs searches on fee basis. **Special indexes:** California biography; California subject; Western outlaws and sheriffs; collected biography; American Indians; family history; local history; coats of arms; photograph collection (accessed on microcomputer). **Remarks:** Electronic mail address: laplgene@class.org (Internet).

Los Angeles Public Library
Social Sciences, Philosophy and Religion Department

630 W. 5th St. Phone: (213)228-7300
Los Angeles, CA 90071 Fax: (213)228-7319
Marilyn C. Wherley, Department Manager

Staff: Professional 6.5. **Subjects:** Philosophy, religion, psychology, social problems, government, foreign affairs, international relations, law, criminology, education, women's movements, family relations, ethnic groups, interpersonal relations. **Special collections:** California, U.S., and U.N. documents depository; African-American history and culture; Mexican-American Affairs. **Holdings:** 400,000 volumes. 10 CD-ROMs. **Subscriptions:** 2850 journals and other serials. **Services:** Interlibrary loan; copying; department open to the public. **Computerized services:** DIALOG Information Services, EasyNet. Internet (electronic mail service). Performs searches on fee basis. **Remarks:** Electronic mail address: laplsocs@class.org (Internet).

Oakland Public Library
Asian Branch

449 9th St. Phone: (510)238-3400
Oakland, CA 94607 Suzanne Lo, Branch Head Librarian

Staff: Prof. 3, other 12. **Description:** Public library providing books, newspapers, magazines, records, cassettes, and videos in Chinese, Japanese, Korean, Philipino, Vietnamese, Thai and Cambodian, and English for all ages. **Founded:** 1975. **Holdings:** 40,000 books. **Subscriptions:** 17 newspapers, and 81 periodicals. **Services:** Interlibrary loan, open to public. **Computerized services:** Online catalog: uses the Dynix system.

Oakland Public Library
History/Literature and Oakland History Room

125 14th St. Phone: (510)238-3136
Oakland, CA 94612 Sherrill Reeves, Senior Librarian

Staff: Professional 5; Other 3. **Subjects:** History, travel, biography, English and foreign languages and literature, genealogy, maps. **Special collections:** Schomburg Collection of Black Literature and History (in microform); Negroes of New York, 1939 (Writers Program; in microform); Sutro Library Family History and Local History Subject Catalogs (in microform); Index to Biographies in State and Local Histories in the Library of Congress (in microform). **Holdings:** 100,663 books; genealogy microfilms. **Subscriptions:** 114 journals and other serials. **Services:** Interlibrary loan; copying; division open to the public. **Special indexes:** Local History. **Publications:** *New Releases*.

Richmond Public Library
Special Collections

325 Civic Center Plaza Phone: (510)620-6561
Richmond, CA 94804 Adelia Lines, Director

Founded: 1905. **Special collections:** Local history; Afro-American history; Hispanic geographical areas. **Services:** Interlibrary loan; collections open to the public. **Computerized services:** DIALOG Information Services; CLSI (internal database); OnTyme Electronic Message Network Service (electronic mail service). Performs searches on fee basis. Contact Person: Douglas Holtzman.

Santa Barbara Historical Museums
Gledhill Library

136 E. De La Guerra St. Phone: (805)966-1601
Box 578 Fax: (805)966-1603
Santa Barbara, CA Michael Redmon, Head
 93102-0578 Librarian

Staff: Professional 1; Other 8. **Founded:** 1967. **Subjects:** Local history and genealogy. Growing collection concerning Hispanic families of Santa Barbara and the surrounding area. **Holdings:** 5000 books; 30,000 photographs; 360 oral history tapes. **Subscriptions:** 20 journals and other serials. **Services:** Copying; photograph reproduction; library open to the public.

University of California, Berkeley
Asian American Studies Library

3407 Dwinelle Hall Phone: (510)642-2218
Berkeley, CA 94720 Fax: (510)642-6456
 Mrs. Wei Chi Poon, Head
 Librarian

Staff: Prof. 1; Other 2.5. **Founded:** 1970. **Subjects:** Asians in the U.S., past and present. **Special collections:** Chinese American Research Collection (archival materials in English and Chinese; 38,113 items). **Holdings:** 63,579 volumes; 5000 slides; 106 videotapes; 26 16mm films. **Subscriptions:** 167 journals and other serials; 134 newspapers. **Services:** Library open to the public with restrictions on circulation. **Publications:** *A Guide for Establishing Asian American Core Collection; Directory of Asian American Collections in the United States.*

University of California, Davis
Michael and Margaret B. Harrison Western
Research Center

Department of Special Phone: (916)752-1621
 Collections Michael Harrison, Director
Shields Library
Davis, CA 95616

Staff: Professional 1. **Founded:** 1981. **Subjects:** History and development of the trans-Mississippi West, mid-19th century to present; American Indians; ethnic studies; military, local, and economic history; sociology; census records; Forbes Collection (Native American studies organized by tribe); religious studies, especially the Catholic and Mormon churches; literature; art and architecture; history of printing. **Holdings:** 19,689 volumes. **Subscriptions:** 107 journals and other serials. **Services:** Center open to the public by appointment only.

University of California, Los Angeles
Asian American Studies Center Reading
Room

3230 Campbell Hall Phone: (310)825-5043
Los Angeles, CA 90024-1546 Marjorie Lee, Coordinator

Staff: 3. **Subjects:** Asian American studies. **Holdings:** 4000 volumes; 450 slides; 8 multimedia kits; 150 sound recordings; 2 filmstrips; 10 maps; 160 manuscripts; 3000 pamphlets; 60 government documents; 5 video recordings. **Subscriptions:** 30 journals and other serials; 25 newspapers. **Services:** Room open to the public. **Publications:** *Asian American Library Resources at University of California, Los Angeles,* available upon request.

University of the Pacific
Holt-Atherton Department of Special
Collections

Stockton, CA 95211 Phone: (209)946-2404
 Fax: (209)946-2810
 Daryl Morrison, Head, Special
 Collections

Staff: Professional 1; Other 2. **Founded:** 1947. **Subjects:** Californiana, Western Americana, Pacific Northwest, Northern San Joaquin Valley, gold mining, Western authors, Native Americans, economic development of the West, ethnic history in California. **Special collections:** Early California exploration. **Holdings:** 30,000 books; 2928 bound periodical volumes; 75 linear feet of VF pamphlets; 45,000 photographs; 1670 maps; 2670 linear feet of manuscripts. **Subscriptions:** 116 journals and other serials. **Services:** Interlibrary loan (limited); copying; library open to the public. **Computerized services:** OCLC. **Also known as:** Stuart Library of Western Americana and Pacific Center for Western Studies. **Publications:** Monographs; *Bibliographic Guides to Archives.*

Colorado

Colorado (State) Division of State Archives
and Public Records

Dept. of Administration Phone: (303)866-2358
1313 Sherman St., Rm. 1B20 Fax: (303)866-2257
Denver, CO 80203 Terry Ketelsen, State Archivist

Staff: 11. **Founded:** 1943. **Subjects:** Noncurrent official public records and printed publications of the Territory and State of Colorado. **Holdings:** 80,000 cubic feet of public records. **Services:** Copying; certification; open to all who wish to consult records for legitimate purposes. **Publications:** *Guide to the Resources of the Colorado State Archives* (loose-leaf), updated periodically; brochures.

Colorado State Library
Colorado State Publications Library

State Office Bldg., Rm. 314 Phone: (303)866-6725
201 E. Colfax Ave. Fax: (303)866-6940
Denver, CO 80203 Maureen Crocker, Librarian

Staff: Professional 1; Other 2. **Founded:** 1980. **Subjects:** State publications. **Holdings:** 12,000 volumes. **Services:** Interlibrary loan; copying; library open to the public. **Computerized ser-**

vices: OCLC. **Publications:** Accessions checklist; microfiche checklist; Selective Bibliography Series; *Colorado State Publications Classification Schedule.*

Denver Public Library
Genealogy Department

1357 Broadway
Denver, CO 80203

Phone: (303)640-8870
Fax: (303)640-8818
James Jeffrey, Collection
Specialist

Staff: Professional 8. **Founded:** 1910. **Subjects:** County, state, town histories; census schedules, 1790–1910; genealogy; military rosters; heraldry. **Special collections:** Denver obituaries, 1939 to present (21 reels of microfilm; 15 volumes; 15 file drawers; 34 microfiche); genealogical manuscripts and clippings (13 VF drawers); genealogical charts (2 map cases); Draper Manuscript Collection (134 reels of microfilm); Corbin Collection (New England; 60 reels of microfilm); Barbour Collection (Connecticut; 98 reels of microfilm); Archives of the Catholic Archdiocese of Santa Fe, 1678–1976 (90 reels of microfilm); Spanish Archives of New Mexico, 1621–1821 (22 reels of microfilm); Mexican Archives of New Mexico, 1821–1846 (42 reels of microfilm); Territorial Archives of New Mexico, 1846–1914 (189 reels of microfilm); Hale Collection of Connecticut Vital Records (358 reels of microfilm); Enrollment card collection of the five civilized tribes, 1896–1914 (93 reels of microfilm); Registers of signatures of the depositors in branches of the Freedman's Savings and Trust Company, 1865–1874 (32 reels of microfilm). **Holdings:** 40,000 books; 3250 bound periodical volumes; 5200 reels of microfilm of census schedules and other material; 30,000 microcards and microfiche; vital records; census indexes; 7 VF drawers of Denver Tramway personnel records; 150 audiocassettes. **Subscriptions:** 450 journals and other serials. **Services:** Interlibrary loan; copying; genealogical research. **Special catalogs:** FHLC Family History Library Catalog. **Special indexes:** Index to obituaries published in 2 major Denver newspapers (1939–present); index to anniversary announcements published in 2 major Denver newspapers; family name file; coat of arms file; IGI (International Genealogical Index) (all on microfiche); index to the Freedman's Savings and Trust Company registers (on microfilm).

University of Denver
Penrose Library
Special Collections

2150 E. Evans Ave.
Denver, CO 80208-0287

Phone: (303)871-3428
Steven Fisher, Curator

Founded: 1864. **Special collections:** Miller Civil War Collection (1000 items); Davidson Folklore Collection (1000 items). **Services:** Interlibrary loan; copying; collections open to the public. **Computerized services:** Online systems.

Connecticut

Connecticut State Library

231 Capitol Ave.
Hartford, CT 06106

Phone: (203)566-4971
Fax: (203)566-8940
Richard G. Akeroyd Jr., State
Librarian

Staff: Professional 43; Other 94. **Founded:** 1854. **Subjects:** Connecticut, local history and genealogy, state and federal law, politics and government, legislative reference. **Special collections:** Barbour Index of Connecticut Vital Records to 1850; indexes to original sources of genealogical data; Connecticut newspapers, town documents; State Archives (includes records of Judicial Dept., Governor's Office, General Assembly, and several executive branch agencies); local government records; land records; selectmen's records; non-government records from individuals, families, businesses, and organizations. **Holdings:** 715,000 books; 34,000 bound periodical volumes; 28,000 cubic feet of archival records; newspaper clipping files, 1927 to present; 26,000 reels of microfilm; 6000 maps; regional federal documents depository of 1.5 million documents; state documents depository of 50,000 state documents. **Subscriptions:** 9053 journals and other serials; 100 newspapers. **Services:** Interlibrary loan; copying; library open to the public. **Computerized services:** OCLC, DIALOG Information Services, InfoPro Technologies, RLIN; internal database. **Publications:** *Checklist of Publications of Connecticut State Agencies; Agency Newsletter.*

Indian and Colonial Research Center, Inc.
Eva Butler Library

PO Box 525
Old Mystic, CT 06372

Phone: (203)536-9771
Kathleen Greenhalgh,
Librarian

Staff: Professional 2; Other 15. **Founded:** 1965. **Subjects:** Indians, genealogy, colonial history. **Special collections:** Elmer Waite collection of glass plate negatives of the area; rare American school books, 1700–1850 (300). **Holdings:** 2000 books; 954 manuscripts; 90 maps and atlases; 2000 early American notebooks; 69 boxes of bulletins and pamphlets; 2000 photographs. **Subscriptions:** 2 journals and other serials. **Services:** Copying; library open to the public. **Remarks:** Also maintains a museum. **Publications:** *Our Woodland Indians* (coloring book).

Kent Historical Society
Library

R.D. 1
Box 321
Kent, CT 06757

Phone: (203)927-3055
Emily Hopson, Information
Director

Staff: 3. **Founded:** 1935. **Subjects:** Local history, settlement, development; Scaticook Indians; iron industry; genealogy. **Special collections:** Photographs of early Kent (1000). **Holdings:** 20 VF drawers; ledgers. **Services:** Library open to the public.

Delaware

Delaware (State) Division of Historical & Cultural Affairs
Delaware State Archives

Hall of Records
Dover, DE 19901

Phone: (302)739-5318
Fax: (302)739-6710
Howard P. Lowell, State
Archivist/Records
Administrator

Staff: Professional 4; Other 2. **Founded:** 1905. **Subjects:** Delaware history and government, county and city records.

Florida

Florida State Archives

R.A. Gray Bldg.
500 S. Bronough St.
Tallahassee, FL 32399-0250

Phone: (904)487-2073
Fax: (904)488-4894
Jim Berberich, Chief

Staff: Professional 12; Other 6. **Subjects:** Florida history. **Special collections:** Florida Photographic Collection (history and culture of Florida; 750,000 photographic images); Florida Genealogical Collection (6000 volumes; 5000 reels of microfilm). **Holdings:** 25,000 cubic feet of state historical records, 1822 to present; 1250 cubic feet of manuscripts. **Services:** Copying; archives open to the public. **Computerized services:** Internal database. **Remarks:** Contains the holdings of the former Florida Photographic Collection.

St. Augustine Historical Society Library

271 Charlotte St.
St. Augustine, FL 32084

Phone: (904)824-2872
Sheherzad Navidi, Library
Director

Staff: 7. **Founded:** 1883. **Subjects:** History of St. Augustine and environs, history of Florida, genealogy. **Special collections:** Cathedral Parish records, St. Augustine, 1594–1763 and 1784–1882 (marriages, baptisms, burials); archives (manuscripts; city papers; St. Johns County court records); East Florida Papers, 1784–1821 (175 reels). **Holdings:** 10,000 books; photocopies; manuscripts; documents; microfilm; 10,000 photographs; 1000 maps; pictures; card calendar of Spanish documents, 1512–1821; card index of St. Augustine people, 1594 to present. **Subscriptions:** 12 journals and other serials. **Services:** Copying; library open to the public for reference use only. **Publications:** *El Escribano*, annual—by subscription; *East Florida Gazette* (periodical).

State Library of Florida

R.A. Gray Bldg.
500 S. Bronough St.
Tallahassee, FL 32399-0250

Phone: (904)487-2651
Fax: (904)488-2746
Barratt Wilkins, State
Librarian

Staff: Professional 32; Other 37. **Founded:** 1845. **Subjects:** Florida, history, social sciences, library science. **Special collections:** Floridana (21,809 items). **Holdings:** 272,067 books; 8503 bound periodical volumes; 115,972 Florida public documents; 140,636 U.S. documents; 18,549 reels of microfilm; 278,846 microfiche; 4801 films; 3574 videotapes. **Subscriptions:** 827 journals and other serials; 13 newspapers. **Services:** Interlibrary loan; copying; SDI; library open to the public. **Computerized services:** OCLC; DIALOG Information Services, Mead Data Central; Internet (electronic mail service). **Special indexes:** KWIC Index to Florida Public Documents, semiannual. **Remarks:** Electronic mail address(es): WILKINB@FIRNVX.FIRN.EDU (Internet). **Publications:** *Florida Library Directory with Statistics*, annual—free to libraries; *Florida Public Documents*, monthly.

Georgia

Atlanta-Fulton Public Library
Special Collections Department

1 Margaret Mitchell Sq.
Atlanta, GA 30303

Phone: (404)730-1700
Fax: (404)730-1989
Janice White Sikes, Manager

Staff: Professional 5; Other 3. **Founded:** 1925. **Subjects:** African-American studies, genealogy, Georgia history and literature, oral history, Margaret Mitchell. **Special collections:** Hattie Wilson High Memorial Genealogical Collection (6800 books, 372 bound periodical volumes, 129 unbound periodicals, 214 city directories, 1200 maps, 160 reels of microfilm); Samuel Williams Collection of materials by and about Afro-Americans (40,000 books, 1600 bound periodical volumes, 2100 reels of microfilm, 1000 microfiche); Atlanta-Fulton Public Library Archives; rare books. **Holdings:** 54,300 books; 3930 bound periodical volumes; 4396 reels of microfilm; 11,000 microfiche; 300 audiocassettes; 790 other cataloged items. **Subscriptions:** 350 journals and newsletters; 15 newspapers. **Services:** Copying; department open to the public for reference use only. **Publications:** Bibliographies and guides.

Georgia (State) Department of Archives and History
Reference Services

330 Capitol Ave. SE
Atlanta, GA 30334

Phone: (404)656-2393
Fax: (404)651-9270
Brenda S. Banks, Dir., Ref./
Preservation

Staff: Professional 9; Other 4. **Founded:** 1918. **Subjects:** Georgia, southeastern U.S., genealogy. **Special collections:** Federal records include population schedules 1800–1820, the Negro in the Military Service of the U.S. 1639–1886, schedule of slave owners 1850 and 1860, African slave trade and Negro colonization records 1854–1872; Georgia state records (82,000 cubic feet); county records (7500 cubic feet; 20,000 reels of microfilm); private papers (2500 cubic feet). **Holdings:** 20,000 volumes; 2000 reels of microfilm of newspapers; 10,500 maps; 2000 manuscript volumes; 20,000 prints and photographs. **Subscriptions:** 425 journals and other serials; 91 newspapers. **Services:** Copying; services open to the public. **Computerized services:** RLIN; BITNET (electronic mail service). **Special catalogs:** Civil War Pension Index (microfilm); Family Surname File; descriptive inventories for individual official record groups and of manuscript collections. **Remarks:** Electronic mail address: GSP@RLG (BITNET). Contains the holdings of the former Georgia (State)

Department of Archives and History—Land Records Office. **Publications:** List of publications of the Georgia State Department of Archives and History—free upon request.

Sara Hightower Regional Library
Special Collections

205 Riverside Pkwy.   Phone: (706)236-4607
Rome, GA 30161   Fax: (706)236-4605
             Jacqueline D. Kinzer, Curator

Staff: 2. **Founded:** 1911. **Subjects:** Cherokee Indians, Georgia and local history, genealogy, Southern history, Civil War. **Special collections:** J.F. Brooks Cherokeeana Collection (401 books); Ellen Louise Axson Wilson Collection; John L. Harris Papers (3 VF drawers); George M. Battey, III, Papers (5 VF drawers); Civil War collection; Yancey Lipscomb Collection (4 VF Drawers); Rome News-Tribune Resource Collection. **Holdings:** 14,000 books; 30 VF drawers; 350 maps; 7800 microforms; 600 unbound periodicals. **Subscriptions:** 71 journals and other serials. **Services:** Interlibrary loan; copying; collections open to the public with restrictions.

Hawaii

Bernice P. Bishop Museum
Library

1525 Bernice St.   Phone: (808)848-4147
Box 19000-A   Fax: (808)841-8968
Honolulu, HI 96817-0916   Duane E. Wenzel, Library
                    Chairman

Staff: Prof 4; Other 2. **Founded:** 1889. **Subjects:** Hawaiiana, history, linguistics, immigration. **Special collections:** Fuller Collection of Pacific Books (anthropology; 2500 volumes); 19th century Hawaiian language newspapers; Carter Collection of Hawaiiana (1500 volumes); early Pacific voyages; Pacific island language texts. **Holdings:** 100,000 volumes; 1500 microfiche; 1000 reels of microfilm; 17,000 pamphlets. **Subscriptions:** 1100 journals and other serials. **Services:** Copying; library open to the public. **Computerized services:** OCLC; Internet.

Family History Center, Hilo

1373 Kilauea Ave.   Phone: (808)935-0711
Hilo, HI 96720

Description: Branch of the Family History Library of the Church of Jesus Christ of Latter-day Saints. **Subjects:** Genealogy, family history, church and civil records, local history. **Remarks:** Access to main library microfilm.

Family History Center, Honolulu

1723 Beckley St.   Phone: (808)841-4118
Honolulu, HI 96819

Description: Branch of the Family History Library of the Church of Jesus Christ of Latter-day Saints. **Subjects:** Genealogy, family history, church and civil records, local history. **Remarks:** Access to main library microfilm.

Family History Center, Honolulu

1560 S. Beretania St.   Phone: (808)955-8910
Honolulu, HI 96826

Description: Branch of the Family History Library of the Church of Jesus Christ of Latter-day Saints. **Subjects:** Genealogy, family history, church and civil records, local history. **Remarks:** Access to main library microfilm.

Family History Center, Kaneohe

46-117 Halaulani St.   Phone: (808)247-3134
Kaneohe, HI 96744

Description: Branch of the Family History Library of the Church of Jesus Christ of Latter-day Saints. **Subjects:** Genealogy, family history, church and civil records, local history. **Remarks:** Access to main library microfilm.

Genealogical Resource Center
Alu Like
Native Hawaiian Libraries Project

1024 Mapunapuna St.
Honolulu, HI 96819-8940

Hawaii Chinese History Center
Library

111 N. King St., Ste. 410   Phone: (808)521-5948
Honolulu, HI 96817-4703   Chow Loy Tom, Librarian

Staff: Professional 1. **Founded:** 1970. **Subjects:** History of Chinese in Hawaii — genealogy, traditions, historic sites, biographies of early and contemporary leaders. **Holdings:** Books; 16 VF drawers; tape recordings of early Chinese residents; information on Chinese societies in Hawaii; maps of the Kwangtung/Guangdong Province of China, with emphasis on the Chungshan and Zhongshan districts; genealogies and family histories of Hawaiian Chinese families. **Services:** Library open to the public by appointment on a limited schedule; provides genealogical reference and referral to national, state, and other historical or genealogical centers or archives. **Publications:** Books; newsletters; publications on the history of Chinese in Hawaii.

Hawaii State Archives

Iolani Palace Grounds   Phone: (808)586-0329
Honolulu, HI 96813   Fax: (808)586-0330
             Jolyn G. Tamura, State
                    Archivist

Staff: Professional 10; Other 4. **Founded:** 1906. **Subjects:** Hawaiian history and government. **Special collections:** Captain Cook Collection (Cook and discovery of the Hawaiian Islands); historic photograph collection (Hawaiian monarchs, major towns, Waikiki, sugar and pineapple industries, and historic events, 1800s–1980s; 107,000 photographs and negatives). **Holdings:** 4038 books; 160 bound periodical volumes; 589 cubic feet of private manuscript collections; 9450 cubic feet of official archives; 3210 microforms; 11,000 aerial photographs; 1855 maps. **Services:** Copying; archives open to the public.

Leeward Community College Library
Special Collections

96-045 Ala Ike
Pearl City, HI 96782-0379

Phone: (808)455-0379
Christine Tomoyasu, Head
Librarian

Founded: 1968. **Subjects:** Asia, Asian Americans. **Special collections:** Hawaiian/Pacific Collection; selected regional federal government depository.

University of Hawaii
Hamilton Library
Asia Collection

2550 The Mall
Honolulu, HI 96822

Phone: (808)956-8116
Fax: (808)956-5968
Lynette M. Wageman, Acting
Head

Staff: Prof. 11; Other 1. **Founded:** 1962. **Subjects:** East, Southeast, and South Asia. **Special collections:** Sakamaki Collection (Ryukyus): Kajiyama Collection (Japanese language); Tun Huang Manuscripts (Chinese language); Imanishi Hakushi Shushu Chosenbon (Korean historical resources); Kyujunggak Collection (archival material from the Yi Dynasty Royal Library); United Presbyterian Mission Correspondence of the 19th and early 20th centuries from and to missions in East Asia, South Asia, and Southeast Asia; despatches from U.S. Consuls and Ministers to East Asia, South Asia, and Southeast Asia (19th and early 20th centuries). **Holdings:** 609,370 volumes; 40,180 reels of microfilm; 278,225 microfiche. **Subscriptions:** 9102 journals and other serials; 112 newspapers. **Services:** Interlibrary loan; copying; collection open to the public. **Computerized services:** RLIN, OCLC.

University of Hawaii at Manoa
Center for Pacific Island Studies

School of Hawaiian, Asian, &
 Pacific Studies
1890 East-West Rd.
Moore Hall 215
Honolulu, HI 96822

Phone: (808)956-7700
Fax: (808)956-7053

Subjects: Pacific Islands, history of the Hawaiian island of Ni'ihau, Pacific Island dance forms, Japanese economic aid to the Pacific. **Holdings:** 66,000 books; 7500 reels of microfilm; 3000 microfiche. **Subscriptions:** 1200 journals and other serials; 33 newspapers.

Idaho

Idaho State Library

325 W. State St.
Boise, ID 83702

Phone: (208)334-2150
Fax: (208)334-4016
Charles Bolles, State Librarian

Staff: Professional 20; Other 30. **Founded:** 1901. **Subjects:** Idaho and Pacific Northwest, library science, public administration. **Holdings:** 103,000 books; 5200 phonograph records and cassettes; 3000 films and videotapes; federal and state document depository. **Subscriptions:** 1100 journals and other serials. **Services:** Interlibrary loan; copying; library open to the public. **Com-**

puterized services: DIALOG Information Services. **Special catalogs:** Film and video catalog, biennial—to Idaho librarians. **Publications:** *Newsletter*, monthly—to Idaho librarians and trustees; *Idaho Library Directory*; *State Documents Checklist*.

Illinois

Illinois State Archives

Archives Bldg.
Springfield, IL 62756

Phone: (217)782-4682
Fax: (217)524-3930
John Daly, Director

Staff: Professional 31; Other 16. **Founded:** 1921. **Subjects:** Illinois history and official records. **Holdings:** 52,000 cubic feet of state agency reports, land patents, manuscript records, county and state agency records. **Subscriptions:** 3 journals and other serials. **Services:** Copying; genealogical, war records, historical, and land record research; archives open to the public, mental health records closed by law. **Computerized services:** Internal databases. **Publications:** *A Descriptive Inventory of the Archives of the State of Illinois*; *Illinois Public Domain Land Sales*; *A Summary Guide to Local Records in the Illinois Regional Archives*; *A Guide to County Records in the Illinois Regional Archives*; *Windows to the Past, 1818–1880*; *Early Chicago, 1833–1871*; *From the Ashes 1871–1900*.

Illinois State Historical Library

Old State Capitol
Springfield, IL 62701

Phone: (217)782-4836
Janice A. Petterchak, Head

Staff: Professional 15; Other 7. **Founded:** 1889. **Subjects:** Illinois history, Lincolniana, Civil War history, Midwest Americana, Mormon history, Indian history, genealogy. **Special collections:** Picture and Print Collection (250,000). **Holdings:** 170,000 volumes; 9 million manuscripts; 70,000 reels of newspapers on microfilm; 3000 maps; 3500 broadsides. **Subscriptions:** 600 journals and other serials; 300 newspapers. **Services:** Interlibrary loan (limited); copying; library open to the public. **Computerized services:** OCLC. **Remarks:** Maintained by Illinois (State) Historic Preservation Agency.

Illinois State Library

300 S. 2nd St.
Springfield, IL 62701-1796

Phone: (217)782-2994
Fax: (217)785-4326
Bridget L. Lamont, Director

Staff: Professional 60; Other 66. **Founded:** 1839. **Subjects:** U.S. and Illinois state government, business. **Special collections:** State documents (475,000); federal documents (1.6 million); U.S. patents; maps (140,000). **Holdings:** 5 million items. **Subscriptions:** 2250 journals and other serials; 27 newspapers. **Services:** Interlibrary loan; copying; current awareness; library open to the public. **Computerized services:** InfoPro Technologies, DIALOG Information Services, OCLC, ILLINET. **Remarks:** Headquarters of the network ILLINET. **Publications:** *Illinois Libraries*, 10/year; *Insight*, 12/year.

Newberry Library

60 W. Walton St.
Chicago, IL 60610

Phone: (312)943-9090
Charles T. Cullen, President &
Librarian

Staff: Professional 42; Other 60. **Description:** Private reference and research library containing one of the most extensive collections of local history and genealogy in the U.S. Has resources for research in the Midwest, New England, mid-Atlantic, Southern, and border states as well as other regions of the U.S. and Canada. **Founded:** 1887. **Subjects:** Genealogy; European, English, and American history and literature; local and family history; church history; bibliography; history of cartography. **Special collections:** Western Americana; American Indian; Midwest manuscripts; over 16,000 printed family histories; county and town histories and published local records (birth, marriage, death registers; tax lists; land records); U.S. census records and city directories; military records; Darcy McNichol Collection (Native Americans). **Holdings:** 1.4 million volumes; 5 million manuscripts; 225,000 microforms. **Subscriptions:** 1500 journals and other serials. **Services:** Copying; library open to the public with identification. **Computerized services:** OCLC, Association of Research Libraries (ARL). **Publications:** *An Uncommon Collection of Uncommon Collections*; *Newberry Library Center for the History of the American Indian Bibliographical Series*; *Catalog of the Edward E. Ayer Collection of American Indians in the Newberry Library;*newsletter; bulletins.

Northern Illinois University
Donn V. Hart Southeast Asia Collection

Founders Memorial Library
DeKalb, IL 60115

Phone: (815)753-1808
Fax: (815)753-2003
May Kyi Win, Curator
Lee Dutton, Librarian

Staff: Prof. 2; other 1. **Founded:** 1963. **Subjects:** Southeast Asia, including history, art history, business, economics, geography, politics, sociology, anthropology, and languages of Thailand, Philippines, Indonesia, Malaysia, Burma, Singapore, Indochina. **Special collections:** Thai Collection (11,093 volumes in Thai); Burma Collection (12,254 uncataloged monographs; rare and contemporary books); Philippine American Collection; modern Indonesia microfiche collection; Southeast Asia Children's Book Collection; N.P.A.C. holdings for Malaysia, Singapore, Brunei, Indonesia, Thailand. **Holdings:** 55,115 volumes; 10,461 pamphlets and reports; Southeast Asian newspapers on 3080 reels of microfilm; 796 maps and atlases. **Subscriptions:** 883 journals and other serials; 18 newspapers. **Services:** Interlibrary loan; copying; collection open to the public with restrictions. **Computerized services:** OCLC, BRS Information Technologies, DIALOG Information Services, WILSONLINE, BITNET (electronic mail service). **Publications:** *A Guide to the Southeast Asia Collection,* 1972; *Newspapers in the Southeast Asia Collection,* 1976; *Southeast Asia Collection Bibliographic Notes,* irregular.

Indiana

Allen County Public Library
Fred J. Reynolds Historical Genealogy
Collection

900 Webster St.
PO Box 2270
Fort Wayne, IN 46802

Phone: (219)424-7241
Fax: (219)422-9688
Curt B. Witcher, Manager

Staff: Professional 5; Other 11. **Founded:** 1961. **Subjects:** North American genealogy and family history, Indiana history, heraldry. **Special collections:** Collection of passenger and immigration records, including thousands of rolls of ships' passenger lists for major U.S. ports; collection of North American historical and genealogical society serial publications; U.S. Census population schedules, 1790–1910; Soundexes, 1880–1910 (microfilm); North Carolina Core Collection (county records through 1868; 4500 reels of microfilm); Canadian census schedules, 1825–1891; ships passenger lists, 1820–1945; Black American family history; Native American family history. **Holdings:** 183,000 books; 8500 bound periodical volumes; 500 vertical file materials and clippings; 210,000 microforms; 9 AV programs; 273,000 clippings and pamphlets. **Subscriptions:** 3182 journals and other serials. **Services:** Interlibrary loan; copying; collection open to the public. **Computerized services:** DIALOG Information Services, InfoPro Technologies, CompuServe Information Service, OCLC, OCLC FirstSearch Catalog; internal database. Performs searches on fee basis. Contact Person: Susan M. Riehm, Online Services Coordinator. **Special indexes:** Subject index to genealogical periodical literature. **Remarks:** Is said to house the largest group of genealogical materials in a North American public library. **Publications:** Bibliographies; pathfinders; *Periodical Source Index*.

Indiana Historical Society
William Henry Smith Memorial Library

315 W. Ohio St.
Indianapolis, IN 46202-3299

Phone: (317)232-1879
Fax: (317)233-3109
Bruce L. Johnson, Director

Staff: Professional 17; Other 5. **Founded:** 1934. **Subjects:** History of Indiana and Old Northwest. **Special collections:** Black history (including Mme. C.J. Walker, Elijah Roberts, and Herbert Heller manuscript collections, Emmett Brown photograph collection; 6000 items); Indiana in the Civil War (including Lew Wallace, D.E. Beem, and Jefferson C. Davis manuscript collections; 15,000 items); Old Northwest Territory history (600 manuscripts); William Henry Harrison and Indiana Territory history (500 manuscripts); visual collection (1.5 million of graphics works, paintings, and photographs). **Holdings:** 65,000 books; 150 bound periodical volumes; 4 million manuscripts; 1000 maps; 1600 reels of microfilm. **Subscriptions:** 360 journals and other serials. **Services:** Limited photocopying; photographic reproductions; preservation consultations; library open to the public. **Computerized services:** OCLC. Performs searches free of charge. **Publications:** Indiana Historical Society annual report (accessions); *Black History News and Notes,* quarterly.

Indiana State Library

140 N. Senate Ave.
Indianapolis, IN 46204

Phone: (317)232-3675
Fax: (317)232-3728
C. Ray Ewick, Director

Staff: Professional 44; Other 40. **Founded:** 1825. **Subjects:** Genealogy, Indiana history, federal and state documents, library science. **Special collections:** Indiana Manuscript Collection. **Holdings:** 1.6 million items; regional depository for federal documents; state documents. **Subscriptions:** 15,792 journals and other serials. **Services:** Interlibrary loan; copying; library open to the public. **Computerized services:** DIALOG Information Services, OCLC, STATIS, Library of Congress Information System. **Special indexes:** Index of Indianapolis newspapers since 1898 (card); genealogical indexes; newspaper, biographical, picture, and map holdings index (card). **Publications:** *Indiana Libraries*, quarterly; *Focus on Indiana Libraries*, monthly; *Hoosier Highlights*.

Notre Dame University Archives

c/o University of Notre Dame
Notre Dame, IN 46556

Iowa

Iowa State Archives

Capitol Complex
East 12th St. and Grand Ave.
Des Moines, IA 50319

State Historical Society of Iowa Library/Archives

402 Iowa Ave.
Iowa City, IA 52240-1806

Phone: (319)335-3916
Fax: (319)335-3924
Christie Dailey, Bureau Chief

Staff: Professional 7; Other 4. **Founded:** 1857. **Subjects:** History—Iowa, the frontier, agriculture, railroad, women, education, American Indians; genealogy. **Special collections:** Robert Lucas papers; Jonathan P. Dolliver papers; Gilbert Haugen papers; Cyrus Carpenter papers; labor collection historical Iowa photographs (265,000); historical Iowa maps (3000). **Holdings:** 130,000 books; 10,000 bound periodical volumes; 15,000 pamphlets; 17,000 reels of microfilm; 10,000 bound newspapers; 25 VF drawers of newspaper clippings; 1800 oral history interviews; 4000 linear feet of manuscripts. **Subscriptions:** 575 serials. **Services:** Interlibrary loan; copying; library open to the public. **Special catalogs:** Manuscript catalog; Fire Insurance Maps of Iowa Cities and Towns. **Special indexes:** Indexes to selected history and genealogy serials. **Publications:** *Bibliography of Iowa Newspapers, 1836–1976; Iowa History and Culture* (bibliography of materials published between 1952 and 1986); bibliographies on immigrant groups.

State Historical Society of Iowa Library/Archives

600 E. Locust
Des Moines, IA 50319

Phone: (515)281-5111
Fax: (515)282-0502
Jerome Thompson, Bureau Chief

Staff: Professional 2; Other 6. **Founded:** 1894. **Subjects:** History—Iowa, agriculture, railroad, regional Indians; historic preservation; genealogy. **Special collections:** State Archives (17,000 cubic feet); historical Iowa photographs (100,000 images); Iowa historical maps (3000); Manuscript collections—Grenville Dodge, Charles Mason, Albert Cummins, William Boyd Allison, John A. Kasson. **Holdings:** 70,500 books; 2500 linear feet of manuscripts; 30,000 reels of microfilm; 42 VF drawers of pamphlets and clippings. **Subscriptions:** 200 journals and other serials; 300 newspapers. **Services:** Interlibrary loan; copying; library open to the public. **Special indexes:** Index to Iowa GAR file (microfilm); index to selected newspapers (microfilm).

State Library of Iowa

E. 12th & Grand
Des Moines, IA 50319

Phone: (515)281-4118
Fax: (515)281-3384
Sharman B. Smith, Administrator, Div. of Library Services

Staff: Professional 14; Other 22. **Founded:** 1838. **Subjects:** State government, public policy, law, medicine, library science. **Special collections:** State Documents Collection; Federal Documents Depository; State Data Center. **Holdings:** 312,232 books; 10 cabinets of vertical files about Iowa; 16,841 reels of microfilm; 630,000 microfiche. **Subscriptions:** 2224 journals and other serials. **Services:** Interlibrary loan; copying; library open to the public. **Computerized services:** DIALOG Information Services, PFDS Online, InfoPro Technologies. **Special catalogs:** Audio-Visual Catalog; *Iowa Documents Catalog* (book). **Publications:** *Iowa Locator* (compact disc), quarterly; *Footnotes*, monthly; *Iowa Library Directory*, annual.

Kansas

Kansas Heritage Center Library

PO Box 1275
Dodge City, KS 67801

Phone: (316)227-1616
Fax: (913)227-1640
Jeanie Covalt, Research Librarian

Staff: 4. **Founded:** 1966. **Subjects:** Frontier and pioneer life, Kansas, the West, Indians of North America, cowboys, cattle trade, transportation, agricultural history, folklore. **Special collections:** Historical collections from the states of Kansas, Missouri, Colorado, and New Mexico. **Holdings:** 10,000 volumes; clippings; pamphlets; microfilm; filmstrips; slides; tapes and phonograph records; 16mm films; videotapes. **Subscriptions:** 6 journals and other serials. **Services:** Interlibrary loan; copying; assembles mini-kits on various subjects; programs and workshops; library open to the public. **Computerized services:** Dodge City Newspapers abstracted 1877–1929; Ford County census 1875, 1885 (internal databases). **Special catalogs:** Reference Materials and Resources. **Publications:** *Sentinel to the Cimarron; The Frontier*

Experience of Fort Dodge, Kansas (1970); *Up From the Prairie* (1974); *The Process of Oral History* (1976); *Dodge City* (1982); *West by Southwest* (1984); *Indians in Kansas* (1987); *Adventures with the Santa Fe Trail* (1989); bibliographies; *399 Kansas Characters* (1992).

Kansas State Historical Society Library

Historical Research Center	Phone: (913)296-3251
120 W. 10th St.	Fax: (913)296-1005
Topeka, KS 66612-1291	David A. Haury, Acting Director

Staff: Professional 6; Other 11. **Founded:** 1875. **Subjects:** Kansas history, local history of other states, genealogy, American Indians, the West, American biography, Civil War. **Special collections:** Kansas (21,529 books; 130,139 pamphlets); genealogy and local history (18,584 books; 7476 pamphlets); American Indians and the West (5006 books; 2140 pamphlets). **Holdings:** 135,119 books; 25,892 bound periodical volumes; 74,086 bound volumes of Kansas newspapers; 12,373 bound volumes of out-of-state newspapers; 1977 volumes of clippings; 51,706 reels of microfilm; 194 titles on microcard. **Subscriptions:** 300 journals and other serials. **Services:** Interlibrary loan; copying (both limited); library open to the public. **Special catalogs:** Guide to the Microfilm Collections of Kansas State Historical Society (1991).

Kansas State Library

300 SW 10th Ave., Rm. 343	Phone: (913)296-3296
Topeka, KS 66612-1593	Fax: (913)296-6650
	Duane F. Johnson, State Librarian

Staff: Professional 11; Other 13. **Founded:** 1855. **Subjects:** Public administration, census, Kansas government and legislation. **Special collections:** Federal and state documents depository. **Holdings:** 60,000 books; 10,000 bound periodical volumes; 60,000 other cataloged items. **Subscriptions:** 250 journals and other serials; 10 newspapers. **Services:** Interlibrary loan; copying; SDI; library open to the public. **Computerized services:** DIALOG Information Services, InfoPro Technologies, PFDS Online, Library Information Service (LIS). Performs searches on fee basis. **Special catalogs:** Kansas Government Documents Catalog. **Publications:** *State Data Center News*, quarterly; *Kansas Libraries*, monthly.

University of Kansas
Kansas Collection

220 Spencer Research Library	Phone: (913)864-4274
Lawrence, KS 66045-2800	Sheryl K. Williams, Curator

Staff: Professional 3; Other 3. **Founded:** 1892. **Subjects:** Kansas and Great Plains social movements, business and economic history, social and cultural history, politics, travel; regional African-American history. **Special collections:** Overland diaries; Kansas State documents depository; J.J. Pennell Collection of photographs and negatives, 1891–1923 (40,000 items); Wilcox Collection of Contemporary Political Movements, 1960 to present (6500 books; 6000 serials; 84,000 pieces of ephemera); Jules Bourquin Collection of photographs, 1898–1959 (30,000); J.B. Watkins Land Mortgage Company Records, 1864–1946 (627 linear feet); regional African-American history. **Computerized services:** OCLC; BITNET (electronic mail service). **Remarks:** Electronic mail address: SWILLIAM@UKANVM (BITNET).

Wyandotte County Historical Society and Museum
Harry M. Trowbridge Research Library

631 N. 126th St.	Phone: (913)721-1078
Bonner Springs, KS 66012	

Staff: Professional 1; Other 5. **Founded:** 1956. **Subjects:** Wyandotte County and Kansas City history; Wyandot, Shawnee, and Delaware Indians. **Special collections:** Early, Conley, and Farrow Family Collections, 1763–1960 (30 cubic feet of papers, books, photographs). **Holdings:** 4000 books; 1000 bound periodical volumes; clippings; 150 reels of microfilm; 5000 photographs; maps. **Subscriptions:** 10 journals and other serials. **Services:** Copying; library open to the public with restrictions.

Kentucky

Kentucky (State) Department for Libraries & Archives
Public Records Division

PO Box 537	Phone: (502)875-7000
Frankfort, KY 40602	Fax: (502)564-5773
	Richard N. Belding, Director/ State Archivist

Staff: Professional 20; Other 48. **Founded:** 1958. **Subjects:** Kentucky—history, genealogy, government, politics, health services. **Holdings:** 91,000 cubic feet of state and local government records, including those of the judicial and legislative branches; 35,000 reels of microfilm; 1000 microfiche; 100 videocassettes; 200 audiocassettes; 25,000 photographic negatives. **Subscriptions:** 15 journals and other serials; 5 newspapers. **Services:** Copying; archives open to the public. **Computerized services:** Internal database. **Publications:** List of publications available on request.

Louisiana

Archives of the Parish of East Baton Rouge
Genealogy Section

Public Service Department	Edward O. Cailleteau,
B1 Governmental Bldg.	Archives Department Head
222 St. Louis St.	Doug Welborn, Clerk of Court
Baton Rouge, LA 70802	

Staff: Professional assistance available. **Description:** Contains one of the most extensive county records collections in the southern U.S. Holds land records from 1799; court records from 1808 (original and microfilm); possesses the 19 volume *Spanish West Florida Records* of the Baton Rouge Post, dating from 1782–1810 (originals and translations on microfilm); *American State Papers*, containing legislative and executive documents relating to public lands (1789–1834); marriage license records, 1840–; criminal records, 1814–.

Le Comite des Archives de la Louisiane

116 Main St.
PO Box 44370
Capitol Station
Baton Rouge, LA 70804

Special collections: Ship passenger lists of the French and Spanish arriving in Louisiana.

Louisiana (State) Office of the Secretary of State
Division of Archives, Records Management, and History

PO Box 94125   Phone: (504)922-1206
Baton Rouge, LA 70804   Fax: (504)925-4726
     Dr. Donald J. Lemieux, State
     Archivist/Director

Staff: Professional 10; Other 25. **Founded:** 1956. **Subjects:** State and local government records, Louisiana history, genealogy. **Special collections:** Louisiana Confederate government records (80 volumes and 8 cubic feet); Records of Board of Confederate Pension Commissioners (147 cubic feet); Louisiana Legal Archives (85 cubic feet); original acts of the Louisiana Legislature, 1804–1964 (121 bound volumes); oral history tape library (930); graphics collection (2379 images); New Orleans birth records, 1790–1893; New Orleans death records, 1804–1943; New Orleans marriage records, 1831–1943; Statewide Death Records, 1900–1943. **Holdings:** 11,100 books; 19,200 cubic feet of archival government records; 53,400 reels of microfilm. **Subscriptions:** 7 journals and other serials. **Services:** Copying; microfilming; conservation laboratory; division open to the public. **Special indexes:** *1898 and 1913 Louisiana Voter Registration Index* (book); *Records of the Opelousas Post, 1766–1803* (book); Confederate pension applicants index (book); collections indexes (card).

State Library of Louisiana

PO Box 131   Phone: (504)342-4913
Baton Rouge, LA 70821   Fax: (504)342-3547
     Thomas F. Jaques, State
     Librarian

Staff: Professional 28; Other 41. **Founded:** 1925. **Special collections:** Louisiana (70,113 cataloged items; 119,493 state documents; 225 VF drawers); genealogy (5238 items); U.S. Government documents (209,478). **Holdings:** 392,949 volumes; 3088 maps; 10,000 photographs; 18,730 reels of microfilm. **Subscriptions:** 1575 journals and other serials; 25 newspapers. **Services:** Interlibrary loan; copying; library open to the public. **Computerized services:** OCLC, DIALOG Information Services, DataTimes, InfoPro Technologies, EPIC, LEAP; Internet (electronic mail service). Contact Person: Margaret Schroth, Head, Reference/Bibliographies, (504)342-4913. **Special catalogs:** Louisiana Union Catalog (card, microfiche). **Remarks:** Electronic mail address: michael-mckann@solinet.net (Internet). **Publications:** *Searching for Your Ancestors on Microfilm* (brochure)—free upon request; *Recent Acquisitions*; *LaGIN Directory of State Agency Information Resources*; *LaGIN Information Resources Exchange.*

Tulane University
Howard-Tilton Memorial Library
Louisiana Collection

New Orleans, LA 70118   Phone: (504)865-5643
     Fax: (504)865-6773
     Joan G. Caldwell, Library
     Head

Staff: 2. **Founded:** 1952. **Subjects:** Louisiana history and culture from colonial times to present. **Special collections:** Louisiana State, Louisiana Territory, and La Louisiane region maps and charts. Books; pamphlets; maps; photographs; newspapers; vertical file of clippings and ephemeral material arranged by subjects; bibliography file, citation file. **Holdings:** 35,000 titles. **Services:** Copying; collection open to the public.

Tulane University
Howard-Tilton Memorial Library
Rare Books

New Orleans, LA 70118-5682   Phone: (504)865-5685
     Fax: (504)865-6773
     Sylvia Verdun Metzinger,
     Rare Books Librarian

Staff: Professional 1; Other 1. **Founded:** 1952. **Subjects:** Southern history, Civil War, literature, water transporation, natural history, English county history, Romanov Russian history and travel, American Revolution, science fiction, 19th–20th century English language first editions. **Holdings:** 50,000 rare books titles. **Subscriptions:** 20 journals and other serials. **Services:** Copying; open to the public with identification. **Computerized services:** OCLC. **Special catalogs:** Favrot Library catalog; rare book catalog. **Formerly:** Tulane University—Manuscripts, Rare Books and University Archives.

University of New Orleans
Earl K. Long Library
Archives & Manuscripts/Special Collections Department

Lake Front   Phone: (504)286-6543
New Orleans, LA 70148   Fax: (504)286-7277
     D. Clive Hardy, Archivist,
     Head of Department

Staff: Professional 3; Other 16. **Founded:** 1968. **Subjects:** New Orleans—ethnic groups, labor unions, legal records, businesses, history, culture. **Holdings:** 4800 volumes; 11,000 linear feet of manuscripts and archival records. **Subscriptions:** 12 journals and other serials. **Services:** Interlibrary loan (limited); copying; department open to the public. **Computerized services:** DIALOG Information Services, InfoPro Technologies, STN International, ORBIT Search Service, OCLC. **Special catalogs:** Special Collections at the University of New Orleans.

Maine

Maine State Archives

State House Sta. 84
Augusta, ME 04333-0084

Phone: (207)287-5790
Fax: (207)287-5739
James S. Henderson, State
Archivist

Staff: 14. **Founded:** 1971. **Subjects:** Maine. **Holdings:** 20,000 cubic feet of judicial, legislative, and executive branch records, land office records, military (Civil War) records, censuses, and vital statistics records. **Services:** copying; archives open to registered researchers. **Computerized services:** Computer databases for patron use only. **Remarks:** Electronic mail address: ubrown@ saturn.caps.maine.edu (Internet). Maintains a Bulletin Board System: (207)287-5797. **Publications:** List of publications available upon request.

Maine State Library

Cultural Bldg.
State House Sta. 64
Augusta, ME 04333-0064

Phone: (207)287-5600
Fax: (207)287-5615
J. Gary Nichols, State
Librarian

Staff: Professional 18; Other 42. **Founded:** 1839. **Subjects:** Maine—history, genealogy, state, county, and local histories. **Special collections:** Maps; manuscripts; town reports, 1892 to present (includes city directories and Maine Registers, 1820 to present); Maine newspapers (*Bangor Daily Whig and Courier*, 1836–1900; *Eastern Argus*, 1803–1921; *Le Messager*, 1880–1946); Maine Vertical File. **Holdings:** 400,000 volumes; federal and state government documents. **Subscriptions:** 200 journals and other serials; 31 newspapers. **Services:** Interlibrary loan; copying; library open to the public. **Computerized services:** OCLC, DIALOG Information Services. Performs searches free of charge. Contact Person: Emily Herrick, Reference Librarian. **Publications:** *The Maine Entry*, quarterly; *Libraries in Maine*, annual.

Maryland

Maryland State Archives Library

350 Rowe Blvd.
Annapolis, MD 21401

Phone: (410)974-3915
Fax: (301)974-3895
Shashi P. Thapar, Library
Director

Staff: Professional 1. **Founded:** 1935. **Subjects:** History—Maryland, American, Black, other states; genealogy; biography. **Special collections:** Works Project Administration Historical Records Survey Publications; Maryland State Publications and Reports. **Holdings:** 15,000 books; 450 bound periodical volumes; reports; manuscripts; archives. **Subscriptions:** 100 journals and other serials. **Services:** Copying; library open to the public for reference use only. **Computerized services:** Internal databases. Performs searches on fee basis. **Publications:** Irregular publications; serials and periodicals list.

Massachusetts

Connecticut Valley Historical Museum Library and Archives

194 State St.
Springfield, MA 01103

Phone: (413)732-3080
Fax: (413)734-6158
Guy A. McLain, Head,
Library & Archival
Collections

Staff: Professional 4; Other 2. **Founded:** 1988. **Subjects:** Connecticut Valley history, Springfield history 1636 to present, New England genealogy, Springfield business history. **Special collections:** Roger Putnam papers (1920–1972; 96 linear feet); 17th–20th century Springfield and Connecticut Valley manuscripts. **Holdings:** 23,000 books; 2000 bound periodical volumes; 35,000 photographs; 2800 linear feet of archival records; 300 feet of vertical files, atlases, and maps; 5000 microform records. **Subscriptions:** 40 journals and other serials; 15 newspapers. **Services:** Copying; department open to the public. **Special indexes:** Springfield History Index (card). **Publications:** Pathfinders for African American genealogy; archives guides for all archives collections.

Jones Library, Inc. Special Collections

43 Amity St.
Amherst, MA 01002

Phone: (413)256-4090
Fax: (413)256-4096
Daniel J. Lombardo, Curator

Staff: Professional 1; Other 3. **Founded:** 1921. **Subjects:** Local and regional history, Amherst authors, genealogy. **Holdings:** 15,000 books; 50,000 historical photographs; 20,000 other cataloged items; 240 reels of microfilm. **Subscriptions:** 11 journals and other serials. **Services:** Copying; collections open to the public. **Special indexes:** Index of local newspapers (online). **Publications:** Finding aids.

Massachusetts (State) Archives at Columbia Point

220 Morrissey Blvd.
Boston, MA 02125

Phone: (617)727-2816
Fax: (617)727-8730
Dr. Albert H. Whitaker Jr.,
State Archivist

Staff: Professional 17; Other 3. **Subjects:** Massachusetts state and local government and history. **Special collections:** Judicial Archives: Superior Court of Judicature Records, 1692–1780 (dockets, record books, and file papers), Supreme Judicial Court Records, 1780–1859 (dockets, record books, and file papers), trial courts and their predecessor courts, 1634–1859, selected county probate records, selected Superior Court naturalization records; Massachusetts Archives (328 volumes of colonial and Revolutionary-era manuscripts); enacted and unenacted legislative documents, 1630 to present; gubernatorial records; maps and plans, 1630 to present; case files for Department of Correction, Mental Health and Public Health, 19th and 20th centuries. **Holdings:** 30,000 cubic feet of archival records; 9000 microforms; 24,000 photographs. **Subscriptions:** 10 journals and other serials. **Services:** Copying; archives open to the public with restrictions. **Computerized services:** RLIN. **Publications:** Collections bulletins and information sheets.

New England Historic Genealogical Society Library

99-101 Newbury St.   Phone: (617)536-5740
Boston, MA 02116   Fax: (617)536-7307

Staff: Professional 4; Other 31. **Founded:** 1845. **Subjects:** Genealogy and family history, local history, vital records, heraldry. **Special collections:** New England family and local histories; Eastern Canadian family and local histories; genealogical research materials; American Antiquarian Society newspaper index. **Holdings:** 135,000 volumes; 7000 reels of microfilm; 3500 linear feet of manuscripts; city directories; vital records; diaries; regimental histories; church histories. **Subscriptions:** 420 periodicals. **Services:** Copying; research; lectures and seminars; library open to the public on a fee basis. **Computerized services:** OCLC, Sydney Library Systems, MARCIVE. **Remarks:** Major center in the eastern United States for Canadian and Canadian American genealogy. **Publications:** *New England Historical and Genealogical Register*, quarterly; *Nexus* (newsletter), 5/year; monographs.

State Library of Massachusetts

341 State House   Phone: (617)727-2590
Boston, MA 02133   Gasper Caso, State Librarian

Staff: Professional 12; Other 20. **Founded:** 1826. **Subjects:** Public law, public affairs, Massachusetts legislation, government, politics, U.S. and Massachusetts history. **Special collections:** Massachusetts history (books; prints; photographs; broadsides; manuscripts); city directories; 18th and 19th century newspapers; maps and atlases. **Holdings:** 825,000 volumes; 12,170 reels of microfilm; 294,855 microfiche; official depository for Massachusetts publications; selective depository for federal publications. **Subscriptions:** 2465 journals and other serials; 97 newspapers. **Services:** Interlibrary loan; copying; library open to the public for reference use only. **Computerized services:** OCLC, CARL; CD-ROMs. Performs searches. **Special indexes:** Boston Newspapers, 1879–1937, 1962–1981, 1983 to present; Index and Guide to Massachusetts Legislative Documents, 1802–1882; Legislative Biographical File, colonial times to present; Guide to Massachusetts Legislative and Government Research. **Publications:** *Commonwealth of Massachusetts Publications Received*, quarterly and annual.

University of Massachusetts Library
Special Collections and Archives

Amherst, MA 01003   Phone: (413)545-2780
                                      Fax: (413)545-6873
                                      Linda Seidman, Acting
                                      Library Head

Staff: Professional 1; Other 2. **Founded:** 1867. **Subjects:** History of botany and entomology to 1900; historical geography and cartography of Northeastern United States to 1900; history of Massachusetts and New England; antislavery movement in New England; travel and tourism in New England, New York, and eastern Canada; Massachusetts; African-American studies; labor and business history. **Holdings:** 19,000 books; 8000 linear feet of records, manuscripts, clippings, photographs, maps, building plans, microfilm, audiotapes. **Services:** Copying; collections open to the public. **Computerized services:** OCLC. **Remarks:** Electronic mail address: linda.seidman@library.umass.edu (Internet).

Michigan

Detroit Public Library
Burton Historical Collection

5201 Woodward Ave.   Phone: (313)833-1480
Detroit, MI 48202   Noel S. VanGorden, Chief

Staff: Professional 8; Other 2. **Founded:** 1914. **Subjects:** History—Detroit, Michigan, Old Northwest, local, Great Lakes, New England, New France; genealogy. **Special collections:** Edgar DeWitt Jones—Lincoln Collection. Canadian material and early French records. **Holdings:** 260,000 volumes; 12,000 pamphlets; 4800 bound volumes of newspapers; 5060 feet of manuscripts and personal papers; 10,500 feet of archival materials; 20,000 reels of microfilm; 10,000 microfiche; 1100 microcards; 50,000 pictures; 4000 maps; 5000 glass negatives; 6800 scrapbooks; 1000 color transparencies; 1000 lantern slides; 4050 maps; 325 broadsides. **Subscriptions:** 500 journals and other serials. **Services:** Copying (limited); collection open to the public. **Special indexes:** Manuscripts reported in National Union List of Manuscripts. **Publications:** *Guide to the Manuscripts in the Burton Historical Collection, Detroit Public Library*; *Genealogical Guide to the Burton Historical Collection*.

Library of Michigan

717 W. Allegan   Phone: (517)373-1580
PO Box 30007   Fax: (517)373-3381
Lansing, MI 48909   James W. Fry, State Librarian

Staff: Professional 38; Other 70. **Description:** One of the top ten genealogical libraries in the United States. Genealogy/Local History Collection focuses on Michigan and areas from which most of the state's earlier settlers came, including Great Lakes, New England, Mid-Atlantic, and Southern states as well as Ontario and Quebec. **Founded:** 1828. **Subjects:** Public policy and management, politics and government, automation. **Special collections:** Special Michigan collection; regional depository for federal documents; official depository for State of Michigan documents; genealogy; Michigan vital records indexes; Michigan newspapers on microfilm (75,000 reels); 250 genealogical and historical periodicals; Martich black history collection. **Holdings:** 850,000 books; 50,000 bound periodical volumes; 5 million microforms; 300 AV items; 2 million pieces of ephemera. **Subscriptions:** 2500 journals and other serials; 57 newspapers. **Services:** Interlibrary loan; copying; library open to the public. **Computerized services:** DIALOG Information Services, InfoPro Technologies, OCLC; internal databases. **Special indexes:** Michigan Documents, quarterly. **Publications:** *Access*, bimonthly; *Michigan Library Directory*, annual; *Michigan Cemetery Atlas*, 1991; *Genealogy Update*, periodic bulletin listing new acquisitions and highlighting various subjects in the genealogy area.

State Archives of Michigan

717 W. Allegan   Phone: (517)373-1408
Lansing, MI 48918-1837   Fax: (517)373-0851
                                      David J. Johnson, State
                                      Archivist

Staff: Professional 8; Other 4. **Founded:** 1913. **Subjects:** Michigan history and government. **Special collections:** Historical photograph collection (300,000 images of Michigan); historical map collection (500,000 cartographic expressions). **Holdings:** 1000 books; 100 bound periodical volumes; 6000 reels of microfilm; 80

million documents (24,000 cubic feet of state and local government records; private papers). **Services:** Copying; archives open to the public (appointments recommended). **Publications:** *A Guide to the State Archives of Michigan: State Records*; published finding aids (1–20); circulars (1–45); genealogical information; *Michigan's Memory* (pamphlets).

University of Michigan
Asia Library

Hatcher Graduate Library, 4th Fl.	Phone: (313)764-0406
Ann Arbor, MI 48109-1205	Fax: (313)763-5080
	Weiying Wan, Head

Founded: 1947. **Subjects:** East Asian humanities and social sciences, including anthropology, archeology, calligraphy, communism, drama, theater, economics, education, ethics, fine arts, geography, history, journalism, linguistics, phonology, library science, military history, military science, music, political science, religion, sociology. **Special collections:** Union Research Institute Classified Files on China; Red Guards materials and classified files on the Cultural Revolution; rare editions of Chinese fiction in Japanese collections; Ming local gazetteers and literary collections; National Peking Library Rare Book Collection on microfilm; British Public Record Office Archives on China; Tun-huang materials from Beijing, Taipei, the British Museum, and the Bibliotheque Nationale: Japanese local history, materials on the Occupation of Japan; Japanese Literature; Japanese Diet Proceedings; Bartlett Collection of Botanical Works and Meteria Medica; Kamada Collection of Pre-war Japanese Works. **Holdings:** 276,832 volumes in Chinese; 222,033 volumes in Japanese; 4,782 volumes in Korean; 21,999 reels of microfilm and 21,968 sheets of microfiche in Chinese; 8,751 reels of microfilm and 5,458 sheets of microfiche in Japanese. **Remarks:** Electronic mail address(es); 141.211.190.10 (Internet).

Minnesota

Minnesota Historical Society
Library & Archives

345 Kellogg Blvd. W.	Phone: (612)296-2143
St. Paul, MN 55102-1906	Fax: (612)297-7436
	Denise Carlson, Head, Reference

Staff: Professional 10; Other 11. **Founded:** 1849. **Subjects:** Minnesota, Upper Midwest, genealogy, Scandinavians in North America, ethnic groups in U.S. and Canada, transportation, agriculture, arts, commerice, family life, industry, Indians (Ojibway, Chippewa, and other Minnesota tribes). **Special collections:** Minnesota newspapers, 1849 to present; Minnesota State Archives (40,000 cubic feet); St. Paul and Minneapolis newspaper negatives (1 million); MHS manuscript collections. **Holdings:** 500,000 monographs, government documents, and microform volumes; 100 VF drawers; 250,000 photographs; 35,000 maps; 1300 atlases; 4.5 million issues of 3000 titles of newspaper volumes; 37,000 cubic feet of manuscripts. **Subscriptions:** 3000 journals and other serials; 436 newspapers. **Services:** Interlibrary loan; copying; library open to the public for reference use only. **Computerized services:** DIALOG Information Services, OCLC. **Remarks:** Absorbed holdings of Minnesota Historical Society—

Archives and Manuscripts Collections. **Publications:** Pathfinders and guides, irregular.

Mississippi

Mississippi (State) Department of Archives and History
Archives and Library Division

PO Box 571	Phone: (601)359-6850
Jackson, MS 39205	Fax: (601)359-6905
	H.T. Holmes, Division Director

Staff: Professional 15; Other 7. **Founded:** 1902. **Subjects:** Mississippiana, genealogy, Confederate history, colonial history of Southeast United States. **Special collections:** Federal records include mortality and population schedules; territorial census for 1805, 1810, and 1816; special census 1890. **Holdings:** 58,000 volumes; 17,000 cubic feet of documents; 2000 manuscript collections; 24,000 nonbook items; 6000 cubic feet of manuscripts; 11,000 cubic feet of official state archives; 7095 maps; 12,500 reels of microfilm; 50,000 photographs; 3 million feet of newsfilm; 2203 architectural drawings; 158 VF drawers. **Subscriptions:** 370 journals and other serials; 137 newspapers. **Services:** Copying; library open to the public for reference use only. **Computerized services:** Informix, Bibliofile (internal databases). **Publications:** List of publications—available on request.

Missouri

Mid-Continent Public Library
Genealogy and Local History Department

Spring and 24 Highway	Phone: (816)252-0950
Independence, MO 64050	Fax: (816)252-0950
	Martha L. Henderson, Department Head

Staff: Prof. 2, other 16. **Description:** Genealogy collection with national and regional focus. Some coverage of African and Native Americans, minor coverage of Hispanic and Asian Americans. **Founded:** 1965. **Special collections:** Federal Census Population Schedules, 1790–1920, for all states with accompanying Soundex; AFRA/MoSGA Genealogy Circulating Collection, over 4,000 titles available on interlibrary loan, free of charge, nationwide. **Holdings:** 30,000 books, 1,000 bound periodical vol., 60,000 microfiche, 50,000 microfilm, 300 periodicals, and 1,000 maps. **Services:** Interlibrary loan, list of researchers for hire, genealogical assistance (inhouse limited mail assistance), and educational programs. Open to public. Developing a pedigree database with access via a bulletin board system. **Publications:** *Genealogy from the Heartland,* (a catalog of titles in the genealogy circulating collection) 1992; *Genealogy Records on Microfilm,* 1994; *Genealogy Records on Microfiche and Electronic Media,* 1994.

Missouri Historical Society
Library

PO Box 11940
St. Louis, MO 63112-0040

Phone: (314)746-4500
Peter Michel, Director of
Library and Archives

Staff: Professional 3; Other 5. **Founded:** 1866. **Subjects:** History—St. Louis, Missouri, Western United States, Missouri and Mississippi Rivers; fur trade; biography; genealogy; selected city and county of St. Louis censuses; theater; music; Thomas Jefferson; early Mississippi travel; steamboats; Lewis and Clark expedition; American Indians. **Special collections:** Western Americana; maps; scrapbook collection; Missouri Gazette newspaper (complete file). **Holdings:** 70,000 book, pamphlet, and periodical titles; 2000 bound newspaper volumes; 2500 maps. **Subscriptions:** 241 journals and other serials. **Services:** Copying; library open to the public. **Publications:** *Gateway Heritage*, quarterly.

Missouri State Archives

600 W. Main
Box 778
Jefferson City, MO 65102

Phone: (314)751-3280
Fax: (314)526-3857
Kenneth H. Winn, State
Archivist

Staff: 12. **Founded:** 1965. **Subjects:** Missouri history, genealogy. **Special collections:** Federal census schedules (microfilm); some partial state censuses; municipal records; French and Spanish land grants, 1790–1803; United States Land Sales, 1818–1903 (26 volumes); Township School Land, Seminary and Saline Land, Swamp Land, and 500,000 Acre Grant indexes; Missouri State Penitentiary indexes, 1837–1933 (microfilm); pardon records, 1837–1901 (microfilm); Reference & Manuscript Collection (city directories, maps, reference books, church records, George Washington Carver papers, A.P. Morehouse collection); Military Records Collection (War of 1812, Black Hawk War of 1832, Heatherly War of 1836, Seminole War of 1837, Osage War of 1837, Mormon War of 1838, Iowa or Honey War of 1839, Mexican War of 1846, Civil War 1861–1865, Spanish American War of 1898, Missouri Militia 1865–1866); county records (microfilm); Supreme Court Records of Missouri, 1804–1940. **Holdings:** 1250 linear feet of books; 20,000 cubic feet of archival material; 55,000 microfiche; 30,000 reels of microfilm. **Services:** Copying; library open to the public. **Publications:** *Researching Family & Community History at the Missouri State Archives*; *Guide to County Records on Microfilm*; *Historical Listing of Missouri Legislatures, 1812–1986*; *The Record*.

Missouri State Library

PO Box 387
Jefferson City, MO 65102

Phone: (314)751-2751
Fax: (314)751-3612
Monteria Hightower, State
Librarian

Staff: Professional 19; Other 28. **Founded:** 1907. **Subjects:** State government, social services, human services, personnel administration, taxation, statistics. **Holdings:** 80,000 books; 365,000 microforms; federal and Missouri state documents. **Subscriptions:** 402 journals and other serials; 22 newspapers. **Services:** Interlibrary loan; copying; library open to the public. **Computerized services:** DIALOG Information Services, InfoPro Technologies; MCAT (Missouri statewide database) (internal database). **Publications:** *Show-Me Libraries*, quarterly; *Population & Census Newsletter*, quarterly; *Directory of Missouri Libraries*, annual; *Missouri Libraries Newsletter*, bimonthly; *Info To GO*;

Update (current awareness bibliography); *Wolfner Library Newsletter*.

St. Joseph Museum
Library

11th at Charles
St. Joseph, MO 64501

Phone: (816)232-8471
Fax: (816)232-8482
Richard A. Nolf, Director

Staff: 1. **Founded:** 1927. **Subjects:** Local and area history, Western movement, ethnology, natural history. **Special collections:** American Indian Collection; Civil War period local history collection; Nusom's Biography of Iowa Indians of Kansas and Nebraska. **Holdings:** 6500 volumes. **Subscriptions:** 40 journals and other serials. **Services:** Copying; library open to the public by appointment. **Publications:** *Happenings of the St. Joseph and Pony Express Museums*.

St. Louis Genealogical Society
Library

9011 Manchester Rd., Ste. 3
St. Louis, MO 63144

Phone: (314)968-2763
Lorraine C. Cates, Librarian

Staff: 2. **Founded:** 1969. **Subjects:** Genealogy, family histories. **Special collections:** Daughters of the American Revolution Collection (lineage books and indexes; bound volumes of DAR Magazine, 1896 to present). **Holdings:** 30,000 volumes; 500 reels of microfilm; 250 microfiche; 100 cassette tapes. **Subscriptions:** 275 journals and other serials. **Services:** Copying; limited genealogical research (fee based); library open to the public. **Special indexes:** Index to 1860 St. Louis City & County Census (book). **Remarks:** Library is located at University City Public Library, 6701 Delmar Blvd., University City, MO 63130. **Publications:** List of publications—available on request.

St. Louis Public Library
History and Genealogy Department

Central Library
1301 Olive St.
St. Louis, MO 63103-2389

Phone: (314)539-0385
Fax: (314)539-0393
Joseph M. Winkler,
Coordinator of Research
Collections

Staff: Professional 2. **Founded:** 1973. **Subjects:** U.S. history; genealogy of Missouri, Illinois, and most states east of the Mississippi River; heraldry; maps. **Special collections:** Complete set of St. Louis city directories; early printed records of Eastern States; American Colonial and State Papers: passenger lists and indexes of the 19th century (microfilm); St. Louis newspapers; Boston Evening Transcript: Genealogical Queries (microfiche); U.S. state and county histories and genealogical materials; Missouri Union and Confederate service records and indexes (microfilm); federal population censuses (microfilm) and indexes; territorial papers of U.S.; family histories (4000). **Holdings:** 143,000 volumes; 1150 genealogy files; 8482 reels of microfilm; U.S. Geological Survey depository for topographic maps; U.S. Army maps of foreign countries; U.S. and foreign gazetteers. **Subscriptions:** 395 current journals and other serials. **Services:** Interlibrary loan; copying; department open to the public. **Computerized services:** CD-ROMs (Biography Index, Place Name Index, U.S. History on CD-ROM). **Special indexes:** Heraldry Index of the St. Louis Public Library, 1980 (4 volumes); Genealogy index (card); heraldry index supplement (card); map index; surname and locations file. **Publications:** *Genealogical Materials and Local Histories in* *the St. Louis Public Library* (bibliography of holdings), 1965, 1st supplement, 1971.

St. Louis University
Pius XII Memorial Library
Vatican Film Library

3655 Pine Blvd.
St. Louis, MO 63108

Description: Collection of microfilmed documents of the Hispanic Southwest as well as Baja California Mission registers. Also on microfilm are records (including genealogical information) of the expulsion of the Spanish Jesuits from Mexico in 1769 as well as film of the Spanish Jesuits in China (the Phillipines) and Japan. **Remarks:** Published articles and guides about their Vatican microfilm collection.

Western Historical Manuscript Collection
University of Missouri, Columbia

23 Ellis Library
Columbia, MO 65201

Phone: (314)882-6028
Nancy Lankford, Associate Director

Staff: Professional 13; Other 3. **Founded:** 1943. **Subjects:** History—Missouri, political, economic, agricultural, urban, labor, black, women's, frontier, religious, literary, social, science, steamboating, social reform and welfare, business. **Holdings:** 13,100 linear feet of manuscripts; 7300 reels of microfilm; 3725 audiotapes and audiocassettes; 700 phonograph records; 190 video materials. **Services:** Interlibrary loan; copying; collection open to the public. **Computerized services:** Internet (electronic mail service). **Remarks:** Electronic mail address: whmscoll@ext.missouri.edu (Internet). Collection contains the manuscript holdings of both the University of Missouri and the State Historical Society of Missouri. Offices are located at the four branches of the University of Missouri. Materials may be loaned among the four branches. **Publications:** *Guide to the Western Historical Manuscripts Collection*, 1952; supplement, 1956; finding aids (index, shelf list, and chronological file).

Western Historical Manuscript Collection
University of Missouri, St. Louis

Thomas Jefferson Library
8001 Natural Bridge Rd.
St. Louis, MO 63121

Phone: (314)553-5143
Ann Morris, Associate Director

Staff: Professional 3; Other 2. **Founded:** 1968. **Subjects:** History—state and local, women's, Afro-American, ethnic, education, immigration; socialism; 19th century science; environment; peace; religion; Missouri politics; social reform and welfare; photography; journalism; business; labor. **Special collections:** Oral History Program (1000 tapes); Photograph Collection (200,000 images); African American Journalism; Afro-Americans in St. Louis; *Limelight Magazine* (black-oriented newspaper); New Age Federal Savings and Loan Association, St. Louis, 1915–1967 (first black-owned financial institution). **Holdings:** 5500 linear feet of manuscripts, photographs, oral history tapes, and university archives. **Services:** Interlibrary loan (limited); copying of manuscripts and photographs; library open to the public with restricted circulation. **Special indexes:** Unpublished inventories to collections in repository. **Remarks:** Collection contains the manuscript holdings of both the University of Missouri and the State Historical Society of Missouri. Offices are located at the four branches of the University of Missouri. Materials may be loaned

among the four branches. **Publications:** *Western Historical Manuscript Collection—St. Louis* (1993 Guide).

Montana

Bitter Root Valley Historical Society
Ravalli County Museum
Miles Romney Memorial Library

Old Court House
205 Bedford Ave.
Hamilton, MT 59840

Phone: (406)363-3338
Helen Ann Bibler, Director

Staff: Professional 1. **Founded:** 1979. **Subjects:** Pioneer and Indian history. **Special collections:** Indian Collection; Granville Stuart Collection; Western News Files, 1890–1977; Ravalli Republican Files, 1899 to present; Northwest Tribune Files, 1906–1950; Stevensville Register Files, 1906–1914; western history (two private libraries). **Holdings:** 500 books. **Subscriptions:** 219 newspapers. **Services:** Copying; library open to the public for reference use only.

Montana Historical Society
Library/Archives

225 N. Roberts
PO Box 201201
Helena, MT 59620

Phone: (406)444-2681
Fax: (406)444-2696
Robert M. Clark, Head, Library and Archives Division

Staff: Professional 9; Other 5. **Founded:** 1865. **Subjects:** Lewis and Clark Expedition; George Armstrong Custer; Charles M. Russell; military history of the Montana Indians; Montana biography/genealogy; mining; cattle and range; homesteading. **Special collections:** T.C. Power papers; F.J. and Jack Ellis Haynes Northern Pacific Railroad and Yellowstone National Park Photograph Collection; state government archives (5500 cubic feet). **Holdings:** 50,000 books; 5000 bound periodical volumes; 50,000 state publications; 6500 cubic feet of private papers; 200,000 photographs; 14,000 reels of microfilm of Montana and other newspapers; 16,000 maps; 4000 broadsides and ephemera; 1500 oral history interviews. **Subscriptions:** 300 journals and other serials; newspapers. **Services:** Interlibrary loan; copying (both limited); library open to the public for research and reference use only. **Computerized services:** Internal database; CD-ROM (Lasercat). **Special catalogs:** Union List of Montana Newspapers in Montana Repositories; Catalog of the Map Collection (microfiche). **Special indexes:** Index to archival collections (online); History of Montana, 1739–1885; Contributions to the Montana Historical Society; Montana obituary index, 1864–1930 (card); Montana biographies index (card); F. Jay Haynes Photo Collection Index (microfiche)—for sale. **Remarks:** Alternate telephone number(s): (406)444-4775 (Archives); (406)444-4739 (Photo Archives). **Publications:** *Montana: The Magazine of Western History*, quarterly; *Montana Post* (newsletter), quarterly.

Montana State Library

1515 E. 6th Ave.	Phone: (406)444-3004
Helena, MT 59620	Fax: (406)444-0581
	Richard T. Miller Jr., State Librarian

Staff: Professional 7; Other 29. **Founded:** 1946. **Subjects:** General collection. **Special collections:** Federal government publications (partial depository); state government publications (complete depository). **Holdings:** 69,592 books; 502 periodical titles; 20,635 state publications; 259,137 federal publications. **Subscriptions:** 502 journals and other serials; 15 newspapers. **Services:** Interlibrary loan; copying; library open to the public. **Computerized services:** DIALOG Information Services, InfoPro Technologies, OCLC; Natural Resource Information System (internal database); Internet (electronic mail service). Performs searches free of charge. Contact Person: Darlene Staffeldt, Program Manager, Information Resources. **Remarks:** Electronic mail address: staffeld@class.org (Internet). **Publications:** *Montana State Library News*, irregular; *Montana Library Directory*, annual.

Nebraska

Custer County Historical Society Library

445 S. 9th	Phone: (308)872-2689
PO Box 334	Mary Landkamer, Researcher
Broken Bow, NE 68822-0334	

Staff: Professional 3; Other 3. **Founded:** 1960. **Subjects:** History—state, local; genealogy. **Special collections:** Census of the 81 cemeteries in Custer County, Nebraska. **Holdings:** 200 books; 110 volumes of bound newspapers; 700 photographs; 50 maps; 221 reels of microfilm; 24 VF drawers of obituaries and biographical materials. **Subscriptions:** 2 journals and other serials. **Services:** Copying; library open to the public. **Special indexes:** Index to Butcher Photograph Collection, city and county histories, obituaries, and cemeteries, 1874 to present. **Publications:** *Custer County Times Newsletter*, 2/year—to members.

Nebraska State Genealogical Library

PO Box 5608	Phone: (402)371-3468
Lincoln, NE 68505	Bob Plisek, President

Staff: 1. **Description:** Some coverage of all ethnic groups, with national and regional scope. Collection is held at the Beatrice Public Library, Beatrice, NE. Members may rent books by mail. **Holdings:** 300 microfilms and 110 periodicals. **Services:** Genealogical assistance. **Special catalogs:** Large special publications catalog available.

Nebraska State Historical Society Library/Archives Division

1500 R St.	Phone: (402)471-4771
Box 82554	Fax: (402)471-3100
Lincoln, NE 68501	Andrea I. Paul, Associate Director, Library and Archives

Staff: 18. **Founded:** 1878. **Subjects:** Nebraska—history, politics, agriculture; Indians of the Great Plains, archeology, Great Plains history, genealogy. **Holdings:** 80,000 volumes; 563 sets of San-

born Fire Insurance maps of Nebraska; 2000 maps and 400 atlases relating to Nebraska, 1854 to present; 2500 photographs in Solomon D. Butcher Photograph Collection of Sod Houses; 465 photographs in John A. Anderson Photograph Collection of Brule Sioux; 247,000 other photographs; Nebraska state government publications repository, 1905 to present; 15,000 volumes of genealogical materials; 15,000 cubic feet of state and local archival materials; 8000 cubic feet of manuscripts; 28,000 reels of microfilm of newspapers, 1854–1991. **Subscriptions:** 930 journals and other serials; 200 newspapers. **Services:** Interlibrary loan (copies only); copying; library/archives open to the public. **Publications:** *Guides to the State Archives*, issued periodically.

Nevada

Nevada Historical Society Library

1650 N. Virginia St.	Phone: (702)688-1190
Reno, NV 89503-1799	Fax: (702)688-2917
	Peter L. Bandurraga, Director

Staff: 7. **Founded:** 1904. **Subjects:** Nevada history, mining, Indians, agriculture, water, gambling, transportation and communication, censuses (Nevada), newspaper index. **Holdings:** 30,000 books; 5000 bound periodical volumes; 3000 manuscript collections; 5000 reels of microfilm; 250,000 photographs; 50,000 maps; manuscripts; photographs; government documents. **Subscriptions:** 260 journals and other serials. **Services:** Copying; limited written research by mail; library open to the public. **Special indexes:** An Index to the Publications of the Nevada Historical Society, 1907–1971. **Publications:** *Nevada Historical Society Quarterly*.

Nevada State Library and Archives

Capitol Complex	Phone: (702)687-5160
Carson City, NV 89710	Fax: (702)887-8330
	Joan G. Kerschner, State Librarian

Staff: Professional 13; Other 15. **Founded:** 1859. **Subjects:** Public administration, history of Nevada, business. **Special collections:** Nevada Collection; state, county, and municipal documents (55,000). **Holdings:** 47,627 books; 12,596 bound periodical volumes; 250,000 U.S. Government publications; 15,233 reels of microfilm of Nevada newspapers. **Subscriptions:** 504 journals and other serials; 60 newspapers. **Services:** Interlibrary loan; copying; archives open to the public. **Computerized services:** DIALOG Information Services, RLIN, VU/TEXT Information Services, OCLC, WILSONLINE, DataTimes. Performs searches. Contact Person: Joyce C. Lee, Assistant State Librarian. **Special catalogs:** Nevada Statewide Union catalog. **Publications:** *Info Connection*.

New Hampshire

New Hampshire (State) Department of State
Division of Records Management & Archives

71 S. Fruit St.　　　　　　　Phone: (603)271-2236
Concord, NH 03301　　　　　Fax: (603)271-2272
　　　　　　　　　　　　　Frank C. Mevers, State
　　　　　　　　　　　　　　　　　　　Archivist

Staff: Professional 2. **Subjects:** State and county archives. **Services:** Copying; archives open to the public for reference use.

New Hampshire State Library

20 Park St.　　　　　　　　Phone: (603)271-2397
Concord, NH 03301-6303　　Fax: (603)271-2205
　　　　　　　　　　　　　Kendall F. Wiggin, State
　　　　　　　　　　　　　　　　　　　Librarian

Staff: Professional 18; Other 41. **Founded:** 1716. **Subjects:** New Hampshire—history, government, political science, law. **Holdings:** 450,100 books; 16,011 manuscripts; 5271 scores; 12,500 reels of microfilm; 71,770 microcards; 114,000 microfiche; 653 motion pictures; 500 sound recordings. **Subscriptions:** 850 journals and other serials; 44 newspapers. **Services:** Interlibrary loan; copying; library open to the public. **Computerized services:** DIALOG Information Services, OCLC; internal database; Internet (electronic mail service). **Remarks:** Electronic mail address: k__ wiggin@uhh.unh.edu (Internet). **Publications:** *Granite State Libraries*, bimonthly to library community; *Reference Roundtable*, quarterly.

New Jersey

Bridgeton Free Public Library
Special Collections

150 E. Commerce St.　　　　Phone: (609)451-2620
Bridgeton, NJ 08302-2684　　Fax: (609)455-1049
　　　　　　　　　　　　　Grace M. Stirneman, Library
　　　　　　　　　　　　　　　　　　　Director

Staff: Professional 2; Other 8. **Subjects:** Cumberland County history, local genealogy, Woodland Indians. **Special collections:** New Jersey reference; Woodruff Museum books. **Holdings:** 2000 volumes, including newspapers, 1881 to present, bound and on microfilm; 20,000 Indian artifacts, 10,000 B.C. to circa 1700 A.D., collected within a 30-mile radius of the library. **Services:** Interlibrary loan; copying; collections open to the public.

Danforth Memorial Library

250 Broadway　　　　　　　Phone: (201)357-3000
Paterson, NJ 07501　　　　　Fax: (201)881-8338
　　　　　　　　　　　　　Kwaku Amoabeng, Director

Staff: Professional 10; Other 50. **Founded:** 1985. **Subjects:** Applied science, business, career information, computers, adult literacy, literature. **Special collections:** African-American studies collection; Spanish-language collection; local history/genealogy collection; New Jersey Government Documents Depository. **Holdings:** 357,000 books; 20,500 reels of microfilm; 1394 AV materials. **Subscriptions:** 300 journals and other serials; 44 newspapers. **Services:** Interlibrary loan; copying; library open to the public. Fee for non-resident loans. **Computerized services:** OCLC, DIALOG Information Services, InfoTrac; Internet (electronic mail service). Contact Person: Usha Regy, Head of Reference Servicess. **Special indexes:** Obituary Index. **Remarks:** Electronic mail address: patersonpl@hslc (Internet). **Publications:** *Resources of Paterson History: An Annotated Bibliography* (Centennial Publications).

New Jersey State Library

185 W. State St.　　　　　　Phone: (609)292-6220
CN 520　　　　　　　　　　Fax: (609)984-7900
Trenton, NJ 08625-0520　　　Louise Minervino

Staff: Professional 38; Other 65. **Founded:** 1796. **Subjects:** Law, New Jersey history and newspapers, political science, public administration, genealogy. **Special collections:** New Jerseyana; New Jersey State Government Publications; U.S. Government documents selective depository. **Holdings:** 750,000 volumes. **Subscriptions:** 2800 journals and other serials. **Services:** Interlibrary loan; copying; library open to the public by appointment. **Computerized services:** OCLC, RLIN, LEXIS, NEXIS, InfoPro Technologies, DIALOG Information Services; CompuServe Information Service; Internet (electronic mail service). Performs searches on fee basis. **Special catalogs:** Genealogy: New Jersey Family Names. **Remarks:** Electronic mail address: hadunn@pilot.NJINNet (Internet). Library coordinates a statewide, cooperative multitype library network. **Publications:** *Checklist of Official New Jersey Publications*, bimonthly— limited distribution; *Impressions* (newsletter), monthly.

Newark Public Library
Humanities Division

5 Washington St.　　　　　　Phone: (201)733-7820
Box 630　　　　　　　　　　Fax: (201)733-5648
Newark, NJ 07101-0630　　　Sallie Hannigan, Supervising
　　　　　　　　　　　　　　　　　　　Librarian

Staff: Professional 6; Other 1. **Founded:** 1889. **Subjects:** Literature, language, literary criticism, biography, bibliography, religion, philosophy, history, geography, psychology, librariana, travel, film, theater, television, sports and recreation, encyclopedias, dictionaries. **Special collections:** Black literature, history, and biography. **Holdings:** 130,000 books; 1000 bound periodical volumes; 1000 maps; dictionaries and encyclopedias in Spanish, Italian, French, German, Russian; information file. **Subscriptions:** 630 journals and other serials. **Services:** Interlibrary loan; copying; telephone and in-person reference available in Spanish; division open to the public. **Computerized services:** InfoPro Technologies, DIALOG Information Services, ORBIT Search Service, OCLC EPIC; CD-ROMs. Performs searches on fee basis.

Rowen College of New Jersey
Savitz Library
Stewart Room

201 Mullica Hill Rd.　　　　Phone: (609)863-6303
Glassboro, NJ 08028　　　　Fax: (609)863-6313
　　　　　　　　　　　　　Clara M. Kirner, Special
　　　　　　　　　　　　　　　　　Collections Librarian

Staff: Professional 1; Other 1. **Founded:** 1948. **Subjects:** New Jersey history, early religious history, genealogy, Indians of North

America, Revolutionary War, War of 1812, Grinnell Arctic expedition. **Special collections:** Family papers: Howell, Inskeep, Haines, Lippincott; Frank H. Stewart Collection (8000 volumes); Charles A. Wolverton Papers (10 boxes); Satterthwaite Genealogical Collection (24 VF drawers). **Holdings:** 16,300 books; 422 bound periodical volumes; 5000 manuscripts; 13 VF drawers of college archives; 4200 volumes of masters' theses; rare books; deeds; surveys; marriage licenses; acts of assembly. **Subscriptions:** 28 journals and other serials. **Services:** Copying (limited); room open to the public for reference use only. **Formerly:** Glassboro State College. **Publications:** *Guide to the Special Collections*—available on request.

New Mexico

New Mexico State Library

325 Don Gaspar
Santa Fe, NM 87503

Phone: (505)827-3800
Fax: (505)827-3888
Karen J. Watkins, State
Librarian

Staff: Professional 17; Other 42. **Founded:** 1929. **Subjects:** Public administration, management, education, social sciences, environment. **Special collections:** Southwest/New Mexico collection. **Holdings:** 70,000 books; 900,000 federal and state documents (Federal Regional Depository). **Subscriptions:** 463 journals and other serials; 57 newspapers. **Services:** Interlibrary loan; copying; library open to the public. **Computerized services:** DIALOG Information Services, OCLC. Performs searches on fee basis for New Mexico libraries. **Publications:** *Hitchhiker*, weekly.

New Mexico State Records Center and Archives

404 Montezuma St.
Santa Fe, NM 87503

Phone: (505)827-7332
Fax: (505)827-7331
J. Richard Salazar, Chief,
Archive Services

Staff: Professional 4; Other 2. **Founded:** 1960. **Subjects:** New Mexico state history, Southwestern history. **Special collections:** Spanish and Mexican Archives of New Mexico; New Mexico Territorial Archives; New Mexico Statehood Archives. **Holdings:** 4000 books; 300 bound periodical volumes. **Subscriptions:** 4 journals and other serials. **Services:** Copying; archives open to the public. **Special indexes:** Photograph index. **Publications:** *Spanish, Mexican, Territorial Archives of New Mexico*.

New York

Cayuga County Historian
Library

Historic Old Post Office Bldg.
157 Genesee St.
Auburn, NY 13021

Phone: (315)253-1300
Thomas G. Eldred, County
Historian

Staff: 4. **Founded:** 1969. **Subjects:** Local history, genealogy. **Special collections:** Cayuga County Records. **Holdings:** 300 books; 500 bound periodical volumes; 50 boxes and 27 VF draw-

ers of reports, manuscripts, letters, broadsides, clippings; 700 reels of microfilm of newspapers; 1500 reels of microfilm of records; photographs. **Subscriptions:** 16 journals and other serials. **Services:** Copying; library open to the public for reference use only. **Publications:** *Cayuga Gazette*.

Columbia University

300 Kent Hall
116th St. & Amsterdam Ave.
New York, NY 10027

Phone: (212)854-4318
Fax: (212)662-6286
Amy Vladeck Heinrich,
Acting East Asian Librarian

Founded: 1902. **Subjects:** China, Japan, Korea—humanities, history, social sciences, art history. **Special collections:** Chinese local histories and genealogies; Korean collection of Yi Song-ui. **Holdings:** Chinese—273,306 bound volumes; Japanese—211,991 bound volumes; Korean—36,957 bound volumes; Western languages—55,005 bound volumes; 13,253 reels of microfilm; 10,905 microfiche.

New York Genealogical and Biographical Society
Library

122 E. 58th St., 4th Fl.
New York, NY 10022

Phone: (212)755-8532
Fax: (212)754-4218
Peter Gordon B. Stillman,
Trustee Librarian, Policy

Staff: Professional 3; Other 4. **Founded:** 1869. **Subjects:** Genealogy, biography, local history. **Special collections:** New York State church, town, and other records; family and Bible records. **Holdings:** 70,182 volumes; 23,011 manuscripts; 3174 reels of microfilm; 7859 microfiche; 30 CDs. **Subscriptions:** 1190 journals and other serials. **Services:** Copying; library open to the public with restrictions. **Publications:** *New York Genealogical and Biographical Record*; *The NYG & B Newsletter*; *Collections of the New York Genealogical and Biographical Society*.

New York Public Library
The Research Libraries
United States History, Local History and Genealogy Division

5th Ave. & 42nd St., Rm.
315S
New York, NY 10018

Phone: (212)930-0828
Ruth A. Carr, Chief

Staff: Professional 5; Other 1.5. **Subjects:** U.S. history; county, city, town histories of the United States; European and American genealogy and heraldry; works on names and flags of the world. **Special collections:** Photographic views of New York City (54,000); postcards and scrapbooks of U.S. local views; Lewis W. Hine Collection (443 prints and negatives); local history ephemera; American Antequarian Society newspaper index; U.S. election campaign materials. **Holdings:** 154,000 volumes. **Subscriptions:** 1254 journals and other serials. **Services:** Copying; division open to the public. **Computerized services:** DIALOG Information Services; CD-ROM (Family Search).

New York State Library

Cultural Education Center   Phone: (518)474-7646
Empire State Plaza   Fax: (518)474-5786
Albany, NY 12230   Jerome Yavarkovsky, Director

Staff: Professional 79; Other 107. **Founded:** 1818. **Subjects:** Education, science, technology, art, architecture, economics, sociology, current affairs, bibliography, New York State documents (also original documents for California), New York State newspapers, law, medicine, state and local history, genealogy, heraldry. **Special collections:** Almanacs; New York State documents. **Holdings:** 8.2 million books, bound periodical volumes, manuscripts, pamphlets; patents; microfilm; microcards; pictures; maps. **Subscriptions:** 18,582 journals and other serials; 111 newspapers. **Services:** Interlibrary loan; copying; library open to the public. **Computerized services:** InfoPro Technologies, DIALOG Information Services; ALANET (electronic mail service). **Remarks:** Electronic mail address: ALA0198 (ALANET). **Publications:** *Bookmark*, quarterly; *Checklist of Official Publications of the State of New York*, monthly.

Rochester Public Library
Local History and Genealogy Division

115 South Ave.   Phone: (716)428-7338
Rochester, NY 14604   Fax: (716)428-7313
    Wayne Arnold, Head

Staff: Professional 3; Other 1. **Subjects:** History of Rochester and Genesee area, genealogy (primarily New York and New England). **Special collections:** Local newspapers. **Holdings:** 25,000 books; 15 cases and 400 volumes of manuscripts; 1800 maps; 500 scrapbooks; 145 VF drawers of newspaper clippings; 80 VF drawers of pamphlets and ephemera; 20 VF drawers of pictures; 12 drawers of postcards; 638 reels of microfilm; 120 films. **Subscriptions:** 200 journals and other serials; 78 newspapers. **Services:** Copying (limited). **Remarks:** The majority of the holdings of the Rochester Historical Society are on permanent loan to the Local History Division.

Staten Island Institute of Arts and Sciences Archives and Library

75 Stuyvesant Pl.   Phone: (718)727-1135
Staten Island, NY 10301   Fax: (718)273-5683
    Vince Sweeney, Curator of History

Staff: Professional 2; Other 1. **Founded:** 1881. **Subjects:** Natural history, Staten Island history, archeology, black history, women's history, urban planning. **Special collections:** Photographs and prints of old Staten Island; local black history; complete list of special collections available on request. **Holdings:** 12,000 books; 22,000 bound periodical volumes; 3000 maps; 1200 prints; 50,000 photographs; 1500 cubic feet of manuscripts, letters, and documents; 80 reels of microfilm of Staten Island newspapers. **Subscriptions:** 200 journals and other serials. **Services:** Copying; library open to the public by appointment. **Special indexes:** Guide to Institute Archives, 2 volumes; indexes to newspapers, iconography of Staten Island, special collections (all on cards). **Publications:** *Guide to Special Collections*, 16 volumes.

University of Rochester
Asia Library
Rush Rhees Library

River Campus   Phone: (716)275-4489
Rochester, NY 14627   Datta S. Kharbas, Librarian

Founded: 1965. **Subjects:** Chinese, Japanese, and Indian history and philosophy; Japanese, Chinese, Sanskrit, Hindi, and Marathi language and literature. **Special collections:** Asahi Shinbum on microfilm; *Times of India,* 1861–1889 (Indian gazetteers on microfilm); India censuses, 1881–1971. **Holdings:** 105,000 books; 15,000 bound periodical volumes.

North Carolina

North Carolina (State) Department of Cultural Resources
Division of Archives and History
Archives & Records Section

109 E. Jones St.   Phone: (919)733-3952
Raleigh, NC 27601-2807   Fax: (919)733-1354
    David J. Olson, State Archivist

Staff: Professional 38; Other 39. **Founded:** 1903. **Subjects:** Official records, especially county records, of the state of North Carolina and its subdivisions. **Special collections:** Federal records include mortality schedules 1850–1880, population schedules 1800–1880; manuscript collections, colonial times to present; maps; photographs; audiovisual materials; microfilm. **Holdings:** 39,800 cubic feet of archive material; 135,000 reels of microfilm. **Services:** Copying; search room and archives open to the public Tuesday–Saturday. **Computerized services:** MARS (Manuscript and Archives Reference System; internal database); Internet (electronic mail service). **Publications:** List of publications—available on request.

North Carolina (State) Department of Cultural Resources
Division of the State Library

109 E. Jones St.   Phone: (919)733-2570
Raleigh, NC 27601-2807   Fax: (919)733-8748
    Sandra M. Cooper, Director/ State Librarian

Staff: Professional 33; Other 81. **Founded:** 1812. **Subjects:** Public policy, Southern history, library science. **Special collections:** Genealogy; North Carolina state documents (123,441). **Holdings:** 200,000 volumes; 600,000 state and federal documents; 33,126 reels of microfilm; 35 titles on microfiche; 166,000 containers of talking books; 7177 16mm films; 2644 videocassettes. **Subscriptions:** 646 journals and other serials; 119 newspapers. **Services:** Interlibrary loan; copying; library open to the public with circulation of materials limited to state employees. **Computerized services:** DIALOG Information Services, InfoPro Technologies, OCLC, LC Direct, U.S. Bureau of the Census; LINC (Log Into North Carolina); BITNET, Internet (electronic mail services). Performs searches for state employees and libraries. Contact Person: David Bevan, Chief, Information Services Section, (919)733-3683. **Special catalogs:** North Carolina Union Catalog (microfilm); North Carolina Online Union Catalog; North Carolina Online Union List of Serials. **Also known as:** State Library of North Carolina. **Publications:** *Tar Heel Libraries*, bimonthly; *News Flash*, monthly—to public libraries; *Selected Acquisitions*; *Checklist of Official North Carolina State Publications*, bimonthly.

North Dakota

North Dakota State Library

Liberty Memorial Bldg.
Capitol Grounds
604 E. Boulevard Ave.
Bismarck, ND 58505-0800

Phone: (701)224-2492
Fax: (701)224-2040
William R. Strader, State
Librarian

Staff: Professional 7; Other 18. **Founded:** 1907. **Subjects:** North Dakota, state government, library science, music, education. **Special collections:** Last Copy Repository. **Holdings:** 126,928 books; 14,233 tape cassettes; 72,059 state documents, 1889 to present; 15,904 federal documents; CD-ROMs. **Subscriptions:** 241 journals and other serials; 15 newspapers. **Services:** Interlibrary loan; copying; library open to the public. **Computerized services:** DIALOG Information Services, OCLC; EasyLink, Internet (electronic mail services). **Remarks:** Electronic mail addresses: 62755117 (EasyLink); strader@sendit.nodak.edu (Internet). **Publications:** *Flickertale Newsletter*, bimonthly.

State Historical Society of North Dakota State Archives and Historical Research Library

Heritage Center
612 E. Boulevard
Bismarck, ND 58505

Phone: (701)224-2668
Fax: (701)224-3710
Gerald Newborg, State
Archivist/Division Director

Staff: Professional 8; Other 2. **Founded:** 1895. **Subjects:** North Dakota and Dakota Territory; social, cultural, economic, and political history; early exploration and travel; fur trade; plains military history; Northern Plains region—archeology, prehistory, ethnology, ethnohistory; historic preservation; genealogy. **Holdings:** 100,400 volumes; 2198 cubic feet of manuscripts; 11,740 cubic feet of state and county archives; 100,000 photographs; 12,500 reels of microfilm of microfilm of manuscripts, records and newspapers; 1421 titles of North Dakota newspapers; 2100 titles of periodicals; 1843 oral history interviews; sound recordings; maps; videotapes; motion pictures; newsfilm archives. **Subscriptions:** 300 journals and other serials; 103 newspapers. **Services:** Interlibrary loan (limited); copying; library open to the public for reference use only. **Computerized services:** OCLC. **Special catalogs:** The North Dakota Newspaper Inventory, 1992. **Publications:** *North Dakota History: Journal of the Northern Plains*, quarterly; *Plains Talk* (newsletter), quarterly; *Guide to the North Dakota State Archives*, 1985; *Guide to Manuscripts*, 1985.

University of North Dakota Elwyn B. Robinson Department of Special Collections

Chester Fritz Library
Box 9000
Grand Forks, ND 58202

Phone: (701)777-4625
Fax: (701)777-3319
Sandra Beidler, Head,
Archives & Special
Collections

Staff: Professional 2; Other 1. **Founded:** 1963. **Subjects:** History—North and South Dakota, Northern Great Plains, Plains Indian, environmental; agrarian radicalism; Nonpartisan League (North Dakota); genealogy; oral history; ethnic heritage and family history (North Dakota); Norwegian local history. **Special collections:** North Dakota Book Collection (17,661 volumes); Fred G. Aandahl Book Collection (1477 volumes); Family History/Genealogy Collection (3429 volumes); North Dakota State Documents (4000); Orin G. Libby Manuscript Collection (12,289 linear feet). **Holdings:** 21,400 books; 11,000 linear feet of manuscript material; 4150 reels of microfilm; 44,500 photographs; 3500 AV items; 6514 theses and dissertations. **Subscriptions:** 71 journals and other serials; 4 newspapers. **Services:** Copying; department open to the public for reference use only. **Computerized services:** OCLC, DIALOG Information Services, IAC; Internet (electronic mail service). **Special catalogs:** Subject Guide to the Orin G. Libby Manuscript Collection, 1979; Guide to Genealogical/Family History Sources, 1986. **Publications:** Reference Guide to North Dakota History and Literature, 1979; Reference Guide to the Orin G. Libby Manuscript Collection (Volume 1, 1975; Volume 2, 1983; Volume 3, 1985; Volume 4, 1990).

Ohio

Allen County Historical Society Elizabeth M. MacDonell Memorial Library

620 W. Market St.
Lima, OH 45801-4604

Phone: (419)222-9426
Anna B. Selfridge, Curator,
Archives and Manuscripts

Staff: Professional 1. **Founded:** 1908. **Subjects:** Local history and genealogy, Ohio history, railroading, American Indian. **Holdings:** 8271 books; 585 bound periodical volumes; Lima, Ohio newspapers, 1840s to present; Lima directories, 1876 to present; 1938 reels of microfilm of newspapers and census records. **Subscriptions:** 40 journals and other serials. **Services:** Copying; library open to the public. **Remarks:** Library is part of Allen County Museum. **Publications:** *Allen County Reporter*, 3/year; newsletter, bimonthly—both to members.

Cleveland Public Library History and Geography Department

325 Superior Ave.
Cleveland, OH 44114-1271

Phone: (216)623-2864
JoAnn Petrello, Department
Head

Staff: Professional 4; Other 6. **Founded:** 1869. **Subjects:** History—ancient, medieval, modern; archaeology; local history; genealogy; heraldry; geography; black history; exploration and travel; numismatics. **Special collections:** Photograph Collection (904,206). **Holdings:** 171,338 volumes; 11,738 bound periodical volumes; 18,800 Cleveland pictures on microfiche; 6000 maps and brochures with current travel data; local history clipping file; 919,526 photographs; 35 vertical files; 4750 microfiche. **Subscriptions:** 411 journals and other serials. **Services:** Interlibrary loan; copying; department open to the public. **Computerized services:** OCLC, DIALOG Information Services, InfoPro Technologies, OhioPI (Ohio Public Information Utility), Hannah Information Systems, PFDS Online; CD-ROMs. **Special indexes:** Photograph Collection index (movie stills and posters captured on an optical disk).

Ohio Genealogical Society Library

34 Sturges Ave.	Phone: (419)522-9077
PO Box 2625	Fax: (419)522-0224
Mansfield, OH 44906-0625	Thomas S. Neel, Office Manager

Staff: Prof. 1, other 1. **Description:** Nonprofit library collection on Ohio pioneer materials including census, court records, county histories, Bible records, and family accounts. Both national and regional focus with some African and Native American coverage, minor Hispanic and Asian American coverage. **Founded:** 1959. **Special collections:** First Families of Ohio, lineage society to pre-1820 Ohio settlers; Ohio ancestor card file, nearly 300,000 cards tying surnames to researchers; Ohio Bible records, everyname index. **Holdings:** Two rooms of archival material, 15,000 books, 200 periodical titles, 16 file cabinets of reports, microfiche (IGI), 1500 rolls of microfilm, with active subscriptions; old newspapers. **Services:** Copying, list of researchers for hire, genealogical assistance. Open to public with fee of $3 per day for nonmembers. **Computerized services:** Phone Disk, Social Security Index, Census Indexes. **Publications:** *The Report,* quarterly, $25.00, circulation: 6350; *Ohio Records and Pioneer Families: Cross Road of our Nation,* quarterly, $18.00, circulation: 1400; *The Ohio Genealogical Society Newsletter,* monthly (with *The Report*), circulation: 6,350.

State Library of Ohio

65 S. Front St.	Phone: (614)644-7061
Columbus, OH 43266-0334	Fax: (614)466-3584
	Richard M. Cheski, State Librarian

Staff: Professional 39; Other 92. **Founded:** 1817. **Subjects:** Management, social sciences, education, public administration, Ohio history. **Special collections:** Genealogy (14,000 items); Ohio and federal documents (1.5 million). **Holdings:** 622,101 books; 495,914 microforms; CD-ROMs. **Subscriptions:** 449 journals and other serials; 26 newspapers. **Services:** Interlibrary loan; copying; faxing; library open to the public. **Computerized services:** DIALOG Information Services, OCLC, LIBRIS, Library Control System (LCS), OHIONET. Performs searches for state agencies. Contact Person: Catherine Mead, Head, Reference, (614)644-6952. **Publications:** *Directory of Ohio Libraries,* annual; *Ohio Documents,* quarterly; *Recent Acquisitions,* irregular.

Western Reserve Historical Society Library

10825 East Blvd.	Phone: (216)721-5722
Cleveland, OH 44106	Fax: (216)721-0645
	Kermit J. Pike, Director

Staff: Professional 7; Other 7. **Founded:** 1867. **Subjects:** Ohio history, American genealogy, Civil War, slavery and abolitionism, ethnic history, African and Native Americans. **Holdings:** 235,950 books; 25,500 volumes of newspapers; 50,300 pamphlets; 6 million manuscripts; 32,500 reels of microfilm. **Subscriptions:** 325 journals and other serials; 50 newspapers. **Services:** Interlibrary loan; copying; library open to the public. **Special catalogs:** Catalogs to manuscript, genealogy, and Shaker collections (all on cards).

Oklahoma

Museum of the Great Plains
Great Plains Research Library and Archives

601 Ferris	Phone: (405)581-3460
Box 68	Steve Wilson, Director
Lawton, OK 73502	

Staff: Professional 2; Other 1. **Founded:** 1960. **Subjects:** Great Plains—history, natural history, archeology, anthropology, agriculture. **Special collections:** Original documents and photographs dealing with the settlement of southwestern Oklahoma and Southern Plains. **Holdings:** 25,000 books; 725 bound periodical volumes; 700 cases of manuscripts, 1880–1940, Comanche County newspapers, 1901 to present, and City of Lawton Journals; 30,000 photographs; hardware; agricultural catalogs and periodicals. **Subscriptions:** 260 journals and other serials. **Services:** Copying; library and archives open to the public. **Special indexes:** Index to photograph collections (card); index to articles in regional journals; index to agricultural catalogs and periodicals; index to collections described in *Great Plains Journal,* volume 17, 1978.

Oklahoma Historical Society
Archives and Manuscript Division

Historical Bldg.	Phone: (405)521-2491
Oklahoma City, OK 73105	Fax: (405)525-3272
	William D. Welge, Director

Staff: Professional 5; Other 8. **Founded:** 1893. **Subjects:** Oklahoma and Indian territories, Indian tribes of Oklahoma, pioneer life, missionaries, territorial court records, explorers. **Special collections:** Records from all state Indian agencies, except Osage Agency (3.5 million document pages; 6000 volumes); Dawes Commission Records (48 cubic feet; 242 bound volumes); Indian-Pioneer History (interviews; 112 volumes); Whipple Collection (8 cubic feet); Joseph Thoburn Collection (20 cubic feet). **Holdings:** 2900 reels of microfilm of Indian and Oklahoma affairs; 265,000 historical photographs; 28,000 reels of microfilm of newspapers; 4500 oral history tapes. **Subscriptions:** 10 journals and other serials. **Services:** Copying; archives open to the public. **Special catalogs:** Catalog listing films for sale. **Special indexes:** Inventories of Five Civilized Tribes documents; card index of Indian-Pioneer History. **Publications:** Microfilm of original materials for sale.

Oklahoma Historical Society
Division of Library Resources

2100 N. Lincoln Blvd.	Phone: (405)521-2491
Oklahoma City, OK 73105	Fax: (405)525-3272
	Edward Connie Shoemaker, Library Director

Staff: Professional 1; Other 8. **Founded:** 1893. **Subjects:** Oklahoma and American Indian history, American west, Oklahoma genealogy. **Holdings:** 62,593 books; 10,600 reels of microfilm of

U.S. Census, 1790–1920; 25,000 reels of microfilm of Oklahoma newspapers, 1893 to present. **Subscriptions:** 300 journals and other serials; 280 newspapers. **Services:** Copying; library open to the public for research use only. **Computerized services:** OCLC. **Publications:** *Oklahoma History: A Bibliography*; *Five Civilized Tribes: A Bibliography*; *Family Histories: A Bibliography*; *Oklahoma Cemeteries: A Bibliography* (1993).

Oklahoma (State) Department of Libraries

200 NE 18th St.	Phone: (405)521-2502
Oklahoma City, OK 73105	Fax: (405)525-7804
	Robert L. Clark Jr., Director

Staff: Professional 40; Other 45. **Founded:** 1890. **Subjects:** Law; legislative reference materials; Oklahoma government, history, authors; librarianship; juvenile evaluation collection. **Special collections:** Oklahoma Collection (11,500 titles). **Holdings:** 320,000 books; 27,000 cubic feet of state archives and manuscript collections; 25,000 cubic feet of state records; 40,000 linear feet of U.S. Government documents (regional depository); 45,000 Oklahoma document titles; 66,000 reels of microfilm; 488 videotapes; U.S. Government documents on microfiche (270,432 linear feet); 290,840 maps; 37,000 microfiche titles; 250 file drawers of pamphlets and clippings. **Subscriptions:** 2400 journals and other serials; 18 newspapers. **Services:** Interlibrary loan; legislative and law reference; archival and state research assistance; department open to the public for reference use only; loans made to state agency personnel only. **Computerized services:** OCLC, DIALOG Information Services, Mead Data Central, InfoPro Technologies. **Publications:** *Annual Directory of Oklahoma Libraries*; *ODL Archives*, quarterly; *Oklahoma Almanac*, biennial; *GPO: Government Publications for Oklahoma*, bimonthly; *ODL Source* (newsletter), monthly; *Oklahoma Government Publications* (checklist), quarterly; *Informacion*.

Oregon

Douglas County Museum
Lavola Bakken Memorial Library

Box 1550	Phone: (503)440-4507
Roseburg, OR 97470	Fax: (503)440-6023
	Frederick R. Reenstjerna,
	Research Librarian

Staff: Professional 1. **Founded:** 1969. **Subjects:** Douglas County history, Umpqua Indians, logging, sawmills and grist mills, marine history, mining, development of area towns, railroads, agriculture. **Special collections:** Photography collection (15,000 photographic prints copied from glass-plate negatives); Catholic church records. **Holdings:** 2500 books; 350 vertical files of letters, diaries, manuscripts, census, cemetery records; 400 oral histories; 175 genealogies. **Subscriptions:** 30 journals and other serials. **Services:** Copying; library open to the public for reference use only. **Computerized services:** Argus Museum Automation System.

Family History Center, Eugene

3550 NW 18th Ave.	Phone: (503)343-3741
Eugene, OR 97402	

Description: Branch of the Family History Library of the Church of Jesus Christ of Latter-day Saints. **Subjects:** Genealogy, family history, church and civil records, local history. **Remarks:** Access to main library microfilm.

Family History Center, Portland

2215 NE 106th St.	Phone: (503)252-1081
Portland, OR 97220	

Description: Branch of the Family History Library of the Church of Jesus Christ of Latter-day Saints. **Subjects:** Genealogy, family history, church and civil records, local history. **Remarks:** Access to main library microfilm.

Family History Center, Portland

1975 SE 30th Ave.	Phone: (503)235-9090
Portland, OR 97214	

Description: Branch of the Family History Library of the Church of Jesus Christ of Latter-day Saints. **Subjects:** Genealogy, family history, church and civil records, local history. **Remarks:** Access to main library microfilm.

Klamath County Museum
Research Library

1451 Main St.	Phone: (503)883-4208
Klamath Falls, OR 97601	Fax: (503)883-5163
	Patsy H. McMillan, Museum
	Director

Staff: 2.5 **Founded:** 1954. **Subjects:** Oregon and local history, Modoc and Klamath Indians, Modoc Indian War. **Special collections:** Modoc Indian War collection; oral history collection. **Holdings:** 1650 books; photo/document archives; microfilm. **Subscriptions:** 5 journals and other serials. **Services:** Copying; library open to the public by appointment for reference use only; user fee. **Publications:** Research books on local history; *Guardhouse, Gallows, Graves* (Modoc Indian War information); *Old Fort Klamath*.

Oregon State Archives Division

800 Summer St. NE	Phone: (503)373-0701
Salem, OR 97310	Fax: (503)373-0963
	Timothy Backer, Supervisor,
	Reference Archives

Staff: Professional 3. **Founded:** 1946. **Subjects:** Oregon government—provisional, territorial, state, county, municipal, special districts. **Special collections:** Records of Oregon state and county government departments and agencies dating from the territorial period. **Holdings:** 25,000 cubic feet of records. **Services:** Copying; archives open to the public for reference use only. **Computerized services:** RLIN; internal database. **Publications:** *Guide to Provisional & Territorial Government Records*.

Oregon State Library

State Library Bldg.	Phone: (503)378-4277
Summer & Court Sts.	Fax: (503)588-7119
Salem, OR 97310	Jim Scheppke, State Librarian

Staff: Professional 14; Other 30. **Founded:** 1905. **Subjects:** Oregon history and government, business, librarianship, social sciences, humanities, science and technology. **Special collections:** Oregoniana. **Holdings:** 1.5 million books and government documents; 1585 video cassettes; 23,893 maps; clippings; pamphlets. **Subscriptions:** 633 journals and other serials. **Services:** Interlibrary loan; copying; SDI; library open to the public. **Comput-**

erized services: DIALOG Information Services, InfoPro Technologies, OCLC EPIC, OCLC; Internet, ALANET, OnTyme Electronic Message Network Service. **Special indexes:** ORULS; Oregon index; Subject and biography index to Salem daily newspaper and other publications. **Remarks:** Electronic mail addresses: CLASS.OSL (OnTyme Electronic Message Network Service); INFO@OPAC.OSL.OR.GOV (Internet). **Publications:** *Letter to Libraries* (online); *Directory and Statistics of Oregon Libraries*, annual—to all Oregon libraries.

Pennsylvania

Fulton County Historical Society
Library

PO Box 115   Phone: (717)485-3207
McConnellsburg, PA 17233   Hazel Harr, Librarian

Staff: 1. **Founded:** 1976. **Subjects:** Local history and genealogy. **Special collections:** Fulton Republican newspaper, 1865–1900; Fulton Democrat newspaper, 1866–1983; old school photographs; local family histories; county histories; church records. **Holdings:** 300 books; microfilm collection; 100 volumes of Pennsylvania Archives. **Services:** Copying; library open to the public on a limited schedule. **Special indexes:** Cemetery file (card); Index to 1850 and 1860 Fulton County census (book). **Publications:** *Annual Research Booklet*.

Genealogical Research Library
Erie Branch

1244 W 22nd St.
Erie, PA 16502

Description: Genealogical materials available for research.

Historical Society of Pennsylvania
Library

1300 Locust St.   Phone: (215)732-6201
Philadelphia, PA 19107   Fax: (215)732-2680
                                    Lee Arnold, Library Director

Staff: Professional 16. **Founded:** 1824. **Subjects:** History—U.S., 1783–1865, Colonial, Revolutionary, Pennsylvania; genealogy; Afro-Americana. **Special collections:** Slavery records. **Holdings:** 564,000 volumes; 16 million manuscripts; 2800 microcards; 17,200 microfiche; 14,700 reels of microfilm; maps; prints; drawings; paintings; newspapers; ephemera. **Subscriptions:** 4000 journals and other serials. **Services:** Copying; library open to the public on fee basis. **Computerized services:** OCLC, RLIN. **Publications:** *The Pennsylvania Magazine of History and Biography*, quarterly; *Guide to the Manuscript Collections of the Historical Society of Pennsylvania*; *The Pennsylvania Correspondent* (newsletter), 5/year—to members.

Lehigh County Historical Society
Scott Andrew Trexler II Memorial Library

Old Court House   Phone: (610)435-1072
5th & Hamilton Sts.   Fax: (610)435-9812
Box 1548   June B. Griffiths, Librarian/
Allentown, PA 18105   Archivist

Staff: Professional 2. **Founded:** 1904. **Subjects:** Pennsylvania and Lehigh County history, genealogy. **Special collections:** Allentown Newspapers, 1810–1916; family genealogies; photographs; Civil War; Allentown imprints; native Indians. **Holdings:** 8000 books; 200 newspaper volumes; 2000 pamphlets; 200 manuscripts, archives, records of local families and businesses; deeds; maps; church records. **Subscriptions:** 12 journals and other serials. **Services:** Copying; library open to the public on fee basis. **Publications:** *Proceedings*, biennial; quarterly newsletter; *Allentown 1762–1987: A 225-Year History* (2 volumes); occasional papers.

Library Company of Philadelphia

1314 Locust St.   Phone: (215)546-3181
Philadelphia, PA 19107   Fax: (215)546-5167
                                    John C. Van Horne, Librarian

Staff: Professional 13; Other 8. **Founded:** 1731. **Subjects:** Pre-1860 Americana, Philadelphia and Pennsylvania, pre-1820 medical material, black history before 1906, women's history. **Special collections:** Early printed books from Girard College and Christ Church (on deposit). **Holdings:** 450,000 books; 50,000 prints and photographs; 160,000 manuscripts. **Subscriptions:** 130 journals and other serials. **Services:** Interlibrary loan; copying; library open to the public for research. **Computerized services:** RLIN. **Special catalogs:** Afro-Americana, 1553–1906 in collections of the Library Company and the Historical Society of Pennsylvania; The Library of James Logan; Quarter of a Millennium: The Library Company of Philadelphia, 1731–1981; occasional catalogs of special exhibitions. **Publications:** Annual reports; newsletters—both free to libraries and individuals on request.

Pennsylvania (State) Department of
Education
Commonwealth Libraries

PO Box 1601   Phone: (717)787-2646
Harrisburg, PA 17105   Fax: (717)783-5420
                                    Sara Parker, Commissioner of
                                                        Libraries

Staff: Professional 40; Other 53. **Founded:** 1745. **Subjects:** Government, law, education, public welfare and administration, Pennsylvania history and biography, Central Pennsylvania genealogy, social and behavioral science, economics, library science. **Special collections:** Early Pennsylvania Imprints; Colonial Assembly Collection. **Holdings:** 983,949 books; 900,000 federal and Pennsylvania government publications; 2.752 million microforms, including Congressional Information Service and American Statistics Index microfiche series; Newsbank, 1977 to present; ERIC microfiche. **Subscriptions:** 3881 journals and other serials; 162 newspapers. **Services:** Interlibrary loan; copying; library open to the public. **Computerized services:** DIALOG Information Services, InfoPro Technologies; Internet (electronic mail services). Contact Person: Susan Payne, Head, Main Reading Room, (717)783-5950. **Special catalogs:** Pennsylvania Imprints, 1689–1789. **Remarks:** Electronic mail addresses: parker@hslc.org; wolfe@hslc.org; hoffmand@hslc.org; emerick@hslc.org (Internet). **Publications:** *Directory-Pennsylvania Libraries,* annual; *Pennsylvania Public Library Statistics,* annual.

Pennsylvania (State) Historical & Museum Commission
Division of Archives and Manuscripts

William Penn Memorial   Phone: (717)783-3281
   Museum & Archives Bldg.   Harry E. Whipkey, State
Box 1026   Archivist
Harrisburg, PA 17108-1026

Staff: Professional 8; Other 6. **Founded:** 1903. **Subjects:** Archives of Pennsylvania and historical manuscripts. **Special collections:** Record groups of the holdings of state agencies and political subdivisions (57); manuscript collections (425); census material beginning in 1782, lists free blacks and slaves. **Holdings:** 17,500 books; 27,000 cubic feet of archival materials; 21,000 cubic feet of personal papers; 15,000 reels of microfilm; 4500 maps. **Subscriptions:** 180 journals and other serials. **Services:** Interlibrary loan (limited); division open to the public. **Computerized services:** OCLC, RLIN; internal databases. **Publications:** List of publications—available on request; Finding Aids.

Rhode Island

Rhode Island State Archives

337 Westminster St.   Phone: (401)277-2353
Providence, RI 02903   Fax: (401)277-3199
                      Timothy A. Slavin, State
                                   Archivist

Staff: 1. **Subjects:** Rhode Island history. **Holdings:** Acts and resolves of the General Assembly; colony records; Revolutionary War records; petitions and reports to the General Assembly; military and maritime charters. **Services:** Copying; archives open to the public with restrictions.

South Carolina

South Carolina (State) Department of Archives & History
Archives Search Room

Box 11669, Capitol Sta.   Phone: (803)734-8577
Columbia, SC 29211   George L. Vogt, Director

Staff: 110. **Founded:** 1905. **Subjects:** History of South Carolina—political, constitutional, legal, economic, social, religious. **Special collections:** Noncurrent public records of South Carolina, including: land records of the colony and state; Revolutionary War accounts; confederate service records; executive, legislative, and judicial records of the colony and state; special census 1890; probate records of the colony; county records (23,000 cubic feet of records; 15,000 reels of microfilm). **Holdings:** 2000 books; 250 bound periodical volumes. **Subscriptions:** 200 journals and other serials. **Services:** Copying; search room open to the public for reference use only. **Special catalogs:** Catalog of reference library (card). **Special indexes:** Published Summary Guide to Archives; consolidated computer output microfilm index to documents;

bound volume indexes to land plats and grants, marriage settlements and other records; map catalog (card); Revolutionary and Confederate War service records (card). **Remarks:** Library is located at 1430 Senate St., Columbia, SC 29201. **Publications:** *Colonial Records of South Carolina,* 16 volumes; *State Records of South Carolina,* 10 volumes; *South Carolina Archives Microcopies,* 16 series; *New South Carolina State Gazette* (newsletter), 2/year; *Guide to Local Records in the South Carolina Archives;* historical booklets; curriculum resource materials; historical and technical pamphlets and brochures; *On the Record* (newsletter), quarterly; *News & Notes* (newsletter), quarterly.

South Carolina State Library

1500 Senate St.   Phone: (803)734-8666
PO Box 11469   Fax: (803)734-8676
Columbia, SC 29211   James B. Johnson Jr., Director

Staff: Professional 21; Other 32. **Founded:** 1943. **Subjects:** Reference, government, business, political science, education, history, fine arts, South Caroliniana. **Holdings:** 247,077 books; 2276 bound periodical volumes; 50,064 South Carolina state documents; 16,892 reels of microfilm of periodicals; 457,743 ERIC microfiche; 246,555 government documents; 2584 videotapes; 2384 films; 10,696 large print books. **Subscriptions:** 2636 journals and other serials; 27 newspapers. **Services:** Interlibrary loan; copying; library open to the public. **Computerized services:** DIALOG Information Services, OCLC, InfoPro Technologies; Internet (electronic mail service). Performs searches on fee basis. Contact Person: Mary Bull, Reference Librarian. **Remarks:** Electronic mail address: SOUTHCAR@CLASS.ORG (Internet). **Publications:** *News for South Carolina Libraries,* bimonthly—to public, school, and academic libraries and trustees; *New Resources*—to state government agencies and libraries.

South Dakota

Black Hills State University
E.Y. Berry Library-Learning Center
Special Collections

1200 University   Phone: (605)642-6361
Spearfish, SD 57799-9511   Fax: (605)642-6298
                     Dora Ann Jones, Special
                          Collections Librarian

Staff: Professional 1. **Founded:** 1925. **Subjects:** Local and regional history, biography, Dakota Indians, western industry, transportation, North American Indians. **Special collections:** Black Hills State University Archives; Leland D. Case Library for Western Historical Studies; Library of American Civilization (microfiche); Wagner-Camp Collection (microcard); Cox Library (microfilm). **Holdings:** 12,607 volumes; 949 manuscript boxes; 54 VF drawers; 85 drawers of maps and photographs; 12,888 titles on 14,548 microforms. **Subscriptions:** 60 journals and other serials; 7 newspapers. **Services:** Copying; collections open to the public with restrictions. **Computerized services:** OCLC.

Dacotah Prairie Museum
Archives

21 S. Main St.   Phone: (605)622-7117
Box 395   Fax: (605)225-6094
Aberdeen, SD 57402-0395 Merry Coleman, Director

Staff: 5.5. **Founded:** 1969. **Subjects:** History of Brown County and the northeastern region of South Dakota, 1797 to present. **Holdings:** Ledgers; photographs; school records; oral histories; records of organizations and businesses; letters and manuscripts of missionaries in the area, 1860–1880. **Services:** Copying; archives open to the public by appointment. **Computerized services:** Internal databases.

South Dakota State Historical Society
Office of History
South Dakota State Archives

900 Governors Dr.   Phone: (605)773-3804
Pierre, SD 57501   Fax: (605)773-6041
                        Linda M. Sommer, State
                        Archivist

Staff: Professional 4; Other 4. **Founded:** 1986. **Subjects:** South Dakota history, culture and government; Great Plains; government administration. **Holdings:** 26,000 volumes; 6000 cubic feet of records; 70 cubic feet of photographs; 12,000 maps. **Subscriptions:** 174 journals and other serials; 140 newspapers. **Services:** Interlibrary loan; copying; office open to the public. **Computerized services:** OCLC.

South Dakota State Library

800 Governors Dr.   Phone: (605)773-3131
Pierre, SD 57501-2294   Fax: (605)773-4950
                        Jane Kolbe, State Librarian

Staff: Professional 10; Other 33.5. **Founded:** 1913. **Subjects:** General collection. **Special collections:** South Dakota; large print books; South Dakota documents; Native Americans (particularly Lakota). **Holdings:** 160,190 volumes; 192,961 documents; 6147 pictures; 581 maps; 8147 films, filmstrips, videotapes, and other media; 34,000 talking book titles; 481,775 microfiche; 8294 reels of microfilm. **Subscriptions:** 1244 journals and other serials; 32 newspapers. **Services:** Interlibrary loan; copying; library open to the public. **Computerized services:** DIALOG Information Services, PFDS Online, InfoPro Technologies, ALANET, OCLC, RLIN, Western Library Network (WLN); Internet (electronic mail service). **Remarks:** Electronic mail address: SDSL@ CHARLIE.USD.EDU (Internet). **Publications:** *South Dakota State Government Publications.*

Tennessee

Chattanooga-Hamilton County
Bicentennial Library
Local History and Genealogical Collections

1001 Broad Street   Phone: (615)757-5317
Chattanooga, TN 37402   Clara W. Swann, Department
                        Head

Staff: Prof. 1; Other 4. **Founded:** 1888. **Subjects:** Southeast U.S. genealogy; local and state history. **Holdings:** 25,047 books; 312

manuscript collections; 160 VF drawers of clippings and photographs; 9,448 reels of microfilm of county records and local newspapers; 8,793 microfiche. **Subscriptions:** 128 journals and other serials. **Services:** Copying; collections open to the public for reference use only. **Computerized services:** Computerized cataloging; OCLC; member of SOLINET. **Special indexes:** Family surname index for materials in the department (card); local newspaper obituary indexes, 1897 to present.

Lawson McGhee Library

500 West Church Avenue   Phone: (615)544-5744
Knoxville, TN 37902   Steve Cotham, Head

Staff: Prof. 4; Other 9. **Founded:** 1921. **Subjects:** History and genealogy of Knoxville, Knox County, Tennessee and other southern states. **Special collections:** Knoxville and Tennessee newspapers, 1791 to present; 1982 World's Fair Archives (750,000 manuscripts); local architectural plans; Thompson Photographic Collection. **Holdings:** 35,416 books; 4,173 BPV; 1 million manuscripts; 1,341 maps; 8,948 reels of microfilm; 33,854 microfiche; 135 VF drawers of photographs and clippings. **Subscriptions:** 240 journals and other serials; 10 newspapers. **Services:** Copying; collection open to the public for reference only. **Computerized services:** Member of SOLINET. **Special catalogs:** *A Guide to the Manuscript Collections of the Calvin M. McClung Historical Collection of Knox County Public Library System.* **Remarks:** Collection located in East Tennessee Historical Center, 314 W. Clinch Ave., Knoxville, TN 37902-2203. The East Tennessee Historical Society, organized in 1925, has its headquarters in the East Tennessee Historical Center as well; gifts to the Society become part of the McClung Collection's holdings.

Memphis-Shelby County Public Library and
Information Center
Memphis Room Collections

1850 Peabody Avenue   Phone: (901)725-8821
Memphis, TN 38104-4025   Fax: (901)725-8883
                         James R. Johnson, Head

Staff: Prof. 8; Other 6. **Subjects:** Memphis/Shelby County, genealogy, Mardi Gras/Cotton Carnival, yellow fever, Blues and Beale Street, Mississippi steamboats. **Special collections:** Many, including Memphis/Shelby County Archives (18,000 volumes), Wassell Randolph Genealogical Collection, E.M. Sharp Genealogical Collection, Ida Cooper Genealogical and Historical papers. **Holdings:** 11,120 books; 1,250 bound periodical volumes; 1,200 maps; 500,000 newspaper clippings; 11,000 photographs; 3,000 pages of oral history transcripts; 250 manuscript collections; 7,500 reels of microfilm. **Subscriptions:** 135 journals and other serials. **Services:** Interlibrary loan; copying; collections open to the public. **Special catalogs:** Several. **Special indexes:** Indexed guide to the collections; index to Shelby County Probate Records, 1820–1876; to Memphis City Council minutes, 1826–1855; to oral histories; to Memphis newspapers, 1975–1989; to death records, 1848–1939; marriage records, 1820–1976. **Remarks:** Maintains the second largest genealogical collection in the state.

Nashville and Davidson County Public
Library
Metro Archives

1113 Elm Hill Pike
Nashville, TN 37210-3505

Remarks: Maintains extensive genealogical collection.

Nashville and Davidson County Public Library
Nashville Room

Eighth Avenue North and
  Union
Nashville, TN 37203-3585

Remarks: Maintains extensive genealogical collection.

Tennessee State Library and Archives

403 7th Ave. N
Nashville, TN 37243-0312

Phone: (615)741-7996
Fax: (615)741-6471
Edwin S. Gleaves Ph.D.,
  Librarian & Archivist

Staff: Professional 32; Other 52. **Founded:** 1854. **Subjects:** Tennesseana, U.S. and local history, state and local government, law and public administration, genealogy. **Special collections:** Papers of Jacob McGavock Dickinson, James Robertson, Andrew Jackson, George P. Buell, Henry Shelton Sanford, Richard Ewell; land records, 1777–1903 (600 volumes); state agency records and governors' papers, 1796 to present; legislative records and recordings, 1796 to present; state Supreme Court records, 1815–1955; Owsley Charts, records of farms, slaves, and equipment for Tennessee and other states in the south from the federal censuses of 1840, 1850, and 1860; petitions to Tennessee State Legislature 1796–1869; voter registration rolls; county records on microfilm; Tennessee newspapers. **Holdings:** 526,193 books; 4 million manuscript items; 22 million archival documents; 127,647 reels of microfilm; 265,193 sheets of microfiche; 47,774 audiotapes; 103,927 photographs. **Subscriptions:** 1541 periodicals; 200 newspapers on 34,670 reels of microfilm. **Services:** Interlibrary loan; copying; library open to the public. **Computerized services:** OCLC (Online Computer Library Center). **Special indexes:** Index to City Cemetery Records of Nashville; Index to Questionnaires of Civil War Veterans. **Publications:** *List of Tennessee State Publications*, quarterly; *Writings on Tennessee Counties*; *Tennessee Newspapers on Microfilm*; producers of manuscript materials; checklist of microfilm; *Guide to the Processed Manuscripts of the Tennessee Historical Society*; *Guide to Microfilm Holdings of the Manuscripts Section*. **Remarks:** The Manuscript Division is located in the archive's 7th Ave. building.

Texas

Dallas Public Library
J. Erik Jonsson Central Library
Genealogy Collection

1515 Young St.
Dallas, TX 75201

Phone: (214)670-1433
Lloyd DeWitt Bockstruck,
  Supervisor, Genealogy
  Section

Staff: Professional 1; Other 7. **Subjects:** Genealogy, heraldry, onomatology, local history. **Holdings:** 59,533 books; 26,530 reels of microfilm; 1237 microcards; 46,372 microfiche. **Subscriptions:** 700 journals and other serials. **Services:** Copying; collection open to the public.

Houston Public Library
Clayton Library
Center for Genealogical Research

5300 Caroline St.
Houston, TX 77004-6896

Phone: (713)524-0101
Maxine Alcorn, Manager

Staff: Professional 8; Other 10. **Founded:** 1921. **Subjects:** Genealogy. **Special collections:** Federal census, 1790–1900 (complete), 1910 (complete); 1900 Soundex (complete); 1910 Soundex (partial); military records; state and colonial records; county records; family histories. **Holdings:** 40,000 books; 2000 bound periodical volumes; 35,000 reels of microfilm; 50,000 microfiche; VF material. **Subscriptions:** 285 journals and other serials. **Services:** Copying; center open to the public. **Publications:** In-house Finding Aids.

Panhandle-Plains Historical Museum
Research Center

Box 967, WT. Sta.
Canyon, TX 79016

Phone: (806)656-2260
Fax: (806)656-2250
Claire R. Kuehn, Archivist/
  Librarian

Staff: Professional 2; Other 2. **Founded:** 1932. **Subjects:** Texas and Southwest history; ranching; Indians of the Great Plains; archeology of Texas Panhandle; ethnology; clothing and textiles; fine arts; antiques; museum science. **Special collections:** Interviews with early settlers and other citizens collected over a period of 63 years. **Holdings:** 16,000 books; 13,000 cubic feet of manuscripts; 20 VF drawers of pamphlets; 800 maps; 1600 reels of microfilm; 45 cubic feet of manufacturers' trade literature; 300,000 historic photographs. **Subscriptions:** 250 journals and other serials; 12 newspapers. **Services:** Copying; center open to the public. **Special indexes:** Index to the Panhandle-Plains Historical Review (card); Index to the Canyon (Texas) News. **Remarks:** Center is the Regional Historical Resource Depository for noncurrent county documents for 24 Texas Panhandle counties (a Texas State Library program).

San Augustine Public Library

413 E Columbia
San Augustine, TX 75972

Southmost College
Arnulfo L. Oliveira Memorial Library

Hunter Room
83 Fort Brown
Brownsville, TX 78520

Southwest Genealogical Society and Library

412 W College St., A
Carthage, TX 75633-1406

Texas State Library
State Archives Division
Sam Houston Regional Library and
Research Center

PO Box 310   Phone: (409)336-8821
Liberty, TX 77575-0310   Robert L. Schaadt, Director/
                                                Archivist

Staff: Professional 2; Other 5. **Founded:** 1977. **Subjects:** Southeast Texas history. **Special collections:** Journal of Jean Laffite; Herbert Bolton's manuscript for Athanase de Mezieres & the Louisiana-Texas Frontier, 1768–1780; French Colony Champ D'Asile, 1819; Tidelands Papers; early Texas newspapers, 1846–1860; Jean Houston Baldwin Collection of Sam Houston (591 items); private executive record of President of the Republic of Texas Sam Houston, 1841–1844 (1 volume); early Texas maps; Trinity River papers (8 feet); H.O. Compton Surveyors Books; Captain William M. Logan Papers; O'Brien Papers; Hardin Papers (52 feet); Julia Duncan Welder Collection (150 feet); family photograph collections; original and microfilm material from the 10 counties of the old Atascosito District of Southeast Texas, 1826–1960; Encino Press Collection; Carl Hertzog books; many individual family papers and collections. **Holdings:** 9729 books; 859 reels of microfilm; 20,029 photographs; 16,000 cubic feet of manuscripts, government records, and archives; county records. **Subscriptions:** 17 journals and other serials; 9 newspapers. **Services:** Interlibrary loan (microfilm only); copying; center open to the public. **Special indexes:** Llerena B. Friend card index on Sam Houston; inventories of collections in books. **Publications:** *Sam Houston Regional Library and Research Center News*, 2/year.

University of Texas at Austin
Center for American History

General Libraries, SRH 2.101   Phone: (512)495-4515
Austin, TX 78713-7330   Fax: (512)495-4542
                          Dr. Don E. Carleton, Director

Staff: Prof. 8; Other 15. **Subjects:** Texas history, literature, and folklore; Texas state documents; University of Texas publications and history; Southern and Western history. **Special collections:** Sound archives (2352 audiocassettes; 29,995 phonograph records; 4964 audiotapes; 1028 videocassettes; 85 videotapes); dime novel collection; Kell Frontier Collection; Austin papers; Bexar Archives; Bryan papers; T.S. Henderson papers; James S. Hogg papers; Ashbel Smith papers; John Henry Faulk papers; Pompeo Coppini-Waldine Tauch papers; Jesse Jones papers; James Wells papers; Martin M. Crane papers; Luther M. Evans collection; James Harper Starr papers; James Farmer papers; True West Archives; Field Foundation Archives; Natchez Trace Collection; Russell Lee Photograph Collection; R.C. Hickman Photograph Collection; Robert Runyon Photograph Collection. **Holdings:** 147,917 volumes; 3000 linear feet of university records; 34,987 linear feet of manuscripts and archives; 29,736 maps; 3,800 titles of historic Texas and Southern newspapers; 767,326 photographs; 12,387 slides; 100 VF drawers of clippings; 1500 scrapbooks; 22,223 reels of microfilm; 1501 microfiche; 4293 tapes of oral recordings. **Subscriptions:** 548 periodicals; 673 other serials. **Services:** Interlibrary loan; copying; center open to the public. **Formerly:** University of Texas at Austin-Barker Texas History Center. **Remarks:** Publishers newsletter, archives guide, and library guide.

Utah

Brigham Young University
Harold B. Lee Library

Provo, UT 84602   Phone: (801)378-4995

Description: Third largest collection of genealogical materials in the U.S.A.

Southern Utah University
Library
Special Collections Department

351 W. Center St.   Phone: (801)586-7945
Cedar City, UT 84720   Blanche C. Clegg, Archivist/
                                                Curator

Staff: Professional 1; Other 6. **Founded:** 1962. **Subjects:** Southern Paiute Indians history, local history, college history, Shakespeare. **Special collections:** William Rees Palmer Western History Collection; Document Collection (various donors); Howard Smith Collection; Homer Jones Photo Collection. **Holdings:** 7000 volumes; 925 oral history tapes; 457 phonograph records; 1445 linear feet of manuscript collections; 51,000 photographs and negatives; 804 linear feet of archives; 7530 microforms; 1743 maps. **Services:** Interlibrary loan; copying; department open to the public for reference use only. **Computerized services:** DIALOG Information Services; internal database. **Special indexes:** Document collection index; oral history index; photo collection index; index to Palmer Western History Collection.

Utah State Archives

Archives Bldg.   Phone: (801)538-3012
State Capitol   Fax: (801)538-3354
Salt Lake City, UT 84114   Jeffery O. Johnson, Director

Staff: Professional 16; Other 19. **Founded:** 1951. **Subjects:** Public records of the State of Utah and its political subdivisions. **Special collections:** Military records. **Holdings:** 85,000 cubic feet of semi-active and historically valuable records; 85,000 cubic feet of records in paper copy; 95,000 reels of microfilm; 90,000 microfiche. **Subscriptions:** 35 journals and other serials; 2 newspapers. **Services:** Copying; archives open to the public. **Computerized services:** RLIN. **Special catalogs:** Records Series Catalog. **Publications:** *Records Retention Schedule*.

Utah State Historical Society
Library

300 Rio Grande   Phone: (801)533-3536
Salt Lake City, UT   Fax: (801)533-3503
  84101-1182

Staff: Professional 5. **Founded:** 1952. **Subjects:** History—Utah, Mormon, Western, Indian. **Holdings:** 25,000 books; 50,000 bound periodical volumes; 500,000 photographs; 22,000 pamphlets; 33,000 maps; 1500 oral history tapes; 3500 linear feet of manuscripts; 6000 reels of microfilm; 160 feet of clippings files; 5500 museum objects. **Subscriptions:** 220 journals and other serials. **Services:** Copying; library open to the public. **Computerized services:** RLIN. **Special indexes:** Utah History Index (card). **Publications:** *Guide to Unpublished Materials*.

Utah State Library

2150 South 300 West, Ste. 16   Phone: (801)466-5888
Salt Lake City, UT 84115   Fax: (801)533-4657
    Amy Owen, Director

Staff: Professional 15; Other 12. **Founded:** 1957. **Subjects:** State and federal government. **Holdings:** 39,811 volumes; 49,987 federal documents; 25,892 state documents. **Subscriptions:** 105 journals and other serials. **Services:** Interlibrary loan; library open to the public with restrictions. **Computerized services:** DIALOG Information Services, OCLC, FirstSearch, Mead Data Central, Deseret News; Internet (electronic mail service). **Remarks:** Electronic mail address: lgr@usl.gov (Internet). **Publications:** *Utah Undercover*, annual; *Directory of Public Libraries in Utah*, annual.

Vermont

Vermont State Agency of Administration Department of General Services Public Records Division

Drawer 33   Phone: (802)828-3700
Montpelier, VT 05633-7601   Fax: (802)828-3710
    A. John Yacavoni, Director

Staff: Professional 1; Other 17. **Subjects:** Vermont town and city land records prior to 1900s, Vermont town vital records prior to 1875, Vermont probate record volumes prior to 1850. **Special collections:** Field forms and draft material of Historical Records Survey inventories of Vermont town records and church records; Vermont Vital Record File, 1760–1982. **Holdings:** 1642 boxes of archival holdings; 31,990 reels of microfilm; 246,921 microfiche; 46,152 boxes of semiactive records center material. **Services:** Copying; division open to the public.

Vermont State Archives

26 Terrace St.   Phone: (802)828-2308
Montpelier, VT 05602   Fax: (802)828-2496
    D. Gregory Sanford, State
    Archivist

Staff: Professional 2; Other 1. **Founded:** 1777. **Subjects:** Governors' official papers, legislative records, election records, surveyors' general papers, original acts and resolves, Vermont state papers, (1744 to present), municipal charters. **Special collections:** Stevens Collection of Vermontiana (60 feet); Houston Studio/Country Camera Photograph Collection. **Holdings:** 500 books; 250 volumes of bound manuscripts; 60 volumes of maps, surveys, and charters; 1700 cubic feet of government records. **Services:** Copying; archives open to the public. **Computerized services:** Minaret (internal database). **Special catalogs:** Inventories for manuscript collections. **Publications:** *State Papers of Vermont.*

Virginia

Virginia State Library and Archives

11th St. at Capitol Square   Phone: (804)786-8929
Richmond, VA 23219   Fax: (804)225-4035
    Dr. John C. Tyson, State
    Librarian

Staff: Professional 71; Other 65. **Founded:** 1823. **Subjects:** Virginiana, Southern and Confederate history, genealogy, social sciences, U.S. colonial history. **Special collections:** Population schedules; special census 1890; Virginia newspapers; Virginia public records; Virginia maps; Confederate imprints. **Holdings:** 640,549 volumes; 86,576 maps; 50,591 cubic feet of manuscripts; 15,522 microforms. **Subscriptions:** 896 journals and other serials; 104 newspapers. **Services:** Interlibrary loan; copying; library open to the public. **Computerized services:** OCLC, RLIN; Virginia Tech Library System (internal database); ALANET (electronic mail service). **Special catalogs:** CAVALIR, statewide union list (microfiche and CD-ROM). **Remarks:** Electronic mail address: ALA1166 (ALANET). **Publications:** *Virginia Cavalcade*, quarterly, available by subscription; *Virginia State Library Publications*, available by subscription and exchange; *Directory of Virginia Libraries*—free.

Washington

Family History Center, Bellevue

10675 NE 20th St.   Phone: (206)454-2690
Bellevue, WA 98004

Description: Branch of the Family History Library of the Church of Jesus Christ of Latter-day Saints. **Subjects:** Genealogy, family history, church and civil records, local history. **Remarks:** Access to main library microfilm.

Family History Center, Seattle

5701 8th Ave. NE   Phone: (206)522-1233
Seattle, WA 98105

Description: Branch of the Family History Library of the Church of Jesus Christ of Latter-day Saints. **Subjects:** Genealogy, family history, church and civil records, local history. **Remarks:** Access to main library microfilm.

Family History Center, Seattle

14022 SW Ambaum Blvd.   Phone: (206)243-4028
Seattle, WA 98166

Description: Branch of the Family History Library of the Church of Jesus Christ of Latter-day Saints. **Subjects:** Genealogy, family history, church and civil records, local history. **Remarks:** Access to main library microfilm.

Lewis County Historical Museum Library

599 NW Front Way   Phone: (206)748-0831
Chehalis, WA 98532   Brenda A. O'Connor, Director

Staff: Professional 3; Other 4. **Founded:** 1978. **Subjects:** History of Lewis County, Chehalis Indians, genealogy. **Special collections:** *Chehalis Bee-Nuggett*, 1883–1930; Lewis County cemetery history; Chehalis Indian Archival Files; genealogy research books and records; Ernst Bechley History Collection; Lewis County voting records, 1870–1930; *Daily Chronicle* newspapers, 1930–1964. **Holdings:** 12,000 photographs; 400 oral history cassette tapes; 36 feet of archival papers and newspaper clippings; 3 feet of family histories; 200 maps. **Subscriptions:** 400 journals and other serials. **Services:** Family research upon request; copies and transcripts of oral history tapes; library open to the public—must have staff present. **Special indexes:** Photograph index by subject; index of oral histories by subject (both card); index to obituary files. **Publications:** Periodical Genealogy & History books; *Lewis County Log*, quarterly—to members.

Seattle Public Library Humanities Department

1000 4th Ave.   Phone: (206)386-4625
Seattle, WA 98104   Fax: (206)386-4632
      Norma Arnold, Managing
      Librarian

Staff: Professional 13; Other 14. **Founded:** 1891. **Subjects:** History, politics, biography, travel, law, literature, languages, philosophy, religion, poetry, fiction, government, general bibliography. **Special collections:** Northwest history; Genealogy Collection; maps. **Holdings:** 452,000 books, and bound periodical volumes; microrecords; newspapers. **Subscriptions:** 1657 journals and other serials; 129 newspapers. **Services:** Interlibrary loan; copying; CD-ROM stations for public use; department open to the public. **Computerized services:** DIALOG Information Services. Performs searches free of charge. **Special indexes:** Northwest Index (300 drawers, subject index of local newspapers).

Skagit County Historical Museum Historical Reference Library

501 S. 4th St.   Phone: (206)466-3365
PO Box 818   Mari Anderson-Densmore,
La Conner, WA 98257   Librarian

Staff: Professional 7. **Founded:** 1959. **Subjects:** Skagit County—history, statistics, demographics, industry, social, economic, community life, transportation; pioneer family genealogies; local Indian histories. **Special collections:** Diaries of Grant Sisson, W.J. Cornelius, Arthur Champenois, and others, 1844–1964; Darius Kinsey Photographs. **Holdings:** 1500 books; 308 bound periodical volumes; 8000 photographs; 700 newspapers; 700 business documents; 200 letters; 200 district school accounts/records; 100 maps; 700 clippings and clipping scrapbooks; 300 programs/announcements; 80 pioneer diaries; 220 oral history tapes with transcripts; American popular music, 1866–1954; local newspapers, 1900 to present. **Subscriptions:** 4 journals and other serials; 7 newspapers. **Services:** Copying; library open to the public by appointment. **Publications:** Newsletter.

Society of Jesus, Oregon Province Archives

Foley Center, Gonzaga   Phone: (509)328-4220
   University   Fax: (509)484-2804
E. 502 Boone Ave.   Stephanie Edwards
Spokane, WA 99258

Staff: 1. **Founded:** 1931. **Subjects:** History—Northwest Church, Alaska Church and missions, Doukhobor, local; Alaskan and Indian languages. **Special collections:** Joset Papers; Cataldo Papers; Crimont Papers; Neil Byrne Papers; Monaghan Papers; Cowley Papers; Prando Papers; Jesuit Mission Papers. **Holdings:** 3600 books; 800 bound periodical volumes; 123,000 manuscripts; 25,000 photographs. **Subscriptions:** 35 journals and other serials; 18 newspapers. **Services:** Copying; library open to those with scholarly credentials. **Publications:** *Guides to Microfilm Editions of the Oregon Province Archives of the Society of Jesus Indian Language Collection: (1) The Alaska Native Languages; (2) The Pacific Northwest Tribes; The Alaska Mission Papers; Guide to Microfilm Editions of Papers on Pacific Northwest Jesuit Missions & Missionaries.*

University of Washington East Asia Library

322 Gowen Hall, DO-27   Phone: (206)543-4490
Seattle, WA 98195   Fax: (206)685-8049
      Min-chih Chou, Head

Staff: Prof. 7; Other 6.5. **Founded:** 1937. **Subjects:** Social sciences, humanities, literature and language, history, religion and philosophy, arts. **Special collections:** Works in Chinese, Japanese, Korean, Tibetan, Vietnamese, Mongolian, and Manchu. **Holdings:** 377,201 volumes; 11,777 reels of microfilm; 7563 microfiche; 4589 pamphlets. **Subscriptions:** 2830 serials. **Services:** Interlibrary loan; copying; library open to the public for reference use only. **Computerized services:** OCLC, LC MARC: Contributed CJK Books; InterNet (electronic mail service). **Publications:** *Twenty-five Dynastic Histories Full Text Retrieval Database; Current Japanese Serials in East Asia Library; Current Korean Serials in East Asia Library.* **Special catalogs:** University of Washington East Asia Library 1990 catalog of yearbooks on China.

Washington State Library

PO Box 42460   Phone: (206)753-5590
Olympia, WA 98504-2460   Fax: (206)586-7575
      Nancy Zussy, State Librarian

Staff: Professional 58; Other 70. **Founded:** 1853. **Subjects:** Public administration, applied sciences, medicine and health, behavioral sciences, transportation, ecology, energy. **Special collections:** Pacific Northwest History (13,906 items). **Holdings:** 409,988 books; 75,750 bound periodical volumes; 1.56 million U.S. documents; 117,297 Washington state documents; 20,534 other state documents; 42,734 reels of microfilm; 483,069 microfiche; 26 VF drawers; 8744 AV titles, including 16mm films. **Subscriptions:** 7550 journals and other serials; 160 newspapers. **Services:** Interlibrary loan; copying; library open to the public. **Computerized services:** DIALOG Information Services, OCLC; ALANET (electronic mail service). **Special catalogs:** Periodicals Holdings (microfiche). **Remarks:** Electronic mail address: WSLADMIN ALA0719 (ALANET). **Publications:** List of publications—available on request.

Washington State Office of Secretary of State
Division of Archives and Record Management

Archives & Records Center
12th & Washington
Olympia, WA 98504

Phone: (206)753-5485
Fax: (206)664-8814
Sidney McAlpin, State Archivist

Staff: Professional 12; Other 12. **Founded:** 1909. **Subjects:** State and local government records. **Special collections:** Land records, 1858 to present. **Holdings:** 8000 bound public records; 50,000 cubic feet of state and local archives; 165,000 cubic feet of records; 200,000 reels of security microfilm. **Services:** Copying; research; division open to the public. **Computerized services:** Gencat Archival Control System (internal database). **Remarks:** Territorial District Court records and other county records are held at five regional depositories operated by the division. **Publications:** *General Guide to the Washington State Archives*; list of other publications—available on request.

West Virginia

West Virginia (State) Division of Culture and History
Archives and History Library

1900 Kanawha Blvd. E.
Charleston, WV 25305-0300

Phone: (304)558-0220
Fax: (304)558-2779
Fredrick H. Armstrong, Director

Staff: Professional 6; Other 7. **Founded:** 1905. **Subjects:** West Virginia archives, history, genealogy; history—U.S., Civil War, colonial, military. **Special collections:** Mortality and population schedules; special census 1890; manuscripts (1510 linear feet); agency records; state documents (22,200); county court records (6620 reels of microfilm); newspapers (16,900 reels of microfilm and clippings); military and land records (2500 reels of microfilm). **Holdings:** 35,800 books; 5,400 bound periodical volumes; 7050 linear feet of state archives; 180 linear feet of special collections; 28,056 reels of microfilm; 65,000 photographs; 6000 maps; 24 VF drawers of clippings. **Subscriptions:** 135 journals and other serials; 95 newspapers. **Services:** Copying; library open to the public for reference use only. **Publications:** *West Virginia History*, annual; Checklist of State Publications, semiannual.

Wisconsin

State Historical Society of Wisconsin
Archives Division

816 State St.
Madison, WI 53706

Phone: (608)264-6450
Fax: (608)264-6472
Peter Gottlieb, State Archivist

Staff: Professional 17; Other 9. **Founded:** 1846. **Subjects:** Wisconsin history; American frontier, 1750–1815; labor and industrial relations; socialism; mass communications; theater; agricul-

tural history; civil rights; contemporary social action movements. **Special collections:** Draper Collection (frontier). **Holdings:** 53,141 cubic feet of Wisconsin state and local public records; 42,670 cubic feet of nongovernmental archives and manuscripts; 15,000 unbound maps; 2000 atlases; 500 titles on 3100 audiotapes; 110 titles on 3500 phonograph records; 1.5 million visual materials; 50 machine-readable data files of state government records. **Services:** Copying; photo and film reproduction and dubbing of recordings for television. **Computerized services:** RLIN; Internet (electronic mail service). **Remarks:** Electronic mail address: Peter.Gottlieb@MAIL.ADMIN.WISC.EDU (Internet). Administers the Wisconsin Area Research Center Network. **Publications:** Accession reports in *Wisconsin Magazine of History*, quarterly; guides and inventories.

State Historical Society of Wisconsin
Library

816 State St.
Madison, WI 53706-1482

Phone: (608)264-6534
Fax: (608)264-6520
R. David Myers, Director

Staff: Professional 20; Other 13. **Founded:** 1846. **Subjects:** History—American, Canadian, Wisconsin, local, labor; radical/reform movements and groups in the U.S. and Canada; ethnic and minority groups in North America; genealogy; women's history; military history; religious history. **Special collections:** African American History Collection (newspapers; periodicals); Native American History Collection (12,000 items; government documents; Native American publications); Lyman Draper Collection of correspondence, etc. gathered by Draper, former director of the Historical Society, which contains a great deal of information about Indian leaders and frontiersmen. **Holdings:** 1.6 million books and bound periodical volumes; 100,000 cubic feet of archives; 1.4 million microfiche and reels of microfilm. **Subscriptions:** 8500 periodicals; 500 newspapers. **Services:** Interlibrary loan; copying; library open to the public. **Computerized services:** OCLC; CD-ROMs; America: History & Life (internal database); Internet (electronic mail service). **Special indexes:** Indian Culture and History (micoform); Index to Wisconsin Native American Periodicals, 1897–1981; Index to names in Wisconsin federal census, 1820–1870 and 1905 state census; Wisconsin necrology index; index of names in Wisconsin county histories. **Remarks:** Electronic mail address: maureen.hady@mail.admin.wisc.edu (Internet). The library is said to be the largest in the world devoted to North American history. This library is a U.S. Federal Government regional depository, a Wisconsin State official depository, and a Canadian Federal Government selective depository for government publications. **Publications:** *Native American Periodicals and Newspapers, 1828–1982*; *Wisconsin Public Documents* (checklist of state government documents)—free upon request; bibliographies; guides.

Outside the U.S.

Family History Center, British Columbia

5280 Kincaid
Burnaby, BC, Canada

Phone: (604)299-8656

Description: Branch of the Family History Library of the Church of Jesus Christ of Latter-day Saints. **Subjects:** Genealogy, family history, church and civil records, local history. **Remarks:** Access to main library microfilm.

Genealogical Research Library

20 Toronto St., 8th Fl.
Toronto, ON, Canada M5C
2B8

Description: Genealogical materials available for research.

National Central Library

60-1 Banpo-dong   Phone: 82-2-838-4142
Feicho-gu
Seoul 137-702, Republic of
Korea

Description: Contains printed genealogies, examination rosters, dynastic records, and other information on Korean families.

Seoul National Library
Royal National Library

Shinrim-Dang
Kwanak-Gu
Seoul 151, Republic of Korea

Description: Contains royal records of the Yi dynasty. **Also known as:** In Korean, Changsogak.

Private and Public Organizations

⊘ This chapter lists those organizations of national and state significance which can provide assistance to those doing genealogical research, and a description of their various activities and services. They are arranged here categorically by scope; national/ regional, followed by state listings. Organizations which either have an international scope or are located outside of the United States, if present, appear at the end of the chapter. All listings are arranged alphabetically within each category.

commissioner of the Bureau of Refugees, Freedmen, and Abandoned Lands, records for the emancipation of slaves in the District of Columbia, naturalizations of foreign protestants in American and West Indian colonies. **Publications:** Three catalogs: vol. I lists all U.S. Federal Population Census Schedules; vol. II covers military and ship passenger lists; and vol. III lists locality, surname, ethnic, and special collections, $12.50 each or $30.00 for set.

National and Regional

Alice's Ancestral Nostalgia

PO Box 510092
Salt Lake City, UT 84151

Description: Genealogical materials available for sale.

American Antiquarian Society (AAS)

185 Salisbury St.   Phone: (508)755-5221
Worcester, MA 01609-1634   Ellen S. Dunlap, President

Staff: 45. **Description:** Gathers, preserves, and promotes serious study of the materials of early American history and life. Maintains research library of nearly 5 million books, pamphlets, broadsides, manuscripts, prints, maps, and newspapers; the collection specializes in the period of American history through 1876. Sponsors fellowships, educational programs, and research. **Founded:** 1812. **Members:** 564.

American Genealogical Lending Library (AGLL)

PO Box 244   Phone: (801)298-5358
Dept. M
Bountiful, UT 84011

Description: State-by-state genealogical materials available for rent. Over 100,000 items available on film or fiche. **Remarks:** $2.75 per roll or fiche title for a full month. Rolls can also be purchased. Holdings include U.S. census records, military records, ship passenger lists, Indian censuses, Indian claims, Indian payment and annuity rolls, enrollment cards of the five civilized tribes (1898–1914), other Indian records, state mortality schedules, slave schedules, Freedman's Savings and Trust Company records, Negro military service records, records issued by the

Ark-La-Tex Genealogical Association (ALTGA)

PO Box 4462   Phone: (318)687-3673
Shreveport, LA 71134-0462   Victor Rose, President

Description: Genealogists whose interests lie in the South, especially in the states of Arkansas, Louisiana, and Texas. Purposes are to collect, preserve, and make available genealogical materials, documents, and records; to encourage interest in genealogy and to sponsor educational programs for its development; to promote and publicize the city of Shreveport, LA, as a major genealogical research center for genealogists and historians interested in records of the Ark-La-Tex area; to cooperate with and assist all other genealogical-historical societies and libraries in furtherance of these purposes. Supports and contributes to the Genealogy Room of the Shreve Memorial Library in Shreveport, LA. **Founded:** 1955. **Members:** 500. **Publications:** *The Genie,* quarterly.

Association of Memoirists and Family Historians (AMFH)

PO Box 44268   Ethel Jackson Price, Director
Tucson, AZ 85733

Staff: 3. **Description:** Promotes genealogical and historical research and documentation of family history. Encourages interaction of generations through memoirs. Maintains biographical archive not open to the public. **Founded:** 1991. **Members:** 835. **Remarks:** Speakers bureau, children's services, research and educational programs. **Publications:** *The Linchpin,* quarterly newsletter containing book reviews, announcements of reunions, and genealogical search requests, $10.00/year, circulation: 835; annual directory.

Augustan Society Inc.

PO Box P
Torrance, CA 90501-0210

Publications: *Spanish-American Genealogist.*

Borderlands Bookstore

PO Box 28497
San Antonio, TX 78228

Description: Genealogical materials available for sale.

Buddhist Churches of America

1710 Octavia St.
San Francisco, CA 94109

Description: Headquarters of 59 branch temples across the United States. Resource for Buddhist death registers.

Bureau of the Census

Federal Office Building   Phone: (301)763-4040
3 Silver Hill & Suitland Rds.
Suitland, MD 20746

Description: Maintains census records.

Bureau of the Census
Personal Census Service Branch

1600 North Walnut Street   Phone: (316)231-7100
Pittsburg, KS 66762

Description: Searches the confidential records from the Federal population censuses and issues official transcripts of the results for a fee. Transcripts may contain information on a person's age, state or country of birth, relationship to householder, etc. **Remarks:** A BC-600 form, *Application for Search of Census Records,* providing the name of the household head and geographic location of the household is required for each search and is available from the Pittsburgh office, the Census History Staff in Washington, D.C. (telephone 301-763-7936), or any of the Census Bureau Regional Offices in Atlanta; Boston; Charlotte, NC; Chicago; Dallas; Denver; Detroit; Kansas City, KS; New York; Philadelphia; Seattle, WA; or Los Angeles, CA. Information services specialists are available to answer inquiries about census publications and other Bureau products. Fee is $25.00 for a search of not more than two censuses. Searches may take two months. Applicant must be a direct blood relative, surviving spouse, executor of the estate, or a beneficiary of a deceased person and must provide proof of death if birth date of ancestor is less than 100 years ago.

Closson Press

1935 Sampson Dr.
Apollo, PA 15613

Description: Genealogical materials available for sale.

Everton Publishers, Inc.

PO Box 368
Logan, UT 84321

Description: Genealogical materials available for sale.

Family History Land

6061 E Broadway, Ste. 128
Tucson, AZ 85711-4020

Description: Genealogical materials available for sale.

Family Tree Genealogical Society

450 Potter St.   Phone: (419)335-6485
Wauseon, OH 43567   Howard V. Fausey, Editor

Description: Publishes *Family Tree Digest,* which features genealogical information and responses to queries on a national basis.

Frontier Press

15 Quintana Dr., Ste. 167
Galveston, TX 77554-9350

Description: Genealogical materials available for sale.

Genealogical Books in Print

6818 Lois Dr.
Springfield, VA 22150

Description: Genealogical materials available for sale.

Genealogical Publishing Co.

1001 N. Calvert St.
Baltimore, MD 21202-3897

Description: Genealogical materials available for sale.

Genealogy Books and Consultation

1217 Oakdale
Houston, TX 77004-5813

Description: Genealogical materials available for sale.

Genealogy Booksellers, Ltd.

208 George St.
Fredericksburg, VA 22401

Description: Genealogical materials available for sale.

Gensoft, Ltd.

13215-C SE Mill Plain, No.
   307
Vancouver, WA 98684

Description: Genealogical materials available for sale.

Heritage Books, Inc.

1540 E Pointer Ridge Pl.
Bowie, MD 20716

Description: Genealogical materials available for sale.

Higginson Book Co.

14 Derby Sq.
PO Box 778
Salem, MA 01970

Description: Genealogical materials available for sale.

Immigration and Naturalization Service

Chester A. Arthur Bldg.   Phone: (202)514-2783
425 Eye St. NW
Washington, DC 20001

Description: Maintains immigration records for genealogical research.

International Genealogical Fellowship of Rotarians (IFRG)

5721 Antietam Dr.   Phone: (813)924-9170
Sarasota, FL 34231   Charles D. Townsend,
                                               Secretary

Description: Interested in recreational, avocational, or vocational genealogy activities. Promotes increased understanding and goodwill through the exchange of genealogical backgrounds. Furthers interchange of genealogical research ideas; develops awareness of the need for open records to aid in family research. **Founded:** 1980. **Members:** 300. **Remarks:** Provides research assistance. Sponsors programs and speakers on the subject of genealogy and genealogical research. **Publications:** *Rota-Gene,* bimonthly magazine, includes queries, news notes, book reviews, location of genealogical records, and other research information, $15.00/year, ISSN: 0730-5168; brochure.

Japanese American Citizen's League (JACL)

1765 Sutter St.   Phone: (415)921-5225
San Francisco, CA 94115   Fax: (415)931-4671
                                      William Yoshino, National
                                                        Director

Staff: 24. **Description:** Educational, civil, and human rights organization. Works to defend the civil and human rights of all peoples, particularly Japanese Americans. Seeks to preserve the cultural and ethnic heritage of Japanese Americans. Resources include library and audiovisual materials. **Founded:** 1929. **Members:** 28,000. **Local groups:** 114. **Publications:** *Pacific Citizen,* weekly.

Korean National Association

545 S. Serrano Ave.   Phone: (213)735-0424
Los Angeles, CA 90020

Description: Promotes research into the history of Koreans in the United States. **Founded:** 1909. **Also known as:** In Korean, Kook Min Hoe.

Lineages

PO Box 417
Salt Lake City, UT 84110

Description: Genealogical materials available for sale.

Mountain Press

PO Box 400
Signal Mountain, TN
   37377-0400

Description: Genealogical materials available for sale.

Mountain Press Research Center

PO Box 400   Phone: (615)886-6369
Signal Mountain, TN   James L. Douthat, Owner
   37377-0400

Staff: 2. **Description:** Genealogical and historical research center. Promotes genealogical and historical research in the mid-Atlantic and Southeastern regions of the U.S. Provides research materials and information. Conducts workshops and training events. Maintains 4,500 volume library; arranges displays of genealogical and historical materials. **Founded:** 1980. **Members:** 30,000. **Publications:** *Appalachian Families,* quarterly; *Southern Genealogical Index,* quarterly; books.

National Genealogical Society (NGS)

4527 17th St. N   Phone: (703)525-0050
Arlington, VA 22207-2399   Fax: (703)525-0052

Description: Publishes *NGS Newletter* which features news of the Society and the genealogical community, articles on genealogical methods, sources, repositories, NGS's library acquisitions, and members' queries. Recurring features include a calendar of events.

R & M Publishing Co.

PO Box 1276   Phone: (803)738-0360
Holly Hill, SC 29059   Mack B. Morant, Publisher

Description: Publishes books for students and laypersons on U.S. history, politics, socio-psychology, curriculum development, art appreciation, and genealogy. Also offers a mailing list. Accepts unsolicited manuscripts. Reaches market through direct mail, trade sales: Baker & Taylor Books, Key Sea Press, and Quality Books, Inc.

Southern Historical Press, Inc.

PO Box 1267
Greenville, SC 29602-1267

Description: Genealogical materials available for sale.

Southern Society of Genealogists (SSG)

RFD 5, Box 12   Phone: (205)447-2939
Piedmont, AL 36272   Mrs. Frank Stewart, President

Staff: 1. **Description:** Genealogists; other individuals interested in southern families. Seeks to encourage genealogical research. Conducts seminars; maintains library. **Founded:** 1962. **Members:** 50. **Publications:** *SSG Bulletin,* annual. Also publishes a weekly column in the *Cherokee County Herald.*

Storbeck's Genealogy & Computers

16515 Dane Ct. E.
PO Box 891
Brookfield, WI 53008-0891

Description: Genealogical materials available for sale.

U.S. Department of State
Passport Services
Records Services

One McPherson Sq.   Phone: (202)326-6124
1425 K St., NW
Washington, DC 20005

Description: Maintains passport records for genealogical research.

Ye Olde Genealogie Shoppe

PO Box 39128
Indianapolis, IN 46239-3330

Description: Genealogical materials available for sale.

Alabama

Alabama Genealogical Society Inc.
American Genealogical Society Depository
and Headquarters
Samford University Library

Harwell G. Davis Library   Phone: (205)870-2749
Special Collections Dept.
800 Lakeshore Dr.
Birmingham, AL 35229

Alaska

Alaska Genealogical Society

7030 Dickerson Dr.
Anchorage, AK 99504

Anchorage Genealogical Society

c/o Barbara Samuels
PO Box 212265
Anchorage, AK 99521

Arizona

Arizona Society of Genealogists

6565 E Grand Rd.
Tucson, AZ 85715

Arizona State Genealogical Society

PO Box 42075
Tucson, AZ 85733-2075

Remarks: Holdings include some Mexican census records.

Family History Society of Arizona

PO Box 5566
Glendale, AZ 85312

Genealogical Society of Arizona

PO Box 27237
Tempe, AZ 85282

National Park Service
Hubbell Trading Post

PO Box 150
Ganado, AZ 86505

Arkansas

Arkansas Genealogical Society

PO Box 908   Phone: (501)262-4513
Hot Springs, AR 71902-0908

California

California Genealogical Society

300 Brannan St.   Phone: (415)777-9936
PO Box 77105   Frederick Sherman, President
San Francisco, CA
94107-0105

Staff: 2. **Description:** Oldest genealogical society in the state of California. Helps people trace and compile their own family histories. Gathers and preserves vital records, and provides education through meetings, seminars, workshops and Computer Interest Group. Maintains reference library open to public consisting of books, periodicals, clippings, and A/V material. Some coverage of African, Hispanic, Native, and Asian Americans on both a national and regional level. **Founded:** 1898. **Members:** 700. **Remarks:** Genealogical assistance, research, and educational programs. Annual Family History Fair. **Publications:** *Index to San Francisco Marriage Returns 1850 to 1858; Member Surnames; The Nugget,* semiannnual, ISSN: 1059-9711, circulation: 700; *CGS News,* bimonthly, circulation: 700; also publishes family history books and book reviews.

California State Genealogical Alliance

PO Box 401   Phone: (714)678-1231
Wildomar, CA 92595-0401

Chinese Culture Foundation of San
Francisco

750 Kearny St. 3rd Flr.
San Francisco, CA 94108

Professional Genealogists of California

5048 J Parkway
Sacramento, CA 95823

Remarks: Register professional genealogists. No archives.

Sonoma State University

1801 E Cotati Ave.
Rohnert Park, CA 94928

Remarks: Instrumental in the publishing of genealogical records of Sonoma County, including cemetery records.

Colorado

Colorado Council of Genealogical Societies

PO Box 24379
Denver, CO 80224-0379

Colorado Genealogical Society (CGS)

PO Box 18221   Phone: (303)333-3482
Denver, CO 80218   Sharon Boatwright, President

Description: Promotes genealogy in Colorado. Seeks to locate, preserve, and index historical records; assists and supports state libraries. Sponsors Black Sheep Writing Contest. **Founded:** 1924. **Members:** 471. **Affiliated with:** Colorado Council of Genealogical Societies; Colorado Preservation Alliance; Colorado Society of Archivists; Federation of Genealogical Societies; National Genealogical Society. **Publications:** *CGS Membership Directory,* annual; *CGS Newsletter,* 10/year; *Colorado Genealogist,* quarterly.

Connecticut

Connecticut Society of Genealogists (CSG)

PO Box 435   Phone: (203)569-0002
Glastonbury, CT 06033   Dorothy Armistead, President

Staff: 4. **Description:** Promotes genealogical research. **Founded:** 1968. **Members:** 4500. **Publications:** *Connecticut Nutmegger,* quarterly.

Florida

Florida Genealogical Society

PO Box 18624   Phone: (813)254-3045
Tampa, FL 33679-8624

Florida Society for Genealogical Research

8415 122nd St. N   Phone: (813)867-4735
Seminole, FL 34642   Dorothy M. Boyer, President

Description: Individuals interested in genealogical research. Maintains book collection and sponsors field trips. **Founded:** 1972. **Members:** 100. **Publications:** *Pinellas Genealogist,* periodic; newsletter.

Florida State Genealogical Society

PO Box 10249
Tallahassee, FL 32303-2249

Southern Genealogist's Exchange Society

PO Box 2801   Phone: (904)387-9142
Jacksonville, FL 32203   Faye Irvin, President

Description: Individuals interested in genealogy. Conducts seminars. **Founded:** 1967. **Members:** 225. **Publications:** *Newsletter,* bimonthly.

Georgia

Georgia Genealogical Society (GGS)

PO Box 54575   Phone: (404)475-4404
Atlanta, GA 30308-0575   Bonnie Dubberly, President

Founded: 1964. **Members:** 1,024. **Publications:** *The Cemetery Book: Cemetery Preservation, Restoration, and Recording; GGSQ,* quarterly, comes with membership; *Newsletter,* quarterly; *Subject Index to 25 Years of the GGS Quarterly, 1964-1989;* and several others.

Hawaii

Diocese of Honolulu, Chancery Office

1184 Bishop St.
Honolulu, HI 96813

Description: Contains church records of those immigrants who converted to catholicism.

Hawaii County Genealogical Society

PO Box 831
Keaau, HI 96749

Hawaiian Sugar Planter's Association (HSPA)

PO Box 1057   Phone: (808)487-5561
Aiea, HI 96701   (808)486-5020
                        Don J. Heinz, President

Staff: 120. **Description:** Sugar companies raising sugarcane and manufacturing sugar; individuals connected with these firms. **Founded:** 1882. **Members:** 150. **Formerly:** Planters Labor and Supply Company.

Hongwanji Temple Headquarters

1727 Pali Hwy.
Honolulu, HI 96813

Description: Headquarters of the Hongwanji Buddhist temples where death registers can be researched.

Japanese Consulate General

1742 Nuuanu Ave.
Honolulu, HI 96817

Description: Contains over 50,000 index cards covering many Japanese immigrants who lived in Hawaii from 1885 to the present. Index cards include Hawaiian address; birth, death, marriage, and adoption dates; and notes on entry and departure from households. **Remarks:** Access is limited to family members and descendants.

Jodo Sect Temples Headquarters

1429 Makiki St.
Honolulu, HI 96822

Description: Buddhist temple of the Jodo Sect where death registers can be researched.

Idaho

Idaho Genealogical Society, Inc.

4620 Overland Rd., No. 204   Phone: (208)384-0542
Boise, ID 83705-2867   Jane Walls Golden, President
Jolyn R. Lockhart-Lawson,
Board Secretary

Staff: 10. **Description:** Furnish aid in genealogical research, preserve Idaho records, stimulate interest among members and others in the science of genealogy, acquire materials and publications which are of genealogical value. Maintain Friends of Idaho State Genealogical Library. Reference collection donated for public access which consists of 10,000 books, 200 periodicals, clippings, A/V material, 8,000 roll of microfilm, and 15,000 microfiche. Books and census records from all states, foreign reference works, and international materials. **Founded:** 1953, incorporated June 1961. **Members:** 360. **Regional groups:** 1. **State groups:** 1. **Local groups:** 5 chapters (inactive). **Computerized services:** Library: Western Library Network (WLN); and on CD-Rom the Social Security Death Record Index and the Family Search files. **Affiliated with:** Oregon Trail Project, 4620 Overland Rd., 204, Boise, ID 83705-2867, phone 208-384-0542. **Remarks:** Museum (as part of Idaho Archives have access to archival records), genealogical assistance, research and educational programs, annual conferences and workshops. **Publications:** *Idaho Genealogical Society Quarterly,* quarterly, $12.50, ISSN: 0445-2127, circulation: international, U.S. and Canada; *Footprints Through Idaho: Volumes of Idaho Pioneers,* volumes I and II (vol. III near publication); *Oregon Trail Travelers Database,* $10.00.

Illinois

Illinois State Genealogical Society (ISGS)

PO Box 10195   Phone: (217)789-1968
Springfield, IL 62791   Joyce Standridge, Executive
Secretary

Description: Individuals interested in genealogy. Seeks to further genealogical research. **Founded:** 1968. **Members:** 3000. **Publications:** *Illinois State Genealogical Quarterly; Newsletter,* monthly.

Indiana

Northwest Territory Genealogical Society (NTGS)

Lewis Historical Library,   Phone: (812)885-4330
LRC22   Donna Beeson, Editor
Vincennes University
Vincennes, IN 47591

Description: Persons involved in genealogical research. Seeks to advance research in area records, preserve historical documents, and make such information more accessible to the public. Maintains library including oral histories. **Founded:** 1980. **Members:** 215. **Publications:** *Northwest Trail Tracer,* quarterly; *Index of Declarations and Naturalizations;* censuses.

Iowa

Iowa Genealogical Society

6000 Douglas
PO Box 7735
Des Moines, IA 50322

Kansas

Kansas Council of Genealogical Societies

PO Box 3858
Topeka, KS 66608-6858

Kansas Genealogical Society, Inc.

Village Square Mall, Lower   Phone: (316)225-1951
Level, 2601 Central   Doris D. Rooney, Executive
PO Box 103   Manager
Dodge City, KS 67801

Staff: All volunteer society. **Description:** To create interest in genealogy; preserve genealogical data; encourage an adherence to accuracy and thoroughness in research; foster careful documentation; and to require a standard of excellence and accuracy in writing of published matter sponsored by the Society. Maintain library open to public which consists of books, periodicals, clippings, and A/V material. National and regional focus. Some coverage of Hispanic and Native Americans, minor coverage of African and Asian Americans. **Founded:** 1958. **Members:** 450. **Remarks:** Biographical archives, genealogical assistance, research and educational programs, and quarterly seminars. **Publications:** *The Treesearcher,* quarterly, $15–$20, circulation: approximately 450.

Kentucky

Kentucky Genealogical Society

PO Box 153
Frankfort, KY 40602

Phone: (502)875-4452
Brian D. Harney, President

Staff: 1. **Description:** Maintains reference library open to public consisting of books, periodicals, and clippings. **Founded:** 1973. **Members:** 2200. **Computerized services:** Kentucky Genealogical Index, 2.3m records, restricted access. **Publications:** *Bluegrass Roots,* quarterly, $15/yr, on microfilm, 1973–1984.

Louisiana

Louisiana Genealogical and Historical Society (LGHS)

PO Box 3454
Baton Rouge, LA 70821-3454

Phone: (504)766-1555
Barbara C. Strickland, President
Nell T. Boersma, Editor

Staff: 19. **Description:** Seeks to preserve genealogical and historical records in Louisiana. Encourages documented genealogical research. Some coverage of all ethnic groups, with regional and national focus. **Founded:** 1953. **Members:** 600. **Remarks:** Books sent to the Society for review are donated to the Louisiana State Archives or the Louisiana State Library, where they are available to researchers. **Publications:** *Louisiana Genealogical Register,* quarterly journal, $25.00, included with membership; *Diary in Gray,* $12.50 postpaid; *Bible Records-vol. 5,* $15.00 postpaid; several others.

Maine

Maine Genealogical Society

PO Box 221
Farmington, ME 04938-0221

Maryland

Maryland Genealogical Society

201 West Monument St.
Baltimore, MD 21201

Maryland Historical Society

201 W Monument St.
Baltimore, MD 21201

Phone: (410)685-3750

Remarks: The Society houses the Peabody Genealogical Collection which consists of 5,000 books (expected to be inventoried and available for use by the end of 1994). It includes materials added to the Peabody Library (Johns Hopkins Univ.) after World War II and consists of genealogical guides; bibliographies; compendia; indexes to and abstracts of genealogical sources; family histories; patriotic society publications; and genealogical journals as well as a vertical file collection of originals and microforms.

Massachusetts

Massachusetts Genealogical Council
c/o New England Historic Genealogical Soc.

101 Newbury St.
Boston, MA 02116

Massachusetts Society of Genealogists Inc.

PO Box 215
Ashland, MA 01721

Michigan

Association for Asian Studies
University of Michigan

1 Lane Hall
Ann Arbor, MI 48104

Michigan Genealogical Council (MGC)

PO Box 30007
Lansing, MI 48909

Description: Genealogical societies. Coordinates activities of members; promotes genealogical research; protects genealogical data. **Founded:** 1972. **Members:** 80. **Publications:** *Directory,* annual; *MGC Newsletter,* quarterly; *1850 Index Census; First Land Owners of Ingham County; First Land Owners of Ogemaw County; First Land Owners of St. Clair County; Michigan Surname Index;* family trees.

Minnesota

Minnesota Genealogical Society

PO Box 16069   Phone: (612)645-3671
Saint Paul, MN 55116-0069   P. Warren

Description: Non-profit, educational organization whose purpose is to foster and increase an interest in genealogy by providing an association of those interested in family, state and local history; collect, preserve and publish genealogical records and information; hold meetings and workshops to educate its members on current genealogy-related topics. Maintains reference library open to public at 1650 Carroll Avenue, Saint Paul, consisting of 5500 books, periodicals, and clippings. Regional focus, some national coverage. Major coverage of Native Americans (Midwest/Eastern Canada), some coverage of Hispanic Americans, minor coverage of African and Asian Americans. **Founded:** 1969. **Members:** 1600. **Local groups:** 9 branches. **Remarks:** Speakers bureau, genealogical assistance, and research and educational programs. **Publications:** *The Minnesota Genealogist,* quarterly, included with membership, ISSN: 0581-0086, circulation: 1700; *M.G.S. Newsletter,* quarterly, included with membership, circulation: 1800. *Minnesota Place Names: Now and Then,* $12.00; *Minnesota Genealogical Periodical Index: A County Guide,* $4.00; Oakland cemetery records: Oakland, Fairview, and Brown cemeteries, prices range from $10 to $15.

Mississippi

Historical and Genealogical Association of Mississippi

618 Avalon Rd.
Jackson, MS 39206

Mississippi Genealogical Society

PO Box 5301
Jackson, MS 39206

Montana

Montana State Genealogical Society

PO Box 555
Chester, MT 59522

Nebraska

Nebraska State Genealogical Society

PO Box 5608   Phone: (402)266-8881
Lincoln, NE 68505

Nevada

Nevada State Genealogical Society

PO Box 20666
Reno, NV 89515

New Hampshire

New Hampshire Society of Genealogists (NHSOG)

PO Box 633   Phone: (603)432-8137
Exeter, NH 03833-0633   George F. Sanborn Jr.,
                                                           President

Description: Educates the public about genealogical records. **Founded:** 1978. **Members:** 800. **Remarks:** Offers assistance in conducting genealogical research. **Publications:** *New Hampshire Society of Genealogical Record,* quarterly journal; *New Hampshire Society of Genealogists Newsletter,* quarterly.

New Jersey

Genealogy Club of the Library of the New Jersey Historical Society

230 Broadway
Newark, NJ 07104

New Mexico

New Mexico Genealogical Society

PO Box 8283
Albuquerque, NM 87198-8330

Remarks: Has published genealogical records including early censuses, family genealogies.

New York

China Institute in America

125 East 65th St.
New York, NY 10021

New York Genealogical and Biographical Society

122-126 E 58th St.　　　　Phone: (212)755-8532
New York, NY 10022-1939　　William P. Johns, Exec. Dir.

Staff: 11. **Description:** To discover, procure, preserve, and perpetuate information and items relating to genealogy, biography, and family history, especially of the state of New York. Maintains research library of 68,000 books, 25,000 manuscripts, and 10,000 microforms. Maintains portrait collection; conducts educational programs. **Founded:** 1869. **Members:** 1,500. **Remarks:** Also publishes source records from New York; offers list of publications; magazine available on microform. **Publications:** *The New York Genealogical and Biographical Record,* quarterly, included in membership dues, circulation: 2,000; *NYG&B Newsletter,* quarterly.

New York State News Vital Records Index Search Service

New York State Archives　　　Phone: (518)474-8955
Cultural Education Center
　11D40
Albany, NY 12230

Description: Searches the Department of Health microfiche indexes to marriages and deaths 1880/1-1943 and births 1880/1-1918. Covers all of the state except New York City and (prior to 1914) Albany, Buffalo, and Yonkers. Once the index entry is found, a copy may be requested from the appropriate local registrar. **Remarks:** Fee is $5 per request; there is no refund for unsuccessful searches. For a marriage or birth record, the applicant must sign a statement that the individual named is deceased. Contact the NY State Archives for the request form. Each form may be used to request a search of one index (birth, marriage, or death) for one name for up to three specific years.

Ohio

Chinese American Cultural Association

8122 Mayfield
Chesterland, OH 44026

Ohio Genealogical Society (OGS)

PO Box 2625　　　　　　Phone: (419)522-9077
Mansfield, OH 44906　　　Mary Bowman, President

Staff: 2. **Description:** Genealogists, historians, libraries, and other interested individuals from throughout the U.S. Promotes genealogical research and the preservation of historical records in Ohio. Facilitates the exchange of ideas and information. Sponsors educational programs on family lineage in Ohio; conducts student essay contest. Maintains 15,000 volume library. **Founded:** 1959.

Members: 6,350. **Regional groups:** 3; Chapters: 102. **Remarks:** Speakers bureau. **Publications:** *Chapter Directory,* periodic; *The Ohio Genealogical Society Newsletter,* monthly, includes calendar of events, chapter announcements, library acquisitions, queries, and membership information, $25.00, circulation: 6,350; *Ohio Records and Pioneer Families,* quarterly, contains cemetery and family records, court abstracts, and genealogical articles, $18.00, circulation: 1,025; *The Report,* quarterly magazine, price included in membership dues; *Ohio Cemeteries,* and *First Families of Ohio Roster.*

Oklahoma

Federation of Oklahoma Genealogical Societies

PO Box 26151
Oklahoma City, OK 73126

Genealogical Institute of Oklahoma

3813 Cashion Pl.
Oklahoma City, OK 73112

Oregon

Genealogical Council of Oregon

PO Box 628
Ashland, OR 97520-0021

Genealogical Forum of Oregon Inc. Headquarters and Library

2130 SW 5th Ste. 220　　　　Phone: (503)227-2398
Portland, OR 97201　　　　Eileen Chamberlin, President

Staff: All-volunteer. **Description:** Purpose is education, collection and publication of historical materials. Largely state and regional in focus; some national coverage. Maintains library open to public for small fee consisting of books, periodicals, clippings, and A/V material. Lends materials to members only. Minor coverage of African, Hispanic, and Native Americans. **Founded:** 1946. **Members:** 1217. **Computerized services:** CD-ROM with databases. **Remarks:** Speakers bureau, biographical archives, and genealogical assistance. **Publications:** *Oregon Donation Land Claims,* volumes 1–5, vol 6: Index and vol 1–3 (1 vol): *Oregon Provisional Land Claims,* $7.25–$20.00; *Idaho Rejected Land Claims,* volumes 1–5 from BLM record; *Multnomah County Marriage Records, 1853–1890,* vol's 1–5, $6.25–$12.00; *The Bulletin,:* quarterly $25/year (included with membership), circulation: 1217; *The Forum Insider,* 8 times a yr. (monthly between publication of *The Bulletin,* $25 yr. included with membership).

Genealogical Heritage Council of Oregon

Douglas County Courthouse,
　Rm. 111
PO Box 579
Roseburg, OR 97470

Oregon Genealogical Society

PO Box 10306   Phone: (503)746-7924
Eugene, OR 97440-2306   Nancy Hodgkinson, President

Staff: All volunteer. **Description:** To promote interest in genealogy, to maintain & staff genealogical research library, to publish genealogical & historical information in a quarterly periodical & other appropriate publications. Meets monthly, except December. Maintains a reference library which is open to public. Library holds books, periodicals, clippings, and A/V materials. Some coverage of all groups, African Americans, Hispanic Americans; extensive coverage of Native Americans; and little coverage of Asian Americans. National and regional scope. **Founded:** 1962. **Members:** 365. **Computerized services:** Some. **Telecommunications services:** Some. **Remarks:** Offers genealogical assistance, research programs, and education programs. Has large Oregon collection, and issues Oregon Pioneer Certificates. **Publications:** *OGS Quarterly,* 4 times per year (Jan., April, July, Oct.), included in dues; *OGS Newsletter,* 6 times per year; also publishes several Oregon census sources and other miscellaneous documents. List available from the Society.

Pennsylvania

Genealogical Society of Pennsylvania (GSP)

1300 Locust St.   Phone: (215)545-0391
Philadelphia, PA 19107   Antoinette J. Segraves,
     Executive Director

Description: Genealogical researchers in Pennsylvania and the Delaware Valley area of Delaware and New Jersey. Collects and preserves genealogical records. Conducts abstracting, indexing, and microfilming of newspapers and records. **Founded:** 1892. **Members:** 2000. **Remarks:** Maintains library. **Publications:** *Journal,* periodic; *PENN In Hand,* quarterly newsletter; *Pennsylvania Genealogical Magazine,* periodic; special publications.

Rhode Island

Rhode Island Genealogical Society

13 Countryside Dr.
Cumberland, RI 02864-2601

South Carolina

South Carolina Genealogical Society (SCGS)

PO Box 20266   Phone: (803)766-1667
Charleston, SC 29413-0266   Kay Manning, Vice President

Description: Persons interested in genealogy. Maintains library. **Founded:** 1972. **Members:** 1,800. **Local groups:** 16. **Publications:** *Carolina Herald,* biennial; *Newsletter,* 4/year.

South Dakota

South Dakota Genealogical Society (SDGS)

PO Box 1101   Marilyn Heesch, President
Pierre, SD 57501

Staff: Volunteers. **Description:** Purpose is to promote an interest in genealogy; encourage, educate, and instruct members in the art and practice of genealogical research; maintain and elevate genealogical standards; stress the importance of accuracy through careful documentation; locate, preserve, and index public and private genealogical records and make such records available to members and the general public; raise funds for any of the foregoing purposes and to accept donations, gifts, legacies, and bequests. Collection of genealogical materials housed at the Alexander Mitchell Library in Aberdeen. **Remarks:** Genealogical assistance. **Publications:** *The South Dakota Genealogical Quarterly,* $15.00 (included with membership), circulation: 150; *No Year Index* (Consists of alpha name index of 10 yrs. of quarterlies), $35.00.

Texas

Texas State Genealogical Society

Rte. 4, Box 56   Phone: (903)885-3523
Sulphur Springs, TX 75482

Description: Individuals interested in the genealogy of Texas. Conducts annual lecture series. Issues Texas Pioneer certificates. **Founded:** 1960. **Members:** 800. **Publications:** *Stirpes,* quarterly journal; *TSGS Newsletter,* periodic.

Utah

Genealogical Society of Utah

35 NW Temple   Phone: (801)240-2331
Salt Lake City, UT 84150

Utah Genealogical Association (UGA)

PO Box 1144   George Jordan, Vice-Pres/
Salt Lake City, UT 84110   Chmn. Publication
     Committee

Description: Promote active interest in genealogy; compilation of accurate, complete pedigrees; preservation of genealogical records; foster genealogical education and training; conduct seminars, conferences, workshops, and chapter meetings; locate genealogical source materials and records and make them available to genealogists and historians; actively disseminate information on research techniques and procedures; provide research assistance to aid people with their pedigree searches. International, national, and regional coverage. Direct access to holdings of the Family History Library in Salt Lake City. **Founded:** 1971. **State groups:** 3. **Local groups:** 4. **Remarks:** Speakers bureau, genealogical assistance, research and educational programs. **Publications:** *U.G.A. Journal,* quarterly (included with membership),

$25.00/year, circulation: approximately 750, available on microform from University Microfilms, 300 North Zeeb Road, Ann Arbor, MI 48106; *U.G.A. Newsletter,* quarterly, included with membership.

Vermont

Genealogical Society of Vermont

46 Chestnut St.   Joann H. Nichols, President
Brattleboro, VT 05301

Description: Individuals interested in their Vermont ancestors and in promoting genealogical activity. Assembles, preserves and makes available genealogical records. **Founded:** 1971. **Members:** 1300. **Remarks:** Offers research assistance. **Publications:** *Branches and Twigs,* quarterly.

Vermont Genealogical Society

PO Box 422   Phone: (802)483-2957
Pittsford, VT 05763

Virginia

Genealogical Research Institute of Virginia

PO Box 29178   Peter Broadbent, President
Richmond, VA 23242-0178

Staff: All volunteer. **Description:** Promotes, fosters and encourages serious and accurate genealogical and historical research by all means possible, including instruction, seminars, workshops and fieldtrips. No library. Some regional coverage. **Founded:** 1981. **Members:** 350. **Remarks:** Answers queries. **Publications:** *News 'n Notes* 10/year; $10/yr; 450.

Virginia Genealogical Society

5001 W Broad St., Ste. 115   Phone: (804)285-8954
Richmond, VA 23230-3023   Emily Rusk, Executive
                                           Director

Staff: 1. **Description:** Minor coverage of African-Americans. No library. **Founded:** 1961. **Members:** 2800. **Remarks:** Educational programs. **Publications:** *Magazine of VA Genealogy*; quarterly; $23/yr.; ISSN: 0734-8095; 2,800. *VGS Newletter*; 6/year; $23/yr.; ISSN: 0734-8095; 2,800.

Washington

Washington State Genealogical Society

PO Box 1422   Phone: (206)352-0595
Olympia, WA 98507

Wing Luke Asian Museum

407 7th Ave. S   Phone: (206)623-5124
Seattle, WA 98104   Fax: (206)623-4559
                                   Ron Chew, Director

Staff: 16. **Description:** Pan-Asian museum devoted to the collection, preservation, and display of Asian Pacific American culture, history, and art. Little genealogical information on Asian Americans. **Founded:** 1966. **Members:** 1,130. **Holdings:** Books, periodicals, clippings, and audio/visual materials. **Services:** Maintains a speakers bureau, biographical archives, and research and educational programs. **Formerly:** Wing Luke Memorial Foundation. **Publications:** Membership Newsletter, free with membership, quarterly; *Executive Order 9066: Fifty Years Before & Fifty Years After,* $10.00; *Reflections of Seattle's Chinese Americans: The First 100 Years,* ISBN: 0-295-97412-5, $18.00.

West Virginia

West Virginia Genealogy Society Inc.

PO Box 249
Elkview, WV 25071

Wisconsin

Wisconsin Genealogical Council, Inc.

Rte. 3, Box 253   Phone: (608)378-4388
Black River Falls, WI   Fax: (608)378-3006
   54615-9405   Carolyn Habelman, President

Description: Sponsors annual state educational conference; ''Beginners Handbook.'' Largely regional focus. **Founded:** 1986. **Members:** 120. **State groups:** 9. **Remarks:** Speakers bureau, genealogical assistance, and educational programs. **Publications:** Newsletter, quarterly, included with membership.

Wisconsin State Genealogical Society

2109 20th Ave.   Phone: (608)325-2609
Monroe, WI 53566

Print Resources

This chapter provides information on printed materials (books, magazines, newspapers, etc.) which aid those researching an ancestral line. Each resource is arranged here categorically by scope; national and regional, followed by state listings. Sources with an international scope, if present, appear at the end of the chapter. Listings are arranged alphabetically within each category.

National and Regional

American Family Records Association— Member Directory and Ancestral Surname Registry

American Family Records Association
PO Box 15505
Kansas City, MO 64106

Phone: (816)373-6570

Covers: Nearly 300 member family historians and genealogists; 4,300 surnames. **Entries include:** Name, address, member number, ancestral surnames with geographic locations and approximate time period. **Arrangement:** Alphabetical. **Frequency:** Annual. **Remarks:** To be available on CD-ROM only, starting late 1993.

American Genealogist

American Genealogist
PO Box 398
Demorest, GA 30535-0398

Phone: (706)865-6440
David L. Greene, Editor and Publisher

Description: Scholarly genealogical journal. **First published:** 1922. **Frequency:** Quarterly. **Circulation** 1,600. **Subscription:** $20.00; $39.00, two years; $58.00, three years. **ISSN:** 0002-8592.

American Newspapers, 1821–1936: A Union List of Files Available in the United States and Canada

Kraus Reprints
Rte. 100
Millwood, NY 10546

Phone: (914)762-2200
Toll-Free: 800-223-8323
Winifred Gregory

Publication date: 1937. **Price:** $198.00.

Ancestry's Red Book: American State, County & Town Sources

Ancestry
PO Box 476
Salt Lake City, UT
 84110-0476

Phone: (801)531-1790
Toll-Free: 800-531-1790
Fax: (801)531-1798
Alice Eichholz, Editor

Covers: Genealogical resources in every state and the District of Columbia, including names and addresses for county seats and parent counties; definitive maps and map listings; vital records; census records; local history collections; land records and maps; probate, court, and tax records; cemetery and church records; military records; periodical, newspaper, and private manuscript collections; archival, library, and genealogical and historical society collections; ethnic collections with unique emphasis; immigration and naturalization resources; and bibliographic references. **Description:** Provides county and town listings within an overall state-by-state organization. **Type:** Book. **Arrangement:** Geographical. **Indexes:** General. **Pages:** 858. **Frequency:** Irregular; previous edition 1987; latest edition January 1992. **Price:** $39.95 (Members, $33.95). **ISBN:** 0-916489-47-7.

Archives: A Guide to the National Archives Field Branches

Ancestry
PO Box 476
Salt Lake City, UT
 84110-0476

Toll-Free: 800-531-1790
Fax: (801)531-1798
Loretto Dennis Szucs, Author
Sandra Hargreaves Luebking, Author

Covers: American Expeditionary Forces; World War I; U.S. Attorneys and Marshals; Bureau of Census; Continental and Confederation Congresses and the Constitutional Convention; U.S. Courts of Appeals; Farmers Home Administration; Federal Housing Administration; Foreign Service Posts of the Department of State; U.S. Housing Corporation; Immigration and Naturalization Service; Bureau of Indian Affairs; Office of the Judge Advocate General; Naturalization Records; Bureau of Refugees, Freedmen, and Abandoned Lands; Selective Service System; Office of the Surgeon General; War Department Collection of Revolutionary War Records; and Work Projects Administration. **Publication includes:** Descriptions of the individual field branches, listings of microfilm copies held by all branches, printed descriptions and inventories, histories of the agencies and their records, cross-references to microfilm holdings, suggestions for research topics, etc. **Description:** Discusses the holdings of the National Archives. **Pages:** 340. **Publication date:** 1988. **Price:** $35.95; (Members $30.50). **ISBN:** 0-916489-23-X.

Computer Genealogy: A Guide to Research through High Technology

Ancestry   Phone: (801)531-1790
PO Box 476   Toll-Free: 800-531-1790
Salt Lake City, UT 84110   Paul Andereck
      Richard Pence

Description: Illustrated. **Pages:** 280. **Publication date:** 1991. **Price:** $12.95 (paper). **ISBN:** 0-916489-02-7.

County Courthouse Book

Genealogical Publishing Co.   Phone: (410)837-8271
1001 N Calvert St.   Toll-Free: 800-296-6687
Baltimore, MD 21202-3897   Elizabeth Petty Bentley

Description: Furnishes the names, addresses, phone numbers, and dates of organization for over 3,300 county courthouses. Over fifty percent of the courthouses provide further information on record holdings, personnel, and services. **Type:** Book. **Arrangement:** Geographical. **Pages:** 386. **Publication date:** 1990. **Price:** $29.95 (paper).

CrossCurrents

Asian American Studies   Phone: (310)825-2974
  Center   Fax: (310)206-9844
University of California, Los
  Angeles
3232 Campbell Hall
Los Angeles, CA 90024

Directory of East Asian Libraries

Association for Asian Studies   Phone: (614)292-3502
Committee on East Asian   Fax: (614)292-7859
  Libraries
c/o Maureen H. Donovan
Main Library, Rm. 310
1858 Neil Ave. Mall
Columbus, OH 43210-1286

Covers: Over 100 library collections concerned with China, Japan, and Korea. **Entries include:** Collection name, institution name, address, names and titles of personnel, phone, fax, electronic mail address. **Pages:** 70. **Frequency:** Irregular; latest edition 1993. **Price:** $10.00, postpaid.

Directory of Family Associations

Genealogical Publishing Co.,   Phone: (410)837-8271
  Inc.   Toll-Free: 800-296-6687
1001 N. Calvert St.   Fax: (410)752-8492
Baltimore, MD 21202

Covers: Over 4,000 organizations, each devoted to the study of a family name. **Type:** Book. **Entries include:** Family name, related family names, organization name, address, phone, contact name, publications. **Arrangement:** Alphabetical. **Pages:** 318. **Frequency:** Biennial, odd years. **Price:** $29.95 (paper). **ISBN:** 0-8063-1319-6.

Everton's Genealogical Helper

The Everton Publishers, Inc.   Phone: (801)752-6022
PO Box 368   Fax: (801)752-0425
Logan, UT 84323-0368   George B. Everton Jr.,
      Publisher

Description: Genealogy magazine. **First published:** 1947. **Frequency:** 6 times/year. **Circulation** 48,000. **Subscription:** $21.00/year. **Former titles:** The Genealogical Helper (1992).

Everton's Genealogical Helper—Genealogy & the Public Library Issue

Everton Publishers, Inc.   Phone: (801)752-6022
3223 S. Main St.   Toll-Free: 800-443-6325
Logan, UT 84321   Fax: (801)752-0425

Covers: More than 200 public libraries nationwide which have separate genealogical collections or a special interest in such materials. **Entries include:** Library name, address. **Arrangement:** Geographical. **Frequency:** Annual. **Price:** $4.50, postpaid, payment with order.

Family Associations, Societies and Reunions

Ye Olde Genealogie Shoppe   Phone: (317)862-3330
PO Box 39128   Toll-Free: 800-419-0200
Indianapolis, IN 46239-0128   J. Konrad, Editor

Covers: About 2,000 family associations, societies, and regularly scheduled reunions; includes Scottish clan associations; coverage includes Canada. **Entries include:** Group name, address of contact, variant names. **Arrangement:** Alphabetical by surname. **Pages:** 100. **Frequency:** Annual. **Price:** $8.00, plus $3.00 shipping. **Remarks:** Formerly published by Summit Publications.

Family Tree Digest

Family Tree Genealogical   Phone: (419)335-6485
  Society   Howard V. Fausey, Editor
450 Potter St.
Wauseon, OH 43567

Description: Features genealogical information and responses to queries on a national basis. **First published:** 1978. **Audience:** Genealogical societies in approximately 40 states. **Frequency:** Monthly. **Price:** $7.50/year for individuals; free for institutions. **ISSN:** 0742-9045.

Genealogical and Local History Books in Print

Genealogical Books in Print   Phone: (607)786-0769
PO Box 394
Maine, NY 13802-0394

Publication includes: List of over 3,600 suppliers of genealogical books, microform, and computer software. **Entries include:** Organization or personal name, address, name and title of contact, product. **Arrangement:** Alphabetical, by publisher name. **Pages:** 1,700. **Frequency:** Every 10 years, with two interedition supplements; latest base edition 1985; first supplement February 1990; second supplement January 1993; new edition expected 1995. **Price:** $37.50, for base edition; $21.95, first supplement; $21.60, second supplement; $75.00, set. **Remarks:** Principal content is a description of genealogical and local history books, reprints, microform collections, and specific surname publications.

Genealogical Periodical Annual Index

Heritage Books, Inc.
1540 E. Pointer Ridge Pl.
Bowie, MD 20716

Phone: (301)390-7708
Toll-Free: 800-398-7709
Fax: (301)390-7153

Publication includes: List of about 260 periodicals published by genealogical societies and genealogists and used in indexing surnames, place names, and related topics for this book. **Entries include:** Name of publication, name of publisher, address, issues indexed, title abbreviation used in book. **Arrangement:** Alphabetical by title abbreviation. **Frequency:** Annual, August. **Price:** $22.50. **Remarks:** Publication mainly consists of a list of 14,000 genealogical citations (surnames, place names, etc.).

Genealogical Research and Resources: A Guide for Library Use

American Library Association
 (ALA)
50 E. Huron St.
Chicago, IL 60611

Phone: (312)944-6780
Toll-Free: 800-545-2433
Fax: (312)440-9374

Publication includes: List of genealogical organizations and societies. **Arrangement:** Alphabetical. **Frequency:** Latest edition 1988. **Price:** $15.00. **Remarks:** Principal content of publication is information on genealogical research publications.

Genealogical Research in the National Archives

Ancestry
PO Box 476
Salt Lake City, UT
 84110-0476

Toll-Free: 800-531-1790
Fax: (801)531-1798

Covers: Principal genealogical record groups within the National Archives including population, military, ethnic, land, court, and civilian records. **Description:** A resource that explains the research potential of genealogical materials in the National Archives of the United States. **Type:** Book. **Pages:** 299. **Price:** $35.00; (Members, $29.95). **ISBN:** 0-911333-00-2.

Genealogical Societies and Historical Societies in the United States

Ye Olde Genealogie Shoppe
PO Box 39128
Indianapolis, IN 46239

Phone: (317)862-3330
Toll-Free: 800-419-0200

Covers: About 3,000 groups in the United States. **Entries include:** Society name, address. **Arrangement:** Geographical. **Pages:** 80. **Frequency:** Annual. **Price:** $8.00, plus $3.00 shipping. **Remarks:** Formerly published by Summit Publications.

Genealogist's Handbook for New England Research

NEHGS Sales Dept.
101 Newbury St.
Boston, MA 02116

Marcie Wiswall Lindberg,
Compiler

Description: For each of the six New England states, lists towns, sections on vital, census, probate, land, church, military, and immigration records, plus libraries with significant or unique genealogical holdings; genealogical societies; journals; and a bibliography of how-to guides and surveys of state-wide records. Covers over 90% of the genealogical repositories and sources in New England, with many revisions and more coverage of ethnic genealogical societies. Also lists all Mormon New England libraries

with Family Search on CD-ROM. **Pages:** 178. **Publication date:** 1993. **Price:** Soft: $15.00, plus $2.50 P&H; Hard: $20.00, plus $3.50 P&H. **Send orders to:** Publisher. **Remarks:** Third edition.

Genealogy & Computers for the Complete Beginner

Clearfield Company
200 E Eager St.
Baltimore, MD 21202

Phone: (410)625-9004
Karen Clifford

Subtitled: A Step-by-step Guide to the PAF Computer Program, Automated Databases, Family History Centers & Local Sources. **Pages:** 269. **Publication date:** 1992. **Price:** $29.95 (paper). **ISBN:** 0-685-60307-5.

Going to Salt Lake City to Do Family History Research

Marietta Publishing Co.
2115 N Denair Ave.
Turlock, CA 95380

J. Carlyle Parker, Author

Description: Designed to prepare researchers for a visit to the world's largest genealogical library, the Family History Library at Salt Lake City. The three parts of the book address preparation for the trip, making the most of your time while you are there, and reviewing your research once you return home. **Indexes:** Subject. **Pages:** Over 200. **Frequency:** First ed., 1989; latest ed., 1993. **Price:** $12.95 (paper), plus $1.50 P&H. **Send orders to:** Publisher. **Also includes:** Maps, information on transportation and lodging, floor plans, a discussion of finding aids, and an appendix which lists Family History Centers. **Remarks:** Second edition.

Guide to Genealogical Research in the National Archives

National Archives Trust Fund
NEPS Dept. 630
PO Box 100793
Atlanta, GA 30384

Toll-Free: 800-788-6282
Fax: (404)501-5239

Publication includes: Information about individuals whose names appear in census records, military service and pension files, ship passenger arrival lists, land records, and many other types of documents. **Description:** Revised. Explains what types of records are preserved in the National Archives and what specific information about individuals is included in each type of record. **Type:** Guide. **First published:** 1982. **Pages:** 304. **Publication date:** 1982. **Price:** $35.00; $25.00 (paper). **ISBN:** 0-911333-00-2, 0-911333-01-0 (paper).

Guide to Multicultural Resources

Praxis Publications, Inc.
2215 Atwood Ave.
PO Box 9869
Madison, WI 53715

Phone: (608)244-5633
Toll-Free: 800-558-2110
Fax: (414)563-7395
Charles Taylor, Editor

Description: Over 4,000 minority and multicultural organizations, including libraries, media, fraternities and sororities, historical societies, and religious and women's organizations, all involved with the Asian, Hispanic, African, and Native American communities. **Type:** Directory. **Entries include:** Organization name, address, phone, fax, year founded, purpose, services and service area, funding, budget, staff, and publications. **Arrangement:** Classified by racial/minority group. **Indexes:** Subject, geographical. **Pages:** 500. **Frequency:** Biennial, January of odd years. **Price:** $49.00. **Remarks:** Published jointly with Highsmith Press.

Guide to the National Archives of the United States

National Archives Trust Fund   Toll-Free: 800-788-6282
NEPS Dept. 630   Fax: (404)501-5239
PO Box 100793
Atlanta, GA 30384

Description: Provides a general description of the basic records of the three branches of the federal government of the U.S. from the first Continental Congress within the context of the government agencies that created them or received them in the course of official business. **Type:** Guide. **First published:** 1974. **Pages:** 928. **Publication date:** 1987. **Price:** $25.00. **ISBN:** 0-911333-23-1. **Also includes:** Appendix containing additional record group descriptions.

Handbook for Genealogical Correspondence

The Everton Publishers, Inc.   Toll-Free: 800-443-6325
PO Box 368   Fax: (801)752-0425
Logan, UT 84323-0368

Covers: The problems and procedures involved in genealogical correspondence including essentials of letters, postmaster and mails, geography, relatives, libraries, church record keepers, public officials, advertising, filing, opportunities. **Pages:** 274. **Price:** $20.00. **Remarks:** Prepared by Cache Genealogical Library. Reprint.

Handy Book for Genealogists

Everton Publishers   Toll-Free: 800-443-6325
PO Box 368   Fax: (801)752-0425
Logan, UT 84323-0368

Publication includes: A chapter on each of the fifty states in the U.S. In each chapter is an alphabetically arranged table of counties which is keyed to a corresponding state map found at the back of the volume. **Description:** New Eighth Edition. Provides researcher with at-a-glance genealogical guidance for every county in the U.S. **Type:** Book. **Entries include:** For each county, a table furnishes a map index number, the date of the county's creation, the parent county(ies) or territory(ies) from which it was created, and the address and phone number for the appropriate county court. **Arrangement:** Arranged alphabetically by state. **Pages:** 382. **Publication date:** 1991. **Price:** $31.95. **Also includes:** Special section, with maps, pertaining to migration routes throughout the eastern half of the U.S. Fold-out map of the U.S.

Heritage Quest

Heritage Quest   Phone: (801)298-5446
PO Box 392   Fax: (801)298-5468
Bountiful, UT 84011-0329   Bradley W. Steuart, Publisher

Description: Contains how-to articles on locating genealogical information. **First published:** 1985. **Frequency:** 6 times/year. **Circulation** 10,000. **Subscription:** $28.00, U.S.; $40.00, other countries. **ISSN:** 0886-0262.

How to Locate Anyone Who Is or Has Been in the Military

Military Information   Phone: (512)828-4054
  Enterprises   Richard S. Johnson
PO Box 340081
Fort Sam Houston, TX 78234

Subtitled: Armed Forces Locater Directory. **Description:** 4th, rev. ed.; illustrated. **Pages:** 176. **Publication date:** 1991. **Price:** $12.95 (paper). **ISBN:** 1-877639-07-9.

Immigration History Newsletter

Immigration History Society   Phone: (215)853-1363
c/o Balch Institute   M. Mark Stolarik, Editor
18 S 7th St.
Philadelphia, PA 19106

Description: Concerned with the field of immigration-ethnic history. Promotes study concerning the U.S. and Canada and the history of emigration from all parts of the world. Includes study of regional groups in the U.S., Native Americans, and forced immigrants. Aims to promote understanding of the processes of acculturation and of conflict. Recurring features include information on research, organizations, and publications in the field of immigration history. **First published:** 1968. **Pages:** 24. **Frequency:** Semiannually. **Circulation** 600. **Price:** Included in membership. **ISSN:** 0579-4374.

Japanese American History

Facts on File, Inc.   Phone: (212)683-2244
460 Park Ave. S   Toll-Free: 800-322-8755
New York, NY 10016   Fax: (212)213-4578
    Brian Niiya, Editor

Subtitled: An A-to-Z reference from 1868 to the present. **Covers:** People, organizations, and events pertinent to Japanese Americans. **Publication includes:** Historical overview, chronology, and eighty black-and-white illustrations from the archives of the Japanese American National Museum in Los Angeles. **Description:** Detailed essays of significant events as seen from the Japanese perspective. Extensive use of oral histories and anecdotes. **Type:** Encyclopedia. **Entries include:** Information on individuals, events, and organizations ranging from a few paragraphs to several pages. **Indexes:** General index. **Pages:** 416. **Audience:** General. **Publication date:** 1993. **Price:** $45.00. **ISBN:** 0-8160-2680-7. **Also includes:** Bibliography.

Journal of American Ethnic History

Transaction Periodicals   Phone: (908)932-2280
  Consortium   Fax: (908)932-3138
Rutgers—The State University   Ronald H. Baylor, Editor
  of New Jersey
Dept. 3092
New Brunswick, NJ 08903

Description: Journal addressing various aspects of American immigration and ethnic history including background of emigration, ethnic and racial groups, native Americans, and immigration policies. **First published:** 1981. **Frequency:** Quarterly. **Circulation** 1,200. **Subscription:** $30.00; $60.00 institutions; $100.00 other countries (airmail). **ISSN:** 0278-5927.

The Library: A Guide to the LDS Family History Library

Genealogy Unlimited, Inc. Phone: (801)226-8971
PO Box 537 Toll-Free: 800-666-4363
Orem, UT 84059-0537 Johni Cerny, Editor
Wendy Elliott, Editor

Covers: Holdings of the Family History Library, the time periods they cover, and how they can be accessed. **Description:** The largest single collection of genealogical information and sources in the world is described. **Pages:** 746. **Price:** $40.00.

Library of Congress: A Guide to Genealogical & Historical Research

Ancestry Toll-Free: 800-531-1790
PO Box 476 Fax: (801)531-1798
Salt Lake City, UT James C. Neagles, Author
84110-0476

Pages: 382. **Publication date:** 1990. **Price:** $35.95. **ISBN:** 0-916489-48-5.

List of 96 Ethnic and Religious Genealogical and Historical Societies and Archives

Summit Publications
Box 222
Munroe Falls, OH 44262

Frequency: Irregular; latest edition March 1989. **Price:** $4.00, postpaid.

Locating Your Immigrant Ancestor, A Guide to Naturalization Records

The Everton Publishers, Inc. Toll-Free: 800-443-6325
PO Box 368 Fax: (801)752-0425
Logan, UT 84323-0368 James C. Neagles
Lila Lee Neagles

Description: Reference book for naturalization records of the United States documenting the present location of records created prior to 1906. **Pages:** 153. **Price:** $12.95.

Managing a Genealogical Project

Genealogical Publishing Co., Phone: (410)837-8271
Inc. Toll-Free: 800-296-6687
1001 N. Calvert St. William Dollarhide
Baltimore, MD 21202-3897

Publication includes: Set of master forms: relationship chart, reference family data sheet, compiled family data sheet, master data sheet, research log, ancestor table, pedigree ancestor index, research journal, and correspondence log. **Description:** Focuses on a particular method of organizing research materials, starting with the preliminary note-gathering stage and ending with the final presentation of all research in the form of a book or report. **Type:** Paperback. **First published:** 1988. **Pages:** 96. **Publication date:** 1991, includes a revised and expanded chapter on genealogical software. **Price:** $14.95. **ISBN:** 0-8063-1222-X.

Midwest Research

Carlberg Press Phone: (714)772-2849
1782 Beacon Ave. Nancy E. Carlberg
Anaheim, CA 92804

Description: Illustrated. **Pages:** 110. **Publication date:** 1991. **Price:** $10.00 (paper). **ISBN:** 0-944878-11-3.

Minority Organizations: A National Directory

Garrett Park Press Phone: (301)946-2553
PO Box 190B Robert Calvert Jr., Editor
Garrett Park, MD 20896

Description: Over 9,700 groups composed of or intending to serve members of minority groups, including Asian, Hispanic, African, and Native Americans; coverage includes cultural & historical museums, professional associations, minority newspapers and periodicals, professional associations, religious organizations, etc. **Type:** Directory. **Entries include:** Organization name, address, description of activities, purpose, publications, etc. **Arrangement:** Alphabetical. **Indexes:** Organizational name, geographical, program, defunct organizations. **Pages:** 514. **Frequency:** Irregular: Previous edition 1987; latest edition 1992. **Price:** $50.00. **ISBN:** 0-912048-30-1.

National Archives and Records Administration Staff Guide to Genealogical Research in the National Archives

National Archives and Phone: (202)501-5235
Records Administration Toll-Free: 800-788-6282
Publications Division
NECR Room G9
7th St. & Pennsylvania Ave.
NW
Washington, DC 20408

Description: Illustrated. **Pages:** 304. **Publication date:** 1985. **Price:** $35.00 (casebound); $25.00 (paper). **ISBN:** 0-911333-00-2 (casebound); 0-911333-01-0 (paper).

National Genealogical Society Newsletter

National Genealogical Society Phone: (703)525-0050
(NGS) Ann Crowley, Editor
4527 17th St. N
Arlington, VA 22207-2399

Description: Features news of the Society and the genealogical community, articles on genealogical methods, sources, repositories, and NGS's library acquisitions; and members' queries. Recurring features include a calendar of events. **First published:** 1975. **Frequency:** Bimonthly. **Indexed:** Annually. **Circulation** 11,000. **Price:** Included in membership. **ISSN:** 0887-1353. **Former titles:** National Genealogical Society Newsletter.

National Genealogical Society Quarterly (NGSQ)

National Genealogical Society Phone: (703)525-0050
4527 17th Street N Fax: (703)525-0052
Arlington, VA 22207-2399 Elizabeth S. Mills, Editor

Description: Genealogy journal. **First published:** 1912. **Frequency:** Quarterly. **Circulation** 13,000. **Subscription:** $25.00/year. **ISSN:** 0027-934X.

New England Historical and Genealogical Register

New England Historic
Genealogical Society
101 Newbury St.
Boston, MA 02116

Phone: (617)536-5740
Fax: (617)536-7307
Jane F. Fiske, Editor

Description: Focuses on history and genealogy. **First published:** 1847. **Frequency:** Quarterly. **Circulation** 14,000. **Subscription:** Free to qualified subscribers; $45.00. **ISSN:** 0028-4785. **Remarks:** Subscription rate includes NEXUS newsletter.

Newspaper Genealogical Column Directory

Heritage Books, Inc.
1540 E. Pointer Ridge Pl.
Bowie, MD 20716

Phone: (301)390-7709
Toll-Free: 800-398-7709
Anita Cheek Milner, Editor

Covers: About 150 columnists appearing in over 250 newspapers and periodicals, offering help to researchers in nearly 250 counties and 30 states. **Entries include:** Columnist name, publications carrying column, mailing address, counties covered, frequency, fees, whether columns are compiled or indexed. **Arrangement:** Geographical. **Pages:** 112. **Frequency:** Irregular; previous edition June 1989; latest edition November 1992. **Price:** $14.00. **Also includes:** Notes on discontinued columns. **Former titles:** Newspaper Genealogy Columns: A Preliminary Checklist (1979).

Newspapers in Microform, United States, 1948–1983

Library of Congress
101 Independence Avenue SE
Washington, DC 20540

Phone: (202)707-5000

Description: Two volumes. **Publication date:** 1983.

Quick Step in Genealogy Research: A Primer for Blacks, Other Minorities and the Novice in this Area

North Star and Day Publishing
Co.

Johnnie M. Day, Author

Records of Genealogical Value for Country

Family History Library of The
Church of Jesus Christ of
Latter-Day Saints
35 NW Temple
Salt Lake City, UT 84150

Phone: (801)240-2331

Description: The Family History Library (formerly known as ''The Genealogical Library'' and ''The Genealogical Society'') is perhaps the world's leading genealogical research library, with over 240,000 volumes, 1,800,000 rolls of microfilm, and 300,000 microfiche that can be loaned to over 1,800 Family History Centers. The library publishes a series of 8–50 page research outlines for numerous countries, provinces, and states. Each research outline describes the types of records available, time period these records cover, contents of the records, and how to obtain them. Outlines emphasize records available at the Family History Library, and include addresses and descriptions of records at other archives and repositories. The outlines sell for $.25 to $3.50 and are available from the library and at the family history centers. **Frequency:** Irregular.

Soundex Reference Guide

Precision Indexing
PO Box 303
Bountiful, UT 84011

Phone: (801)298-5468
Bradley W. Steuart, Editor

Pages: 253. **Publication date:** 1990. **Price:** $29.95 (lib. bdg.); $19.96 (paper). **ISBN:** 1-877677-12-4 (lib. bdg.); 1-877677-09-4 (paper).

The Source: A Guidebook of American Genealogy

Ancestry Publishing
440 S. 400 W., Bldg. D
PO Box 476
Salt Lake City, UT 84101

Phone: (801)531-1790
Arlene Eakle, Co-Editor
Johni Cerny, Co-Editor

Description: Comprehensive guide to U.S. genealogical records. Part one covers cemetery, church, census, and legal records. Part two identifies published sources with indexes, newspapers, and biographies. Part three focuses on ethnic resources and includes a chapter on computer databases. Sample records are included throughout. **Pages:** 786. **Publication date:** 1984. **Price:** $39.95. **ISBN:** 0-916489-00-0. **Also includes:** Glossary of genealogy terms, bibliographical index, subject index.

State Census Records

Genealogical Publishing Co.
1001 N. Calvert St.
Baltimore, MD 21202-3897

Phone: (410)837-8271
Toll-Free: 800-296-6687
Ann S. Lainhart, Author

Description: Comprehensive list of state census records listed state by state, year by year, often county by county and district by district. **Pages:** 116. **Publication date:** 1992; reprinted 1993. **Price:** $17.95.

Survey of American Church Records: Major Denominations before 1860

The Everton Publishers
PO Box 368
Logan, UT 84323-0368

Phone: (801)752-6022
E. Kay Kirkham

Description: 4th ed. **Publication date:** 1978.

United States Census Compendium

The Everton Publishers, Inc.
PO Box 368
Logan, UT 84323-0368

Toll-Free: 800-443-6325
Fax: (801)752-0425
Jack Stemmons, Author

Covers: Published census records in addition to any type of document that can be used as a census such as tax lists, petitions, oaths of allegiance, directories, poll lists. **Publication includes:** An abbreviated reference to the publisher or compiler of each record within each entry as well as a complete listing of these references. **Arrangement:** Geographic, by state. **Pages:** 143. **Price:** $12.50.

Using the Family History Library Computer System: Including the Library Catalog, Ancestral File, International Genealogical Index.

Carlberg Press
1782 Beacon Ave.
Anaheim, CA 92804

Phone: (714)772-2849
Nancy E. Carlberg

Pages: 120. **Publication date:** 1994. **Price:** $15.00 (paper). **ISBN:** 0-944878-08-3.

Where to Write for Vital Records: Births, Deaths, Marriages and Divorces

National Center for Health
  Statistics
6525 Belcrest Rd., Rm. 1064
Hyattsville, MD 20782

Phone: (301)436-8500

Covers: Vital statistics offices in each state. **Entries include:** Name and address of office, cost of full copy, cost of short form, any special requirements, dates of records held. **Arrangement:** Geographical. **Pages:** 20. **Frequency:** Irregular; previous edition April 1991; latest edition 1993. **Price:** $2.25 (S/N 017-022-01109-3). **Send orders to:** Superintendent of Documents, U.S. Government Printing Office, Washington, DC 20402-9371 (202-783-3238). **Former titles:** Where to Write for Vital Statistics.

Arkansas

Arkansas Family Historians

Arkansas Genealogical
  Society, Inc.
PO Box 908
Hot Springs, AR 71902-0908

Phone: (501)262-4513
Margaret Harrison Hubbard, Editor

Description: Offers genealogical information on citizens of Arkansas. Contains primary and secondary source materials and family data. Recurring features include news of research. **Frequency:** Quarterly. **Price:** Included in membership.

Historical and Genealogical Source Materials

Arkansas History Commission
One Capitol Mall
Little Rock, AR 72201

Remarks: Write to the Arkansas History Commission for this brochure.

Researching Arkansas History

Rose Publishing Co.
2723 Foxcroft Rd., Ste. 208
Little Rock, AR 72207

Phone: (501)227-8104
Tom W. Dillard, Editor
Valeria Thwing, Editor

Publication includes: List of archives, libraries, government offices, and other repositories which hold materials significant in the study of Arkansas history and genealogy; includes sources for Black history and genealogy. **Entries include:** Institution or department name, address. **Arrangement:** Classified by type of source. **Frequency:** Published 1979. **Price:** $5.00, postpaid.

Connecticut

Connecticut Sources for Family Historians and Genealogists

Everton Publishers, Inc.
PO Box 368
Logan, UT 84321

Phone: (801)752-6022
Toll-Free: 800-443-6325
Fax: (801)752-0425
Kip Sperry, Author

Publication includes: Lists of manuscript collections, genealogical and historical libraries and societies, public libraries, and other sources. **Entries include:** Library or collection name, address, holdings. **Arrangement:** Geographical. **Pages:** 112. **Frequency:** Irregular; latest edition 1980. **Price:** $9.95, plus $1.50 shipping, payment with order. **Also includes:** Bibliographies, indexes, finding aids, etc., concerned with Connecticut history and genealogy.

District of Columbia

Lest We Forget: A Guide to Genealogical Research in the Nation's Capital District of Columbia

Annandale Stake
Church of Jesus Christ of
  Latter-day Saints
Box 89
Annandale, VA 22003

Phone: (703)780-1290
H. Byron Hall, Editor

Covers: Facilities available for genealogical research in Washington, D.C., primarily at various units of the National Archives (including information on regional archive offices) and the Library of Congress, and the libraries of the Daughters of the American Revolution and the National Genealogical Society. **Type:** Directory. **Entries include:** Facility or unit name, address, phone, hours, types of material available, and, in separate sections, detailed information on what materials are available, where and how to secure access, and notes on scope, content, limitations of the materials. **Indexes:** General subject-collection name-locality index. **Pages:** 154. **Frequency:** Irregular; previous edition December 1986; latest edition (eighth) 1992. **Price:** $12.60 National Genealogical Society members, $14.00 nonmembers, plus $3.00 shipping. **Send orders to:** NGS Special Publications, 4527 17th Street North, Arlington, VA 22207-2399.

Florida

Searching in Florida

ISC Publications
Independent Search
  Consultants, Inc.
PO Box 10857
Costa Mesa, CA 92627

Diane C. Robie, Author

Subtitled: A reference guide to public & private records. **Publication date:** 1982. **Price:** $10.95. **ISBN:** 0-942916-01-8.

Georgia

Georgia Genealogical Research

Ancestry   Toll-Free: 800-531-1790
PO Box 476   Fax: (801)531-1798
Salt Lake City, UT   George K. Schweitzer, Author
  84110-0476

Description: Presents information about most of the principal sources used by anyone begining to search for an ancestor who lived in Georgia. **Type:** Book. **Pages:** 238. **Price:** $12.00; (Members, $10.50). **ISBN:** 0-913857-10-6.

Hawaii

Chinese in Hawaii: An Annotated Bibliography

Books on Demand   Phone: (313)761-4700
300 N Zeeb Rd.   Toll-Free: 800-521-0600
Ann Arbor, MI 48106-1346   Nancy Foon Young

Publication date: 1973. **Price:** $43.50. **ISBN:** 0-8357-2766-1.

Filipinos in Hawaii: An Annotated Bibliography

University of Hawaii Press   Phone: (808)956-8255
2840 Kolowalu St.   Ruben R. Alcantara
Honolulu, HI 96822   Nancy S. Alconcel

Publication date: 1977. **Price:** $8.00. **ISBN:** 0-8248-0612-3.

Japanese in Hawaii: An Annotated Bibliography

University of Hawaii Press   Phone: (808)956-8255
2840 Kolowalu St.   Mitsugu Matsuda, Author
Honolulu, HI 96822

Pages: 304. **Publication date:** 1975. **Remarks:** Part of the Hawaii Series, no. 5.

Illinois

Genealogical Index of the Newberry Library (Chicago)

GK Hall & Co.   Phone: (617)423-3990
70 Lincoln St.   Toll-Free: 800-343-2806
Boston, MA 02111

Description: 4 vols. **Publication date:** 1970. **Price:** $380.00 (Set, lib. bdg.). **ISBN:** 0-8161-0498-0.

Guide to Local and Family History at the Newberry Library

Ancestry   Toll-Free: 800-531-1790
PO Box 476   Fax: (801)531-1798
Salt Lake City, UT   Peggy Tuck Sinko, Author
  84110-0476

Description: A user-oriented guide to the Newberry Library's books, maps, atlases, journals, orginal sources, finding aids, etc. **Type:** Book. **Pages:** 202. **Publication date:** 1987. **Price:** $16.95; (Members, $14.00). **ISBN:** 0-916489-24-8.

Searching in Illinois

ISC Publications   Gayle Beckstead, Author
Independent Search   Mary L. Kozub, Author
  Consultants, Inc.
PO Box 10857
Costa Mesa, CA 92627

Subtitled: A reference guide to public & private records. **Pages:** 210. **Publication date:** 1984. **Price:** $12.95. **ISBN:** 0-942916-05-0.

Indiana

Genealogist's Guide to the Allen County Public Library

Watermill Publications   Phone: (219)493-1735
2238 Cimarron Pass   Karen B. Cavanaugh
Fort Wayne, IN 46815

Pages: 100. **Publication date:** 1989. **Price:** $16.95 (paper). **ISBN:** 0-3184-3234-X.

Manual for Indiana Genealogical Research

Genealogy Unlimited, Inc.   Phone: (801)226-8971
PO Box 537   Toll-Free: 800-666-4363
Orem, UT 84059-0537   Pat Gooldy
                                          Ray Gooldy

Covers: History, federal, and state sources; land, military, church, and vital records; published county histories; newspapers; libraries; societies; colleges and universities; Black history. **Pages:** 94. **Price:** $15.00.

Searching in Indiana

ISC Publications   Mickey D. Carty, Author
Independent Search
  Consultants, Inc.
PO Box 10857
Costa Mesa, CA 92627

Subtitled: A reference guide to public & private records. **Pages:** 278. **Publication date:** 1985. **Price:** $14.95. **ISBN:** 0-94916-06-9.

Kentucky

Blue Grass Roots

Kentucky Genealogical
   Society, Inc.
PO Box 153
Frankfort, KY 40602

Landon Wills, Editor
Ilene Wills, Editor

Description: Publishes transcriptions, abstractions, and annotations of Kentucky public records of genealogical research value, as well as information on research sources, tips, and techniques. **First published:** 1973. **Audience:** Society members, libraries, and other societies. **Frequency:** 4/yr. **Indexed:** Annually. **Circulation** 2,150. **Price:** Included in membership. **Remarks:** Also available in microform. Cumulative index (1973–1984) is available for $15. Original issues (1973–1984) available on a roll of microfilm for $15.

Kentucky Ancestry

Ancestry
PO Box 476
Salt Lake City, UT 84110

Roseann Reinemuth Hogan,
   Author

Subtitled: A guide to genealogical and historical research. **Covers:** Kentucky. **Description:** Outlines resources in Kentucky libraries and archives, special subjects (vital records, county tax records, women's records, African-American records, secondary sources). **Indexes:** General. **Pages:** 388. **Publication date:** 1992. **Price:** $19.95 plus $2.50 shipping and handling. **Send orders to:** Publisher. **Also includes:** Maps; an inventory of microfilmed county records available at the Kentucky Department of Libraries and Archives, the Kentucky Historical Society, and the University of Kentucky Library; and a county-by-county survey of existing records types, including categories of records destroyed by fire, flood, etc.

Kentucky Genealogical Research

Ancestry
PO Box 476
Salt Lake City, UT
   84110-0476

Toll-Free: 800-531-1790
Fax: (801)531-1798
George K. Schweitzer, Author

Description: Presents information about most of the principal sources used by anyone beginning to search for an ancestor who lived in Kentucky. **Type:** Book. **Pages:** 156. **Price:** $12.00 (Members, $10.50). **ISBN:** 0-913857-02-5.

Maryland

Genealogical Research in Maryland: A Guide

Maryland Historical Society
   Genealogical Committee
201 W. Monument Street
Baltimore, MD 21201

Phone: (301)685-3750
Mary K. Meyer, Author

Covers: Describes vital records, tax lists, military records, and various libraries and archives Maryland and their holdings. **Publication includes:** All the addresses of genealogical and historical societies in the state and a bibliography of Maryland genealogical source records. **Pages:** 117. **Publication date:** 1992, fourth edi-

tion. **Price:** $12.50. **Remarks:** Also available from Pipe Creek Publications, 5179 Perry Road, Mount Airy, MD 21771, (410)875-2824.

Maryland Genealogical Society Newsletter

Maryland Genealogical
   Society
201 N Monument St.
Baltimore, MD 21201

Phone: (301)685-3750
Ella Rowe, Editor

Description: Publishes news of the Society, its members, and its activities. Contains information on the location and availability of genealogical research resources such as tombstone inscriptions, wills, marriage records, and materials available in specific collections or regions of the U.S. Recurring features include news of other genealogical societies. **First published:** January 1974. **Frequency:** 4/yr. **Circulation** 1,400. **Price:** Included in membership.

Massachusetts

Massachusetts Genealogical Research

Ancestry
PO Box 476
Salt Lake City, UT
   84110-0476

Toll-Free: 800-531-1790
Fax: (801)531-1798
George K. Schweitzer, Author

Description: Presents information about most of the principal sources used by anyone beginning to search for an ancestor who lived in Massachusetts. **Type:** Book. **Pages:** 281. **Price:** $12.00 (Members, $10.50). **ISBN:** 0-913857-12-2.

Michigan

Genealogical Guide to the Burton Historical Collection, Detroit Public Library

Ancestry
PO Box 476
Salt Lake City, UT 84110

Phone: (801)531-1790
Toll-Free: 800-531-1790
Joseph Oldenburg, Author

Pages: 128. **Publication date:** 1988. **Price:** $7.95.

Michigan Ethnic Directory

Michigan Ethnic Heritage
   Studies Center
60 Farnsworth/Rackham Bldg.,
   Ste. 120
Detroit, MI 48202

Phone: (313)832-7400
Fax: (313)831-5633
Otto Feinstein, Editor-in-Chief

Description: About 2,000 ethnic organizations and institutions in Michigan, including churches, clubs, consulates, fraternal and political organizations, and media. **Type:** Directory. **Entries include:** Organization name, address, phone, name and title of contact, description of activities and purpose. **Arrangement:** Classified by ethnic group. **Indexes:** Organization name. **Pages:** 118. **Frequency:** Irregular; previous edition October 1991; latest edition 1994. **Price:** $15.00. **Remarks:** Supersedes *Peoples of Michigan: A Two Volume Guide to Ethnic Michigan.*

Michigan Genealogy Sources and Resources

Genealogical Publishing   Phone: (301)837-8271
1001 N. Calvert St.   Toll-Free: 800-296-6687
Baltimore, MD 21202   Fax: (410)752-8492
    Carol McGinnis, Author

Frequency: Irregular; latest edition fall 1989 (now out of print); new edition expected 1994. **Price:** $18.00 (1989 edition), postpaid.

Missouri

Missouri Genealogical Records & Abstracts

Heritage Books   Toll-Free: 800-398-7709
1540-E Pointer Ridge Pl.   Fax: (301)390-7153
Bowie, MD 20716   Sherida K. Eddlemon

Publication includes: Information on specific counties, and the state as a whole, i.e., marriage records, Spanish censuses, tax lists, estrays, letters at the post office, wills and bonds, jury lists, indictments, Indian trade records, cemetery listings, petitioners, animal marks and brands, slave bills of sale, French and Spanish land grants, military records, disaster victims. **Description:** Vol. 1: 1766–1839, 34 counties; Vol. 3: 1787–1839, 43 counties; Vol. 4: 1741–1839, 49 counties; Vol. 5: 1755–1839, 52 counties. **Type:** Book. **Indexes:** General. **Pages:** 336 (Vol. 1); 253 (3); 272 (4); 275 (5). **Publication date:** 1990 (Vol 1); 1991 (3); 1992 (4); 1993 (5). **Price:** $23.00 (Vol. 1); $20.00 (3); $21.00 (4); $23.00 (5); all paper.

Nebraska

Nebraska Local History and Genealogy Reference Guide

Sylvia Nimmo, Publisher   Phone: (402)331-2384
6201 Kentucky Rd.   Sylvia Nimmo, Editor
Omaha, NE 68133   Mary Cutter, Editor

Publication includes: Lists of about 450 genealogical archives and societies, libraries, and museums for genealogists in Nebraska. **Entries include:** Name, address or location. **Arrangement:** Geographical by county. **Frequency:** Published December 1986. **Price:** $35.00, postpaid. **Also includes:** Maps of Nebraska counties. **Former titles:** Guide to Nebraska Research. **Remarks:** Principal content includes citations to vital records, directories, historical publications, and other sources useful to Nebraska genealogists.

New Hampshire

Directory of Repositories of Family History in New Hampshire

Clearfield Co.   Phone: (410)625-9004
200 E Eager St.   Scott E. Green
Baltimore, MD 21202

Description: Provides a list of the major genealogy and local history collections throughout the state of New Hampshire. **Type:** Book. **Entries include:** For each of New Hampshire's ten counties, the addresses and phone numbers of the Register of Deeds and Registrar of Probate are given. Information listed under the towns and cities consists of the community date of foundation, mailing address and phone number of the clerk, prior names for that community, and a succinct listing of the prinicipal genealogy repositories. **Arrangement:** By county and immediately thereunder by municipality. **Indexes:** General. **Pages:** 61. **Publication date:** 1993. **Price:** $10.95 (paper).

New Hampshire Genealogical Research Guide

Heritage Books   Toll-Free: 800-398-7709
1540-E Pointer Ridge Pl.   Fax: (301)390-7153
Bowie, MD 20716   Laird C. Towle
    Ann N. Brown

Publication includes: Several appendices which provide data on depositories within the state, a listing of manuscript sources, and the contents of several major series and periodicals published on the state. **Description:** Contains instructions on how to pursue research on New Hampshire families using sources both inside and outside the state. **Type:** Book. **Indexes:** General. **Pages:** 98. **Publication date:** 1983. **Price:** $20.50 (paper). **Also includes:** Maps.

New Jersey

Complete Public Records Guide: Central and Northern New Jersey Region

REyn, Inc.   Fred D. Knapp
Publishing Division
140 Huguenot St.
New Rochelle, NY
10801-5208

Description: Covers Bergen, Essex, Hudson, Hunterdon, Mercer, Middlesex, Monmouth, Morris, Passaic, Somerset, Sussex, Union, and Warren Counties. Begins with a basic description of types of records/indexes available throughout the state (land, court, corporate, election, etc.) and then explains where and how they are filed in each county. Contains detailed floor plans of each repository and explains computer systems where applicable. **Pages:** Over 178. **Publication date:** 1993. **Price:** $39.95. **Also includes:** Illustrations. **Remarks:** Also contains information on accessing motor vehicle/license information from all states.

Genealogical Resources in Southern New Jersey

Gloucester County Historical
  Society
17 Hunter St.
PO Box 409
Woodbury, NJ 08096

Phone: (609)845-4771
Edith Hoelle, Editor

Covers: Historical societies, public libraries, colleges, and other sources of records and information for genealogical research. **Entries include:** Name, address, phone, description of collection/records available, contact name, hours and days open, whether fee is charged, whether copier is available. **Arrangement:** Geographical by county. **Pages:** 30. **Frequency:** Irregular; previous edition 1989; latest edition 1993; new edition expected 1994. **Price:** $6.00, postpaid.

General Index to the New Jersey Archives

Genealogical Publishing Co.
1001 N. Calvert St.
Baltimore, MD 21202-3897

Phone: (410)837-8271
Toll-Free: 800-296-6687
Frederick W. Ricord,
  Compiler

Covers: References to about 7,500 individuals and to hundreds of special subjects relating to the founding and settlement of colonial New Jersey. **Description:** Index to the first ten volumes of New Jersey Archives; key to the historically important colonial documents published in NJA. **Pages:** 198. **Publication date:** 1888; reprinted 1994. **Price:** $22.50. **ISBN:** 0-8063-1445-1.

New Jersey: Digging for Ancestors in the Garden State Genealogy

Detroit Society for
  Genealogical Research, Inc.
c/o Burton Historical
  Collection
Detroit Public Library
5201 N. Woodward Ave.
Detroit, MI 48202

Phone: (313)833-1480
Dr. Kenn Stryker-Rodda,
  Author

Pages: 40. **Frequency:** Latest edition 1984. **Price:** $5.00.

New York

Genealogical Resources in the New York Metropolitan Area

Ancestry
PO Box 476
Salt Lake City, UT
  84110-0476

Toll-Free: 800-531-1790
Fax: (801)531-1798
Estelle M. Guzik, Editor

Covers: More than 100 facilities, including fifty-two government agencies and courts, thirty-two libraries, and twenty archives. **Description:** Discusses the records available for New York City's five counties, Long Island, Westchester, northern New Jersey counties, and the state capitals of Albany and Trenton. **Type:** Book. **Entries include:** Address, telephone number, and hours of operation; travel directions; geographic scope and time span of records; finding aids and access. **Pages:** 648. **Price:** $24.95 (Members, $21.00). **ISBN:** 0-9621863-0-9.

Guide to Records in the New York State Archives, 2nd ed.

New York State Archives and
  Records Administration
10D45 CEC
Albany, NY 12230

Description: Lists 3,200 records series, from colonial times to the present including land, military, probate, and state office records. Some records can be accessed on film, but many are only available at Albany. Appendix B lists all microfilm copies of local government records available at Archives. **Pages:** Over 500. **Frequency:** Previous edition 1981. **Publication date:** 1993. **Price:** $12.95, plus $3.00 P&H. Make check payable to SARA publications.

New York Atlas of Historical County Boundaries

Simon & Schuster
Academic Reference Division
15 Columbus Cir. 26th Fl.
New York, NY 10023

John H. Long, Editor
Kathryn Ford Thorne,
  Compiler

Description: The second volume of the Newberry Library's project to produce a 40-volume series of more than 3,000 U.S. counties. Introduction explains laws which have shaped county boundaries. Maps show changes and counties which are no longer in New York. No town boundaries are covered. Particularly valuable for northern, central, and western New York. **Pages:** 242. **Publication date:** 1993. **Price:** $50.00. **Also includes:** Bibliography; maps.

New York Genealogical and Biographical Record

122 E 58th St.
New York, NY 10022-1939

Phone: (212)755-8532
Henry B. Hoff, Editor

Description: Focus on New York state. **Type:** Magazine. **First published:** December 1869. **Frequency:** Quarterly. **Circulation** 1,950. **Subscription:** $25.00. **ISSN:** 0028-7237.

New York Genealogical Research

Ancestry
PO Box 476
Salt Lake City, UT
  84110-0476

Toll-Free: 800-531-1790
Fax: (801)531-1798
George K. Schweitzer, Author

Description: Presents information about most of the principal sources used by anyone beginning to search for an ancestor who lived in New York. **Type:** Book. **Pages:** 254. **Price:** $12.00 (Members, $10.50). **ISBN:** 0-913857-11-4

Searching in New York

ISC Publications
Independent Search
  Consultants, Inc.
PO Box 10857
Costa Mesa, CA 92627

Kate Burke, Author

Subtitled: A reference guide to public & private records. **Covers:** Approximately 1,000 repositories of public and private records in the state of New York. **Entries include:** Record source name and address. **Arrangement:** Geographical. **Pages:** 270. **Publication date:** 1987. **Price:** $15.95, postpaid. **ISBN:** 0-942916-10-7.

North Carolina

North Carolina Genealogical Research

Ancestry
PO Box 476
Salt Lake City, UT
  84110-0476

Toll-Free: 800-531-1790
Fax: (801)531-1798
George K. Schweitzer, Author

Description: Presents information about most of the principal sources used by anyone beginning to search for an ancestor who lived in North Carolina. **Type:** Book. **Pages:** 192. **Price:** $12.00 (Members, $10.50). **ISBN:** 0-913857-03-3.

Ohio

Cleveland Ethnic Directory

Nationalities Services Center
  of Cleveland
1715 Euclid Ave., Ste. 200
Cleveland, OH 44115

Phone: (216)781-4560

Description: Several thousand ethnic organizations, societies, cultural and political organizations, and performing groups in the Cleveland, Ohio area. **Entries include:** Organization name, address, phone, names, and titles of key personnel, subsidiary and branch names and location. **Arrangement:** Classified by nationality. **Indexes:** Subject. **Frequency:** Irregular; latest edition 1989.

Ohio Genealogical Guide

Carol Willsey Bell, C.G.
4649 Yarmouth Ln.
Youngstown, OH 44512

Phone: (216)782-8380
Carol Willsey Bell, Editor

Covers: Location, content, etc., of land, tax, census, church, military, and other records in Ohio; includes lists of libraries, periodicals, etc. **Entries include:** Name of source, address, description of holdings. **Arrangement:** Classified by type of source or record. **Pages:** 120. **Frequency:** Irregular, latest edition 1990. **Price:** $16.25, postpaid.

Ohio Genealogical Periodical Index: A County Guide

4659 Yarmouth Lane
Youngstown, OH 44512

Phone: (216)782-8380
Carol Willsey Bell

Publication includes: List of publishers of about 110 genealogical periodicals. **Type:** Index. **Entries include:** Title of publication, publisher name, address, rates, and dates covered. **Arrangement:** Geographical by county. **Indexes:** Subject. **Frequency:** Biennial, spring of odd years. **Price:** $12.75, postpaid. **Remarks:** Primary content is a cumulative index of articles published on Ohio's counties and Bible and family records.

Ohio Genealogical Society Newsletter

Ohio Genealogical Society
PO Box 2625
Mansfield, OH 44906

Phone: (419)522-9077
Sunda Anderson Peters, Editor

Description: Fosters interest in people who helped to establish and perpetuate the state of Ohio. Connects the Society's 6,300 members and 100 chapters. Acts as a clearinghouse for genealogical information on Ohio families. Recurring features include news of research, a calendar of events, reports of meetings, news of educational opportunities, and notices of publications available. Also includes financial reports, listings of library acquisitions, computer genealogy articles, chapter addresses, and queries. **First published:** 1970. **Audience:** Genealogists and historians with Ohio interests. **Frequency:** Monthly. **Indexed:** Annually. **Circulation** 6,000. **Price:** $25.00/yr., U.S.; $33.00 elsewhere. **ISSN:** 1052-858X. **Remarks:** Only accepts member queries.

Ohio Guide to Genealogical Sources

Genealogical Publishing Co.
1001 N. Calvert St.
Baltimore, MD 21202-3897

Phone: (410)837-8271
Toll-Free: 800-296-6687
Carol Willsey Bell, Author

Publication includes: Records of the State Auditor, Clerks of Court, Court of Common Pleas, Children's Homes, Coroner, County Homes, County Commissioners, Probate Court, Recorder, Sheriff, Soldier's Relief Commission, and Treasurer; census records available for each county, a listing of the county's records on microfilm in the State Library, manuscript collections, newspapers, tax records, articles from periodicals, and published sources for that county. **Description:** Comprehensive guide to the genealogical records and sources in Ohio. **Entries include:** County creation date and the name(s) of the parent county; the county seat; the name and address of the county courthouse, library, historical society, genealogical society, archival district, and health department; a list of relevent land surveys (for land and deed research); the surrounding counties; and the names of all townships in the county. **Pages:** 372. **Publication date:** 1988; reprinted 1993. **Price:** $30.00.

Wyandot Tracers

Ohio Genealogical Society
PO Box 414
Upper Sandusky, OH
  43351-0414

Nira Beaschler, Editor

Description: Provides historical and genealogical information on individuals who lived in Wyandot County, Ohio. Recurring features include news of research, a calendar of events, and notices of publications available. **First published:** March 1983. **Audience:** Genealogical societies and libraries. **Frequency:** Bimonthly. **Circulation** 350. **Price:** Included in membership.

Oklahoma

Guide to the Historical Records of Oklahoma

Heritage Books
1540-E Pointer Ridge Pl.
Bowie, MD 20716

Toll-Free: 800-398-7709
Fax: (301)390-7153
Bradford Koplowitz

Covers: Oklahoma's earliest white settlement and Native American records from the state's eastern counties. Commissioners' minutes, land records, probate records, civil records, divorces, marriages, criminal records, adoptions, elections, tax rolls, school records, oil and gas leases. **Description:** Identifies and describes public records which span the 1880s through 1920 for all county governments, all municipal governments for cities over 5,000 people, and for smaller cities of historical significance. **Type:** Book. **Pages:** 189. **Publication date:** 1989. **Price:** $20.00 (paper).

Pennsylvania

A Genealogist's Guide to Pennsylvania Records

Genealogical Society of Pennsylvania
1300 Locust St.
Philadelphia, PA 19107-5661

Phone: (215)732-6201
Helen Hutchison Woodroofe, Compiler

Description: Originally published over 17 issues of the *Pennsylvania Genealogical Magazine.* Arranged alphabetically by county. **Pages:** 464. **Publication date:** 1995. **Price:** $39.95, plus $4.00 S&H. **Also includes:** Appendix of county information (date organized, county seat, etc.).

Guide to Genealogical Sources at the Pennsylvania State Archives

Genealogy Unlimited, Inc.
PO Box 537
Orem, UT 84059-0537

Phone: (801)226-8971
Toll-Free: 800-666-4363
R.M. Dructor

Pages: 129. **Price:** $9.00.

Guide to the Manuscript Collections of the Historical Society of Pennsylvania

Historical Society of Pennsylvania
1300 Locust St.
Philadelphia, PA 19107

Phone: (215)732-6201

Description: Second edition. **Publication date:** 1949.

Guide to the Record Groups in the Pennsylvania State Archives

Pennsylvania Historical and Museum Commission
Box 126
Harrisburg, PA 17108

Phone: (717)787-2891
Frank M. Suran, Author

Pages: 84. **Publication date:** 1980.

Pennsylvania Genealogical Research

Ancestry
PO Box 476
Salt Lake City, UT 84110-0476

Toll-Free: 800-531-1790
Fax: (801)531-1798
George K. Schweitzer, Author

Description: Presents information about most of the principal sources used by anyone beginning to search for an ancestor who lived in Pennsylvania. **Type:** Book. **Pages:** 227. **Price:** $12.00 (Members, $10.50). **ISBN:** 0-913857-09-2.

Rhode Island

Rhode Island Sources for Family Historians and Genealogists

The Everton Publishers, Inc.
PO Box 368
Logan, UT 84323-0368

Toll-Free: 800-443-6325
Fax: (801)752-0425
Kip Sperry, Author

Covers: Getting started; historical chronology; evolution of Rhode Island; counties and major towns; sources of information. **Arrangement:** Alphabetical. **Pages:** 146. **Price:** $9.95. **Also includes:** Appendices.

South Carolina

Guide to South Carolina Genealogical Research and Records

Brent Howard Holcomb
Box 21766
Columbia, SC 29221

Phone: (803)772-6919
Brent Howard Holcomb, Author

Pages: 65. **Frequency:** Latest edition 1991. **Price:** $15.00, postpaid. **Also includes:** Maps of South Carolina counties, parishes, and district boundaries.

South Carolina Genealogical Research

Ancestry
PO Box 476
Salt Lake City, UT 84110-0476

Toll-Free: 800-531-1790
Fax: (801)531-1798
George K. Schweitzer, Author

Description: Presents information about most of the principal sources used by anyone beginning to search for an ancestor who lived in South Carolina. **Type:** Book. **Pages:** 192. **Price:** $12.00 (Members, $10.50). **ISBN:** 0-913857-08-4.

Tennessee

Guide to County Records and Genealogical Resources in Tennessee

Genealogical Publishing
1001 N. Calvert Street
Baltimore, MD 21202

Phone: (301)837-8271
Toll-Free: 800-296-6687
Fax: (410)752-8492
Richard Carlton Fulcher, Editor

Covers: Archives and libraries in Tennessee with genealogical records and statewide reference materials. **Entries include:** County seat, names and addresses of libraries and genealogical societies, public records, manuscripts, church records, etc. **Arrangement:** Geographical. **Pages:** 200. **Frequency:** Irregular; latest edition fall 1989. **Price:** $23.00, postpaid.

"Research in Tennessee"

National Genealogical Society
Quarterly
National Genealogical Society
4527 17th St. N
Arlington, VA 22207-2309

Phone: (703)525-0050
Fax: (703)525-0052
Gale Williams Bamman,
Author

Covers: Emphasizes the genealogical holdings of the Tennessee State Library and Archives and lists a variety of sources available elsewhere in Tennessee and the United States. **First published:** Volume 81:2, June 1993, issue of *National Genealogical Society Quarterly.* **Pages:** 99-125.

Tennessee Genealogical Records

Genealogical Publishing Co.
1001 North Calvert St.
Baltimore, MD 21202-3897

Phone: (410)837-8271
Toll-Free: 800-296-6687
Edythe Rucker Whitley,
Author

Subtitled: Records of Early Settlers from State and County Archives. **Description:** Information abstracted from Tennessee records covering over 18,000 settlers. **Type:** Book. **First published:** 1985. **Indexes:** General. **Pages:** 393. **Publication date:** 1989, reprint. **Price:** $25.00.

Tennessee Genealogical Research

Ancestry
PO Box 476
Salt Lake City, UT
84110-0476

Toll-Free: 800-531-1790
Fax: (801)531-1798
George K. Schweitzer, Author

Description: Presents information about most of the principal sources used by anyone beginning to search for an ancestor who lived in Tennessee. **Type:** Book. **Pages:** 138. **Price:** $12.00 (Members, $10.50).

Texas

Genealogical Records in Texas

Genealogical Publishing Co.
1001 N Calvert St.
Baltimore, MD 21202-3897

Phone: (410)837-8271
Toll-Free: 800-296-6687
Fax: (410)752-8492
Imogene Kennedy
Leon Kennedy

Description: Covers nearly 200 years of genealogical records in Texas; describes what the records are and where they are located. **Type:** Book. **First published:** 1987. **Pages:** 248. **Publication date:** 1992, reprint. **Price:** $35.00.

Livingston's Directory of Texas Historical and Genealogical Organizations

Bee Tree Press
Box 135
Lake Jackson, TX 77566

Phone: (409)265-6342

Covers: Nearly 300 active historical and heritage societies, preservation, archeological, religious, ethnic, and genealogical groups within the state. **Entries include:** Organization name, mailing address, membership fees, titles of periodicals and other publications or transcriptions, projects completed or underway; listings may also include phone, hours for museum (if any). **Arrange-**

ment: Alphabetical. **Indexes:** Geographical (including references to locations covered by an organization in addition to its own location). **Pages:** 60. **Frequency:** Irregular; first edition November 1984; new edition expected late 1989. **Price:** $12.50, plus $.69 shipping, payment with order. **Also includes:** County and town name cross-reference.

Virginia

Virginia Cemeteries: A Guide to Resources

University Press of Virginia
Box 3608, University Sta.
Charlottesville, VA
22903-0608

Phone: (804)924-6064
Fax: (804)982-2655
Anne M. Hogg, Editor
Dennis A. Tosh, Editor

Covers: About 1,300 cemeteries, cemetery recording projects in progress, and published and unpublished records in Virginia. **Entries include:** For cemeteries—Name, location, name of record keeper. For recording projects—Organization or researcher name, address. For published records—Title, publisher, location, bibliographic details. For unpublished records—Type of record, location. **Arrangement:** Geographical. **Indexes:** Geographical, cemetery name. **Pages:** 319. **Frequency:** Irregular. **Price:** $12.95.

Virginia Genealogical Research

Ancestry
PO Box 476
Salt Lake City, UT
84110-0476

Toll-Free: 800-531-1790
Fax: (801)531-1798
George K. Schweitzer, Author

Description: Presents information about most of the principal sources used by anyone beginning to search for an ancestor who lived in Virginia. **Type:** Book. **Pages:** 196. **Price:** $12.00 (Members, $10.50). **ISBN:** 0-913857-06-8

Virginia Genealogical Resources

Detroit Society for
Genealogical Research, Inc.
c/o Burton Historical
Collection
Detroit Public Library
5201 N. Woodward Ave.
Detroit, MI 48202

Phone: (313)833-1480
Robert Young Clay, Author

Publication includes: Lists of libraries, court houses, etc., that are of use in genealogical research in Virginia. **Frequency:** Published 1980. **Price:** $5.00, postpaid, payment with order.

Virginia Genealogical Society Newsletter

Virginia Genealogical Society
5001 W. Broad St., Ste. 115
Richmond, VA 23230-3023

Phone: (804)285-8954
Chris Hooper, Editor
JoAnn Nance, Editor

Description: Includes news of research, a calendar of events, news of educational opportunities, book reviews, notices of publications available, queries, and a column titled "Acquisitions at the Virginia State Archives." **Audience:** Historians, genealogists, and interested individuals. **Frequency:** Bimonthly. **Indexed:** Annually. **Circulation** 2,700. **Price:** Included in membership.

Virginia Genealogy: Sources & Resources

Genealogical Publishing Co.
1001 N Calvert St.
Baltimore, MD 21202-3897

Phone: (410)837-8271
Toll-Free: 800-296-6687
Carol McGinnis, Author

Description: Describes the types of resources available, where they may be found, and what they contain for Virginia as a whole, for all 95 counties, and for all 41 independent cities. **Type:** Book. **Indexes:** General. **Pages:** 505. **Publication date:** 1993. **Price:** $35.00. **ISBN:** 0-8063-1379-X.

West Virginia

West Virginia Genealogy: Sources and Resources

Genealogical Publishing Co.
1001 North Calvert St.
Baltimore, MD 21202-3897

Phone: (410)837-8271
Toll-Free: 800-296-6687
Carol McGinnis, Author

Description: Describes which West Virginia records are available and how they can be located. **Type:** Book. **Indexes:** General. **Pages:** 135. **Publication date:** 1988. **Price:** $18.50.

Wisconsin

"Research at the State Historical Society of Wisconsin"

Minnesota Genealogical
  Society
PO Box 16069
Saint Paul, MN 55116-0069

Phone: (612)645-3671
Paula Stuart Warren

Description: In-depth guide to the library of the State Historical Society of Wisconsin. **First published:** September 1993 in *Minnesota Genealogist,* volume 24:3.

Searching for Your Wisconsin Ancestors in the Wisconsin Libraries

Genealogy Unlimited, Inc.
PO Box 537
Orem, UT 84059-0537

Phone: (801)226-8971
Toll-Free: 800-666-4363
Carol W. Ryan

Pages: 100. **Publication date:** Second edition, 1988. **Price:** $8.50.

Outside the U.S.

Canadian Genealogical Handbook: A Comprehensive Guide to Finding Your Ancestors in Canada

Wheatfield Press
506 King Edward St.
Winnipeg, MB, Canada R3J
  1L8

Phone: (204)885-5731
Eric Jonnsson, Author

Publication includes: Illustrations, facsimiles, and maps. **Description:** Revised 2nd edition. **Pages:** 352. **Publication date:** 1978.

Everton's Genealogical Helper—Directory of Genealogical Societies, Libraries, and Periodicals Issue

Everton Publishers, Inc.
3223 S. Main St.
Logan, UT 84321

Phone: (801)752-6022
Toll-Free: 800-443-6325
Fax: (801)752-0452

Publication includes: Lists of genealogical societies, libraries, and periodicals throughout the world. **Entries include:** All entries include organization or individual name and address; periodical listings include frequency and price. **Frequency:** Annual, July–August issue. **Price:** $4.50, postpaid, payment with order.

Everton's Genealogical Helper—Directory of Professional Researchers Issue

Everton Publishers, Inc.
3223 S. Main St.
Logan, UT 84321

Phone: (801)752-6022
Toll-Free: 800-443-6325
Fax: (801)752-0425

Publication includes: List of professional genealogical researchers, worldwide; a listing fee is charged. **Entries include:** Researcher name, address, specialties; some listings may include additional detail. **Frequency:** Annual, September/October. **Price:** $4.50, postpaid, payment with order. **Remarks:** Researchers were formerly listed in "Genealogical Helper—Directory of Genealogical Societies and Professionals Issue," now split into this issue and ". . . Societies, Libraries, and Periodicals Issue," (see separate entry).

Genealogical Computing

Ancestry, Inc.
440 South 400 West, Bldg. D.
Salt Lake City, UT 84101

Phone: (801)531-1790
Toll-Free: 800-531-1790
Fax: (801)531-1798

Covers: Genealogical computer databases, bulletin boards, and interest groups in the United States, Australia, and Great Britain. **Entries include:** Company name, address, phone, requirements for membership, and description of service. **Arrangement:** Geographical. **Pages:** 48. **Frequency:** Quarterly. **Price:** $8.50 per issue; $25.00 per year. **Also includes:** Articles and information on using computers and genealogy.

Genealogy in Ontario: Searching the Records

Ontario Genealogical Society
40 Orchard View Blvd., Ste. 102
Toronto, ON, Canada M4R 1B9

Phone: (416)489-0734
Brenda Merriman, Author

Publication includes: Maps. **Pages:** 168. **Publication date:** 1988.

International Vital Records Handbook

Genealogical Publishing Co., Inc.
1001 N Calvert St.
Baltimore, MD 21202-3897

Phone: (410)837-8271
Toll-Free: 800-296-6687
Fax: (410)752-8492
Thomas Jay Kemp, Author

Covers: Vital records offices for 67 countries and territories in North America, the British Isles and other English-speaking countries, and Europe. **Entries include:** Office name, address, phone, application fees, method of payment, description of holdings, actual application forms to use in obtaining copies of records, and alternative record locations. **Arrangement:** Geographical. **Pages:** 404. **Frequency:** Biennial, even years. **Price:** $24.95, plus $2.50 shipping. **ISBN:** 0-8063-1264-5. **Former titles:** Vital Records Handbook.

Inventory of Ontario Newspapers, 1793–1986

Micromedia Ltd.
20 Victoria St.
Toronto, ON, Canada M5C 2N8

Phone: (416)362-5211
J. Brian Gilchrist, Editor

Pages: 74. **Publication date:** 1987.

List of Genealogical Societies Outside of the United States

Summit Publications
Box 222
Munroe Falls, OH 44262

J. Konrad, Editor

Covers: More than 350 genealogical societies in 26 foreign countries. **Entries include:** Association name, address, phone. **Arrangement:** Geographical. **Pages:** 25. **Frequency:** Published 1990. **Price:** $3.00, plus $1.00 P&H.

Other Media

⌀ This chapter provides the names and producers of other media sources of information, including on-line databases, CD-ROM products, and microfiche, which provide guidance or records of value to researchers whether interested in genealogy in general or in a specific ethnic group. Listings are arranged alphabetically by product name.

Ancestral File

The Church of Jesus Christ of   Phone: (801)240-2331
  Latter-day Saints   Jay Roberts, Ancestral File
Family History Library   Specialist
35 N West Temple St.
Salt Lake City, UT 84150

Description: Directory contains genealogical information on 15 million individuals throughout the world, linking individuals into pedigrees indicating ancestors and descendants. Enables the user to search by similar last name spelling, exact last name spelling, and Ancestral File number. Includes the names and addresses of people who have contributed information. Comprises six individual compact disks. Typical record items: name, gender, birth date, christening date, death date, burial date, parents, spouse. Can show in one entry several events, unlike IGI which shows single events. The information in Ancestral File is GEDCOM compatible. Users can print in several different formats or download information onto diskette from Ancestral File for their own family records. The names and addresses of submitters are also available for records in Ancestral File so that research efforts may be coordinated and shared between genealogists. Users are encouraged to contribute their own efforts and findings so that they may be included in future updates. **Languages:** English. **Type:** CD-ROM. **Subjects:** Genealogy. **Updating:** Regularly. **Online availability:** Producer. Available as part of the Family Search system, which is made publicly available through the Family History Library and other family centers operated by the LDS.

City Directories of the United States, 1861–1881

Research Publications   Phone: (203)397-2600
  International   Toll-Free: 800-444-0799
12 Lunar Dr., Drawer AB   Fax: (203)397-3893
Woodbridge, CT 06525

City Directories of the United States, 1882–1901

Research Publications   Phone: (203)397-2600
  International   Toll-Free: 800-444-0799
12 Lunar Dr., Drawer AB   Fax: (203)397-3893
Woodbridge, CT 06525

Family History Library Catalog

The Church of Jesus Christ of   Phone: (801)240-2331
  Latter-day Saints   Jay Roberts, Ancestral File
Family History Library   Specialist
35 N West Temple St.
Salt Lake City, UT 84150

Description: Contains descriptions of records, books, microforms, and microfiche held in the Family History Library. Features information on census records, birth records, family histories, church registers, immigration, military, probate and vital records. Typical Record Items: Author; title; publication date; publication year; publisher; notes; content. CD version allows searching by key words and spelling variations, locality, family name, or film number. 1992 list included 235,000 books; 1.75 million microfilms and 325,000 microfiche; maps, and other materials. **Languages:** English. **Subjects:** Genealogy. **Online availability:** CD-ROM: Producer. Rates/Conditions: Available as part of the Family Search system, which is made publicly available through the Family History Library and other family history centers operated by the LDS. **Alternate electronic formats:** Microform: Family History Library Catalog.

FamilySearch

The Church of Jesus Christ of   Phone: (801)240-2331
  Latter-day Saints
Family History Library
35 N West Temple St.
Salt Lake City, UT 84150

Description: Contains five CD-ROM packages: Ancestral File, International Genealogical Index, Family History Library Catalog, Social Security Death Index, Military Index. Information on millions of names from around the world, since the Middle Ages. **Languages:** English. **Type:** CD-ROM packages. **Subjects:** Genealogy. **Price:** Approximately $2,000.00. **Updating:** Regularly. **Remarks:** See separate entries on: Ancestral File, International Genealogical Index, Family History Library Catalog, Social Security Death Index, and Military Index.

Genealogical Collection

Library Preservation Systems Phone: (213)538-2662
4209 Woodcliff Rd.
Sherman Oaks, CA 91403

Description: Early California records. 3 rolls. Individual records available. 16 mm microfilm. **Price:** $75.00.

Genealogical Index of the Newberry Library (Chicago)

GK Hall & Co. Phone: (617)423-3990
70 Lincoln St. Toll-Free: 800-343-2806
Boston, MA 02111 Fax: (617)423-3999

Description: 8 reels of records or 109 microfiche, available in 35 mm film (ISBN: 0-8161-1317-3) or 4 x 6 microfiche (ISBN: 0-8161-1771-3). **Price:** $345.00 ($415.00 export).

Genealogy Forum

CompuServe Information Phone: (614)457-8600
  Service Toll-Free: 800-848-8199
5000 Arlington Centre Blvd. Fax: (614)457-0348
PO Box 20212 Dick Eastman, Forum
Columbus, OH 43220 Administrator

Description: Provides text files equipped with appropriate information on starting or continuing a family history search. Includes shareware programs to help trace birthdates, baptismal records, and marriages. Contains a message board, forum libraries, a surname exchange, and a member directory. **Languages:** English. **Type:** Bulletin board. **Subjects:** Genealogy. **Online availability:** CompuServe Information Service (ROOTS: $12.80/connect hour (1200 and 2400 baud); $22.80/connect hour (9600 baud)).

Genealogy RoundTable

GE Information Service Phone: (301)340-4000
  (GEIS) Toll-Free: 800-638-9636
GEnie (General Electric
  Network for Information
  Exchange)
401 N Washington Blvd.
Rockville, MD 20850

Description: Provides a forum enabling participants to share genealogical information and family anecdotes. Includes the Genealogy KnowledgeBase, which contains descriptive items on where to write for further information on a particular genealogical topic. **Languages:** English. **Subjects:** Genealogical and historical societies, family or surname associations, family or surname newsletters, books and magazines, publishers, professional researchers, sources of vital records and other information, computer interest groups, software, and research libraries. **Online availability:** GEnie (General Electric Network for Information Exchange) (GENEALOGY: prime-time rates: $18.00/connect hour; non-prime-time: $5.00/connect hour (300 baud), $6.00/connect hour (1200 baud), $10.00/connect hour (2400 baud)).

Guide to the Holdings of the Archives of Ontario

Ontario Ministry of Culture Phone: (416)314-7611
  and Communications Fax: (416)314-7635
77 Bloor St., W., 3rd Fl. Barbara L. Craig, Co-editor
Toronto, ON, Canada M7A Richard W. Ramsey, Co-editor
  2R9

Description: 9 microfiches. **Publication date:** 1985.

International Genealogical Index (IGI)

The Church of Jesus Christ of Phone: (801)240-2331
  Latter-day Saints Jay Roberts, Ancestral File
Family History Library Specialist
35 N West Temple St.
Salt Lake City, UT 84150

Description: Provides more than 200 million names of deceased persons with the majority of names dating from the early 1500s to 1875. Comprises a parent index, marriage and birth index, and a similar and exact surname section. Typical Record Items: Name, event type, event year, event place, relative name, parent's name, child's name, birth/christening year and place, source information, description, batch and sheet numbers, and printout call number. Individual entries can be printed or downloaded. **Geographic coverage:** Over 30 individual disks containing information from every region of the world. **Online availability:** CD-ROM: Producer. Rates/Conditions: Available as part of the Family Search systems, which is made publicly available through the Family History Library and other history centers operated by the LDS as well as through the genealogical and history sections of public libraries.

Military Index

The Church of Jesus Christ of Phone: (801)240-2331
  Latter-day Saints Jay Roberts, Ancestral File
Family History Library Specialist
35 N West Temple St.
Salt Lake City, UT 84150

Description: List of almost 110,000 servicemen and women who died while serving in the United States Armed Forces in Korea (1950–1957) and Vietnam (1957–1975). Birth and death dates, residence, place of death, rank and service number, and, in the case of those who served in Vietnam, religion, marital status, and race are provided. This index is on the fourth disk of the Social Security Death Index.

Searching U.S. Census Records: An Invaluable Aid for Locating and Tracking Families

Family History Unlimited Phone: (801)375-2841
3507 N University Ave, Suite Jimmy B. Parker, Presenter
  350 B
Provo, UT 84604

Description: Genealogical course presented on four audiocassettes. Includes workbook containing dozens of illustrations extracted from historical documents. **Subjects:** Content and availability of censuses, search strategies, and sources of additional information. **Price:** $75.00.

Social Security Death Index (SSDI)

The Church of Jesus Christ of
  Latter-day Saints
Family History Library
35 N West Temple St.
Salt Lake City, UT 84150

Phone: (801)240-2331
Jay Roberts, Ancestral File
  Specialist

Description: Contains the names of 39.5 million deceased people who had social security numbers and whose deaths were reported to the U.S. Social Security Administration (and whose families collected death benefits) primarily from between 1962 and 1988; some records date from 1937 to 1989. Comprises four individual compact disks. Typical Record Items: name, birth date, Social Security number, state of issuance of Social Security number, death date, state of residence at death and zip code, state where death benefit was sent and zip code. The Social Security Number will allow the researcher to obtain additional information from the Social Security Administration. On-line the researcher will find information on how to order a civil death certificate from the appropriate state. **Languages:** English. **Subjects:** Genealogy. **Updating:** Regularly. **Online availability:** CD-ROM: Producer. Rates/Conditions: Available as part of the Family Search system, which is made publicly available through the Family History Library and other family history centers operated by the LDS.

Using U.S. Military Records: A Rich Source of Information for Genealogists and Family Historians

Family History Unlimited
3507 N University Avenue,
  Suite 350 B
Provo, UT 84604

Phone: (801)375-2841
Jimmy B. Parker, Presenter

Description: Genealogical course consisting of four audiocassettes. Includes a workbook containing several illustrations extracted from historical documents. **Subjects:** History of conflicts in North America; discussion of the probability that an ancestor served in the military; content and availability of colonial, state, and national military records; and search strategies. **Price:** $75.00.

Part III
Indexes

Author Index

Title & Organization Index

Subject Index

Author Index

Title and Organization Index

⌀ This index provides an alphabetical, word-by-word arrangement of all titles, products, organizations, archives, and libraries listed in Part II.

Subject Index

Subject Index